Reflections on ART

Fifth Edition

Janet LeBlanc

Cover Art: *The Gates, Central Park, by Christo and Jeanne-Claude 1979-2005*, photo copyright: Janet LeBlanc

ISBN 0-89308-843-9

Preface

Reflections on Art is the product of my many years of teaching Art and Architecture History survey courses, especially one-semester courses designed for non-majors pursuing their first and possibly only introduction to the history of art. Brief courses of this type are nearly always problematic in ways that students may not envision. It is challenging to scale material down to a digestible amount of information that can be absorbed in the span of a single semester, while not sacrificing the intellectual merit of the course. This edition of the book is an interim custom book between the rough draft and the final textbook which will include images of the art and architecture.

Art can be approached in at least two distinctly different ways within an academic setting. Art Appreciation addresses simple connoisseurship. The student is coached toward an understanding of styles and themes in art, without much emphasis on development over time or ways in which art is distinguished by place. As such, portraits might be compared to other portraits for example, as ends in themselves without the burden of understanding why they were created as they were. Art Appreciation is frequently offered through museum Saturday afternoon programs for the general public, and in many ways it is appropriately suited to that environment more than to a rigorous university setting. Art History presumes that the student will develop an appreciation for the art, but the focus of the education is founded in a deeper exploration of historical context. *Reflections on Art* is an Art <u>History</u> book, with as much or more emphasis placed on the history behind the art as on the physical art product itself. As a teacher and as an author, my particular objective is to provide a solid grounding in historical context for the visual images discussed. I want you to understand *why* things were as they were and are as they are; what makes it all tick?

There are dozens of Art History books on the market, and believe me when I say that over the years I have tried them all. The problem with one-semester courses is that the big tomes provide way too much material for a short course. No student regardless of how brilliant will get through a 1200 page book in a few weeks. The flip side of this dilemma is a substantial number of smaller books, but these have proved to be lightweights in terms of content, as they too frequently sacrifice the meaty historical context and drift toward the "appreciation" end of the spectrum. Beyond that, virtually all the textbooks are written in "professorspeak," the pretentious language of academia which most students find deadly dull to read. For *years* my students complained time and again that the solution would be for me to write my own textbook, one that paralleled my style of teaching. And so, here it is, albeit still evolving from a rough draft to the final version. *Reflections on Art* does not presume to be the definitive Art History book, but it does aspire to fill a niche for an overview with some meat on the bones.

I would like to recognize and thank my husband, Christian for his support and help toward completing this project. He read every word, catching errors I missed and making suggestions for improvement. Christian also did all the maps along with help from my 17-year old son, also named Christian, to whom I am likewise grateful. Finally, I would like to dedicate *Reflections on Art* to the thousands of students I have taught over the years, who in turn taught me how to teach.

Janet LeBlanc
January 2007

Author's Survival Guide

Surviving Art History: Part One: Learning Data

Every semester I hear from students who swear they have put in hours upon hours of studying for a test, only to fail. Some of them are bluffing of course, but many are not. It is frustrating to say the least to put in lot of time studying and then make a poor grade. Sometimes it's a simple matter of procrastination and they tried to do too much too fast. But often that's not the problem. When I dig deeper, I almost always discover that these students have no system for studying, they just read and reread their material so many times that after awhile, their minds drift off on vacation while they stare at their notes or at the book.

Perhaps at some point in your life you may have taken an MBTI (Myers Briggs Type Indicator) personality test. Tests of this type can be useful in assessing a number of things about yourself, among them a good predictor of how you learn. While some students are naturally inclined to do equally well on all types of tests, most are not. Some students are what Myers Briggs would define as "sensors." Sensors are usually pretty sharp at getting the details. They gravitate toward specific data, and are often stronger at remembering small points rather than seeing the giant sweep of trends, which require them to make comparisons and see relationships between different, unrelated things. Folks in this camp often prefer multiple-choice tests.

At the other extreme there are what Myers Briggs calls "intuitives". These people excel at abstract thinking. They see the big picture effortlessly and seem to comprehend how things influence each other, however remotely. They are often casual about remembering small details. People who favor intuitive thinking often loathe multiple-choice tests and believe they do much better on essay exams. Frequently they are right! Multiple-choice tests that are poorly written often favor sensors. Essay tests that are not well graded will favor intuitives. For better or worse, the problem is not with the student when this happens, it is with the teacher! Teachers who write multiple choice tests must be sure that half the test screens for abstract thinking instead of pure data, and teachers who read essays must be prepared to hold students accountable for a set volume of data in addition to their ability to blather on in platitudes about the topic in general.

For the record, I have taken the MBTI several times, always with the same results. I score off the charts in the intuitive range, while not answering a single question with a sensor response. I am 100% a big picture person, the one who sees the entire forest clearly but is not naturally inclined to get caught up thinking much about trees. So how is it that I managed to learn all these snippets of detailed information you might wonder ... I can lecture for hours without ever using a single note card. That is a sensor skill ... but I have already told you that I have zippo aptitude in that department. That's right; I don't. So if I can do it, so can you.

I have had to develop systems to force my brain to learn data, which it is not naturally inclined to do. I developed the following study system way back when I was an undergraduate trying to survive art history myself. To learn data, I suggest you create a spreadsheet. I did mine by hand on legal pads, but you could probably do it on a computer nowadays; some students have used Excel successfully for example. For every work of art or architecture, you need to have a complete ID which includes **title, artist / architect** (if known), **patron** (if known, this category might also include other "who" information like who used it or who discovered it), **location, period,** and **date.** That is six units of data per work of art or architecture, with some being blank if the information is unknown (more common the earlier in history something was created). Writing only on one side of each sheet, create your headings:

Title   **Artist/Architect**   **Patron ("who")**   **Location**   **Period**   **Date**

Now, one by one, you begin to fill in your chart with data. When you don't know a slice of information, you leave that spot blank for that entry. For example, under the above headings, an entry might look like this:

Zoser's Pyramid   **Imhotep**   **Zoser**   **Saqqara, Egypt**   **Old Kingdom**   **3000-2200BC**

With this system, you create your study list as you read along, no need to wait for the last minute. When you finish a chapter, update your spreadsheet to include the newly introduced data. Most of the information you need can be conveniently found on the Image Lists for each unit. Always write out the location, period and date for every entry, even when it is the same as the one above. The repetition helps reinforce the data in your mind. To learn the information so you are prepared for the test, keep the sheets in a binder (always in their correct order) and quiz yourself one sheet at a time. When you begin to feel confident that the IDs are sinking in, cut a sheet of scrap paper to cover all the dates. Can you remember the dates to go with each period? When you know all the dates, hide the next column from the right. Do you remember where on your list the Old Kingdom ends and New Kingdom begins? Now cover three columns. Can you tell where Egypt ends and the Minoans begin? Keep this up until you get to where all you need to see is the list of titles and you can spit out the rest of the ID. Matching the titles to the pictures is the final step, and not the thing that most people find difficult.

How long will this take? That will vary from person to person. Be sure to leave yourself enough time. It is never a matter of the system didn't work. Assuming you have no errors of incorrect information on your study spreadsheet, if you didn't learn it all, you didn't allow enough time. Some people are quick studies once they get organized. Other people need a jackhammer to pummel the data into their brains even with a good system. I haven't a clue where your rate of retention falls, but if you employ this system, you'll find out on your own. I used to drive my college roommates crazy with my manic studying, BUT, by the day of the test, I could recite every image we had seen, with complete ID, in the order in which the images were presented, 100% from memory while driving in for the exam - I didn't even need the list of titles! Guess what? I could still do that now – from memory, itemize every example of art or architecture discussed in this book in the order in which they will appear with complete ID. And remember, I am the one with zero natural ability in this department. If I can train myself to do it, you can too.

Surviving Art History: Part Two: Learning Broad Concepts

I have to admit that learning the big picture was never difficult for me when I was in school, so I never had to resort to special study techniques. That said, every semester I have students who can identify every image with a correct ID, but they get completely confused and can't seem to keep any of the rest of the material straight. I call this "scrambling." Usually they have the right information in tiny bytes, but they don't get it put together right ... sort of like trying to fit a puzzle piece of Snow White into a puzzle of Sleeping Beauty. An exaggerated version of scrambling might be something like this:

> *The first pharaoh of the New Kingdom was Akhenaten who was married to Hatshepsut. Hatshepsut actually ran the show during this time because Akhenaten was from Crete, as evidenced in the Minoan style art associated with the Amarna style of Akhenaten. The king was presented to the people as being the Son of God and average Egyptians were in awe of Akhenaten even though he was different from most Egyptians. The high priests knew something was wrong, and they murdered him as a young king, which left Hatshepsut free to develop trade with the Mycenaeans who had invaded Egypt during the Middle Kingdom. Her successor, Rameses reversed Hatshepsut's policies of peace and trade and enslaved the Hebrews to build the pyramids.*

You get the idea. The paragraph is full of half-truths, errors and the occasional tidbit of correct information in the right place at the right time. To set the record straight, the first successful pharaoh of the New Kingdom was Hatshepsut, not Akhenaten. Hatshepsut wasn't married, but her "boyfriend" was Senmut, while Akhenaten, who came later, was married to Nefertiti, who quite possibly did run the show during Akhenaten's reign. Akhenaten wasn't from Crete, although his court artists were. He was presented to the people as the Son of God. The high priests probably did know something was wrong, but nobody murdered Akhenaten. They waited, and murdered his successor, King Tut in order to destroy the family line. Hatshepsut didn't develop trade with the Mycenaeans, who by the way never invaded Egypt. She may have hired the Mycenaeans to fight the Mesopotamians who had invaded Egypt, and she did later developed trade with Mesopotamia. Rameses came along about a hundred years after Akhenaten who was already a hundred years or so after Hatshepsut, and while Rameses did enslave the Hebrews, it was to build temples, not pyramids, which were obsolete by almost a thousand years by that time. You see how you can have all the right pieces of information in a completely wrong order!

Usually scrambling occurs in one of two situations:

1) The student procrastinated on starting his or her studying, and then discovered that it was all more complicated than he or she thought. With great cramming zeal, the student tries to compensate for the late start, but by the time he or she is sitting in the test, all that information is like a plate of spaghetti on the brain. It becomes impossible to keep it all straight, and the student cannot discern correct answers from incorrect on the test. SOLUTION? Start way early!

2) The student may have started early (or maybe not), but just cannot let go enough to get a good night's rest before the test. He or she burns the candle at both ends into the wee hours of the morning and then sits the test completely fried. In that condition, he or she is completely incapable of logically working through complex questions and answers. This is the person who is almost reduced to tears when he or she gets a bad grade because "I KNEW that; I don't know why I picked that answer." SOLUTION? This one is easy: *GO-TO-BED*. Be sure you get a decent night's rest the night before a test (any test) because your brain is worthless if you are overtired.

But what about the person who honestly starts early and doesn't stay up half the night before the test and still has trouble keeping ideas straight? If this might be you, try this. First, consider how you read the chapters. Do you just pick up the book and read it as though it were recreational reading with no test staring you down? Never pick up a textbook unless you pick up a pen and highlighter at the same time. As you read, overline key points, including names of important people and special vocabulary and ideas that appear in bold italics in your book (an obvious clue that you need to know the material. Make margin notes, that is jot a word or two in the margins that identify the main theme in that section of the chapter so you can easily locate information later. Once you finish reading a chapter … STOP. Do not go on to the next chapter until you make study note cards on the material you just read while that information is still fresh in your mind. Let me hasten to add that I do NOT mean creating 457 flash cards where you copy half the text onto 3x5 cards and then hypnotize yourself shuffling through the stack over and over again. I can think of few LESS effective ways to study! You create one card (4x6 is a good size) for every period / location in all the units, and from Renaissance to Modern, another card for each artist. For example, you would have a card for Old Kingdom Egypt, one for Minoans / Crete and Thera, one for Classical Greece, one for Julio-Claudian Rome and so forth. You then go through your book and notes and write bullet points (quick notations – a single word or short phrase rather than full sentences), distilling the information into a few key words. For example, if I were making a card for Old Kingdom Egypt, I might include:

Pharaohs - Narmer, Zoser, Khufu, Khafre, Menkaure

Pyramids / Mastabas / Necropolis

Death Orientation

Funerary Statues

Pictographs

You get the idea. If when you study, you realize that you can't remember how big funerary statues are or what they are made of, you can go back to your original source and look that up easily enough, and you may want to flag some additional things in the book by more overlining and extra jotted notes in the page margins. Study note cards are also a good place to note other cultures that occur at the same time elsewhere - for example, on all your Greek cards from the Classical period through Hellenistic you might note that the Republic was alive and well in Rome, and vice versa. Keep an eye out for connections between cultures that occur at the same time, or for influences of earlier civilizations/ periods / artists on later generations.

The advantage of making cards like this is that it condenses the material into a quick study - you should only have somewhere between maybe a dozen cards to no more than fifty tops for any given test. The exercise of making the cards is already a giant step toward organizing your thoughts, and the exercise of making useful note cards is enhanced by good making margin notes and overlining while reading. It is also easy to ask someone to help you study - it doesn't even need to be anyone involved with the course. A friend can offer you a bullet and you identify on what card it is found:

Your study mate says: Perikles = You reply: Classical Greece

Your study mate says: Pax Romana = You reply: Julio-Claudian Rome

Your study mate says: Death Orientation = You reply: Old AND New Kingdom Egypt

Your study mate says: Perfect male nude statues = You reply: Classical AND Late Classical Greece

Your study mate says: Senmut = You reply: New Kingdom, Egypt

Alternatively, your friend can ask you to cite the "x" number of bullets on the Republican Rome card for example, and you test yourself to see how many you can remember. With the information reduced to the basics, you can easily absorb all the high points while keeping your book and notes for reference to bulk up the information as necessary. Set the cards aside as you feel confident with one period or another; you should have an easier time keeping the right rulers, artists, architects and more in the right time and place, doing the right things for the right reasons.

Contents

Unit One

The Awesome Ancient World:

Prehistory to Pagan Antiquity

1. Abu Simbel
2. Akkad
3. Akrotiri
4. Assyria
5. Athens
6. Babylon
7. Deir el Bahari
8. Giza
9. Knossos
10. Lascaux
11. Mycenae
12. Ostia
13. Persia
14. Pompeii
15. Rome & Veii
16. Saqqara
17. Sparta
18. Stonehenge
19. Sumer
20. Tarquinia & Cerveteri
21. Tel el Amarna
22. Valley of the Kings
23. Willendorf

The Ancient World

Image List for Unit One

Paleolithic (dates for all prehistoric need to be learned for individual art)

    1. Venus of Willendorf (c.30,000 BC - Austria)
    2. Lascaux Cave Painting (c.15,000 BC - France)
    3. Lascaux Cave Painting

Neolithic

    4. Stonehenge (c.2000 BC – England)
    5. Stonehenge

EGYPT

Old Kingdom 3000 - 2200 BC

    6. Palette of Narmer
    7. Palette of Narmer
    8. Geese of Medum
    9. Necropolis
    10. Mastabas
    11. Zoser's Pyramid *by Imhotep*
    12. Pyramids at Giza
    13. King Khafre
    14. Menkaure and his Queen
    15. Rahotep and Nofret
    16. Seated Scribe

MESOPOTAMIA

Sumerian c. 3800 – 2300 BC

    17. Cylinder Seals
    18. Ziggurat as it appears today
    19. Reconstruction of the Ziggurat at Ur
    20. Votive Figures
    21. Bull Lyre

Akkadian c. 2300-2150 BC

    22. Victory Stele of Naram-Sin

Babylonian c. 1900-1600 BC

    23. Stele of Hammurabi

EGYPT

New Kingdom c.1500 - 1000 BC

24. Hatshepsut
25. Mortuary Temple of Hatshepsut @ Deir-el-Bahari *by Senmut*
26. Akhenaten
27. Nefertiti
28. Amarna Relief
29. Amarna Bust (Head)
30. Gold Mask of Tutankhamun
31. Mortuary Temple of Rameses II @ Abu Simbel
32. Egyptian Temple Plan (happens to be Temple of Horus @ Edfu FYI)
33. Pylon (also Temple of Horus @ Edfu FYI)
34. Hypostyle Hall (happens to be Temple of Amun-Re @ Karnak, FYI)
35. Hypostyle Hall (Karnak again)

MESOPOTAMIA

Assyrian c. 900 – 612 BC

36. Citadel of Sargon II at Khorsabad
37. Winged Human-Headed Bulls
38. Ashurnasirpal Hunting Lions

Neo-Babylonian 625 – 538 BC

39. Ishtar Gate

Persian Empire 539 – 331 BC

40. Great Audience Hall of Darius
41. Darius and Xerxes Receiving Tribute

MINOAN (period) 1750 - 1400 BC

On Crete (location):

42. Palace at Knossos
43. Palace at Knossos
44. Dolphin Fresco (Palace at Knossos)
45. Toreador Fresco (Palace at Knossos)

On Thera (location):

46. Akrotiri
47. Flotilla Fresco

MYCENAEAN (period), Southern Greece (location) 1600 - 1200 BC

48. Mycenae
49. Lion Gate
50. Treasury of Atreus
51. Treasury of Atreus
52. Mask of Agamemnon

GREECE

Archaic 600 - 480 BC

53. Metropolitan Kouros
54. Anavyssos Kouros
55. Peplos Kore

Classical 480 – 404 BC

56. Acropolis
57. Parthenon *by Iktinos and Kallikrates*
58. (know info) Greek Orders
59. (know info) Doric and Ionic Orders
60. (know info) Greek Temple Plan
61. Parthenon Frieze *by Phidias*
62. Erectheion *by Mnesikles*
63. Porch of Maidens (caryatids) from the Erectheion
64. Warrior (artist not known)
65. Doryphoros *by Polykleitos*

Late Classical 404 - 323 BC

66. Hermes and Dionysos *by Praxiteles*
67. Aphrodite of Knidos *by Praxiteles*
68. Theater of Epidauros *by Polykleitos the Younger*
69. Theater of Epidauros *by Polykleitos the Younger*

Hellenistic 323 – 147 BC

70. Aphrodite de Melos (Venus de Milo)
71. Barberini Faun

72. Old Market Woman
73. Laocoon *by Hagesandros, Polydoros, and Athanadoros*
74. Nike of Samothrace

ROME

Etruscan c.700-509 BC

75. Etruscan Temple
76. Apollo
77. Musicians and Dancers (tarquinia)
78. Sarcophagus
79. Burial Chamber @ Cerveteri

Republic 509 – 44 BC

80. Temple of Fortuna Virilis
81. House of Faun
82. House of Faun
83. Insula @ Ostia
84. Patrician with the Busts of His Ancestors
85. Republican Bust

Julio-Claudian 30 BC – 68 (AD)

86. Ara Pacis Augustae
87. Ara Pacis Augustae
88. Ara Pacis Augustae
89. Augustus of Prima Porta
90. Theater of Marcellus
91. Theater of Marcellus
92. Roman Arch with Centering (understand concept)
93. Roman Arch showing weight distribution (understand concept)

Flavian 69 – 96

94. Colosseum
95. Colosseum
96. Arch of Titus
97. Arch of Titus (Spoils of Jerusalem relief sculpture detail)
98. Young Flavian Woman

Philosopher Kings 96 – 180

99. (FYI) Roman Forum
100. (FYI) Trajan's Forum

101. Basilica Ulpia
102. Basilica Ulpia
103. Column of Trajan
104. Column of Trajan
105. Pantheon *by Hadrian*
106. Pantheon *by Hadrian*
107. Pantheon *by Hadrian*
108. Equestrian Statue of Marcus Aurelius

Late Empire 180-325

109. Head of Constantine
110. Arch of Constantine

1. Prehistoric Art and Architecture

The study of art and architecture is best understood if one goes back to its earliest beginnings. The term "prehistoric" describes human society before the advent of written communication. As such, it does not describe a set period of time so much as it does a level of development. The reality is that there are still isolated pockets of the world that remain prehistoric to this day in that there are small, illiterate tribes of people which time has passed by. It is too broad to suggest that prehistoric culture lasted from 30,000 BC to the present day; accordingly, for prehistoric art and architecture only, you should be familiar with a specific round date for specific artifacts, painted images and monuments.

Period designations within the vast scope of prehistory will describe in better detail the level of development of the "artists" and "architects." The first is

Paleolithic

Paleolithic means Old (paleo) Stone (lith) Age. Paleolithic people can be characterized by two important facts. First, they had only stone tools; metalworking of all types had yet to be invented. Second, they had no understanding of agriculture and relied on hunting and gathering to provide food. Common sense would suggest that people who live off found food and hunting would be *nomadic* (people who move around). They would have to follow the food supply, either moving with herds of wild game, or at worst, finding new plants in a new region after they had devoured all the plants someplace else. Common sense would further suggest that people who live as nomads, constantly on the move, would probably not get around to developing architecture. How silly would it be for a tribe of wandering bushmen to design buildings, only to abandon their enterprise before they could even move in? European Paleolithic people were cavemen. Just as they relied on luck as much as skill to find food, they also had to hope for the best in finding natural shelter in the form of caves big enough to house their group. Again, relying on common sense, they probably lived in small groups, as large communities would be both problematic to house and to feed in a Paleolithic world.

Hopefully you have spotted the "common sense" factor being repeated here. The fact is that without proper written records, we really *know* very little about any prehistoric society. We piece together our understanding of these people with a small number of facts that can be proved, often through archaeology, and by developing theories extrapolated from ... well ... good old common sense.

The first work of art we will consider is an artifact discovered in Austria that has been dated as early as 30,000 BC, which date we will use for our purposes. The **Venus of Willendorf** is a good example of a generic type of sculpted artifact that was evidently produced in substantial numbers. We don't have many that survive in good condition today, but plenty of fossils have been found of similar statues where the original piece is long gone. The Venus of Willendorf is small, about the size of the palm of your hand, which makes good sense given that it would have to be easily portable. What sense would it make for nomads to carve a gigantic statue that could not be moved? It is made of a soft grade of stone. Given that the artist had only stone tools, he could not consider carving any material harder than his tools. We presume that most of these little figures were probably made of wood, which accounts for why we might have a fossil today instead of the original statue.

We have considered the physical properties of the statue, but why were these statues popular in Paleolithic communities? Think for a minute. Does it make sense to you that people would be concerned about art in a culture where everyone is constantly on the move, and nobody knows where their next meal might come from? Can you picture a group of prehistoric guys loafing around the cave discussing the merits of some beautiful statue they saw at a gallery show? Probably not. Odds are they had zero concept of "art" as we think of it today. An individual's time would have to be spent doing something that offered a practical benefit to the group – either picking berries, or hunting, or cooking, or sewing furs into coats and mukluks. Who had time to make fancy little statues of big-breasted women just for the heck of it? These little sculptures must have been perceived as useful in some capacity. Look at the Venus of Willendorf; what do you see? Little attention is paid to her face or limbs, but the artist seemed quite preoccupied with her breasts and hips. Although we do not know this for certain because we have no records to prove it, common sense among the majority of educated guessers dictates that these were fertility figures – that is, objects carried by young women as good luck charms for conceiving and bearing healthy babies to insure their clan's survival.

A second glimpse at Paleolithic culture is seen in the **Lascaux Cave Paintings**. These were discovered in France just a few decades ago, and they are typical of many similar cave paintings found across southern France and Spain. Radiocarbon dating was employed to fix the Lascaux Cave Paintings at approximately 15,000 BC. Time out. Before we explore cave paintings, consider the dating, especially relative to us today. The Venus of Willendorf is as much earlier than the cave paintings, as the cave paintings are to you and me today, if the paintings were from about 15,000 years ago (give or take a few thousand years), and the fertility figure dates as early as 30,000 BC. In fact, the next level of development, Neolithic, doesn't even show up on the planet's radar until around 8000 BC. This means that for 20,000 years, nobody got around to figuring out how to control the food supply. Nobody figured out that if you bury a seed, a plant will grow. Nobody figured out how to build a simple fence to keep animals corralled. It's an amazing thought given that nowadays, you go to bed at night thinking your car, computer and everything else is state-of-the-art up-to-date, and by morning you discover it's all obsolete!

Since we are dealing with Paleolithic "artists" again, it is reasonable to presume that the paintings must have had some practical application. Surely they were not created to decorate the cave! Their location alone would dispel that error. The images found in Paleolithic cave dwellings are not located in the mouth of the cave actually inhabited by people. They are found in deep crevices, inconvenient if their purpose was linked to visual enjoyment. The fact is, we don't know for certain what the purpose was behind these scenes, but we can pose educated theories. The subject of Paleolithic cave paintings almost always revolves around animals. Seldom are people present at all, and when they do find their way into the art, people are represented as rudimentary stick figures compared to the more careful, realistic portrayals of animals.

The most popular theory is that these images were linked to the hunt. Scholars propose that cavemen produced images of the animals they hoped to kill during the hunt, and then in a primitive ritual ceremony, they would attack the paintings as if thrusting some sort of voodoo hex onto the actual animal, thus giving the hunters a good luck edge in their quest for food. A second theory is that these animals had nothing to do with the hunt at all, but were sacred images of gods. We don't know if Paleolithic people had religious beliefs in 15,000 BC, but it is interesting to note that every culture that figured out how to write later on brought a fully developed religion along with them from their prehistoric roots. Primitive religions frequently employ animal imagery for gods, so it is not unreasonable to guess that "secret" images tucked away in secure passages in the cave where most people would never see them might be the "holy of holies" accessible only by a high priest or shaman. Recent archaeology has shown that the animals depicted in the paintings seldom match the remains of the actual animals the cavemen ate. Charred bones found buried beneath the floors of caves indicate that cavemen ate small animals like rabbits, while the paintings depict large game like bison, bulls, wild horses, gazelles and antelope. The folks who support the hunt theory aren't giving up easily, though. They suggest that just because the caveman wanted to capture and kill an antelope, doesn't mean he was so fortunate. When it is getting late in the day, you are hungry and there is no large game to cook up for dinner, those trapped rabbits begin to look pretty tasty.

A third possibility could be a primitive attempt to document information without the benefit of written language ... sort of like a visual library. Carbon 14 dating has disclosed that the Lascaux Cave Paintings were actually produced over a span of several centuries around 15,000 BC, painted by many different groups of Paleolithic people who made those caves their temporary home. This helps to explain why the animals, all individually rendered so realistically, are portrayed with gross disregard for *scale*. For example, a cow might be twice the size of a horse. The reason, it appears, is because the cow and horse were painted by two different artists a hundred or more years apart. Perhaps the gallery of animal images was an attempt to let those who would follow know what animals lived in the area. The new guy painting in the cave, though, considered *your* animals old news, so he didn't pay attention to details like scale (relative size) when he painted his pictures on top of yours. One way or the other, whether the pictures were produced to generate good luck in the hunt, or to pay homage to animal gods, or to document regional wild game, later generations of artists evidently were keen to find the right part of the cave to do their animal pictures, but once located, the "old" pictures were not valued in any way as "new" pictures were superimposed as if the old ones didn't exist.

Neolithic

The other level of prehistoric development we will consider is Neolithic. You should recognize the "lith" part of the word, and therefore know that these people were also a Stone Age culture dependent entirely on stone tools. The "neo" or "new" in this case indicates that Neolithic people had finally figured out agriculture. Learning how to plant crops and contain and control herds of animals meant that for the first time, man could control his food supply. This in turn meant that he did not have to limit the size of his communities; in fact, there were advantages to establishing larger communities that could be organized to defend and protect farmland. To do so, though, they also had to develop architecture to supplement whatever supply of natural caves could be found to house their population. As a general rule, the development of architecture tends to go hand in hand with the development of agriculture, for these (common sense) reasons.

Neolithic development creeps onto the scene round about 8000 BC. The earliest type of architecture is called *subtractive*. It is nothing more than removing earth away to create more caves, like a child digging tunnels in the sand, and you don't have to be much of an engineer to figure it out. *Additive* architecture is a little more demanding, given that you start with ground zero and must figure out how to build something that will stand up and not fall in on your head. The earliest and most simple form of architecture is called *Post and Lintel*. First, two upright members are put in place (posts), and then a horizontal beam (lintel) is set on top. This building practice dates all the way back to Neolithic builders, yet we still use it today, as easily witnessed looking at any door jamb where a pair of uprights topped by a horizontal beam frame the opening to a door.

The most famous Neolithic post and lintel architecture structure is **Stonehenge**, built on the Salisbury Plain in southern England sometime around 2000 BC. Although we do not know for certain what the purpose was for this structure (it would make a lousy house as it had no roof), it is generally believed that it once served as a calendar. If it was not designed to be a calendar, it is all the more remarkable that it coincidentally functions as one! By lining up the sun with different observation stones, it was possible to predict the equinoxes and solstices. Basically, Stonehenge permitted illiterate farmers to predict with good accuracy when the seasons would change so they could plan their planting and harvesting according to the calendar, rather than relying on the weather which can prove quite fickle.

Stonehenge has baffled and awed generations ever since it was constructed, and part of the mystique is that we don't really know how these Neolithic builders pulled off such a fabulous building feat. For example, the stone employed on Stonehenge was sarsen stone, known to be the most durable and hard in Britain. We can easily understand why sarsen stone would appeal to the builders – it would be most likely to last a long time, and this structure is pretty big and complicated to have to rebuild it every few years. The problem is, how did they quarry sarsen stone, if all they had were stone tools? These are immense, multi-ton blocks of stone; imagine trying to chisel them out of the quarry wall, and the best instruments you could hope to have would be stone ax-like tools made of the same sarsen stone! Unless they figured out something rather clever, we might wonder why we aren't all still employed on that end of the project to this day. Our best guess, because remember, there are no records to prove or disprove this theory, is that workers wore away grooves in the rock deep enough to slam in wooden wedges, then they poured water on the wood to make it swell, and the pressure helped to break huge slabs of stone away from the quarry wall. The theory is plausible given that it doesn't require tools or know-how that Neolithic people wouldn't have. Still, although quicker than trying to do all the stone-cutting by hand, it would nevertheless take a very long time, generations perhaps, to get the quarrying completed.

The next problem was transportation. The quarries were located over by Wales, while the selected construction site was miles away in south-central England. Nowadays we could load them on a truck and off we would go, but there is no evidence that the wheel had been invented in England by 2000 BC (the Chinese had discovered the principle of the wheel quite early on, but unfortunately, there were no Chinese consultants on hand to offer these builders advice). Our best guess is that they cut down thousands of trees, skinned them of their bark, and created a very long road made of wooden rollers from the tree trunks, over which these massive *megaliths* (big stones) could be slowly shoved along from the quarry to the Salisbury Plain. Again, the prospect of such a campaign isn't beyond the knowledge of Neolithic builders, but it would take a very long time.

Once the megaliths were at the building site, how did they get them to pop upright? If they had understood pulleys and levers, like the Chinese, it might not have been much of a problem, but of course, there is no evidence that Englishmen were that far along the learning curve in 2000 BC. Our best guess is that they created great dirt-mound ramps, then topped those with a conveyer path of wooden rollers, shoved the posts up the gradual incline on the rollers, then finally let them plop over the side, upright. They probably got a pair of posts in place and set the lintel, before tearing down the dirt slope and rollers to move the operation a few feet to the right or left to begin the process again.

All and all, as astonishingly advanced as Stonehenge appears, and as often as loony stories appear about aliens visiting Earth to stupefy us dummies with their sophisticated architecture, there is nothing about Stonehenge which cannot be explained relying on common sense, ingenuity, and limiting ourselves otherwise to what we know to be the abilities of the folks who were locally on hand to build such a monument in 2000 BC. In truth, what might be the single most amazing feat about Stonehenge is that they managed to produce such a technically sophisticated observatory, which demanded that each stone be placed just so for it to do its job, and these measurements were precisely memorized and passed down through what would have had to have been many many generations of workers … without any written records. Nowadays this would be inconceivable. People considered quite clever in today's society require shopping lists to go to the super market and actually remember to purchase milk *and* bread at the same time, without having to make a second trip to the store. This is because we have become very dependent on the written word. Back in prehistoric times, before there were any written words, people were accustomed to listening much more closely, and their minds were trained to memorize important information, word for word, so it could be passed on down through the generations.

A particularly good example, not so far removed chronologically from Stonehenge either, would be the Torah, or the original five [Old Testament] books of the Bible. These and all the books that followed were learned verbatim through oral tradition. There was no such thing as sitting down to read the books. Even if your rabbi had scrolls, it wasn't like you could *read* them, as they were written as one, long, unbroken string of consonants with no divisions into chapters and verses, and not even divisions into words, for that matter. The only way anybody could "read" the sacred texts was to recite what they had already memorized, using the sacred scroll only as an aid in that a few letters might trigger a word in your memory, if you got stuck. Now you figure if average men and women learned texts as long and complicated as the Bible, how much harder (or easier) would it have been to memorize how tall and wide a few dozen stones needed to be, and how far apart to place them?

England and Europe in general remained prehistoric later than regions along the southern and eastern coasts of the Mediterranean. If <u>Stonehenge</u> was indeed produced sometime around 2000 BC, then they were running at least a thousand years behind places like Egypt and Mesopotamia where written language and metallurgy were well established by this time. This reinforces why it is important to think of prehistoric "periods" like Paleolithic and Neolithic, not so much in terms of a finite dated time period, but rather as a level of development. Usually there is a begin date, where we can safely say that nobody prior to a given date had made certain discoveries, but it is extremely difficult to determine at what point everyone left the primitive lifestyle behind.

2. Egypt and Mesopotamia

While European culture remained prehistoric, the eastern Mediterranean advanced much more rapidly. There, two civilizations developed parallel cultures around the same time: Egypt and Mesopotamia. Egypt is familiar as it has always been in the same place and known through history by the same name to us. Mesopotamia was a region centered in what is now the country of Iraq, with adjacent territory reaching across the Middle East.

Neolithic civilization appeared first in Mesopotamia with evidence of farming and domesticated dogs dating back as early as 8,000 BC. The ancient city of Jericho mentioned in the <u>Bible</u> was a fortified Neolithic settlement. By the time the Old Testament hero Joshua got there, millennia had passed since its founding day, however. There were a number of independent farming communities during prehistoric times, starting first in the hill country and later moving into the "*fertile crescent*" between the Tigris and Euphrates rivers, and finally to other similarly fertile valleys sprinkled from Turkey over to Iran. Houses were built out of mud bricks, and towns were frequently protected by walls to keep foreigners out. Archaeologists have discovered that the early citizens of Jericho and other Neolithic communities buried their dead beneath the floor of their house, which may indicate some sort of ancestor cult. Unfortunately, we know very little about the religious beliefs of the Neolithic residents in the region. What alienates us from a better understanding of their society is that the indigenous people of prehistoric Mesopotamia were apparently superseded by outsiders, and the new guys were the ones to develop written language.

Unlike Mesopotamia, Egypt is one of the easier ancient cultures to illustrate the transition from prehistory to a developing literate society. Originally there were two groups of people living in the land which would become Egypt. In the southern inland region, which was heavily forested thousands of years ago, there lived the Upper Egyptians; while along the Mediterranean coast in the north the Lower Egyptians lived. If you think they got themselves turned upside down with the Uppers living geographically south of the Lowers, bear in mind that these folks didn't have maps; they based their understanding of where they were on the flow of the Nile River which begins deep in the heart of Africa and flows downstream (north) toward the sea.

The Upper Egyptians remained a Paleolithic Stone Age people who hunted to provide food for their tribes, while in the delta region of the Nile, the Lower Egyptians moved on to a Neolithic society much earlier (early 20th century excavations suggest at least as early as 4000 BC) given their easy access to excellent farmland. The Upper Egyptians were nomads who worshipped several gods. Among the most important and probably the first Egyptian deity was **Hathor**, the goddess of the Moon, and by some accounts the entire sky. She was depicted as a horned cow. Hathor was the supreme deity of all creation, the universe being contained in her great belly. **Ra** was the sun god, and creator of all on Earth within the great universe of Hathor. He was depicted alternatively as a hawk or as a hawk-headed man.

The Lower Egyptians were more stable; they lived in communities of built houses, and their religion developed parallels to agriculture. The chief deities were *Osiris*, who was often depicted as a bull, and who was a sort of grand patriarch of all the gods. He was associated with sexual creative power, including rather optimistically prominent genitalia in much of the art. *Isis* was his all-purpose companion / wife / sister. She was frequently depicted as a bird, and as mother to all, she could conquer even death through her love. Since the farmers had more time on their hands to reflect on life's mysteries over the course of the year than their hunter-gatherer counterparts, their religion became more elaborate. Every spring there was a festival to celebrate the birth of Osiris, which corresponded conveniently with planting season. In the autumn, a harvest festival marked the death of Osiris. Because the farmers had observed that after the death of a crop (harvest), life was resurrected the following year in the form of another crop, their religion likewise incorporated the concept of rebirth.

According to legend, Osiris was killed, dismembered and cast to the wind coinciding with the harvest, just as the crops were likewise taken from the earth and divided among the people. Every winter Isis, upset that her husband had been chopped to bits, flew throughout the universe collecting all the pieces of her beloved. Then in the spring, as the goddess of life-giving fertility, she would breathe life back into Osiris at the festival celebrating his birth. So it was that Osiris became the God of the Underworld of Death and Regenerated Afterlife. He and Isis had a son, *Horus*, who was depicted as a hawk, and who was associated with the sun and later blended with Ra as the great creator. Horus was perceived as being the prototype of the *pharaoh*, or Egyptian king, sort of a mythical first pharaoh reaching far back in time before history. In later times, Isis and Hathor were also frequently conflated into one entity.

These ideas of birth, death and regeneration probably began from observing nature, but in time, they permeated the Lower Egyptian's understanding of his own mortality. It was understood that everyone had a soul, called the *ka*, and it was believed that while the body died, the ka lived on. As it was in Mesopotamia, it became customary for Egyptian families to bury the body of the family patriarch, also known as Grandpa, beneath the floor of his house, on the assumption that the soul would hang around where the body was buried. It was their belief that the ongoing presence of Grandpa's soul would help protect the family and bring them good fortune. Perhaps some similar belief prevailed in Mesopotamia to explain why they also buried their dead beneath the house.

Early Egypt

Old Kingdom *c. 3000-2200 BC*

Now presumably everything went along fine until the combination of increasing population among the farmers, and the hunters seeking new territories with plenty of untapped herds of wild game eventually brought the two groups into contact with one another. This unfortunate clash of disparate cultures happened sometime well before 3000 BC, and the result was many years (centuries, possibly) of war between them.

Sometime shortly before 3000 BC, there was one particular warrior who was so formidable that he managed to bully both sides of the conflict into honoring him as the boss-man over everyone. This was King Narmer, who was probably one in the same with the legendary God-King Menes, a tale from the Upper Egyptians about a great king who conquered all of Egypt. His reign ushered in a new era for Egypt as a unified nation with a strong central government. Although Narmer technically predates the assorted dynasties of pharaohs that ruled Egypt as kings, and although he undoubtedly lived slightly before 3000 BC, we are going to simplify matters by calling Narmer the start of the Old Kingdom period, for which we will use the round dates of 3000-2200 BC.

We know next to nothing about Narmer, but most scholars believe he was an Upper Egyptian, both based on imagery of Upper Egyptian gods on artifacts from his reign, and also because common sense would suggest that a skilled hunter might have better military instincts than a farmer. The most famous artifact from the days of King Narmer is the **Palette of Narmer**, which is a two-sided carved slate palette, about 25" tall. It was probably used for mixing cosmetics, as evidenced by the small, indented dish in the center of one side.

The palette illustrates stories about King Narmer through the use of *pictographs and registers*, which is a pre-literate form of communicating information. The principle is simple. Small images, or pictographs tell the story, with the images being separated by horizontal bars called registers. The concept is not unlike comic strips we see today where boxes of pictures read across, and then we go to the next line down and continue with the story. Because written language had not yet been developed in Egypt, although it soon would be during the Old Kingdom, in this piece the artist must clearly communicate the whole story without using any written words. King Narmer himself shows up on both sides of the palette. On one side he wears the crown of the Upper Egyptians and is shown pummeling some poor guy into submission, while on the other side he sports the crown of the Lower Egyptians, and seems to be in a procession to inspect the dead (we know they are dead because their heads have been removed and placed neatly between their legs); we can only guess that these men died at the hands of Narmer's minions. All in all, Narmer is shown to be one tough guy, in charge or else. Notice that he towers over everyone. This doesn't mean that Narmer was actually a physical giant. It is a way of making sure the viewer recognizes that he is the most important person in the scene. This quickly became tradition in Egyptian art: size = status. The largest person in the scene is the most important, and lesser people's status may be determined by simply observing their smaller size.

Also notice how stiff and unnatural Narmer and his cohorts appear. Devotees of more realistic art sometimes see Egyptian painting and sculpture as primitive, suggesting that the artists for some reason never learned their craft very well. This could not be further from the truth. Egyptian artists were highly skilled, and could produce photographically realistic art when the subject called for this. The point is that realism was reserved for unimportant subjects. Observe the **Geese of Medum**. Animals are less important than people, and accordingly, see how the artist has flawlessly presented these humble birds as they appear in life, doting on realistic detail.

Important subjects, however, were supposed to be idealized and perfected. Let's use Narmer as our case study. He was a man, and men are supposed to have narrow hips. You certainly don't want the esteemed pharaoh to look fat! Usually men's hips will appear slimmer in profile than from the frontal view, so Narmer's hips are shown in profile. The problem is, without the clarity of writing, someone might mistakenly think Narmer was missing a leg if only one were shown in profile, so the pharaoh is depicted with legs splayed, as if going for a stroll. By the way, check out his feet – they both show the big toe, as a clutter of little toes would look untidy. Unfortunately, a profile chest and shoulder view might make this he-man pharaoh look too scrawny, so he is twisted at the waist to make his upper torso appear grander in a frontal pose. This enabled the artist to easily include both arms also. The face is tricky. It must look like the pharaoh so there is no confusion, and the best way to capture a likeness is in profile so the line of the chin and nose might be shown. Unfortunately, eyes need to be viewed straight-on to get the best point of view. No problem – the artist simply dragged Narmer's eye around his head to show it frontally on an otherwise profile face. It isn't realistic because that was not the artist's intent. His objective was to illustrate every aspect of the pharaoh from its most flattering perspective. We see this first with Narmer, but it seemed like such a swell idea, that for a thousand years artists in Egypt plugged along using the same formula. The Egyptians worshiped stability; "if it ain't broke, don't fix it" might have been a good motto for them.

Over time during the Old Kingdom the people adopted the customs of the Lower Egyptians regarding their ideas on the soul. They had well-developed agriculture, and were rich in natural resources such that Egypt felt no pressing need to venture beyond her borders. For a thousand years the Egyptians stayed home. They were wealthy, comfortable and extremely static. Nothing much ever changed in Egypt. The Nile flooded. The floods receded. The crops were planted. The crops were harvested. Everyone you ever met looked like you, spoke like you, followed the same religion as you, and wore clothes like you … frankly, it was probably a little boring. Position in society was fixed like a caste system, so you couldn't work toward upward mobility especially. In the end, the one big change from the same old monotonous routine that everyone got to look forward to was … death. The Old Kingdom became Death Oriented. Their religion developed around the Book of the Dead, and was lived in practice more like wizardry. No particular emphasis was placed on morality; "salvation" if you will, in the form of a contented afterlife, was thought to be achieved more through buying charms and mumbling magic incantations than it was in adjusting one's lifestyle. Since nobody from the dead ever came back to contradict popular opinion, it was believed that death held whatever fabulous goodies you could imagine. People lived their lives looking forward to the passage from this world to the next on the double assumption that whatever tedium, pain or disappointment they suffered in this life would be left behind, BUT whatever pleasures they enjoyed could be carried along for the ride into afterlife. That's a pretty good deal; small wonder the Egyptians held death in such high regard.

The catch was that to benefit from this great afterlife program, you had to preserve a physical environment for your soul to inhabit. The Egyptians were more concrete than abstract in their thinking on these matters. Even though they knew the body died, and even though they believed that the soul was now free to come and go, weaving in and out of whatever luxurious paradise they could imagine, they nevertheless held fast to the notion that when the soul required rest, it had to come home to an earthbound residence. The Egyptians went to great lengths to develop their knowledge of chemistry, motivated largely by a burning need to preserve dead bodies so that their souls could come home to nap. The results are still around today in the form of Egyptian mummies, which are a bit spooky in that they look alarmingly life-like with skin and hair, even thousands of years later.

Mummies needed a final resting place. In prehistoric times you will recall that the Lower Egyptians buried Grandpa beneath the floor of his house. During the Old Kingdom this practice was upgraded. They built a brand new house for Grandpa's afterlife; bigger and better than anyplace Gramps lived during his life. In fact, during the Old Kingdom, Egypt was divided down the middle, with the east side of the Nile River reserved for the living (the sun rises in the east, hence it marks beginnings), and the west side of the Nile was reserved exclusively for dead folks (the west hosts the setting sun, or passing on from day to night.) Whole cities for the dead were constructed. Such a place is called a *necropolis* (necro = death / polis = city). An individual "house" found inside a necropolis is called a *mastaba*. **Mastabas** were huge, mesa-shaped mounds made of limestone blocks. They were mostly solid construction, with a burial chamber for the mummy located underground, hence the dead were still buried beneath the floor of the house in a manner of speaking, and inside the structure there was an offering chamber. The offering chamber was a storage room where the deceased was able to pack along all the goodies from the world of the living that he desired to accompany him into the afterlife. This might include everything from beloved pets (also mummified), to food to furniture to pretty much anything you might imagine.

After a few centuries, the pharaohs became disenchanted with mere mastabas for their final resting place. In the rigid social structure of Old Kingdom Egypt, pharaohs were born into royal families at the top of the food chain. The pharaohs had come to believe that not only were they superior people, they were divine - descendants of Osiris and Isis, just like the great god, Horus who was believed to be the first of their line. They served as kings during life, and were promoted to gods in the afterlife. In life they lived in the most elaborate and expensive luxury, yet after they died, their remains were shuttled off to mastaba tract housing … it just didn't seem right. King Zoser was the first pharaoh to finally do something about this gross injustice. He commissioned his architect, Imhotep, to design for him a tomb that was befitting of his elevated status. The result was the stepped **Pyramid of King Zoser**.

The principle behind the stepped pyramid was simple and straightforward: it was a stack of mastabas, starting with a massive, oversized mastaba for a base and successive tiers of smaller mastabas reaching up to the sky. The mountain-like appearance reinforced notions that Zoser was a god, given that gods tend to reside in the sky or at the very least, on top of great mountains. The Pyramid of King Zoser was constructed from huge limestone blocks, like mastabas, and it was solid except for offering chambers inside where the pharaoh had packed away a mountain of wealth to keep him comfortable in the afterlife. The burial chamber was beneath the floor of the pyramid, underground, and along the perimeter of the pyramid there were several shaft graves for members of the pharaoh's family so that their souls might keep him company forever. Imhotep didn't stop with the pyramid, however; he built an entire private necropolis, called *Saqqara* just for Zoser, with the tomb located "downtown" amidst other buildings, most notably a mortuary temple designed to resemble the pharaoh's palace where the high priests might worship the god-king for all eternity.

The most famous of the Egyptian pyramids, built midway through the Old Kingdom time period, are the **Great Pyramids at Giza**. There were three successive pharaohs buried here, Khufu (also known as Cheops), the first and the one who laid out the necropolis plan, Khafre (also known as Chefren), and finally Menkaure (also known as Mycerinus). Giza includes the three pharaonic pyramids, smaller pyramids and mastabas for extended family burial, a mortuary temple adjacent to each big pyramid, a valley temple for each pharaoh, connected by long causeways out to the banks of the Nile, and accessible by boat during flood season so that regular people could visit to worship the god-kings (regular people being otherwise forbidden access to the pharaoh's necropolis), and the great sphinx, a lion-shaped body sporting Khafre's face, provided to remind everyone who they were dealing with over here, and that they'd best behave themselves if they knew what was good for them.

The Great Pyramids at Giza were more sophisticated than Zoser's earlier tribute to himself. For starters, they were enormous. Khufu's pyramid, the largest of the three, was constructed of 2.5 million limestone blocks, each individually weighing anywhere from 2.5 to 150 tons; the structure covers 500,000 square feet and rises 481 feet, or roughly as tall as a 48 story skyscraper, into the air. The pyramids were now smooth-sided, mostly solid structures, and they were completely sheathed in smooth marble, and then plated with electrum – a mixture of gold and silver – such that they gleamed in the arid sun and could be seen for miles. These pyramids were carefully oriented to the points of the compass for reasons not entirely known to us today although theories abound.

Scholars have noted that the relationship of the pyramids to one another appears to mimic a pattern of stars seen in the constellation Orion. The research along this theme began with Robert Bauval in the 1980s when he first noticed the similarity between the alignment of the three pyramids at Giza and the stars in Orion's belt. Presuming this to be a conscious effort on the part of the Old Kingdom pharaohs, he began researching the subject, and has published a number of books and articles since the early 1990s on the subject. Bauval's theory is that the pyramids at Giza were not just tombs, but were also vehicles to assist the kings' souls to fly back to the "First Time," or their origins with the gods. In 1964, Virginia Trimble and Alexander Badawy discovered and published their findings that the great pyramid of Khufu had airshafts pointed directly at Orion when the pyramids were built, and these shafts in turn lead to a secret chamber within the pyramid. Building on the earlier research, Bauval's *Orion Correlation Theory* suggests that the pharaohs prepared their whole life for their trip to the First Time, that is that their soul would project back into space (and time?) to Orion, origins of Osiris and the Egyptian gods. Each king was a living renewal of the covenant between the gods and man; the pharaoh would be born in the flesh in this world, then be reborn with the gods, fully divine himself. Bauval based his studies on many ancient Egyptian texts, including the Book of the Dead and an earlier collection of writings called the Pyramid Texts.

Inside the pyramids there were the required offering chambers containing every imaginable wealth – gold, jewels - as well as big ticket items like yachts and other must-haves for a comfy lifestyle in the next world. There were also lavatories provided for the comfort of the deceased pharaoh, and either real food or at the very least, painted images of food so the soul would remain well fed into eternity. Curiously, at Giza the burial chambers were no longer underground, but were moved up into the pyramid itself, dead center and about a third of the way up from ground level. Perhaps this was to alleviate even the remotest possibility that if the Nile floodplain ever changed that water damage could ever be a threat to the mummy.

Controversy has surrounded the Great Pyramids at Giza since at least the days of the Greeks as to how exactly these monuments were constructed. Hearsay has offered colorful theories that modern man may have discounted long ago, except that we still had problems trying to solve the mystery ourselves. What we have known all along is that they were built by Egyptians, not foreign slaves and not extra-terrestrials either. Although we do not have the building plans or specific information on their techniques, we have payroll information, and what we know for sure is that there was a paid Egyptian labor force. We know how many people were on the payroll and about how long they took to complete the project, which happened to be within the lifetime of the pharaoh to eventually be entombed there. The problem until recently was that even with the benefit of computers, scholars could not make the numbers work. Given what we know about their tools and building knowledge, either they needed more men to complete the projects in 20-40 years, or they needed more time for the limited number of employees on the payrolls we have to do the work.

Recent archaeology seems to be finally putting to rest all the far-fetched theories about the pyramids. Mark Lehner of the Oriental Institute at the University of Chicago has been working for some time in Egypt with Zawi Hawass, Director General of Giza, trying to solve these questions. His team has now discovered a whole support city where workers on the pyramids were housed and fed, barracks-style during the Giza projects. Lehner's theory first recalls that Egypt was well known for having a strong sense of community as well as a profound respect for the pharaohs and for religion. He believes that Egyptians served on the building crews in a manner that might parallel military service to one's country. They would have rotated on and off the project for a period of a few years at a time – long enough to do their duty and pay homage to the king, but not so long as to destroy their real life-long career back home. The work force could have been conscripted or volunteer, and the men may well have been paid in addition to room and board through different payrolls; Lehner assumes the payrolls we have refer to the skeleton crew of highly trained architects and artisans who were career men in the service of the pharaohs' pyramid project. Lehner notes that recently discovered graffiti inscriptions suggest that the men worked in crews or gangs that seem to have had fun names, like the Friends of Khufu Gang, and they appear to have had ongoing friendly competitions to see who could get their job done the fastest and best. Based on Lehner's research model, the updated theory is that 20,000-36,000 men worked on the project at any given time, including both permanent employees and temporary Egyptian workers. We now have the housing, bakeries and other support facilities being excavated to prove these crews were onsite, with all the evidence confirming it was a large Egyptian workforce from start to finish.

Pharaohs, like other Egyptian citizens, had their mummies laid to rest in their tombs. By Zoser's time, however, the pharaohs had become concerned not only about their relative status in afterlife housing accommodations, but also about the security of their soul's survival if something ever happened to their mummy. Any number of perils might attack that security, from eventual decomposition, to something more dramatic like a flood or fire. As insurance against these potential threats, pharaohs began commissioning funerary statues. The statue accompanied the mummy into the tomb, and was on hand to pick up the slack of providing a safe haven for the soul if anything were to happen to the mummy. A good example is the **Funerary Statue of Khafre**, found in his pyramid at Giza. Pharaoh's statue is approximately life-size, because presumably his soul would be the same size as the pharaoh was during his life. The face was a portrait likeness, although an idealized version along the lines of a high school senior picture; funerary statues looked enough like the person to be easily identified by the soul, but were an improved version compared to their probable day-to-day appearance. The body was completely idealized. No need to carry that potbelly and flabby behind into the afterlife! They were made out of a durable material in order to last for eternity; this one is diorite, which is a very hard stone. They were also blocky and solid in appearance, with less interest in making them graceful and realistic, and more interest in keeping the solid block of stone as intact as possible to reduce the possibility of breakage. Further, the pharaoh wears a big hat to reinforce his neck; it would be one thing for his arm to break off, thus amputating an arm from the soul, but having one's head fall off? That would be a disaster! The pharaoh wears an artificial beard – more of a goatee really. The beard was a symbol of supernatural power, acknowledging the pharaoh's elevated rank of god status in the afterlife.

Menkaure and his Wife (Queen Khamerernebty) illustrates the standing variation of pharaonic funerary statues, compared to the seated pose of the Khafre. Like the earlier example, Menkaure is a portrait likeness, and it is made of durable material, in this case, slate. Now look at **Rahotep and Nofret**. Is Rahotep a pharaoh? If you guessed "no," you are right. The first clues you would have are no beard and no hat. Another clue to suggest non-pharaonic position in society is that Rahotep and Nofret are made of limestone instead of the more durable and expensive diorite or slate. In funerary statues, the lower the status, the lesser grade the material. A quick way to tell the difference is to recognize that Khafre and Menkaure were polished stone, while Rahotep and his wife were painted. High quality materials were customarily polished in Egypt while lesser quality materials were painted, rather like how we today would polish an expensive mahogany dining room table, but might choose to paint an inexpensive pine cupboard.

Notice that both Queen Khamerernebty and Nofret are portrayed the same size as their husbands. Would you guess this was regular or irregular? In the case of Rahotep and Nofret, this was conventional. Husband and wife were from the same strata of society, and would therefore have been represented in the same scale. Menkaure was the pharaoh, so in his case, his wife was by necessity a lower station and should have been depicted in a slightly smaller than life-size scale. Menkaure must have thought a lot of his beloved wife. In order to have her rest in peace with the same dignity as himself, he appears to have had both of them created slightly under life-size, assuming Menkaure was not remarkably shorter than his father, Khafre. This sort of "humanizing" of the pharaoh is very rare in the Old Kingdom.

Our last sample of Old Kingdom funerary statues is the **Seated Scribe**. Predictably it is made of painted limestone, and the figure does not wear a hat or a beard. From looking at the figures of Rahotep and the scribe, can you tell which one is the more important person in society? If you guessed Rahotep, you are right. Notice how his body and face are more idealized than the scribe. The more real something looks, the less important it is. While the scribe would have been a very important member of the court,

Rahotep may have been Khafre's brother (Menkaure's uncle), or at least he was related to the royal family. Rahotep and Nofret are also about the same scale as Menkaure and his wife, while the scribe was considerably under life size. His soul was presumably life-size the same as royalty, but remember, in Egyptian art since the days of Narmer, the pharaoh was always represented the biggest because he was the most important person, and everyone else was smaller according to his or her station in society. In the case of funerary statues, this meant that while the pharaoh got to have a perfect fit for his soul, lesser persons were obliged to be slightly cramped in smaller quarters in their afterlives so as not to insult the pharaoh, or presume too much status for themselves. Better to have a pair of shoes a size too small rather than to have no shoes at all. Finally, notice how both Rahotep and the scribe look tan, while Nofret seems alabaster pale. This convention of painting men dark and women white was popular throughout the ancient world, perhaps suggesting that men were virile and took on life outdoors while women were delicate and to be maintained indoors. It in no way represents different races.

Early Mesopotamia

Sumerian *c. 3800 - 2300 BC*

What was happening in Mesopotamia during the Old Kingdom in Egypt? Sometime around 3800 BC, seemingly out of the blue the old, established Neolithic farming communities were superseded by a new group of people who migrated from somewhere further east into the Mesopotamia region. These newcomers were the Sumerians. We don't know for sure where they originally called home. Scholars believe they came from the coastal areas of the Caspian Sea to deep in Persia or even further east than that. One thing is certain though; they did not so much evolve out of the indigenous population already in Mesopotamia as plant themselves on top of the locals, arriving as a fully developed nation of people with at least the foundations for a sophisticated written language called *cuneiform* already in place.

Society during the Sumerian period agriculture-based; they settled in the fertile farmlands of southern Mesopotamia. Farming in Mesopotamia was not as predictable as Egypt where the Nile conveniently flooded regularly to feed the soil. In Mesopotamia, there were frequent droughts that made irrigation necessary, and the flip side of the coin was that sometimes violent storms would drown crops with too much water. Life offered less stability here. As time went on, the Sumerians also developed extensive trade and commerce both by land with neighboring city-states to the north for stone and wood, and by sea in the Mediterranean for tin and copper. In this regard they differed from the Old Kingdom Egyptians who were rich in natural resources and did not feel the necessity to venture outside their own nation to meet their needs. **Cylinder Seals** were used to create small clay tablets that could be used in much the same way we might have an invoice or packing slip today. The cylinder was made of a hard material which was *incised* (cut) with a design usually showing people or animals. When the cylinder was rolled across a soft clay surface, it created a relief impression that was distinctive, and each *seal* would look the same as any other rolled from the same cylinder, rather like a company logo today, or letterhead stationery that identifies who sent the package. These small tablets were packaged with goods in trade, or used to sign documents or mark storage containers.

Unlike the Egyptians who formed a unified nation ruled by god-kings, the Sumerians built substantial city-states, which were largely autonomous and self-ruled through a limited democracy. While society was largely governed by the priestly class, other less important positions were established by popular consensus among the people rather than by appointment from a supreme ruler. Sumerian citizens were among the most devoutly religious anywhere in the ancient world. They were *polytheistic*, meaning that they worshipped many gods, with each city-state placing greater emphasis on one or another according to its own local customs. Most of their gods held identities connected to nature: *Anu*, god of the sky, *Bel*, creator and ruler of earth, *Sin*, the moon god, *Shamash*, the sun god, and *Ishtar*, goddess of love, fertility and later associated with battle as well. They believed that man was created to serve the gods. All good things were perceived as gifts from the gods, and bad things were seen as punishment for sin, a concept rather foreign to the Old Kingdom Egyptians.

Sumerian cities were designed with a particular urban-planning program that was both practical and helped to maintain a sense of focus within the community. Their cities were designed around an enormous building called a ziggurat set in the heart of downtown. Consider the **Ziggurat at Ur** as one of just a few surviving examples. Ur was a city that developed late in Sumerian culture, reaching a population of about 24,000, and it was the home of Abraham of Old Testament fame. Even as a very late example, notice what poor condition this structure is in today. Southern Mesopotamia was not blessed with stone quarries, and as a result, builders relied on mud bricks as their staple construction material. Unfortunately, mud brick erodes badly over time, and even immense, solid structures like ziggurats have gradually wasted away into so much sand and dust. The ziggurat was created to be a towering man-made mountain, stepped toward the heavens with massive ramps of stairs leading up to a rather modestly scaled chamber at the pinnacle of the structure. The room at the top was the town temple, high above the city where the gods lived. Only the priests customarily went there, while ordinary citizens remained earthbound, yet in a state of perpetual awe and respect for the gods. There is no evidence that the Sumerians practiced a form of worship requiring participation in formal services like we might think of today; indeed their temples were not designed to accommodate indoor worship.

The base of the ziggurat was the equivalent of the town square, with markets, trade, and administrative activities. Presumably education was also conducted there. The residential village, often a walled community, surrounded the ziggurat, and the farmlands formed an insulating doughnut beyond the city limits around the people's homes. The layout was quite practical in a variety of ways. First, the ziggurat was the central focal point for everyone in the city. It was easily accessible to all the citizens, which made good sense when you recall that all basic services for the community were housed at the base of the ziggurat. It also kept Sumerian citizens focused on the gods since the temple on top could be easily seen from any point in the city. Finally, Sumerian cities were designed to be easily defended. If invaders approached a city, they would be seen from miles away. Sumerian citizens could aggressively defend their turf by engaging the enemy before he even reached the farmland. Failing that, Sumerians could try to repel their enemies in the fields while sparing their homes, and in the worst case scenario, fight in the streets of their city before an enemy would stand any chance of getting to the ziggurat in the city center. Planning for defense was part of life in Mesopotamia. Whereas Egypt had natural defense boundaries with jungles to the south, deserts east and west, and the sea to the north, Mesopotamia was wide open, and it was easy for anybody who wanted what you had to attack your city and try to take it.

Sumerians were profoundly dedicated to their religion, yet we find no evidence of group worship. How then, did they practice their religion? In addition to presumably modifying their personal behavior to reflect the precepts of their faith, Sumerians were expected to live every moment of their lives from birth to death in a state of constant prayer and devotion to the gods. To them, the notion that a couple hours a week at church would do the trick would have seemed altogether inadequate. The problem is, praying 24/7 makes it difficult to survive in a human world. Even taking time off to sleep would have been considered sacrilegious, much less time off to eat, go to the bathroom or wash clothes, work in the field or go to school. In order to practice the faith flawlessly, while also managing to get along in day-to-day life in the real world, the Sumerians invented **Votive Figures** to practice the faith for them.

Votive Figures were small statues designed to stay in the temple praying on behalf of their owners around the clock day in, day out... year after year. Votive figures could be as small as the Venus of Willendorf, or for a really important person like a priest, as much as 30" tall. Many were made of clay as that was locally available and inexpensive, although some of the more impressive figures were made of imported stone, and were therefore more expensive so presumably owned by rich folks or important officials. Each person was probably given a votive figure at birth, and the figure stayed in the temple to stand in for that individual all his or her life. Many of these figures have been dug up in what appear to be large dumps, suggesting that perhaps the priests continued to present new figures onto shelves inside the temple until the temple was overflowing, at which point some sort of ceremonial housecleaning took place where all the old statues were chucked (many probably there left over from people who were long dead anyway), and new ones were installed for everyone still around and in need of this ongoing vigil up at the temple.

Votive Figures have uniform features created from carved cylinders rather than rectangular blocks like the Egyptians preferred. They were generic, like Barbie and Ken dolls rather than portrait likenesses of real people. The male figures were bearded and bare-chested with long skirts, while the females did not have beards (reassuring...) and their skirts included a bodice drape covering the shoulder. Most importantly, they all have enormous, over-sized eyes. The artists may have used pedestrian materials like ordinary clay to make the figure, but the eyes were treated as special, often being made of inlaid shells with dark limestone pupils. The eyes were perceived as "windows to the soul" and it was believed that the figures used their immense, unblinking eyes to maintain constant communication with the gods through prayer.

In addition to their preoccupation with religion, the Sumerians were accomplished musicians and storytellers. The **Bull Lyre** pays tribute to both. It is a small harp found in a tomb in the ancient city of Ur, made of wood, with inlaid gold, lapis lazuli and shell decoration on the sound box. The images are depicted in registers like we saw in the Palette of Narmer, and they seem to illustrate scenes from the most famous tale handed down by the Sumerians, the *Epic of Gilgamesh*. Amazingly, as we saw in prehistoric societies, this 3,000 line poem was passed down by oral tradition through the generations for centuries before it was ever written down. In fact, this small harp was created nearly 700 years before the poem was first written down.

Akkadian *c. 2300- 2150 BC*

The Sumerians from all accounts were basically a peaceful people. They lived in harmony and respect with their neighbors, and while they were perfectly capable of defending what was theirs when need be, they do not appear to have been unnecessarily aggressive toward others. In the end, they were toppled by a more belligerent people who lived among them: citizens of neighboring city-states known today as the Akkadians. We don't know much about the early history of the Akkadians, although many scholars believe they came from somewhere in the Arabian Peninsula and migrated over toward southern Mesopotamia (Iraq today). By the time they waged war on the Sumerians, the Akkadians had adopted much of the Sumerian culture while living side-by-side in southern Mesopotamia. They were originally from different stock, however, as the majority of the Akkadian gene pool came from Semitic tribes, and they spoke a different language from the Sumerians.

The Akkadian period began sometime around 2300 BC when the city-state of Akkad came under the rule of a despot named Sargon, and unlike the more mild-mannered, egalitarian and orderly Sumerians, Sargon wanted power. It's no surprise then that Sargon conquered his Sumerian neighbors. He introduced the idea of royal power, which up until this time was unknown in this part of the world, and he expected everyone to toady up to him rather than show allegiance to the abstract concept of the city-state. His son and then grandson followed in his footsteps, the grandson, Naram-Sin, being the bossiest of the bunch. Naram-Sin insisted that all his governors serving in captured cities were his slaves, and he referred to himself as "King of the Four Quarters," which is to say, the supreme ruler of earth.

Naram-Sin's ego is memorialized in the **Victory Stele of Naram-Sin**. It is a large tablet (about 6' 6" tall) with a relief carving showing Naram-Sin climbing a mountain, trampling over the heads and bodies of others as he goes. At the top, he is greeted by two gods, presumably Shamash the great sun god, and either Sin, god of the moon or Ishtar, now exercising her role as the goddess of battle and war. Naram-Sin is depicted taller than everyone else, which was a popular convention in Mesopotamia the same as Egypt as a way to pay homage to the most important person in the scene.

The villainous domination of Akkad was short-lived. Perhaps in an act of divine retribution for their own reign of terror, the Akkadians were overrun by hordes of barbarian invaders flooding down from the mountain regions nearby, and this in turn opened a window of opportunity for the Sumerians to collect their wits and reassert themselves as the regional culture of choice in southern Mesopotamia. Ur, where the great ziggurat we considered earlier was located, became the capital city during the waning days of Sumerian civilization, sometimes dubbed the "neo-Sumerian" period. The region was soon invaded again, and the brief experiment with central government fell by the wayside, with every city in southern Mesopotamia once again establishing itself as an autonomous city-state. One of these many independent city-states was Babylon, which in time would rise to become the new leader in the region.

Babylonian *c. 1900 – 1600 BC*

Babylon, like Sumer, Ur, Akkad and other city-states in southern Mesopotamia was just one of many similar towns with (by this time) a gene pool mix of old Sumerian stock, the blood of Semitic tribes from the region and presumably whatever people were left over from prehistoric times who had long since assimilated into the local culture. Like the others, Babylon had been completely autonomous until the rise of an uncommonly good administrator named Hammurabi. Hammurabi was perhaps the most famous king from all of Mesopotamia in ancient times, remembered especially for his codified laws which took the mishmash of confusing, disorganized and sometimes even conflicting laws and customs of the peoples of that region and established instead an organized and clearly spelled-out codification of laws by which all could live in a civilized world. Have you heard the expression an eye for an eye and a tooth for a tooth? That is straight out of the Hammurabi Code. In fact, much of the thinking and attitude found in Hammurabi's Code was centuries later reiterated in the Laws of Moses. Hammurabi was much respected, and he elevated Babylon to become the new capital of southern Mesopotamia, filling the role established however briefly by the former great city of Ur a couple hundred years earlier.

The **Stele of Hammurabi** is the most famous example of Babylonian art. It is quite large, standing over 7' tall with the complete code of the law spelled out for all to read. The stele is made out of sturdy basalt, which would have been expensive, especially such a large chunk of rock that hard, in this region without natural quarries available. Obviously it was important to create the stele large enough to include all the laws everyone was expected to know, and made to last over time lest people start to forget right from wrong. At the top of the stele, there is a relief carving of Hammurabi receiving the code of law from a representative of the gods; it seems to be Shamash the sun god, judging by the flames of the sun that shoot out from his shoulders.

Babylon ruled southern Mesopotamia until sometime around 1600 BC, when the region was invaded by the Hittites, a particularly vicious people hailing from Anatolia, which corresponds roughly to modern-day Turkey. After these marauders sacked Babylon, they mowed their way through Egyptian territory too, and generally made a nuisance of themselves wherever they went. With no power center left in the southern realms of Mesopotamia, the door was now opened for domination from the north.

Later Egypt

New Kingdom *c. 1500-1000 BC*

Meanwhile, what was happening back in Egypt? The Old Kingdom ended around 2200 BC, not long after the fall of the Sumerians to the Akkadians. The upper classes in Egypt, which controlled the agriculture based economy, had become increasingly disenchanted that they held no real power. Eventually they challenged the pharaohs' supreme authority to grab power for themselves. With the crumbling of the central government in Egypt came a weaker national image on the world scene, and the result was waves of invasion coming out of Mesopotamia, and eventual domination under the Hyksos. The Hyksos knew how to use the wheel, which the Old Kingdom for all their accomplishments had yet to discover, and they were from a land where war was common, producing skilled and determined armies. They had speedy chariots and sophisticated crossbows. The Egyptians were completely unprepared to defend themselves against such a military giant, and while their civilization limped along, for several centuries Egyptian society was in trouble compared to the good old days. The borders which had previously insulated Egypt from outside influence became porous, allowing assorted Mesopotamians of various ethnic heritages to wander in and set up housekeeping. It was during the Hyksos occupation that the Old Testament hero Joseph, with his coat of many colors, was brought in as a slave and over time became the right hand man of a (Hyksos?) pharaoh.

The New Kingdom was born around 1500 BC, and lasted until about 1000 BC (round dates). It was a period that produced some of the most fascinating political personalities found in history. One of the earliest and most interesting pharaohs was **Hatshepsut**. The small statue that survives is not a funerary statue, which is long gone. Perhaps because it is not, it is more recognizable as the figure of a young woman. Hatshepsut was the first female pharaoh of Egypt. She was the daughter of one of several of the weakened pharaohs during the transition from the turmoil of the Middle Kingdom, Thutmose I and his royal wife, Queen Ahmose. By the way, mom was always the one who carried the royal lineage in Egypt, although on the surface of things the women were certainly not in charge. In the case of Hatshepsut's pedigree, some evidence suggests that her father was an illegitimate heir to the throne, which would have made his marriage to Ahmose especially critical. How exactly their daughter Hatshepsut came to rule is not entirely clear since the concept of a female pharaoh was unprecedented, and Egypt certainly didn't have a track record for bucking the status quo when it came to tradition.

Some suggest that her father, Thutmose I, raised her to equal power to himself in the waning years of his reign. This is possible, given that Hatshepsut was only 15 when her father died, and she was the only surviving child of his marriage to Queen Ahmose. This made her the only heir with royal blood, even if she was a girl. She had a 12 year-old half brother, Thutmose II who was illegitimate and apparently had some physical handicap and may also have been retarded. In any event, it seems that Hatshepsut and Thutmose II may have been married to keep things kosher with him being given the official title of pharaoh, but Hatshepsut was the one running affairs of state while her kid half-brother was kept out of the public eye. Thutmose II died four years later. Enter Thutmose III. This could have been yet another illegitimate child of her father, or it may have been a child born to Hatshepsut (by Thutmose II? By somebody else?), we don't really know, but this child was now appointed heir to the throne with Hatshepsut as his regent running things until he came of age. Apparently over the next few years Hatshepsut eased herself into the title of full pharaoh, with the backing the royal priesthood it seems. That's one version of Hatshepsut's story.

Others have suggested that Hatshepsut yearned for power, but that as a female she had difficulty persuading her family to take her seriously. It is possible that after her father died, she had a hand in the demise of Thutmose II in order to establish herself as pharaoh. Regardless of how she got to power, once Hatshepsut seized control of Egypt, she was smart enough to realize that while she may hold the power, the Egyptian people would probably not accept being ruled by a queen. She concocted a myth about her mother conceiving wee Hatshepsut during an extramarital visit from the great god, Amon, but even that was not likely to put her squarely in the good graces of the public. Therefore, she simply had herself legally declared male, and ruled as king! She dressed in men's attire in public, and wore the popular fake beard associated with pharaohs to prove her point.

Hatshepsut was successful where her predecessors had failed. She whipped Egypt back into shape without resorting to tyranny, and after restoring the strong central government, she opened Egypt to broad international trade. One important question is when exactly the Hyksos departed Egypt, since the New Kingdom was clearly out from under Mesopotamian occupation by the time Hatshepsut rose to glory. Many scholars agree that they got the heave ho around 1550 BC after they lost a decisive battle at Tanis and were driven out of the country. That said, during her reign, Hatshepsut spent a lot of money having temples restored, and at one of them there is an inscription where she bragged about kicking the Hyksos out of Egypt herself. The problem is the dating, given that Hatshepsut came to power in 1473 BC, about 80 years after the Hyksos were presumably already gone if we accept that the Battle at Tanis brought on their demise, and we assume that the date on Tanis is correct. One way or the other, Hatshepsut set forth to visit Egypt's neighbors under a policy of peace and prosperity, sometimes leading the excursion herself (her successful expedition to Punt was quite famous), or sending emissaries to establish trade agreements.

She ruled for 22 years, giving birth to two daughters, one of whom she apparently groomed to succeed her. Her eldest daughter was married to Thutmose III, as would be the custom to keep those nasty commoner cooties out of the royal bloodline. But when Thutmose III reached his majority, he was keen to take control of the country away from Hatshepsut whom he believed had stolen his birthright. When he staged his political coup, she mysteriously disappeared without a trace. Thutmose III was less charitable toward other nations, and reversed Mom's /Sissy's friendly policies. During his reign, Egypt saw wars and more wars, with Thutmose III taking particular delight in making slaves of other nations, especially throughout Mesopotamia. He hated Hatshepsut, and tried to eradicate her memory by destroying many public monuments, but he never found one site in particular … the site where that little statue was found.

Hatshepsut had planned to be buried in the Valley of the Kings in a secret rock-cut grave, although the tomb prepared for her was apparently never used. By the fall of the Old Kingdom, pyramids had already become obsolete. The irony was that for as much as the grand tombs celebrating the immortality of the god-king were huge ego boosts to the ruling class, they quickly served to defeat the presumed immortality they were designed to enhance. Why? Because they were like massive advertisements to the public showing where untold treasure was located. Every single pyramid was ransacked within a few years of the pharaoh's burial. Thieves would find the offering chambers and steal all the goodies, such that the pharaoh would be broke in his afterlife instead of rolling in luxury. To make matters worse, clever thieves (did stupid ones ever figure out how to bypass the mazes to get to the treasure?) knew that the pharaoh was now a god … a god who would live forever *as long as his soul had a resting place*. Common sense would suggest that the best way to finish the job would be to destroy the mummy (and statue if possible) before departing so the god-king couldn't make problems for you later. It was bad enough for the pharaoh to have his wealth stolen, but to have his afterlife ended … now that really is going too far.

Not only were New Kingdom pharaohs buried in secret graves, but they built their mortuary temples far away from their graves so as to avoid tipping off robbers. Hatshepsut's chief architect, Senmut, designed the **Mortuary Temple of Hatshepsut**, built at Deir-el-Bahari, Egypt. In fact, Senmut appears to have been not only Hatshepsut's architect, but also her lover, primary advisor, and frequent foreign ambassador. The mortuary temple is mostly a rock-cut structure, subtractive architecture dug out of the side of a natural cliff. The *façade*, or face (front entrance) of the building is post and lintel design. Inside there were assorted large halls and smaller chapels. During the New Kingdom, mortuary temples were built during the lifetime of the pharaoh to be used privately for his (or her) private worship, then after the pharaoh died the temple would be opened to the public to come pay homage to the god-king. At this point they became busy, both with worshipping admirers of the late pharaoh and also tourists as they were designed to include parks suitable for public recreation. Senmut secretly built his eventual final resting place beneath the floor of the Mortuary Temple of Hatshepsut. This is where the statue of Hatshepsut was found, perhaps provided for the benefit of conjugal visits in the afterlife. Much as Thutmose III tried to find Senmut's tomb so it could be destroyed, it never occurred to him to look under the floor of Hatshepsut's temple. In many ways it would be the last place Senmut should have considered. For starters, the whole point of separating the mortuary temples from burial sites was to protect the secrecy of the tomb locations. Beyond that, the building was so open to the public that one might consider security to be constantly compromised – rather like burying treasure at a busy airport today. It is an ironic twist of history that Senmut's "badly" located tomb turned out to be the most secure storage of information about Hatshepsut, as her successor discovered and desecrated nearly everything else.

A couple generations after Hatshepsut, another interesting pharaoh came on the scene. Amenhotep IV, who renamed himself Akhenaten, became pharaoh in 1380 BC. Akhenaten was like no other pharaoh before him. He is best remembered as the heretic king who abolished the old pantheon of Egyptian gods (or tried to), and introduced *monotheism* to Egypt. His one god was Aten: the great spirit of the universe and great creator who had no form but could be witnessed in the sun. Akhenaten proposed that he had been sent from this divine god - the son of god – to bring Egypt the good news. This development rendered the royal priesthood redundant as their services were not needed any longer so long as the son of god was on hand to divine the true religion. As king, Akhenaten was soft-spoken and gentle, inclined more to peace, poetry and quiet contemplation than the sort of grand heroics of his forefathers. Akhenaten was wildly popular with the common man, but despised by the priesthood for obvious reasons.

As you consider the statue of **Akhenaten**, notice how different he appears when compared to other pharaohs. His facial features are elongated, almost rubbery, and his body appears quite effeminate with narrow shoulders and broad, curvy hips. Clearly he is not being represented according to the idealized standards of the past, and if he is not shown as idealized, then we must presume that the art of his reign was more realistic. If this was how Akhenaten really looked, then he was one peculiar looking fellow! Many scholars have observed this, and some have suggested that Akhenaten may have suffered from a genetic disorder called Klinefelter syndrome. Klinefelter syndrome is when the individual has an extra chromosome such that instead of being XX (female) or XY (male), the child is born XXY. Klinefelter babies seem like normal male infants at birth. As they develop, the first clue that something is wrong comes when it is discovered that the child is mentally slow; degrees of mental retardation vary, as they might with other chromosome anomalies like the more common Down syndrome. As time passes, though, the real problems set in, and at puberty the child develops secondary female, not male, characteristics (breasts and hips instead of beards and broad shoulders). Finally, Klinefelter individuals are sterile.

So if Akhenaten had Klinefelter syndrome (remember, it is a theory, not proven fact), then who ran the show during his reign? Enter Nefertiti, his exquisitely beautiful wife, who, by the way, was also his sister. It had been the custom since Old Kingdom days for pharaohs to marry their sisters in an effort to keep the divine bloodline pure. We understand today what havoc inbreeding causes to a gene pool, but evidently in Egypt this was either not known, or assumed to not apply to the "gods." It may be no accident that **Nefertiti** is such a famous visage in Egyptian history, given that she was never a pharaoh herself. IF Akhenaten had Klinefelters, then presumably Nefertiti would have known from the time she was a girl that the job of protecting her brother, and by extension the rule of her family name, would fall to her. Monotheism, with the provision that her brother was the son of the only true god, may have been Nefertiti's idea. After all, why would the son of god be expected to look and behave like any Joe Lunchbucket off the street? Why shouldn't he be like no other human being you had ever seen before? Akhenaten could only be referenced against himself.

Nefertiti had seven daughters. Demonstrating that Akhenaten was a "regular guy" in terms of virility may have come in handy if there were rumors circulating about the pharaoh being unfit to rule. Akhenaten may or may not have biologically fathered the children (certainly not if he had Klinefelters), but he was a loving and doting husband and father regardless. He and Nefertiti were extremely close; he did not revel in concubines like his predecessors (in fact, he deplored immorality), and he was open in his affections toward his family both in public as well as private, as seen in an **Amarna Relief** (Tel el-Amarna was the name of the palace city where Akhenaten and Nefertiti lived, and art from that district is referred to as "*Amarna*" style art). In the carved relief, Akhenaten sits on the left, offering his young daughter a big kiss. Nefertiti is on the right, with one child on her lap, and another being cuddled on mommy's shoulder. The disk above represents Aten, who is shown blessing the royal family with rays ending in little hands. This relief carving differs from the much earlier Palette of Narmer in a significant way (beyond the nature of the subject matter), in that written language is being used to tell the story such that one illustration can be employed with additional written text. Egyptian written language is called *hieroglyphics*, and is seen here as pictograph-shaped images in oval frames called *cartouches*. Despite the visual similarity between pictographs and hieroglyphics, the latter was a phonics-based language with each of the images representing a sound, not the subject of the image itself.

Significantly, there were no sons among Akhenaten's children. IF Akhenaten had Klinefelters, there may have been other boys in the family just like him such that the family determined they couldn't afford to wait and see if a male heir were healthy and normal. By only having daughters (or destroying any male babies so that only the girls survived), a male heir would have to be married into the family. Akhenaten's reign, while promoting peace and harmony, brought destruction to the Egyptian empire of power. Akhenaten was not inclined to support military actions to enslave his neighbors, and as a result, they wriggled out from under Egyptian domination. The money coming in from foreign taxes dwindled as the possessions broke free of Egyptian control, and Akhenaten left behind a bankrupted nation. He was only 30 when he died, of natural causes as far as we know. A postscript of sorts is a rare **Amarna Bust** from Akhenaten's reign. Notice how the skull is distended. It became fashionable at this time to bind babies' heads such that they grew into a deformed cone-head shape. IF Akhenaten had Klinefelters, his skull would have been malformed as this is characteristic of the disorder; it is curious that during his reign only, not before and not after, it became a fad in Egypt for parents to deform their babies' skulls to resemble Klinefelters. Sculptures like this one help to confirm the probability of Akhenaten's secret.

After Akhenaten, Tutankhamun came to the throne. Despite his fame today, in fact King Tut was a nobody. He was around nine years old when he was married to Akhenaten's daughter, Ankhesenpaaten (who was only slightly older than her young husband) and through marriage he became pharaoh. During most of his reign Tutankhamun was too young to run the country, so the task fell to two high officials at court, Ay (who may actually have been his young wife's grandfather) and Horemheb who was commander in chief of the Egyptian army. The young king and queen time tried to appease a hostile, displaced priesthood by reverting Egypt back to her old pantheon of gods, thereby reinstating priests to their old positions of importance and authority. All the same, Tutankhamun died in his late teens; quite possibly he was assassinated by those close enough to the royal family to strongly suspect that there was something wrong with the family line. He was secretly buried in great haste to protect his tomb from vandalism. Unlike other pharaohs' tombs that were ransacked shortly after burial, Tut's was not discovered until the 1920's disclosing the vast wealth with which pharaohs were packed off to the next world. The **Gold Mask of Tutankhamun** was originally placed over the face of his mummy so his soul would recognize the handsome young king forever. Presumably all pharaohs were entombed with similar insurance to guarantee that each soul could always find its own body.

The last great pharaoh of the New Kingdom was Rameses II, who ruled for 90 years and who left no fewer than 100 sons and 50 daughters by his assorted wives (some of whom were incestuously recycled daughters) to carry on the family line. He rebuilt the empire and made slaves of Egypt's neighbors, among them the Jews from Palestine. Rameses II is believed to have been the pharaoh during the days of Moses and the great Exodus of the Hebrew people back to their promised land. The pharaoh undertook massive building campaigns, among them a great mortuary temple to honor himself. The **Mortuary Temple of Rameses II**, located at Abu-Simbel was Rameses' personal temple for worship, later opened to the public as was the custom during the New Kingdom. It is rock-cut, with the old post and lintel façade seen on Hatshepsut's temple replaced with enormous statues of Rameses (not to be confused with funerary statues which are found in tombs) cut out of the living rock.

Like Hatshepsut, Rameses placed great emphasis on building and restoring temples to the gods, all of which followed a basic Egyptian *temple plan*. These could be constructed on a modest scale, or blown up to heroic proportions depending on the budget and labor force. Usually the temple would be approached along an avenue lined with small sphinxes or comparable statues to impress upon the citizen that this was a special district. The façade of the temple was a *pylon*, or massive gate. Ordinary people were not welcome beyond the pylon. Inside, there was a large courtyard, where the upper echelons of society congregated during religious festivals. From the courtyard, one entered the ***hypostyle hall***. Only the pharaoh and priests were permitted into this enclosed area. One stepped up to a grand platform, and the ceiling was painted to resemble the heavens full of stars. The structure was post and lintel in design, with the uprights being large, lavishly painted columns forming a sort of forest in which the priests and pharaoh could confer about important matters. The columns in the central section of this great hall were taller than those lining the perimeter, allowing for a row of grated "windows" called a *clerestory* above the outer columns. Finally, the hypostyle hall led to the *sanctuary*, which was the holy place where the statue of the deity was kept. The floors of the sanctuary were elevated from the hall, and the ceiling dropped such that the effect was akin to entering a sort of secret womb. Normally the sanctuary was reserved for the priestly class only. Their job was to attend the god, and of course, interpret oracles of wisdom, which the priests could then use for leverage to maintain their control over even the pharaoh himself. The Egyptians, with their very physical approach to life and death, believed that the statues ate like real people, so the best food was sent to the temple, often while the general population went hungry. And whom do you suppose ate the food? The priests were responsible for dressing the statue daily, and on special holidays, the priests would bring the statue-deity out in all its regalia to be paraded around so that regular citizens could pay their proper respects.

You may recall that the Babylonians fell around 1600 to the Hittites, who hailed originally from Anatolia (Asia Minor). Well the Hittites were apparently keen to control all of Mesopotamia, because they had been bumping up against the Egyptian territories as well since the days when Thutmose III took over Syria in his bid to muscle in on Mesopotamia himself. These on again off again battles continued until the days of Rameses II when following a huge battle in 1276 BC, the Egyptians and Hittites negotiated and signed what is often believed to be the first peace treaty in history. One of the primary motivations for the treaty was that a new civilization was rising in Mesopotamia that posed a threat to everyone else in the region: the Assyrians.

Later Mesopotamia

Assyrian *c. 900- 612 BC*

The Mesopotamian societies we have looked at so far was from the south. Further north there were also numerous city-states… perhaps not as culturally developed as those in the south in the early days, but engaged in their own power struggles to and fro just the same. They had abundant rock quarries in the north, so cities were usually encased by fabulously massive stone walls. This was Assyrian country. The Assyrians were a Semitic people closely related to the old Akkadians who toppled the Sumerians over a thousand years earlier. In fact, the Assyrians had been in northern Mesopotamia since that time also (c.2400 BC), but aside from the quick rise and fall of the Akkadian period under Sargon and his successors, nobody heard too much from their relatives up north for quite awhile.

Around 1365 BC, during Akhenaten's tenure of weak influence abroad, the Assyrians set about creating an empire for themselves as the Akkadians had done earlier. It only lasted until approximately 1248 BC, but it was enough to get the attention of their neighbors from across Mesopotamia to Egypt; remember Rameses' II decision to quit fighting the Hittites and negotiate a peaceful alliance instead? Assyria was the reason. The Akkadian conquests around 2300 BC and the early Assyrian power trip around 1300 BC were mere dress rehearsals for their real quest for power which began around 900 BC and lasted until their defeat in 612 BC. The Assyrians were brutal, power-hungry savages who ripped their way across northern Mesopotamia, and then, finding Babylon weakened after the Hittite invasions, the Assyrians washed their way across the south displacing other authority and culture to dominate the entire Middle East under a cruel and merciless military dictatorship. They successfully quelled revolts by forcing conquered populations to migrate to new territories, mixing up nationalities into a disoriented mish-mash of lost cultural traditions. There were three major Assyrian centers of power as military command centers and capitals of political power: Nimrud, Khorsabad, and Nineveh. The atrocities committed against humanity by the Assyrians would rival anything the world has seen since. Put mildly, they were NOT very nice people.

Consider the **Reconstruction Drawing of the Citadel of Sargon II at Khorsabad**. This was one of the palace cities. First, it was a citadel surrounded by thick walls to keep enemies out (as if anyone from the south were going to take them on). The city interior measured about a square mile, and the palace took up about 25 acres of that, reminding everyone else in town that Sargon II was an awesome king to be admired… and feared. The palace was raised up on a huge platform above the rest of the city – some 50 feet in the air (5 stories above ground level) which both elevated the king's status and also made it that much easier to defend his sovereignty against any malcontent who might be stupid enough to pick a fight with the king. There was also a huge ziggurat adjacent to the king's palace, seven stages high with each of the seven stages being two stories tall, and each story was painted a different brilliant color creating a visual spectacle far exceeding anything seen in the south up until this point. Besides, it was made of stone – built to outlast all those puny ziggurats made of lousy old mud brick in southern Mesopotamia.

The entrance to the palace was guarded by **Winged Human-Headed Bulls**, presumably portrait likenesses of the king attached to weird monster bodies that resemble massive bulls (often associated with power and fertility) and sporting eagle wings. It would seem reasonable to guess that these monsters were designed to scare off any would-be intruders, and to reinforce paralyzing fear of the king's power. It is interesting that while from the front, these monsters might give the illusion of being freestanding statues (and colossal statues at that – nearly 14' tall), but in reality they are glorified relief carvings. It is curious that a nation swimming in abundant stone quarries never developed a talent for freestanding sculpture. Each figure appears to be standing squarely on all fours when seen from the front, but from the side, an additional leg is introduced to make the monster assume a walking stance.

Much of the art associated with the Assyrian empire is relief carvings found in the various palace complexes. An example is **Ashurnasirpal Hunting Lions**. In this relief sculpture the king is seen hunting lions, a popular sport and one that would impress a spectator that the king was a man of such immense power that even wild lions were no match for him. Other hunting scenes depict Assyrian kings hunting people, shooting them full of arrows and crushing them beneath the wheels of their chariots like so much insignificant litter along life's path. Small wonder the Assyrians were both feared and hated by all who knew them. It was only a matter of time before somebody somewhere would come along and do whatever it took to eliminate these vile aggressors. Ashurnasirpal was the last of the great Assyrian monarchs, and while he was associated with great cruelty, he was also responsible for assembling a great library of Mesopotamian tablets and literature. After he died in 626 BC the empire began to crumble. To the south, the Babylonians had long been adversaries of the Assyrian / Akkadian people. With Assyria in a weakened state, Babylon joined forces with the Medes from Persia; they marched on Nineveh and burned it to the ground.

Neo-Babylon *625-538 BC*

The Assyrians didn't go away overnight, but their influence over southern Mesopotamia was broken. Babylon rose very briefly to power once again in the south, and this time around it was not so much a period of restraint, law and order as it had been under Hammurabi, as it was a time of glamour and exotic culture. The grand pooh-bah of this generation was King Nebuchadnezzar, a flamboyant fellow whose reign is recorded in some detail in the Old Testament Book of Daniel. Babylon was refashioned into a gorgeous city of fabulous architecture so marvelous it was considered one of the great wonders of the ancient world. They had the ziggurat to beat all ziggurats – known to us today by way of the Hebrews as the great Tower of Babel. It was in fact a ziggurat dedicated to their god Bel, creator and ruler of earth. It was magnificent! The ramp of stairs wound around the rising tiers, eight in all, complete with resting places for the faithful (or tourists) with seating provided along the way up, and the temple at the top was much larger than usual with a exquisite throne where they claimed the god came down from heaven to hold audiences in person and a massive couch where he purportedly slept. There were very grand, solid brass gates at the entry to the ziggurat, and the ziggurat complex was adorned with the spectacular "hanging gardens" of Babylon, which were evidently unsurpassed for their beauty. All in all, it was an experience to behold.

Most of the extraordinary treasures from Babylon are of course long gone, but we do still have a beautiful gate that marked the entrance to the temple district, called the **Ishtar Gate**. It is now completely restored and reconstructed in a museum setting in Berlin. It was made of beautiful blue glazed brick, and originally was the focus of elaborate processions on the way to the ziggurat. It should be noticed that the Babylonians were familiar with the arch, as seen here. In fact, Mesopotamian architects often employed the arch instead of post and lintel design in their architecture. It should be understood however, that while Mesopotamian architects figured out how to build arches, they did not fully understand the engineering capacity of the arch. It would be the

Romans, centuries later, who would rediscover the arch, and figure out how to use it to take architecture to new levels of engineering magnificence not seen before in the ancient world.

Persian Empire *539-331 BC*

In the end, all of Mesopotamia fell to the Persians, who hailed from the region of what is today Iran. Although the Persians had also paid dues in their time being governed by others in the region, in the mid-6th century BC they fought for and won independence as a nation under the leadership of King Cyrus II. The Persians then went on to conquer one neighbor after another until they dominated the entire region, their empire surpassing even the Assyrians. Unlike the Assyrians who went to great lengths to disenfranchise their conquered subjects by destroying their cultural heritages, the Persians were inclined to be more tolerant of those they governed, allowing for diversity in customs and religions which resulted in a more eclectic culture.

The Persians didn't go in much for grand temple architecture or tombs, preferring to lavish their resources on palace architecture instead. The **Great Audience Hall of Darius** built at Persepolis is an excellent example. The palace was begun by King Darius around 520 BC to be the new capital of Persia, and completed by his son Xerxes. Darius appears to have picked up some design pointers from Assyrian palaces like the one from Khorsabad. The entire palace complex was raised up on a huge platform some 4 stories high accessed by a wide staircase of shallow steps. The audience hall itself was a huge ballroom-sized chamber supported by 100 towering columns where the king could meet with foreign delegations.

Relief carvings decorated the stairway and the walls. **Darius and Xerxes Receiving Tribute** illustrates the seated king and his son standing behind as they greet visitors who come to pay them homage. Compare the style you see here with other relief sculpture from Egypt and Mesopotamia. Like the Palette of Narmer and the Victory Stele of Naram-Sin, the more important people are presented larger than everyone else. We didn't see that in the Amarna Relief or Ashurnasirpal Hunting Lions. This can be explained as the difference between official art meant to impress others, and art that was perhaps more for the pleasure of the ruling family. Notice that the Persians and the Assyrians who were chronologically later were more likely to show bodies in profile, while the Egyptians and Akkadians went in for the twisted physique to show off broad shoulders alongside narrow hips, although all of them favored a frontal eye. The Persians and Assyrians were also more interested in detail in the form of highly stylized hairstyles and beards. Finally, observe how each relief sculpture was carved. The Palette of Narmer is the earliest. It is a very shallow low relief where the images were presumably drawn on a flat slice of slate, and then the background was carved away. The images are barely raised from the background at all. The Amarna Relief, done in the same region only quite a bit later is still a shallow relief, but notice how this time the images have been carved into the limestone rather than removing the background. The artist has also offered some modeling, making the figures slightly rounded, as if three-dimensional set inside the stone. The Assyrian example is also very low relief. Like the Palette of Narmer the background has been chiseled away, and while there is considerably more detail in the Ashurnasirpal relief, it is barely incised into the alabaster surface. The

Akkadian and Persian examples are both slightly higher relief than any of the others, meaning that the figures stand out from the background just a little more. Although both show less detail than the Assyrian relief, they attempt to show the figures as rounded and three-dimensional in the same way the Amarna Relief does, only now the figures stand out from the wall rather than being imbedded in it as Akhenaten and Nefertiti are.

The Persians were eventually conquered by Alexander the Great, as were the Egyptians, and so it was that both of these giants of the ancient world passed from great glory. Mesopotamia had been a region populated by competing giants – great peoples of different ethnic heritages who often failed to get along and who spent millennia fighting with one another to control the Fertile Crescent between the Tigress and Euphrates Rivers and beyond. Through it all they developed many principles of mathematics; they wrote epic poetry and created great libraries. Early democracy was practiced here. On the other hand, so were vicious military practices designed to strip people of their freedom and dignity. Egypt also stands apart as a nation of achievements from antiquity. Her agriculture, engineering and metallurgy were rivaled by few. Her citizens lived in comfortable dwellings with furniture, they dressed well and enjoyed a comfortable life, compliments of an orderly, peaceful government and good education, including primary, secondary, technical training and advanced studies in literature, science and medicine. The first widespread monogamy started here. Her architecture is still considered among the wonders of the world. Apparently even the beer was pretty good in Egypt. In many ways, Egypt is the stable and timeless grand dame of early Western civilization, like an elegant grandmother respected for her wisdom and her sophisticated, classy style by many generations to follow. Later civilizations would learn from both Egypt and Mesopotamia, borrowing ideas initiated by both of these early civilizations.

3. Minoans and Mycenaeans

The Minoan and Mycenaean civilizations (periods) chronologically overlap New Kingdom Egypt and the turbulent centuries immediately preceding when the Hyksos ruled, as well as the decline of Babylon in Mesopotamia. Both the Minoans and Mycenaeans lived in the Aegean Sea region, with the Minoans being island dwellers, and the Mycenaeans calling the Peloponnesus area of southern mainland Greece home. The Minoans were the more ancient people, having been around since the earliest days of ancient Egypt and Mesopotamia. Their communities appeared and disappeared in the Greek islands over the centuries, apparently the repeated victims of natural disasters. Their last flowering, which is the only period to be considered here, began around 1750 BC and lasted over three centuries; we will use 1400 BC as the round close date. The Mycenaeans arrived on the scene a little later. They appeared around 1600 BC and remained a viable civilization until at least 1200 BC.

Minoans *c. 1750-1400 BC*

The Minoans were a seafaring nation, largely out of necessity as island dwellers. Their central island, where the seat of their government was located, was the large island of Crete which is only 150 miles long by 36 miles wide. Smaller island settlements were sprinkled throughout the Aegean Sea. All evidence suggests that the Minoans were a sophisticated society, but sadly we do not know as much about these people as we might. They were highly literate, but we are as yet unable to translate their primary language called Linear A. Accordingly, most of what we know about the Minoans we have learned either through commentary from their neighbors like the Egyptians or Mesopotamian peoples, or from archaeology.

Most Minoan families were tied to maritime occupations. Their primary livelihood was fishing. They appear to have produced enough food to feed their people through local agriculture, so trade was primarily fish and whatever grain, fruit, cattle and sheep they could afford as surplus in exchange for metals, especially copper and tin which were made into bronze tools and luxury goods. As time went on, they turned their mercantile savvy into trading service for goods as well, offering to carry the products of others to different ports of call for a price. Evidence of Minoan trade has been found as far away as Scandinavia, so it is clear they were well traveled and well known abroad. If papa wasn't a fisherman, or a maritime merchant, odds were that he was in the navy. The Minoans were the supreme naval power in the Mediterranean world at this time in history. We do not find records of them being aggressive toward their neighbors, despite the fact that they could have used their navy for war. They seem to have been happier patrolling the waters around their islands as a matter of defense, although in truth, a foreigner would have been pretty bold to take on such a formidable force. The Minoans appear to have enjoyed and promoted peaceful relations with other people, which after all was good business for a trading nation. Records from other countries reinforce this picture by portraying the Minoans as an easy-going pleasant people, perhaps given to drink excessively at times, but otherwise good folks you could trust in business. They had plenty of friends, and not many (if any) enemies among those who knew them.

The archaeologist who discovered and began excavation of the great palace of the Minoan king(s), located at Knossos, Crete, was Sir Arthur Evans from England. In 1893 Dr. Evans was in Athens, Greece where he purchased some amulets with a peculiar style script that no scholar could read. Tracing the origins of the amulets, Evans traveled to Crete. Two years later in 1895 he purchased the land which he believed held the palace site of Knossos buried deep below, and in a manic 9-week season that spring with 150 workers, he dug out enough of the site to learn that his hunch was correct. He worked for many years on the site and published his findings in 1936 in a 4-volume report called *The Palace of Minos.* The **Palace at Knossos** is still under excavation, and is gradually being reconstructed as a tourist attraction.

Look at a reconstruction drawing depicting how it probably appeared at the time the kings lived there. Notice first how enormous the palace was (it covered 6 acres; the king must have been very rich), but perhaps more importantly, notice how open the building design was. The palace was as much open balconies and verandas as it was a solid building. There were no surrounding walls to enclose the open structure, either. What does this tell us? We can assume that security was not a problem. We already know the navy protected the island from threats of foreign invasion. But what about the common man on the street who lived on Crete? There was evidently no fear that Minoan citizens were going to break in and steal from the king, because the building was designed with absolutely no concern for security. The only logical conclusion is that average people must have lived comfortably themselves, and they must have recognized that in part at least they could thank their good government for this privilege. If the people had not been content with their lot in the world, the king's wealth would not have been safe in that palace, and perhaps not even his life could have been protected. Other nations, like Egypt, were known for their great wealth, but most of the big bucks rested with the ruling class. The Minoans as a whole civilization seemed to have been at the top of the food chain with a certain level of luxury enjoyed by everyone, not just kings and queens.

The Palace at Knossos was magnificently decorated with frescoes. *Fresco* is a painting technique where pigment is applied directly to wet plaster such that the picture dries as an integral part of the plaster wall or ceiling. Frescoes are well suited to hot, dry climates where they were often popular in the ancient world because of their durability. The **Dolphin Fresco** is typical of the sort of images found on the palace walls. It depicts a marine subject, in this case, dolphins. Other subjects might include fish, sea horses, octopi, seaweed, or pretty much anything likely to live in the sea. Notice how the dolphins appear to move through the water creating a rhythm of curving and flowing lines. This is in stark contrast to the more angular art we usually associate with Egypt and Mesopotamia. Notice also how this room in the palace, which was part of the queen's apartment, was apparently redecorated at some point, as you can see how a new layer of plaster was applied over the earlier design in order to repaint the trim around the door.

One of the frescoes discovered at the Palace at Knossos is very unusual compared to the others. The **Toreador Fresco** has nothing to do with marine motifs. Instead, it depicts a bull situated between young women (notice their fair skin), and there is a young man apparently vaulting over the bull's back. For some time this fresco has attracted interest, especially since we cannot translate the Minoan records left behind, and are not entirely sure what this picture represents. One theory is that it shows some ceremonial event where a youth of a certain age must participate in a daring ritual to mark the passage from boyhood to adult status. Another theory is that it may depict a religious sacrifice. We don't know that the Minoans believed in human sacrifice, but on the other hand, we don't know that they did not either. A third possibility may be that it represents some sort of contest, like a forerunner of the Olympic Games that would be found in Greece several hundred years later. The Minoans were part of the ancient gene pool which contributed to the Greek people who inhabited the region later on, and perhaps the Greek concept of formal games originated on Crete.

One way or the other, we suspect that the Toreador Fresco depicts a real event and not a storybook fantasy. An enormous labyrinth where large animals were housed has been discovered beneath the palace, and it is generally assumed the animals in question were bulls because archaeologists have also dug up massive bull masks, which they assume were worn at these events. Students of the _Iliad_ and _Odyssey_ have traditionally believed these were fantastic fiction tales – novels written by Homer, a late Mycenaean / pre-Greek, around 900 BC. Recent archaeology at Knossos has shed new light on this classic literature, suggesting that perhaps it wasn't so much myth as oral history, albeit a bit distorted and augmented. In his writing, Homer describes the great Minotaur – a frightening beast that was half man and half bull. The Minotaur has been customarily depicted as a bull with a human upper torso and head. Perhaps instead, it was a Minos (king) Taurus (bull), or the king presented as a bull wearing a great mask as he served as master of ceremonies at … well, at the Minoan version of a bar mitzvah, or perhaps at a holy human sacrifice, or maybe at the start of Olympic-style games. If you have read Homer, you know that his "memory" of what happened centuries earlier, as conveyed through oral story telling, involved the evil King Minos sacrificing boys to the Minotaur. Okay, what really happened? Probably some, or even many boys did die in whatever event is recalled in the Toreador Fresco, but what we may never know is whether the king sacrificed these boys as part of some strange cult, or whether they were simply casualties from the process of boys undertaking a dangerous act to prove they were men, or in the course of pursuing a challenging sport.

A second Minoan site, this time not on Crete, has proved generous in the amount and importance of the archaeological finds. That is the city of **Akrotiri** on the ancient island of Thera, called Santorini today. A Greek ship history buff named Spyridon Marinatos first published in 1939 his theory that a Minoan settlement had been located on Thera. He had reached this conclusion by studying ships of the ancient world. He knew the Minoans were great mariners, but he also understood that the idea of a galley where one prepares food on board had not yet been invented in the days of the Minoans. Accordingly, common sense suggested that while the Minoans had no fear of traveling far and wide, they could only set sail for a single day at a time. By the end of that day, they would need to put into port to prepare food to feed the crew. Marinatos knew the Minoans had active contact with her neighbors the Mycenaeans who lived in southern Greece. He also knew the currents and trade winds in the Aegean and Mediterranean. He concluded that it would have been impossible for a Minoan sailing vessel to reach

Mycenae in a single day from the ports on Crete. They must have had a harbor town somewhere along that route where they could pull into shore and eat. The most logical choice, geographically, was Thera.

Finally in 1967 Marinatos put together an archaeology team and the funding to start digging on Thera, and they discovered the ancient city of Akrotiri. Marinatos died in 1974, but not before publishing his research and theories on Akrotiri. The excavation is ongoing to this day under the direction of Professor Christos Doumas.

The city of Akrotiri was a fabulous find because it was not connected with a royal palace in any way, and thus represented how regular citizens lived; it was a merchant city. The houses found there were large. One Minoan house was discovered to have 23 rooms on the only surviving floor, and many homes were multi-story affairs. They were also opulently decorated with frescoes, something we simply never see anywhere else in the ancient world. While in other cultures the king might have had access to wondrous art, the average guy on the street had nothing so grand to call his own. In Minoan society, ordinary people apparently could afford splendid art that would make a king proud in other parts of the world.

Of the many frescoes found here, perhaps the most famous is the **Flotilla Fresco**. It was discovered in the "West House," so named because at the time it was discovered it was at the western perimeter of the excavation, although the dig has now moved considerably west of this particular home. It was not one of the largest houses, although evidence suggests that the West House was probably owned by a ship's captain. The Flotilla Fresco is important, first because it is our primary source for understanding ship structure and rigging from Minoan times. Lucky for posterity, the fresco was more of a catalogue of many different styles of Minoan ships and boats than it was a depiction of a unified fleet of like vessels. Prior to this discovery, scholars were obliged to rely on cartoon-simple images found on Minoan coins and seals (cylinders carved such that they could be rolled onto wet clay to imprint a message). For the first time it was possible to clearly see how the sails were rigged, how many oars a ship had, and from this information, determine how many men were required to operate the ship.

Another reason this fresco is both unique and significant lies in the teensy people seen onboard the ships. Curiously, many of the larger ships have two distinct groups of people on the boat, as differentiated by their style of dress. The majority of the men were Minoan – the captain was Minoan and so were all the sailors. Yet there was another contingent of men who were dressed in Mycenaean garments. Keep this tidbit of information handy, as we will explore the relationship between the Minoans and Mycenaeans after the Mycenaeans are introduced.

Thera, which like Minoan settlements through history had suffered earthquakes and managed to rebuild, was ultimately destroyed in a massive volcanic eruption. Unfortunately, the island was actually the top of a dormant volcano, which burst to life and buried Akrotiri under a multi-story blanket of volcanic ash. Scholars agree that the magnitude of the eruption has not been paralleled in the past four or five millennia; even the famous Mount Vesuvius which buried Pompeii wouldn't hold a candle to the devastation that occurred at Akrotiti. Ash from the eruption has been found as far away as Great Britain! The force of the earthquakes associated with the eruption sheered off huge sections of the island which then sunk to the bottom of the sea. Some scholars believe that the stories of the devastation of Thera were the foundation for Plato's writings on the lost civilization of Atlantis.

When exactly all this took place remains an unresolved question. Marinatos dated the destruction of Thera close to 1500 BC based on his evidence. He further suggested that a storm of tidal waves or tsunamis like the world witnessed in 2004 in Indonesia and Thailand were unleashed from this cataclysmic volcanic blast. His theory was that these tsunamis followed by earthquakes and uncontrolled fires brought the downfall of Minoan civilization across the Aegean, including Crete which seems to have limped along for several more decades before collapsing entirely. Other scholars have employed a variety of different dating systems, and have put forth their own theories ranging from earlier dates of 1645 BC and 1626 BC, and still others have dated it later: 1420 BC and even 1390 BC. The jury is still out on the exact chronology.

One interesting point, regardless of whose date is correct and regardless of whether the demise of Knossos was the result of the volcano on Thera or if the two events were unrelated was this: no bodies have been found at Akrotiri. None. Nada. This indicates that for as unimaginably devastating as the volcanic eruption was, folks on the island had advanced warning that something was terribly wrong, and they got on their boats and sailed away. All evidence is that they emigrated to Mycenae where they melded into the local population over time. Knossos was destroyed sometime between 1500 and 1400 BC, also by natural disasters on a catastrophic scale, and on Crete many people did lose their lives. Some who survived the attacks of nature on their homeland lingered on trying to rebuild, until sometime around 1400 BC when they were possibly invaded (by whom is not entirely clear) and petered out as a society. Many others however didn't hang around for the grand dénouement of their world; they emigrated to Egypt. The Minoans were well accepted in Egypt, although they remained separate from Egyptian culture rather than assimilating. The artists at King Akhenaten's court were Minoan immigrants who were held in high regard by the royal family for their beautiful art. This probably contributed to the increase in flowing, curvilinear forms seen in "Amarna" art.

Mycenae *c. 1600-1200 BC*

Mycenae is the sister culture to the Minoans, in part because their written languages were related. Minoans used Linear A as their primary mode of recorded information. They also had Linear B, a less important language in Crete, but which happened to be the written language used by the Mycenaeans. Linear B was translated in the early 1950s; it turned out to be a very ancient relative of Greek. Sadly the information gleaned from these documents isn't as useful as one might hope. The Minoans used Linear B for inventories of stored goods, but not for documents that might inform us about their culture beyond what they ate. For their part, the Mycenaeans were not especially literate at all, and there isn't much to work with even with Linear B translated. In many ways, although they were a bronze-age society like the Egyptians, assorted Mesopotamians and Minoans, the Mycenaeans functioned more like a Stone Age culture that just happened to have better grade tools. They relied primarily on oral tradition, which might help explain why tales of the Mycenaeans were recorded centuries later by the locals living in the region; Homer's epics would be among such accounts. They were avid hunters, both for food and sport, and they were agriculturally inclined, but only as necessity required to feed their population.

The archaeologist who discovered Mycenae was Heinrich Schliemann. Schliemann's father read Homer's *Iliad* and *Odyssey* to his son as a child, which so inspired the young German lad that by the age of 10, he vowed he would devote his life to finding the remains of this lost civilization. In 1836 Heinrich left school at the ripe age of 14 to start his career working as a grocer's apprentice, then moved on to become a clerk earning a whopping $150 a year. He continued to read read read, spending half his salary on books. He worked hard, such that by age 25 he was an independent merchant, and by 36 he was so wealthy he figured he could retire and spend the rest of his life pursuing archaeology. He was passably fluent in English, French, Dutch, Spanish, Portuguese, Italian, Russian, Swedish, Polish, Arabic and Greek in addition to his native German, thanks to his practice of learning the languages of all the people he had done business with during his years as a merchant. He lacked a formal education in a strict sense, but certainly nobody would argue that he was anything less than a well-read intellectual who happened to be consumed with a true vocation to find the lost worlds of Homer and prove it was all real.

In 1876, he arrived in southern Greece after "successfully" digging up Troy in Turkey. Actually, he dug up nine Troys in all; Schliemann, for all his monumental contributions to archaeology, has been criticized for his excavation techniques which often blasted right through what he was seeking down to an earlier civilization, and he'd have to fumble his way back to the correct level, all too frequently messing up the *stratigraphy* (layers of rock and sediment used by archaeologists to determine time periods of found artifacts) so one couldn't be absolutely sure that each article found was from the same time period. Schliemann completed his dig at Mycenae in eight quick years, and in 1884 he moved on to a second Mycenaean city, Tiryns. In 1886 Schliemann visited Crete and located the site where he believed Knossos lay. He entered into negotiations for the right to excavate, but the landowner tried to cheat him, and the businessman side of Schliemann walked out on the deal in a huff. He died shortly thereafter, leaving Knossos for Arthur Evans who would arrive nine years later and just buy up the land rather than try to win legal battles to excavate somebody else's backyard.

Consider the reconstruction illustration of **Mycenae**. Notice that unlike the Minoan palace at Knossos, or the city of Akrotiri, there are massive stone walls enclosing the entire community. The Mycenaeans lived in cities that might be better understood as impenetrable citadels. They developed their cities this way to protect them from barbarians, who seemed to arrive in periodic waves from the north and who were a constant threat to security. The problem with huge, thick walls surrounding everything was the challenge of designing entrances that would enable the locals to come and go, while barricading the unsavory interlopers out. The Mycenaeans opted for small "gates," or openings in the wall that could be easily defended. The **Lion Gate** is a good example. What you want is a hole in the wall big enough for your people to get in and out a few at a time, but not so big that an enemy army can pour through the gate and mow your city down. The problem is, if you rely solely on post and lintel architecture to frame the gate, and then continue to build that heavy wall above the lintel, sooner or later the weight of all those huge rocks will be too much for the lintel, and it will snap in the middle and cave in … on your head. To alleviate this problem, the Mycenaeans developed the *corbelled arch*. They would start with a regular post and lintel opening, but when the wall was built to the level of the lintel, instead of placing the next course of stones all the way across the lintel, they would cantilever two rocks just a smidgen over the two posts, but otherwise leave a gap. The next course of stones would follow the same pattern, with two stones slightly cantilevered beyond the lower two, but otherwise leaving a gap, albeit a smaller gap than the last row. In this way, the builders inch each course of stones closer together until they meet again. Over the lintel there is a triangle of open space, called a *relieving triangle*, while above the relieving triangle, the massive wall continues to its proposed height without further interruption. A relieving triangle allows the lintel to do its job, without having to carry any weight from the wall above. Perhaps for security reasons (to plug the hole so nobody could throw stuff inside) or perhaps for aesthetics, the Mycenaeans often filled the relieving triangles with a lightweight stone or clay insert on which they would carve an image which presumably helped them to keep the different gates separate (the lion gate, as opposed to the hippo gate or monkey gate).

Fighting for one's survival in a hostile environment made the Mycenaeans tough. They had a rigidly ordered society, with the upper echelon caste being the warriors. In essence, the Mycenaeans became known as the thugs of the Mediterranean for their generation. They thrived on fighting and could be brutally vicious. They were not initially great mariners, but they managed enough sailing to terrorize their neighbors along the coast as pirates, and in general, they pretty well took what they wanted rather than conduct business in a mannerly, polite fashion.

Time out. Back track to that Flotilla Fresco again. Remember that the ships had both Minoans onboard, and also Mycenaeans? The Mycenaeans are easy to spot because they are dressed as warriors rather than bare-chested, Minoan-style sailors. Had the Mycenaeans captured these ships? Nope. The scenes appear friendly, with the Minoans and Mycenaeans getting along just fine, thanks. Evidently they were working together on some joint venture that required, we must presume, excellent sailors, and excellent warriors. They weren't fighting in Mycenae because the warriors wouldn't have to sail to that destination. They weren't fighting on Crete – the navy patrolled those waters well enough to scare off outside forces. Where were they going? Where were the obliging Minoan nautical navigators taking the soldiers? If Marinatos' dating is correct, that these paintings were created sometime around 1500 BC, then who in the Mediterranean world might have been in need of mercenaries for hire? For that matter, who had enough money (gold) to lure the Minoans and Mycenaeans into working for a foreign power?

Egypt, that's who, and if the original dating offered by the archaeologist who discovered the site is right, then it would have been right around the same time as the Hyksos were booted out of Egypt. So many of the records from that transitional time through the reign of Hatshepsut were destroyed by her malcontent successor Thutmose III that it is difficult to prove, what with destroyed records in Egypt, untranslated records from Crete and Thera, and high testosterone illiterates for the most part coming out of Mycenae. But it makes sense. Egypt had a crummy army as much as anything because historically they had not needed one. That would change of course, but probably not by 1500 BC, give or take a few years. Further, goldmines had been operational from early in Egyptian history.   Gold had always been locally available and plentiful. Isn't it curious, then, that during Hatshepsut's reign especially, Egypt opened international trade in no small part to get more gold, and lots of it? She imported vast reserves from Sudan, Ethiopia, Djibouti, Somalia and probably also Zimbabwe. Who needs that much gold? Perhaps someone paying a king's ransom for highly skilled military privateers and for their maritime chauffeur service to and from Egypt across the great sea, that's who.

Probably the most spectacular architecture from Mycenae was their tombs, like the **Treasury of Atreus**. These were colossal, hollow beehive shaped structures that were built, and then buried to disguise them from enemy vandalism. The building principle for these beehive, or *tholos* tombs was simple corbelling like we saw with the Lion Gate, only this time in three dimensions. A large circle of stones was laid out, with each successive course of stones a tad smaller in diameter until the circle closed in on itself at the top. Think a minute. What type of people would be likely to build big tombs? Presumably, the more focused on death and afterlife you are, the more a tomb might be important. Do the Mycenaeans strike you as a death oriented people? Do you suppose that people who were into killing and being killed (it's one or the other) languish in bed at night wondering what their souls will be doing in a million years? Probably not. Death orientation is a luxury of people who have a lot of time on their hands. Everything about the Mycenaeans suggests a life-oriented people. So where would they have gotten the idea to build these big tombs? There is only one place they could have gone and been exposed to colossal tombs: Egypt. Imagine the Mycenaean warrior arriving in Egypt, with the gleaming Pyramids at Giza there to greet him. Pretty impressive, eh? Nothin' like that back home! So he asks his more savvy Minoan friend what those things are, and he's told they are special houses for dead kings. Whoa, what a concept! The Mycenaeans had to be impressed with Egypt; who wouldn't be? The country was so beautiful, and rich, and the people were sophisticated and just plain classy. They had some bizarre ideas, but it probably made them seem all the more exotic.

So the Mycenaeans got back home, and by golly, they'd like to have some of those nifty tombs for their important people too. Of course, they did't know how to build pyramids, but they knew how to corbel, so they used that technology instead. What is particularly curious is that while they built huge tombs, suggesting an interest in death orientation, their *use* of the tombs was anything but. Mycenaean tholos tombs were reusable! Granny would be laid out with gifts, presumably with some sort of funeral farewell. A caretaker would baby-sit the corpse periodically to determine when Granny had rotted away (no embalming in Mycenae, of course), at which point Gran's bones were swept away like so much trash into the square chamber adjacent to the tomb called the *grab* (which means grave in German). The gifts were presumably returned to their rightful owners (not Granny of course, because the woman is dead after all), and the process would begin again with the next dead candidate ready for a fancy send-off … into oblivion.

The inside of the Treasury of Atreus is completely gold-plated. That's a lot of gold, and there were no goldmines close by in Mycenae. Further, gold masks like the **Mask of Agamemnon** (it may or may not be that – Schliemann was infatuated with Homer's world and saw specific Homer references in everything he found, regardless of whether it could be substantiated) confirm that the Mycenaeans must have been exposed to Egypt early in their tenure in the Mediterranean, as there is no place else where they could have gotten the idea of placing a gold mask over the face of the deceased.

In later years the Mycenaeans gave up pirating and looting to become more involved in respectable international trade, perhaps inspired by the more congenial people they had met on their sojourns with the Minoans to Egypt. Their increased expertise on the sea may have also been closely linked to the fact that after Thera was destroyed, a substantial number of Minoans relocated from Thera to Mycenae to take advantage of their business partner's hospitality. With accomplished sailors marrying into the local population over time, it's reasonable to assume that the Mycenaeans would learn Minoan skills. For 200 years after the collapse of the Minoans as a distinct civilization, the Mycenaeans became increasingly accomplished seafarers alongside others, like the Phoenicians who had improved their maritime skills as well, and trade flourished throughout the Mediterranean. It is still unclear why exactly the Mycenaean society died. Evidence suggests that they were attacked in one final blow that undid their defenses and decimated their population. Many scholars believe the aggressors were the Dorians, who arrived in the Balkan Peninsula about this time, although this is still being debated. The Mycenaeans, with the Minoan sub-culture intact, lived on. The society crumbled, but the survivors stayed put, quietly holding their own in the region and eventually contributing to the gene pool that would produce the Greeks.

4. Greece

In many ways, the Greeks were the founders of Western thinking. Unlike their predecessors, who more often than not found great virtue in long-standing stability, the Greeks liked change. They were the first Western culture to seek development in everything they did. There was a sense that I can do things better than my Dad (anything you can do, I can do better). Contrast this to someplace like Egypt, where a more likely mantra would be: if it was good enough for my Granddad, then it's good enough for me. This positive Greek attitude toward growth and development led to a society that shifted gears more rapidly than earlier cultures seemed to do. For the first time in Western history, we will begin to see cycles of development. The Greeks would start with a very simple idea, whatever it might be. They would strive to perfect the idea, and then get bored with their perfection. To keep it interesting, they would find ways to make it more and more complex. We will explore this phenomenon in the artistic expression of the Greek people; look for the pattern to be repeated throughout history in the West. The biggest change from the days of the Greeks compared to our world today is not the pattern of cyclical change, but rather the rate of change. In antiquity, a cycle took several hundred years to run its course, while nowadays the cycles are moving so fast you could miss the pattern altogether if you were not attuned to it.

The people whom we call "The Greeks" first appeared around the 8th century BC. In reality, they didn't so much arrive, given that they had been there all along, as they did evolve out of the hodge-podge of folks living in the Balkan Peninsula. We know the Mycenaeans were there, and they had already absorbed the remnant of surviving Minoan culture. Add to the mix the Dorians, who moved in from parts north sometime around 1200 BC, and the Ionians, who were islanders living off the west coast of Greece in the Adriatic Sea who had been mingling with the locals in the Balkan Peninsula for some time. There was great political unrest for a few hundred years after the collapse of Mycenae, which is often referred to as a dark age in the history of this region. We know that during this time they developed into city-states, each with its own character, and ruled by kings.

By the 8th century BC, they were experiencing problems with overpopulation given that everyone lived off the land, and the barren soil of Greece is not especially generous. It was the old custom for families to will their land evenly divided between their children, such that after awhile, many families found that the parcels were too small to farm with any success. As a result, many families began to leave the land only to the older children, and younger children had to relocate outside their hometown. They began to travel more in search trade, and they established colonies on foreign soil. Perhaps in their adventures of meeting people from other nations, they set about improving their own. Not much in the way of art survives from the 8th and 7th centuries BC other than some examples of pottery and a few rare small sculptures. One particularly important achievement was the Greeks fine-tuned their alphabet at this time, borrowing heavily from the Phoenicians.

Archaic *±600-480 BC*

The Archaic Period in Greece was the 6th century BC, or more correctly from approximately 600 – 480 BC, and it was during this time that the Greeks set about building their culture with the art and architecture still with us today. Thanks to their recently improved alphabet, we also have more written accounts describing their world available to us than during the Dark Age. The system of city-states remained, with each community exceedingly proud of its own citizens while remaining suspicious of folks from other towns, and everyone uniformly viewing all non-Greeks as "barbarians" (barbaros means "babblers" – people who spoke languages the Greeks didn't understand) regardless of how enlightened these other civilizations might be. Some of the city-states moved gradually and peacefully toward a shared rule among the citizens; others went through a more violent upheaval to rid themselves of their old-style kings.

Greece is often credited as the birthplace of democracy, although our concept today of what that means is often a far cry from their reality. In fact, only aristocrat landowners were allowed to participate in the government at all, and only the crème de la crème top echelon of wealthy men were permitted to hold public office. Furthermore, the notion of representing the needs and desires of economic underdogs was unheard of. The rich ruled because it was generally believed that they were better suited to the task, plus their wealth afforded them the luxury of owning a sword and shield, which spoke well of their ability to fight for themselves and presumably for the protection of others while they were at it. The fact is, unfortunately, the rich landed gentry often tended to look out for themselves, sometimes at the expense of the less fortunate. Further narrow the field by excluding women from the ranks of power and politics, and you have a handful of country-club types participating in an exclusive enterprise for gentlemen only.

Most of the architecture of this period is long gone on mainland Greece, compliments of the Persian Wars when the invading army had the bad habit of razing everything in sight. We will instead focus our attention on the sculpture, beginning with the **Metropolitan Kouros**. Kouros statues, or kouroi (plural) were free-standing male nude figures standing at least life size, with many twice that large. Most were carved from marble, which was locally available in plentiful quantity and conveniently an attractive, good quality material. Kouroi have been largely found in cemeteries, where they were evidently used as grave markers. Initially you might be fooled into thinking that these were funerary statues. Not so! Stylistically they do resemble the stiff, walking pose of Egyptian funerary figures, and it is quite possible that this much at least may have been inspired by Egyptian influence. The Greeks were trading with the Egyptians by this time, but recall also that funerary statues in Egypt were usually hidden away in tombs and not on public display. Regardless of any possible stylistic inspiration coming from Egypt, there is no evidence that the life-oriented Greeks had the slightest interest in housing souls. Greek kouros statues are something quite different. First, some are considerably larger than life size which sort of defeats the Egyptian concept where funerary statues were close in size to the deceased in order to comfortably accommodate a life-size soul. Also, they were not carved as solid blocks, leaving too many opportunities for breakage, and then they were left out in the open where they could deteriorate or be vandalized. Another significant difference between kouros statues and funerary statues is that the former are nude. Prehistoric fertility figures aside, no other ancient civilization in the

West had taken an interest in portraying their subjects nude. So if they were not intended to be funerary statues, what were they?

Scholars initially assumed they were statues of gods, which made sense in light of the fact that in other ancient civilizations, the only "people" represented larger than life were deities, either bona fide gods, or kings that were believed to have had divine powers. When the **Anavyssos Kouros** was discovered, the figure was still attached to its original base on which there was an inscription telling about the statue. Apparently the sculpted figure represented a real person, a young man named Kroisos, presumably the fellow buried beneath the kouros. It seems these statues were not supposed to represent gods; in fact, during the Archaic period, there appears to have been only a minor interest in creating religious art at all compared to other ancient civilizations. Kouroi represented society's heroes. It seems that the qualifications for being admired as a hero (mind you, admired larger than life, in a very open, public area, and buck naked too) were that one be young and handsome, and if the guy happened to have been brave too, well, so much the better. Essentially, it was a sort of cult of the glamorous hero, not too much different from the Hollywood celebrity phenomenon we see in our own times.

The female counterpart of the kouros was the *kore*. A good example is the **Peplos Kore**, so named because of the peplos blouse she wears. These were produced in fewer numbers than the kouros, they were usually under life-size, they were clothed, and usually housed indoors, specifically inside temple districts where it is presumed the figures served as handmaidens of the gods. What does all this tell us about the Greeks? First, it tells us that the most important thing to the Greeks was … well … ME. There is a popular adage often applied to the Greeks: *man is the measure of all things.* The Greeks had religion, but the gods were no more than immortal versions of themselves with the same overall lack of morality. It could be said that the gods' job was to serve the needs of men, rather than men being obliged to serve the gods. The Greeks perceived themselves as the absolute center of the universe, and while we may nostalgically think of them as being somehow open-minded and fair (that popular misunderstanding of "democracy" creeping into our sentiments), in fact their primary interest tended to be what's good for ME, followed by what's good for my town, followed by occasionally considering what might be good for all Greek people, and no concern whatsoever for the greater world of barbarians out there who don't rate caring about at all.

The differences between the kouros and kore also illustrate the difference between men and women in Greece. Men were important, good looking and to be admired in all manner (especially me …), while women barely showed up on the radar as real people in most regions. Females were perceived as so much chattel, a bit of a burden if one happened to have any as dependents. Females were not allowed to receive an education, except the highest level of prostitutes, called hetaerae, who were imported from Ionian territories offshore and who had bleached blonde hair to distinguish themselves from "regular" women. These high rent hookers were allowed to learn to read, one might guess so they would prove less boring to their customers. There were an isolated few women who managed against the odds to make their mark in the world. The poet, Sappho from the island of Lesbos is an example. But in the end, the men were solidly in charge. In most regions of ancient Greece, women were viewed a little like cows. We have cows around because we like hamburgers and milk, but nobody takes cows very seriously. People don't spend their time wondering what opinions cows have on important issues. We don't hold cows among our circle of close, personal friends. Most folks would not consider it even possible to have a meaningful relationship with a cow. In Greece, women were necessary to produce sons. They were also handy in that they could be trained to cook, clean and sew. It didn't seem probable to many men that women would be terribly useful for much else.

In ancient Greece it was possible to rid yourself of unwanted children through laws of exposure. The game plan was simple enough. If your wife gave birth to a child you found inconvenient, it was socially acceptable and politically correct to place the newborn on a pot, and leave it on the steps of the temple. Anyone who happened along was welcome to take the child home if he or she felt so inclined. Male infants had a decent shot at informal adoption, but girls usually passed away and were discarded like so much rubbish. This tended to create a lopsided society heavy on males. Homosexuality (or at best bisexuality) was probably closer to the norm than the exception, and even those men who clearly preferred the opposite sex for carnal gratification, would turn to men for companionship.

Looking again at the Peplos Kore, notice that colored paint remains on parts of the statue. In fact, all ancient Greek statues, and for that matter their buildings as well were garishly painted with vivid colors. Look at me! Nowadays we imagine Greek art as pristine and white, but it did not look this way in the days of ancient Greece. Statues were painted to resemble life, and life in bright colors at that. The kouros statues would have been painted also, but since they were left outdoors, the paint has long since worn away. The Greeks were the first ancient society to place less emphasis on art that represented tyrannical rulers, and more emphasis on its handsome citizens, people like you and me. They invested less in art that promoted submission to religion, and more on art that promoted beauty for the sake of itself. The art represented a beautiful version of you and me, and the goal was to make it as realistic and good looking as possible. Toward this end, notice also that all three of the statues wear a welcoming smile, often dubbed the "archaic smile."

Finally, compare the Metropolitan Kouros to the Anavyssos Kouros. They were sculpted within the same time period, but the former at the start of the period and the latter at the end, about a hundred years apart. Can you see how much more realistic the body and face of the Anavyssos Kouros seem? The chest and abdomen muscles seem more natural, and the face looks more like a real person. In Greece, the highest glory in art was realism ... which shouldn't come as a surprise because of course, it makes the art look more like ME. Consider Egypt, where for a thousand years art hardly changed at all. In Greece, even within the span of a single century there was growth and development.

Classical *480-404 BC*

The Classical Period dates from 480 – 404 BC. This is the time often referred to as the "Golden Age;" it was the pinnacle of Greek society and culture, and the period most likely emphasized when one thinks of "ancient Greece." Ironically perhaps, the entire period only spanned a couple generations – no more than three quarters of a single century. The boundaries of the Classical Period were established by wars ... and politics. The Greek city-states had always been both autonomous and competitive. While Greeks were quick to distinguish themselves as a whole from non-Greeks, the reality was that they seldom got along very well with their neighbors just down the road. There was such an emphasis on the individual "me," and from there, to "my" town with the assumption that anything that is an extension of me must certainly be inherently superior to anything less closely related to me. Early Greek history was marred by an ongoing series of petty squabbles among neighboring Greeks. Even the Olympic Games were at least in part a chance to demonstrate for everyone to appreciate that I am superior to you, and people from my city or village are better than dolts from your neck of the woods. To be fair, one should note that the Greeks were a composite of different ethnic groups if you dug deep enough into their history, and some regions did still have more of one gene pool than another. Still ...

Two cities that are frequently compared are Sparta and Athens. Sparta, located down in the Peloponnesus region which the Mycenaeans once called home, developed largely from Dorian stock. These were the marauders who arrived at the demise of Mycenae, and may well have had a hand in upsetting that apple cart. The Dorians were true barbarians, in that they were more ferocious thugs than even the Mycenaeans, less civilized, BUT they had iron weapons rather than bronze, and they could wallop just about every group of people they encountered. The people of Sparta developed a rigid society where military fitness was a religion. Young boys were removed from their parents' home as little kids to be raised by the state, which subjected them to extremely harsh conditions. They seldom were given appropriate clothes to wear for the weather, they were expected to sleep outside on the bare ground, and they were deliberately shortchanged on food, all the while being expected to maintain a boot camp regimen of grueling challenges for years on end that would make military training today look like a holiday for pantywaists. This, in their opinion, turned out real men. Even the girls were expected to exercise nude in public so people could see plainly whether they were fit. Nobody cared whether anybody learned much of anything intellectual. Sissy stuff! What mattered was whether you lived in a constant state of readiness for war and severe deprivation. Even after children grew up (no sooner than 30) and married, the men were never permitted to dine with their wives; instead they would trudge off to the mess hall, where they would be underfed bad food with the other tough guys, lest they grow soft and domesticated from family life.

Herodotus and others credit the invention of this "Spartan Code" to a man named Lycurgus, and while we don't have dates for this legend of a man, we do know he lived prior to 600 BC. He promoted infanticide (a father's duty) for any child that did not appear to measure up, and babies born with any perceptible "defects" were routinely thrown off a cliff to die on the jagged rocks below. Because the emphasis was on producing a superior race of people, men were expected to share exceptional wives with the best men in the city such that superior children might be produced. Breeding was viewed as just that, and there was no room for personal feelings. While celibacy was a crime and virtually everyone was expected to marry or be excluded from the community, monogamy was also ridiculed. The pleasures of sex were typically both homosexual and heterosexual, starting early as boy toys and little Lolitas submitting to the (pedophile?) older generation, then returning the favor later on. Formal prostitution for money was more rare here than in other cities. For as dismally bleak as all this might sound to most of us today, the good news was that Spartans were known to be uncommonly attractive and healthy, men and women alike. No surprise there, if for no other reason other than everyone was built like he or she lived at the gym, plus they had ruggedly handsome features to begin.

Athens was completely different from her southern neighbors. The Athenians were erudite poets, philosophical and contemplative by nature. They arose from what was probably a mingling of leftover Mycenaean stock combined with Ionian genes from the Adriatic islanders. They built an orderly society around the concept of first the individual, then the family, then the clan or extended family, and finally the tribe, which was more-or-less the folks in their town whom they attributed as having descended from one god or another. It was here that the notion originated that a landed aristocracy running things via a limited democracy, or by Assembly, would be better than accepting dogmatic rules and laws from a king. Essentially society was marked by 3 basic economic classes: the rich people at the top of the food chain; the craftsmen, or traders and other free laborers who worked as professionals, made a decent living but did not hold political power; and finally the peasants groveling to make ends meet, usually by farming small patches of the poorest land. Outside the class structure altogether were slaves, who owned nothing and served their masters in exchange for the basics of survival. In general, it was considered somehow distasteful for "real men" to do any work in Athens, so those who could, made a point of being idle, while exploiting the less well off to do the labor as the rich business or land owner siphoned off the cream of the profits.

Athenians for the most part were completely amoral. They did not have the strong discipline that the boot camp Spartans did, and they were not bound by as many rigid rules of absolute conduct. Prostitution was rampant, and was taxed as a legitimate business. The young boys who offered up sexual favors for pocket money, however, were outside the taxation loop, and the self-righteous whores in the city often publicly denounced homosexual relations as "immoral," based more on their anger over having to share the easy money made in illicit sex with boys who didn't have to pay taxes, rather than any real concern over who slept with whom. Most people who got around to getting married were expected to have children, but small families were preferred and society demanded that "excess" conceived babies be aborted. Otherwise infanticide was always an option, especially if there was anything about the new baby that didn't suit you. "Religious" festivals were customarily accompanied by orgies. Honesty was perceived as a good thing in theory, although hardly anybody ever practiced it. They were kind to animals, but cruel to humans, admirers of abstract philosophy, who lived their day-to-day lives consumed by lapsed morals, sensual fetishes and a self-indulgent preoccupation with how special they were.

An avid interest in politics practiced by an assortment of characters over the years, some good and some bad, made Athens a place where new ideas and reforms were welcomed to correct past political mistakes, or to move society forward. The leader in power at the turn of the 5th century BC was Themistokles. It was he who laid the groundwork for Athens becoming the superpower of his generation. He was an aristocrat who maintained popularity with the common people. According to the ancient historian Thucydides, Themistokles was witty, far-sighted and deep thinking. He was a man who could solve problems, which was a good thing, because he was destined to face a time of crisis, not just for Athens, but for all Greeks everywhere.

Persia, off in the Middle East approximately where Iran is today, had been gaining power and prestige by conquering its neighbors through a long series of successful military campaigns. Under her commander and king, Darius, Persia attacked the Ionian Islands, which scared the Greeks into temporarily trying to put aside their differences to consider a plan of action if Persia attacked the mainland. The attacks did come, first from the north, and gradually working their way south. While the Greeks were not fighting one another for a change, neither were they always helping each other fend off the Persians. Finally in 490 BC the Persians landed at Marathon, a coastal city near Athens. The Athenians fought Persia alone after their request to Sparta for help went unanswered. Sparta claimed it was a religious holiday and they couldn't come, although it is also true that there were pro-Persian supporters in Sparta, or at least pro-Persia insofar as the rest of Greece was concerned. Against the odds, Athens won the battle, in part because the Persians had to fight uphill while the Athenians could more easily maneuver their ranks downhill. This put Athens on the map as a potential leader among the Greeks, which was very annoying to Sparta.

Themistokles seemed to realize the threat was not over, and he advised Athens to build up her otherwise modest navy fleet with an additional 200 ships. In 486 BC the Persian pooh-bah, Darius died, leaving control of the army to his son, Xerxes, who was young, brash and eager to prove himself. By 480 BC Xerxes had rebuilt his army and he was ready to rumble. He must have had troops numbering close to 200,000 at least; some Greek accounts (probably embellished) put the numbers at a million. On the advice of Themistokles, the Athenians with their impressive new fleet of ships retired to the small island of Salamis located in the straits between the main Greek peninsula and the Peloponnesus to wait for the Persians, thus escaping the devastating sack of Athens by the Persian Army. Themistokles knew that Xerxes had his ships anchored just outside the straits. He wanted to force the Persians into the narrow straits, which would reduce their maneuverability, so he pretended to be a traitor and sent Xerxes a letter saying that the Greeks had a plan to escape before Xerxes attacked. Taking the bait, Xerxes situated himself comfortably on land to watch the great victory as he sent his fleet crowding in around the Greeks. As it happened, the Greeks were better sailors, and they out-maneuvered the clumsy Persian fleet. Their new ships were also heavier, and when they rammed into the Persian boats, the latter tended to break apart faster than their Greek counterparts. The final ingredient, which favored Greek victory, was that the Athenians knew how to swim, and the Persians did not! Every time a Greek ship went down, the men swam to another boat and kept fighting. But every time Persian ships sank, all the men on board drowned.

The Battle of Salamis in 480 BC was the final major victory against Persia, and it brought to Athens (thanks to Themistokles) a new status of being the leader among all Greeks. Sparta, trying to imagine the limp-wristed Athenians as leaders of anything more demanding than a poetry reading, continued to be *not* amused. Sparta's disgust over Athens being admired as heroes was exacerbated by the fact that Sparta had been clobbered by Persia at Thermopylae shortly before the Battle of Salamis. The tough guys were attacked at both their front lines and from the rear, thanks to other Greeks who betrayed them to the Persians. Sparta inflicted more damage man for man on Persia than the other way around, but as their army was so much smaller than Xerxes' forces, in the end almost the entire Spartan force was killed. It was galling to have fought valiantly and lost, only to see the Athenians, who weren't nearly as rough and tough as Sparta, win through luck and clever wit rather than brute strength.

The Classical Period is more about Athens than it is about all of Greece. Shortly after the victory at Salamis, the Athenians formed a new "league of nations" called the **Delian League**, formed initially with the Greek islands but including many city-states on land as well ... but not Sparta. The Delian League was a straightforward agreement among neighbors. Everyone in the League acknowledged the contribution Athens and her navy had made toward beating the Persians. Instead of returning to their old ways of bickering, they agreed to pay an annual tribute, or tax to Athens for her to build up her navy, and in exchange, Athens promised to protect her contributing neighbors if ever again they faced a formidable foe like the Persians. In addition to ushering in a period of peace for Greece, the Delian League brought a financial windfall to Athens. They were able to build a fabulous navy, and with the vast sum of money left over, they rebuilt their city.

See the view of the **Acropolis** (acro = high / polis = city) in Athens as it appears today. Every city in Greece had an acropolis, although the one in Athens is what most people recognize. The "high cities" were temple districts, built on the highest promontory in the city, as gods live in high places. While it cannot be said the Greeks were a devout people compared to others in the ancient world, their temple districts were very important to them, as much for civic pride as anything else. Everyone living in town, and many a distance away could see the buildings there. In keeping with the Greek natural inclination toward competition, there was a feeling of pride that "our acropolis is more beautiful than your acropolis," religion aside. The Persians destroyed the entire old acropolis, so once the money was available, the city took on the task of rebuilding it more lovely than ever.

Athens' new political leader, Perikles, rebuilt the Acropolis. Perikles was a child during the days of the Persian War, although his father had distinguished himself in battle at Salamis. Perikles seemed to understand early in his career that there was a political shift happening in Athens away from the old rule limited to the upper classes, to a new day where the free labor force would have its say. The decision to build the fleet of 200 ships before Salamis contributed to this because rather than owing victory to the army, which had always been an aristocrat organization (remember how important it was for aristocrats to own a shield and sword?), Greeks owed their victory over Persia to the navy, which had traditionally been more of a blue collar outfit. More citizens were given the vote, and Perikles aligned himself more with the workers than the aristocracy, despite his own aristocratic heritage. He was voted into the position of commander (one of ten for the city) in 467 BC, and was re-elected repeatedly to extend his career in public office until 428 BC making him the primary man in charge during most of the great golden age.

Perikles had a vision for Athens, and the excess money sloshing around from the Delian League seemed the ideal source of funds to tap for the project. Initially the citizens were wary of spending money designated for defense on architecture and art, but when Perikles embarrassed the people by saying that if the city would not pay to rebuild, he would have to pay for it himself, he was given the okay to proceed using Delian League funds. Looking again at the Acropolis, there is one temple that is larger than all the rest. This is the **Parthenon**, which was the primary temple in Athens as it was dedicated to the city's patron deity, Athena (or more fully, Athena Parthenos – the

"Virgin Athena"). The temple was built by the premiere architect team working in Athens during the 5th century BC: Iktinos and Kallikrates. The Greeks were not so much interested in cutting edge engineering to develop newfangled building techniques. They preferred to construct buildings using the old reliable stand-by of post and lintel, but placed their creative energy into making it the most perfect specimen of post and lintel ever conceived.

It is helpful to understand the vocabulary used when discussing Greek architecture. First, Greek temples were designed with slight variations on the post and lintel theme called orders. The first and earliest is the *Doric* order. The Doric order was employed during the Archaic Period and remained popular into the Classical Period. The Parthenon is a Doric temple. The easiest way to keep the orders straight is to look at the *capitals,* or decorative tops of the *columns,* or upright posts in the construction. Doric capitals look like cereal bowls. Doric temples have a heavy, masculine feel to them with stocky columns and simple designs. The second order is *Ionic.* Ionic capitals look like scrolls, or rams' horns. This style became popular as interior design during the Classical Period (the interior columns inside the Parthenon were Ionic) then later during the Late Classical period the Ionic style became increasingly popular on temple exteriors. The last order is *Corinthian*. These temples look much like Ionic, but the capitals are quite ornate, looking like a salad of swirling vegetation. Corinthian columns came into vogue for interior design during the Late Classical Period, and were popular on temple exteriors during the Hellenistic age.

Architecture may be understood in *plan*, as if you were a bird flying overhead and looking down on a map of the building, or in *elevation*, which is a flattened view of a wall section seen straight on. The elevation of the Doric and Ionic orders labels all the parts of the building seen from that point of view. The floor of the temple was called a *stylobate*. Doric columns rest directly on the stylobate, while Ionic columns sit on a *base*. The column is composed of the *shaft* and *capital*, with the capital being the decorative cap on top. Resting on top of the capitals is the equivalent of a double lintel, called an *entablature*. The first lintel (bottom) is the *architrave*. It is plain, and recalls the old days when Greek temples were probably constructed with a simple wood lintel sitting on wood columns. The apparent second lintel stacked on top of the architrave is called the *frieze*. On an Ionic temple, the frieze is a continual band of sculpted design, but on the Doric temple (and only Doric) the frieze is composed of a checkerboard pattern of alternating *triglyphs* and *metopes*. Triglyphs are squares of vertical grooves, while the metope would have been filled with small, sculpted images. The Doric temple gives the best clue to explain why Greek post and lintel design came to have this double lintel. When the temples were made of wood in the old days, above the regular lintel (architrave) you would have seen the butt ends of the beams supporting the gabled roof above. The triglyphs recall the butt ends of beams, while the metopes, once plain and now filled in with sculpture, recall the open spaces between the support beams. At either end of the building there was a *pediment* that was a triangular space, usually decorated with sculpture, framed by the gabled roof above and the entablature below.

In plan, you can see that even a large temple in terms of stylobate area actually had only a modest interior space; clearly nobody ever intended for people to use these temples for indoor religious services. The interior room was called a *cella* or *naos*. The cella only needed to be large enough to accommodate a statue of the deity. The statue of

Athena from the Parthenon is long gone, but in its day it must have been spectacular as it filled almost the entire space. The cella was supposed to have a front porch called a *pronaos*. Often there was a bogus back porch too, that didn't go anywhere; it's only purpose was to make the plan formally balanced with the same amount of "stuff" on the front and back. Surrounding the cella was a *colonnade*, which is a row of columns together. A colonnade may be freestanding, or when it surrounds a building or courtyard and supports a roofed area like we see with temple architecture, it is called a *peristyle*.

The Parthenon is the perfect example of Classical design. The proportions recognized as making the most pleasing rhythms in architecture of this type follow a formula that can be expressed as $L = 2W + 1$. Count the number of columns along the short end of the building. The length of the building will have twice that many plus an extra column for good measure. Iktinos and Kallikrates were keen to make the proportions of the temple look perfect; in order to do so, they incorporated several optical illusions. What appears to be "regular" is in reality anything but. The stylobate looks flat. It isn't though. It is raised in the center and slopes off slightly toward the perimeter of the structure (good for water drainage), and further, it slopes even more toward the four corners of the building, humping the stylobate up slightly toward the center of each side. This was done to counter the illusion that a long horizontal line will appear to sag in the center. Because intuitively we expect rectangular buildings to be supported at the corners, the columns at the corners are just a little fatter than those closer to the center of each side, and they are slightly closer together too. Even more curious, the columns were designed to look as though they were bulging under the weight of the heavy roof. The circumference of each column about a third of the way up from the floor is bigger than the measurement at its bottom resting on the stylobate. This illusion of swelling under weight is called *entasis*. To compensate for the top-heavy design of the temple, the columns all tilt slightly inward, the roof area being smaller than the stylobate, although to the naked eye they appear to be the same size.

The Parthenon serves as a good example of Greek architecture as a whole. First, the emphasis was on beauty. There was little concern for whether the building happened to be practical, as in the case here where a very grand and expensive building had such a modest interior space that it was barely usable at all. The architecture was exterior oriented. This means that it was best appreciated from outside, even at a distance. Given that people weren't especially expected to *use* the building, it was almost more like a large sculpture – a monument to the significance of Athens more than anything more pragmatic. It was also large enough to be impressive, but never so huge as to dominate man and make him feel small. Remember that man was the measure of all things in Greece. He wanted temples that were big enough and gorgeous enough to make MAN feel important. He did not however wish to feel like a lowly peon, being compared to anything all that much grander than himself. This is in complete contrast to important architecture in most ancient cultures, where the norm seemed to be to dwarf the common man and impress upon him that he is a nobody compared to great powers in the world and beyond.

Perikles' personal favorite artist was hired to decorate the Parthenon with sculpture: Phidias. Phidias created the massive statue of Athena that originally filled the cella. It is long gone, sadly, but much of the relief sculpture that embellished the walls of the building survives. See the **Parthenon Frieze**. Think about this a minute, where would you expect to find most of the decoration, on the outside or inside of the temple? Outside, right? But the Parthenon was a Doric temple, so we know that above the architrave, the frieze on this temple should be alternating triglyphs and metopes. Correct. The triglyphs and metopes are there right where they should be. Then where was this frieze of unbroken sculpture located? The Parthenon Frieze ran around the exterior of the cella walls, so you'd have to peer through columns to see it. The subject of the Parthenon Frieze is a *Panathenic Procession*. The Panathenic Procession took place every 4 years, dating back to 566 BC. In theory one could argue that it was a religious festival, given that part of the pomp and circumstance was to deliver a new cloak to the statue of Athena. The fact of the matter was that the religious part of the festival paled when compared to the real reason everyone turned out: the Panathenic Games! Similar to the larger and older Olympic Games which date all the way back to 776 BC, the games sponsored by Athens attracted predominantly regional competitors but were nevertheless a BIG deal in Athens where sport and the cult of the body beautiful was closer to the true religion of the people.

Phidias' claim to fame was the *wet drapery technique*. He was renowned for his ability to sculpt wet fabric in such a way that it revealed the anatomy beneath. Phidias almost always dressed his models in togas that looked like the artist hosed them down before starting work. Female figures, which everyone expected to be clothed anyway, were his favorite, giving a furtive glimpse of a shoulder here and the curve of a breast there under the wet clothing. Even with male figures, Phidias would offer up a scarf or loincloth or cape that would alternatively flap in the wind and cling to the body with the ripple of muscle visible through the cloth.

Beyond the specifics of Phidias' style, the Parthenon Frieze serves as an excellent example of Classical art as a whole. Classical Greek art was generic. It doesn't matter that the faces of these women are long gone, because they were never meant to be identifiable citizens of Athens or anyplace else anyway. This was not a depiction of a specific Panathenic Procession, and these were not intended to be portraits of anybody in particular. It is a generalization of what a Panathenic Procession was more or less like: it is a department store window version of the beautiful good life with mannequins filling in on behalf of real people. Classical Greek art is about an idealized version of reality. Here we can make a comparison to Egypt. In Egypt, the artist set about depicting real people, but he was obliged to make the real person look better than he did in reality – the artist idealized ordinary-looking people. In Greece, the artist had little interest in depicting real people (mannequins were preferred), but he started with the most perfected body he could find in the form of a model, and then did his best to realistically depict Mr. or Ms. Workout Champ as a "stand in" on behalf of the less glamorous real world out there. Greek art is a collection of Barbies and Kens, or perhaps we could even think of it as a slice of Garrison Keillor's Lake Wobegon, where all the women are strong, all the men are good-looking, and all the children are above average. The men in Classical Greek art are handsome and fit; the women are slender and beautiful. Nobody is old, or fat, or skinny. There are no bratty kids, or grumpy grandpas. Everyone is young and lovely. Notice also that the scene is never overcrowded. Classical Greek art always erred on the side of simplicity. What did it matter that a Panathenic Festival was a crowded frenzy of activity? It will be forever memorialized as an elegant event promoting a mood of calm and dignity, which is exactly how the Greeks would want to be remembered.

Employing the same wet drapery style of Phidias, we have a group of female figures standing in a row as they function as columns on a building. These are *caryatids*. We first saw something similar at the Mortuary Temple of Rameses II in Egypt, but the difference is that those huge statues of Rameses were rock cut out of the side of a cliff – they did not support a roof at all. True caryatids are statues that function as columns in post and lintel architecture. These caryatids are part of the Porch of Maidens (south porch) on another famous building from the acropolis in Athens: the **Erectheion**. If the Parthenon is a typical Greek temple, the Erectheion is one of the most unique. Although both date from the Classical period, the Erectheion was built at least fifteen years later, and we can see that the architect, Mnesikles, was already looking forward to the Ionic order rather than employing the Doric order again. The second largest temple at the Acropolis, it honored both Athena and Poseidon, who according to legend, fought a battle on this site. Although the temple is smaller than the Parthenon, it is considerably more complex. The plan is asymmetrical and built on staggered levels due to the uneven site. The eastern porch is dedicated to Athena as patron of the city, while the north porch was a shrine to Poseidon. Finally, the temple also offered tribute to Erectheus, a legendary king of ancient Athens dating back to the days when the gods were in the habit of dropping by to offer first hand advice on how to manage affairs.

Phidias and his admirers excelled at presenting elegant, clothed figures, but most sculptors during the Classical period continued to study the male nude. The **Warrior** is a very early Classical statue that was discovered by a diver off the coast of Riace, Italy. Two statues were found together, suggesting they may have been pitched overboard in a storm to keep a heavily burdened ship from sinking. The statue is at the upper end of life size (6'6"), and made of cast bronze which was gaining popularity at this time in Greece. The *lost-wax method* of casting was employed. First the artist created the piece in a soft material like clay or plaster that was easier to fashion than sculpting stone. Then the figure was completely covered with hot wax, and once that had cooled, another coat of the soft clay or plaster material was applied. The wax was then melted away as molten bronze was poured in its place. Once it cooled the outer shell could be cracked away, and the artist could work the bronze to add additional details. One advantage of cast bronze was that it helped artists work on getting the anatomy right without having to deal with a material as unyielding as marble. Notice how compared to the two kouroi, the Warrior looks more realistic, muscled and fit. Artists also experimented with cast bronze to determine ways to make the figures look super real, since unlike marble, these statues were not painted. Instead they might add colored glass or stone eyes and ivory or silver teeth. This statue even had eyelashes attached!

The most famous sculptor from the Classical period (or at least tied with Phidias) was Polykleitos. He produced freestanding male nude statues of athletes, and his life-size (again around 6'6") figures followed a formula. The **Doryphoros** is a good example. It is generic, as Classical art would most always be, and clean shaven as most mature art of this period tends to be. The artist has employed an athlete for his model (in this case, a javelin thrower – doryphoros means spear bearer), but the objective of the statue was to demonstrate ideal beauty, not to pay tribute to a specific man. The figure is more natural and relaxed in appearance compared to kouros statues.

Both the Warrior and Doryphorus demonstrate the same pose called *contrapposto*, which is the shifting of weight from 2 feet to 1 foot. Contrapposto creates an "s" curve to the body, such that the hip of the supporting leg is slightly raised, and in more exaggerated examples, the corresponding shoulder is slightly drooped. Polykleitos was consumed with the goal of producing the ideal male body-type, and toward this end, he developed a standard canon of proportions for male anatomy which reduced the task of determining proportions to a series of ratios. How big is the head in relationship to the height of the figure, how long should an arm be compared to a leg, how big around should the chest be compared to the hips, and so forth. This canon of proportions made it easy to copy Polykleitos, and many artists did just that rather than create their own style. It should be noted that the sample of Polykleiton statues we have with us today are all Roman copies from Greek originals, although we still refer to them as Polykleitos pieces. Polykleitos worked in both marble and cast bronze, and the copies likewise come down to us in both mediums. You can easily identify a Roman copy by looking for one of two telltale clues. First, if you see that the nude is sporting a strategically placed fig leaf, it is almost certainly a Roman copy produced after Christianity was widely accepted, encouraging greater modesty. Another quick test is to see if there is any sort of odd looking object slapped up against the leg. Here, for example, the Doryphoros has a peculiar worm like … thing … slithering up his leg and looking for all the world like it is about to meld into his behind (Freud would have a heyday … .) What *IS* that? Plain and simple, it is a support system created to brace the leg so the statue would be more stable at the base and less likely to topple over. The Romans were a practical lot, and it seemed reasonable to them if they were going to invest in a big statue, they ought to make it sturdy. The Greeks would have been aghast! Their goal was to create the most beautiful art possible, and they wouldn't dream of compromising perfection with something as tacky as leg braces that distract our attention from the figure itself.

Late Classical *404-323 BC*

The Late Classical period was ushered in with the fall of Athens following her defeat in the Peloponnesian Wars. Sparta had never accepted that Athens was the new military powerhouse, and throughout the 5th century BC, Sparta had initiated niggling disputes with Athens in order to flex those Spartan muscles. In balance, it wasn't all Sparta's fault. Athens' pride and lust for power had compromised her attitude toward her colleagues in the Delian League. Increasingly Athens used her allegiances for personal gain, amassing wealth at the expense of her immediate neighbors through colonization and trade with rich nations like Egypt. When Sparta made her move, it was not in isolation because many other cities joined forces against Athens. Finally in 404 BC, Sparta beat Athens after a series of battles, bringing down her reign of glory, as well as destroying the only period in ancient Greek history where there was a successful stretch of international (or at least inter-city and inter-island) peace. Sparta for all her military acumen, however, hadn't the slightest interest in assuming the role of cultural leader of the greater Hellenic (Greek) society once Athens was knocked off her pedestal.

Athens was bankrupted by the wars, but did in part manage to salvage some wealth through redoubled business interests, trade and mining (silver mostly). Even so, she was in moral decline, and considering where she started, it's almost remarkable that she could fall even lower. Family loyalty declined, as did marriage as an institution, and motherhood as an honorable vocation. Sex with everything short of the livestock was considered not only okay, but almost preferable to anything resembling monogamy and fidelity. Athenians were not even faithful to their old state religions, opting to follow whatever new cult was imported along with goods from foreign ports. Civic pride tapered off along with any feelings of patriotic duty.

Off to the north in Macedonia, this newly weakened state of affairs in Greece did not pass unnoticed. Macedonia was an unlettered region, although traditionally on friendly terms with the Greeks, they were never up to the intellectual snuff of their southern neighbors. Philip became king of Macedonia in 359 BC. He was a hearty sort of fellow, given to drinking and no stranger to the pleasures of the flesh, with his taste for the boys surpassed only by his lust for the girls. He had a violent temper, but was known to be uncommonly generous also. He thrived on military life, and enjoyed nothing more than the company of fighting men who lived in the fast lane. Philip watched as Greece reduced itself to squabbling siblings, each town investing only in its own best interests, and even within the towns, each person looking out primarily for himself. Philip had visions of building an empire, starting first by unifying the petulant Greeks, then spreading his largess as far afield as Persia. What Philip started, his son and successor Alexander finished. The Late Classical Period was the age of Macedonian conquest, and the star to emerge as the great hero was Alexander the Great. The period ends with the death of Alexander in 323 BC.

During the Late Classical Period, the arts flourished. This may come as a surprise, because it would be easy to imagine that the great Golden Age in Athens would have produced the largest supply of gifted artists. Not so. It is ironic perhaps, but often throughout history we do *not* always find our best talent and most prolific art being produced in times of peace and prosperity. Unfortunately perhaps, strife often jump-starts the status quo in many ways, including creative expression. Whereas during the 5th century BC there were a handful of biggies like Phidias and Polykleitos, most of the "also ran" artists were content to copy the great masters of their generation. During the 4th century BC, people were less inclined to follow along. Many significant artists appeared at this time, with each taking his own individual approach to his craft.

Although there were many important artists, perhaps the one best remembered today is Praxiteles. Praxiteles focused his attention on the male nude as a theme, like Polykleitos before him, but Praxiteles presented his body beautifuls as gods rather than the athletes that the original models undoubtedly were. **Hermes and Dionysos** is an excellent example. Like the earlier Classical statues, it is slightly larger than life size (7'1"), and the figure displays contrapposto to make him appear more relaxed and natural. Compared to the <u>Doryphorus</u>, you may realize that the body proportions have changed. During the 4th century BC, another standardized canon of proportions was invented, not by Praxiteles, but by an exact contemporary sculptor named Lysippos. If the old prototype during the 5th century BC resembled a rugby player or wrestler, the new version of ideal perfection during the 4th century BC looked more like a tennis champ, or the star of field and track competitions. During Polykleitos' day, the ideal man was stocky and muscular, tall but not with especially long legs in proportion to his torso. During Praxiteles' day, the ideal man was expected to be a little taller, still muscular, but more streamlined with long legs and an overall lithe expression of fitness.

Compare these two statues. Do you find you prefer one to the other? Putting the basic differences of body types aside, there may be reasons for your preferences. Polykleitos produced his statue with the goal of intellectually distilling the qualities of ideal beauty. Praxiteles certainly started with a similar intention, but for him that was the point of departure, not the end in itself. Praxiteles' preoccupation was to create an emotional response in his viewer. He was subtle. He included the infant and established eye contact between the two so we are inclined to perceive Hermes as a sensitive kind of guy. He exaggerated the contrapposto, jutting the hips toward us with a sensual "in your face" aggressiveness. Finally, he polished his marble to make it shiny, and emphasized this fact by leaving the hair tousled and rough. No other Greek artist up to this time had ever polished marble statues. Shiny surfaces invite a tactile response, or in simple terms, when folks see this statue, they often get the urge to sidle on up next to the guy and pat him on the thigh. This is not by accident; the artist intended for you to be attracted to the piece. Most people find that appealing – the figure draws them in. Other people do not want to feel enticed to pat some naked guy on the thigh, and the statue makes them feel uncomfortable. Either way, people have a gut response to Praxiteles' work, be it favorable or otherwise, in a way that is often not true with earlier Greek art. Praxiteles would be pleased; that is what he was trying to achieve with his art. By the way, the Romans didn't think much of Praxiteles' work, so didn't steal many statues to copy. Hermes and Dionysos was found in a local excavation near Olympia, Greece, and many scholars presume it to be an original statue by the artist.

Praxiteles was the artist who introduced the female nude to Greek sculpture. Perhaps he recognized that while men ruled the day in Greece, lots of men found women physically appealing. His **Aphrodite of Knidos** is a good example. These statues created quite a stir when they were first introduced, with some enthusiasts actually going up and fondling the marble ladies in public! Since there were no athlete models for female nudes, Praxiteles relied on his shapely live-in girlfriend, Phryne for his inspiration.

The Greeks were crazy for theater; through much of their history theater was free admission, and attendance was expected. Theater wasn't just entertainment; it was a method of conscious enculturation where the prevailing morality and religious ideals were reinforced. Remember that the ancient Greek version of morality was not necessarily what we might think of today. Virtues like chastity and honesty weren't so much of an issue, while patriotism and bravery were perceived as the foundations for a virtuous society. Many theaters, like the **Theater at Epidauros** are still around today, and even still functional with excellent acoustics; there isn't a bad seat in the house – everyone can hear! Greek theaters were built outside in the open air such that the surrounding countryside provided a bucolic backdrop for the play. People sat on stone bleachers that were built into the natural, if probably enhanced slope in the land, fanning gradually away from the evening's drama or tragedy in a semicircular arc. They were large too; the Theater at Epidauros could seat up to 14,000 spectators for a single performance, and everyone had an equally good view. The circular area at the base of the *auditorium* seating was called the *orchestra*. The productions were staged here with singing, dancing, reciting poetry, and acting, always performed by an all male cast. Behind the orchestra was a raised structure called a *skene*, or basically scene; which was the equivalent of painted architectural scenery behind the players. Hidden behind the skene was the ***proskenion***, or proscenium, which was a storage area for the actors' props with its raised, flat top meeting the backside of the skene. Over time some of the actors began to conduct part of their performance from this raised platform-roof of the proskenion, using it like a stage, although traditionally Greek theater was performed exclusively in the orchestra.

Hellenistic *323-147BC*

The Hellenistic Period is the grand dénouement of Greek society and culture as a dominant force in the Mediterranean. It began with the death of Alexander the Great in 323 BC, and for our purposes, ended in 147 BC when Rome conquered Greece and took control of the country (the Greeks lived on, but they were increasingly under Roman influence). Alexander was a remarkable man. Although never fully educated, he studied for a time under Aristotle and showed remarkable promise as a scholar. He was a man of morals too, or at least relative to his Greek peers whom, as we have discussed, teetered toward absolute moral bankruptcy. He devoted his brief life almost exclusively to ambition: his goal was to complete what his father had started. In fact, Alexander exceeded even Philip's wildest dreams by extending his empire from the Balkan Peninsula all the way to India.

On his deathbed, Alexander was supposedly asked to whom he would leave his great empire … to which he responded, "to the strongest." There was no one capable of maintaining Alexander's power, and thus the whole thing gradually unraveled. Democracy to a substantial degree had failed in Greece; for as many different people who had wriggled their way into government, most had abused the power of office and tried to stack the deck toward personal gain. There were class wars. Sexual immorality had become so pervasive that nothing even resembling scruples existed in Greece anymore; people of both sexes pretty well indulged their senses with anything that moved. Increasing numbers of healthy babies were left to die of exposure, since childrearing was perceived as a nuisance interfering with obtaining the all-important luxuries in life, and the birth rate plummeted as a result. Avarice was the god of choice. Alexander's ideas of melding the East and West was his one lingering legacy, with Greek, Egyptian and Persian influences bleeding back and forth between the different regions.

In the arts, the cycle of development mentioned at the start of this chapter reached its zenith of complexity during the Hellenistic Period. The Greeks had started with a simple idea. Let's represent man, and let's try to make him look real. The kouros was the initial experiment, with the kore as a second string alternative art form. Because the Greek was naturally inclined to think a lot of himself and believe himself more gifted than those who came before him, the move toward perfection went quickly, and in no time it seems we have Polykleitos who not only seemed to figure out how to make a male nude look perfect, he even reduced the whole process into a mathematical formula that could be duplicated by anyone.

But people got bored with it, and within a hundred years, different artists would find different ways to jazz it up. Praxiteles, for example, decided that intellectual art wasn't enough, there had to be a sensual component as well, and he manipulated the male nude to ring new bells with a viewing audience, and introduced the female nude to spice things up a bit.

The Hellenistic Period would be the same, only more so. If a sprinkling of female nudes were good to spark the imagination in Praxiteles' day, why not make more of them? The **Aphrodite of Melos**, or as she is often better known (by the Roman name) **Venus de Milo** is a perfect example. She looks not unlike a statue by Praxiteles, voluptuous and beautiful. So much for the naked ladies, but what about the naked guys? Check out the **Barberini Faun**! If a little sensuality was good a hundred years earlier, why not opt for raw pornography now? Why leave anything to the imagination? Why be subtle?

Not all art played the sex card, but what it all has in common is that it pays greater tribute to emotions than to intellect. Up until now, the Greeks had devoted themselves to the pursuit of simple beauty. Consider the **Old Market Woman**. She's a pathetic old bag lady; nothing remotely glamorous here! The artist was now willing to break the old rules in order to guarantee the statue will "get to you." There's no telling what exactly you might feel toward this woman, pity perhaps, or disgust, but one way or the other, you probably feel *something*.

Probably the most famous statue from the Hellenistic period is the **Laocoon.** It represents the Trojan priest and his two sons who tried to warn their countrymen of the impending trap of the Trojan horse. Poseidon, god of the sea and ardent supporter of Greece sent serpents to kill the priest so the Greek ruse would not be discovered. The statue is well over life size, and beyond that, the priest looks more like a weight lifter on steroids than a "man of the cloth" in any sense. The figures writhe in pain and suffering. There is no restraint on the part of the artist, no attempt to simplify the piece, or emphasize the dignity of anybody. Whereas Classical art at one extreme is stoic, timeless, simplified and intellectual, Hellenistic art is dramatic, theatrical, complex, and wrought with emotion.

The last statue to be addressed here may be one of the most spectacular and striking of any art that has come down to us from the Greeks: the **Nike of Samothrace**. Like the Laocoon, she stands 8' tall (in the case of the Nike that is without her head). She was discovered in the ruins of the Sanctuary of the Great Gods in Samothrace by a French explorer in 1863. There isn't anything else quite like it in Greek art, no prototype or precedent. We presume she was created to celebrate and memorialize a naval victory, as she appears to have just lighted on the prow of a ship, like a glorious figurehead. She also appeared to have part of a stone ship, long broken away, in her original base. Her gown swirls about her body, whipped by the wind. This is a magnificent statue, and yet we have no idea who the artist was, who paid for such a spectacular piece or even why it was commissioned. And so it was with the decline of Greece. They were gifted artists to the end, but in a crumbling society. It would be Rome that would salvage the fundamentals of Greek art and architecture, and reinterpret the beauty of the past into a new and different expression of national pride.

5. Rome

Rome is often compared to Greece, on the assumption that the two civilizations were little more than two sides of the same penny. While it is true that the clothing, the array of gods, and often art and architecture had common roots, in fact they were very different people.

The Etruscans *c. 700-509 BC*

The Etruscans lived along the western seaboard of Italy between the Arno River to the north and the Tiber River to the south, in the region called Tuscany today. They may have been indigenous to central Italy, or perhaps they came originally from Asia Minor. One way or the other, the Etruscans had been in central Italy dating back as far as 1000 BC, although it was closer to 700 BC when they rose to become a prominent civilization in this part of the world. As you can see from the dates, they were contemporaries of the Archaic Greeks, and the two cultures appear to have been trading partners and well acquainted with one another. The Etruscans were ruled by kings, as were the early Greeks, and also like the Greeks they failed to form a unified country, preferring the autonomy of individual city-states.

Similarities of style are easily seen in both their temple architecture and also some large scale sculpture, suggesting they borrowed ideas back and forth across the Adriatic and Tyrrhenian Seas. Unfortunately, no Etruscan temples survive since they were made of *wattle and daub* (branches of wood filled in with clay and mud) built on top of a raised stone podium, but we have a temple model reconstructed from a Roman description. The **Etruscan temple** was a cella (apparently divided into three chambers) with a front porch, columns and a gabled roof, although there was no pediment. It seems the Etruscans didn't go in for a carved frieze (not surprising given the construction materials), but they decorated the roof with free-standing *terra cotta* (baked clay) statues instead. Still, the basic design recalls Greece … or perhaps it was the other way around. Likewise, the Etruscans produced life-size statues, a little smaller than kouroi in Archaic Greece but not unlike them in some ways. The 5'10" **Apollo** found in the city of Veii illustrates the similarities and differences. Apollo is similar in size, and the walking pose and Archaic smile also resemble kouros statues created at the same time in Greece. It differs from kouroi in that the Etruscan figure is at least partially clothed, and it was made of terra cotta, the material of choice in Etruria, rather than marble

Whatever the similarities one might find between Archaic Greece and Etruria, however, the two societies were quite different. For starters, the Etruscans were the most open-minded ancient civilization when it came to the roles of women, in stark contrast to the Greeks who erred at the other end of the spectrum. Husbands and wives were considered more equal, socializing together and apparently enjoying similar rights under the law. Women had the same opportunities as men to receive an education. While it was still important for women to have a dowry when they married, the Etruscans fully approved of young women working for a few years as prostitutes to earn enough money to secure a good match in marriage. A husband would be proud of such wife; entrepreneurial spirit was admirable and came with bragging rights.

Perhaps like the Minoans, the Etruscans were apparently party people who enjoyed life. Since we cannot read the records that survive (a pity since according to later generations in Rome the Etruscans produced great literature) most of what we know we have learned through archaeology and tomb art. Scenes like the **Musicians and Dancers** fresco found in a tomb in Tarquinia depict the Etruscans living it up and having a good time. Although the information on their religion is sketchy, it seems the Etruscans believed in an afterlife like the Egyptians did. Not all the tomb frescoes show paradise, however. Unlike the Egyptians, the Etruscans believed in hell, and much of the tomb art depicts terrible demons and suffering. Either they decided to live life in the fast lane while they could because what was to come wasn't pretty, or they hoped that whatever judgment lay ahead, they might either escape eternal punishment, or pay their dues in hell then get promoted to paradise.

Whatever their exact beliefs, like the Egyptians they invested in preparations for death and afterlife. Rather than embalming their dead, they either cremated cadavers and put the ashes in an urn, or encased the corpse in a terra cotta **Sarcophagus** (coffin) with no interest in preserving the body. Typically a sarcophagus would depict a husband and wife (both of whose remains would presumably be stored together) shown in happy times, reclining as if attending a supper party. There is nothing somber or sad, or even especially serious about how the couple is depicted for their final send-off. Tombs varied, but some were quite spacious and embellished with both murals of good and evil, and sculpted objects of everyday items the deceased my need in the afterlife (kitchen utensils and that sort of thing). Observe the **Burial Chamber** from Cerveteri. Notice that inside the tomb there are several niche "beds" carved into the walls even including carved pillows. Etruscan tombs were reusable like Mycenaean, the difference being that in the Etruscan world, the tomb was designed for the extended family and folks just "moved in" after they died. Nobody was cast aside to make room, the newly deceased was simply shown to his or her bed and the tomb was resealed until the next guy passed on.

The Republic *509-44 BC*

Prior to 509 BC, central Italy was inhabited by a variety of tribes, people of slightly different ethnic origins who lived in small hamlets. The Etruscans had dominated the region for a couple centuries, but they weren't the only people there. As was true in other locales like Greece and Mesopotamia, these independent city-states frequently had little use for one another. The two other dominant tribes other than the Etruscans were the Latini, whose main city was called Rome after their first king, Romulus (of legendary Romulus and Remus fame – the twins raised by a she-wolf), and the Sabines. After centuries of war given that these two groups lived a stone's throw from each other, their leaders determined that they might do better to pool their resources and devise ways to live together in improved harmony. Another Latin speaking tribe called the Caelians tag-teamed in on the arrangement, as did other minor ethic stragglers in the region, and the Roman Republic was born around 509 BC. They rose up against the Etruscan kings in order to forge a unified nation where all the citizens, no matter their heritage, might live in peace together. Although the proud Etruscans took a little longer to fully assimilate, by the third century BC they were also fully onboard with the Republic

And so, the Republic of Rome was founded in 509 BC, and it lasted until the assassination of Julius Caesar in 44 BC. Unlike Greece, which experimented with a limited democracy, Rome evolved as a republic. For starters, there were too many people to be governed for each person to participate fully in all government affairs and decisions. Thus, they developed a system whereby some people were elected to government posts, and those who were not directly involved relied on these elected officials to represent their interests. At the local level, the people were governed by magistrates, who were elected annually, and who reported to the Senate. The senators in turn selected their leader, called a Rex (or *elected* king), which was a position akin to a prime minister in parliamentary government today.

In Rome, citizens were divided into two basic classes. The upper class people were called **patricians**, and lower class citizens were **plebians**. The prerequisites for patrician status were: 1) most important, the individual had to demonstrate that his or her family line could be traced back to one of the founding tribes of Rome; and 2) the individual had to be a landowner, in essence, one had to own a house. Only patricians were permitted to hold public office, but this did not mean that plebians were disenfranchised. Plebian families attached themselves to patrician families as loyal subjects, supporting them in elections in order to gain representation in government. Moreover, unlike some ancient civilizations where there was little or no social mobility, in Rome, if a plebian family had been faithful supporters of a patrician family over multiple generations, it was considered appropriate to arrange a marriage between members of the two households, at which point the entire plebian family was grandfathered into patrician status. Women also fared better in Rome than elsewhere, especially Greece, as Roman women were permitted to inherit land. Often this privilege improved a woman's prospects at marriage, and while she might not be the one marching off to work in the Senate, her husband, who may have acquired patrician status thanks to his wife's land holdings, was wise to remember who held the behind-the-scenes power in that family.

Romans are sometimes perceived as following in the shadows of glorious Greece, and doing a second rate job at that. This is a sad misunderstanding of Rome. In fact, there were many occasions when Rome did borrow heavily from Greece, but the important thing to understand is that there was always a *reason,* and the reason was always more legitimate than pure copycat motives. At the same time, Roman art and architecture does not usually look *exactly* like Greek art and architecture if you get past the first glance; it is different not due to inferior craftsmanship, but due to different agendas between the two cultures. The only type of Greek art that Romans out and out copied was Classical Greek nudes, like the statues by Polykleitos in particular, and the reason they left them as beautiful nudes was because they were used to decorate the public baths, which is where folks hung out in the buff.

A good introductory exercise to understanding the similarities and differences between Greece and Rome would be Republican temples like the **Temple Fortuna Virilis**. It is easy to spot the similarities to Greek temples. It has Ionic columns, and the same basic presentation with a gabled pediment over an entablature. It looks similar, just not as beautiful. The key here (as always) is to try to put yourself in the other guy's shoes and think like he thinks. The Greeks weren't very practical, and they were happy to spend lots of money for a gorgeous temple, which for the most part would never be actively used. True, it housed a spectacular statue (that many people never saw), but for the most part, temples like the Parthenon sat perched on their pedestals overlooking the city and they served as much as anything as the "image" of the city – a source of civic pride almost more like a huge statue of a building rather than a real building that was ever intended to house many people inside.

The Romans were much too down to earth and sensible to go in for such wasteful extravagance. The Romans would spend great sums for things that made sense and offered a benefit they could understand, but big, expensive architecture that doesn't really have much practical function … hmmmm … not very Roman. Like the Greek religion, Roman religion did not include the concept of group worship the way people might go to a church, synagogue or mosque today. Therefore, since the only day-to-day function of a temple was to house a statue (rather like a fancy mini-warehouse?), it seemed more reasonable to place the building on a regular city lot rather than consuming the prime real estate in town. It also seemed like a waste to put the best architects to work on the project. The best land and the best architects (and the most money invested) should be reserved for buildings people actually used every day. When an architect was given a temple project, it didn't make sense to waste a lot of time trying to invent a new style of building; save the creativity for buildings people were likely to use. So they simply borrowed from earlier models, which were also more or less mini-warehouses to store statues, albeit very large and costly mini-warehouses. Rather than make it so big and expensive, the Romans shrunk the size down to what was actually required, which is basically a cella and little more; this idea probably came from the Etruscans. It wasn't a "bad" building and not entirely unadorned either; for example, three sides of the building were dressed up with relief carved columns, called ***engaged columns***. This added a modest amount to the project cost but was deemed appropriate so the temple wouldn't be a plain box. Roman temple designs were not devoid of art, they were just more thrifty and practical than their Greek prototypes. There is a pronaos, which seemed reasonable because the porch let the odd visitor know where the door was, but no fake back porch. The stairs only went up the side of the building where there was a door; the Greeks put stairs on all four sides of the Parthenon even though three of those expensive flights of stairs led to nothing but blank walls … the Romans figured they could find better ways to spend their money.

So where did the Romans invest their architecture dollars, if not on spectacular temples like the Greeks? Before anything else, they put money into good quality residential housing. The **House of Faun** is a wonderful example of Roman housing at its most luxurious. The actual house is long gone, which is why we have only the plan which was reconstructed from the foundations dug out by archaeologists. We can also create reconstruction drawings of how it may have looked back during the Republic. The House of Faun was discovered in the city of Pompeii. Remember that "Rome" is the name of a country or nation in ancient times. It was also the name of the capital city, but within the realm of Rome, there were many cities. The discovery of Pompeii and her neighbor city of Herculaneum was an archaeologist's dream come true. Over the centuries, the city of Rome went through many makeovers, such that it had become almost impossible to find traces of the old Republic. Pompeii, in contrast to the busy capital, remained a sleepy town with a Republican character well into the early years of the Empire. On August 24th in the year 79, Mount Vesuvius erupted sending forth tons of lava and hot ash, burying the towns lying at her base. Eyewitness accounts tell of the massive black cloud with great tongues of fire consuming the lost towns, where the citizens were caught split-second and frozen in a time capsule of thick volcanic ash. Excavations in Pompeii have been ongoing since the mid-18th century.

The House of Faun was clearly the home of a wealthy patrician as it was larger than a typical house, but big or small, Roman houses shared common characteristics. First, the typical Roman house filled the entire lot, which might cover an acre or more of land. It butted right onto the street, which could have posed a problem with lack-of-privacy except that the "front yard" was converted into shops that were rented out to merchants. In this way, commercial and residential neighborhoods were one in the same, no "bedroom" subdivisions like today where someone might have to drive 15 miles to buy a gallon of milk; everything was close by and convenient. Making money off the "front yard" also meant that the homeowner might afford more house than he could if he were not collecting rent from tenants. There was a long, narrow entrance hall between the shops back to the big living room called an ***atrium***. The House of Faun was so grand that it had two atriums, sort of like a big house today having a formal living room for entertaining company and a den reserved for private family time. An atrium had no windows to the outside as it was surrounded on all sides with other rooms, so the only light source was a hole in the ceiling in the center of the room. This meant that sometimes it rained inside the house! No problem, because beneath the hole in the roof was a pool to collect rainwater called an ***impluvium***. The impluvium collected free water that could be used for cooking, cleaning, washing clothes … just about anything except drinking water, which helped to lower utility bills as homeowners seldom required much purchased water from the aqueducts. Around the sides of the atrium there were modest bedrooms for each member of the family, called ***cubiculae (plural of cubicula)***.

At the far end of the atrium, opposite the main entrance was the ***tablinum***. The tablinum was the most important room in the house, for it was here that the busts of ancestors were kept. Given the extreme importance of being able to document one's family pedigree to maintain patrician status, it was customary to keep sculpted images of dead relatives on hand. These were used to educate the next generation of children in the family, as well as to show off to your guests how important your family was. Beyond the tablinum there was a ***peristyle garden***. This was a lovely, formal garden with a covered veranda (hence we get the peristyle) around the perimeter, and the center open to the sky so it could be enjoyed almost like an outdoor living room in good weather. It was completely enclosed for privacy, being surrounded by either servant's quarters like we see in the House of Faun, or sometimes surrounded by rental apartments (more revenue for the homeowner) that opened to alleys running between the houses, rather than opening into the main house as the servant's quarters do. Out back there was usually a substantial vegetable garden where the owner might have a modest orchard, keep small livestock and grow vegetables, all designed to lower his food expenses at the market, making home ownership more affordable. This particular house is unusual because the owners were evidently so wealthy, and probably so influential, that the standard vegetable garden has been transformed into a massive second peristyle garden, obviously on a scale that suggests hosting enormous receptions.

As time moved on, these huge, sprawling houses gradually became obsolete. Especially in the city of Rome, the population grew to where it got quite overcrowded. Since much of the capital city was built on land near marshes where it was too wet to build, the city couldn't expand indefinitely into the countryside, so it became densely populated. Big one-story houses became residential dinosaurs, and were gradually replaced by apartment buildings called *insulae*. By the close of the first century AD, most people in the city of Rome lived in these apartments. Insulae had been around since the Republic, however, and some of the best early examples were in Ostia. Ostia was the port facility for the city of Rome. Since Rome was not located on the coast, it was necessary to create a port harbor to keep Rome competitive in trade. Ships unloaded their goods in Ostia where they were moved by barge up the Tiber River to the capital. The **Insula at Ostia** is a good example of a Roman apartment building. A typical insula was 5 stories tall, with the first story serving much the same purpose as front yards did for single-family houses. Shops were located here, as well as public toilets that were used by the general public and also by the inhabitants of the apartments. Apartments had no private bathrooms; remember that bathing was done at the public bath. A typical insula contained only 4 apartments, two 2-story apartments on each side of the building, running from the front to the back of the building. They were quite spacious so the people who lived in insulae didn't have to feel like they were getting a bad deal buying an apartment rather than buying a detached house. Obviously, while an apartment owner might share some of the same amenities as regular homeowners, like an atrium, cubiculae, a tablinum, and even a pleasant peristyle garden to be shared by the 4 families, realistically they couldn't possibly have an impluvium in each apartment, and no vegetable garden either.

The **Patrician with the Busts of His Ancestors** and the **Republican Bust** are both examples of the sort of sculpture you would find in a tablinum. When grandpa died, the family would call in an artist immediately to create a hot wax mask from the deceased person's face. This would then be used to create a very realistic sculpture of the dead relative, to be added to the family collection. For as much as Greek art tends to be generic, Roman art is almost always specific. During the Republic, we see that sculpture in many cases was a means to an end, as a way to document family lineage. Greeks were concerned with abstract beauty for its own sake. In contrast, as we look at the images of dead ancestors, we can understand that beauty, as an abstract has no place here. If the statue looks pretty or ugly, it's because the dead person represented really looked pretty or ugly toward the end of life. It has nothing to do with the artist making a statement, be it a sample of ideal beauty (Classical) or trying to get an emotional response from the viewer (Hellenistic). The Roman artist was there to document reality for the sake of history, a concept that would have been quite novel in Greece.

The Republic in Rome lasted for almost 500 years, and while there were certainly changes during that time, the basic form of governance and the basic identity of what it meant to be Roman remained constant. This was not so much true for Imperial Rome. Julius Caesar was assassinated in 44 BC, which brought the old Republic to a close. After a few years of political chaos, Octavian, nephew to Julius Caesar, established the Roman Empire. Julius Caesar may have technically been the Rex of the Roman Senate, but he effectively ruled as a dictator, and he chose his nephew, Octavian to succeed him prior to his death. Octavian was, however, challenged in his bid for power. Following the Battle of Actium in 31 BC, where Mark Antony and his co-conspirator, Cleopatra of Egypt, were defeated, Octavian at last secured his position as head of state in 30 BC. Recognizing that the days of the egalitarian Republic had faded, he had himself retitled Augustus, and he ruled as the first emperor of Rome. Imperial Rome (the Rome ruled by emperors) was unlike the Republic in that the mood of the nation was profoundly influenced by whichever dynasty of emperors happened to be in charge. Accordingly, we do not consider "Imperial Rome" to be a period in history, but rather the empire is subdivided into smaller chunks of history corresponding to the dynasty of emperors in power.

Julio-Claudian *30 BC-68*

The Julio-Claudian period began in 30 BC when Augustus took over the reins of government, and three years later he declared himself Emperor of Rome. The dynasty ended in 68 with the suicide of the emperor, Nero. These emperors were all descendants of Julius Caesar, and are often referred to as the Caesars, although that isn't a family name so much as it is a title. There were five emperors in this line: Augustus, Tiberius, Caligula, Claudius, and Nero. Augustus was the greatest statesman in the group, and it was Augustus who set the standard for what the Julio-Claudian period would project as an image. All the emperors in this extended family were patricians, as one would expect of government officials in Rome, and yet Augustus was very keen to have Rome be the best place on Earth for all her citizens. He had a genuine concern for his people, especially for broad ideals which he considered important toward making Rome a great society. When Augustus assumed leadership of Rome, the country which had taken such pride in its upright, stoic heritage had fallen into immorality and social decay as well as deep financial distress. The money problems were initially alleviated when Rome was able to hijack riches from defeated Egypt. Interest rates fell, and Augustus publicly forgave debts so that citizens had a shot at a fresh start. But these measures would only be a temporary stay from disaster unless Rome modified its behavior. The birth rate had plummeted, with many Romans electing to remain childless through infanticide, abortion and contraception. Meanwhile the only segments of the population that were increasing were slaves who had to be supported and foreigners moving in looking for a free handout from the government. Augustus made it his business to reverse these trends by passing laws that promoted marriage, fidelity and family life. Adultery became a serious offense punished by banishment or death. Penalties were also imposed on celibates (they could not legally inherit), as Roman citizens were expected to marry and raise families as part of their patriotic duty. Divorce was permitted, but both parties were expected to remarry within six months to stay in the good graces of government policy.

His successor, Tiberius, was the son of Augustus' wife by a prior marriage. Augustus was not fond of Tiberius who apparently was secretive and an introvert, but in the end he adopted his stepson when there seemed no other option for a successor. He also imposed his daughter, Julia on Tiberius, insisting that Tiberius divorce his pregnant wife that he loved in order to marry the pretty but promiscuous daughter of Augustus. Unfortunately for Tiberius, Julia was not an easy wife to fathom, much less manage. She was known for her flagrant infidelities with assorted lovers, which caused more than just a little embarrassment to her husband. Roman law allowed (in fact recommended) that cheating wives be dealt with very severely: the custom was for the husband to kill a wife who was unfaithful. This put Tiberius in a difficult position. The more he suffered her humiliations, the more the public perceived him as a weak man not able to handle his domestic life, much less matters of state. In the end, he simply didn't deal with it at all. Tiberius exiled himself to the island of Rhodes, leaving the Julia problem to an aging Augustus to handle. Julia was banished, which broke Augustus' heart, but what could he do? She had so openly defied the laws that he had passed to improve morality; how could he continue to turn a blind eye to her indiscretion? Tiberius was never interested in being emperor; if he had had his way, the Republic would have been restored. Even after reluctantly accepting his fate, he tried to rule more as the leader of the Senate rather than lording over the government, using the Senate more like an occasional advisory board as Augustus had done. Although he was a good emperor, the people were not especially fond of him since he was a stern stoic in a time of epicurean tastes. Tiberius retired to the island of Capri to escape the public eye in Rome, leaving government affairs in the hands of subordinates (Sejanus, the prefect of the Praetorian Guard to be specific). In the end his absence led to power struggles in Rome, and Tiberius was smothered with a pillow to open Rome to new leadership.

Tiberius was succeeded by his great-nephew, Gaius Caligula, who was a bona fide lunatic. Caligula (his nickname from childhood meaning "Little Boot") started off more or less okay, promising to restore the country to the days of the great Augustus. It didn't take long for the power to go to his head, which combined with health problems (epilepsy), insecurity and psychotic delusions wreaked havoc on Rome. Caligula only ruled five years, but caused quite a ruckus for so brief a reign. For example, he was a devoted enthusiast of chariot races, and invited his favorite winning horse to dinner and proposed having the horse appointed to the Senate. He admired the old pharaohs of Egypt and wanted to be treated like a god himself. Toward this end, he began to conflate himself with Jupiter, wearing costumes around the palace and shooting "thunderbolts" with a theater prop he had constructed to appear more convincing. Caligula's lack of morals was legendary. He had affairs with all of his sisters, and was in the habit of "marrying" most of the attractive women in Rome for a few days or weeks to try them all out in bed, after which he would divorce them, sometimes making it illegal for them to remarry. He passed bizarre laws, like ordering that all bald men be imprisoned, executed and fed to animals. He enjoyed inflicting pain, and randomly killed people, often through slow torture, for fun and sport. He bankrupted the treasury with his gross extravagances, this in just five years after inheriting a financially wealthy nation from the boring but prudent Tiberius. Caligula was terrified that people were plotting against him (certainly he gave them plenty of motives), so he was quick to murder his opponents, real and imagined, before they could murder him. In the end the Praetorian Guard assassinated Caligula, and his Uncle Claudius succeeded him.

Claudius came to power by default. He was hastily selected by those who killed Caligula because they assumed Claudius was a simpleton they could control. He had survived Caligula by playing the buffoon while the rest of the family was murdered right and left. Claudius had gimpy legs causing him to walk with a limp and he spoke with a stutter, imperfections he used to his advantage with his nutcase nephew, Caligula.

Claudius would bumble about looking stupid and Caligula took immense pleasure in picking on his uncle as a pathetic but harmless idiot. Caligula never felt threatened by Claudius, which accounts for why Claudius was still alive when Caligula was killed. Much to everyone's surprise, Claudius turned out to be a pretty good statesman, interested in history and particularly attached to the ideals of the old Republic when Rome was less corrupted, at least in theory. His own personal morals left something to be desired, but his biggest flaw perhaps was trusting charlatans, both romantic and political who did him in. Claudius' fourth wife murdered him with poison mushrooms in a plot to undo the order of succession away from Claudius' son (a decent fellow) in favor of her own son by a previous marriage. That was Nero.

Nero, like Caligula, goes down in history as being a bad boy, although his problem wasn't insanity. On the one hand, he was artistically inclined, generous to the poor and a pretty good administrator during his early reign. On the other hand, Nero was breathtakingly immoral and self-indulgent in every possible way. He was also casual about killing people he found inconvenient; Nero had his own mother murdered (that sweet lady who poisoned Claudius so Nero could steal the throne). He moved on to kill his wife so he could marry another woman. When his new wife died (rumor has it after he kicked her in the gut late in pregnancy), he found a boy whose face resembled his dead wife, had him castrated and used him for carnal gratification. Nero disliked all religion, but he especially loathed the Christians, who were at that time a minority cult in the empire. In 64 a massive fire broke out in Rome destroying most of the city. It has never been determined if Nero had the fire set, although it is likely that he had a hand in the disaster. It had been his dream to remake the city according to his own plans, although it is also true that he energetically reached out to help survivors by providing food and shelter, demonstrating that he wasn't completely insensitive to their plight. Looking for a scapegoat to deflect suspicion from himself, he accused the Christians of setting the fire, and to punish them he inflicted the worst possible cruelty. According to the historian Tacitus, some were covered with the hides of wild animals and left to be eaten alive by starved dogs, while others were crucified, or doused with flammable liquids and set ablaze. It was during Nero's reign that Saint Peter and Saint Paul were both executed in Rome, and it is most likely Nero who is referenced in the Book of Revelations in the Bible as the antichrist. Fortunately Nero had the decency to commit suicide in 68. Even before he died, those plotting against him had already selected a successor … from outside that family line.

The art and architecture of the Julio-Claudian period was primarily influenced by the vision of Augustus. Augustus had two goals for the new empire. For one, he wanted to secure international peace for Rome. Augustus had seen war tear apart the country during the latter Republic. It was a drain on the economy too. It seemed to Augustus that if he could achieve a peace treaty with the barbarian neighbors along Rome's boundaries, they could enjoy a better life at home while also bringing the good Roman way of life to other less fortunate people. Toward this end, Augustus achieved the *Pax Romana*, a peace treaty annexing Spain and Gaul (France) to the empire in 13 BC. He considered this to be his crowning glory accomplishment. Secondly, Augustus was deeply concerned for what he perceived as a slight inferiority complex attitude among Romans when they compared themselves to Greeks. Certainly the Romans were already spectacularly successful in complex areas where the Greeks were less remarkable. The

Romans were superb engineers, they had mastered far more sophisticated government, and their society was more unified and fair. And yet, the Romans perceived the Greeks as exuding a sophisticated style that eluded the more pedestrian Romans. The Greeks were artistic and philosophical, while the Romans were methodical and practical. The Greeks were glamorous, especially to the outsider's eye, while Romans saw themselves as hard working, but common, not elite in their manners and disposition. Augustus set out to prove to Rome that she was every bit as classy as Greece in addition to Rome's other stellar qualities. He did this by creating a "culture transfer" in the art and architecture of his generation.

This culture transfer is especially evident in Julio-Claudian sculpture. Let's consider the Ara Pacis Augustae, which was an altar commissioned by Augustus to celebrate the signing of the Pax Romana with Spain and Gaul. Around the exterior perimeter of the altar there are relief carvings called the **Ara Pacis Frieze**. If you look at the sculpture style, you will probably detect a Phidias influence. This is 100% deliberate. What matters, though, is not so much that the Roman artist copied Greek art, what matters is *why* he copied. The Roman artist was just as gifted an artist as Phidias, so his motive would not have been because he couldn't think of any other way to create art. In fact, he borrowed the wet drapery technique from Phidias for two reasons. First, according to Augustus' wishes, he is creating a culture transfer; that is, he was going out of his way to demonstrate to Rome that the home boy could do whatever the Greeks could do every bit as well. No reason to apologize about inferior talent in Rome, thank you very much! Beyond that, it is important to notice that Phidias was selected as the mentor. Artists working for Augustus borrowed heavily from Classical Greek art, but not Greek art from other periods. The reason was that it was only during that brief slice of Greek history when the Delian League flourished that the Greeks enjoyed international peace. Given that Augustus was especially motivated to reinforce his attachment to peace, he avoided aligning his reign to any period of Greek history that failed to measure up to these peace-keeping ideals. Expect to see Julio-Claudian art and temple architecture looking back to the days of Perikles, but don't expect to see art from other Greek periods being recalled.

For as much as the Ara Pacis Frieze looks like the Parthenon Frieze with everyone decked out in wet togas clinging to their bodies, hopefully you would never get the two confused. The Roman frieze has all different types of people – old folks, bald guys and bratty kids, whereas the Greek frieze shows a bunch of perfect mannequins. Remember, Greek art was generic, but Romans went in for specifics. The Ara Pacis Frieze shows the actual people who attended the isolated singular event of the signing of the Pax Romana. They are clearly documented with realistic portrait likenesses of real people who can be individually identified. Furthermore, they are all crowded in together, unlike the more simplified Parthenon Frieze, because the artist was compelled to fit everyone in for the equivalent of this group picture. In order to accomplish this task, notice that the Roman artist has actually had to stretch his talent further than Phidias by incorporating both *high relief*, like Phidias employed, and *low relief*, more like the shallow carving seen in Egyptian and Mesopotamian art, to show more people in the background.

The **Augustus of Prima Porta** does much the same thing. The statue gets its name because it was found near the villa of Prima Porta, a quiet refuge frequented by Augustus' wife, Livia. It is 6'8" tall, so slightly larger than life sized. That little cupid riding a dolphin stuck to his leg serves not only to brace the base of the statue making it more stable, it also makes reference to the Julio-Claudian claim that they were descended from Venus (mother to Cupid), the goddess of love who rose from the sea, which in turn suggests that the emperors were gods themselves. His bare feet indicate that he is a hero, and the breastplate illustrates a variety of propaganda scenes reinforcing the Augustan preoccupation with international peace.

Look for a Classical Greek influence; it *will* be there. The body proportions of this statue are a direct lift from Polykleitos. Again the Roman artist looked to the 5th century BC for a prototype, and found a famous artist who generously left us a standardized canon of proportions for creating a perfect male body ... how convenient! The face of the statue is a portrait likeness of Augustus (albeit a "senior picture" version), but there is no compelling reason that from the neck down Augustus must look like himself, hence the Greek influence applied here. Unlike Greek statues, however, Augustus is not depicted nude, even with his new, better than ever physique. Romans were a pragmatic people, and there is little one can say about the emperor by showing him in his birthday suit. Adding clothes offered an opportunity to make politically correct statements about how wonderful the emperor was in one way or another. In this case, the art was to remind the world that Augustus was the great leader who brought peace to the world.

While Julio-Claudian sculpture owes much to Greek prototypes, this is not always so evident in architecture. The **Theater of Marcellus**, commissioned by Augustus, is an especially good example. Like the Greeks, Roman citizens enjoyed theater, but the theater experience between the two cultures was quite different. In Greece, it was expected that all people should attend the theater, and plays were designed to draw attention to Greek cultural and spiritual ideals, grappling with issues from ethics and morality, family relations and religion. The philosophy du jour was then presented to the public as entertainment. In Rome, the tastes of the public were far more bawdy and unsophisticated. Romans had a taste for blood and gore, making violent public events hosted in giant amphitheaters popular. The alternative was light diversion provided in theaters, like the Theater of Marcellus. Forget uplifting drama with a message to be pondered and discussed later, theater in Rome was more along the line of slapstick comedy. The show was staged by both men and women performers, and usually included the women in the production winding up stark naked on stage by the end of the show, to the leering delight of the rowdy audience. In fact, there are documented cases of female performers who refused to provide the expected striptease being attacked by the audience, forcefully stripped naked, and then thrown bodily out of the theater onto the street! So much for enlightening, cultural entertainment!

Greek theaters, you will recall, were sprawling open-air structures nestled into the rolling topography of the landscape such that views of the countryside were visually important components of the theater experience. That was fine for Greece; they had unlimited supplies of sturdy land and they could afford to take up as much of it as they liked for a single building. Roman architects did not have this luxury as space downtown was at a premium and pricey too. Accordingly, the Romans were obliged to figure out how to build up instead of out to accommodate a large crowd. Post and lintel design had always been the staple of architecture in the past, but the problem facing Roman architects was this: if you pile too much weight on top of a stone lintel, sooner or later it will snap in half and cave in, crushing everyone seated below. They had to devise a structural system that would allow them to stack seating so that a large number of people could be packed into a relatively tight allotment of land. They achieved their goal by developing the Roman arch.

The arch, unlike post and lintel, is designed to accept tremendous weight from above. Construction begins with posts, the same as other building techniques. A wooden structure called **centering** is placed between the two posts, so the arch may be built over the curved centering while under construction (it would otherwise be unstable). The stones composing the curved arch are slightly pie-shaped such that one end is narrow (the inside of the arch) and the other end is wide (the outside of the arch). These are laid up both sides of the arch following the curve of the centering, until the builders reach the top where one last pie-shaped stone must be stuck in the top to complete the arch. This top stone is called a **keystone**. Once the keystone is in place, the arch is stable and the centering may be removed. Since the keystone is pie-shaped, no matter how much weight is placed bearing down on the keystone, the fat end of the stone cannot squeeze through the narrow space of the little end. In principle, it is a little like a bathtub. Water goes through the drain, but a 14-pound baby cannot fit through the drain hole. If you make the child bigger, say 80 pounds, it obviously still cannot fit through the drain. The keystone cannot fall in on your head, even if you had dancing hippos jumping up and down on the keystone; the fat part can never get shoved through the narrow slot.

The weight that bears down on the keystone is diverted down and out along the long sides of the stone. While post and lintel design has all the weight plunging straight toward the ground, with the arch, weight from above is pressed down and out away from the keystone. This means that while the keystone can't fall in on your head, the liability of the arch is that it must be braced from the sides, or it might just do the splits! Bracing can be handled in a couple ways. One way to support an arch is with buttresses. A **buttress** is a big, heavy pier or wall that works like a bookend shoved up against the arch to keep it in place. Another way to brace an arch is with another arch. Two arches that are the same height, the same width, and that carry the same weight from above, will have the same amount of outward thrust. So if two arches so described butt up against each other, they effectively cancel out one another's outward thrust, and brace each other.

Roman theaters relied on the arch to allow them to build compact theaters that would hold a large audience. The <u>Theater of Marcellus</u> illustrates the typical semi-circular plan. Like Greek theaters there is an **auditorium** (or *cavea)* where people sat to watch the show. There is also an orchestra, but unlike Greek theaters, which used this space for the performance, in Roman theaters the orchestra was reserved for special seating for important dignitaries. Instead there is a **stage,** where the old skene and proskenium would have been, and that's where the show was performed, against an elaborate backdrop with scenery since there is no view of the countryside to provide a natural setting like at Greek theaters.

Flavian *69-96*

After the fall of the Julio-Claudian line we have the Flavians, who rose to power in 69, and remained in their position of glory until 96. The Flavian dynasty was composed of a father and his two sons. The first to rule was Vespasian, and like the preceding generation of emperors, the first in the line sets the trend for what to expect of that dynasty. Vespasian *Flavius* (hence the name of the dynasty) was succeeded first by his older son Titus, then by his younger son, Domitian. Vespasian wasn't the overnight choice for emperor; in fact there were three flash in the pan "emperors" who were in and out of office like a revolving door before the Senate settled on Vespasian. The man was a career general in the army with a distinguished career. He was also a plebian, which was a real first for Rome. Up until this point, patrician class was required to hold any public office, much less emperor, so you can imagine how desperate Rome must have been for good leadership for a patrician Senate to admit that they might be better governed by a plebian.

Vespasian was viewed by Rome almost as a savior. He was so unlike his spendthrift predecessors who had managed to bankrupt the nation with their personal extravagances. He had proved himself in the army as someone who could make things happen, and accomplish a lot with limited resources. When Vespasian was appointed to the title of Emperor, he was off on a military campaign putting down a revolt by the Jews in Palestine. He turned his command over to Titus who finished the job in devastating style, and Vespasian returned to Rome to assume his new command post: running the country.

Vespasian never lost sight of his plebian heritage, and never lived a fancy life or put on airs of being better than other people. He was a down-to-earth grandpa type who fostered a feeling of trust among the citizens. He did exactly what he set out to do, which was to rebuild the economy, and start rebuilding Rome. This task was critical due to the massive fire in Rome that during Nero's reign created misery for thousands of displaced people. He pumped up the economy by beefing up taxes, especially on "provincials," those non-citizens whom all Romans believed benefited from Roman rule … such as the unruly Jews who challenged Roman control of Palestine for example. Provincials paid taxes at a higher rate than Roman citizens. He also invented new taxes; the pay toilet, which many of us have endured at one point or another, was one of Vespasian's brilliant ways to collect extra revenue. The trophy real estate properties that once belonged to Nero and his predecessors were liquidated for cash or torn down and rebuilt with an eye toward serving the larger population. To his credit, Vespasian didn't squander the cash on himself; it went toward making Rome a nicer place to live for everybody.

The most famous monument commissioned by Vespasian was the **Colosseum**. It was an enormous amphitheater built in the heart of bustling downtown Rome, using the same building principles of the arch that we saw with the <u>Theater of Marcellus</u>. It could accommodate 50,000 spectators for a single event. The <u>Colosseum</u> was built on the site of a former artificial lake Nero had made for his personal pleasure. Vespasian drained the lake and replaced that monument to a single man's self-indulgence with a monument created to serve the common man. It originally had grand awnings to protect people from the glare of the hot sun so that the entertainment never stopped: some events went on for weeks! The spectacles offered here ranged from a naval battle where the arena was flooded and miniature boats staged a battle at sea, to gory gladiator fights, to the ever-popular contests between Christians and hungry lions (the lions always won). What all these pastimes had in common, of course was that they were profoundly violent. Romans seemed to have had a taste for blood and guts, but beyond that, the government also took advantage of this preoccupation as a way of defusing social unrest. If tens of thousands of spectators managed to exhaust themselves being grossed out at these "games," they were less likely to pick fights and get into trouble outside the Colosseum in the real world.

You may notice that the Colosseum is in poor condition today, and may wonder how this came about given that in many ways, it is the perfect structural design: an oval with all the arches supporting one another. During the Middle Ages at the time of the Crusades, when there was little respect for old pagan architecture, sections of the Colosseum were taken apart to collect the metal dowels that were originally used like pegs to hold the blocks of stone together. These dowels were valuable because they could be melted down and refashioned into suits of armor and weapons to help support the Crusades. The problem was, once a few arches were removed, it created an unstable situation. The arch left exposed when its next-door arch was dismembered now became subject to collapse (remember the splits?), and like falling dominoes the arches were inclined to collapse one by one until the whole building could wind up leveled. The Italian government has attempted to arrest this damage by building immense buttresses adjacent to the exposed arches to help them remain stable.

Titus succeeded his father, Vespasian to become the second emperor of the Flavian line. His reign was short (only two years) as he died young, so he is best remembered for his military career prior to his stint as emperor. Titus was the Roman general in charge of sacking Jerusalem in 70, when the Temple of Solomon was completely destroyed. His victory over the Jews was absolute and complete, and while folks in the Middle East may not have thought he was a great guy, in Rome he was a hero of Herculean proportions. The **Arch of Titus** was erected spanning his route of entry back into Rome from the Holy Land. Triumphal Arches are a trademark of Imperial Rome, all periods. They were built as glorious tributes to the conquests of society's great leaders. This particular arch is heavily embellished with relief sculpture detailing the destruction of Jerusalem, like the **Spoils from the Temple in Jerusalem**. Titus was a popular emperor, but his shortcoming was that he overspent, and much of the economic headway his father had made on behalf of the empire was quickly frittered away by Titus.

After Titus died, his younger brother, Domitian took the reins of government. Domitian has been compared to Tiberius in that for the most part he was a decent administrator, at least in the beginning, but the public didn't like him because he didn't have the down-to-earth regular Joe personality of Vespasian or the reputation of a being a generous war hero like Titus. He was a stickler for laws against adultery and child prostitution, he rebuilt damaged temples and he organized public programs to provide employment for the underprivileged in an attempt to distribute wealth equitably between the citizens. But through all his attempts to make Rome a better nation, Domitian suffered setbacks in war and faced rebellions abroad. He also had a poor relationship with the Christians and killed those who would not make sacrifices before his statues. As his reign progressed, Domitian became increasingly caught up in his own power trip, basking in his role as a god. He feared plots of conspiracy against him, depended on the unreliable advice of informers and his penchant for executing those he didn't trust escalated. In the end, his reign of terror frightened even his own household, leading his wife and servants to help assassinate the emperor. When he died, the Senate smashed all his statues and destroyed many of his records. Good-bye and good riddance! It was time to abandon all faith in this family line, and move on to something new.

Despite the difficulties of Domitian's reign, portrait sculpture in particular flourished while he was in power. Once classical art was perfected, whether it was the Doryphorus in Greece or the Augustus of Prima Porta in Rome, artists seemed anxious to move onto something with a little more pizzazz. The **Young Flavian Woman** could be seen as Rome's answer to Praxiteles. Again the artist has experimented with varied textures between hair and skin. Whereas Praxiteles played roughly textured hair off polished flesh, the Flavian artist juxtaposed the simplicity of a smooth but unpolished complexion against ornately coifed curls that must have cost her patron hours of preparation, what with the braiding in back topped by a halo of meticulously arranged, individually curled locks. This hairstyle was all the rage by the way, popular with the ladies, but often the brunt of good-humored jibes from the men.

Philosopher Kings 96-180

The period designation of "Philosopher Kings" was coined by historians Will and Ariel Durant, who in turn borrowed it from Plato. The Senate had by now made it clear that no more family dynasties could maintain a stranglehold on Rome, so each emperor following Domitian would have to be chosen on his own merit. In practice, the Senate chose the first and those who followed were "adopted" by the current ruler, such that each was chosen by his emperor (not the Senate) to be the next successor. The Philosopher Kings included Nerva who barely took office in 96 before he died of old age two years later, Trajan (98-117), Hadrian (117-138), Antoninus Pius (138-161), and Marcus Aurelius (161-180). Trajan didn't have the slightest business being chosen for the prestigious position of emperor given that not only was he not a patrician, he wasn't even a plebian! Trajan was a provincial. Although he had Italian blood in his ancestry, he came from the boondocks by Roman standards: his family lived in Spain. It is difficult to express how peculiar this would have been, what an upset to the status quo of power and the chain of command. In America, by comparison, for someone to be elected president, s/he must have been born here. It isn't good enough to be a naturalized citizen who immigrated from elsewhere; you have to be a native born citizen. Let's call that our "patrician" requirement. If that were true, then Vespasian as a plebian would be tantamount to a Canadian, who moved here as a young man and became a citizen after doing a stint as a registered alien with a green card, being chosen president. It would be outside the rules. Even more irregular would be if a man from Guam, which is a US territory but not a state, who had never set foot in the USA, suddenly found himself drafted into becoming the next president. Now that's *really* outside the rules!

Trajan was chosen for many of the same reasons as Vespasian. They were both generals in the Roman army who had distinguished themselves as good fiscal managers and strong leaders. Trajan was on a military campaign in Germany when he was called to Rome to serve as the new emperor. Trajan was a remarkable ruler, one of the greatest Rome ever had. He was highly intelligent and had an unusual combination of civic vision and military wisdom. The Romans loved him! His nickname was "Optimus Princeps," which means "the best chief." He was an imperialist bent on expanding the influence of Rome which he did by annexing more territories during his tenure as head of state than any other emperor. His building campaigns were legendary. He vastly improved public facilities, including special attention to public baths and markets, which served the most common of Roman citizens. Everything was done on a magnificent scale, sure to impress his followers and reinforce in them a feeling that all was well in Rome. He even initiated a program (or at least implemented it – the basic idea was Nerva's) called *alimentia* to offer financial support to families raising children in an effort to increase the birth rate. Perhaps most amazing of all, he managed to produce this phenomenal rate of growth while lowering taxes! Between his conquests of foreign lands (which frequently came with riches), careful spending practices and promoting population growth which in turn could be expected to feed the work force and productivity over time, tax rates dropped while the economy boomed.

Trajan added onto the Roman Forum, as several emperors from Augustus to Nerva had done before him. The difference is that his "addition" almost doubled the size of the place. There were spectacular markets open to the public fanning off the open forum's town square. But the crown jewel was the **Basilica Ulpia**, named after Trajan's family name. *Basilicas* were large buildings with two primary functions. First, they served as a court of law, where judges could be found to hear cases and render judgments. Secondly, basilicas were a type of commodities exchange to facilitate trade; one might compare them to today's textile halls or merchandise marts where people come together in large numbers to do business. The Basilica Ulpia was entered from the Forum. The bulk of the interior was a huge, open hall called a *nave*. Trade was conducted in the nave, with booths and tables most likely. Surrounding the nave there were *side aisles*, which aided in circulation. If you came in the door, and spotted the person you needed to see across the floor, it was bad manners to shove your way through hundreds of people attempting to make their own deals. Instead, you would slip into the aisle and walk around the perimeter of the nave until you were closer to your business associate. Above the side aisles there was an upstairs balcony called a *gallery*. This was provided as a quiet place away from the hubbub of the nave where people might have private discussions, especially heated private discussions since arguing on the main floor was not allowed because it was too disruptive to others trying to do business. At either end of the building there was a semi-circular room called an *apse*. The apses at either end of the basilica served as courtrooms where judges were assigned to hear cases.

There were two libraries attached to the backside of the Basilica Ulpia, one Greek and one Latin. Between them was a decorative pillar called the **Column of Trajan** which was heavily carved with details from the emperor's military career, and across a small courtyard behind the libraries was a temple. Most of the forum is in ruins today, but the Column of Trajan still stands as a tribute to the emperor, which is somehow fitting given that his ashes are buried beneath it. While Trajan's forum was hailed one of the great wonders of the world when it was completed, alongside biggies like the Pyramids at Giza which enjoyed the same fame, even the mere column was a master feat in itself. It was constructed out of eighteen fifty-ton blocks of marble imported from Greece. The finished column was 12 feet in diameter, soaring 97 feet tall (nearly 10 stories) resting on a massive base that was approached by 185 marble steps and the whole thing was topped by a statue of Trajan holding the world in his hands (that statue, now long gone, was later replaced with one of Saint Peter). The relief sculpture scenes spiraling around the column like a gigantic corkscrew depict highlights from Trajan's conquests in Dacia (Romania). Some 2000 figures tell the story in 124 panels of Trajan and his troops crossing the Danube and setting camp, there is a battle and a village is set fire. Women and children beg for mercy, but then retaliate by torturing Roman prisoners. Enemy soldiers are beheaded, while others are treated by surgeons and still others are taken away as slaves. The artists conveyed as best they could all that happened, alternatively showing Trajan as a magnanimous commander of great mercy and again as a heartless despot brutally conquering others to serve the empire's needs; taking Dacia improved Trajan's position for dealing with Germany, and Dacia was rich in silver and gold mines which helped boost the Roman economy.

The style of the relief carvings is worth noting, because it demonstrates again how the Romans, like the Greeks, experienced a developing style that started simple, was perfected, then moved on the greater complexity. Back in the days of the Republic the Romans established that their art would have more to do with documenting real people than abstract concepts of ideal beauty like the Greeks. The busts of ancestors were a good start. With the Julio-Claudian dynasty it seemed like it should be possible to have all the realism of portrait likenesses, but have the beauty of art at the same time, and the frieze on the Ara Pacis Augustae proved the point. It depicted a real event, but attention was paid to the quality of the togas and to the technique of combining high and low relief. Sculpture had graduate from the equivalent of Archaic (the Republic) to Classical (Julio-Claudian). The Column of Trajan emphasizes action, great heroics and the horrors of defeat. Gone is the understated simplicity and charm of classical inspiration; Trajan's art is closer to Hellenistic in style.

Trajan selected his second cousin, Hadrian to succeed him. Or perhaps Trajan's widow did; there were rumors to that effect suggesting a hint of romance there (disappointing if it was true given that unlike his predecessors, Trajan was a faithful husband). Hadrian had Roman ancestors but was born of a Spanish family of "foreigners," so like Trajan, he was an unlikely candidate to be emperor. While Trajan was the emperor with unparalleled military acumen, and the man who did more to expand Rome than any other emperor, Hadrian was less concerned with expansion, and more with consolidation. Hadrian is sometimes remembered for his ill-fated campaign in Great Britain, where he determined that the Scots (Picts) were too fierce to be taken on. He simply built a wall sprinkled with forts from the North Sea all the way across to the Irish Sea to cut Scotland off from England to keep those wild men out of the civilized world (sections of the wall still remain today). In fact, he really disliked war altogether, finding peace more agreeable.

Hadrian traveled widely and was tolerant of outsiders, not the least of which were the Christians who had suffered at the hands of other emperors. He extended many of Trajan's benevolent policies, like alimentia, to families throughout the empire including provincials, not just Roman citizens. Although not particularly happy in his marriage, he was not a hedonist like some of his predecessors. Hadrian was well educated with a special affinity for all things Greek, he wasn't especially religious himself although he supported the old roster of Roman gods and tolerated other people's gods also. He was an avid hunter, loved horses and dogs, and was a proficient artist and author. He died of tuberculosis, possibly combined with other illness. Ironically in view of how many past emperors were assassinated, Hadrian asked to be put out of his misery but nobody was willing to kill him, and so he wasted away suffering until death came naturally.

Hadrian is best remembered today for the magnificent architecture associated with his reign. Many emperors left a legacy of great building, but Hadrian is unique because not only was he the patron, Hadrian was also the architect! He was brilliantly gifted, and his architecture still stands out today as an important influence on design. His most challenging and famous building is the **Pantheon**. Atypical of the usual Roman design, this outstanding building was nevertheless a temple. Normally we think of temples as being redundant architecture in Rome without much new to contribute to the vocabulary of architecture, but the Pantheon is very different. Hadrian determined that he could produce an appropriately economical result (you gotta love those pragmatic Romans), while also indulging his interest in creative, beautiful, and b-i-g buildings, if he simply refrained from building dozens of tiny, trivial temples to this god and that, and produced one glorious temple dedicated to all the gods instead.

The Pantheon was set in the midst of crowded downtown Rome, which is important as the space helped Hadrian to play with visual perception. From the front entrance, it would appear to the unsuspecting passer-by that this is an ordinary temple like any other, perhaps a little larger, but just the same. In fact, this front porch was "recycled" from an earlier temple. Anyone approaching the gabled porch would have every expectation of going through the door into a rectangular cella. Surprise! Once through the doorway, you find yourself standing inside a big ball! The Pantheon is the first building designed around negative space. Let me explain by considering a building you already know, the Parthenon in Athens. When it was designed, the architects used columns outside. When you look at the façade of the Parthenon, what the architects expected you to see were the lovely columns. It did not occur to them that you might instead focus on the rectangular space of open nothing framed by 2 columns on either side, the entablature above and the stylobate below.

Hadrian designed the entire Pantheon around a big invisible ball of space. The building was designed to contain the visual space, as opposed to the usual arrangement where the interior space is almost an accident left over after the architect has designed his building. Hadrian was so far ahead of his time, that we don't see this kind of thinking again for many centuries. To achieve this goal, he designed the interior "ball" to have the same distance from the top of the domed roof to the floor as the diameter of the circular *rotunda*. The curve of the dome was repeated by a slight dip in the floor, such that the floor seems to swoop up into the walls and keep flowing upward all the way into the domed ceiling. The surprise of finding yourself caught up in this spherical space was enhanced by the nonchalant, business-as-usual post and lintel façade.

The spherical interior was encased in a mammoth concrete drum. It is plain and unappealing outside, because the focus of the Pantheon, like so much Roman architecture (houses, baths, basilicas etc.) was on the interior. Inside, the thick walls were decorated with enormous columned niches and huge decorative statues of the gods. The ceiling was *coffered*, that is decorative sunken panels employed to give visual texture to an otherwise large expanse of boring, plain surface while at the same time reducing the weight of the ceiling. There were no windows, so the only light source was the huge *oculus* (27' across!), or hole in the top of the dome. As we saw with the Roman house, leaving a hole in the roof meant that sometimes it rained inside. No problem here, the floors of the <u>Pantheon</u> dipped in the center of the building, where drains were provided to allow water to escape to the sewers. The <u>Pantheon</u> survives today, almost as it was in Hadrian's time, except that it has long since been converted to a Christian church.

Hadrian was succeeded by Antoninus Pius, who also came from non-Patrician stock as his family had relocated to Rome from France just two generations earlier. Just the same, his people were among the richest in Rome, and Antoninus used his personal wealth to improve the imperial treasury by canceling arrears in taxes, making gifts to those in need and personally picking up the tab for games and festivals. He continued Hadrian's policy of tolerance toward the Christians, and improved relations with the Jews. For his own part, Antoninus faithfully observed the pagan Roman religion. He freed the slaves of cruel owners and punished anyone who killed a slave. He encouraged education, especially for girls who lagged behind boys in this area. He was an all round good guy who died peacefully in his sleep during a bout with what was probably the flu.

The last of the Philosopher Kings was Marcus Aurelius, who in addition to being selected by Antoninus to succeed to the throne, also was married to the former emperor's daughter. Marcus Aurelius was both wealthy and extremely well educated and he could have lived in the lap of luxury if that had suited him. Instead, he was dedicated to the study of philosophy, and believed in ideals like modesty, patience, piety and benevolence. His character defined stoicism. He was more than fair with all he met, setting an example by serving others rather than demanding to be served. He continued to reform the laws that Hadrian and Antoninus had initiated, especially in offering alimentia to the largest number of families throughout the kingdom in Roman history. The people adored him. Although he did not care for war, circumstances forced him to take on the Parthians (from Persia), a war which he won. Unfortunately, the aftermath was that his troops brought back a plague – Bubonic Plague from the descriptions - and thousands of citizens died. The emperor was tireless in his efforts to relieve suffering and care for his people, although medicine being what it was, not much could be done until the plague ran its course. To make matters worse, no sooner had the troops returned from one war and they were off to another. German tribes had invaded Dacia, so Rome was obliged to deal with the Germans … again. That region had been a sore spot for Roman endeavors since the foundations of the empire. How ironic that Marcus Aurelius, who did not especially aspire to being a great general, spent most of his career managing military campaigns. Despite these hardships, Rome flourished under his rule; the standard of living was the highest it had ever been.

Marcus is remembered today in a splendid cast bronze statue that was originally also gold-plated. The **Equestrian Statue of Marcus Aurelius** shows the emperor on horseback (equestrian means on horseback), a popular motif in ancient Rome for depicting the emperor as a gallant and virile military hero. Few have survived, it seems because they were melted down during the Middle Ages, especially during the Crusades when needs ran high for metal to make weapons and armor. Apparently Marcus Aurelius was mistakenly identified as an Early Christian emperor, and his statue was spared. Marcus Aurelius chose to succeed him the only surviving son born of his wife, but quite possibly fathered by somebody else, Commodus.

Late Empire *c. 180-325*

Commodus was the beginning of the end for Imperial Rome. He and those who followed lacked the administrative genius of the Philosopher Kings, and they reveled in every possible vice while often ignoring the welfare of the nation they were entrusted to lead. Some were half decent administrators, but the problems of the empire seemed too much for any of these men to handle, so they experimented with subdividing it which only seemed to provoke power struggles between competing rulers. Some were more cruel than others, and but all expected to be treated like gods.

The last emperor of pagan Rome was Constantine, who rose to power in 306, initially sharing power with Maxentius as part of the shared emperorship experiment. The two had built a fabulous new basilica in the Roman Forum, and after Constantine defeated Maxentius in battle, securing the title of emperor for just himself, he installed a colossal statue of himself in the basilica. What remains of the statue is the head and a hand. That **Head of Constantine** is a whopping 8'6" tall; can you imagine how imposing the entire statue must have been presiding over affairs in the basilica? Clearly the emperor was impressed with himself and wanted to make sure that the citizens of Rome were too. Further proof of this was the **Arch of Constantine**, which he had erected to commemorate his victory over Maxentius. Compare it to the <u>Arch of Titus</u>, which at 50' tall, is dwarfed by Constantine's nearly 70' tall triple arch. In fairness to Constantine, not all the sculpture on the arch was a tribute only to himself; in fact, it honored earlier emperors' achievements as well. Marcus Aurelius' victory over the Germans was remembered as well as Trajan's military success over the Dacians, and homage was paid to Hadrian's rule as well.

The <u>Arch of Constantine</u> was one of the last architectural tributes to pagan antiquity. Very soon Christianity would eclipse paganism and other assorted popular philosophies as the religion of choice throughout the Mediterranean world. Rome was born in a world that admired all that was Greek. Yet Athens had only been a regional power for less than a hundred years, while Rome was leader of the entire Western world for over five centuries. Roman society was ever evolving, but the common thread through it all was an emphasis on good government (at least in theory if not always perfect in practice), fairness toward most of the people most of the time, and a practical attitude toward getting the job done regardless of what the job might be. Even the worst of the intolerant and abusive emperors was more patient with foreigners and more inclined to put aside personal prejudice for the greater good of the nation than most Greeks were until after Alexander the Great opened their society to the outside world. Rome would continue on as an important center well into the Middle Ages, only now as the leaders in the rise of Christian culture.

Unit Two

The Splendor of Christian Culture:

Medieval Europe

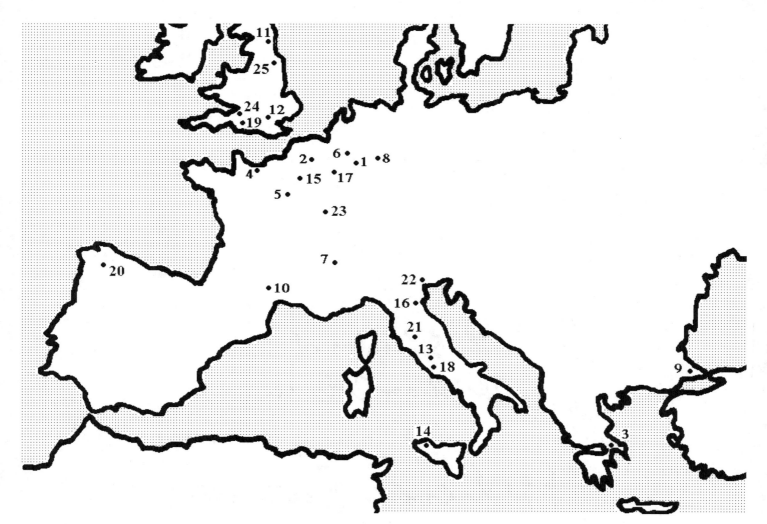

1. Aachen
2. Amiens
3. Athens
4. Bayeux/ Caen
5. Chartres
6. Clairvaux
7. Cluny
8. Cologne
9. Constantinople
10. Conques
11. Durham
12. London
13. Orvieto
14. Palermo
15. Paris
16. Ravenna
17. Reims
18. Rome
19. Salisbury
20. Santiago de Compostela
21. Siena
22. Venice
23. Vezelay
24. Wells
25. York

The Medieval World

Image List for Unit Two

EARLY CHRISTIAN PERIOD: 313 – 500

1. Menorahs and Ark of the Covenant (FYI – Jewish)
2. Old Saint Peter's Church (***Rome, Italy***)
3. Old Saint Peter's Church (plan)
4. Old Saint Peter's Church (interior)
5. Church of the Holy Sepulchre (***Jerusalem, Israel***)
6. Church of the Holy Sepulchre (plan)
7. Santa Sabina (***Rome, Italy***)
8. Santa Sabina (interior)
9. Santa Maria Maggiore (interior) (***Rome, Italy***)
10. Annunciation Mosaic (inside Santa Maria Maggiore)
11. Coronation of the Virgin (inside Santa Maria Maggiore)

BYZANTINE PERIOD: 395 – 1054

12. San Vitale (***Ravenna, Italy***)
13. San Vitale (plan)
14. FYI San Vitale section showing gallery – understand concept
15. San Vitale (apse view)
16. Justinian Mosaic (inside San Vitale)
17. Theodora Mosaic (inside San Vitale)
18. Hagia Sophia *by Anthemius of Tralles & Isadorus of Miletus* (***Constantinople, Turkey***)
19. Hagia Sophia (interior)
20. FYI Pendentive Illustration – understand concept
21. Hagia Sophia (plan)
22. Virgin Enthroned Icon (***Mt. Sinai, Egypt***)
23. Monastery of the Dormition at Daphni *(near **Athens, Greece**)*
24. Monastery of the Dormition at Daphni (interior)
25. Pantocrator (inside Monastery of the Dormition at Daphni)
26. Nativity (inside Monastery of the Dormition at Daphni)
27. San Marco (***Venice, Italy***)
28. San Marco (detail of entrance)
29. San Marco (plan)
30. San Marco (interior)
31. San Marco (interior dome)
32. Anastasis (inside San Marco)
33. Cathedral of the Assumption *by Aristotele Fioravanti* (***Moscow, Russia***)
34. Cathedral of the Assumption (interior)
35. Cathedral of the Annunciation (***Moscow, Russia***)
36. Cathedral if the Annunciation (interior)
37. Saint Basil's *by Barna & Postnik* (***Moscow, Russia***)
38. FYI – Iconostasis

39. FYI – Iconostasis in situ
40. Saint Basil icon (***Moscow, Russia***)

HIBERNO-SAXON PERIOD: 432- c.900

41. Saint Matthew page from the Lindesfarne Gospel (***Scotland***)
42. Saint Matthew page from the Book of Kells (***Ireland***)

CAROLINGIAN PERIOD: 732 – 936

43. Saint Matthew page from the Coronation Gospel (***Germany***)
44. Saint Matthew page from the Ebbo Gospel (***France***)
45. Palatine Chapel (today) *(**Aachen, Germany**)*
46. Palatine Chapel (9ᵗʰ century) *by Odo of Metz*
47. Palatine Chapel in context
48. Palatine Chapel (plan)
49. Palatine Chapel (interior)
50. San Vitale (FYI interior for comparison)
51. Plan for the Abbey of Saint Gall (***Switzerland***)

OTTONIAN PERIOD 936-1002

52. Saint Michael's Hildesheim (***Germany***)
53. Saint Michael's Hildesheim (interior)
54. Saint Michael's Hildesheim (plan)
55. Bronze Doors Saint Michael's Hildesheim

ROMANESQUE PERIOD: c.1000 – 1200

56. Sainte Foy (***Conques, France***)
57. Sainte Foy (plan)
58. Last Judgment tympanum (from Sainte Foy at ***Conques, France***)
59. Last Judgment tympanum (Sainte Foy) detail
60. Last Judgment tympanum (from Saint Lazare at ***Autun, France***)
61. Santiago de Compostela (plan) (northwest ***Spain***)
62. Santiago de Compostela (nave)
63. San Miniato al Monte (***Florence, Italy***)
64. Christ between the Virgin and St. Minas (façade of San Miniato al Monte)
65. Abbey at Cluny (***France***)
66. Sainte Madeleine *(**Vezelay, France**)*
67. Sainte Madeleine (façade tympanum)
68. Mission of the Apostles tympanum (from Sainte Madeleine at ***Vezelay, France***)
69. Sainte Madeleine (interior)
70. Abbey Church at Fontenay (near ***Clairvaux, France***)
71. Abbey Church at Fontenay (interior)
72. Fontenay Madonna (from Abbey at Fontenay)

73. Mont Saint Michel (Normandy region of ***France***)
74. Mont Saint Michel (closer)
75. Mont Saint Michel (interior – refectory/ dining hall)
76. FYI La Grande Rue @ Mont Saint Michel
77. Saint Etienne *(**Caen, France**)*
78. Saint Etienne (nave)
79. Bayeux Tapestry (***Bayeux, France***)
80. Bayeux Tapestry: Harold's Audience with Edward the Confessor
81. Bayeux Tapestry: Guy Turns Harold Over to William
82. Bayeux Tapestry: Harold Saves Soldiers in Quicksand
83. Bayeux Tapestry: William's Troops Arrive at Pevensey
82. Durham Cathedral *(**Durham, England**)*
85. Durham Cathedral (nave)
86. Capella Palatino (***Palermo, Sicily***)
87. Capella Palatino (Pantocrator dome detail)
88. Monreale Cathedral (near ***Palermo, Sicily***)
89. Monreale Cathedral (interior)
90. FYI Monreale Cathedral (nave arcade) – understand concept
91. Sacrifice of Isaac (inside Monreale Cathedral)
92. Christ Pantocrator (inside Monreale Cathedral)
93. Christ Blessing King William (inside Monreale Cathedral)
94. FYI ceiling detail inside Monreale Cathedral – understand concept

GOTHIC PERIOD: c.1150 – 1400

95. Chartres Cathedral *(**Chartres, France**)*
96. Chartres Cathedral (Royal Portal tympanum)
97. Chartres Cathedral (jamb statues)
98. Chartres Cathedral (Charlemagne window detail, covered later in chapter)
99. Paris Cathedral (***Paris, France***)
100. Amiens Cathedral, *by Robert de Luzarches* (***Amiens, France***)
101. Amiens Cathedral (aerial view)
102. Amiens Cathedral (plan)
103. Amiens Cathedral (choir)
104. FYI Amiens Nave Wall – understand concept
105. FYI: ribbed groin vaulting – understand concept
106. FYI: flying buttress – understand concept
107. Reims Cathedral (***Reims, France***)
108. Annunciation and Visitation Jamb Statues (on Reims Cathedral)
109. Sainte Chapelle (***Paris, France***)
110. Sainte Chapelle (interior)
111. Cologne Cathedral
112. Wells Cathedral (***Wells, England***)
113. Wells Cathedral (nave)
114. Salisbury Cathedral
115. York Minster (***York, England***)

116. York Minster (nave)
117. Great East Window (inside York Minster)
118. Westminster Abbey (**_London, England_**)
119. Eilean Donan Castle (**_Scotland_**)
120. Orvieto Cathedral (**_Orvieto, Italy_**)
121. Orvieto Cathedral (side view)
122. Assumption on the Virgin (façade @ Orvieto Cathedral)
123. Coronation of Mary, Queen of Heaven (façade @ Orvieto Cathedral)
124. Orvieto Cathedral (nave view)
125. Madonna and Child Enthroned *by Cimabue* (**_Florence, Italy_**)
126. Ognissanti Madonna *by Giotto* (**_Florence, Italy_**)
127. Arena Chapel (located in **_Padua, Italy_**, frescos by *Giotto* from **_Florence_**)
128. Lamentation by *Giotto*, from the Arena Chapel frescos
129. Annunciation *by Simone Martini* (**_Siena, Italy_**)

6. Early Christian

Jewish Roots

First things first. It's hard to appreciate the development of Christianity in Western history, much less Christian art and architecture, without first considering its historical foundation which was Judaism. The ancient Hebrews were one of the many ethnic groups to evolve out of Mesopotamian civilization. They were originally Semitic nomads who differed from their polytheistic neighbors in that they believed in only one God, whom they called Yahweh. Their religion was based on oral tradition, in that it was passed on through the generations by memorizing the information as it was told to you. According to Jewish tradition, God made a covenant with Abraham, whom you will recall was a citizen of the ancient Sumerian city of Ur, to grant the land of Canaan (Palestine) to the Hebrew people for their homeland. This is recalled in the first book of the Old Testament, called Genesis.

Many generations later, things hadn't gone so well for the Hebrew people, and they found themselves in Egypt working as slaves for the pharaohs. Toward the end of the New Kingdom, another Hebrew was singled out by God to renew His covenant with the Jews. Moses was given the power and authority through God's grace to lead His people back to the Holy Lands. It was presumably sometime considerably after the time of Moses that Scripture was first written down, and the initial result was the **Torah**. The Torah is the first five books of the Old Testament, Genesis (the original ancient history by way of oral tradition), Exodus, Leviticus, Numbers, and Deuteronomy. In Jewish tradition these five books are called the Torah and they constitute the Hebrew Law, while in Christian tradition these same five books (the first five of the Bible) are called the **Pentateuch**. Different name … same books.

Over the centuries, other texts were added to the Jewish collection of books. Some were historical narratives, while others offered wisdom, and still others were prophetic in nature. Jewish Scripture was never compiled in a book like we think of the Bible today; instead they were individual scrolls, more like a library. Jews were still expected to commit Scripture to memory, which was critical because the scrolls could not be read like today's library book anyway. Back then, a "book" was one long, run-on sentence of consonants (no vowels) so that if you didn't already know what it said, odds are you'd be in trouble trying to wing it.

We don't have much in the way of surviving ancient Jewish art and architecture. For one thing, they started out as nomadic tribes and nomads generally do not produce much art and virtually no lasting architecture. Beyond that, we don't have all that much still around from any Mesopotamian society (say compared to Egypt which was more stable), and to further complicate matters the ancient Babylonians destroyed the original Jewish Temple when they sacked Jerusalem in 568 BC, the Jews rebuilt and then the Romans came in and sacked the place again in AD 70.

Probably the most famous object from Jewish antiquity was the Ark of the Covenant. We know from Exodus 25 in the Old Testament that the Ark was about four and a half feet long and nearly three feet wide. It was made of acacia wood, lined in gold and decorated with sculpture of *cherubim* (an order of angels usually represented in art as large winged children – erring on the side of chubby babies or toddlers more than older-looking children). The Ark was the prize procession of the ancient Jews as it contained the tablets given to Moses from God with the Commandments. Unfortunately it was lost many centuries ago, but it was sometimes visually recorded from memory in ancient Jewish art. **Menorahs and Ark of the Covenant** is a wall painting from a tomb found in a Jewish *catacomb* (subterranean cemetery of rooms with niches for sarcophagi (plural of sarcophagus: caskets/ coffins of dead people). This particular catacomb was from Roman times, dated sometime between the first to third centuries. The decorated box in the center would be the Ark, with a veil draped above (also described in Exodus) and it is flanked by two menorahs. A *menorah* is a 7-branched gold candelabra ("golden lampstand") used in Jewish worship, the original being created to light the Ark according to God's instructions in Exodus 25:31-40.   Remember the Arch of Titus? The relief carving of the Roman soldiers carrying off the spoils of Jerusalem after they sacked the Temple prominently features the menorah as prized booty. Sadly, the Ark had already gone missing before Titus arrived, and nobody knows for sure what happened to it.

Early Christian *313- c. 500*

Jewish history is important because it was here that the Christian religion was born. Judaism has always taught that God's people would be delivered by a Messiah. While the Jews still await this savior, Christians believe that Jesus of Nazareth, a well-documented historical person who lived roughly two thousand years ago, was and is the long awaited Messiah, or Christ. Jesus was a Jew from the family lineage of King David, fulfilling ancient messianic prophesy. He was born sometime around 4 BC (after adjusting for calendar inaccuracies) by our best estimates today, to a young woman named Mary whom Christians believe was a virgin. Like Judaism, Christianity is monotheistic, with one God who is manifest as the Great Creator (God the Father), and who came to live among men as their Redeemer (God the Son, Jesus Christ), and the Holy Spirit (God the Paraclete or Advocate) who resides in those who receive His grace. The mystery of God's triune nature is called the Holy Trinity. Jesus lived an outwardly unremarkable life as far as we know until He started His public ministry at age thirty. Then for three years Jesus preached and performed miracles, attracting both devoted disciples who believed He was the Christ, and negative attention from some Jewish leaders who were expecting perhaps a different kind of savior. He was crucified at the age of thirty-three. According to Christian faith, Jesus resurrected three days after He was killed, and lives on in heaven where He advocates for the salvation of all believers until the end of time.

The Early Christian period began in 313. That may come as a surprise because presumably Christianity began with Jesus, and given that our dating system revolves around the life of this man, it might seem more logical that the Early Christian period would start something more like "0," or at least by 30 when one might assume the ministry of Jesus began, or even 33 when he presumably died. While it is quite true that Christians in the first, second and third centuries were "early Christians," in the study of art and architecture the Early Christian period doesn't begin until 313. Why? Before 313, while Christianity was flourishing, it remained an underground movement for the most part because those in political power scorned it. The Jews certainly didn't think very highly of Jesus and His followers, whom they perceived as heretics, and the pagan Roman government looked askance of Christians because they didn't fit in very well in pagan Rome. They weren't troublemakers; if anything they were annoying in their pacifism which was hardly the respected norm for Roman patriotism. The problem was, they weren't in awe of the emperors and they refused to pay homage to pagan rituals. Christians also placed themselves above the common morality (or lack of morality) that the average Roman pagan considered normal. Okay, fair enough. But so far, the objections stated against Christians would have applied equally well to Jews. The Jews also refused to worship the emperor, they would not make sacrifices to pagan gods, and the Jews lived by the same commandments of moral behavior that the Christians held dear. Further, while the Romans may have disliked the Jews alongside the Christians (and undoubtedly other minority groups too), Rome had survived centuries as a world power in part because they were pretty good at ruling a diverse population which required patience with folks who were "outsiders." So why were the Christians frequently singled out as scapegoats, while more often the Jews were just ignored? What was it about the Christians that Romans found so deeply objectionable, to where Nero (the sultan of decency...) denounced Christians for their detestable evil practices, and the citizens of Rome found his disgust plausible and understandable?

Unlike the Jews, Christians told weird stories about their Messiah rising from the dead, which every sensible pagan determined was ridiculous, and what was even more bizarre, they claimed to eat the body and drink the blood of this dead but also somehow miraculously alive Christ, and cannibalism was clearly against the civilized laws of the respectable Romans. Incidentally, those charges of cannibalism against the Christian community can be reviewed with some amusement in a second century document called the _Octavius_ written by Minicius Felix. Obviously the author, along with many other self-respecting pagan Romans, misunderstood the Christians, perhaps from hearing the prayers spoken during their worship without a proper understanding of what it all meant.

Hippolytus, who was a bishop, scholar and finally in 235, a Christian martyr, recorded in detail their service, or **Liturgy of the Eucharist**. It seems the bishop was critical of how sloppy the Christian rite had become in some circles, and he wanted to set the record straight on how things had been done since the foundation of the Church so that Christians would clean up their act. Hippolytus wrote that the priest would give thanks to God while laying hands on the offering of bread and wine, and asking all present to lift their hearts to the Lord and give thanks. Following a series of prayers in which the passion of Christ was retold, the priest would lift the bread and say, "_Take and eat, this is my body_ which shall be broken for you." Then raising the cup, the priest would say, "_This is my blood_ which shall be shed for you; when you do this, do it in memory of me." While the Christians _did_ believe they were eating the body and blood of their Christ during communion (many were willing to die for the privilege), their understanding was that they were consuming the risen Christ by way of a mystery of faith set forth by Jesus. Christians were certainly not sneaking around eating dead people, but rumors to that effect were rife in pagan circles. From a pagan point of view, clearly these Christians were an altogether suspicious lot. Some emperors turned a blind eye to them, while others were quick to persecute Christians. At any point in their brief history up to this time, Christians had always followed an illegal religion, whether the civil authorities punished their actions or not.

All this changed in 313. The emperor in power at that time was Constantine, who was introduced to you in the chapter on Rome. He was as pagan as any of his predecessors through most of his life, although his mother, Helena was a Christian convert. On October 27, 312, according to the historian, Eusebius, Constantine was facing the decisive battle with Maxentius, his pagan co-emperor in Rome, when he had a vision of a flaming cross in the sky, and with it the message "in this sign conquer." Constantine then heard a voice in a dream early the following morning commanding him to have his soldiers mark their shields with the *Chi-Rho*, a commonly used symbol to represent Christ. The Greek letter chi (X) superimposed over the Greek letter rho (P) form the Chi-Rho; chi and rho are the first two letters in "Christ" when it is spelled in Greek. Constantine obeyed and won the battle. Following these events, and presumably after allowing a little time to mull things over, in early 313 Constantine called a meeting in Milan with his colleagues to discuss issues regarding national governance, and it was then that he set forth the *Edict of Milan*. The Edict of Milan declared that for the first time in history, religious toleration would be extended to all religions. Further, persecutions of Christians in particular would cease immediately, and those who had been deprived of their rights and properties during past persecutions would have these restored to them. Thus for the first time since the birth of Christianity it was legal for Christians to join together and worship publicly as a community. The Early Christian period began in 313 with the Edict of Milan, but it does not ever really end, although one might suppose over time that the word "early" would fade away. Following the Edict of Milan, it is reasonable to say that the old *pagan* Roman Empire died. The nation was no longer "Rome" so much as it was Italy, with the city of Rome being the capital, and neighboring regions outside Italy once under pagan Rome's control that were gradually gaining their own independent identities. We will use a close date of 500, not so much because the Early Christian period ended, but because it gradually morphed into a more mature Christian society

Following the Edict of Milan, one of the first priorities of the Christian community was to build churches. The form of Christian worship had been well established for centuries by now, but the practice had been for just a few people to gather together in a private home for fear of discovery by the authorities. Justin Martyr wrote one of the earliest accounts of how Christians worshipped way back in 150. Christians, many of whom initially maintained their ties to the Jewish Temple and observed the Hebrew Sabbath on Saturday, would come together in a Christian home to celebrate their worship of Jesus on Sunday. The pattern of Sunday worship also dovetailed symbolically with the fact that Jesus' resurrection took place on a Sunday. A bishop (episkopos) was the leader within a regional Christian community. Every bishop had been ordained through the laying on of hands by a bishop, who in turn had been blessed before that by a bishop, carrying the blessing all the way back through the centuries to the Apostles, and ultimately to Christ himself. The ability to trace a bishop's *ordination* directly back to Christ in an unbroken line of blessings carried out through the laying on of hands is called *Apostolic Succession*. The local bishop would be on hand to celebrate the Liturgy of the Eucharist by consecrating the bread and wine offerings. If the bishop could not be there, given that he was obliged to cover a large territory, he had a local priest (presbuteros), who was likewise blessed through Apostolic Succession to preside in his place.

The service was divided into two parts. The first part was the *Liturgy of the Word.* At this time, the priest or bishop would recite a passage from Scripture, which is to say at this point in history, the Old Testament. Following this there might be a psalm, then usually either a letter written by Paul might be read, or another letter from a Christian written during Apostolic times, or in many cases when no copy of any letters were on hand, the basic content of such an epistle was recalled from memory. Finally, the presiding official would recount the story of Jesus, or what we would today call the *Gospel*, which means "good news." Once the direct teachings of Jesus had been reviewed, the service moved on to the Liturgy of the Eucharist, which was the ceremony for blessing the bread and wine mentioned earlier in this chapter. Following the prayers and blessings, the offering was divided so that everyone ate the consecrated bread and drank from the cup. A portion of the *communion*, or Lord's Supper was set aside for the benefit of any Christian who was unable to be present (say if somebody was sick at home), and kept safe in a special box called a *tabernacle*. As time went on, the combined Liturgy of the Word and Liturgy of the Eucharist was often called the *Mass*, a term first used by Ambrose, the Bishop of Milan, in 385.

Now that Christianity could be practiced in the open, there was a strong desire to get as much of the extended Christian family together for worship as possible. The problem was nobody had a preconceived idea of what a church ought to look like. Certainly it had to be a big building capable of holding lots of people at one time. This ruled out the old Greek or Roman temple prototype, as pagan temples were never intended to accommodate crowds of people. Besides that, buildings that looked like classical temples recalled pagan persecution, which was unlikely to sit well with the Christians. In the end, the Roman basilica was selected as a prototype, and modified to fit the needs of Christian worship. Incidentally, Jews, who were now also more free to exercise their faith publicly, also chose the Roman basilica as the model of choice for synagogue design. Early Christian churches were built large, and they were almost always urban – located in areas with substantial populations so that most people could get there easily, while folks living out in the smaller villages and countryside would have to travel in to attend Mass.

Constantine may not have been Christian himself in 313 (he officially converted and was baptized on his deathbed nearly a quarter century later), but he extended a genuine effort to assist Christians in making up for lost time on church construction both by funding the building campaigns, and in the case of churches being built in the city of Rome, it is said he even pitched in and physically helped with the construction. Perhaps this was at the behest of his mother who was a Christian convert, or perhaps he simply considered it politically expedient to be seen as supportive given that the number of Christians had grown so large. The first Christian basilica built immediately following the Edict of Milan was Saint John Lateran which served as the *seat*, or home church of the Bishop of Rome, who by now was already being called the *pope*, meaning "papa," or the "father" of the Church. Saint John Lateran may have been first, but it was not the most famous church built during the 4th century.

The two most famous churches built during the 4th century were **Old Saint Peter's** in Rome, and the **Church of the Holy Sepulchre** in Jerusalem. Both of these churches were originally built as a **martyrium**, which is a type of church unique to the Early Christian period. Martyrium churches were built on sites that were either associated with the death or burial of a Christian martyr. Old Saint Peter's was built over the old Jewish cemetery (catacombs) where Saint Peter was buried. The 4th century church no longer exists, however [new] Saint Peter's Cathedral in Rome (the "Vatican") is built over the foundations of the Early Christian basilica, which is still over Saint Peter's grave of course, and with special permission, it is possible to this day to go beneath Saint Peter's, down through the ruins of the old church, and all the way down to those catacombs where Early Christians scrawled on the walls near his grave, "Saint Peter, pray for us" … pretty impressive to say the least. The Church of the Holy Sepulchre was built spanning two sites: it contains both the rock of Golgotha where Jesus was crucified, and it also enshrines the nearby tomb where His body was placed when He was taken down from the cross. It was nearly destroyed twice, once by fire and once by Muslims, but it has been rebuilt and still retains some of the architectural features of the original church.

Martyrium churches were built primarily as shrines, where people would travel great distances to pray. The Church of the Holy Sepulchre also served as the seat of the Bishop of Jerusalem, so Masses were celebrated there from the start. In Rome the faithful attended Mass at Saint John Lateran, so Old Saint Peter's was strictly a shrine. During the 4th century, these shrines were left with dirt floors as it was considered a huge honor for a devout member of the Church to be buried in the floor of the martyrium. As time went on, though, martyriums began to stink with all those shallow graves and poor ventilation indoors, so the floors were sealed. After this point, Old Saint Peter's became the official seat of the Bishop of Rome, although Saint John Lateran is still referred to as the Pope's (Bishop of Rome) church.

The Early Christian basilica became the model for Christian churches to follow so it is wise to become familiar with the basic parts of the church. In fact, most churches today still have at least part of the same vocabulary applied to their design. Let's start with the plan for Old Saint Peter's since it was in many ways the standard for church design. Upon climbing the steps to the front door, one entered an enormous enclosed courtyard called an **atrium**. The atrium had a double function, and it is nearly impossible to determine which was the higher priority. For one, the atrium provided a safe haven for travelers. Remember these churches were urban, and crime was always a possibility, especially for the unwary traveler who might be camping out by the church for a few days on his stay. Usually there was a well in the atrium where fresh water could be obtained for drinking, washing up or even preparing food. In addition to providing a safe haven for travelers, the spacious atrium was used for assembling the clergy and faithful for processions into the church during Mass.

Beyond the atrium there was a covered, and later enclosed, hall called the **narthex**. The narthex was a sort of lobby or foyer area where one collected one's thoughts before the service began. Nowadays you might find hymnals in a church narthex, or a coatroom or bathrooms off to one side. It was also a dry alternative to the open atrium if it poured rain and you happened to arrive early for the service. From the narthex, one entered into the **nave**, which is where the congregation stood during the Mass. The modern idea of sitting down during a Christian service would have been unthinkable during the Middle Ages. You might kneel or stand, but in the presence of

God, traditionally one would not sit. On either side of the nave there were 2 side *aisles* in Old Saint Peter's. This would be true of all martyrium churches, but "regular" Early Christian basilicas often had only 1 aisle flanking each side of the nave. The first (or only) aisle next to the nave was for circulation. If you arrived late and the back of the church was too crowded for your small children to see, you might slip into the aisle and move closer to the front. The outer aisle in a martyrium was provided for the display of coffins rather like one might find today at a funeral parlor, because martyrium churches were frequently hosting funerals for Christians destined to be honored with burial in the floor of the church.

At the far end of the church there was a small, usually semi-circular area called an *apse*. This was the holy place within the church, and normally only clergy would go there. The apse contained the two most important furnishings for the Early Christian basilica. First was the altar, which was the equivalent of the prepared table used in the old days when the Liturgy of the Eucharist was celebrated in people's houses. The altar is where the priest would offer up thanksgiving and consecrate the bread and wine. Usually right behind the altar was the tabernacle where the Eucharist was held in reserve for anyone who might receive communion at a later time. Old Saint Peter's apparently did not have an altar during the 4th century since it was not being used for formal church services at that time (remember Saint John Lateran); the altar was installed when the floors were sealed and the pope began celebrating Mass there. Both Old Saint Peter's and the Church of the Holy Sepulchre had the apse in the west due to the lay of the land, but this would not be the norm as time went on. Most medieval churches, were later oriented such that the apse was in the east end of the basilica, so that the first of God's light each day would bathe the altar and tabernacle before the rest of the church. Between the apse and nave, in some churches there was a perpendicular hall called the *transept*. The transept formed a cross when combined with the apse and nave, which reinforced a Christian sensibility in the design. Beyond that, the transept was used during the communion part of the Mass. The priest would come down from the altar in the apse and give the Lord's Supper to the people, who were coming forward from the nave to receive. In Old Saint Peter's there was a canopy placed in the crossing of the transept and the nave to mark Saint Peter's grave below.

Old Saint Peter's was the largest Early Christian church built, measuring an estimated 700' from the entrance into the atrium to the apse, with the church alone being closer to 475' without the courtyard. The Church of the Holy Sepulchre was smaller, although it could still accommodate a crowd at an estimated 475' long, with the actual church part being closer to 250' and the shrines located out beyond the apse. The Church of the Holy Sepulchre had a unique plan due to the peculiar circumstances of incorporating two separate, albeit related shrines. The church was built on a pre-existing street which made it necessary to slightly skew both the shape and angle of the entrance into the enclosed atrium in order to accommodate the street, the lay of the land, and the location of the two shrines to be encompassed in the church. From the atrium, one entered directly into either the nave or the immediate side aisles used for circulation (no narthex here). The transept was also omitted, with the apse jutting out into the nave. The building from the atrium to the apse was designed to be used by the Bishop of Jerusalem for celebrating Mass. The martyrium shrine was out back behind the apse. Looking at the plan, you can see that on the left side of the apse one could enter a small shrine enclosing the top of the rocky outcropping of Calvary where the crucifixion took place. Then beyond that, there is a large enclosed peristyle courtyard, similar to the atrium at Old Saint Peter's only not in its usual location in the plan. Finally the church culminated in a spacious domed rotunda usually called the *Anastasis* (Resurrection) *Rotunda* (round structure) which marks the tomb where Jesus was laid, and from which Christian tradition holds that He was raised from the dead.

The interior of Old Saint Peter's must have been spectacular in its day. The nave was flanked by a row of magnificent columns, all recycled from ancient buildings by the way. Columns or piers used to divide the nave from the aisles are called either a *nave colonnade* when the columns support a flat lintel or a *nave arcade* when the columns support a series of arches. Since the nave would be taller than the aisles, above the nave arcade, windows were added to allow natural light directly into the nave. This is called a *clerestory*. Typically Early Christian churches had exposed wooden rafters spanning the nave, but otherwise there was no ceiling; you could look right up into the interior roof structure from the floor of the nave. In fact, over the centuries, these exposed wooden rafters posed a serious hazard as they dried out, making them ripe for fires with the multitude of candles usually burning inside a church. This is why so few Early Christian churches survive today, most burned down hundreds of years ago. Look at the interior reconstruction drawing of Old Saint Peter's Church. Do you see the arch that separates the nave from the transept, and another separating the transept from the apse? Structurally Early Christian churches were basically post and lintel design; these arches are no more needed here than they would be the entire length of the nave. Why are the arches there? A huge *triumphal arch* separated the body of the church where the faithful stood from the apse of the church, where presumably God was present during the consecration at Mass, and also later in the tabernacle. The triumphal arches symbolize the triumph of Jesus and Christianity in the world.

While these two magnificent 4th century churches are now gone and have been replaced (in part or in full) by later churches in the same sacred locations, a handful of original Early Christian basilicas are still standing with few changes from their original appearance. One of the best examples from the 5th century is **Santa Sabina** in Rome. From the outside, Santa Sabina still looks much the same as it probably did when it was first built between 422 and 432, with its plain brick exterior. Inside, this very simple basilica had only a single side aisle separated from the nave by a nave arcade comprised of Corinthian columns supporting arches and clerestory windows above. There is no narthex or transept, but the triumphal arch remains. Nowadays a flat wooden ceiling has been added, but Santa Sabina had exposed wooden rafters through most of its history.

Another excellent example is **Santa Maria Maggiore**. It is no longer the simple Early Christian basilica it once was after centuries of chapel additions and façade facelifts, but the nave still retains much the same character that it did when it was first built. The original church on this spot was begun in 358, when according to legend, the pope had a dream that Mary told him to build a church dedicated to her on the spot where snow would fall the next day. Given that it was summer, it was strange indeed that snow did fall in a single location in Rome the following day on August 5th, and accordingly the church was built. The original church built by Pope Liberius didn't last (like the snow?), and the church that stands today was commissioned by Pope Sixtus III in 432 to preside over the same site. "Santa Maria Maggiore" means the "major (or big) Saint Mary's" which is fitting because while there were several churches dedicated to Mary in the city, this was the grand dame. There was a particular incentive for building such a church at this time. The previous year, in 431, the collective bishops of the Church were called together to judge the teachings of a man named Nestorius. Nestorius had been teaching that while Mary gave birth to the human nature of Jesus, the God part of Jesus was something separate. The *Council of Ephesus* condemned the Nestorian Heresy affirming that Christ was both fully human and fully divine, both truly God and truly man, and that these two natures of Christ were indivisible. Taking that one step further, then if Jesus Christ is fully God as well as fully man, then His mother, Mary, must also be accepted as the Mother of God – the *Theotokos*, or "God-bearer." This did not mean to imply that Mary came before God and the creation of the universe, but it did mean that she gave birth to the totality of who Jesus was, and if Christians accept that He is the Lord, then she must by extension be the Mother of that manifestation of God... it would have been humanly impossible for her to give birth to part of Christ's nature as opposed to the totality of who and what He was. Heavy stuff, but the point is that in 431, more than a few theologians, clergy and even regular people on the street were pretty impressed with this thinking, and it seemed fitting that amidst churches dedicated to this saint or that, maybe they should build a really lovely church to dedicate to the Mother of God.

Santa Maria Maggiore was designed along the same lines as Santa Sabina with a roomy nave, no narthex or transept and a single side aisle, in this case separated from the nave by an Ionic columned nave colonnade. The apse was framed by a triumphal arch, and originally the rafters up to the roof remained visible. One change over the years which is significant, and may help to explain why this church is still standing today when so many Early Christian churches were lost, is the updated coffered ceiling which was added much later to protect the tinderbox timbers from catching fire. From the start this church was decorated with beautiful mosaics making it more gloriously elaborate than Plain Jane Santa Sabina. Pope Sixtus commissioned a series of *mosaics* for the church interior illustrating both Old Testament scenes and images related to the incarnation of Christ. Mosaics had been popular in antiquity, especially in Greece and Rome, but earlier mosaics were customarily found on floors. They were made of colored stone and ceramic tile, with tiny pieces called *tesserae* grouted in place, not unlike tile or stone floors we might have today. They were attractive, and also extremely durable. Early Christian and Byzantine mosaics, in contrast, are found on ceilings and walls, but never floors. The tesserae are made of colored glass, with a thin veneer of real gold sandwiched between two slivers of glass. The tesserae are mounted into the plaster wall or ceiling in a jagged, uneven way such that each individual tessera reflects light off the gold, or shows itself as a rich color depending on the angle reflecting light from the many windows.

Among the more beautiful mosaics inside Santa Maria Maggiore are those paying homage to the high points in Mary's life as she accepted her role in God's plan. The triumphal arch over the altar showcases several scenes involving Mary taken from the Bible, among them the **Annunciation**. In the scene, a most glamorous Virgin Mary sits on a throne looking more like an empress than a young Jewish maiden. She wears jeweled golden robes, earrings and a crown. It would seem that the artist, or more likely the *patron* (the person paying for the art) was influenced by the recent Council of Ephesus clarification on the role of Mary and wanted to be extra sure that she was given proper respect. The Virgin is attended by numerous angels, and one flies overhead apparently directing the Holy Spirit in the form of a dove the size of a dog toward Mary. Off to the far right Joseph appears; he's the one wearing what looks like candy cane striped socks (a peculiar fashion statement to be sure). Another angel is filling Joseph in on God's plan so he won't leave Mary high and dry once he discovers she is pregnant. Passing from the triumphal arch where the <u>Annunciation</u> mosaic is found, we focus on the spectacular mosaic serving as the final focal point of the apse: the **Coronation of the Virgin**. Inspired by a passage from the Book of Revelation the scene depicts Mary, Queen of Heaven, enthroned next to Christ who places the crown on his mother's head. This image perhaps more than any other emphasizes the importance of Mary, with Jesus elevating her above other mortals to be his right hand man (well … more accurately his right hand *wo*man) in heaven.

It would be impossible to over-emphasize the impact of Christianity on the art and architecture of the West starting in the 4th century and continuing through at least the 17th century (Christianity didn't end at that point, but other subjects rivaled religion in the arts more during the 17th century and beyond). Just as it makes sense to become familiar with the vocabulary of church architecture because you will see it again and again, so too should you get to know the basic themes in Christian art that will be often repeated through many centuries. *Iconography* is the study of a subject matter in art. It includes and understanding of the narrative, or what story the picture represents, and the *iconology* which is the study of the deeper, symbolic meaning that sometimes is not immediately apparent to the untrained eye. Certain stories in the Life of Christ will appear often in art, so it's a good idea to know them. Here are some handy reference notes for you to become acquainted the cycles in Christian iconography. If you should encounter an account you do not recall, odds are you can look it up here.

The Incarnation Cycle
The first cycle illustrates how Jesus came into the world, and tells us the stories of His childhood, about which little information appears in the <u>Bible</u>.

The Annunciation: The archangel Gabriel is sent to visit a young virgin named Mary to tell her God's plan that she conceive the Christ, and Mary accepts. In addition to the Virgin Mary and the angel Gabriel, usually some symbolic reference is made to the *incarnation* (the union of divinity and humanity in Christ). Most often this is shown as a dove standing in for the Holy Spirit, flying directly at Mary as if to miraculously enter her. Sometimes a teensy infant might be employed in the same way, as if flying toward Mary from God.

The Visitation: Gabriel also tells Mary that her kinswoman, Elizabeth is pregnant. This is unexpected since Elizabeth is past childbearing age, reflecting that this is once again a miracle. Elizabeth is carrying John the Baptist, who would be a distant cousin of Jesus and who was born about six months before Jesus. Mary elects to visit Elizabeth to help with her pregnancy. When Mary arrives, Elizabeth knows immediately that young Mary is carrying the Christ.

The Nativity: Joseph has now married Mary, and they are obliged to travel to Bethlehem for the census (each man was required to return to his family's hometown to be counted). There is no room at the inn, so Mary and Joseph wind up staying in a stable (sometimes depicted as a cave). Mary goes into labor, and Jesus is born in these humble circumstances. The child is laid in a manger (food trough for the animals). In addition to baby Jesus, Mary and Joseph, the scene will usually have animals present, normally an ox and donkey. Sometimes a couple of midwives are also included.

The Annunciation to the Shepherds: Sometimes this scene is included in the background of a Nativity. It depicts shepherds out tending their flocks of sheep late at night, with a brilliant star overhead. Suddenly an angel appears, frightening the men. They are told to find the Messiah in the stable in Bethlehem, and off they go to pay Him homage.

The Adoration of the Shepherds: Sometimes this scene and the previous one or the one following are folded into one. The shepherds arrive at the stable and pay their respects to the Holy Family.

The Adoration of the Magi: Three Wise Men from the East follow the Star of Bethlehem to find the prophesied great King. This event may have taken place later than the birth, but in art it is customarily depicted with the Magi (kings) showing up at the stable shortly after Jesus was born. They bring Jesus precious gifts of gold, which symbolizes that Christ is king, frankincense which is expensive incense used to "assist" prayers rising to heaven thus symbolizing Christ's divinity, and myrrh, a bitter resin used in the preparation of the dead for burial, symbolizing Christ's eventual sacrifice on the cross.

The Presentation at the Temple: According to Jewish tradition, Jesus must be presented to the high priest for ritual circumcision. Mary and Joseph take Jesus to the Temple, and along the way they encounter Simeon, an elderly man who has waited his whole life to see the Messiah. He recognizes Jesus immediately, proclaiming that He is the long awaited Savior. Simeon also prophesizes that Mary will have her heart pierced in sorrow.

The Massacre of the Innocents: King Herod is undone at the prospect of a King of the Jews being born to upset his rule, so he orders his men to kill all male children under the age of two throughout the kingdom. Fortunately, Jesus escapes.

Flight into Egypt: An angel warns Joseph about Herod's plans and tells him to pack up the family and flee to Egypt where Jesus will be safe. The scene usually shows Mary holding Jesus while riding a donkey, with Joseph walking along beside them.

Jesus Preaching in the Temple: We don't know much about Jesus' life after he returned to Nazareth from Egypt after Herod's death. Presumably His childhood must have been relatively uneventful growing up as the son of a carpenter and his wife. Some artists have created homey scenes of Jesus as a child, but the imagery is not inspired from passages in Scripture. The one event that is recalled in the <u>Bible</u> took place when Jesus was twelve. His extended family had traveled to Jerusalem for the Passover as was their custom. Apparently on the way home, Mom and Dad lost track of Jesus, each assuming the other knew where He was and both presuming He was probably off with His cousins. By the time they realized He was missing, they were quite a ways from Jerusalem. The panicked parents rushed back to the city and scour the place for their son. Lo and behold, they discovered Jesus in the Temple leading a discussion with the elders on Scripture. He seemed to think His parents should have known He would be about His Father's business. This is the first sign mentioned in the Bible foreshadowing Christ's ministry.

The Public Ministry Cycle

These scenes illustrate Jesus establishing His circle of Apostles, His preaching, and performing miracles to demonstrate His divinity.

The Marriage at Cana: Jesus and His friends are invited to a wedding, but the unlucky bride and groom run short on wine. Mary mentions this to Jesus, who initially shrugs it off, pointing out that He has not yet started His ministry. Mary knows well that Jesus will come around and answer her unspoken request that He do something about it. She says nothing more to Him, but instructs the men serving at the wedding to do whatever Jesus tells them. And so, Jesus turns water into wine and saves the day. It is Christ's first public miracle, prefiguring the Eucharist. It also establishes the precedent that Mary is one who has Jesus' ear, demonstrating that even when He was not especially inclined to do what she asked, He did it anyway to honor His mother.

Cleansing the Temple of Moneychangers: Jesus is outraged that those hoping to make an easy buck have set up shop in the Temple selling animals for sacrifice. In His anger, Jesus upsets their stalls and boots them out ranting that they have turned the house of prayer into a den of thieves.

The Baptism: Although Jesus is without sin, He elects to be baptized by John the Baptist alongside other *penitents* (people sorry for their sins) at the Jordan River. At that moment the Holy Spirit is made apparent (usually seen as a dove in art) and God's voice from heaven proclaims that Jesus is His son with whom God is well pleased.

The Temptation of Jesus: Filled with the Holy Spirit, Jesus retires to the desert to fast and pray for forty days, where the devil tempts Him to forego His ministry and accept gifts from the Prince of Darkness instead. Jesus perseveres.

The Sermon on the Mount: Although there are multiple accounts in the Bible of Jesus preaching to great crowds, and there are plenty of parables, often the scene that shows up in art to cover the whole shebang is the Sermon on the Mount found in Matthew 5 and Luke 6.

Miracles of Healing: Take your pick; there are several that show up in art. Among the most popular would be Christ healing the Demon Possessed Youth, Healing the Blind Man, Healing the Paralytic, and Healing the Leper.

The Miraculous Draft of Fishes: After a lousy night fishing where the men caught nothing, Jesus persuades Simon (Peter) to put out their nets again, and they catch such a huge haul that men in other boats have to come help pull in the nets. Jesus uses the opportunity to tell the men that they will become fishers of men.

Calming the Storm at Sea: Again the men are out fishing and a violent storm blows up. Jesus is with them, calm and unperturbed while everyone else is terrified. He rebukes the winds and the sea, stopping the storm to the amazement of everyone present.

The Calling of Saint Matthew: Of all the Apostles, the Calling of Saint Matthew is the story most often recalled in art. Matthew (called Levi before his conversion) was a despised tax collector, a sinner of the worst kind. Jesus decides to have dinner at this man's house to the disgust of the other Apostles. Throughout the course of dinner, Matthew comes to see the errors in his ways; he has a change of heart and leaves his old life behind to become an Apostle.

The Parable of the Prodigal Son: Although Jesus told many parables, few show up as frequently as a theme for art as often as the Prodigal Son. The moral of the story is that God forgives those who repent their sins.

The Multiplication of the Loaves and Fishes: During Christ's public ministry there are accounts of him feeding thousands of people by miraculously multiplying what little available food was on hand. In two Gospels, a boy had five barley loaves and two fish which miraculously fed five thousand men (not including the women and children) leaving twelve baskets of leftovers after the meal. In another version of what may have been the same story but recalled by a different evangelist, seven loaves and a "few" fish fed four thousand with seven baskets of leftovers. Any way you look at it, a whole lot of people were fed with hardly any food, constituting a miracle.

Jesus Walks on Water: This passage comes a little later in Scripture, although sometimes in art it is conflated with Jesus calming the sea from a fishing boat during a storm. In this account, Peter sees Jesus walking on water coming out to greet the men in their fishing boat. Peter jumps out to greet Jesus and also starts walking on water in his enthusiasm, but when he realizes what he is doing he starts to sink. Jesus saves Peter and chastises him for his weak faith.

Christ gives the Keys of the Kingdom to Peter: Jesus asks the Apostles who they think He is. Of all the assorted replies, only Peter seems to understand that Jesus is the Messiah. Jesus says that Peter is blessed by the Holy Spirit. ("Simon son of Jonah" Mt 16:17 – but Simon Peter's earthly father was named John – see John 1:42 and John 21: 15-17. "Bar Jonah" or "son of Jonah" does not refer to Peter's biological father but rather to his being the son of the Spirit. Jonah means Spirit just as Adam means Man and Peter means Rock; frequently Bible names carry special meaning.) Jesus then gives Peter the keys to the Kingdom (heaven) which is a reference back to the Old Testament book of Isaiah (Is 22:22), the "Key to the Kingdom" implying authority over others.

The Transfiguration: Jesus climbs a mountain with Peter, James and John to pray, and to the amazement of the Apostles, suddenly Jesus becomes luminous and they see him talking to Moses and Elijah who appear out of the blue. While this is happening, a bright cloud casts a shadow over them, and the Apostles hear a voice say, "This is my beloved Son with whom I am well pleased, listen to Him."

The Tribute Money:

The Apostles are expected to pay a temple tax but have no money. Jesus tells Peter he will find the appropriate coin in the mouth of a fish. Sometimes this account is conflated with another account where Jesus is questioned whether it is right to pay taxes to a pagan oppressor like Rome. Jesus asks whose face is on the coin. It is Caesar, to which Jesus says to give to Caesar what is Caesar's and to God what is God's.

The Raising of Lazarus: Lazarus and his family are friends of Jesus. Lazarus dies, but not before Jesus was summoned in the hope Lazarus would be healed. When Jesus arrives four days after Lazarus has already died and been laid in his tomb, the family is upset. Jesus then raises Lazarus from the dead, asking him to walk out of the tomb still wrapped in his death shroud. This account occurs in the Gospel of John at the close of Jesus' public ministry, and is a foreshadowing of Christ's resurrection.

The Passion Cycle
The third cycle of imagery associated with the life of Jesus deals with the end of His life including establishing the Eucharist, His death on a cross and finally His resurrection and eternal role in heaven.

The Entry into Jerusalem: Jesus and the Apostles enter Jerusalem for the Passover. Jesus is riding on a donkey, and the crowds turn out to welcome Him. Palm fronds are placed in His path (the Entry into Jerusalem is celebrated in Christian tradition on Palm Sunday).

The Last Supper: This is the *Passover Seder* (the feast to commemorate the Jews' exodus out of Egypt with Moses to enter their promised land). Jesus offers hints of what lies ahead although the Apostles do not fully understand. He discloses that one of them will betray Him. Finally, Christ initiates His new covenant through the elements of the Seder meal. After blessing the unleavened bread and wine, Jesus tells his Apostles that these are His body and blood, which they are to eat in remembrance of Him, thus establishing the Eucharist. The Last Supper is recalled anytime communion is shared by Christians, but most especially on Holy Thursday, or Maundy Thursday (Maundy means "command," coming from Jesus' command at the Last Supper to love one another) a few days before Easter.

Jesus Washing the Apostles' Feet: This theme isn't quite as popular in art, but it does occasionally show up. At the Last Supper, Jesus washes the feet of each Apostle to set an example of humility. Initially Peter is not keen on the idea, but when Jesus insists (telling

Peter he cannot remain an Apostle otherwise), Peter says to wash his hands and head also. Sometimes this act is also part of Maundy Thursday Christian worship.

The Agony in the Garden: Following the Last Supper, Jesus and the Apostles retire to the Garden of Gethsemane where Jesus asks them to pray with him, but they all manage to fall asleep. Jesus is intensely troubled at the prospects of his impending gruesome death since He is well aware of what lies ahead. He has the power to refuse, but He accepts His sacrifice on behalf of the salvation of humanity.

The Betrayal of Judas: The Apostle Judas Iscariot has become disillusioned with Jesus and elects to accept thirty silver pieces from the chief priests in exchange for revealing the location of Jesus and the Apostles. Judas arrives on the scene with an armed guard, and singles Jesus out from the others with a kiss. Peter attempts to defend Jesus, only to deny Him later in the same night, showing His own weakness. While Peter seeks forgiveness for his lapse in judgment, Judas does not and later hangs himself, presumably from regret.

Jesus before ... Caiaphas, Pilate, and Herod: Jesus is first brought before the High Priest Caiaphas, who declares that Jesus is a blasphemer and must be sentenced to death. But under Roman Law, the Jewish religious leaders do not have the authority to kill one another. So Jesus is taken to the Roman governor of Judea, Pontius Pilate. Pilate is befuddled by Jesus, but finds him harmless enough. He would prefer not to get involved, so cleverly recalls that Jesus was from Nazareth, so technically not under Pilate's jurisdiction. He passes Jesus on to Herod Antipas who governs Galilee. Herod dismisses Jesus as fool, sending him back to Pilate. Pilate *really* has a bad feeling about this, but the mob is being stirred up by the high priest's entourage and is worrisome. In the end Pilate acquiesces to the crowd's demands, but he publicly washes his hands of the whole affair stating that the blood of Jesus would not be on his hands, but on those who demanded Jesus' death.

The Flagellation: Sometimes called the ***Scourging at the Pillar***. In an attempt to mollify the mob demanding Jesus' death, Pilate has Jesus flogged as punishment for His "crimes."

Jesus Crowned with Thorns: Sometimes also called the ***Mocking of Christ***. The soldiers in charge of flogging Jesus get carried away. Not only do they beat Jesus severely, they dress him up in robes like royalty and weave a wreath of thorns that they jam onto his head like a crown, all the while laughing at Jesus and making fun of him as King of the Jews.

Carrying the Cross to Calvary: Jesus is finally sentenced to death by crucifixion, and is obliged to carry his cross outside the city walls to Calvary. Medieval artistic tradition depicted fourteen "Stations of the Cross," and these are still observed by many Christians up to modern times, especially during Lent which is the forty day period preceding Easter. Expect to see elements of the Stations of the Cross in art. They are: 1) Jesus is condemned to death; 2) Jesus takes up His cross; 3) Jesus falls the first time; 4) Jesus meets His grieving mother; 5) Simon of Cyrene is asked to help Jesus carry the cross; 6) Veronica wipes Jesus' face with her veil; 7) Jesus falls a second time; 8) Jesus tells the women of Jerusalem to weep not for Him, but for their children; 9) Jesus falls a third time; 10) Jesus is stripped of his clothes; 11) Jesus is nailed to the cross; 12) Jesus dies on the cross; 13) Jesus is taken down from the cross; and finally; 14) Jesus is placed in the tomb.

The Crucifixion: Jesus is nailed to the cross and after approximately three hours of agonized suffering, He suffocates and dies. Christ is depicted wearing a loin cloth, often bearing dreadful wounds from the scourging. Sometimes three crosses are shown with Jesus flanked by two criminals, one of whom repents on the cross and Jesus promises He will take him to paradise. Usually included in the scene are the Virgin Mary accompanied by Saint John the Evangelist and Mary Magdalene. The presiding Roman soldiers are customarily depicted as coarse. They cast lots for Christ's clothes and continue to mock him while others mourn. Sometimes an artist will include a sponge of wine being lifted to Christ's lips just before He dies. Other artists might include a skull at the foot of the cross which is a reference to Golgotha, the name given the exact site on top of the Hill of Calvary where the crucifixion took place.

The Descent from the Cross: Christ's body is taken down from the cross. The Virgin Mary, Saint John the Evangelist and Mary Magdalene are devastated by grief. A couple wealthy Jews are also on hand to assist with Christ's burial. Joseph of Arimathea is there since he was the one who asked Pilate for Christ's body and donated his nearby tomb (prepared for himself, but offered to Jesus instead). Nicodemus is included also. He was a Pharisee known to have an interest in Jesus' teachings. Their discourse on baptism is included in the New Testament, and he also stuck up for Jesus in the kangaroo court held in the secret of night at the Sanhedrin when Jesus was found guilty by the high priest. Joseph of Arimathea and Nicodemus wrap Jesus' body in a linen shroud and prepare the body with a hundred pounds of myrrh and aloe purchased by Nicodemis. Often other mourners are included in the scene.

The Lamentation: or its close cousin, *the Pieta*. After Jesus is taken down off the cross, His mother, Saint John and Mary Magdalene mourn over his prostrate body. This motif is popular in Italian art. The French preferred another style of the same scene called a pieta. Here Christ is draped over the Virgin Mary's lap and she is usually shown praying over His body.

The Entombment: Christ is placed in a tomb and a large stone is rolled in place. Roman guards are sent to be sure nobody steals Christ's body over the Jewish Sabbath.

The Resurrection: Three days after His death, Jesus is resurrected and departs the tomb while the guards sleep. This imagery is not terribly common in Western art tradition as it proves to be quite challenging. Perhaps the most compelling image of the Resurrection was painted by Matthias Grunewald during the Renaissance (stay tuned, more on that later). In Eastern art traditions, the Resurrection is called the ***Anastasis*** and includes images of Christ rescuing souls from hell.

The Three Marys at the Tomb: Following the Sabbath, on Sunday morning the Virgin Mary, Mary Magdalene and Mary the mother of James all come to the tomb to attend the body since it had been hastily prepared before entombment due to the onset of the Sabbath. They discuss among themselves who will roll back the big stone for them, only to discover it has already been rolled away. When they peak inside, they discover the tomb is empty. An angel dressed in white is there, and tells them Christ has risen from the dead. Everyone is frightened and confused.

Noli Me Tangere: which means touch me not. Christ first appears to Mary Magdalene. At first she thinks He is the gardener because she doesn't recognize Him. After she asks where they took the body of Jesus, she suddenly realizes who He is and reaches out to Him. He tells her not to touch Him since He has not yet ascended to heaven (after He resurrected, the first stop was hell or some in-between limbo where Jesus freed those destined for heaven but who had to wait for the arrival of the Messiah first). This is called the ***Harrowing of Hell***. In Byzantine art, the Harrowing of Hell is usually conflated with the ***Anastasis*** as part of the same theme.

Supper at Emmaus: The story here is similar to the one above. This time a couple of Jesus' disciples are walking along to the village of Emmaus (seven miles from Jerusalem) and as they talked about Jesus, a stranger comes along and walks with them. It is Christ, but they do not recognize Him. He asks about Jesus, and the disciples are amazed that the stranger doesn't seem to know all that has happened. They invite the stranger to join them for supper and as Christ says the blessing over the bread, the men suddenly understand who it is. Immediately Christ vanishes before their eyes.

The Ascension: After forty days appearing to the Apostles and other disciples, Christ is swept up to heaven in clouds.

Pentecost: Although strictly speaking Jesus is not present at Pentecost as He is in almost all of the other scenes in all three cycles, a postscript is that He promised the Apostles that God would send a helper, the Holy Spirit, to assist them in their ministry of spreading the Good News. Images of Pentecost frequently appear alongside the Passion Cycle, showing the Apostles and often the Virgin Mary with tongues of fire descending on their heads as they receive the Holy Spirit.

The Last Judgment: Again this theme is not part of the Passion Cycle, since it is our turn to be judged rather than Jesus, but the subject is a popular one in art and should be included in this list. Last Judgment scenes normally depict Christ enthroned, often with Saint Michael the Archangel assisting by weighing souls. Bodies rise from the earth to be judged. Those deemed worthy are escorted off to heaven, often welcomed by a host of angels and Saint Peter checking them in at the gate. The less worthy souls are cast into hell which is always depicted as a horrific place of burning fires, hideous demons and an eternity of relentless suffering.

The Early Christian period is significant as this passage in history established models for both Christian architecture and Christian themes in art. It was also an important period of intellectual growth and spiritual development by way of Church Councils that took place during the 4th and 5th centuries. The Council of Ephesus was mentioned in conjunction with Santa Maria Maggiore, but it was certainly not the first big meeting where the bishops ironed out important issues of the day. The Roman government merely recognized as legitimate the Christian Church as it was already functioning in 313. Once Christianity was legalized and completely out in the open, it became increasingly evident that while most Christians professed a common set of beliefs, there were some who seemed to be lurching off in the wrong direction. The bishops contacted Emperor Constantine, and requested permission to hold a special meeting to iron out some of these heretical ideas that had been brought to their attention. The result was the *First Council of Nicaea*, held in 325.

The issue that most preoccupied the council was the Arian Heresy, which seems to weave in and out of Christian history, and in many ways might be considered the all time most challenging heresy Christianity has withstood. It was started by a Greek priest in Alexandria, Egypt called Arius. Arius argued that Christ and God the creator were not one, but rather that Jesus was a creation of God, but not God Himself. He argued that Jesus was less than God and that the Holy Spirit was even less than Jesus, and that all three aspects of the Trinity were not one, but separate. The outcome of the First Council of Nicaea was that the Nicene Creed was formally written so that all Christians everywhere would confess the same, uniform set of beliefs, hopefully without "creative interpretation" leading people away from the faith. The council set a precedent that would be revisited often in Christianity: if it ain't broke, don't fix it. Christianity, like Judaism before it, was established through Oral Tradition. Historically there has been a pattern of not spelling out every detail in official written documents *unless / until* there is a problem where a significant number of believers have forsaken the Oral Tradition … then a council is ultimately called so that the Oral Tradition may be clearly set forth in writing as non-negotiable.

The other 4th century council that had a major impact on Christianity, and ultimately on the development of the West, was the *Council of Rome* in 382. This is when the Bible was created as a *book*. Mind you, up to this point there wasn't even an Old Testament book, much less an Old and New Testament. The ancient texts of the Old Testament had been translated into Greek in 200 BC so they actually could be read. Remember, since the days of Alexander the Great, the ancient lands of the eastern Mediterranean where Judaism thrived were more Greek speaking than Hebrew, but whether in Greek or Hebrew, there was still no single book you could pick up and read. The problem with the Christian texts, which included letters mostly, along with accounts of the life of Jesus, was that there were a slew of them floating around, and not all of them were equally good sources to learn the faith.

Prior to 382, there had been considerable disagreement among Christians over which written material was legitimate, and what was not. For example, in 140, a Roman businessman named Marcion put forth what he thought the Bible ought to be. He wanted to see 2 separate Gods, Yahweh, the mean God from the Old Testament and Abba, the nice God from the New Testament. In fact he was all for tossing out the Old Testament altogether, and for a New Testament, he wanted to see just the *Gospel of Luke* and 13 letters of Paul because he thought everything else was "too Jewish." Another do-it-yourself version was introduced in 200, the Muratorian Canon, which hits closer to the final version in that all 4 gospels were included, *Acts of the Apostles*, and 13 letters written by Paul, but *Hebrews* got the heave ho, and so did 4 of the other 7 epistles not written by Paul (*1-2 John* and *Jude* were retained), and then the ringer: the *Apocalypse of Peter*, as opposed to the *Apocalypse of John*, which is the one that ultimately was included in the Bible.

The Council of Rome undertook the task of determining which texts were inspired, and therefore which texts would be officially included in Scripture, putting the Old Testament and New Covenant together. The Old Testament was not a problem, by the way; they just grandfathered in the ***Septuagint***, which were the texts compiled and translated into Greek by the famed 70 scholars in Alexandria in 200 BC, as that was the Scripture in use at the time Jesus lived.

The litmus tests applied to the New Testament written material were as follows. First and foremost, every word in the text had to conform, without exception, to Oral Tradition. If 99% of the text was perfect, but there was one passage that didn't jive with Oral Tradition, it was deemed ***apocrypha***, meaning that it might be some pretty good stuff, but deemed to be less than 100% inspired by God and therefore not officially Scripture. By the way, all the apocrypha texts, such as the *Gospel of Thomas* or that *Apocalypse of Peter* for example, can be easily located online these days, and they make for an interesting read. The second consideration was who wrote it and when. The author had to either be an Apostle or someone deemed to have worked directly with an Apostle, and it had to have been written during the lifetime of the Apostles, which is to say, during the 1st century AD. The Bible was compiled so that texts that were not up to snuff would no longer be used in worship, potentially risking leading Christians astray. Oral Tradition remained alive and well, but now for the first time, a significant portion of that Oral Tradition would be available in a single book. The roster of inspired texts was authoritatively determined at the Council of Rome in 382, confirmed at the Council of Hippo in 393, and finally ratified at the Council of Carthage in 397. The Bible was first translated from Greek, and much of that from original Hebrew, into a "vulgar" or vernacular language spoken by everyday people so that it could be read in the year 400, when Saint Jerome translated it into Latin which at that time was a less scholarly language and more "popular" for regular people than Greek. That translation is called the *Vulgate* … and it is still around today.

7. **Byzantine**

395 - 1453

As the predominant influence on the Middle Ages in the West, Christianity went on for a time as a completely unified religion. Curiously perhaps, the first seeds of what was to come can be traced back to a completely innocent, non-religious series of political events. Rome, which had been the supreme experiment in unified political power for the first 200 years of the Empire, grew to such a size that in 285 it was partitioned into East and West empires. There was an emperor for each, although most of the time these men coordinated their efforts so that there remained a strong sense of central government and absolute authority, despite having two capitals. The Senate in Rome continued on, business as usual, while the second capital was assigned to the ancient city of Byzantium, which was located in Asia Minor, and is called Istanbul today. This made sense because the Empire was growing faster in the East than in the West, so a presence near the "eastern frontier" was useful. To make a long story short, Constantine came to power in 306, and after defeating his co-emperor, Maxentius in 312, he unified the East and West together again with a single capital back in Rome.

Unfortunately though, Rome had become a crime-ridden city, it wasn't all that clean, it was chronically subjected to barbarian invasions from malcontents up north who were outside the Roman umbrella of civilization, and as time went on, Constantine simply wanted someplace a little nicer to live. In 330 he moved his base of government operations to Byzantium, rebuilding much of the city to suit his needs, and renaming it Constantinople, after himself. Located on the Bosphorus straits with fabulous views out over the water, and at least in the old days, plenty of fresh air, Constantinople in Constantine's day was like a glorified Camp David might be to America in contemporary times. The basic government, such as the Senate was still located in Rome, but the executive branch spent a fair amount of time off at the splendid retreat further east. Constantine died (being baptized on his deathbed) in 337 … and his successors (his sons) redivided the Empire again into East and West parcels. Perhaps the Early Christian Church had enough to manage during this time just getting churches built, sorting out the <u>Bible</u> and all, but one way or the other, politics didn't seem to play a part in Church affairs during the 4th century.

Theodosius ascended to the emperor's throne in 379. He reunited the Empire again, in no small part because he spent a lot of time running to and fro between Rome and Constantinople instead of staying primarily in one city. Theodosius died in 395, leaving the Empire to his two sons who divided it yet again, and it was from this point on that problems began to pester the Church. The son in Constantinople did a pretty good job of managing government business, while his brother off in Rome was a lousy administrator, and Rome set into a period of decline. And what impact would this have on Christianity you might wonder?

In the Christian Church, the bishops held their positions of authority through Apostolic Succession, and like the Apostles back in the 1st century, they had a leader. Peter was leader of the Apostles. On many occasions Jesus gave instructions to Peter that were not extended to the other Apostles, in much the same way as the Apostles as a group received instructions and blessings that exceeded what Jesus offered to the average guy on the street. There was a pecking order, and if nothing else, a tally of the number of times each Apostle is mentioned by name in the <u>Bible</u> illustrates rather clearly that Peter was the grand pooh-bah of the group. Peter, for those who are interested, gets mentioned by name 195 times in Scripture, and the other Apostles, combined, only score 130 together! Second to Peter is John with 29 references, and even the name James (remember, there were two of them with this name) share 38 hits between them. Peter completed his ministry in Rome and was the first Bishop of Rome. All subsequent Bishops of Rome are the descendants of Peter's office, and throughout the early centuries, the other bishops, while in charge of their own regions, nevertheless continued to recognize to the Bishop of Rome as the first among equals on Christian matters.

Looking back to the days of Jesus and Apostolic times, Byzantium was nowhere special back then. As the early Church grew, major cities where Apostles had carried out their ministries or where there had been large Christian communities in Apostolic times had bishops that were considered more authoritative than the bishops who did not directly succeed the office of an Apostle or who presided in smaller Christian communities. For example, Saint James was the Apostle in Jerusalem (Bishop of Jerusalem), and Saint Peter was the Apostle in Rome (Bishop of Rome), and Saint John was the Apostle in Ephesus (Bishop of Ephesus). Those cities traced their roots back to a specific Apostle. Likewise, the Christian communities in Antioch and Alexandria were large and had been early on. Peter was active in Antioch before going to Rome, and Matthew was probably there also, and the Church Alexandria was established by the evangelist Mark, who was a companion and secretary to Peter.

The leading bishops who filled an office in direct succession to an Apostle and who led the faithful in the larger Christian communities were called *patriarchs* or in the case of the patriarchal city of Rome, the special "nickname" of *pope* ("papa" – the father). The first three cities to receive patriarchal status were Rome, Antioch and Alexandria with Jerusalem added later. Byzantium had not been a locale where one of the Apostles established his ministry nor had there been a substantial Christian community there, so there was no patriarch historically in this region unlike the "big" patriarchal centers. After the Edict of Milan and Council of Nicaea, when it seemed more and more like Christianity was the new up and coming religion of choice for the Empire, Constantine felt there was a need for patriarchal status for the bishop in his newly chosen quasi-capital city of Constantinople, so he selected the man of his personal choice for the new post. This was a bit unorthodox given that the leadership within the Church customarily decided such assignments, but the collective bishops in the Church approved Constantine's choice and offered the appropriate blessings for this bishop to assume his station as a patriarch in the Church.

In time the Patriarch of Constantinople wanted greater power and recognition within the Church. While he continued to defer to the pope, he desired to be considered the "second in charge" right behind him. This position was first introduced at the First Council of Constantinople in 381. In the now famous third canon of that council, the Patriarch of Constantinople declared that because Constantinople had become a "New Rome," the bishop of that city should have preeminence of honor after the Bishop of [the "old"] Rome. Constantinople's argument was increasingly based on politics. If the only strong arm of the government was now in Constantinople, it seemed to make sense for the Patriarch of Constantinople to have more authority, in order to work closely with the secular government for the overall benefit of the Empire. He wanted to see a shift in power away from the dying city of Rome (and likewise away from the pope) over to his camp in Constantinople. In contrast, the pope's view was that Jesus had established these offices, and frankly it didn't matter where the government called home, because secular governments had nothing to do with the Christian religion. This empire would come and go, and other empires in history would follow and fade, but the Church would not pass away and it was the job of the Church to stay faithful to what Jesus established, whether that always seemed "logical" to the eyes of men or not. The point here is to understand that both church leaders made their arguments based on what seemed best for the Church. They may have had a different understanding of what the priorities should be, but their positions were based more on doing what is right for Christianity rather than on massaging individual inflated egos.

The start date for the Early Byzantine period is 395 since this is when the patriarch in Constantinople began to officially pull away from the authority of the pope in Rome. The period ends in 1453 when Constantinople fell to the Ottoman Turks, which is to say, Islam. Even after the Byzantine Empire fell (politics), the Byzantine *style* of art and architecture continued on.

In summary then, the Byzantine Church was in the East, based out of Constantinople, and it enjoyed a close relationship with the government. The Byzantine Church is the ancestor of the Eastern Orthodox religion today, which continues to be associated with national churches such as Greek Orthodox and Russian Orthodox. Each branch of the Orthodox faith has "holy fathers" who are called ***patriarchs***, and the patriarchs oversee broad regional religious leaders called ***metropolitans***, who oversee regional ***bishops*** who oversee ***priests*** in their region. The Early Christian Church is the ancestor of the Catholic Church - it was being called this already at the Council if Nicaea; "catholic" means "universal." It was historically in the West (although worldwide nowadays), based out of Rome, and independent of national affiliation. There is one "holy father," who is called the ***pope***, who also oversees broad regional religious leaders called ***archbishops*** who oversee regional ***bishops*** who oversee ***priests*** worldwide. It is also important to remember that these positions within the church build on one another. Archbishops, metropolitans, patriarchs and popes are also ordained bishops; they are bishops with elevated seniority and authority who oversee a broad region with other bishops under their supervision.

Theologically these two branches of Christianity are very similar, with the biggest difference being that the Eastern patriarchs no longer recognize the authority of Peter's office. Although the disagreements between the assorted bishops started in 395, they all hung in there for several centuries before conceding that a schism was inevitable. The actual ***schism*** (split) occurred in 1054, which was well after the Early Christian period had developed into Early Medieval in the West, and midway through the Byzantine Empire in the East.

Byzantine churches and Early Christian churches are frequently, although not always, quite different. Early Christian architects modified the old basilica design to meet their needs, while in the East, the ***central plan*** became more popular. These churches are round (or if not always perfectly circular, close to it – ovals or octagons). Usually Byzantine churches were also smaller in scale as more often they were designed to serve smaller communities, like a neighborhood church, rather than large regional areas. They can be rural or urban. Keep in mind we are making broad, generalized statements here; there were Byzantine basilicas, and there were Catholic central plan churches, but the *norm* was rectangular design for Catholic, and round design for Byzantine.

A splendid sample of Byzantine design is the church of **San Vitale**, commissioned by the 6th century Emperor Justinian, or to be technically correct, the local bishop issued the commission, but it was built to promote Justinian and the Byzantine Church in Italy. By the time Justinian came to power in Constantinople, the two divisions of the Christian Church had been voicing their differences of opinions on where the central authority for Christianity should be based for almost two centuries. Justinian made it a priority to try to reunite Christians under one common banner before further separation could take place. Toward this end, he commissioned San Vitale in particular to promote Christian unity, built on Italian soil in the city of Ravenna, near Venice on the Adriatic. Italy had been invaded repeatedly during the 5th century by Germanic tribes out of the north (still a nuisance after so many years; remember that the Romans had struggled with German barbarians since the early days of the Empire). Finally in 476 Rome fell to the Ostrogoths. Half a century later Justinian managed to conquer Italy back, and he established Ravenna (not Rome) as his "western" capital for Byzantium as it was convenient for facilitating trade with Constantinople. Justinian hoped to dazzle the Christians in Italy, who were loyal to the pope in Rome with the splendor of the Eastern Church, and hence bring them in line with the patriarch in Constantinople.

Notice that San Vitale does not have an atrium. Because most Byzantine churches were scaled to accommodate a local population, there was no need to have a big courtyard for travelers. Instead, there is a large narthex, big enough to hold lots of people in bad weather, and also big enough to coordinate processions indoors. From the narthex, one crossed over the aisle, which was used for circulation, into the round nave in the center of the church, which in plan resembles the hole in a big doughnut-shaped building. As we saw with basilica churches, the faithful would stand in the nave during the service. In Byzantine times, only men were expected to stand in the nave; women and small children were obliged to go upstairs into a balcony area over the aisle called a *gallery*. Men and women were not separated in Catholic churches. Central plan churches do not have transepts, but instead we find the apse leading off the nave. The holy sanctuary in the apse end of a Byzantine church will always be considerably deeper than the apse in a Catholic church. In addition to the altar and tabernacle, there must also be room for the *iconostasis* (stay tuned, more on that later).

Why were most Byzantine churches designed in the round? The interior of the church quickly shows us why. Byzantine churches were lavishly decorated with beautiful mosaics, which were provided both to enhance the atmosphere and remind you that you were in church, and they also helped to educate the illiterate faithful by depicting a selection of religious subjects. While Early Christian churches put their efforts and resources into size, with the idea that they could always come back later and make the interior fancier with more art (and they did), Byzantine churches were usually smaller, with a budget set aside for lots of art from the get go. The round design made it easy to stand in the nave and see all the spectacular mosaics at one time. Additionally, having windows running full circle around the nave allowed for maximum natural light to show off the mosaics to their best advantage. As we saw with Early Christian mosaics, they were made of small pieces of colored glass, with a thin veneer of real gold sandwiched between two slivers of glass. These *tesserae* were mounted into the plaster wall or ceiling in a jagged, uneven way such that each individual tessera reflected light off the gold, or showed itself as a rich color depending on the angle reflecting light from the many windows. Byzantine mosaics sparkle as one moves through the nave and as the light angles change from moment to moment reflecting either color or a glitter of gold. It is as if the walls and ceiling were encrusted with glittering jewels. Breathtakingly beautiful to be sure!

There are two mosaics in the apse of San Vitale that are particularly famous. Looking from the nave, to the left of the altar is the **Justinian Mosaic**, and to the right is the **Theodora Mosaic**. The Justinian Mosaic depicts the emperor in the center, dressed in the purple robes of a king and sporting a halo. He is surrounded by a dozen attendants, and he holds a basket of bread in his arms. It seems rather obvious that Justinian is being presented as a Christ figure, complete with his Apostles and the Eucharistic bread to be consecrated and offered during the *Divine Liturgy*, which is what the service is called in the Eastern Church; "Mass" and "Divine Liturgy" mean the same thing. Flanking the altar on the other side is Justinian's wife, Theodora. She also wears a halo as she offers an attendant the chalice, which recalls the Blood of Christ. On her robes there are three well-dressed kings on camels, all of them with gifts in hand. Surely these are the three wise men. The only woman they called on was the Virgin Mary, so we presume that a parallel is being made between the empress and Mary. What's going on here? Justinian was evidently trying to make the point that he and his wife were devout Christians, which in turn would serve as a sort of testimonial of support for the Eastern Church given that his loyalties lay with Constantinople. How might you guess this art would be received? Imagine if you walked into a church or synagogue or mosque today, and there at the front, in whatever part of the building you would consider to be the most holy, were larger than life images of the president depicted as Jesus (or Moses, or Muhammad), and the First Lady as Mary or a comparably holy woman in the religion of your choice. Do you suppose most people would see imagery like that in a sacred context, and think to themselves, "Gee, I didn't realize the president was such a holy guy; I must become a more devoted follower of the president." Or do you suppose many might be offended? The Justinian and Theodora Mosaics may have seemed like a good idea to Justinian at the time, but rather than spread unity between the Catholic and Byzantine churches, the divisions widened.

Justinian built San Vitale in Ravenna to encourage unity between the Western Christians and the Church in the East. He built the **Hagia Sophia**, which means Holy Wisdom, in Constantinople for his home base church, where he and the empress attended the Divine Liturgy, and where visiting officials might join the pomp and circumstance of royal patronage at church. Hagia Sophia is several times larger than the petite San Vitale due to its relative importance in the expression of harmony between church and state in the East. Also due to its unique role, the church had an atrium (now gone) provided both to accommodate travelers and also to coordinate processions in its day. The church was designed by two eminent architects prone to innovative design, Anthemius of Tralles and Isadorus of Miletus. The result was not only an immense church, but a complicated design experimenting with architectural and engineering features not seen in Early Christian basilicas or smaller Byzantine churches like San Vitale.

Inside the church is dominated by a spectacular colossal dome which appears to float on a halo of forty windows. This is not a simple dome like we saw at the Pantheon where a shallow, solid dome rested on a massive, equally solid concrete drum. Instead it was built as a tall, thin shell resting on four massive piers that frame the nave. To make this work, the architects employed *pendentives*. By definition, pendentives are curved triangular supports that are part of a groined vault … which probably means absolutely nothing to you as you try to figure out what you are looking at. Pendentives can be tricky to explain because they are derived from understanding geometry principles that you can't see and immediately comprehend from just looking at the finished product. So if you will, consider a little experiment. You will need a grapefruit and an orange and a sharp knife. Cut your grapefruit in half, and place one half juicy side down. There you have a big dome, yes? But it's wider than your nave and it isn't as tall as you would like the dome to be either, so you would like to perch half an orange on top. To support your half orange, trim the grapefruit down to a square by slicing off four "sides" (leaving just a small wedge of grapefruit at each corner) then slice off the top of the grapefruit dome so the half-orange rests on a flat surface. Can you see that rising from the piers (the four corners of the square grapefruit) there are four curved triangles that rise to meet the base of your (orange) dome? Those are your pendentives. Now if you take the other half of your orange, cut that in half again and tack those orange wedges back on to either end or your square grapefruit, you have **conch domes** or half domes at either end of the nave making it oval. Compare your fruit "structure" to the plan of <u>Hagia Sophia</u> to see how it worked.

<u>Hagia Sophia</u> once had glorious interior mosaics. Sadly, many centuries ago it was converted to an Islamic mosque, and as a result, the spectacular mosaics that once graced the interior have been largely destroyed as Islam prohibits human imagery in religious art. Nowadays <u>Hagia Sophia</u> is a museum.

Recall that the apse in Byzantine churches had to be deeper than in Catholic churches because Byzantine churches needed room for the *iconostasis*? An iconostasis is a screen which divides the apse in half, such that part is visible from the nave, and part is hidden. The Byzantine Divine Liturgy places great emphasis on mystery, and toward that end, the parts of the Divine Liturgy involving the consecration are celebrated by the priest behind the screen. The iconostasis displays dozens of individual painted images called *icons*. Icons traditionally are painted in *tempera* (pigment mixed with egg yolks) paint on wooden panel. They depict Apostles, saints, or scenes from the life of Christ. Byzantine churches (and Eastern Orthodox today) are required to have icons as part of the church architecture. The **<u>Virgin Enthroned Icon</u>** is a very early example dating back to the 6th century around the time of Justinian. It is still in its original location in the Monastery of Saint Catherine on Mount Sinai in Egypt. Here we see the Virgin Mary seated on a throne holding the infant Jesus, a theme that would become popular during the Middle Ages and remain so through the Renaissance. Mother and Son are flanked by two saints: Saint Theodore is the bearded fellow, while Saint George is the fair-haired young man.

To understand icons and how they are used, it is necessary to become familiar with a concept called the *Communion of Saints*, an idea familiar to all Christians at this time in history. Christians have always been taught to pray for one another, and in fellowship with other Christians. The <u>Bible</u> makes it clear in several verses that people are supposed to pray for each other, and it also states that when two or more are gathered in God's name, that God is present and hears the prayers. Most people easily understand this to mean that if your Grandma is sick, you ask your friends to keep Grandma in their prayers. When you pray for your Grandma, what aspect of you is communing with God? Most people would agree that it is the soul of a person in prayer which God knows and hears; it isn't your mouth, or nose or your knee cap that keeps you in touch with God.

Let's take this a step further. Let's say that Grandma's husband, also known as Grandpa, died 2 years ago. From a Christian perspective, what part of Grandpa died? A Christian would say it was his body. And his soul? Christians assume the soul is as alive as it ever was, and if we give Grandpa the benefit of the doubt that he was a good man, devout in his faith and moral in his behavior, then one hopes for the best that Grandpa went to heaven. If Grandpa's soul is alive, and if it is the soul which prays to God, and if Grandpa's soul is in heaven, then why not ask Grandpa to pray for Grandma? Just because his body died doesn't mean his soul is dead also, and if he's in heaven, he is probably closer to God right now than you and your friends might be. All Christians living in Early Christian and Byzantine times would have taken for granted that the souls of the people who were in heaven could put in a good word for the folks slogging it out on Earth. Who else would be in heaven along with Grandpa? Christians would assume that the saints and Apostles would be there too, and probably to the degree that there might be preferential status in heaven, the Apostles and saints would be even closer to God than Grandpa. So maybe it might be a good idea to ask one of these good souls to pray with you for Grandma's speedy recovery. The point is, you never want to pray by yourself if you can ask others to pray with you, you ideally want those praying with you to be on good terms with God (the Bible also states that the prayers of the *righteous* are answered), so calling on a saint or Apostle to pray with you seems to cover the bases.

Icons in Byzantine churches served (and continue to serve today) as catalysts in prayer. Since the faithful will ask a saint or Apostle to join them in prayer, the icon is available to assist them in focusing their attention, and they pray *through* the icon asking that saint or Apostle to pray also so that two or more are gathered in God's name, lending strength to the petition placed before God. Note that people do not pray *to* icons. Painted pictures do not do magic tricks and no icon can make Grandma's health improve. Furthermore, although someone might say they are praying "to" the saint, this means that they are *asking* the saint to help them with their petition to *God*. All Christians believe that the saints and Apostles have no intrinsic power (any more than your friends do when they join you in prayer), in heaven or otherwise that is not God working through them. Ultimately, all the prayers are directed to God, and it is God who responds to prayer. Icons are mandated in Eastern Orthodox churches today, as they were in the old Byzantine churches. Icons are not and never were required in Catholic churches, *but* it should be understood that the understanding of the Communion of Saints is the same between these two branches of Christianity, whether an iconostasis is part of the church architecture or not. The precedent for sacred images dates all the way back to Apostolic times when images of scenes of the life of Christ, the Apostles and the early saints were used to help counter the impact of pagan Roman imagery. This should not be confused with graven images, like the ancient Hebrews worshipping the Golden Calf; Christians do not worship art anymore than tourists visiting Washington DC worship the Lincoln Memorial or those in New York worship the Statue of Liberty. Churches since the beginning might have icons, or they might have other types of paintings or statues, and people may kneel before these and pray. In no case are they praying to the object, anymore than when someone kneels at his bed to say prayers in the evening that he is praying to his mattress.

As the Byzantine Church evolved into what we call today the Eastern Orthodox Church, the basic Byzantine style of central plan churches with domes also evolved. Just as the different regions had regional church affiliations, one style of dome evolved in the western regions of the Orthodox world (the western East?) and another became popular farther to the East (eastern East?). The western style of Byzantine design is more closely associated with the Greek Orthodox Church and other national Orthodox Churches in the West. A good excellent example of Greek Orthodox design is the **Monastery of the Dormition at Daphni** near Athens, which is dedicated to the *Dormition of the Virgin*, which means the end of Mary's life on earth (her "sleep"). The church stands on what was originally a temple to the Greek God Apollo which was destroyed in 395. In the 6th century a small monastery was built there, which later was abandoned and fell into disrepair. Then in the 11th century the monastery we see today was rebuilt on the same site. Unfortunately, the <u>Monastery of the Dormition at Daphni</u> has not always been well maintained over time. During the Crusades when some European troops occasionally attacked their fellow Christians in the East, this region was occupied by the Franks (inhabitants of northern France and regions of Germany) and in 1207 the operation and care of the monastery was turned over to Cistercian monks (they will be covered in the chapter on Romanesque). Later the region was taken by the (Muslim) Turks, driving out the Catholic monks and leaving the monastery vacant. Finally in 1458 the Greek Orthodox Church regained control of the monastery. But then later during subsequent wars it was used as a barracks for military troops, and at one point it was even used as a lunatic asylum! All these reassigned uses of the building have taken their toll. Just the same, there are good reasons to give this church a look.

It is a central plan church with a narthex and dome similar to most others in the Greek Orthodox style, as you can see from the exterior picture. The interior offers good examples of mature Byzantine mosaics. A mid-20th century Austrian scholar named Otto Demus wrote about Byzantine churches stating that in his opinion, the mosaic designs were meant to be appreciated from the top down rather than starting at the ground level and raising our eyes upward. In the center of the dome there is a magnificent mosaic depicting Christ as the Almighty Lord and Creator of All, called the **Pantocrator**. *Pantocrator* images of Christ show Him looking directly at the viewer, bearded, wearing and stern expression and usually blessing with his right hand while he holds the Gospels in his left. These images were the decoration of choice in Byzantine domes, as if to represent God in all His majesty and power looking down on us from heaven. In Catholic art the adult Christ is more often than not depicted as humble or suffering, whereas the Byzantine tradition favored a more sober, authoritative looking Christ. According the Demus, the all-powerful Lord in heaven is the first zone.

The second zone, found immediately below the dome, represents a stage in between heaven and earth. At the monastery in Daphni those scenes are taken from high points in the life of Christ including scenes like the Annunciation, Nativity, Baptism and Transfiguration. Consider the **Nativity** mosaic from Daphni. Notice that baby Jesus is tucked away in a manger inside a cave which is typical of Byzantine art; more often Catholic artists opt for a stable instead. A petite cow and donkey peek over the side of the manger to check out the new arrival, as streams of light from the Star of Bethlehem (sadly now gone) beam in on the child. Mary reclines next to the manger, looking considerably more humble than the last time we saw her in the <u>Annunciation</u> and <u>Coronation</u> mosaics in Santa Maria Maggiore (presumably by now her recognition as

Theotokos was old news). Joseph sits off to the right, seeming a little less engaged in the moment than his wife. A host of angels are peering in on the Holy Family, although the one of the far right has been distracted by a pair of shepherds whom he greets. For their part the shepherds behave like they run into angels every day. "Oh hi there, it's good to see you. A Messiah's been born? Gee, thanks for the tip; we'll stop by when we get off work."

Below scenes like the Nativity is the third zone which would includes images of saints, sometimes full length and sometimes half-length, similar to icons, and still above eye level so we are obliged to pay proper respect by looking up to the Church's heroes. At Daphni as at many other Byzantine churches, the depictions of saints circle around the nave in the order of their saint feast days on the *liturgical calendar*. Saint feast days are observed in both the Orthodox and Catholic churches, as they always have been. Initially they started as special tributes to martyrs, although in time saints who were not martyred were also included. A feast day is a specific date that is set aside every year as a special day to reflect on the contribution to Christianity made by that saint. It might be his or her birthday, or the date of the saint's death, or even just a day that was free on the calendar and set aside for this honor. Early saints starting with Saint John the Baptist, the Apostles, and many others are common to both the Church in the West and the Church in the East. As time moved on, some saints were observed more in the East or in the West according to where the person lived and which branch of Christianity felt the greater impact from a given saint's life.

The concept of a liturgical calendar is common to both Catholic and Byzantine tradition. The year is divided into seasons. Starting with *Easter Sunday*, which marks the beginning of the Church year, the calendar moves through the season of Easter, which extends from the *Resurrection* (Easter) through the *Ascension* (forty days after Easter) to *Pentecost* (fifty days after Easter; the feast marking the gift of the Holy Spirit coming to the Apostles) celebrated the eighth Sunday after Easter. Then the calendar moves into "*ordinary time*" through the remainder of spring summer and most of the fall. Four Sundays before Christmas begins the season of *Advent*. This is a period of prayer and preparation for the *Nativity* of Jesus celebrated at *Christmas*. The Christmas season lasts through the celebration of the *Baptism* of the Lord, which feast day is observed in mid-January. Then it is back to ordinary time again until forty days before Easter, which begins the season of *Lent*. Lent is a time of fasting and prayer to prepare for the Crucifixion and Resurrection of Christ once again at Easter. The images of saints in many Byzantine churches are presented in the order of their feast days throughout the liturgical calendar, reminding the faithful of the flow of the Christian observances each year. Finally the fourth and lowest level of Byzantine interior design, at eye level, there are fine veneers of veined marble.

A particularly splendid example of mature western Byzantine design is **San Marco** located in Venice, Italy. The church was originally built in the 9th century to house the *relics* (bones) of Saint Mark, which had been acquired by the city. Saint Mark died in Egypt back in the first century and his remains were salvaged and buried by the Christian community there. Eventually the Christians arranged a shrine for the bones in Alexandria. Many years later in 828 the church containing Saint Mark's bones was under Muslim control, and two Venetian merchants presumably fearing for the safety of the relics, smuggled Saint Mark's bones back to Italy. Supposedly they packed them in with slabs of pork to sneak them past the Muslim officials in control of Alexandria who would be loathe to touch the pork as it is forbidden in their religion. Once the bones were safely in Venice, it seemed fitting to build an appropriately beautiful church to house such important relics.

Although a Catholic church, San Marco was expanded and remodeled into a Greek Orthodox style Byzantine design during the 11th century after the emperor in Constantinople granted Venice special status to dominate maritime trade in the Adriatic in an effort to bolster commercial rapport between the East and West. The church was designed with a *Greek cross* plan. Notice on the plan that there is a central crossing connecting four arms of nearly equal length, sort of like a big plus sign in plan. One "arm" is the apse, the two to the sides were chapels, and the one opposite the apse serves as an extension of the nave when connected to the center of the church. The exterior of San Marco was embellished over the centuries, adding beautiful mosaics above the entrance portals (they tell the story of Saint Mark and his being welcomed to Venice, with a Last Judgment scene in the middle over the main door). The updating also included constructing an outer shell over each of the multiple domes to make them appear taller from outside than they really are. Without the bolstered second shell poofing up the roofline at San Marco, the actual dome structure, which can be seen on the inside of the church, is similar to the dome at the Monastery of the Dormition.

Shall we step inside? Now this is what a gorgeous Byzantine Church is supposed to look like! As you look at the church interior, see that the four arms and the center are all topped by domes connected by arches, each dome resting on pendentives just like we saw at Hagia Sophia. Moreover, San Marco glimmers from the dazzling array if beautifully intact mosaics covering almost every inch of the ceilings and walls. Let's look at one in particular that is a subject popular in Byzantine art that never caught on so much with Catholic artists: the **Anastasis**, or what is more commonly called the Resurrection in the West. Sometimes it is also referred to as the *Harrowing of Hell* since after Christ rose from the dead, his first task was to descend into hell, or some antechamber of hell to rescue righteous souls who could not enter heaven until after Christ's sacrifice had been offered to redeem mankind. In the West, the Resurrection isn't portrayed with the same popularity as say the Annunciation, or Nativity, or Crucifixion. When the Resurrection is painted, usually the image is of Christ rising from the tomb, then from there artists seem to jump ahead to Mary Magdalene seeing Jesus but not recognizing Him at first (called Noli Me Tangere). In the East, it was more common to skip the actual Resurrection imagery, and fast forward to Christ in the netherworld pulling those destined for heaven from their graves. Here, as is typical in this narrative, Christ arrives on the scene and crushes a shackled Satan under His feet while yanking Adam out of his crypt. Eve arises from the same tomb, raising her hands to Christ in homage and thanksgiving while others in limbo look on, awaiting their invitations to heaven.

The Greek Orthodox architecture style, with its round hemispheric domes has remained dominant in the West. Traditionally in the East, the Russian Orthodox style gravitated to the more elaborate *onion dome*. Let's turn our attention to Moscow for some good examples. Choosing Moscow is not by accident, while many cities in the East have beautiful Byzantine style churches, Moscow is also important for other reasons.

Remember at the start of this chapter it was mentioned that at the First Council of Constantinople in 381 that the Bishop of Constantinople put forth that he wanted to be recognized as second only to the Bishop of Rome as leader of the Church? In 451 there was another council (Chalcedon) where the Bishop of Constantinople was promoting his authority again. This time the papal delegation left at the beginning of the session, being displeased with how the proceedings were going. After their departure, the Bishop of Constantinople further expressed his hierarchal superiority in the Church. When the results of the council were forwarded to Rome to be ratified by the pope, there were protests registered by a number of the delegates that it violated the authority of the bishops of Alexandria, Antioch and Jerusalem established at the Council if Nicaea (the first council back in 325), and in general it put too much emphasis on Constantinople, even to where it began to challenge the pope's own office as the Bishop of Rome. The pope did not sign off on the canons introduced by the Bishop of Constantinople.

By now it seems clear that the Bishop of Constantinople saw his city as the "Second Rome" with him being a sort of "new pope" or leader of the Church. Remember, that in the East, authority in the Church was usually linked to politics in that church and state were united. When the secular government in Rome fell apart (especially after Rome was sacked by barbarians), it just seemed logical to Constantinople that the Church should shift attention to wherever the government was strong.

Look ahead a few hundred years, and lo and behold, Constantinople was sacked by the Muslims in 1453. This did not go unnoticed further east in Russia, where the understanding of how power is established in the Church closely matched the political viewpoint typical of Byzantine thinking everywhere (in contrast to the West where authority is tied to the office or Peter which doesn't move around). If the "Second Rome" was also sacked, then it seemed reasonable to Christian Russia that God didn't want the leadership of the Church there either, so in 1510 a monk from Pskov, Russia named Filofei wrote,

"All Christian realms will come to an end and will unite into the one single realm of our sovereign, that is, into the Russian realm, according to the prophetic books. Both Romes fell, the third [Moscow] endures, and a fourth there will never be."

From this point on the Russian Orthodox Church popularized the notion of Moscow being the "Third Rome," including the concept borrowed from Constantinople that the political head of state was elevated to a position of both spiritual and secular preeminence. One might wonder how this notion has been affected by the various sackings of Moscow since 1510, not to mention the ravages of Communism which tried to eradicate Christianity altogether… The point is that once things got politically shaky in Constantinople, the Bishop of Moscow began to flex his ecclesiastic muscles in the same way as the Bishop of Constantinople had done centuries earlier. Meanwhile back in Constantinople the Greek Orthodox Church survived the challenges of Islam, and in Rome, the Catholic Church plugged along regardless of secular politics.

The **Cathedral of the Assumption** was built in the 15th century, commissioned by Grand Prince Ivan III on the heels of the fall of Constantinople. It is located inside the Kremlin which is the citadel-style city center of Moscow and the heart of the national government. Its dedication to the Assumption of the Virgin Mary is a theme popular to both the Orthodox and Catholic faith. After Mary died, it is believed that Christ took her body and soul to heaven where she is today glorified as all true believers will be one day following the Last Judgment (sometimes the Assumption is conflated with the

Dormition). The grand Cathedral of the Assumption was built to serve the people and was considered the most important public building in all of Russia, sort of a "national cathedral." It replaced an earlier church which had fallen into disrepair and which also had long been the burial church of metropolitans and patriarchs. With the rising consciousness of Moscow being the Third Rome, the Russian church and government alike were keen to see themselves as being the visible glory of God on earth.

Curiously perhaps, they hired an Italian (most likely Catholic?) architect from Bologna named Aristotele Fioravanti for the design. The cathedral took over a year to build and another two years to decorate the interior. The exterior of hard-fired brick was sheathed with beautiful white limestone with decorative pilasters creating the illusion that the façade was a gigantic arcade of rounded arches, and it was crowned with five magnificent *gilded* (gold-plated) domes, a larger one in the center surrounded by four more.

The interior was quite unique in that it was designed as a large, open hall with no gallery like we customarily find in Byzantine churches to separate men and women during the service. This made it even easier to see all the art. The same hierarchy appears here that was discussed earlier. The central dome has Christ the Pantocrator and the lesser domes have other traditional images of Christ. The domes rest on elevated drums, and between the windows in these drums are figures of patriarchs and prophets. The pendentives illustrate the Apostles and evangelists (Gospel authors) with New Testament subjects completing the rest of the ceiling. The walls illustrate themes ranging from the life of the Virgin Mary, to images recalling church councils. Much of the interior art here is fresco rather than mosaic, although it is no less compelling.

A few years after The Cathedral of the Assumption was completed, a smaller church was commissioned next door to serve the royal heads of state: the *czars* (see more on that below). The **Cathedral of the Annunciation** petite compared to the larger church built to accommodate the citizens of Moscow, but no less was spent on both its magnificent cupolas plated in real gold or the spectacular interior, including a magnificent iconostasis featuring icons produced by the leading religious painters in Russia.

The last church we will consider is the 16th century church of **Saint Basil's Cathedral** located in Red Square in Moscow, Russia (Barna and Postnik – architects). It may be slightly outside our Byzantine period, but who could pass up an opportunity to marvel at this flight of architectural fancy? If Hansel and Gretel were real, and if they lived in Russia, surely they would have gone to church here! Once Moscow came to see itself as the Third Rome, the princes came to believe that they should be Caesars, just like Rome had during the height of its pagan empire. The first to rename himself "Caesar," or *Czar* was Ivan the Terrible. He commissioned this church to commemorate great Russian conquests in war, rather like a memorial to Russians who had died trying to liberate their country from foreign overlords. By the way, it was originally named the Cathedral of Intercession of the Virgin Mary (intercession, as in thanks Mary for helping with your prayers to set Russia free), but later dedicated to Saint Basil the Blessed. Although it looks like a gingerbread church today with the fanciful brightly painted domes, the colors were changes introduced later; originally the church was painted white topped by gold domes, similar to both the Cathedral of the Assumption and the Cathedral of the Annunciation. Saint Basil's employed several onion domes exhibiting an array of surface patterns: twisted strips, zig-zag chevrons and reticulated (pineapple textured). In the center of the domes is a tall pointed tower called a *shater* which has been embellished with scallops and topped by a small gold onion dome. Curiously, while you might expect that the inside would reflect the same extravaganza of color, in fact it was always quite plain compared to other Russian churches. From its beginnings as a memorial, Saint Basil's was more of an "object" to ponder than it ever was a house of worship. It was almost like the entirety of Red Square might be the "church" for special festivals or services, and indeed, even the icons were carried outside for such occasions and placed in front of the church rather than inviting the public indoors.

Let's revisit the tradition of icons one last time, focusing our attention on Saint Basil since we just looked at a splendid cathedral dedicated to this saint. Basil the Great is the Patron Saint of Russia and the Patriarch of Eastern Monks. As such, he is one of the most important and most popular saints in Russia. He was born in 329 in Caesarea, capital of Cappadocia in Asia Minor. He studied in the newly rebuilt Constantinople and Athens, then returned to Cappadocia to teach rhetoric. It seems before his career got off the ground, he decided to drop out of the "real world" and withdrew to the wilderness where he lived in poverty. Basil soon attracted other men to his way of life, and in time, he and his brother formed the first monastery in Asia Minor. His way of life became the model for Eastern monasticism. Basil was ordained to the priesthood in 363, and his orthodox preaching helped defeat lingering pockets of the Arian Heresy which had been denounced at the Council of Nicaea in 325. He went on to become a bishop and then an archbishop. Throughout his life and ministry Basil actively helped the sick and the poor, for example he built a hospice to meet the needs of the critically ill, and he was a champion of morality, both fighting corruption among the clergy (simony in particular: when someone tries to buy a position in the clergy) and among those he served (for example, he excommunicated Christians discovered to engage in illicit sex). Basil is considered one of the giants of early Christianity in both the East and the West; he is a "Doctor of the Church" which is a title reserved only for a select few Christians who made a profound impact on the spread and development of Christianity.

Here is an icon of **Saint Basil** dating from right around the same time as Saint Basil's Cathedral was built. Notice that he is bearded, dressed as a priest and he holds a Gospel book. Icons adhere to a strict code of presentation. By tradition they are never painted realistically; the figures are elongated and flat as realistic art was too closely associated with paganism in the early centuries of Christianity. A typical *iconostasis* would have numerous scenes from the life of Christ, and usually an array of individual saints, like Saint Basil, that the faithful could select to assist in offering up prayers and petitions. It might be a saint that the person especially admires, or perhaps something about that saint strikes a chord with the type of petition being requested. In the Eastern Church, icons have always been a mandated part of the architecture to reinforce the habit of praying in union with others close to God. In the West, a church might have an altarpiece in the apse as opposed to an iconostasis, or statues of saints to likewise inspire prayer to God in union with others. In the West the art has never been required, although most churches traditionally have expected art to be part of the interior design.

For the first seven centuries of Christianity, everyone was more-or-less on the same page when it came to sacred imagery inside churches (or before that, inside homes which doubled as make-shift churches). During the 8th century, however, the *iconoclast* movement was born. *Iconoclasm* was an effort to rid Christianity of sacred images; it was initiated in Constantinople in 726 by Emperor Leo III who decreed that all religious images were idols and should be destroyed. Wholesale destruction of icons, statues, mosaics and other Christian art followed, and those who attempted to defend images of Jesus, Mary, and the Apostles and saints were persecuted. What motivated the Emperor to initiate the destruction of Church property? On the one hand, there were pockets of Christians, especially in the East who disliked sacred imagery. In part this may have been influenced by fear that poorly informed Christians might imagine that the images themselves had powers, as opposed to being conduits used by God to offer His power. In part it may have also been the influence of a heretical group of that time called the Paulicians, who were promoting the idea that all matter was bad and that all external religious forms, be it art or relics or sacraments (things like baptism and marriage) should be abolished.

On the other hand, it could also have been the influence of Islam. As it happened, shortly before the story unfolded with Emperor Leo III, there had been a similar persecution in Damascus under the influence of the Muslim Khalif in that city. Khalif Yezid I first initiated a purge of religious images between 680-683, and this was reinforced by his successors, especially Yezid II between 720 and 724. Meanwhile back in Constantinople, it was no secret that Leo had certain sympathies with Islam. Khalif Omar II had tried in earnest to convert the Emperor to Islam between 717-720, and while Leo III didn't buy into the whole program, he seemed to develop an appreciation for the Islamic attitude toward imagery in art. It didn't hurt that the Muslims under the Emperor's rule applauded the iconoclast movement, making the government popular in circles where it often fell short of support. Further, it appears that Leo had a larger agenda. The campaign against images was part of a larger plan by the emperor to centralize authority of the state and the Church throughout the Empire, with the emperor being the big man of the hour and the patriarchs being somewhat diminished in the process.

In the year 787, a Church council was called in Nicaea to address the question of the iconoclast movement. The Seventh Ecumenical Council was significant because it was the uniform decision of the bishops, including the Bishop of Rome (the pope) *and* the Bishop of Constantinople working together in unity for the first time in centuries, to uphold the *veneration* of sacred images, and the Empress Irene who succeeded Leo III came on board supporting the Church position in 843. Veneration is a word that nowadays sometimes gets confused with worship. It needs to be emphasized that at no point did either the Church in the East or the Church in the West condone worship of art. What was accepted and promoted was the respect and admiration of sacred images as reflections of the faith held dear. For those who believe in the Communion of Saints, having images of saints would be like having pictures of your deceased grandmother on the mantle. Presumably you don't confuse Grandma with God, and even more absurd is the notion that you imagine her photograph is God. But you do hold your grandmother close to your heart, even after she has departed this world. She will always be a cherished member of your family. So too are the saints; for the Christian, these men and women are like the generations of grandmothers and grandfathers that have gone before and are now in heaven. They are family, and they are remembered as such with art that is treated with the same respect one pays to the family portrait of a beloved Grandma.

8. Early Medieval

Early Medieval culture in Europe was based in the Mediterranean region. Italy, Greece, Asia Minor and Egypt were all active Christian centers, and where Christianity flourished, culture followed. Everything we have seen so far of Early Medieval Christian art and architecture was centered around the Mediterranean. The Catholic Church was based out of Rome, with her art stretching from Italy to Greece then across the Middle East and into northern Africa. The Byzantine Church was based out of Constantinople, and her influence extended over the same territories, with a little less in Italy, but then in time extending further east into Russia. The rest of Europe, however, had nestled into a barbaric Dark Age since the decline of the pagan Roman Empire. Given that these pagan tribes seldom trusted anyone outside their own group, and given that they tended to fight each other for what they wanted rather than build a society of cooperation where they might work together to achieve common goals, each posed a threat to another who might have more than they did. Naturally the sophisticated folks living down south along the Mediterranean enjoyed a higher standard of living than the uncivilized barbarians, so it doesn't come as much of a surprise to learn that barbarians frequently invaded these realms of the good life to steal what they could, and in general make a nuisance of themselves. This had long been a problem in Italy in particular. It wasn't that the barbarians were picking on Catholic Christians while leaving the Byzantine Christians to their wealth and creature comforts; the Christians in Italy were just geographically closer and made an easier target than people living as far away as Asia Minor.

It didn't take long before the Church in the West decided that there was much to be gained by trying to make Christians of these people. If the barbarians could be brought into the faith, and their circumstances upgraded through a change in attitude and lifestyle, everyone would be the better for it. From the earliest days of Christianity, even before it was legalized with the Edict of Milan, there had been scattered Christians throughout northern Europe. It just wasn't anywhere near as pervasive as it had become in Italy and the Middle East.

Hiberno-Saxon *432- c. 900*

The first real presence of widespread Christianity outside the Mediterranean cradle of Christian culture was the Hiberno-Saxon period centered in Ireland and spreading to Scotland from the 5th century forward. The person most responsible for the early spread of Christianity in this region was Saint Patrick. Patrick was born near Dunbarton, Scotland in 387. His father's family was originally of Roman stock, and they were Christians. When Patrick was 16, he was kidnapped and sold into slavery in Ireland. He lived as a slave tending sheep for 6 years in Ireland, and learned to rely on prayer to sustain him in these times of trouble. According to his autobiography, the *Confessio*, he then had a vision from an angel telling him to flee his circumstances, so he escaped and traveled about 200 miles to the sea where he caught a ship to Gaul (France). Over the next few years, he returned to Scotland to visit his family, but otherwise studied for the priesthood, mostly likely in Auxerre, France. He was ordained sometime around 417. We know that he traveled to Rome and met the pope. We also know he distinguished himself early in his career by assisting in the fight against the Pelagian Heresy. (Pelagius taught that there was no original sin, that Adam's transgressions affected only Adam, and that mankind neither carries the sin of Adam (requiring Baptism), nor is man offered life through the Resurrection of Jesus. These ideas conflict with Scripture (see Romans 5:17; reading the whole passage puts it into broader perspective). All along, though, Patrick felt compelled to return to Ireland, home of his captivity, and bring Christianity to the Druid people living there.

Sometime around 432 Patrick arrived back in Ireland, having been ordained as bishop to serve that region. He spent the rest of his life traveling throughout Ireland, ministering to the Irish people, preaching and converting large numbers of the population to Christianity. He built monasteries, churches and schools; in fact, some of the Catholic churches built by Saint Patrick are still around today, albeit much changed from their earlier days. Despite his great success as a missionary in Ireland, Patrick never let it go to his head. Here is a direct quote from his *Confessio*,

"I, Patrick, a sinner, and the most ignorant and of least account among the faithful, despised by many... I owe it to God's grace that so many people should through me be born again to Him."

Saint Patrick died in 493, leaving Ireland predominantly Christian. Meanwhile, Scotland and England still had pockets of Christianity, but after Patrick's success in Ireland, the tables were now turned to where most of the Christians were in Ireland and not the "big island." Saint Columba is largely credited with increasing the numbers of Christian converts in Scotland and Northern England. Columba was born in Donegal, Ireland in 521. He was educated early on by a local priest, and like Patrick, he is associated with multiple miracles starting early in his religious career. He established a monastery in Derry is 548 that became quite famous for its illuminated manuscripts. In 563, Columba sailed to the Scottish island of Iona (off the coast of Glasgow) to found a monastery disconnected from his native Ireland and all he had known. Some sources suggest this may have been a self-imposed penance, stemming from a copy of the Book of Psalms he secretly made for himself (their work at the abbey was supposed to be for the benefit of others). In any event, Columba elected to become a missionary to the pagan people of Scotland, the Picts. Some 60 years later, one of the monks from his abbey at Iona, Aidan, set out to establish another abbey on the far side of Scotland on the island of Lindesfarne (off the coast of Newcastle, now northern England). Saint Columba died at the abbey on Iona in 597. A curious aside about Saint Columba (trivia 101...) is that he apparently witnessed up close and personal the so-called Loch Ness monster on at least one of his many travels around Scotland as a missionary, as the incident was chronicled by one of his fellow monks (Adomnan) in his biography shortly after Columba passed away.

As the Bishop of Ireland, Patrick reached most of his converts through preaching, sometimes on his travels around the country and sometimes in the churches he built. Monks like Columba and Aidan were living off in remote retreats, so you might wonder how they could expect to spread the faith to the greater population. This was a critical issue not only in Britain, but everywhere across Europe. Picture a couple monks setting out to convert pagans. How would they reach the people? Nowadays someone might pass out written material ... but who could read it back in those days? And even if they could read by some miracle, would they? Hmmmm ... probably not. The monks could try delivering lectures. This worked pretty well for Patrick who apparently was a charismatic speaker. Just the same, the problem is that often people who are not interested in the subject won't waste time coming to listen. So how do you captivate the interest of people? You use pictures and tell stories. And what subject matters might the monks want to show in these pictures? Well, they would definitely want scenes from the life of Christ to illustrate the story of Jesus. And from there, it would be helpful to have pictures of the Apostles to pick up with the story of the Church. And finally, pictures of the saints would be useful to set an example of how good Christians live their lives. What have we just described? Icons! But wait, aren't icons a Byzantine thing, and these missionaries were Catholic? This is true. Just because the Catholic Church never required icons in their churches, does not mean these images were not very useful for the education of non-believers. It was also quite convenient that these modest wooden panels traveled well.

Monks like Columba and Aidan established themselves in pagan territories, and gradually began the task of converting the local people. Sooner or later, the initial images were not enough. Either converted chiefs of pagan tribes wanted their own copies of the images, or converts in their zeal wished to follow in the monks' footsteps and carry on in the next village; in fact, Aidan fits that description as he became a monk to carry on Columba's work. Sooner or later, the monks had to start making copies of the images to make them more available. They did this on vellum (specially treated calf's skin – prohibitively expensive) or parchment (made from split lamb skin, and while not as pricey as vellum, still costly) so they would be lightweight and could be bound together, and the result was a rise in the production of Christian *manuscripts*, or handwritten books. The most popular category of manuscript during medieval times was *Gospel Books.* These would include the books of Matthew, Mark, Luke and John, the first 4 books of the New Testament, which are the only ones that deal directly with the life of Christ. Second were *Psalters*, which were the collection of Old Testament psalms. Psalters were popular because they offered good guidelines for upright behavior, and were easy to commit to memory. Finally, few <u>Bibles</u> were produced because the cost was off the charts.

A <u>Bible</u> cost about the same as building a big church at this point in history, which was well beyond the means of most individuals to afford. It has been estimated that a single <u>Bible</u> would take a monk at least 10 months to copy (that's assuming the monk kept his nose to the grindstone with no goofing off), which has been estimated at a rough cost of $5,000 in "medieval dollars" per book. To put that in perspective for you, there is currently near Monmouth, Wales a *scriptorium* (large room or facility where manuscripts are made) where several calligraphers and artists are producing a real <u>Bible</u> using all the same tools and techniques employed in monasteries during the Middle Ages. The project was suggested by one of Queen Elizabeth's personal scribes, renowned calligrapher, Donald Jackson, and it is being largely underwritten by Saint John's College in Minnesota, where Jackson taught calligraphy (beautiful writing) for two decades. It is expected that when the project is completed, the book will run 1,150 pages with 160 illustrations ... and the anticipated final price tag in *today's* dollars is estimated at $4,000,000 (it could run higher) ... for *one* book. Perhaps that might fit Bill Gates' budget, but it is probably just a wee bit too expensive for the rest of us. Besides the cost factor, hardly anybody outside the clergy during the Middle Ages could read anyway, so it would have been a lot of money spent on a luxury with limited practical use. Most knowledge of the <u>Bible</u> still came from oral teaching and preaching.

Let's look at the **Saint Matthew Page from the Lindisfarne Gospel** which was produced around 700, not so long after Aidan himself presided at the Scottish monastery. Hopefully you can see that the picture of Saint Matthew closely resembles an icon in that it is not very realistic and it is flat, although it is also colorful which would draw the viewer in to take a closer look while s/he listed to the stories of Jesus told in the Gospel of Matthew. A second Hiberno Saxon manuscript page, this time from Ireland, is the **Saint Matthew Page from the Book of Kells**. These two Gospel Books were produced about 100 years apart, and what you should notice is that while neither is realistic, the later one is *less* realistic than the earlier one. We don't expect this; our innate sense of development in the West expects later work to be more polished than earlier examples. Stop and think for a moment. Can you imagine monks attending life drawing classes back in the Middle Ages? Do you suppose that fellows like Columba and Aidan took turns stripping down to their birthday suits so the other monks could sketch them naked and learn how to render human anatomy? It's comical to even think of such things. The point is that icons started out unrealistic to begin with, but over time, when monks who had no formal training as artists copied them, the manuscript illustrations became even less recognizable as images of people. At the same time, the extraordinary colors and decorative patterns, including Celtic interlace patterns borrowed from earlier regional art, increased as realism decreased. The sheer beauty of the pictures kept the viewer engaged while learning the Life of Christ from hearing the accounts read to them by monks and priests from the Gospels. Sadly, the original monasteries at Iona and Lindesfarne are long gone, both the victims of repeated Viking raids. There is now a lovely Benedictine Abbey used for Christian retreats on Iona where Columba's monastery once stood. Lindesfarne's ruins remain as a testimony to the hardships faced by many Christians during the Middle Ages.

Christianity throughout Britain and Ireland was spawned largely by the influence of one man, Patrick. As Bishop of Ireland, his influence stretched across the Emerald Isle, and his followers carried the Christian faith across the Irish Sea to Scotland. Throughout most of Western Europe, Christianity was introduced into pagan territories by Benedictine monks. Hiberno-Saxon period aside, Western monasticism was born shortly after the year 500 under the direction of Benedict of Nursia (a small town in Italy), commonly called Saint Benedict today. Born in 480, Benedict was educated in Rome, but grew weary of the corruption he found in everyday life there. Around the year 500 he chose to remove himself from society and live alone in solitude as a hermit ... rather like a John the Baptist of his day. In time, he attracted followers not so much because they viewed him as a prophet, but more because they wished to devote their lives to God, and Benedict seemed to have the answer to "getting away from it all" to a simple life of prayer and personal sacrifice. By 530 Benedict began to build a monastery for his modest community. The Benedictine Order, often called the Benedictine Rule or simply the Benedictines, was born. This 6th century order established the basic format for most of Western monasticism. The monks were men (or women living separately as nuns) who lived in a celibate community away from the general population such that they be less distracted by the material and moral (or lack thereof) trappings of society. The monks took vows of obedience, stability, chastity and individual poverty (the Benedictine Order was allowed to own land, buildings and related property, but the individual monks did not). They lived their lives to serve God, dividing their time between manual labor and prayer. Each monk was expected to be obedient to God first and foremost, but as an extension of that respect for authority, obedient to the pope and precepts of the Church, and finally to the abbot, or leader of their individual community. They were stable in that each monk lived in a specific monastery and the general rule was that they were expected to stay tied to that place. The monks might be sent to establish a new monastery in a new region, but once built, the monastery was home and they lived out their lives there. It was the Benedictine monks serving as missionaries who first assumed the task of Christianizing most of pagan Europe during the early Middle Ages.

Carolingian *732 - 936*

The Carolingian Period was a time of great awakening in northern Europe, revolving especially around the life of one man: Charlemagne. The period began in 732 during the reign of Charlemagne's grandfather, Charles Martel (Charles the Hammer). In this year Charles and his fierce countrymen repelled the Muslim invasion of Gaul at Poitiers, establishing themselves as a dynasty of rulers to lead all of Europe. His son, Pepin the Short followed Charles Martel, then in 768, Pepin's son, Charlemagne (Charles the Great) came to power. Charlemagne ruled until his death in 814, after which the Carolingian Empire set into a gradual decline as nobody could fill the shoes of Charles the Great. Finally in 936 the divided Carolingian Empire fell into Ottonian hands. The Carolingians were Franks, a Germanic people, although the territory ruled by them extended over vast sections of Europe including the "low countries" (Holland and Belgium today), northern Spain, northern Italy, and Switzerland as well as France and Germany.

Charlemagne was a devout and dedicated Christian. His personal morals were a vast improvement over past generations of northern European rulers, although he did manage to accumulate a few overlapping wives with an occasional girlfriend on the side. Despite his own personal lapses in Christian morality, Charlemagne made it his goal to help spread Christianity throughout his empire, and while he was at it, to upgrade the level of general learning in northern Europe to an intellectual standard more closely aligned with that of Italy. He was very supportive of the Benedictine monks, and funded the construction of many monasteries with large scriptoriums where hundreds of monks worked together diligently copying manuscripts. Charlemagne encouraged the copying of both religious texts and secular literature from the past. The Vulgate <u>Bible</u> was copied many times over, with special provisions made to correct any errors that had occurred in the centuries since the translation first appeared in 400. It was agreed that part of the problem in the past was that lettering had never been standardized, making it difficult to read the penmanship of others. The solution was simple; handwriting was formally standardized at this time, so that once the effort had been made to make corrections on those sloppy texts, the same type of errors would not be repeated in the future. The writings of the Early Church Fathers were copied and made available for study. Likewise, nearly all manuscripts of Latin poetry and prose still in existence were copied in Carolingian monasteries and thus preserved for posterity.

In addition to supporting education within monasteries, Charlemagne also invited several top scholars of his day to live in residence at his palace city of Aachen. Among the most notable was a Saxon scholar of famed reputation named Alcuin who came from York, England. Alcuin of York was glad for the opportunity to leave his homeland, which was under attack from the Danes (recall the assorted Norsemen and Vikings who sacked the Scottish monasteries at Lindesfarne and Iona), and he settled in at Charlemagne's court to run a school there. Aachen became a small city of great learning in the North, with Charlemagne being among the most eager students. Rhetoric, grammar, literature, music, arithmetic, astronomy, Latin and Greek were taught here, and at many *cathedral schools*, which were organized and sponsored through churches where a bishop was in charge. Some bishops even made sure that schools were available in every parish (any church, whether it is run by a priest or the bishop), and the schools were strictly free of charge to encourage all people to learn. Many of these schools became the seeds from which universities would grow later on. Sadly, for all his enthusiasm for education, Charlemagne found that running such a vast empire kept him away from his studies much more than he would have preferred. He learned to speak Greek and Latin reasonably well, could read some, but never did master writing, to his eternal disappointment.

Two samples of Carolingian manuscript illustration point to a change toward greater realism in art at this time: The **Saint Matthew Page from the Coronation Gospel**, and the **Saint Matthew Page from the Ebbo Gospel**. Both illustrate the front page for the first Gospel, and both demonstrate an effort by the artist to make the figure of Saint Matthew look more realistic than Hiberno-Saxon examples. Unlike Byzantine art, which retained an interest in "protecting" Christianity from too much realism in art, once the monks in the West improved their skills, they made steady gains on greater realism. This new interest in making the pictures realistic expressed the hope that by making the illustrations more real, ideally the message of Scripture might likewise become more real to the reader. Artists were encouraged to make their figures look less flat, so we see hints of the body under the clothing. The Coronation Gospel was Charlemagne's personal book. Although he could never read well enough himself to make it through a Gospel book, he had the Gospels read to him regularly so he knew Scripture well. He thought so highly of his Gospel book that he had it buried with him. Later, when his body was exhumed and relocated to a new burial site, the book was retrieved. The Ebbo Gospel was the personal copy of Scripture owned by the Bishop of Reims.

Charlemagne was a generous promoter of the Church. His support of the Benedictines was legendary, although he also made demands of the clergy, and insisted on piety and moral behavior among priests, nuns and monks. Throughout his reign, he likewise maintained a stream of regular communication with the pope far away in remote Rome, and offered just about as much free advice as he did gifts and financial donations. In 795 a new pope was elected: Pope Leo III ... not to be confused with the Emperor in Constantinople earlier in the same century with the same name! Unfortunately, the Italian people didn't like him very well, and on April 25, 799 they accused him of assorted misdeeds, attacked him, beat him up and threw him in prison! He escaped, and high-tailed it up to Charlemagne's turf for protection. Charlemagne received the pope, and concerned for his safety, had him escorted back to Rome with an armed guard and the provision that he, Charlemagne, would serve as an intermediary if the pope and his accusers would allow him to hear their case in Rome the following year.

Charlemagne arrived in Rome on November 24, 800. A few days later, he heard the charges against the pope. When the pope was asked if he would swear a solemn oath that he did not do whatever it was he was suspected of doing, the Franks and Romans who had made the accusations decided that was good enough for them, and they dropped the charges. Absolving the Church of scandal, everyone was ready to begin the Christmas season with celebration. On Christmas Day, Charlemagne went to Old Saint Peter's Church to pray with the rest of the city's Christians, and was quite surprised when the pope brought out a jeweled crown, and crowned Charlemagne Holy Roman Emperor! Christians in the West were delighted, and the warm relationship between Charlemagne and the Church helped to give his empire the new title of Holy Roman Empire. Needless to say, this news did little to impress the folks in distant Constantinople, who already had their own emperor, thank you very much. There had been only one emperor in office at a time since the late 400's, as opposed to one for the West and one for the East, and he was located in Constantinople. Moreover, their emperor was a pretty holy guy as far as they were concerned too. In fact, it was downright offensive to them to imagine this country bumpkin Frank who was all but illiterate being schmoozed by an educated man of the cloth; it seemed to further discredit the Bishop of Rome that he would lower himself to this standard while the Patriarch of Constantinople and the Byzantine Emperor were more elite.

Charlemagne did not always understand or agree with the Church, but without exception he consistently deferred to the judgment of the Church. One issue where he was initially at odds was the iconoclast movement, as Charlemagne felt strong sympathies with those who frowned of sacred imagery. Just the same, like many Christians, he was encouraged by the show of unity at the Seventh Ecumenical Council just 13 years earlier, where the pope (Bishop of Rome) and patriarch (Bishop of Constantinople), and all the bishops agreed to uphold and support the veneration of sacred images. Despite that his own recently acquired new title wasn't helping to promote unity between the East and the West, Charlemagne encouraged the pope to make every effort to find common ground with Constantinople. His hope was that Christians everywhere might remain part of *one* Church, and not splinter into many (the Church did not officially split until 1054, so in Charlemagne's day it still technically was one Church, however fragmented by certain issues).

During his stay in Italy, Charlemagne took the opportunity to travel and see some of the great art and architecture of the past. The little church of San Vitale in Ravenna especially struck him. He understood that Justinian had commissioned this church in an attempt to bring greater unity among Christians, which impressed Charlemagne even if much of the message left by Justinian was propaganda for the Eastern Church. Upon his return to Aachen, Charlemagne commissioned local architect, Odo of Metz to build a church adjacent to the palace. The result was the Palatine Chapel.

The **Palatine Chapel** was clearly inspired by San Vitale; there simply are no other churches built in this region using so Byzantine a design. During the Gothic period, the Palatine Chapel received a considerable facelift to where it doesn't today resemble much of what it looked like back in the 9th century, but a simple drawing reveals that it was built as a very basic central plan design. Nowadays the church is downtown in Aachen, which has grown into a pleasant border city just inside Germany close to both Belgium and Holland. In its day, the Palatine Chapel was part of the palace complex with little more than a village beyond the royal residence, such that Charlemagne could be at home right up until it was time for Mass, then just scoot across a small courtyard and be in church. The plan reveals that like San Vitale, the church is laid out like a doughnut with a nave in the center, surrounded by an aisle for circulation. The narthex is smaller here than at San Vitale, as much as anything because this was a semi-private chapel attached to the palace, so if it were cold and wet outside, folks would just hang out by the fire at home rather than go early to church and stand around waiting for Mass to begin. The apse is also smaller. Remember, although much of the plan design is similar to San Vitale, the Palatine Chapel was a Catholic Church, never Byzantine, so there was no need for a larger apse as there would be no iconostasis here. Like San Vitale, the Palatine Chapel was built with a gallery, but unlike San Vitale, they had no need for a gallery because men and women were not separated during the service in Catholic churches. Charlemagne had a throne set up for himself in the gallery, sort of like having the ultimate best seat in the house …probably the *only* seat in the house as everyone was still expected to stand or kneel, but not sit down at church. He would frequently attend Mass from the luxury of his throne, which by the way, was visible through the clerestory windows to commoners in the streets below who might swing by the Palatine Chapel to see if they could catch a glimpse of Charlemagne attending church.

When you walk in the front door, then you *know* you are *not* in a Byzantine church. Compare the interiors of the Palatine Chapel to San Vitale. While San Vitale is full of bright light and beautiful mosaics, the Palatine Chapel seems gloomy and dimly lit, and while there are some very handsome mosaics inside the Palatine Chapel that would have made Byzantine artists proud, it's hard to see them very well because the church is so dark inside. Why is it so dark? The walls are much thicker at the Palatine Chapel than at San Vitale, probably because poor Odo of Metz had never built anything like this before, and the concept of a domed structure may have seemed pretty intimidating. It seems he over-reinforced the walls to be sure they could accept the weight from that dome, and he was careful to keep the windows extra small too so as not to weaken the walls with a bunch of big holes. The result: a dreary, dark interior because not much natural light can get in. Notice also that while slender, graceful arches support San Vitale, those at the Palatine Chapel seem stubby and heavy by comparison. It might be easy to also blame this on the architect's lack of experience, but more than likely there was another reason for these particular proportions. Bear in mind that this church was commissioned as much as anything as an architectural statement of unity between the Church of the West, and the Church of the East. We see this already in the basic design: the church is clearly a central plan like we would see in Byzantine churches, but the apse has been modified to be strictly Catholic in its scale. Inside, a gallery that is not required is included anyway, as a sort of tribute to Byzantine style, but the arches have the size and proportion of triumphal arches, like those we would find inside the Early Christian churches and hence would be part of the Catholic tradition in church design.

Following Charlemagne's death, his son Louis the Pious ruled, continuing Pop's interest in supporting monasteries. It was at this time that a basic, standardized design plan for Benedictine monasteries, or *abbeys* was sorted out. The **Plan for the Abbey of Saint Gall** was drawn up by Abbot Haito to illustrate the ideal complete monastery complex. It includes the actual abbey church of course, which in his rendering more closely resembles the old Basilica Ulpia with an apse at each end rather than the Early Christian model with an apse opposite a narthex. One apse was raised up higher than the nave and contained the altar and tabernacle. The opposite apse was accessed from outdoors through the *westwork*, which was a formidable entrance (customarily in the west end of the church as the name implies) flanked by towers. A westwork would have an entrance vestibule, smaller than a traditional narthex but with a gallery or chapel upstairs that offered a pleasing view of the nave. The abbots plan included so much more than just a church, however, because remember that the men would live out their lives here. The plan for Saint Gall is more like a city planners design for an entire planned community. Immediately adjacent to the church there were the living accommodations for the monks, including dormitories, baths and latrines, a *refectory* (dining room), kitchen and storerooms. The *cloister* was a large enclosed outdoor garden where the monks could stroll, pray and spend some quiet time alone. There was a bakery, a brewery, a mill, gardens, barns and chicken coops. The complex included a scriptorium and a school, an infirmary for the monks and a hospital for treating the poor who lived in the area, separate housing for the novices (monks in training) and another separate house for the abbot. There was even a guesthouse for accommodating visitors. Abbot Haito thought of everything, and while his particular plan for Saint Gall was not fully realized, his sketch served many generations of Benedictines as a model for how to set up the physical plan for their communities.

Charlemagne's weak grandsons did not live up to family expectations, and the empire was divided.   In the far west the territory that would become France was its own region, to the south Spain and Italy fell away, and Germany, Switzerland and Austria became the foundation for a new kingdom as the Carolingian period to faded into history.

Ottonian *936 - 1002*

The Ottonian period developed out of the Eastern most territory of what was once the Carolingian Empire; Germany, Switzerland and Austria returned to the Saxons who had swayed influence in those parts before the Carolingian salad days. The period gets its name because there was a succession of three rulers, all named Otto: Otto I, Otto II, and Otto III. If Charlemagne was the great hero of medieval France, Otto I was the equivalent for Germany. He unified the unruly German tribes into a unified state and set about gaining control of the Italian states. The man was clever; he wooed the widow of a powerful Italian king, married her and gained a toehold into Italian nobility. In time, and after assorted intrigues, military and otherwise, Otto I was crowned Holy Roman Emperor in 962, following in Charlemagne's footsteps. The Holy Roman Empire was alive and well... and being managed largely out of Germany. The Ottonians wielded considerable influence over Church matters during their tenure. This may seem like an outrage, but things were already bad in Rome with all kinds of sordid deals going on under the table. Fortunately no major Church business was addressed during those years (no big heresies to counter, or Church Councils to clarify dogma) because the cast of characters and their shenanigans resembled a soap opera more than informed holiness.

Otto I was succeeded by his son, who married the daughter of the Byzantine Emperor, potentially securing the unity of East and West in the Church that both Justinian and Charlemagne had dreamed of in the past. Nothing came of it though. Otto II died young leaving his own 3-year old son as heir with Mom and Grandma served as regents until the boy came of age to rule. Otto III also had visions of uniting all of Christendom with shared rule between the pope and himself as emperor, but he made a mess of things. The citizens of Rome refused to submit to Otto's rule and tried to recreate a version of the old Republic as an alternative to submitting to a German overlord, especially one with maternal ties to the Byzantine Emperor. Otto treated their actions as a rebellion and responded, killing their leader. He should have quit while he was ahead, but he was perhaps young and foolish. So instead, he fell in love with his late adversary's widow, who agreed to be his mistress, and then promptly poisoned him. He was only twenty-two when he died, leaving no son as heir.

The abbey church of **Saint Michael's, Hildesheim** was built toward the end of the Ottonian period. Notice that like the plans for Saint Gall, Saint Michael's looks a great deal like the Basilica Ulpia with double apses, and in this case, the church was even accessed through entrances in the side aisles very much like the old Roman basilica. The church added two transepts to offset the two apses which is something we haven't seen before. The appearance of a transept at either end suggests that the monks must have had occasion to switch back and forth between celebrating Mass in the small apse in the east end of the church, or opting for the larger apse in the west. Inside, notice that the nave resembles a small Early Christian basilica with a nave arcade and small clerestory windows above. The exposed rafters we would expect to see in a typical Early Christian church have been finished into a flat painted ceiling.

More famous than the actual building were the **Bronze Doors at Hildesheim**. Bishop Bernwald of Hildesheim commissioned the entire church project, and the glorious bronze doors were especially dear to him as he was trained in metalworking himself. The doors stand 16' 6" high and illustrate <u>Bible</u> scenes, with the Old Testament being recalled on the left and New Testament stories on the right. Let's start with the left door, which offers highlights from the Book of Genesis, illustrated with registers separating the different scenes. At the top, God has taken a rib from Adam's side to create Eve. Next God introduces the two, who seem pleased to become acquainted. The third scene shows the Temptation, where Eve is taken in by the serpent to eat the forbidden apple, and now she encourages Adam to give it a taste. Uh oh, now they are in trouble; the next scene shows Adam and Eve ashamed as they try to hide their nakedness from God. Below, an angel gives the ingrate couple the heave ho out of Paradise. Alas, Adam and Eve find they have to work for a living in the next scene. In the second from the bottom, their sons offer God (see the big hand?) the first fruits of their labor, Abel on the left offers livestock while Cain hands over a bushel of grain. In the bottom scene, Cain clobbers Able and kills him in a fit of jealousy after God likes Abel's gift better than Cain's.

On the right are scenes from the life of Christ. This time they read from bottom to top. In the lowest relief, the archangel Gabriel visits Mary to say she will conceive the Christ (the Annunciation). Above, we find the Nativity with Mary taking it easy in the bottom of the scene and a rather large infant Jesus looking like he was just catapulted to the stars (artists did not yet understand perspective at this point, so often things that are supposed to be "behind" wind up being "above"). Three wise men visit the baby Jesus in the third scene: the Adoration of the Magi. Above, Jesus is presented to the high priest for circumcision (Presentation at the Temple). Fast forward to Christ being condemned above followed by the Crucifixion in the third scene from the top. Above the tomb is found empty and an angel announces to the three Marys that Christ has risen. Finally at the top is Noli Me Tangere, where Christ encounters Mary Magdelene but tells her not to touch Him as He has not yet ascended to heaven.

Early medieval times are often seen as being a dark age sandwiched between the glories of pagan Rome and the high profile art and especially architecture that will follow in the later Middle Ages, particularly the Gothic period. While it is true that architecture was less sophisticated and art was in transition from a pagan past looking forward to an increasingly Christian future, the centuries of the Hiberno-Saxon, Carolingian and Ottonian periods were not without development and growth. Christianity spread across Europe, promoted by monks as well as the clergy. Schools were established to encourage literacy and learning. Perhaps we might think of it more as a beginning for Europe rather than a dark age, since during the height of the pagan Roman Empire, most of Europe was a cultural backwater held in little regard by the sophisticated elite living along the coasts of the Mediterranean. It was during the Early Medieval periods that Europe came into its own, not as barbarian dependents of better people elsewhere, but as political and cultural leaders who were beginning to make their own contributions to civilization.

9. Romanesque

c. 1000 - 1200

The Romanesque period began at the end of the first millennium and lasted about 200 years. The name Romanesque has been applied to these two centuries in hindsight; nobody living at the time walked around thinking of themselves as being Romanesque or living in Romanesque times. It gets its name from aspects of the life, art, and architecture of these two centuries, which recall ancient Rome, specifically in contrast to the early medieval periods. For one thing, much of the building, church architecture in particular, returned to the lost art of the Roman arch, hence recalling the grandeur of Imperial Rome.

More subtly, but more importantly too, the psychological feel of Europe at this time eased away from the early medieval sensibility of itsy-bitsy fiefdoms, more toward a feeling of commonality that extended beyond national boundaries ... a return to the sense of being part of a greater whole than your own little ethnic group, much as it had been at the height of Imperial Rome. Although this sense of being part of the group had flourished briefly during the reign of Charlemagne, it had once again been lost following his death. There were two very good reasons why this feeling of "wholeness" as opposed to "separateness" arose at this point in history. For one, the Romanesque period is associated with the Crusades. Prior to Muhammad, Christianity flourished throughout Mediterranean Europe; it was the predominant religion in the Middle East and across northern Africa. As we have seen, pockets of Christianity were thriving across northern Europe too. From the birth of Islam in 622 to the close of the 7th century, Christendom had been chopped in half through Islamic political and military conquest in Christian territories. By 633, Jerusalem, Antioch and Alexandria fell to Islamic advances. In 641, Islamic forces took Persia. In 642 they conquered Egypt, Syria and the rest of Mesopotamia and in 697 Carthage fell. By 755 they had such an established presence in southern Spain that they installed a Caliph there. In fact, in 846 Muslims forces even raided Rome and sacked Saint Peter's, so the assaults on Christianity had been ongoing for some time.

Within a hundred years of Muhammad's death, the Muslim empire extended from the Pyrenees to China. Now this was fabulous news if you happened to be Muslim, but it was not a happy development for Christians of either Byzantine or Catholic persuasion. By the 11th century, Byzantine Christians had been fighting Islam on and off for some time, but the Christians in the West were slow to become involved until they felt more directly threatened by Islam themselves. Jerusalem had been captured by Islam centuries earlier, but now at the close of the 11th century there was an act against Christianity that so offended all Christians, that Catholics were prepared to join in the fight. The Church of the Holy Sepulchre, the old Early Christian martyrium built over the site of Golgotha where Jesus was crucified, was confiscated by Muslims and the shrine was desecrated. Further, the Islamic presence in Spain was increasingly perceived as a much more aggressive threat given that followers of Islam had demonstrated pretty effectively over the centuries just how pushy they could be when it came to "manifest destiny." In fairness, it might be true that both the average Christian and the average Muslim were peaceful individuals. At some margin, though, there is a theological difference that can be understood by comparing the texts of the New Testament and the ***Koran (Qu'ran)*** which is the holy book for Islam. When a Christian becomes aggressive to where he attacks another who does not share his faith, he goes against the teachings set forth by Jesus. In contrast, Muhammad taught that while it was good to try to convert others to Islam peacefully when this could be achieved, if an unbeliever proves to be stubborn, then force is acceptable. The uneasy mood over Islam made Christians across Europe feel increasingly united in their faith, regardless of whether they happened to be Italians or Franks or Britons. Finally in 1095, Pope Urban II called the first Crusade, and Christians across the continent came together to defend their faith against the encroachment of Islam into their Christian world.

The second factor, which helped Europeans to view themselves as being part of a community greater than their ethnic divisions, was the dramatic rise of monasticism. The Benedictine order was established during the 6th century, and had mushroomed under the patronage of Charlemagne during the late 8th and early 9th centuries. By the Romanesque period, Benedictine monastic communities were established across all areas of Europe. In addition to the Benedictines, during the 10th and 11th centuries new orders were founded, and there was a substantial increase in the number of monks. Part of the reason this occurred was directly related to the type of economy found across Europe at this time. Romanesque Europe was the height of ***feudalism***, which is an agriculture-based economy where wealth is measured by land holdings. Under feudalism, those who owned the largest tracts of land were called ***lords***, or ***nobles***. Beneath the nobles would be ***vassals***, who owned smaller parcels of land and who were beholden to the big noble in their region, and at the bottom of the food chain were peasant ***serfs*** who owned nothing, and who worked the land for the lord or vassal in return for a modest place to live and hopefully enough to eat. The noble or vassal on whose land the serfs lived and labored owned the serfs like so much chattel. Feudal society is predominantly rural. A ***manor*** could cover a thousand acres or more with the noble's house in the center and a small village of support "industries" like a mill, a brewery or winery, a forge, and modest peasant housing. The sleepy hamlet also provided a small community church for those who lived on the manor. Although the feudal manor was the norm at this point in European history, some people lived outside the system, mostly as peasant landholders who were not beholden to any lord, and were not perceived as a threat to anybody so long as they farmed quietly and minded their own business.

The only way a feudal society can survive beyond a generation or two is to have laws of primogeniture in place. Laws of primogeniture insist that the first-born son in each family inherits EVERYTHING. He gets the real estate, the house, the cows and sheep and chickens, Dad's winter coat – everything. It is critically important that one child inherit the entire estate so that the family's holdings are never divided, thus protecting the status of the family name. If a father had 10,000 acres of land let's say, and four sons whom he loved equally and he wanted them to share the wealth, each son would get 2,500 acres of land, thus reducing the family name to the level of 2,500 acre landowners rather than a family title associated with the full 10,000 acres. Of course, the upshot is that if Junior gets the whole kit and caboodle, there isn't anything for the other kids in the family ... except a good family name. Accordingly, during the 11th and 12th centuries, the second-born son was expected to serve in the military. During the Crusades, that's where most of these second-born sons went, whether they were so inclined or not. Under any set of circumstances, the sons of nobles entered the king's army, and the sons of vassals entered the NOBLE'S army; large landowners maintained their own substantial militias to defend their territories. Second born sons of serfs, unfortunately, like first-born sons and all the younger brothers also were destined to live their lives planting and harvesting turnips. Laws of primogeniture are oriented to families that had possessions, especially land, which was generally a notch beyond the peasants.

The third son in the family was customarily expected to enter the service of the Church. Some of these might become priests, or higher eventually - bishops or cardinals even - but the vast majority became monks. Given that many families might have more than 3 sons, these extra boys more often than not were sent off to the monastery too. Some may have settled for squatting on some wee parcel of land and becoming peasant farmers, but otherwise there was no place else in society for them to go; it wasn't like someone could go out and get a job – there were no jobs. The Church was tantamount to a massive charitable institution. Folks who had "extra" boys frequently dropped Biff and Bubba off at the monastery when they were little kids, 4 or 5 years old sometimes, to let the Church raise them (feed them, clothe them etc.) since they knew the boys would end up being monks anyway. For girls, the options were even more limited. If Mommy and Daddy could produce an attractive dowry, Petunia might stand a good chance of having a marriage arranged for her, given that nobody was going to take Petunia for his wife unless she came with pigs and chickens on the side. If not, then off to the convent she went, again often as a small child, to be raised by nuns at Church expense rather than on Mommy's and Daddy's money. Even if there were no other mitigating factors, the laws of primogeniture alone would guarantee a huge growth in monasticism. Bear in mind also, that *wanting* to be a monk or nun seldom had anything at all to do with whether or not that was to be your destiny in life. Anyone who looks for accounts of scandalous behavior in medieval monasteries or convents will be able to find isolated examples; there *were* men and women trapped in this station of life who might have been better suited to being something else ... had that option been available. The real miracle is that the overwhelming majority buckled down and made the best of the life they inherited.

In addition to primogeniture, another factor influenced the growth of monasticism. This was the introduction of two new monastic orders at this time, which became immensely popular, the Cluniacs and the Cistercians. Many young men enthusiastically wished to become monks in one order or another, some in fact passing their inherited position as first-born or second-born to a younger brother for the privilege of becoming a monk. In the end, this rapid and dramatic increase in the number of monks and nuns served to make society more unified across Europe, as members of a common order viewed other members of the same order as "brothers" and "sisters" regardless of where they lived, in much the same way as members of the same fraternity or sorority or civic organization might feel a kinship to others participating in the same organization elsewhere.

The Romanesque period ushered in two new variations on the Christian basilica favored in the Western church since the fourth century. ***Pilgrimage churches*** were built to accommodate traveling Christians, mostly Crusaders on their way to fight Muslims, either to the Holy Land, or in the south of Spain. The roads traveled by crusaders are called pilgrimage routes, and logically they run east/west (going to Jerusalem), or north/south (going down into Spain). In addition to crusaders on these routes, there would also be pilgrims, in fewer numbers perhaps, but this is where the churches and the routes got their name. Pilgrims were people, individuals or in some cases entire families, who were on the road to visit holy shrines as a measure of their faith. They might be going someplace special as an act of penance to show God how sorry they were for their sins. The point was to not to just *say* you were sorry, but to *do* something that required sacrifice to *show* it. Consider the difference between a boyfriend who mumbles "I'm sorry" and goes on his merry way after he acted like a jerk, and the boyfriend who says he is sorry, and then arrives with flowers to take his fair lady out to dinner to help make up for the offense … one path requires more investment of effort than the other. Alternatively, they might be going on a pilgrimage in thanksgiving to God for answering prayers, or they might find themselves in terrible straits with illness or threatened security, and find that making this sacrifice to God helped them to focus on their faith and prayer life. Whatever the case, many were headed to the Church of the Holy Sepulchre in Jerusalem or Old Saint Peter's in Rome (east/west route), while others who for whatever reason could not go that far, might be headed down to Santiago de Compostela in Spain (north/south route), where the bones of Saint James were housed as relics.

Relics, whether the bones of a saint or a garment or other object directly associated with a saint became a significant focus during the Romanesque period. It began when visitors to the Holy Land (pilgrims and crusaders alike) brought back items purported to be linked to either an Apostle or early saint, or even to Jesus himself. A famous example still around today is the Shroud of Turin, which is said to be the shroud in which Jesus was buried in the tomb. Some of the relics were undoubtedly real, while just as many were probably fakes; in fact, many a charlatan made a fast buck on duped religious "tourists" in a foreign land. That said, it doesn't make any meaningful difference, really, given that these articles served primarily to move people to deeper prayer and devotion to God. Sometimes in today's society, people look back at the Middle Ages as a time in history when folks entertained foolish superstitions that held no merit. Always remember that throughout history, if you want to understand others, you must try to see the world through their eyes.

The reason people were attracted to relics at all can be found in the Bible: passages like Matthew 9:20, Mark 5:27, Mark 6:56 and Luke 8:44 for example, where a woman is healed by nothing more profound than seeking a chance brush with Jesus' cloak. In other accounts, like Acts 19:12 or Acts 5:15, simple objects like a saint's handkerchief offered the same healing mystery, or even the mere shadow of a saint healed the sick and cast out evil spirits. Perhaps better still would be Old Testament passages common to both the Jewish and Christian faiths, like 2 Kings 13:21 where a dead man came into contact with the bones of Elisha and came back to life! Now to a non-believer these may be considered myths, but to the believer, accounts in Scripture were serious business.

Taken at face value, the Bible demonstrates repeatedly that for reasons we might not understand, God apparently chose to use ordinary objects and elements in the world as a means to deliver healing and grace … the conduit was physical, not just a spiritual thing. As it happened many of these relics *were* associated with otherwise unexplained miracles of healing, but the significant thing is not that the relic did magic tricks and the person got better, the significant thing was that the person got better, presumably healed by God, and curiously after making the pilgrimage, where relics were often encountered. Further, many documented healings occurred following years of suffering when God chose not to heal; the healing came only after the pilgrimage. The relics did no more healing than Jesus' robe or Peter's shadow did in the <u>Bible</u>, but the faithful pilgrim could argue that God chose to heal them in response to their faith … accompanied by contact with some physical object they could see or even touch, and which only God can answer as to why. Pilgrimage churches are associated with the display of relics, which the faithful would travel great distances to see, and to be inspired toward greater devotion and prayer to God.

The other kind of church which pops up like mushrooms during the Romanesque period is the *abbey*. Abbeys are monastery and convent churches, designed to serve a religious community, including adjacent living quarters, like we saw in the plan for Saint Gall (Carolingian). In general it is true that Romanesque churches are *large*. Pilgrimage churches had to be huge to accommodate entire armies passing through, and abbeys had to be big to accommodate the ever-growing community of monks (or nuns, just not both together!) in residence. Romanesque churches are almost always *rural*. For one thing, there were no big cities at this time, although small towns did grow up around pilgrimage churches in particular. Those free peasant farmers mentioned earlier often saw the pilgrimage routes with their steady supply of humanity passing through as an opportunity to develop trade. Europe was otherwise sprinkled with small hamlets and peasant villages since pretty much everyone else was tied to a manor owned by a wealthy lord; it was an agrarian world. Pilgrimage churches were originally located out in the boondocks. This made sense because the incentive to carry on to the battle front (or to the sacred shrine) might wane if the travelers weren't reinforced along the way, especially along the stretches of road with no manor villages to offer a meal or a kind word of support. Nowadays towns and even cities have grown up around these big churches, but when they were built, they were in the middle of nowhere. Likewise, abbeys were off by themselves as the whole point of being a monk in those days was to be at least somewhat removed from society.

Pilgrimage Churches

The pilgrimage church of **<u>Sainte Foy</u>** located in the hill country of Conques, France, was situated along the southern pilgrimage route leading down to Spain. It is one of the best surviving pilgrimage churches to examine, although it is petite compared to many. <u>Sainte Foy</u> was run by a small group of Benedictine monks who looked after the pilgrims and soldiers, offering them a place to stay as well the opportunity to attend Mass. As you can see, the town that has grown up around the church presses in closely making it impossible to stand back today and see the church from a distance. Still, you can compare the aerial photograph to the plan to see how a typical pilgrimage church was designed. Notice first of all that it is a basilica, but unlike Early Christian basilicas, it does not have an atrium. While it is true that these churches were designed to serve travelers, just like Early Christian basilicas, unlike Early Christian churches which were usually found in cities, pilgrimage churches were located out in the country. Therefore, if people showed up and needed a place to stay, presumably there were forests or quiet meadows nearby where they could camp out, bathe in a stream, and in general enjoy the pastoral beauty for a few days rest while visiting the church.   Besides, many pilgrimage churches were hosted by a small community of monks who could provide sleeping quarters for at least some guests.

From the great outdoors then, the visitor would enter directly into the *narthex*, which again is a lobby or vestibule area provided to collect one's thoughts before entering the actual church.   Inside, again we find the *nave* where people would stand during the Mass.   The *apse* is located in the east end of the church, and you could expect to find the altar and tabernacle there.   The apse area of Sainte Foy is deeper than we saw on Early Christian church plans.   It includes the apse and a small space just outside the apse called a *choir*, which is where the monks who lived at the abbey would stand during a Mass. The choir will become a more important feature in Gothic churches later on.   The *transept* separates the apse from the nave, and communion would be distributed here.   A pilgrimage church might have one or two side aisles, just like Early Christian.   Notice on the plan of Sainte Foy that the aisle doesn't stop at the transept like earlier churches, but now wraps all the way around the transept, and even behind the apse!   When the aisle curves in behind the apse it is called an *ambulatory*.   The extension of the aisle around the transept, and the new ambulatory in the Romanesque church are provided to allow access to *chapels*, which on the plan look like jelly beans stuck off the ambulatory and east end of the transept.   This is where relics would be placed on display, and the faithful would be invited to visit these chapels for private prayer outside of Mass.   The clever design of Romanesque churches allowed for small groups of pilgrims to arrive, even in the middle of a Mass with a packed church, slip quietly into a side aisle and walk all the way around the church, visiting each of the little chapels, without ever disturbing anyone attending the Mass.   The church of Sainte-Foy was very fortunate to have the bones of Sainte Foy (Saint Faith in English), who was a third century Christian girl who was martyred as a child or refusing to worship pagan gods.

Exterior sculpture on a pilgrimage church is normally limited to relief carvings around the doors, or *portals* provided there to offer a hasty message to the visitor on his or her way into the church.   Usually a pilgrimage church will have double front doors in order to move crowds in and out of the church easily.   Above the double portal at Sainte Foy is a relief sculpture of the **Last Judgment**.   See from the picture that the scene fits into a tidy semi-circular arc over the two doors; this is called a *tympanum*.   The Last Judgment was by far the most popular choice to grace the entrance of pilgrimage churches.   Probably the most famous tympanum from a Romanesque pilgrimage church is the **Last Judgment** from the church of Saint Lazare at Autun, France (also known as Autun Cathedral).   Rare as it is for this period in history, we even know the name of the sculptor on the latter tympanum, Gislebertus, who signed his work.   Let's look at both to see how this popular theme was addressed… and why.   Notice that Christ appears in the center of each tympanum, surrounded by a *mandorla* which is an almond-shaped halo of light; He also has a round halo surrounding His head.   On the Saint Lazare tympanum, Christ fills the entire space, while the figure is smaller on Sainte-Foy, offset by a huge cross behind the mandorla.   By the way, look at the sculpture style of the two. Gislebertus had a very individual and distinct style.   His figures (Christ and others) are elongated with stylized faces, sort of like simplified cartoons compared to the figures on Sainte-Foy which are more realistic.

Traditionally on Christ's right (your left) we find those who have been judged worthy of heaven. The Saint Lazare tympanum shows a small group of elongated figures, hands clasped in prayer, gazing at Christ. On Saint-Foy, the artist has included a repertoire of saints and Apostles, at least one of which can be identified by his *attribute*, which is an object (or color in painting) that identifies who is who. Look closely. Can you see the fellow with the key in his hand to Christ's right? That's Saint Peter, standing right behind the Virgin Mary who looks on at Jesus with complete reverence. These are the lucky souls who will live for all eternity in paradise. Notice how Christ raises his hand in greeting toward those who will join him in heaven. His hand turns down to those on His left, indicating their unfortunate fate. Below, a monster joins in with assorted wild-eyed devils in administering horror to hell's victims. The arrangement is the same on the Saint Lazare tympanum. Grisly demons snatch terrified souls into hell; can you see the pair of hands reaching from the depths of hell to pluck souls for Satan's punishments? Clearly hell is not a fate anyone would choose if it could be avoided.

The purpose of these horrific images is to scare people into doing the right thing. Perhaps this wasn't so much of an issue with pilgrims, other than to suggest that their efforts at penance were well advised, but with the soldiers, it was to be a point well taken. Sadly, crusaders often behaved badly, and the Church was aware of this problem. At some margin, the call for a crusade meant that the Church was already marking a fine line between right and wrong, given that the Church had always taught that the Ten Commandments, including "thou shalt not kill" were serious and not to be taken lightly by anyone seeking salvation. The potential sticky wicket when you suggest that one rule might bend slightly in special circumstances is that those looking for moral guidance might also be inclined to bend another rule or two while they are at it. It's not okay to kill someone, unless that person happens to be a different religion from you. Okay, well maybe it's also wrong to steal, unless I am a soldier fighting for God and I want to eat your cow. And maybe while I am at it, it is wrong to commit adultery, unless I am a soldier fighting for God and I have been away from my wife a long time and your wife is looking pretty good to me. You get the picture. The Church knew that God does not turn a blind eye toward sin, and the Church also knew that many of these men would be facing death, and hence judgment ahead of the natural order because they would die in battle, without in many cases the luxury of time to show God they were sorry for their sins. Accordingly, the Church felt the necessity of emphasizing how horrible hell is in the hope that crusaders would live chaste and moral lives while fighting for the faith, lest their souls be lost for all eternity.

While Crusaders were frequent visitors to pilgrimage churches, and those Last Judgment tympanums were perhaps aimed mostly at them, don't forget that holy pilgrims were also on the road. Those traveling east were going to either Saint Peter's in Rome or the Church of the Holy Sepulchre in Jerusalem, both being Early Christian churches that you know. The church drawing a crowd down in Spain was **Santiago de Compostela**. This church was new, since the shrine was new.

Oral tradition dating back at least as early as the year 400 was that the Apostle Saint James the Greater, the son of Zebedee and brother of Saint John the Evangelist, had traveled to Galicia in northern Spain toward the end of his life. This Saint James is not to be confused with the Apostle Saint James the Lesser (probably meaning he was shorter, not that he was less of a good guy) who was the Bishop of Jerusalem. Anyway, Saint

James supposedly went to Spain, but then nobody knows what happened to him. Certainly if he died there, nobody knew where the grave was. The story goes that in 835 a bishop named Theodomir was "guided by a star" (Compostela basically means "plain of the star") to find the tomb of Saint James, which lo and behold, was conveniently nearby. The truth is nobody really knows whose bones are beneath the altar at Santiago de Compostela. Scholars, including Catholic theologians have indicated there are difficulties validating these relics. For example, Acts 12:2 suggests that Saint James was martyred in the year 44, and the oral tradition of the early Church is that Saint James had not left Jerusalem at that time. Further, Saint Paul wrote in the year 58 that he would not want to build on another man's foundation, and that he was hoping to visit Spain (Romans 15:20 and 24), suggesting that neither Saint James nor any other Apostle had already established a ministry there. Of course, it is always possible that Saint James never preached in Spain, but that his bones were carried there; relics often had a way of migrating when one Christian or another would decide that the current location was unsafe, or even for purely selfish reasons of wanting the saint's shrine closer to home. In fact, more often than you might imagine, the remains of a deceased saint have been divvied up so that I take an arm, you get a leg and his head will go to somebody else. So who knows whose bones are enshrined at Santiago de Compostela? It may be Saint James, or it may be somebody else. The point is it really doesn't matter (beyond sheer curiosity) if the shrine moves visitors to greater faith.

Looking at the plan of Santiago de Compostela you should see that while the basic layout is the same as Sainte-Foy, it is considerably larger. The biggest difference you might notice are additional doors, given that it was a very large church anticipating huge crowds. Beyond the double front door, see the two additional doors offering direct access to the side aisles for those pilgrims who wanted to go directly to the chapels off the transept and ambulatory. There are also double doors provided in both the north and south transept for the same reason. The exterior of the church has received a substantial facelift since its Romanesque beginnings, but the nave of Santiago de Compostela still looks very much like a typical Romanesque church; it is dark, even dreary inside.

Compared to Early Christian and Early Medieval churches, the flat wooden ceiling or exposed wooden rafters has been replaced with a stone ceiling. Fires had been a constant threat to church architecture in the early centuries with all that dry timber inside churches with hundreds of burning candles. It would be impossible to build a flat stone ceiling based on post and lintel design because it would be too heavy to span such a large space without hundreds of intermediate supports poking up here and there throughout the nave. To solve this problem, the architects have rediscovered the old Roman arch seen in Imperial Roman architecture like the Theater Marcellus and the Colosseum. The arch, you will recall, allowed architects to span a substantial space while supporting much weight so long as the sides of the arch were adequately braced to counter outward thrust. When the arch is employed to create a ceiling, one arch next to another next to another and so forth until it creates a kind of tunnel, it is called a **barrel vault**. Most Romanesque churches relied on barrel vaulting in order to make the naves large to pack in a crowd, and to offer better fire protection at the same time. In order to make barrel vaulting stable, so the outward thrust of all those arches doesn't make the walls do the splits, the architects gave the churches very thick walls which worked like fat bookends pressed against the arches to keep them sturdy and sound.

Inside there is a nave arcade, not unlike what we saw in earlier basilicas. Above the nave arcade there is a *gallery*. Up until now we have thought of galleries as being a Byzantine idea to keep men and women separated during the Divine Liturgy. Remember, though, that Santiago de Compostela is a Catholic Church, so the use of the gallery must be different. On occasion people who were not confirmed members of the Church (*catechumens*) might be attending, and since they would not be receiving communion, they were asked to stand upstairs to allow more room in the nave for others who would be receiving. Galleries in Romanesque churches were also provided for crowd overflow. Notice that Santiago de Compostela did not have clerestory windows. In the earlier basilica churches built with post and lintel design, whether they had flat wooden ceilings (like Santa Maria Maggiore) or rafters open to the roof structure above (like Old Saint Peters), the walls were not dealing with outward thrust, and it was easy for the architects to punch holes in the wall to create windows without weakening the structure. With barrel vaulting, the walls need enormous amounts of bracing to remain stable, so architects usually left the windows out rather than weaken the supporting walls. Pilgrimage churches were usually very plain inside. With the barrel vaulting making a clerestory nearly impossible, it was too dark and gloomy to see much art even if it were there. The small chapels off the ambulatory had windows, however, and they were often quite lovely.

Benedictine Abbeys (Italy)

In addition to pilgrimage churches, the 11th and 12th centuries saw many new abbeys built to accommodate the rapid rise in monastic populations. Partly this was in response to the social structure which kept both monasteries and convents filled with young men and women who may not have had other alternatives in life. But that was only part of the equation. All Benedictine monasteries were independent, in that the abbot in charge had a certain amount of leverage over exactly how the men would spend their time between prayer, manual labor like farming (if you don't work, you don't eat), and tasks like copying manuscripts in large scriptoriums. Initially, despite minor individual differences between one abbey and the next, the basic lifestyle was the same for all Benedictines.

Few Italian Romanesque churches were as structurally advanced as churches built elsewhere at this time in that the Italians usually clung to construction features of Early Christian basilica design rather than opting for barrel vaulted ceilings. Instead, they sometimes made up for the lapse with innovative and beautiful church facades. **San Miniato al Monte** in Florence is an excellent example. Built originally as a Benedictine abbey, the church was dedicated to Saint Minias, who was a third century martyr from Florence. Minias probably came from parts further east - Greece or maybe the Levant – but settled in Tuscany where he made a nuisance of himself converting the locals to Christianity, until the pagan Roman government finally put a stop to his ministry by beheading the fellow. According to the story, legend or otherwise, the saint then picked up his own head and carried it to the highest point in Florence where his followers erected a shrine. By the 8th century there was a small chapel on the site, and early in the 11th century construction began on the current church built for the Benedictines. Later it passed to the Cluniacs (see below), and it is still a monastery today serving an small, obscure order founded later in the 14th century.

Unlike Romanesque churches elsewhere, which feature plain, drab facades with at most a decorated tympanum over the front entrance, <u>San Miniato al Monte</u> offers a colorful welcome to visitors. Green and white marble was employed to create pleasing geometric patterns that break up the expanse of the façade with rectangles and rounded arches that are more for show than structural benefit. A mosaic showing **Christ between the Virgin and Saint Minias** decorates the façade above the main entrance and reminds visitors of this obscure saint who helped establish Christianity in Florence.

Cluniac Abbeys (France)

The Romanesque period is also associated with two new monastic orders, both of which developed out of the Benedictine model. Many wealthy families felt sorry that their third sons were destined for what they perceived as a glum life in the monastery, devoid of luxuries enjoyed by the eldest son who would inherit the family estate, and without the shot at glory available to the son marked for military service. In 909 a wealthy nobleman, William, Count of Auvergne and Duke of Aquitaine, donated land and a villa near the village of Cluny to establish a new monastery that would specifically serve the sons of noble families. The arrangement at Cluny was sufficiently altered from the Benedictine Rule such that in 910, the *Cluniacs* became their own new order. Although similar to the Benedictines in that the men lived in a monastery off in the country away from the general public, and they were expected to be obedient and chaste, the Cluniac Order allowed for serfs to do the manual labor of providing for the abbey (farming, laundry, cleaning and more), while the monks themselves spent their time in prayer and labor that did not include dirt under their fingernails. Cluniac monks were known for their splendid manuscript art and ecclesiastic music. They took pride in being intellectual and cultured. These were men accustomed to luxury who did not have to sacrifice their elegant lifestyle when they became monks. The Cluniac Order was wealthy from the start, so they could indulge in fabulous abbeys, all of which were built in and around Cluny (unlike Benedictine abbeys which were scattered all over). Also, all the Cluniac abbeys, although separate buildings, were a single congregation under the authority of a single abbot (again unlike Benedictines where each abbey was independent with its own abbot). Although the great abbeys at Cluny have fallen to ruin, we have renderings of the third **Abbey at Cluny** which was so spectacular that in its day it was considered one of the great wonders of the world. Cluniac abbeys were often enormous, and while plain on the outside, frequently more decorated inside than pilgrimage churches. The monks themselves lived in luxury, wearing robes of the finest fabrics, and in some cases, enjoying a lifestyle better than their brothers who inherited the family manor.

One uniquely lovely example of Cluniac church architecture that is still intact today is **Sainte Madeleine**, located in Vezelay, France. <u>Sainte Madeleine</u> is interesting because it is both a pilgrimage church and also an abbey. The church's location made it a convenient point of departure for *both* the Crusaders and Holy Pilgrims headed east to Jerusalem, *and also* those who were bound for Spain to the south. The monks were delighted with their high visibility role and served as gracious hosts to all who came to visit. The church of <u>Sainte Madeleine</u> was also famous for her relics: the bones of Mary Magdalene.

You might wonder how Mary Magdalene's bones wound up in France. The most probable account of Mary Magdalene following the Resurrection is that once the Apostles dispersed to preach the Gospel, she initially went to Rome where tradition says she was able to obtain an audience with the Emperor Tiberius. According to the account, she was influential in getting Tiberius to recall Pontius Pilate from Palestine, after which he was sent to a post in Gaul where he died in the year 41. Meanwhile, Mary was apparently in Rome when Paul arrived and she left sometime after, returning to Ephesus in the Holy Land to be close to Mary the Mother of Jesus who in turn was staying with Saint John the Evangelist, both of whom were like close family to Mary Magdalene. Some scholars believe she may have contributed to the first twenty chapters of the Gospel of John, which was being written during those years. According to tradition, she died at the ripe old age of 72 and was buried in Ephesus.

In 899, Emperor Leo VI had her body exhumed, and the bones (now considered relics) were moved to the monastery Church of Saint Lazarus in Constantinople. Most credible scholars can agree on that much. As to how the relics got from Constantinople to Vezelay … now that is open for debate. The monks in Vezelay began claiming they had Mary Magdalene's relics around 1050, saying that one of their monks (named Badilo) brought them back from a pilgrimage to the Holy Land. This account may well be true given that it does not conflict with any widely accepted facts. Recall that the Cluniac Order was rich, and the monks themselves often came from rich families. It would not be unreasonable that such a monk on his travels could entice a poor abbey to part with some relics for the right price.

Another version of the story which is considerably less credible suggests that a little later, after the start of the Crusades, the relics were "rescued" from Constantinople, which was increasingly seen as being an unsafe place for a Christian shrine in view of what had happened to the Church of the Holy Sepulchre in Jerusalem. The bones were initially brought to Rome to the Church of Saint John Lateran, and then later taken to Marseilles in the south of France (why they would be taken to Marseilles is not addressed and would at the very least be an illogical choice for a preferred final resting place over Rome), with the monks from Vezelay eventually obtaining the relics from Marseilles. This version of the story, it is worth noting, would put the relics in Vezelay nearly a century after the church dedicated to Mary Magdalene was already built, which doesn't necessarily discredit the account, but it doesn't strengthen it either. Odds are this second version of the story was doctored from legend … read on.

There was a popular myth about Mary Magdalene circulating in the late Middle Ages that introduced the fantasy about her coming to Marseilles. To begin, the legend presumes that Mary Magdalene was the sister of Martha and Lazarus, which is known to be false since Mary Magdalene is so named because she came from Magdala whereas the Mary who was kin to Martha and Lazarus was from Bethany. Anyway, according to this story, after the Resurrection, Mary, Martha, Lazarus and a host of other Christians were shanghaied by some grumpy Jews who set them to sea in a boat that drifted to Marseilles, France. Upon arrival, they all evangelized the local pagans. Lazarus became the bishop of Marseilles, and eventually Mary Magdalene withdrew from the townspeople and moved into a cave in the hills outside the city where she lived as a hermit for several years until her death.

It is worth noting that this tale appears to have originated in the 1100's (no record of it exists before then), and it was probably concocted to bring pilgrim business to Marseilles in the hope of bolstering local fame and fortune. It's possible that Lazarus and his family may have gone to Marseilles, although scholarship has determined that the Lazarus who was a bishop there was in fact a 5th century man. The legend of Mary Magdalene as a hermit was quite possibly inspired by the life of yet another Mary (do we have enough Marys?), the penitent Mary of Egypt who was 5th century woman who lived in the Jordanian desert after abandoning her prior life as a singer and actress of questionable reputation. The story of Mary of Egypt was popular during the Middle Ages, with her life (of which we actually know very little) being embellished with juicy details. In all probability, Mary Magdalene never set foot in France, however appealing such a tale may have been to the medieval citizens of Marseilles. As to whether the relics at Vezelay are genuine … that depends on where the Cluniac monk originally obtained the bones. If they came from the monastery Church of Saint Lazarus in Constantinople, then they are probably the genuine article.

Abbeys were usually rather plain on the exterior, given that the monks were accustomed to spending the better part of the day inside anyway, but Vezelay is more ornate. Over the double front door is a tympanum depicting the ever popular Last Judgment, which should not come as a surprise given that this abbey doubled as a pilgrimage church. The current tympanum is actually a later replacement, as the original façade of the church has weathered badly over the centuries. Above the Last Judgment tympanum is an impressive display of five grand statues (very rare for a Romanesque church) perched above five tall, slender *lancet windows* (narrow arched windows) that are punctuated by the statues of saints. The statues on top are in poor condition today, but they can still be recognized as Christ enthroned in the center, flanked by the Virgin Mary to the left and Mary Magdalene on the right, and an angel stands on the far side of each Mary. The central three figures can be identified in part by their relative locations, even though they are so badly damaged that we might otherwise be left guessing. As we saw with the two Last Judgment tympana from Conques and Autun, the central figure is almost always Christ, especially if that figure is seated on a throne. The Virgin Mary is frequently on the left (Christ's *right* hand side). In this statue grouping the figure of the Virgin Mary is almost a shadow given that the shape of the figure is there, but almost all the details are worn away. Can you see the outline of her standing, shifting her weight as she holds her child and wearing a crown on her head? This image of Mary will be popular throughout the latter Middle Ages and on into the Renaissance. Opposite Mary on the other side of Jesus the figure is so badly damaged that we might guess little about it other than the lower robes appear to be those of a woman. We can surmise who it is by taking stock of the saint for whom the church was named. This church was dedicated to Saint Mary Magdalene, so common sense suggests that is who the mystery woman is figured prominently with Jesus and His Mom.

Once you step inside the door, you find yourself in a narthex which has another set of doors leading to the nave, and above those doors is another tympanum. This latter tympanum was sculpted with a scene called **The Mission of the Apostles**, where Christ commissions the twelve apostles to go forth into the world, illustrating to all the faithful about to depart on a pilgrimage or Crusade that they were doing God's will. Christ dominates center stage again, just as we saw in the Last Judgment scenes. He is shown as a dynamic figure, looking almost like He is about to stand up (or about to start dancing…); he is calling His followers to action. Around the large central image are smaller scenes showing the Apostles getting out there and doing as God wills, and around these images are small roundels containing astrology symbols. It may see peculiar at first to see astrology signs on a church, but in medieval art and architecture, astrology images were often used as a symbolic way to illustrate time, in this case, to suggest that Christ's call to action is for all time.

Inside, the nave of <u>Sainte Madeleine</u> is brighter than Santiago de Compostela with modest clerestory windows replacing the gallery (to do this, the architects used an early experimental form of groin vaulting rather than straight barrel vaulting; more on groin vaulting later with a better example). It was important to get more light into the nave to see the lovely stonework in the nave arches which alternate reddish brown and white voussoirs creating a festive feel inside. We have seen striped arches like this before, at the Palatine Chapel, but the dark interior there didn't showcase the peppy décor as well as <u>Sainte Madeleine</u>.

Cistercian Abbeys (France)

The Cistercian Order was founded in 1098. Unlike the Cluniac Order, which was created largely to accommodate wealthy young men who were either obliged to become monks or desired a monastic life, but who were not keen on the manual labor aspect of the traditional Benedictine Rule, the Cistercian Order was initiated as a reform specifically against the luxuries of the Cluniacs. Robert de Molesme established the first monastery, initially Benedictine, at Citeaux, France. As Benedictine abbeys were always independent and subject to the direction of the abbot, Robert set about making his abbey strict about the rules. One of his monks, an Englishman named Stephen Harding wrote up a new constitution, and in 1119 the Cistercian Order was officially recognized by the Pope Calixtus II, who curiously enough happened to be a Cluniac himself!

Cistercians were men dedicated to a life of self-sacrifice and denial. Unlike the Cluniacs who usually found prime real estate with lovely views for their abbeys, the Cistercians deliberately opted for plain Jane sites, usually remote valleys which had to be cleared but which were near water, perhaps a small river running through a mountain valley. There they would built a completely self-contained monastery complex of no-frills buildings to meet the needs of the monks, always according to the same plan which spelled out in detail not only what buildings need be included, but where they should be in relationship to one another, and always laid out at right angles. The men wore only plain robes, woolen in winter and linen in summer, with no comfortable undergarments or coats. They ate one meal a day of fish, a vegetable and bread but no meat (and certainly no treats). They were expected to follow a rigidly disciplined life of hard work farming the land (they provided all their own food and also raised enough additional food to help feed the poor) and running the abbey (everything from making the wine to spinning the cloth) combined with equally extensive prayer and study. In short, they were ascetics like Saint John the Baptist and Saint Benedict, only instead of being isolated hermits, they lived in a community. Some of the monks remained illiterate, which was fine so long as they strictly observed the Masses and prayers and understood every word, as punishments were strict for anyone who did not know his faith. Others wound up becoming the pre-eminent theologians and scholars of their age due to their extensive studies which frequently resulted in equally extensive writing … not copying and decorating manuscripts so much as writing original work.

One of the young men attracted to Citeaux was the third-born son of a rich family, and just the sort one might expect to prefer the upper crust lifestyle offered at the Cluniac monasteries. The man's name was Bernard de Fontaines, better known today as Saint Bernard. Not only did Bernard become a Cistercian himself, he attracted to the order over time most of the men in his family either as lads, or later in life as widowers. In fact, Bernard so clearly distinguished himself within the new order that the abbot ordered him to build another abbey - Clairvaux - which quickly became the center of the rapidly growing Cistercian order as the motherhouse to sixty-eight additional monasteries. Bernard was a brilliant theologian, often called upon to advise even the pope himself. He also was the voice who called the faithful to support the Second Crusade, which was launched from Sainte Madeleine in Vezelay by the way.

Bernard was especially critical of the Cluniacs, and had plenty to say on the subject. One famous dissertation is his *Apology for William*, written for an abbot named William whose abbey of Saint Thierry was located near Reims, France. "Apology" means a formal justification or defense; it has nothing to do with being sorry … Bernard wasn't sorry at all for what he had to say! In the essay he took great offense at a variety of Cluniac practices and attitudes. He compared their haughty attitude of superiority to the Pharisee who looked down his nose at the publican in Scripture. He disrespected their laziness in having serfs and servants do the manual labor so the monks' lifestyle would be cushy. He had conniptions over their diet of multiple courses of rich foods served several times a day, suggesting that these guys ate to the point of belching and producing "flatulent pulses." Bernard thoroughly disapproved of the Cluniac penchant for coveting relics, then using them to create a sort of tourist attraction, which in turn brought in financial donations from the pilgrims who came to visit. None of the Cistercian abbeys were located on roads where they might attract many visitors. Bernard was also highly critical of the art associated with Cluniac abbeys. Religious themes were fine, although he felt like the Cluniacs made too big a deal out of the art inside their abbeys (many had frescoes and more to dress the church up), and in the end it became a distraction to prayer and study which were more important. He especially went nuts over some of the curiosity margin filler doodles common to Cluniac manuscripts, where a monk might dash off anything from an obscene monkey, a savage lion or tiger or imaginary animals from pagan fiction like centaurs or even weird animals they made up themselves, like putting a dragon's tail on a fish. Bernard perceived droll amusements like these to be offensive to God and completely out of place in Scripture manuscripts.

As you might expect, Bernard expected Cistercian abbeys to be plain, with no frilly frou-frou. One of the abbeys Bernard personally oversaw, built just fifteen years after Clairvaux, was the **Abbey Church at Fontenay**, France. The exterior is stripped down to the bare basics. The Cistercians were known for their superior brick masonry, but there was zero interest in cluttering up the building with a bunch of fancy stuff. There are no towers flanking the entrance like we saw at Sainte-Foy, and there is no exterior sculpture to either scare anybody into going to church, or to make them feel welcome. What there is of a small tympanum over the single set of doors is completely plain. Inside the austerity was continued. Cistercian churches like <u>Fontenay</u> eliminated the narthex (who needs it?) and transept, opting instead for a very simple box with a nave arcade dividing the nave from the aisle. The apse was a continuation of the rectilinear box (love those right angles) compared to the round apse in a typical Cluniac church or pilgrimage church, both with chapels to house relics radiating off an ambulatory. They used no stained glass, but did include plenty of windows since interior light was likened to the presence of God. The barrel vault in Cistercian churches will almost always employ pointed arches instead of round, as they were found to improve the acoustics. It might surprise you to discover in this rather Spartan church there remains to this day a lovely statue of the **Virgin Mary Holding the Infant Jesus**. Such statues were common to many Cistercian monasteries, as they held the Virgin Mary in high regard. Notice how beautifully natural she appears, and see also how similar this typical figure of mother and child is compared to the statue of the Virgin Mary on the facade of the abbey at Vezelay. Both emphasize the tender maternal qualities of Mary, likened perhaps to a loving mother whose job it is to bring all her children closer to Christ.

By the end of the Middle Ages, there were nearly 1500 Cistercian monasteries scattered across Europe in most countries. While the Cluniacs came and went, Cistercians are still around today. Modern day Trappist Monks are a branch of the old Cistercian Order.

Norman Abbeys and Art

(France)

Not all of France was culturally French. Like many European countries during the Middle Ages, France was made up of mixed ethnic stock. The northwest region of the country was settled by Vikings who invaded from Norway or Denmark. These Northmen or "Normans" came in waves during the 9th century, destroying villages and displacing or killing off the locals. Eventually the Normans made peace with the Carolingian rulers in power at that time, and the newly recognized (Norman) Dukes of Normandy converted to Christianity compliments of Benedictine missionary efforts.

Long before there were Cluniacs and Cistercians, Benedictine missionaries had taken on the task of making Christians of the local people across what is now France, and these monks and their monasteries didn't disappear during the Romanesque period with the formation and rising popularity of new monastic orders. One of the most famous Benedictine abbeys in the world is found here: **Mont Saint Michel**. In 708 the local bishop heard the voice of Saint Michael telling him to build an abbey on a spit of rock off the coast of France where the Couesnon River divides Brittany to the south and Normandy to the north. Originally the river flowed such that <u>Mont Saint Michel</u> was situated in Brittany, but over the centuries the course of the river has changed slightly such that nowadays the island church is just over the line in Normandy (to the chagrin of the residents of Brittany I might add). During high tide the dot of land became an island completely surrounded by water, while at low tide it was surrounded by mud flats featuring dangerous stretches of quicksand making it a risky trek to get there on foot or horseback. All in all it would seem like a ridiculous place to attempt building anything at all, but build they did, a small church at first. The original monks it seems were hermits living apart from society, <u>Mont Saint Michel</u> being an excellent location to reinforce solitude, but by 966 the abbey was home to Benedictine monks. The church as we see it today was begun in1017 and was built over a series of crypts designed to serve as a foundation on the otherwise rocky, uneven terrain of the island. Work continued well into the Gothic period, on the apse especially, since the Romanesque apse collapsed and had to be rebuilt. Overall, though, the design of the abbey is Romanesque. A small town with a single street grew up around the abbey and the entire community was walled in, partially to protect the inhabitants from rising water but conveniently also serving to protect them from invaders, which has proved useful during times of war and social upheaval.

Centuries later during the French Revolution, when the notion of monks and churches and Christianity were deemed out of vogue, <u>Mont Saint Michel</u> was confiscated by the French government and used as a prison, ironically at first to house arrested clergy who refused to denounce their vows to the Church. The prison was eventually closed in 1863 and fifteen years later they even built a causeway across the perilous mudflats so that pilgrims and tourists could access the church safely. This in turn silted up the bay, so now there are plans to remove the causeway in the hope of restoring <u>Mont Saint Michel</u>'s island status.   An alternative transport system will be devised to bring people safely to and from the mainland and <u>Mont Saint Michel</u>.

Back in their day, abbeys like <u>Mont Saint Michel</u> housed monks keen to convert the non-Christian newcomers to their neighborhood to the faith. It wasn't an easy transition as many Nordic residents of Normandy felt like their leaders were selling out on their Scandinavian heritage when they chucked the old pagan religion, but with time, the citizens of this region melded into the Christian fold. <u>Mont Saint Michel</u> is unique due to its unusual location, but typical church architecture in Normandy had a style all its own compared to other regions in France, and the abbeys here served as the primary inspiration of Gothic cathedral design later on.

Of all the Norman dukes, perhaps the best remembered is William the Conqueror, who ruled in the mid-eleventh century. The men's abbey of **<u>Saint Etienne</u>** located in Caen, France, in the Normandy district was commissioned by William the Conqueror in 1064, and he was eventually buried at this church. It was a Benedictine abbey, although the Cistercians also built numerous abbeys in the region. <u>Saint Etienne</u> has three small individual portals instead of the frequently seen double portal on Romanesque churches, and it is similar to the abbey at Fontenay in that the portals are small and there is no art in the tympana. Norman abbeys were the first medieval churches to incorporate a symbolic message into the façade design. Look how many times the number three is repeated: there are three doors with three lancet windows above and another three above that. The façade is divided into vertical thirds by buttresses, and horizontally into thirds by a repeated variation in the brickwork called a *stringcourse* separating the level with the doors from each the rows of windows. Even the soaring twin *towers* flanking the façade, although not having special meaning by themselves, were originally divided into three segments almost resembling Lego blocks (the fancy "party hats" atop the towers, called *spires* were a later Gothic addition).   This repetition of the number three is to symbolically recall the Holy Trinity – the Father, Son, and Holy Spirit – a Christian precept passed down by Oral Tradition since the days of the Apostles (no explanation of the Trinity appears in the <u>Bible</u>; the word "trinity" isn't even in the Bible).

The interior of the church originally followed the old Early Christian model of leaving rafters open to the roof structure, which allowed the architects to add a clerestory above the gallery which in turn was above the aisles flanking the nave on either side. With the nave wall divided into three sections – the nave arcade, gallery and clerestory - the symbolic division into three was expressed in the interior as well as on the church façade.   The exposed rafters were an unsatisfactory construction solution in the long run, though, and in 1120 a stone ceiling was constructed using a new architectural technique called ***ribbed groin vaulting***. This style of vaulting, more typical in Gothic churches later on, allowed the architects to keep their clerestory, which had been a problem with the old fashioned barrel vaulting.   This vaulting construction will be explained in the next chapter, as it is more typical of Gothic churches.

Meanwhile over in England, many more churches were being built employing their own version of Norman architecture design.   William the Conqueror invaded England in 1066 and at the Battle of Hastings, William's victory made England a Norman possession.   Politically these ties would endure for some time, and the connection between the two countries also created a cultural bridge across the English Channel when it came to architecture style.

The historical account of this invasion, albeit told from the point of view of the French Normans, is preserved in The **<u>Bayeux Tapestry</u>**. This remarkable artifact is actually not a woven tapestry at all, but rather a 20 inch high by 230 feet long embroidered cloth. For centuries the legend was that William's wife, Matilda created the embroidery with help from her ladies in waiting to honor her husband's military success. Recent scholarship has overturned that romantic tale however and it now seems more likely that the cloth was commissioned by Bishop Odo, who was William's half-brother. It is likely that he commissioned the tapestry around the time his new cathedral in Bayeux was commissioned, and that it was completed in time for the cathedral's dedication in 1077. Further, the tapestry was most likely not created in France but rather in England under the Bishop's instructions, employing Anglo-Saxon artists and relying on local seamstresses to do the needlepoint work. Odo was awarded the title of Earl of Kent, a position of authority and power in southern England following the success at Hastings which would have put him going back and forth across the Channel to attend duties in both France and England.   Additionally, the dyes used in the cloth and embroidery are typical of those used in England, and particular variations in the Latin captions found throughout the scenes telling the story suggest Anglo-Saxon influence.

The story unfolds in 1064 at the Royal Palace of Westminster (London).   The king, Edward the Confessor, is talking to his brother-in-law, Harold, the Earl of Wessex. Harold departs on horseback with hunting dogs and hawk, heading to his family's estate in Sussex. After attending church to pray for a safe voyage, he and his entourage set sail. But their ship is blown off course, and they wind up landing in Normandy by mistake in the territory of fierce Count Guy, who takes Harold prisoner. Duke William (who would later be the story's hero, "William the Conqueror") hears about Harold's arrest and demands that Count Guy, who serves the Duke, release Harold. Guy complies, and he and Harold ride off, both with their hawks, to meet William (Guy is in front, pointing back to Harold as they meet William).   William must have envied their cool hawks, because in the next scene he takes Harold's, and the men ride off to William's palace at Rouen.

Harold next joins William in battle against Duke Conan of Brittany (Mont Saint Michel appears in the scene). Some soldiers start to sink into the quicksand near Mont Saint Michel but Harold rescues them. Duke Conan escapes, but they catch up with him and he surrenders in battle. William rewards Harold for his services by offering Harold his coat of arms. The ceremony would be interpreted as Harold accepting William as his overlord, which is an important detail as the story continues. William and Harold return to Bayeux where Harold swears a solemn oath on holy relics, presumably furthering his allegiance to William. He is then set free and sails back to England.

Harold now goes to visit King Edward who is shown looking sick and frail. He dies on January 5, 1066 and is buried at Westminster Abbey. Two noblemen offer the crown and ax, symbols of royalty and authority, to Harold and he accepts. The next day he is crowned king, with the Archbishop of Canterbury presiding and people cheering. Halley's Comet appears, which everyone assumes is an evil omen and the people are frightened. Meanwhile back in France, William hears that Edward has died and Harold is the new king. William is furious because he believes he should be king since Harold swore to be his loyal subject. He decides to attack England to claim his throne. Bishop Odo appears for the first time here showing his support for William. The boats are loaded and the army sets sail.

The army lands at Pevensey on September 28th and the men stock up on provisions as they march toward Hastings, where they enjoy a magnificent feast. William takes counsel from Odo among others, and a castle-like fort is constructed to strengthen their base. A messenger brings the news of William's arrival to Harold. On October 14, 1066, William's soldiers, dressed in full armor, ride off to meet Harold's army. The battle ensues. Arrows and lances fly every which way and many men fall. The English troops are all on foot while the Norman soldiers ride horses. Brutality and violence rule the day. Curiously, Odo uses a club rather than a sword because bishops were not allowed to spill blood … but apparently it was okay to bludgeon an opponent to death. At one point William's horse is killed and he raises his helmet to show his men that he is still alive and fighting so they will not falter in battle. King Harold is shot in the eye (ouch) and killed, and the English soldiers scatter leaving William the victor. The final scene is lost, but most likely it showed William being crowned King of England.

(England)

William's victory at Hastings was the first step toward ruling England, and bringing Norman influence in architecture to his new realm. The most famous Norman-designed church in England is **Durham Cathedral**. Also built as a Benedictine abbey, the church at Durham was unique because Durham itself was unique. Durham enjoyed a level of independence from the English crown, in that this region, called Northumbria, was recognized as having both religious and secular jurisdiction over itself. This arrangement probably evolved because Northumbria is just south of the Scottish border, and the English, like the Romans before them had learned that the Scots were "difficult" (as in nearly impossible) to rule. The English were just as glad to have Northumbria handle its own problems and serve as a semi-independent buffer zone between Scotland

and the rest of England.   In Northumbria, the **bishopric** (bishop's seat) is located at Durham, and during the Romanesque period, the bishop served as both the leader of the Church and also as effective head of state.   And so it was that Durham Cathedral was at once both a Benedictine abbey, and also the cathedral home church of the bishop.

Durham Cathedral enjoys a dramatic setting as it is perched high on a cliff overlooking a bend in the River Weir below, a location that came in handy as it made attacking the church more difficult than if it had been situated on easily approached flat land.   From the river below, you can see that Durham Cathedral is more ornate than Saint Etienne, but that in England there was no interest in topping the massive square towers with elaborate spires, then or centuries later.   Inside, this huge church displays some of the most unique architectural design of any church of this period, and for this reason it attracts more than its fair share of tourists.   Like English churches in general, Durham Cathedral places greater emphasis on being long rather than on being tall, but in anyone's vocabulary, the church is mammoth in size.

In order to incorporate both clerestory windows and a stone ceiling, in 1133 the architects here employed ribbed groin vaulting like we saw at Saint Etienne, again foreshadowing the ceiling structure of preference during the Gothic period and hence ahead of it time. ‣ Although Durham made use of groin vaulting, which was more sophisticated than the more common barrel vaulting, it is still clearly Romanesque as the outward thrust of the vaulting is still handled primarily through thick, buttressed walls further aided by additional bracing in the gallery.   In fact, the gallery barely has room for anyone to stand for all the structural supports there propping up the nave vaulting; fortunately the church was so large that it really didn't need the extra floor space a gallery might provide anyway.

The nave arcade is both unique and more decorative than other churches of this period.   There are humongous cylindrical piers, all decoratively carved in distinctive and unusual patterns, chevrons, diamonds, and spiral fluting (grooved stripes).   These alternate with massive **compound piers** that are huge supports decorated with colonnettes and which carry the weight from the ribs in the vaulting above.

Durham Cathedral, like many other Benedictine abbeys, houses relics of those long gone, but who have through the centuries served as an inspiration to the Christian community.   It is home to the bones of the Venerable Bede, a beloved English monk who lived around 700 and who is considered one of the most learned men of his day.   He studied and wrote English literature as well as being a scripture scholar, a theologian, and an expert in his time on scientific treatises, historical works and biographies.   His most very famous work, Ecclesiastical History is admired to this day as being the foundation for much of our understanding of early European history.

The remains of Saint Cuthbert, also enshrined at Durham, have an interesting history.   Cuthbert was an early bishop at Lindesfarne, following Saint Aidan in that post some fifty years later in 685.   An extraordinarily virtuous man, after his death he was buried at Lindesfarne.   Eleven years after his burial, Cuthbert's remains were dug up so they could be placed in a more honored spot within the church.   Surprise, surprise ... they expected to find nothing but bones, but old Cuthbert was still completely intact, as if sleeping, pliable joints and all!   The casket was later moved to Durham Cathedral, and in 1104, to quell a dispute over whether the monks had been lying centuries earlier, the casket was opened again and Cuthbert was still *incorrupt*, perfectly preserved, and flexible (say as opposed to mummies which are stiff and unnatural).

During the 16th century Henry VIII broke away from the Catholic Church and among his many enterprises in the realm of religion in England, he confiscated all abbeys both to gradually get rid of monks, and also to take possession of their wealth. In the process, Henry demanded that all relics be destroyed. In 1537 Henry's henchmen arrived at Durham and demanded that the shrines of Cuthbert and Venerable Bede be destroyed. The men dispatched were named Lee, Henley and Blythman, and their records survive describing how Henley demanded that the casket be opened and the bones cast out. The poor monk who was forced to open the casket became upset when the process of prying it open left one of Cuthbert's legs broken, and he further replied that he couldn't throw out the bones because they were still held together in the saint's body. Then Lee stepped up to the casket to see inside, and he told Henley that the saint was entire. Henley didn't believe it so he went up to look too, and he even handled the body.

The men didn't know what to do, so they told the monks to carry the body into the vestry (or sacristy – the room where priests get dressed for Mass) until they could get instructions from the king on how to proceed. Some five years later the few remaining monks at Durham were given permission to bury Cuthbert, but what nobody knows to this day is whether they did what they were told, or whether the monks hid the body of Cuthbert and buried somebody else in Cuthbert's robes instead. In any event, the new tomb was opened again in 1827, but all they found was a skeleton, either Cuthbert having decayed since 1537, or an imposter buried for Cuthbert's protection. If the latter is true, the monks responsible for the ruse took their secret to the grave with them.

(Sicily)

Normally when we think of the Norman conquests we focus on France and England, but as it happens, Sicily not only became a Norman stronghold during the Romanesque period, some of the most unique and distinctively beautiful churches are found there. So how did the Normans wind up in Sicily?

Sicily is a large island off the coast of southern Italy; on a map it resembles a football being kicked by a boot (Italy). Although it is part of Italy today, albeit still retaining its own independent character, over the centuries this island was a prize possession grabbed by a succession of conquerors. It was first settled by Greeks and Phoenicians in ancient times, then the Greeks, Romans and Carthaginians fought over Sicily. In 535 it was captured by the Ostrogoths. These Eastern Germanic people had been absorbed into the Constantinople orbit during the previous century, so they introduced Byzantine Christianity to Sicily. In the 8th century when the Iconoclast Controversy caused a rift between the emperor in Constantinople and the pope in Rome, the emperor yanked Sicily away from the jurisdiction of the Catholic Church and assigned it to the patriarch in Constantinople, thus eliminating the pope's influence over the island. Sicily remained a Byzantine cultural center until the 9th century, when Muslim Arabs living in northern Africa began to settle in Sicily in increasing numbers.

In 965 their occupation was complete, having toppled the last Byzantine stronghold on the island, and Sicily was brought under Muslim rule. Christianity was tolerated, but not encouraged, and many Christians were converted to Islam. So by the start of the Romanesque period, Sicily was a Muslim country in the middle of the Mediterranean, with pockets of surviving Eastern Christian culture quietly getting by.

In 1059, just a few years before the start of the Crusades, the pope decided to intervene in a the hope of discouraging the spread of Islam through the Mediterranean; southern Spain as you already know had fallen to Islam and Sicily was just a little too close to Italian soil to feel comfortable. The pope granted feudal rights to govern the island to a Norman family who moved south to meet the challenge of taking on the Muslim leadership there. By 1091 the Normans had successfully gained control of Sicily on behalf of the pope, and Roger I was named the first Count of Sicily.

The Norman rulers turned out to be broadminded and fair. They may have been the conquering victors bringing Western Christianity to Sicily, but they generously supported the Byzantine Greek Orthodox monasteries to encourage continuation of that culture, and so as not to disenfranchise the Muslims, the government encouraged Muslim communities to continue the peaceful practice of their religion, and the Norman rulers even went out of their way to employ Muslims in government posts, especially the military which showed not just tolerance, but also trust.

The **Capella Palatino** in Palermo, Sicily, was built by Roger II between 1132 and 1189 as a private palace chapel, not unlike Charlemagne's Palatine Chapel centuries earlier. This exquisite architecture jewel illustrates the marriage of Western Norman architecture and Eastern Byzantine art, with some Islamic influence introduced in the form of Muslim 8-point stars employed in clusters to create Christian crosses in the ceiling design, making this chapel truly unique. Just as Charlemagne had a throne set up in the Palatine Chapel, in the Capella Palatino Roger likewise had a special throne installed for himself so he could be surrounded by the glory of all the mosaics while retaining his own importance over others who might join him in worship. The oldest mosaics in the chapel are those in the domed ceiling. There we find a traditional Byzantine Christ Pantocrator surrounded by angels, then further encircled by Apostles and saints. The shimmering images are labeled in Greek, suggesting that the artists were the best Greek Orthodox talent money could buy. The subject of the mosaics in the apse and transept is the Acts of the Apostles. Mosaics further back from the apse illustrate scenes from the Old and New Testaments, These are of slightly lesser quality, and since they offer their inscriptions in Latin rather than Greek, it is assumed that the craftsmen producing these were probably local talent.

While the Byzantine churches we studied earlier were all variations on central plan design, some Byzantine churches even dating from the earliest days were basilicas. The biggest difference between a Byzantine basilica and a typically Catholic one is that most Catholic basilicas end in a single apse, while the Byzantine design favored a main apse at the end of the nave, a smaller apse at the end of the single aisle flanking the nave on either side, creating a triple-apse plan. Norman Sicilian churches favored the Byzantine 3-apse basilica design. While Capella Palatino is a modestly scaled early example of this style of architecture, **Monreale Cathedral** near Palermo is a spectacular example of a full-scale huge cathedral built with all the bells and whistles of Norman Sicilian design.

Work on this church began in 1174 under the direction of a later Norman successor, William II, and in 1182 the church was dedicated to Assumption of the Virgin Mary and elevated to the status of a cathedral. William died in 1189, but not before seeing most of the work completed on his gorgeous church. The exterior is quite modest and plain (the portico is actually a later addition). Clearly the outside was never intended to be the focal point of the church design.

Step inside to appreciate this magnificent cathedral. Almost every surface of the interior is decorated with intricate, colorful mosaics. Along the nave walls there are 130 individual mosaic scenes from the Old Testament. The mosaics lining the narrow aisles, which can be easily seen from the nave, tell the story of Christ's life. In both cases there are mosaic inscriptions in Latin or Greek offering written accounts alongside the images. Consider the **Sacrifice of Isaac**, an Old Testament scene found above the nave arcade at Monreale. The mosaic technique may be Byzantine, but the style of the figures, which are naturally proportioned and show an interest in anatomy, bear little resemblance to the elongated, flat figures associated with true Byzantine style. The artist depicts Abraham in an action pose as he prepares to sacrifice his son, and the ram which will become the actual sacrifice as the story unfolds, is caught in a thicket which has been included in a modest attempt to show a landscape setting.

Above the altar in the apse there is a humungous **Christ Pantocrator**, looking more benign and kind than many Byzantine examples, and there is a smaller but likewise impressive Madonna enthroned holding the Christ Child immediately below. Flanking the Mother of God and Christ Child are angels and Apostles. Saints Peter and Paul get special billing as they presented in the conch domes in the two smaller apses located at the east ends of the two side aisles. Off to the side and well away from being a visual focal point in the church there is a mosaic of **Christ Blessing King William** as the patron of this beautiful church. It's worth noting the differences between this mosaic of a Western king found inside a church, and what might seem at first glance to be a similar mosaic of Eastern emperor Justinian (Justinian Mosaic) found inside the church of San Vitale. Both are secular rulers included in church art, but there the similarities end. While Justinian had his mosaic showcased as the primary art in the holy sanctuary apse of the church, William's mosaic is less prominently displayed. William is portrayed in a smaller scale than Christ and situated physically below the enthroned Christ while receiving a blessing from his Master to whom he pays homage as if to say, "All that I am is by the grace of God." In contrast, Justinian opts to be portrayed as the Messiah himself, halo and all!

There is no gallery in this church, allowing for larger than usual clerestory windows which provide ample natural light to see the art. For as truly awe-inspiring as the embellishment is on these Norman Sicilian churches, do note that complex vaulting in the nave like we might find in French or English Norman churches is absent. The Norman churches built in Sicily mostly favored the old Early Christian model of rafters open to the roof structure above. In the case of <u>Monreale Cathedral</u>, even the rafters and roof interior were lavishly decorated, but from an engineering standpoint the structure is less sophisticated than a church like Durham Cathedral.

Some periods in history end abruptly due to specific events that usher in a new era. Others enter into a period of decline and die a slow death over time. The Romanesque period did neither. It evolved gradually into the Gothic period over several decades between the middle of the 12th century on into the 13th in a nearly seamless transition.

10. Gothic

c.1150 - 1400

The Gothic period began around 1150, while the Romanesque period was still going strong, and the two overlapped for at least a half-century. By 1400, it had given way to the Early Renaissance, so the grand finale to the Middle Ages spanned roughly two and a half centuries. As we saw during other medieval periods, the people living in the late 12th through 14th centuries did not imagine themselves to be "gothic." The term "gothic" was first applied during the 16th century by an artist-author named Vasari, initially as a derogatory expression of contempt for the fancy styles popular at this time. The name stuck, although the negative connotations are long gone.

While many changes took place during this final stage of medieval culture, everything can be linked to one significant factor that started a long chain of reaction: the waning of the Crusades. The Crusades dwindled on into the 13th century, but as they gradually petered out, two resources that were formerly consumed by war in large quantities were now more readily available back home: men and money. Initially the latter had the greater impact. Try to imagine yourself living in a Romanesque world. If you were a nobleman who discovered that you suddenly had a great deal more disposable income, what would you buy with that money? Land! Sure you would, because in a feudal society, status and wealth were measured by landholdings. Accordingly, with the decline of the Crusades, there was a gradual shift in European demographics. Those who could afford it bought out those with less; the richest big landowners offered welcome cash to small landowners for their property. Think about it. If a family owned 100,000 acres, and had the money to double their holdings, graduating to a 200,000-acre landowner status, it should increase their position in society quite a bit. In contrast, if a family owned a 10-acre plot, and could also afford to double their holdings, becoming a 20-acre landowner isn't going to set the world on fire. And so it was that the big nobles bought out the smaller nobles and vassals who really didn't stand much of a shot at the big time anyway.

Over time, a dual society emerged. First, the old feudal system was still alive and well with status measured in landholdings, and an economy based on agriculture. The difference now was that the big shot nobility owned immense landholdings and likewise held vast power as, compliments of primogeniture, they maintained sizable private armies and they also controlled thousands of serfs. At the other end of the spectrum, there was a new and growing culture of people who were displaced from feudal society as they had either sold their land, or they were serfs who had the security of a homestead sold out from under them. These folks had no place in the agricultural world of feudalism, and they moved to towns, which rapidly grew into cities, or in some cases, they created cities from nothing. If there happened to be an old pilgrimage church in the region that was no longer fully used now that crusaders weren't marching through, it made sense to build homes around it as at least the great expense of providing a church for the community was already covered. The Gothic period is associated with the rapid growth of cities, and along with that, a rapid increase in population (that's where having the men back home factors in ... ahem ...). By rough estimates, Paris had mushroomed to a population of 100,000 people by 1200, and a century later it was up to 150,000. London had a population of about 20,000, and Brugge and Ghent in Flanders boasted 50,000 citizens apiece by 1200. In Italy, Milan, Venice and Florence hovered around 100,000 each by 1300.

One of the pressing problems presented with such a dramatic restructuring of society was how these new urban populations would earn a living. Obviously they could not farm, therefore people turned to commerce and industry. Many people had to learn new trades, and toward this end guilds were formed where someone might apprentice to learn skills, then join the guild which would see to it that professional standards were maintained, and the system protected wages as well. The Gothic period is also when universities began to sprout up across Europe, offering people a chance to learn more than simple job skills. Literacy rates improved, and Europe enjoyed an intellectual growth that exceeded anything seen in this part of the world before.

The changes in Europe at this time led to the formation of new monastic orders, created to meet the needs of the people. The Franciscan Order was founded in 1209 under the direction of Saint Francis of Assisi, and the Dominican Order was founded in 1215 under the direction of Saint Dominic. Both of these orders are a departure from the old Benedictine model (and for that matter, they are different from the Cluniac and Cistercian orders for the same reason); neither Franciscans nor Dominicans kept themselves removed from society, living off in monasteries.

Francesco Bernadone, was the founder of the Franciscan Order. Francesco, or Francis as he is called in English, was the son of a wealthy silk merchant in the newly emerging commercial markets in Italy. Papa had every expectation that his only son would inherit the business and prosper, and in his youth, Francis seemed to be heading in that direction. He lived a cavalier lifestyle, until he was in his early 20's and fell seriously ill upon his return from fighting in a minor war. He is said to have seen visions of Christ, who instructed him to rebuild his Church. Francis didn't really "get it" at first, but understood enough to know his merry days of being a wealthy bachelor were over. He renounced his title and all worldly goods, and went off to live as a hermit while rebuilding an old dilapidated church near his hometown. Everyone thought he had lost his mind, including his father who publicly disinherited him in front of the whole town. In one of the most dramatic moments in Christian history, Francis stripped himself of his clothing, which he returned to his father, along with his name. All the while, despite the blight on his reputation, Francis developed a following of like-minded men who had a gut-sense that Francis was on the right track.

In time, Francis discerned that it wasn't so much his efforts as a contractor that God sought, but rather his calling was to rebuild the spiritual Church, which perhaps needed a good nudge. He sought an audience with Pope Innocent III, and while others at Saint Peter's wondered if Francis might be a heretic, the pope saw things otherwise. He gave his blessing to the new order, which set about helping the poor. Franciscans until relatively recently made it a rule to own nothing. Nowadays they are permitted to own the buildings where they reside, but in the old days as *medicants* (religious who combine monastic vows with life outside an abbey, and who do not own personal or community property), these wandering *friars* (brothers) were expected to beg for everything from shelter to food to clothes. The Franciscans cared for the terminally ill of their day that most people avoided, like lepers, and they helped care for the poor. A childhood acquaintance of Francesco's named Clare was very moved by his ministry, and founded a sister order called the Poor Clares. They were quite unique, as nuns in this order frequently worked alongside the men caring for the sick and dying as opposed to being shut away in a convent embroidering altar cloths. As a point of trivia about Francis of Assisi, he is the first documented and verified stigmatist in Christian history. Those who receive the stigmata develop the wounds of Christ – bleeding holes in their hands and/ or feet. Over time the Franciscans gravitated to cities where they lived in the slums helping the poor. They are still around today. You would be most likely to find Franciscans in hospitals where they minister to the sick, in schools, or in underprivileged neighborhoods where they run youth programs.

The Dominican Order was created initially to combat assorted heresies of the day. The most famous of these was the Albigensian Heresy, but there were others too: the Cathars, the Waldensians and more. Some of these groups were basically benign and the Church didn't worry *too* much about them, like the Waldensians who for the most part didn't hurt anybody, but tinkered with how they celebrated the Mass. Others were more of a handful in that some promoted wild promiscuity, and especially problematic were those that got the nifty idea that it was a good thing to assassinate the clergy, a pastime guaranteed to alarm bishops and priests who preferred not to be murdered.

Dominic de Guzman, a Spaniard, was a priest and scholar. While traveling in Southern France, he and his bishop became acquainted with Cistercian monks who were trying to bring the Cathars back into the Church. Dominic believed that he could do a better job of it. He dressed humbly and went among the people preaching the Gospel, but also listening to their concerns and talking to them directly about their faith. Pope Honorius III gave final approval for Dominic to train up a band of mendicant preachers prepared to depend on the goodness of others to get along, and the Dominican Order was founded. Although mendicants, and therefore usually not in residence at an abbey, the Dominicans were granted the Early Christian church of Santa Sabina (see the Early Christian chapter) as a home base for their order. This gift was made by Honorius III, and Santa Sabina remains the mother church of the Dominicans to this day.

Dominican friars would travel town to town like the Apostles did, teaching the faith as they went. Obviously monks with this type of assignment couldn't very well live off in rural abbeys. As time went on, and the heresies subsided, Dominicans took on the task of building universities to provide higher learning for others. Most universities across Europe started out as Catholic Church sponsored institutions. At that point the Dominicans began living in the equivalent of faculty housing, so even if there were a common house where the men lived together, it was hardly fruitful to have it way off in the country someplace. A point of trivia about Dominic: the prayers of the rosary date back to this saint. It is said that the Virgin Mary appeared to him and encouraged him to ask for her prayers to God to assist the monks in their tribulations working with heretics. Dominican monks are still around today, and are often associated with institutions of learning, especially universities.

Obviously, most church construction during the Gothic period was in urban areas. Feudal estates still had whatever chapels were needed to handle the rural populations, but many cities had grown to where churches that had been around at the end of the Romanesque period were inadequate to meet current demand. The churches were built huge to accommodate burgeoning populations that were expected to continue to increase. Many of the largest and most spectacular churches popping up in cities were seats for bishops, and these churches are called *cathedrals.* Gothic churches were designed to house large, local populations, as well as many friars and nuns of the Dominican and Franciscan orders as these *religious* (friars, monks and nuns) would not have their own churches like monks and nuns in other orders customarily had. There was also a philosophical attitude toward church design that originated in France, where it was believed that being in church should be an ethereal experience like a little sliver of heaven on Earth. There was a push to make churches taller and taller, as though they were soaring up to heaven, and a concerted effort to alter the atmosphere inside with colored light filtered through stained glass such that the overall experience might seem otherworldly.

France

The first Gothic church we will consider is **Notre Dame de Chartres**, or as it is more commonly known, **Chartres Cathedral**. The "real" name, translated, means *Our Lady of* Chartres. Many Gothic churches were dedicated to the Virgin Mary, hence there is almost always a Notre Dame church in every town; in this case, the town of Chartres which is located southwest of Paris. For this reason, you must always identify the city, as calling a church simply Notre Dame is seldom enough information since there were so many of them. During the Gothic period there was a general increase of respect toward women. This was the age of chivalry! Why? Partly because the men discovered and had to admit that the women had done a decent job of taking care of business during the height of the Crusades when so many men were away. Women were credited with being more capable, and with that acknowledgment came respect. Thus, by extension, there was an increased interest in female saints. In the past most churches were named after male saints and Apostles, but less frequently female saints. Mary had never been ignored going back to Early Christian times, but devotion to the Virgin rose to immense popularity at this time. In part, this was due to the Dominicans' affection for Mary after Dominic's experience with Mary's apparition and the rosary. Certainly as important women in the Christian tradition go, it's hard to top Jesus' Mom, and Christians exalted Mary as Queen of Heaven with her crown of twelve stars (Revelations 12). Christians had long been in the habit of asking saints to pray with them, and who better than the Queen Mother? After all, the Queen Mum was a popular intercessor in Old Testament times with earthly kings, and Scripture offers testimonial that Jesus likewise honored his mother's request, even if he wasn't especially inclined to do what she was asking (John 2: 1-11).

Chartres Cathedral is a famous church from this period, serving as a bishop's seat and the destination of many pilgrimages since it was home to a cloak of the Virgin Mary which was kept here as a relic. It was built as an Early Gothic Church, although fire damage toward the end of the 12th century ruined parts of the church that had to be rebuilt. When new construction was undertaken, High Gothic elements were introduced. For our purposes, we will focus only on the church in terms of Early Gothic style. The west façade shows strong influence from French Norman abbeys like Saint Etienne.

Notice how the façade has been divided into thirds to recall the Holy Trinity again. There are three portals, with three *lancet windows* above. These tall, narrow windows would soon fall out of fashion as the visual focal point on French Gothic churches. Vertically the façade is divided into thirds with buttresses just the same as at Saint Etienne. Horizontally, above the lancet windows we have a new kind of window, a *rose window*. The rose window is a common feature on French Gothic Cathedrals, especially those dedicated to Mary. In narrow terms, the rose window symbolizes the Virgin Mary. In broad terms, the rose window symbolizes the Church and God's domain on Earth. Above the rose window is a small band of sculpture called the *gallery of kings*, representing Old Testament kings. This was not part of the original design on Chartres, but rather added later. Eventually the gallery of kings became a regular part of exterior design in France, although it would not normally be located in this position.

There are twin towers flanking the façade, with elaborate pointy spires added on top, just like Saint Etienne. On the Romanesque church the towers held no particular symbolic message, but on a French Gothic church they symbolize a strong show of support between the kings of France and the popes in Rome. One could date this cordial rapport back to the days of Charlemagne, but during the Gothic period it became expedient for the French monarchs to beef up the good relationship in case they needed help from the pope. Remember how the big lords and nobles bought out all the little guys, and recall also how these now super big landowners had their own private armies? Well, the king wasn't stupid; he knew well that it wouldn't take much for one of these noblemen to topple the French government if he ever had a mind to do so. The king went ahead and "bought insurance" if you will, by pledging to the pope that if there were ever another crusade, the pope could count on the king of France and his army to fight. In return, the pope, who was still maintaining an army leftover from the Crusades just in case, promised the king that if any of the nobles got too big for his britches and tried to overthrow the government, that the pope would send in soldiers to help defend the king.

Notice that around the doors of Chartres there is much more art than is normally found on Romanesque churches. The three doors at the west entrance on Chartres Cathedral are called the **Royal Portal**. Gone are the old scary images of the Last Judgment seen on Romanesque tympanums. The tympanum on the right shows Mary holding the infant Jesus, and the one of the left depicts the Ascension of Jesus into heaven. The central portal is the main entrance, and above that door we see the glorified Christ enthroned in a mandorla. He is not judgmental and stern like Romanesque sculpture, but more serene. Jesus is surrounded by the symbolic representations of the four gospels. An easy way to remember the four Gospel symbols is ALBE (pronounced like a name – Al-bee). The first Gospel is Matthew, whose symbol is the Angel (A), second is Mark, whose symbol is the Lion (L), then comes Luke, who is likened to a Bull (B), and finally, John, who is the Eagle (E). Although these images come from the Book of Revelation, describing the four beasts attending God on his throne in heaven, often the same symbols stand in for the Gospel authors and their books in the Bible in both medieval manuscripts and sculpture with the artist assuming that you know what it means. Moving down from the tympanum, notice that the doors have numerous statues on either side, almost like a receiving line in stone as you enter the church. These are **Jamb Statues**. Jamb statues were representations of Bible heroes (Old as well as New Testament), Apostles and saints. They are always shown in a friendly disposition and

183

their function is just as it seems, they make you feel welcome as you enter the church. While the Romanesque Church often emphasized a stern God and the punishments inflicted on those who sin, the Gothic Church preferred a more forgiving attitude where the emphasis was on helping the faithful achieve salvation. You could think of the former as negative reinforcement, while the latter offers more positive reinforcement.

Let's turn out attention to another Early Gothic cathedral, **Notre Dame de Paris**, or **Paris Cathedral**. Construction on Paris Cathedral began about 30 years after Chartres, although the site in the heart of Paris had religious connections dating all the way back to a Roman temple to Jupiter. An Early Christian church dedicated to Saint Stephen was built on the site in the 6th century, and it became the city's cathedral in the 10th century. The old church was demolished in 1160 to make way for the grand Gothic church we see today. The west façade is a perfectly developed example of early Gothic style. Like Chartres, the façade of Paris Cathedral is divided both horizontally and vertically into thirds which recalls the Holy Trinity, with twin towers. Notice that the gallery of kings in now below the rose window, which is its correct location. The symbolism now adds commentary on the structure of society. The portals with their welcoming jamb statues stand for the people, folks like you and me at the lowest echelon of society. Above the people is the gallery of kings, which represents Old Testament Kings from the Bible and by extension, the role of all those who govern on earth. Finally, with power over the people *and* their government is the authority of God and the Church, symbolized by the beautiful rose window.

One of the best examples of High Gothic, or the mature version of this style, is **Notre Dame d'Amiens**, or **Amiens Cathedral**, located north of Paris. The original architect who created the overall design was Robert de Luzarches, although as you might imagine, these cathedrals took longer to build than one man's lifetime, so other architects took over as time went on. Hopefully you might notice how much more elaborate Amiens is than Chartres or Paris. You might also pay attention to the comparative scale between Early Gothic and High Gothic. Check out those portals – see how small the people look relative to the size of the building? Gothic churches grew to a mammoth size as city populations continued to mushroom. Looking at the façade in full, it might seem so ornate that the old simple symbolism seen on Chartres or Paris has been replaced by frosting rosettes, ribbons and bows, but it's all still there. There are jamb statues at the doors to greet the public, and the façade is divided both horizontally and vertically into thirds, symbolizing the Holy Trinity and the proper order of society. Finally, there are twin towers, although sadly, they were never finished. Had they been completed, the spires topping the towers would have been so tall that they probably would require flashing red lights nowadays to prevent incoming air traffic from plowing into them! These High Gothic churches took so long to build, and were so fabulously expensive, that few were ever completed before they ran out of steam or money or both. In some cases, construction on these churches dawdled on over many centuries, until they were completed not so long ago in modern times. As for Amiens, it was left in its incomplete state at the close of the Gothic period.

We will use the plan of Amiens Cathedral to discuss Gothic design. Like Romanesque churches, there is no atrium on Gothic cathedrals. While it is true they were urban churches like Early Christian prototypes that did include atriums, remember that most of the people coming to the Gothic churches were local residents and hence not traveling long distances to get here. There was usually an open town square in front the church which was adequate for organizing processions and milling about. Early Gothic churches maintained the separate narthex, but later designs like Amiens have only a modest open space at the entrance before launching directly into the nave. On either side of the nave, Gothic churches usually had only one side aisle used for circulation. There was no need to create a second aisle for crowd overflow because they just made the church big enough to accommodate a huge crowd from the start. At Amiens for example, the entire city could fit into the church for a single Mass! At the east end of the church we find the apse with the altar and tabernacle as we would expect. There is an ambulatory, which allows access to small radiating chapels, some of which might have relics, although many were simply provided for private devotions.

Notice that the transept has moved. It used to be right up next to the apse, but now it is shifted further west such that it appears to cut the nave in half. The segment of the nave that is east of the transept is called the *choir*. This is where friars and nuns stood during the Mass. Nowadays we associate the word choir with people singing. It didn't have that meaning originally, although it is easy to understand how this came about since monks (who live in monasteries), friars (monks who are normally mendicants, without their own abbeys) and nuns would frequently be chanting antiphons, psalms and hymns during the service. Moving the transept made it a good location now to add extra doors. Both the north and south transept on Gothic cathedrals had elaborate entrances almost as magnificent as the main portals in the west. This allowed the church to be filled and emptied relatively quickly considering its large size. A fringe benefit of this new and improved design was that Gothic churches could function as big cathedrals when this was advantageous, like Easter Sunday perhaps, but they could also be "little" for events that did not include the entire city, like weddings, baptisms, or funerals. Since all the friars and nuns would not be attending these private family affairs, the nave might not be used at all. The ceremony could take place entirely in the choir, with its more intimate relationship to the pastor in the apse.

Shall we step inside Amiens? Holy moly, talk about being inside a B-I-G church! The rise from the floor to the ceiling is 13 stories. The church itself is quite a bit taller than that of course, as the roof structure and the towers rise well above the top of the vaulting. In the photo, you are facing the apse, from a vantage point in the choir; the entire nave and narthex would be behind you! You can see that the nave wall has now been divided into three sections to echo the symbolism of three seen on the exterior. There is a tall nave arcade and equally tall clerestory windows, with what appears to be a little gallery in between. In fact, there is no gallery in High Gothic church design as they didn't need extra room What you see is a *triforium*, which is a fake gallery. It is only about as wide as a catwalk and there primarily for visual appeal rather than function. In order to include those colossal clerestory windows, which make Gothic interiors bright and beautiful with all that stained glass compared to Romanesque churches, the architects had to find a better ceiling design than old-fashioned barrel vaulting. Their solution was *ribbed groin vaulting*.

Ribbed groin vaulting functions differently from barrel vaulting. First, it relies on pointed arches rather than the traditional round arch. The advantage of the pointed arch is that it can cheat, and doesn't have to follow all the rules like a round arch does. Roman (round) arches have to be the same height and the same width, while carrying the same weight to do the same job. Pointed arches can be any width at all and do the same job, and that's what the architects needed here. Look at the image of the vaulting taken looking straight up at the ceiling. Notice that first there is a rib spanning straight across the nave, and then two ribs cross like an "X," then another straight across and so forth. In a barrel-vaulted ceiling, even if ribs are introduced, the structure itself is one straight across arch after another after another every linear inch down the nave wall such that the weight is distributed evenly, and there is no convenient place to stop and punch a hole in the wall for big windows. With ribbed groin vaulting, each of those rectangles with an "X" crossing is a *bay*, and the weight from above is being handled by the ribs. The weight comes down on the keystones and is distributed down and out along those ribs. The key factor here is that the arches crossing each other are wider than the ones going straight across. Can you see looking up at the ceiling how they are each a hypotenuse on a right triangle, and therefore longer than the other sides? The weight is being diverted to collective pressure points along the nave walls where more than one rib (typically, three) come together. To visually reinforce that multiple ribs are joining together at the support piers in the nave arcade, see how the piers have attached *colonnettes* (skinny columns) to visually carry the line of each rib to the floor? These are called *compound piers*. Where the ribs come together there is huge outward thrust that must be braced. In between the pressure points, however, there is no weight from above being placed on the walls at all. Therefore, the walls can be opened up with mammoth windows, and the integrity of the walls isn't threatened in the slightest.

The problem becomes how to handle the outward thrust at those pressure points along the nave where the ribs meet. The builders could have handled the problem the typically Romanesque way with colossal buttresses running down between the clerestory windows, and that would have worked just fine. The problem, however, with putting extra thick walls between the windows is that less light would be able to reach the windows at all, and what's the point of spectacular stained glass if there isn't enough light to see the beautiful images and to transform the church interior with a kaleidoscope of color? Instead, they employed *flying buttresses*. These are like arms that allow the walls between the clerestory windows to remain thin, while the flying buttresses carry the outward thrust over to enormous regular buttresses located far enough away from the wall that it doesn't interfere with light getting into the church.

Notre Dame de Reims, or **Reims Cathedral**, located northeast of Paris, is a contemporary church to Amiens Cathedral; they are almost identical in size and display similar elaborate embellishment. At Reims the stone tympanums have been replaced with additional windows of stained glass, but otherwise the two churches are very similar. Take a close look at the facade. Notice anything peculiar about Reims? How about that gallery of kings way up there at the top, and so oversized at that. What's going on here? If it were an earlier church, one might guess that the gallery of kings was a later addition like we saw at Chartres. But Reims is a mature high Gothic church, not transitional from Romanesque; this was the design from the beginning. The question is … why? Reims Cathedral enjoyed a special status among churches of this generation because it was used for the coronation of French kings. Accordingly, it was granted a special dispensation to have the gallery of kings more prominently displayed, even at the expense of the hierarchy usually seen with the rose window on top.

Let's turn our attention to the jamb statues at Reims Cathedral, especially compared to the Old Testament kings we saw flanking the Royal Portal at Chartres. The statues at Chartres Cathedral look like rigid columns with faces and then draped in starchy stiff robes compared to the more natural figures at Reims. Here we see figures representing two popular themes from the Gospel of Saint Luke. The **Annunciation** took place when the Archangel Gabriel came to tell the Virgin Mary of God's plan for her to be the mother of the Christ. The story of the **Visitation** follows when Mary, barely pregnant herself, sets out to visit her kinswoman Elizabeth, who despite being an older matron past the age of childbearing, is pregnant with John the Baptist. Notice how at Reims, unlike Chartres, there appear to have been different artists working on the project, each with a distinctive style. Here for example, there seem to be three different artists at work: one for the angel Gabriel, a different artist for Mary, and another sculptor for Mary and Elizabeth together in the second Bible account. The fact that artists are exhibiting their own individual styles speaks to the increased respect offered such masters in France.

The angel Gabriel is so distinctive and individualized that we call his otherwise unknown sculptor the "Master of Smiling Angels." Gabriel illustrates *International Style* in sculpture. We call it "International Style" because artists across Europe began using a similar style around the late Gothic and Early Renaissance periods. International Style in sculpture emphasized elongated figures with little emphasis on anatomy underneath the flowing garments. Mary in the Annunciation group is apparently not by the same artist as there is no animated quality or elongated torso.

The Visitation figures are clearly classical, recalling statues from ancient Greece and especially Rome. They were created by a particular shop of sculptors working at Reims Cathedral between 1230 and 1235 who appear to have imported influence from Italy. The city of Reims dates back to being a major center in ancient Gaul, which was captured by Augustus Caesar during the 1st century BC. There may have been local examples of classical art in the Julio-Claudian style left behind that served as models for these Gothic sculptors. It is significant because this brief flowering of classical influence predates similar trends in Italy by a full century.

The last French church to be considered is the petite **Sainte Chapelle**, located in Paris. Obviously with its diminutive size, it was not built as a great cathedral. Sainte Chapelle was commissioned by King Louis IX as a palace chapel (in this regard, similar to Charlemagne and the Palatine Chapel) adjacent to what was at that time, the royal palace in downtown Paris. Louis had a large personal collection of relics from Christ's Passion, and what he created in Sainte Chapelle was not so much a church in the conventional sense, as a building-size *reliquary*, or box where relics are kept. Inside, see how the walls melt away so that nearly everywhere you look there is stained glass, with barely any solid structure to hold it together. We call this the *Rayonnant* style. The stained glass windows here illustrate the Nativity and Passion of Christ, and the life of Saint John the Baptist. The king's own story of his quest for sacred relics is also memorialized in stained glass, which is fitting in that Louis IX was canonized to sainthood himself about fifty years later.

Sainte Chapelle may have more stained glass per square foot than other French churches, but the most famous stained glass windows are in Chartres Cathedral. Unlike many other Gothic churches in France, which had to replace broken windows after bombing raids during World War II, the windows at Chartres are original. The townspeople showed great foresight by removing the windows and burying them during the war, so they could be reinstalled in mint condition once peace was restored. The blues and reds in medieval glass are much richer than comparable windows manufactured today. In a detail from the **Charlemagne Window** found in the ambulatory at Chartres, we see Charlemagne supervising Odo of Metz working on the Palatine Chapel.

Germany

Romanesque style prevailed in Germany long past the point when French cathedrals soared to heaven with each church taller than the one built a few years before. **Cologne Cathedral** was begun late in the Gothic period, and the architect on this project, a certain Master Gerhard, was familiar with <u>Amiens Cathedral</u> and also with <u>Sainte Chapelle</u>. His goal was to bring the best of both to his own masterpiece church. <u>Cologne Cathedral</u> is colossal; in fact, the interior is almost a full story taller than Amiens. Only the choir of <u>Cologne Cathedral</u> was completed during the Gothic period. The church was consecrated in 1322 and opened for worship, more-or-less, with construction continuing until 1330. After that the project sort of fizzled out, with construction crews on again, off again piddling away at it until 1560 when they apparently just gave up on ever getting the church finished. In the early 19th century, the original plans for the cathedral resurfaced after being long lost, and there was renewed interest in completing the church according to Master Gerhard's original design.

<u>Cologne Cathedral</u> is a vertically imposing church like the examples we saw from high Gothic in France. The interior employed the same 3-section wall design made popular in France, with a nave arcade, a triforium and a massive clerestory. Unlike Chartres, Amiens, and Reims, however, Cologne filled the triforium with windows to emulate the style of <u>Sainte Chapelle</u> where the walls seem to dissolve into lacy stained glass with minimal structure to hold it all together. The stained glass windows at Cologne were all lost in bombing raids during WWII, but the basic church architecture withstood the attacks and aside from losing the original windows, it is in good condition today.

England

English Gothic churches are quite different from the French prototype, with **Wells Cathedral** being one of the best examples to illustrate exactly how different! French Gothic design emphasized tall, while English Gothic style placed a greater emphasis on long, and in some cases, wide.

<u>Wells Cathedral</u> was begun early in the Gothic period. Curiously, it was built as a cathedral, which is to say, the seat of the local bishop… except that at the time, it wasn't actually the seat of the bishop at all. During the Middle Ages there was an ongoing rivalry between the neighboring towns of Wells and Bath in western England for which town would host the bishop. Wells had enjoyed this privilege until 1088 when the pope moved the "Bishop's Seat" to the great abbey at Bath. The local clergy and townspeople in Wells wanted to persuade the pope to reinstate their town as the home for the local bishop, and with this goal in mind, they undertook building this spectacular church. In

the end, the pope decreed that the local bishop would become the bishop of both Bath and Wells, and then in 1245, Wells was finally granted full cathedral status once again.

The façade of Wells Cathedral is completely covered with hundreds of statues representing saints, many of them larger than life-size. Sitting atop all the figures, at the pinnacle of the center of the façade, is Christ enthroned offering the sign of benediction to bless those entering the church. Directly below Christ, positioned similarly to the gallery of kings on Chartres Cathedral, are twelve statues representing the Apostles. At the time it was built, this display of religious statues was the largest anywhere in the Christian world. Originally the figures were all painted, so it would have been colorful as well as ornate. To add to the impressive atmosphere, the façade had small holes punched through to the church interior, which served as a sort of medieval public address system, allowing folks outside the church to hear the music and singing going on inside. Wells Cathedral, like most English Gothic churches does not have a rose window like we customarily see at this time in France. English Gothic churches also do not usually have a pair of tall towers with party hat spires flanking the façade; they favored a massive tower rising from the crossing of the nave and the transept instead.

Let's peek inside. Although the vaulting at Wells is not as lofty as we might find in France or Germany, the very broad nave began to show signs of cracked supports under the weight of the huge tower over the crossing, and in 1338, master mason William Joy designed the unique *scissor arch* to provide the additional support needed to keep the structure sound. English Gothic churches usually have a *Lady Chapel*, which is found directly behind the sanctuary where the altar is found. Whereas a French church might have several small chapels radiating off an ambulatory, English churches are more likely to skip lots of small chapels, and have just the one large chapel dedicated to the Virgin Mary. Incidentally, English Gothic churches usually have a square-shaped sanctuary, sometimes called a *presbytery*, instead of the semi-circular apse design employed by the French.

Wells Cathedral also has a *cloister*. Cloisters are enclosed gardens or "greens," usually with a covered walkway surrounding the open space. Normally we associate cloisters with abbeys, especially in England (Durham Cathedral, discussed in the previous chapter, was originally an abbey, and it also has a cloister). The cloister was adjacent to the monks' dormitories, and it provided a secluded place for them to walk about quietly and pray. Wells doesn't have dormitories for monks of course, since no monks ever lived there, so the cloister does not have a specific function beyond simply being a pleasant design tradition that could be enjoyed by all who attend church here. Although not near the cloister, like most English Gothic churches, Well Cathedral does have a modest living area provided to house a few priests called a *Chapter House*. The *Dean* (top priest appointed by the bishop to be in charge if the church did not have a bishop in residence) and *Canons* (ordinary priests functioning as a community) lived together in the Chapter House and often prayed as a group rather than always by themselves.

Salisbury Cathedral was built just a few years after Wells. Like Wells Cathedral, but unlike most other Gothic churches, Salisbury was completed with the exception of finishing touches in record fast time - 38 years in this case - keeping the architecture style consistent to Early Gothic design throughout the church. Like Wells, Salisbury was built as a cathedral and never functioned as an abbey. In spite of that the church compound was designed with a chapter house and a cloister, in fact the largest cloister in England. The spire, which was completed a century after the church was begun, is the tallest in England stretching 404 feet into the air. By comparison, Chartres' spire (the taller of the two flanking the façade) is 377 feet tall. Most French Gothic cathedrals were left with stubby towers; the spires that were intended to cap the towers were never built. Cologne Cathedral borrowed heavily from French design, however, and that church did finally complete the architecture project centuries later producing spires soaring to 516 feet.

Salisbury Cathedral has the distinction of being home to one of only four surviving original manuscript copies of Magna Carta. This early 13th century charter, first drafted in 1215 and modified successively over the course of the century is significant because it has served as a foundation for much of common law as we know it today as well as influencing the documents that established the ground rules for democracy in our own country, such as the US Constitution and Bill of Rights. Magna Carta was drafted to curb the authority of the king, both in the secular realm of politics as well as his influence over the Church.

King John of England, through poor management of his realm extending across Britain and into France, angered his noble barons who found themselves losing power to govern locally while their taxes were increasing to finance John's political intrigues. At the same time, centuries before the Reformation, the English king had presumed the right to hand pick his own Archbishop of Canterbury, with the monks at Canterbury simply approving the king's choice. This wasn't just any clergy appointment; an archbishop has authority over all the bishops in his jurisdiction, and those bishops in turn have authority over all the priests in their diocese, and the Archbishop of Canterbury is the grand pooh bah who oversees the entire Church in British realms. Pope Innocent III (the same pope who helped establish the Franciscan Order) balked at King John's selection for Archbishop of Canterbury, sending his own recommendation instead, which the king in turn refused to accept, and to retaliate, the king exiled all the monks. The pope was outraged given that this was a church appointment, not government, and he ordered that no public worship would be allowed in England until the king got with the program, and when the king didn't comply, the pope excommunicated him altogether until the king eventually relented.

The original Magna Carta was forced on the king by a band of malcontent nobles, and it included articles that would reduce the king's power to being little more than a puppet to the nobility. Even the pope, who certainly wasn't the king's biggest fan, agreed that this was taking it too far. Over the course of a few revisions a balance was established which granted rights to the king's subjects, while not eliminating the king's authority to govern his people fairly.

York Cathedral, usually affectionately dubbed **York Minster** by the locals is the largest Gothic Cathedral in England. The term "minster" implies that the church was run by monks. Like Wells and Salisbury, this cathedral was never a monastery, although it is true that a handful of archbishops who served there were Benedictines. York was a Christian town in northern England dating as far back as 314 when its bishop was recognized after the Edict of Milan made Christianity legal in Roman territories. It suffered some ups and downs, but by the early 7th century there was a wood church dedicated to Saint Peter there serving as the cathedral, and a hundred years later York boasted the largest cathedral school and church library in the Christian world. Remember Alcuin of York? This is where he went to school before heading out to the continent and landing a job at Charlemagne's court. Alcuin left to escape the influx of Danes in Britain at this time, but their pagan influence never completely squelched Christian worship in York. The church has been rebuilt many times, including once in the 11th century during the reign of William the Conqueror, when it was designed in the Norman style of Romanesque very similar to <u>Durham Cathedral</u> which is just up the road from York. The church suffered fire damage less than a hundred years later, and what you see today is the rebuilt Gothic church that retained some Norman elements of design, like the elegant twin towers flanking the façade, but featured typically Gothic elements as well. Like Wells, York has a Lady Chapel and a chapter house, but it does not have a cloister.

Since this is the largest Gothic church in England, it might be fun to compare it to <u>Amiens Cathedral</u>, which is the behemoth equivalent in France. While Amiens rises 13 stories from the floor to ceiling, York measures only 9 stories to the vaulting. So Amiens is bigger, right? Not so fast. York is 524 feet long compared to Amiens' 438 foot length, but the real clincher is how wide the churches are: Amiens is a svelte 96 feet wide at the transept, while York measures a whopping 249 feet wide. Yikes! York wins. English Gothic churches are never as towering up to the clouds tall as French Gothic design, but they sure make up for it in length and in width. In fact, like Wells, York required special intervention to span such a wide nave; in this case, special wooden bracing was added to the groin vaulting to reinforce the ceiling.

Finally, <u>York Minster</u> was blessed with clever citizens who like their friends in Chartres, removed all the cathedral windows for safe keeping during the bombing raids of World War II. Not only does she still have her original stained glass windows, including some windows that date back to the older Norman Romanesque church, but she boasts the largest medieval stained glass window in the world, which measures about the size of a tennis court. The **Great East Window** was built at the tail end of the period (1405-08) by master glazier John Thorton who was paid about $93, which in those days was good money (by comparison, a pair of boots might set you back a penny at that time). The window, which looms over the Lady Chapel in the east end of the church depicts an array of <u>Bible</u> scenes. There are Old Testament stories from the creation of the world through the lives of King David and his sons. Other themes are taken from the Book of Revelations depicting the end times. Finally, the lowest row of figures illustrates kings and bishops, with the window's original donor, Bishop Skirlaw of Durham in the center. Bishop Skirlaw was hoping he might be appointed the next archbishop of York when he shelled out the big bucks to pay for this glorious window, but alas, the honor went to somebody else.

The last English church we will look at is the only one that actually was an abbey: **Westminster Abbey**. This London church looks like a gigantic cathedral but it isn't. Westminster *Cathedral* is a short walk away and not nearly so splendid a church by comparison. The site was originally a shrine built back in 616 and dedicated to Saint Peter after a fisherman claimed he experienced a vision of the saint there. In the late 10th century it was dedicated to the Benedictines as an abbey, and a few years later, around the time of the Norman conquest of England under William the Conqueror, King Edward the Confessor built a large, grand stone abbey, where he planned to be buried. That old Norman abbey, consecrated in 1065, was included in the illustrations in the Bayeux

Tapestry. Since that time <u>Westminster Abbey</u> has been the traditional site for royal coronations (like <u>Reims Cathedral</u> in France), and there has been a tradition of burying important people there, not just kings, but all different kinds of famous people.

The old Norman Romanesque church was demolished in 1245 to make way for construction on the High Gothic church we see today. They made speedy progress building from the apse end of the church working down the nave until a pair of double whammy setbacks brought the project to a temporary halt. First, there was a major fire which wiped out most of the monastic out buildings in 1298, and then a horrific wave of Bubonic Plague followed which decimated the monastic population. In time the building program was resumed and slowly construction lurched on into the Renaissance, although the Gothic design was retained. In the end the abbey is distinctively closer to French design that other English Gothic churches, boasting the highest Gothic nave in England.

The monks at Westminster always worked closely with the English kings, and with the government in general, since the abbey is located for all intent and purposes next door to the Palace of Westminster which nowadays houses Parliament. The Benedictines here lived like the luxury-loving Cluniacs in France (remember, the Cluniac Order started out as a subdivision of the Benedictine Order), in that the monks at this abbey got caught up in secular concerns and a privileged lifestyle given their neighborhood. Still, with the monastery being set in an urban location the monks wound up playing a positive role in the local economy both as consumers and also as employers.

Like other abbeys in Britain, Westminster saw her monks dismissed under Henry VIII who initiated the Protestant Reformation here. The monks were welcomed home under his successor, Queen Mary, who was Catholic, but then kicked out again when Mary's half-sister, Elizabeth, took over and reinstated Protestant rule. At that time the "abbey" was designated a "royal peculiar" in that it was an abbey with no monks, its officials became government appointees and from then on it has been exempt from answering to the Church (any church), being its own little island diocese accountable only to the monarch du jour.

A few of the curious bedfellows buried at Westminster Abbey include Saint Edward the Confessor (note the dead king was elevated to saint status before the Church of England disconnected from the Catholic Church), Charles Darwin, Geoffrey Chaucer and Ralph Vaughan Williams, among many others. Nowadays Westminster Abbey is primarily a wealthy collegiate institution involved with high-end education. Officially it is the Collegiate Church of Saint Peter, Westminster, although it is still popularly called Westminster Abbey just the same.

Scotland

All the medieval architecture we have considered so far has been churches, and yet for many readers the Middle Ages is a time they associate with castles at least as much as churches. This is true. Plenty of castles were built during the Romanesque and Gothic periods especially, but many of these were fortresses made of wood that are long gone, or stone but which have nevertheless been reduced to rubble after many wars, or if any part of an old stone castle survived, it has had so many structural changes over the centuries that the original medieval castle is no longer recognizable. One excellent exception is **Eilean Donan Castle** in the western Scottish Highlands. Not only is the castle still essentially as it was, albeit largely rebuilt but with care to keep it true to the period, it is also one of the most photographed castles in the world from popular calendar pictures to a frequent choice for movie-set location.

Eilean Donan Castle was built is 1220 by Alexander II (ruled Scotland 1214-1249). Alexander had married the daughter of the King John of England, and both men were instrumental in developing Magna Carta, the document limiting the authority of the king over nobles. The peace with England was welcome (if not permanent), but Alexander still had to deal with the threat of Vikings attacks. Notwithstanding those Vikings who centuries earlier had settled in Normandy, adopted Christianity and exported their civilized ways to Britain, in the 13th century still more barbarian Norsemen continued to raise havoc invading the Christian world. Eilean Donan Castle was built on an island as a defensive fortress for protection against these rogues from Scandinavia. "Eilean" means island, and according to tradition, Donan was the name of a 7th century monk, originally associated with Saint Columba's monastic heritage, who was said to have become a hermit living on this island. Nowadays the castle is approached by a footpath causeway for the convenience of tourists, but originally the island was safely surrounded by water making an attack more difficult. The design proved successful because in 1263 a vast Viking fleet was so thoroughly trounced in battle at Eilean Donan that the Scots were able to achieve a peace treaty (Treaty of Perth, 1266) with Norway, thus ending the Viking assaults. Other castles from this time that did not have the benefit of being built in the middle of a lake or river often dug a moat around the castle to offer those inside the same defensive advantage.

As it happened, the peace with England didn't last. After Alexander's line died without an heir (Alexander's granddaughter, Margaret, was the only heir and she died young before bearing children), the English crown tried to dominate Scotland again. Among the many freedom fighters for Scottish independence was William Wallace (of *Braveheart* fame for those who have seen the movie). William's favorite for King of Scotland was Robert the Bruce, who did in fact manage to regain the throne out from under English rule. When Scotland was under siege from England, Robert the Bruce took refuge at Eilean Donan Castle, which contributed to his military success.

During later periods in history castles were often quite grand, but medieval castles like Eilean Donan were often little more than military strongholds that would not be confused with luxurious living. Inside the thick walls with few, if any, window openings there were two large main rooms, the billeting room which served as quarters for the men to stow their weapons and often to sleep dormitory-style, and a large hall or banqueting room where the men ate. At Eilean Donan there was an upper level with half a dozen smaller rooms, bedrooms for the important chiefs, or family being protected at the castle. There was a kitchen of sorts and storage within the walled compound, but otherwise not much that would be inviting by today's residential standards.

Italy

Just as we saw during Romanesque times, Italy was not especially progressive in adopting the new style of architecture during the Gothic period, defaulting to models like Santa Maria Maggiore, which by now was pretty old-fashioned, for inspiration rather than looking to the magnificent cathedrals in France or England for new ideas. The

Italians never quite got around to flying buttresses, or ceilings that floated up to the stars, or incredibly complex vaulting, or oceans of stained glass held together by the finest tracery. But just as we saw with San Miniato al Monte, where pleasing designs of colored marble were introduced to dress up the facade, Italian Gothic churches have a style all their own.

One of the most lavishly embellished Italian Gothic churches is **Orvieto Cathedral**. It is a simple basilica not unlike what we have seen since the Early Christian era, but what this church design lacks in innovative engineering and magnificent sculpture and glass, it compensates with extraordinary exterior mosaics. Italian architects did not seem to see the church façade as being an integral part of the overall church design. The facades were often treated like screens – almost like a flat iconostasis to which art could be attached. They look almost like breathtakingly beautiful altarpieces that have been enlarged and glued on the front of an otherwise unremarkable building when compared to Gothic architecture elsewhere. Orvieto's façade has a combination of bas relief sculpture (low relief as opposed to more three-dimensional sculpture on churches elsewhere) combined with colorful mosaics, but once you round the corner there is little to capture visual interest as the rest of the church exterior is simple striped layers of plain white and blue-grey stone.

The church was commissioned by Pope Urban IV to commemorate a miracle said to have occurred in 1264 in the neighboring town of Bolsena. According to the account, a priest there suffered doubts over whether the consecrated hosts at communion were really the body of Christ (a teaching called *transubstantiation*). Then while celebrating Mass one day, the host started to bleed in the priest's hands, so much so that the blood stained the white altar linen below. Whether or not this really happened is left to personal discernment – the Catholic Church does not officially support the "Miracle of Bolsena" which is viewed as being a matter of personal private revelation for the priest who claimed it happened – but the bloodstained altar linen was preserved and remains in a specially dedicated chapel inside Orvieto Cathedral to this day.

Construction didn't begin until 1290, by then under another pope, with Arnolfo di Cambio, a famous architect from neighboring Tuscany, as the architect of record. When he died around 1309, and the project was taken up by Sienese architect, Lorenzo Maitani, who wound up solving the lion's share of the engineering problems on the project negotiating the height and span of the cathedral's nave. As often happens on projects that extend beyond one architect's tenure, the later guy made his fair share of changes to the original design, so the famous façade and most of the interior is actually Maitani's vision. Most of the exterior sculpture was created by the latter architect himself, including the ALBE statues representing the four Gospel Evangelists: and angel for Matthew, lion for Mark, bull for Luke, and eagle for John.

Above the sculpture is a series of golden mosaics depicting scenes from the life of the Virgin Mary. We will look at the two located above the central portal. In the tympanum immediately over the portal we see the **Assumption of the Virgin**, where Mary is raised up to Heaven by angels. See the little guy in the lower left hand corner? That's doubting Thomas, who according to legend was offered Mary's belt as proof of her assumption. Above that, on the highest pediment above the rose window we see the **Coronation of Mary, Queen of Heaven**, where the Blessed Mother is being crowned by Jesus in the company of angels. The theme of respect for the Virgin Mary, always popular during the Gothic period, is carried over into the church interior. The apse is filled with frescoes, now in disrepair, telling the story of Mary's life. Note that the ceiling does not offer the customary vaulting in the nave like we have seen in French, German and English churches of the period. Instead we see simple Early Christian exposed rafters with a clear view up to the inside of the roof.

While Italian Gothic architecture design may not be cutting edge, they made up for this lapse in the art department. In most other European countries at this time, the dominant art outside of church embellishment (sculpture, stained glass) was manuscript illustration. Italy never became too involved in manuscript art, largely because the Church started here and the need for missionaries toting Gospel Books was nil. There were manuscripts produced in Italy, but never on the scale as we might find elsewhere. The Italians put their effort into creating magnificent altarpieces instead.

Cimabue

Italian art had its roots in Byzantine-influenced Mediterranean styles. Since the days of Justinian, Byzantine mosaics and icons had become part of Italian art. As the Catholic Church evolved through the centuries, a large altarpiece would be placed in the apse of a church as a visual focal point in much the same way as an iconostasis serves a Byzantine church. During the Gothic period, these altarpieces were what we might call an *Italo- Byzantine* style, which simply means that this type of painting common to Catholic churches in Italy derived influence from Byzantine art of the past. The late 13th century painter Cimabue was the last famous artist of this tradition. He was from Florence, which during the Gothic period was one of the two biggest art centers along with Siena; both are in the Tuscany region of north/central Italy.

The **Madonna and Child Enthroned** , a huge altarpiece – almost 12' tall - was commissioned for the high altar of Santa Trinita in Florence. The gold background is reminiscent of Byzantine mosaics and icons; in fact Cimabue elaborately incised the background (scratched tiny grooves into the paint) to imitate mosaics. The angels surrounding the throne look almost like they holding it up, or maybe they are stacked on risers like stadium bleachers around the throne. They do not look at Jesus and Mary; instead they look out to us as if they were posing for the picture. Below the throne are Old Testament prophets looking old and grumpy – they hold scrolls, which presumably are scripture references foretelling of the coming Messiah. The Virgin and child both have gold striations on their robes to show folds in the fabric. Looking at the robes falling between Mary's legs, it looks more like curtains draped over the back of a chair than it does clothing on a woman. The figures are more stylized than real; there is no sense of a body underneath flat fabric.

Giotto

Compare Cimabue's altarpiece to the **Ognissanti Madonna**, so named because it was painted for the Church of Ognissanti (All Saints), by Giotto just a few years later. He not only eclipsed Cimabue's fame in Florence, but Giotto became the Gothic mentor to Early Renaissance painting in Florence and throughout Italy. Notice how the angels all turn their heads to focus on Jesus and Mary now. The mother and child both look more natural; their bodies have mass and volume as opposed to being flat. Those gold striations Cimabue employed are long gone with an attempt to show highlights and shadows as they might appear in real life. Their faces look less stylized than earlier examples as well. Even the throne looks a little more solid and sturdy. Giotto paid considerable attention to natural shadowing to make his figures more realistic, although he did not as yet understand the concept of using a single light source in the painting to model figures.

Unlike most artists of his day, Giotto was internationally traveled, throughout Italy and also France in particular, possibly at the invitation of the Avignon popes (between 1305 and 1378 the seat of the papacy was temporarily moved to Avignon, France to escape political turbulence in Rome). Giotto was so famous that Dante even wrote about him. His style rapidly spread across Italy in almost all regions except Venice where the old Byzantine imagery remained popular. In many ways Giotto was THE most important artist of the Gothic period in Italy.

His most famous masterpiece was a series of frescoes for the **Arena Chapel** in Padua, Italy painted from 1304-06. It was this project that solidified his reputation as the greatest of all painters and one of the most famous personalities of his own day. Enrico Scrovegni, a wealthy merchant from Padua (near Venice) commissioned the chapel. The building was a simple barrel vaulted structure which was attached to the patron's palace along one wall, with windows running the length of the chapel along the opposite wall. The barrel vault was painted blue like the heavens with stars. Three registers of frescoes tell the story of Mary and Jesus in comic strip style, with Mary's life on top near the ceiling, and Jesus on the lower two closer to eye level. Chronologically it reads like a book from top to bottom. In the life of Jesus, the scenes depicted by Giotto include:

The Nativity: Scene showing Jesus in a manger
Adoration of the Magi: Three wise men come to pay homage to the infant, Jesus
Presentation at the Temple: Jesus is presented to the priest for circumcision
Flight into Egypt: Jesus and his parents, Mary and Joseph escaping King Herod
Massacre of the Innocents: All the male children under age 2 are killed by Herod
Christ Preaching in the Temple: At age 12, Jesus was "lost" and his parents found him teaching elders
Baptism of Christ: Jesus goes to John the Baptist to be baptized
Marriage at Cana: Jesus' first miracle, at the request of Mary; he changes water into wine.
Raising of Lazarus: Jesus' friend died, but Jesus was able to raise him from the dead
Entry into Jerusalem: Jesus rides into Jerusalem on a donkey. This scene is associated with Palm Sunday
Expelling Moneychangers from the Temple: Jesus got mad at people making money off sacrifices
Last Supper: Jesus shares his last meal with the Apostles and initiates the Eucharist
Christ Washing the Feet of the Apostles: Jesus offers a blessing by humbly washing everyone's feet
Judas' Betrayal: Judas seals his fate by identifying Jesus to the Pharisees with a kiss
Christ before Caiaphas: Jesus is brought before the high priest of the Sanhedrin to be judged
Mocking of Christ: The guards make fun of Jesus, give him a hard time and beat him
Carrying the Cross to Calvary: Jesus must carry his own cross to the place where he is to be crucified
Crucifixion: Jesus dies on the cross – associated with Good Friday
Lamentation: Jesus is taken down from the cross and mourned by Mary and her companions
Noli Me Tangere: After the Resurrection, Jesus appears to Mary Magdalene, but tells her not to touch him
Ascension of Christ: Jesus is taken up to heaven
Pentecost: The Holy Spirit descends on the Apostles like tongues of fire, and they begin their ministry

All these accounts are taken from the Bible. Let's look at the **Lamentation**. Jesus is laid across his mother's lap, while Mary Magdalene caresses Christ's wounded feet, and Saint John the Evangelist expresses his grief with flailing arms. The scene is painted against a blue sky, which was quite innovative at the time, as it replaced the usual gold background like we saw in the big Madonna and Child altarpieces. There is also a crude attempt at landscape with a large rocky crag rising up behind the figures, and one lonely and somewhat anemic looking tree perched on top of the crag. Scholars have wondered if the single tree might have had some special significance. Could it be a reference to the Tree of Knowledge, of Good and Evil mentioned in Genesis, shown withered and dead from the sins of Adam and Eve down to the present day? Or perhaps it could refer to the Legend of the True Cross, which was quite popular at this time, inspiring other artists and poets … possibly suggesting here that the wood of Christ's cross came from this tree. Then again it could also be nothing more than an artist who had no experience painting landscape giving it a somewhat tentative try … a little landscape is better than no landscape at all. Regardless of whether hidden meaning may have been intended, the modest attempt at landscape was innovative. Also cutting edge were the angels, shown in contorted positions and most interesting of all, *foreshortened* such that they appear to be flying in from the background. Finally, notice that again we see Giotto using highlights and shadows to try to make his figures appear bulky and real. This is especially evident in the figure sitting dead center in the middle of the painting, with her back turned to us, which was also highly unusual. The Lamentation has come a long way from Cimabue's Madonna. Now not only do characters in the scene to the left and right turn their heads to face the subject, but those in the foreground disregard the viewer altogether, turning their backs on us in order to focus their attention, and ours, on Jesus.

Simone Martini

While Cimabue recalled Byzantine mosaic art of the past, and Giotto could be described as "proto-Renaissance" anticipating the future, Simone Martini was the Italian artist whose style was the most truly Gothic. A citizen of Siena rather than Florence, Simone followed a different path in painting, opting less for monumental figures and more for the newest vogue of the Gothic period: International Style. His figures are graceful, slender and elongated, with an emphasis on elegant line more than substantial form. His **Annunciation** is the earliest known example of this subject matter presented on its own as an altarpiece, not part of a larger theme. The central Annunciation was painted for Siena Cathedral, while the two attached saint side panels were probably added to the Annunciation when the elaborate Gothic frame was created after-the-fact.

Like Giotto, Simone Martini catapulted to international fame, serving not only a myriad of important patrons in his hometown but also attracting commissions from the nobility of Naples. He may not have been as innovative as the famous Florentine master, but like Giotto, Simone Martini eventually found his way to employment with the popes; in fact he died in Avignon serving the Papal Court there.

This brings us to some final reflections on the Middle Ages, especially on church design. As we saw in the classical world of Greece and Rome, there was a clear cycle of development that started with a very simple premise, which was perfected, then made increasingly more elaborate until society turned another page in history. First, Early

Christians had to come up with an idea of what a church was supposed to be, so they borrowed the Roman basilica and modified it to meet Christian needs. But there were problems with fire safety, and you couldn't see the art very well from any one point in the nave. Perfection? In the West, Romanesque churches like Norman abbeys solved some of the problems. They are big with oodles of space, there are places for crowd overflow just in case, and with some careful modifications, they had fireproofed stone ceilings and even a few windows could be included to allow light into the church. In the East, where the emphasis on art was more critical, central plan churches like San Vitale did the trick. All the basic parts of the church are there, just the shape has changed to make it easier to see the mosaics and iconostasis. But is it enough? Apparently not, because in the West the Church moved on to Gothic Cathedrals, which would be the Medieval answer to the Hellenistic extreme of "more (and more and more) is better." Likewise, in the East, churches like Saint Basil's look more like something out of a fairy tale than they do simple, practical churches. Having run its cycle, the great age of magnificent churches drew to a close. The pattern of simple to complex would start again in the 15th century, but never again in human history would there be such a profusion of exquisite Christian architecture as during the Middle Ages.

The Age of Magnificent Masters, Piety and Plato:

The Renaissance

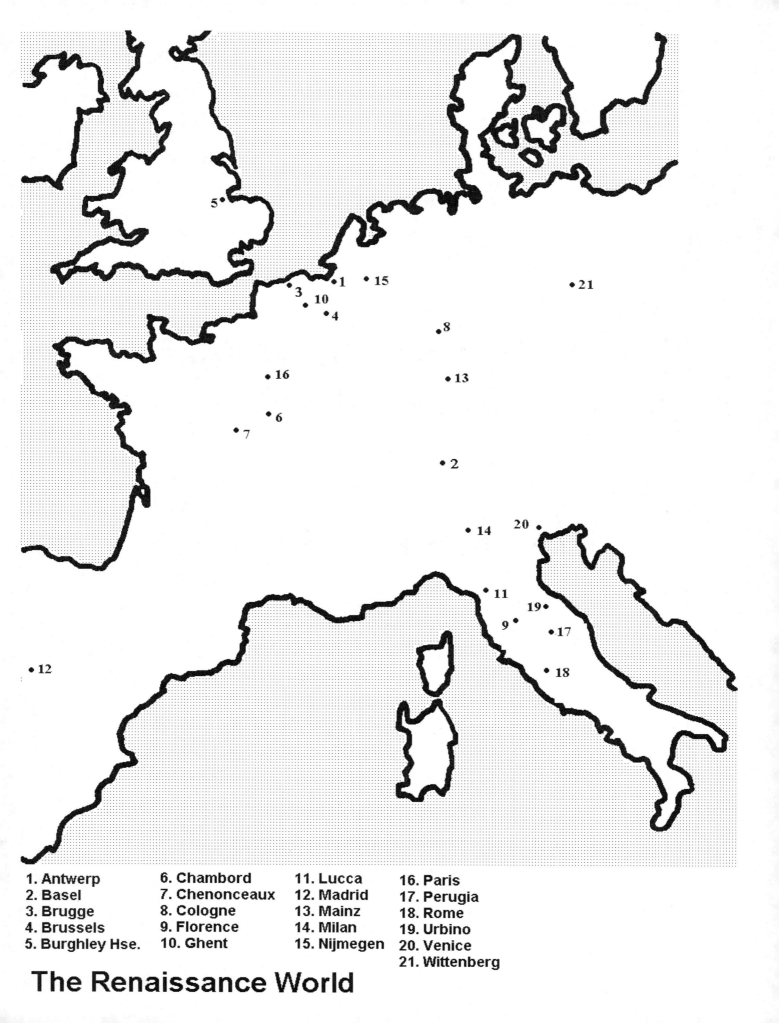

The Renaissance World

1. Antwerp
2. Basel
3. Brugge
4. Brussels
5. Burghley Hse.
6. Chambord
7. Chenonceaux
8. Cologne
9. Florence
10. Ghent
11. Lucca
12. Madrid
13. Mainz
14. Milan
15. Nijmegen
16. Paris
17. Perugia
18. Rome
19. Urbino
20. Venice
21. Wittenberg

Image List for Unit Three

All images are: **RENAISSANCE: 1400-1600** (*Early* = 15th c *High* = 16th c)

FRANCE

Limbourg Brothers

1. January Page from <u>Les Tres Riches Heures du Duc de Berry</u>
2. February Page from <u>Les Tres Riches Heures du Duc de Berry</u>
3. March Page from <u>Les Tres Riches Heures du Duc de Berry</u>
4. April Page from <u>Les Tres Riches Heures du Duc de Berry</u>
5. May Page from <u>Les Tres Riches Heures du Duc de Berry</u>
6. June Page from <u>Les Tres Riches Heures du Duc de Berry</u>
7. July Page from <u>Les Tres Riches Heures du Duc de Berry</u>
8. August Page from <u>Les Tres Riches Heures du Duc de Berry</u>
9. September Page from <u>Les Tres Riches Heures du Duc de Berry</u>
10. October Page from <u>Les Tres Riches Heures du Duc de Berry</u>
11. November Page from <u>Les Tres Riches Heures du Duc de Berry</u>
12. December Page from <u>Les Tres Riches Heures du Duc de Berry</u>

FLANDERS

Jan van Eyck

13. Berlin Madonna
14. Canon van der Paele Madonna
15. Canon van der Paele Madonna (detail)
16. Rolin Madonna
17. Rolin Madonna (detail)
18. Man in the Red Turban
19. Margaret
20. Arnolfini Wedding Portrait
21. Arnolfini Wedding Portrait (detail)
22. Arnolfini Wedding Portrait (detail)
23. Ghent Altarpiece (grisailles)
24. Ghent Altarpiece
25. Adam from the Ghent Altarpiece
26. Eve from the Ghent Altarpiece

Hugo van der Goes

27. Portinari Altarpiece
28. Portinari Altarpiece
29. Portinari Altarpiece
30. Portinari Altarpiece

Hans Memling

31. Mystic Marriage of Saint Catherine Altarpiece
32. Mystic Marriage of Saint Catherine Altarpiece (central panel)
33. Mystic Marriage of Saint Catherine Altarpiece (John the Baptist panel)
34. Mystic Marriage of Saint Catherine Altarpiece (John the Evangelist panel)
35. Saint Ursula Reliquary
36. Saint Ursula Reliquary
37. Saint Ursula Reliquary (Virgin with donors)
38. Saint Ursula Reliquary (Ursula with her companions)
39. Saint Ursula Reliquary (Departure from Cologne)
40. Saint Ursula Reliquary (Disembark at Basel)
41. Saint Ursula Reliquary (Baptism and Marriage)
42. Saint Ursula Reliquary (Departure from Basel)
43. Saint Ursula Reliquary (Arrival in Cologne)
44. Saint Ursula Reliquary (Martyrdom of Saint Ursula)

FLANDERS *and* HOLLAND

Pieter Bruegel

45. Massacre of the Innocents
46. Netherlandish Proverbs
47. Hay Harvest
48. Wheat Harvest
49. Return of the Herd
50. Hunters in the Snow

ITALY

Lorenzo Ghiberti

51. Sacrifice of Isaac by **Ghiberti**
52. Sacrifice of Isaac by **Brunelleschi**
53. Saint John the Baptist

Donatello

54. Saint Mark
55. David
56. David
57. David

Gentile da Fabriano

58. Adoration of the Magi

Masaccio

59. FYI: Brancacci Chapel view
60. Tribute Money

Fra Filippo Lippi

61. Madonna and Child

Fra Angelico

62. Annunciation
63. Last Supper (detail)

Piero della Francesca

64. Federico da Montefeltro
65. Battista Sforza
66. Brera Madonna

Ambrogio Bergognone

67. Virgin & Child with Saint Catherine of Alexandria & Saint Catherine of Siena

Perugino

68. Christ Delivering the Keys of the Kingdom to Peter

Sandro Botticelli

69. Punishment of Korah, Dathan and Abiram
70. Punishment of Korah, Dathan and Abiram (detail)
71. Birth of Venus
72. Calumny

Leonardo da Vinci

73. Madonna of the Rocks (Paris)
74. Madonna of the Rocks (London)
75. Last Supper
76. Mona Lisa
77. Self Portrait

Giorgione

    108. Sleeping Venus
    109. Pastoral Concert (aka: Fete Champetre)

Titian

    110. Assumption of the Virgin
    111. Pesaro Madonna
    112. Pope Paul III
    113. Isabella d'Este
    114. Girl with a Basket of Fruit
    115. Venus of Urbino
    116. Rape of Europa

Arnolfo di Cambio (*Gothic*)

    117. Florence Cathedral

Filippo Brunelleschi

    118. Dome of Florence Cathedral

Donato Bramante

    119. Tempietto
    120. Plan for Saint Peter's Cathedral

Michelangelo

    121. Plan for Saint Peter's Cathedral
    122. Dome of Saint Peter's Cathedral

Michelozzo di Bartolommeo

    123. Medici Palace

Andrea Palladio

    124. Villa Rotunda

FRANCE

Domenico da Cortona (*he's Italian but the chateau is in France*)

    125. Chateau de Chambord

Philibert de l'Orme

    126. Chateau de Chenonceaux

ENGLAND

William Cecil
Capability Brown (*gardens*)

    127. Burghley House

HOLLAND

Herman van Herengrave

    128. Town Hall, Nijmegen

FLANDERS

Cornelius Floris

    129. Town Hall, Antwerp

11. Northern Renaissance Painting

Early Renaissance

The Renaissance began around 1400 across Europe. Outside Italy it was a gradual shift away from medieval thinking and artistic traditions as opposed to a dramatic new style. Nothing changed overnight in northern Europe. The regions which had enjoyed a leadership role in the arts continued to do so, and the types of art made popular during the Middle Ages likewise were as popular as ever in the early 1400's. Accordingly, France initially remained the leader in the arts of northern Europe, as it had been during most of the Middle Ages from Charlemagne's day through the Gothic period. Aside from fabulous churches, during medieval times the manuscript became the premiere art form across northern Europe, and this also remained constant during the first few decades of the 15th century.

The type of manuscript that gained popularity during the early Renaissance was a little different from the Gospel books and Psalters being produced in monastery scriptoriums however. For one, medieval manuscripts were usually produced by monks, while Renaissance manuscripts were produced by professional artists – men who set up shop in town, hung out a shingle and took orders for hand-made books. Secondly, while medieval manuscripts tend to be religious books, Renaissance manuscripts were secular. They might have prayers or hymns or other religious material in them, but they were not Scripture per se.

Limbourg Brothers

The most popular new manuscripts were called *books of hours*, so named because they contained prayers for different hours of the day. Rich people often commissioned books of hours as a show of wealth. They were a sort of status symbol in their day – like a 15th century version of having a couple Bentleys and a Rolls Royce sitting in your circular driveway today. The most famous, and most expensive artists producing books of hours in France at the turn of the century were the (three) Limbourg Brothers.

Books of hours were verrry expensive, and for this pricey investment, patrons expected highly personalized books with plenty of beautiful illustrations. The prayers might be selected from among old favorites learned at church, or they could be do-it-yourself prayers the patron made up himself. After all, it was his book, he was paying for it, and he was going to get whatever he wanted. The prayers would be accompanied by painted illustrations that would be unique and personalized to the patron's family. It wasn't just any family, it was the patron's family because he was paying for it, and he was going to get whatever he wanted. Books of hours commonly included psalms – not the entire Book of Psalms from the <u>Bible</u>, but just a few favorites of the patron. The same goes for songs. These could be hymns, if the patron liked hymns, but they didn't have to be religious at all. After all, it was his book, he was paying for it, and he would get whatever he wanted. Finally, books of hours usually contained a reusable calendar, and it was often here that the very best illustrations are found.

The book of hours we will consider was commissioned by the Duke of Berry, and created by the famed Limbourg Brothers. The Duke of Berry was off-the-charts wealthy. Remember during the Gothic period when all the big lords were buying out all the little lords? Well, the Duke of Berry was from one of those families that became so rich in landholdings that he wound up owning a huge chunk of France. And not a shabby chunk of France either; the Duke of Berry owned the Loire Valley, which is pretty spectacular as real estate goes. Most of the gorgeous French castles and chateaux you may know from picturesque calendars were in his real estate portfolio. The Duke of Berry didn't own just one book by the Limbourg Brothers, he owned two. This would be like deciding that one personal Learjet just isn't enough, you "need" two. He also had books created by less famous artists as well. The particular book we will see is called **Les Tres Riches Heures du Duc de Berry**. The title might be French, but translated it is no more than calling the book exactly what it was: "the very rich (expensive) hours of the Duke of Berry!" It was the most expensive book owned by the Duke, and the last one he ever bought as well as being the last one ever produced by the Limbourg Brothers, who actually left it to be finished by assistants, as the whole lot of them died of Bubonic Plague – the Black Death.

The calendar pages of <u>Les Tres Riches Heures du Duc de Berry</u> illustrate special celebrations associated with different months, or seasonal labor throughout the year. The actual calendar is encompassed in the lunette at the top of each page. Notice that on each page, the lunette is divided into two sides, each containing a zodiac symbol. Frequently during the Middle Ages and Renaissance, zodiac (astrology) images were employed to symbolically illustrate the passage of time through the months and seasons of the year, and for this reason, you should be familiar with their order. Zodiac signs represent a lunar calendar, which of course overlaps a solar calendar, but the months and signs do not start and end on the same days. Therefore, each month on a solar calendar begins under one zodiac sign, but ends under another. January begins under the sign of Capricorn, which is represented as a goat with a fish tail, and the month ends under the sign of Aquarius, which is the water-bearer, a youth pouring an amphora of water. February begins under the sign of Aquarius, and ends under Pisces, the twin fish, usually swimming in opposite directions. March begins in Pisces, and ends under the sign of Aries, which is the ram. April begins in Aries, and then moves on to Taurus, the bull. May starts in the sign of Taurus, and ends in Gemini, the twins, usually a boy and girl holding hands. June starts in the sign of Gemini, and concludes in Cancer, the crab. July begins under the sign of Cancer, and ends with Leo, the lion. August starts off in Leo, and then moves into Virgo, the virgin, usually a beautiful, young maiden. September begins in Virgo, then ends in Libra which is either depicted as scales, or the figure of justice holding the scales. October starts out in Libra, but moves into Scorpio, which is usually depicted by a scorpion, but can also be symbolized by an eagle. November begins with Scorpio, then concludes in Sagittarius which is the archer – usually seen as a centaur raising his bow and arrow. And finally December begins under the sign of Sagittarius and ends in Capricorn.

Look first at the **January page**. It depicts an elegant dinner party, presumably at the Duke's home (one of his many homes) because he is present – the fellow dressed in blue robes who is slightly bigger than everyone else. What feast takes place in January? Although it isn't a big holiday in America today, it's still on most calendars … Epiphany, on the 6th of January. This is the feast of the Wise Men, sometimes called Twelfth Night, as in the Twelve Days of Christmas, which starts on Christmas Day and goes forward into January. Back in the 15th century, Christmas was observed as a religious day of fasting and prayer. Twelve days later, at Epiphany, gifts were exchanged and everyone ate a large meal, not unlike how most Christians would celebrate Christmas Day nowadays. The festivities take place inside, although the lively mural on the wall might lead you to believe it is outside in the middle of some crusade! Any months where cold, wet, or otherwise unpleasant weather might make being outdoors uncomfortable were customarily portrayed as cozy, indoor scenes. The January page is an excellent example of manuscript painting at this time because it exhibits perfect *International Style*. International Style is called as much because it appeared across Europe, both in northern countries and Italy, around the same time although there is no evidence that artists were communicating their ideas with one another. Look for these characteristics in the January page. International Style shows figures that are elongated and flattened. The artists employ lots of patterns (brocades, damask etc.), which make the figures look even flatter. There are lots of bright colors, and plenty of real gold leaf tooled into the pages. Finally, all the figures are squashed together into a shallow space, as though the scene were taking place on a stage.

Compare the January page to the **February page**. First, the February page is very unusual because it illustrates a winter scene outdoors. This is actually one of the earliest snow scenes ever painted in history. We must assume that it was the brainstorm of the artists, which they were obliged to sell to the patron (hey, Duke, we have this really great idea! How about if we tried to paint snow!) In any event, the Duke went along, but notice that he chose not to be included in the February page, just in case it wound up being the only snow scene ever because it was decided to be stupid art … best not to have your face showing up on *that* page. Instead, peasants are employed to illustrate activities and chores associated with the cold winter months. There were good reasons to include peasant scenes in books of hours, and this page is by no means unique in that regard. It gave the artists more latitude to experiment with new ideas, like we see here with the snow. Beyond that, it gave the artist a chance to illustrate labor of one type or another, as surely the ritzy patron would not want to be shown toiling away at some manual task when he had serfs who did that sort of thing. Further, we have to remember that the Duke owned these peasants every bit as much as he owned horses and cows and castles; he is showing off his many possessions. Finally, showing the poverty of peasants makes the Duke look that much more grand by comparison, so it bolsters the ego of the man paying the artists' bills. The February page moves away from International Style, with fewer bright colors, and an increased interest in showing depth of space. Notice that the artists use diagonal lines to make the background appear to recede in space, and objects in the background are smaller in scale, again to increase our ability to believe they are in the background. Mathematical perspective had not yet been invented, but in northern

Europe, many artists were starting to tinker with assorted methods to make backgrounds look far away.

The February page offers us a unique insight into both the Duke and his artists. Look at the three peasants warming themselves by the fire in the shed in the foreground. There are two women dressed in blue, and a man between them. We don't know the relationship between these three, but presumably we might assume that they cannot all be married to one another (ménage a trois? I think not). Okay, now look closely, two of the figures – the man and the woman behind him – have lifted up their garments and are exposing themselves, with private parts clearly on parade! What's going on here? Do you suppose the Duke would expose himself in the presence of ladies? One would hope not. So why are the poor folks doing this? They are being portrayed as depraved as well as deprived. Why, if these were more decent people, God would have made sure they were born into "good" families! There is no need for the Duke to feel guilty that he has all this money and yet provides so little for the poor. They are scumbags who deserve the lousy lot in life they have. Does this reflect the philosophy of the artists? Probably not. Do you suppose that the Duke mandated in his commission that poor people need to appear immoral? Probably not. Most likely, by the time the Limbourg Brothers got around to producing their second manuscript for this patron, they had a pretty clear vision of the man they were dealing with. The Limbourg Brothers didn't get to be the best-paid artists in this line of work by being obtuse. By sussing out their client, and producing work that reinforced his prejudices and attitudes, they could be assured that he would like what he saw and be prepared to pay the artists well.

The **March page** shows peasant labor – tilling the soil for planting. This page shows the artists experimenting with shadows. Incidentally, all the glamorous castles and chateaux in these calendar pages are real places, all owned by the Duke of Berry. The **April page** shows the Duke again, dressed in blue with a red turban. This scene commemorates his niece's betrothal. The **May page** shows members of the court riding off to go hunting – a popular pastime for nobility. The **June and July pages** show peasant labor, first with farming, then with shearing sheep. The **August page** is another curiously different page in that it combines peasants and nobility, although the Duke has taken a powder; he is nowhere to be seen. In the distance the peasants have gone swimming, and we see that the artists have (however unsuccessfully) tried to show distortions in the appearance of objects – in this case the objects are people – when seen in water. **September and October** show autumn work around the Duke's assorted estates.

Then we get to the **November page**. Do you see a difference in style here? Notice how the herder in the scene looks so much more substantial than the people depicted on other pages. His legs look solid and round, not flat like a paper doll. His face is rough and crude with highlights and shadows unlike what we have seen before. Furthermore, look at the landscape. It appears to recede back into space much more successfully than other pages. Notice that the artists used diagonals to lead your eye back into space like we have seen before. They have also altered the colors such that those in the foreground are earthy – browns and greens, while those in the background are bluish grey, which makes the background seem to recede. This is called *aerial perspective*. Why is this page so different? Assistants produced it after the Limbourg masters had all died from the Plague. The **December page** was half and half – started by the Limbourg

Brothers, but evidently completed by assistants. The background is very typical of the Limbourg Brothers, and some of the figures' bodies have the flat, Limbourg Brothers look. The faces, though, are far too burly for the more delicate hand of the Limbourg Brothers, and the one fellow in the back who looks like a lumberjack is clearly the handiwork of somebody new, not the soft style of the Limbourg Brothers. As a postscript on **Les Tres Riches Heures du Duc de Berry**, did you happen to notice the wee church of Sainte Chapelle in the background of one of the pages? Ah … a little exercise for you … see if you can find it!

Gradually over a decade or two the center of culture and art shifted away from France to her northern neighbor, Flanders. Flanders no longer exists as a country; it corresponds geographically (more or less) to where Belgium is today. Flanders and Holland together formed the Netherlandish provinces, which at the time were territories owned by Spain. Art and culture shifted north because that's where the economy was strongest, and the reason the economy thrived at such a high level in Flanders, and to a slightly lesser degree, Holland, was that this region became the center of international trade.

Most trade at this time was processed through maritime shipping. Huge boats with large cargo holds sailed between ports of call carrying goods to and fro. The problem was that most regions specialized in certain commodities, but their trading partners did not require full boatloads of any one or two products. For example, let's say that Holland's specialty was cheese. The Dutch could fill a ship with cheese, but who needs an entire boatload of just cheese? What you want to export is a full boatload of your specialty product. What you want to import is a boatload of mixed goods with a little bit of everything – cheese from Holland, lumber from Norway, woolens from Scotland, brocades from Italy let's say, and so forth. The port facilities in the Netherlandish provinces accommodated this hiccup in trade.

Centrally located for trading partners from Scandinavia to the Mediterranean, and blessed with excellent harbor access, the port cities made big business out of brokering the shipping trade. The way it worked, ships laden with the specialty product of a single region would sail to a Netherlandish port, where brokers representing every possible international concern would break the load down and redistribute the products to fill their orders with a mix of goods from a variety of regions. So in simple terms, a boat might leave Oslo loaded with Norwegian lumber and sail to a port in Flanders, where a broker from the Norwegian firm would have a stack of orders for lumber destined for several different regions. He would supervise reloading the lumber onto a number of other boats, while the rest of those boats would be filled with Dutch cheese, Scottish woolens, Italian brocades and a variety of other goods. Likewise, the boat scheduled to return to Oslo would be filled with a variety of goods from all over Europe. Under this system, the boats always sailed filled to capacity, which makes good economic sense. The deal was, of course, that the Netherlandish ports made good money off ALL international trade. If Norway traded lumber with Scotland in exchange for woolens, Flanders and Holland made money on the deal because the trade filtered through their ports where broker's salaries and commissions made a positive impact on the local economy. With all this money sloshing around, it shouldn't be surprising that folks might have cash on hand to pay for art, which has always been a luxury primarily reserved for the rich.

As noted earlier, Flanders and Holland were not independent countries during the 15th and 16th centuries. As northern territories under the Spanish crown, they had to be governed long-distance by individuals selected by the King of Spain as trustworthy associates. At the turn of the century, the powerful Duke of Burgundy, Philip the Good oversaw the government of the Netherlandish territories. Based out of northern Flanders in the city of Brugge (Bruges in French), the Duke maintained a full court, which included a court artist. In the north, artists more often than not made a living by holding a post as either a court artist for a rich family, or as a town artist. These positions were "tenured" in that once you secured the post, the odds were that you would stay on in your position unless you did an unsatisfactory job. Naturally if you failed to work up to expectations or if another stellar talent arrived on the scene you might be replaced, but under normal circumstances artists did not have to compete on a daily basis for each and every job. Accordingly, while artists may not have felt compelled to change their styles rapidly like we will often see in Italy, nor did each artist seem to feel it was necessary to be uniquely different from the painter next door, they frequently had the opportunity to develop ideas more fully than they might have had they been constantly scrambling to find work. Northern Renaissance painting is sometimes criticized for not producing the range of individuality artist by artist seen in Italy at the same time. The upshot is that it was northern painters, not Italian, who developed oil paint decades before it was introduced in Italy. Likewise we find earlier advancement in portraiture, going from the medieval profile to three-quarter poses, and much more rapid development of landscape painting in the north compared to Italy also.

Jan van Eyck

Jan van Eyck was court artist to Philip the Good, and is the best-documented and most famous artist of the early 15th century in Flanders. Van Eyck is credited with inventing oil painting, although the reality is more likely that this was a collaborative discovery of several artists working together, Van Eyck simply being the most famous of the lot. As court artist to the Duke of Burgundy, Van Eyck was responsible for everything from decorations for fancy balls to banners for parades to official state portraits. He was even dispatched occasionally to visit the King of Spain on official government business, indicating his level of importance within the court. Curiously, we no longer have a single painting by Van Eyck which was an official commission from the Duke, despite him being the artist's primary patron. When Van Eyck was not engaged in official court assignments, he was free to accept commissions from other well-heeled patrons who wished to hire the best artist in town.

A good example of a typical commissioned painting for a patron outside the court (we don't know who this might have been) is the **Berlin Madonna**. It gets its name nowadays because it is housed in the Berlin Museum of Art. The scene is oil paint on wood panel, typical of most Northern Renaissance painting during the 15th century. Note the detail seen in the work. It would be easy to imagine that this painting should be life-sized with such profuse detail, but in fact it is tiny, measuring only 12" x 5." Northern Renaissance painting grew out of a manuscript painting tradition, and the tendency was toward miniature imagery with minute, painstaking detail. The artist would paint the entire scene in black, white and grey opaque base paint, then add layer upon layer of translucent colored oil glazes to build up the color to a rich, bright finished product. Oil painting was far more laborious than the old-fashioned egg-based tempera, but the vivid colors obtainable with oil paint made the effort worthwhile. Jan van Eyck is known for his brilliant colors, and also for his fabulous attention to the tiniest details. He was known to use a single horsehair to capture facets in jewels and reflections sometimes so small they aren't much bigger than a pinhead.

This little painting would be about the right size to sit propped on a tabletop or hang next to a door jamb – certainly not an "important" work. And yet, not only is there great attention paid to physical detail in the scene, it is also imbued with rich symbolism, not blatant and obvious, but hidden such that we must study it in some detail to fully appreciate all the artist is offering his viewer. Mary is depicted standing in a Gothic church interior (note the pointed arches, the triforium and clerestory). She is also huge! Mary and the Gothic church are made to be one in the same – she fills the church. In Northern Renaissance symbolism, Gothic architecture is frequently used to symbolize the Virgin Mary, as it was during that time that Mary enjoyed a particular surge in popularity. Likewise, Gothic architecture is frequently used to symbolically represent the New Testament and Christianity, as Christianity begins with Mary conceiving Jesus. Similarly, the old Romanesque style is used to symbolically remind us of the Old Testament, and of the Jewish world. Look closely at the painting. You are looking toward the apse end of the church, so therefore you must be facing east. If you are facing east, then the light bathing the nave is coming from the clerestory on the north side of the building. Light does not shine through northern exposure windows in the real world. This is not natural light at all, but rather divine light which enters the church according to God's Will, and against all known laws of nature … in just the way that according to Christian belief, Mary conceived by the Holy Spirit while a virgin, also by Divine Will and against the laws of nature.

Most religious commissions by Jan van Eyck were a little grander in scale than the tiny <u>Berlin Madonna</u> because they were intended for display in chapels, but even at that they could not be considered large. The next two paintings are "chapel size," each running just a tad larger than two feet square, and also painted in oil on wood panel. The first, which we will consider only briefly, is the **Canon van der Paele Madonna**. The title suggests to us that the patron was Canon van der Paele, a clergyman who commissioned this painting to hang in a chapel in his hometown church. This painting is a good tutorial on exactly what a typical painting of this type should look like. The subject matter, which happens to be Mary holding the infant Jesus (probably the most popular theme in 15th century painting), is dead center in the middle of the painting, which is where one expects to find the central subject matter in 15th century art. In addition to Jesus and Mary, there are other figures present. The gentleman wearing white is Canon van der Paele himself. It was considered completely appropriate for the patron who was paying for the art to have his portrait worked into the scene, and such a figure is called a *donor figure*. A donor figure is a portrait of the patron within the context of the scene. While it was fine to include the patron, there were certain protocols required to keep it in good taste. The donor figure must be depicted in a pose suggesting humility before Jesus and Mary, and he or she must also sit physically below the heads of the Holy Family. Notice how Mary is sitting higher than van der Paele, allowing both her head and that of Jesus to be above the humble donor.

217

Humility was not enough, though. The donor figure must receive a proper introduction to Jesus and Mary, and toward this end, notice the soldier tipping his helmet and making a formal introduction. This is the *patron saint*; in this case, Saint George has the honors. During the Renaissance, everyone living in the Christian world would have had a patron saint; it was a normal part of being confirmed in the faith. Patron saints were selected in one of two ways: either you chose the saint who shared your name, or you selected the saint that personified some vocation that appealed to you. In this case, the painting was commissioned by George van der Paele, who has chosen Saint George to make his introduction to Mary and Jesus. It happens that Saint George is the customary patron saint for the Boy Scouts, so a Boy Scout named Fred or Paul or Steve might also choose Saint George if he preferred, as opposed to Saint Frederick, Saint Paul, or Saint Stephen. Finally, notice that there is another figure off to the left, wearing spectacularly opulent royal blue robes. This figure is not required for the painting to be in good taste, but when such a figure appears, it indicates the chapel for which the painting was commissioned. In this case, it is a rather obscure late 5th century saint, Saint Donation, indicating that the painting was promised to a chapel honoring Saint Donation.

Turn your attentions now to the **Rolin Madonna**, commissioned by Nicolas Rolin around the same time as the Canon van der Paele Madonna was painted (both dating from the mid 1430's). If the latter painting were textbook typical, surely you should notice problems with the Rolin Madonna right away. Jesus and Mary are scuttled off to one side of the scene, Chancellor Rolin (an official serving in the Duke of Burgundy's court) sits at the same level as Mary, his head even above Jesus, and he doesn't seem to feel the need for a proper introduction ... he looks like he just dropped by for a game of cards rather than to show his respect for the Holy Family! How can this be? Chancellor Rolin was not a particularly religious man; for that matter, he was not particularly Christian in his behavior either until he got old and in poor health and suddenly "got religion" and built a hospital for the poor in his old age with infirm health ... a dramatic departure from his greedy and self-serving attitude through most of his life. Why would a man like this commission a religious painting at all, you might wonder. Here is the twist. Rolin's wife was a devout Catholic, and it was she who wanted the altarpiece for their private family chapel. What is an artist to do? The wife is a holy woman who wants a nice religious painting, but the husband, who will be paying for it and who therefore is the patron, isn't much interested in religion at all. Jan van Eyck solved this problem by using disguised symbolism.

Where would you expect to find the central subject matter? In the center of the painting, which is exactly where it is. There are three arches in the center of the scene (3 = trinity), and it is through these arches that the *real* story unfolds. On the left side of the landscape scene there is a village. It is not a real place, the concept of painting real locations won't be invented for another 200 years, but the vineyards and architecture resemble the Burgundy district in France from where Chancellor Rolin hails. In short, the landscape behind Rolin symbolically represents the man himself. Behind Jesus and Mary is a city composed entirely of splendid Gothic churches. These represent Jesus, Mary, and the new covenant. Are the two worlds, that of Rolin and that of Jesus and Mary connected? No, they are not. They are separated by a river. What brings them together, hence standing in symbolically for a patron saint, is the bridge. Although the average Flemish or Dutch person living in the 15th century would be familiar with popular disguised symbolism, like 3 = trinity for example, bear in mind that the artist had to invent his own symbolism here to satisfy a peculiar commission. Bridges do not always represent patron saints. We can understand therefore that while this painting might have served the Rolin family just fine in their private family chapel, it would have probably offended the general public had it been hung in a public location at the time it was painted.

Jan van Eyck was the premiere portrait painter of his generation. We have two portraits to consider, **The Man in the Red Turban**, considered by most scholars to be a rare self-portrait of the artist, and **Margaret**, a portrait of the painter's wife. The latter painting was lost for many years then rediscovered quite by accident being used on its backside as a cutting board in a local fish market! Northern Renaissance portraits are usually head and shoulder shots set against a plain, dark background. Noteworthy is that they are ¾ views of the patron's face as opposed to the old fashioned profiles seen in earlier work (think of the depiction of the Duke of Berry in the January page of Les Tres Riches Heures du Duc de Berry). Flemish painters like Jan van Eyck were interested in catching every nuance of detail in all their subjects, not just religious ones. Showing a face in ¾ view is considerably more difficult than profile, but this is exactly the level of challenge that appealed to painters like Van Eyck. By the way, if Margaret looks strange to you with that odd hat she is wearing, the Flemish and Dutch were crazy for their elaborate headgear during the Renaissance. Women of high station customarily plucked their hairlines to just behind the ears, giving them absurdly high foreheads (high forehead = upper class), then they would hide all their remaining hair, which was left long, under some form of preposterous hat when in public. Styles in hats changed quickly and in many cases, paintings of women can be dated with good precision based on whatever strange concoction they are sporting on their heads.

A third portrait by Jan van Eyck is actually much more than it seems. **The Arnolfini Wedding** is a celebration of the marriage between Giovanni Arnolfini and Giovanna de Cenami. It is more than a simple portrait, however. It is also a legal document. Nowadays when a couple gets married it is a complicated affair, but years ago it was pretty simple; people married themselves. Marriages were arranged of course, but the actual ceremony was simple and straightforward. The husband and wife "shook hands" on the deal while the groom raised his left hand to repeat an oath; they recited some prayers, and presto, instant marriage. The problem with this system is obvious: where is the accountability? This is why by the time folks got to the 15th century it was considered customary to have witnesses, preferably from the bride's family to hold the husband accountable to his vows. In this case, such an arrangement was likely to prove problematic.

Giovanni Arnolfini was an Italian textile merchant from Lucca, Italy living in Brugge where he served as a broker representing his family's firm. Remember those brokers whose job it was to redistribute shiploads of goods? His arranged marriage was to the young daughter of a competitor textile family, also from Lucca although his bride had spent most of her life based out of France where Daddy promoted the family business abroad. Their marriage was designed to merge the family fortunes and business interests into a mini-cartel. The problem was that while the wedding would take place in Flanders, as that is where Arnolfini was based, it was unlikely that any family from either side would actually be present to witness the ceremony. Hence, Arnolfini commissioned this painting to be given as a gift to his wife's family as testimony of the marriage contract. As you can probably guess, everything in the painting is there for a reason, explaining to the folks back home in precise detail the specifics of their marriage agreement.

First, notice that the scene is divided in half with the groom on one side and the bride on the other. There is a window on the groom's side, indicating that it is agreed that it will be his job to support his family by working outside the home. There is no window on the bride's side, suggesting that while this might be a marriage arranged to merge fortunes, it isn't *her* job to bring in money to support their family. On her side of the room is a bed. This indicates that the bride has agreed to sleep with her husband. It may come as a surprise given that in today's world we generally assume that husbands and wives have an intimate relationship, but during the 15th century this would not be assumed. Marriages were often a matter of convenience between people who didn't know each other at all. They may cooperate to produce heirs to the estate, but otherwise live separate lives. In this case, it appears that bride and groom had a romantic interest in one another in addition to conveniently fulfilling the business objectives of their extended families.

Moving to the bottom of the painting, notice that both bride and groom are standing in their stocking feet. His sandals are off to the left while hers are behind, back by the couch near the wall. This shows that they are "standing on holy ground," a symbolic reference going back to the book of Exodus in the Bible when Moses was asked to remove his shoes in the presence of the burning bush because he was standing on holy ground. In the context of a wedding portrait, it means that the couple has sought the blessings of the Church on their marriage. Between them is a cute dog, again not there by chance. The dog is the traditional symbol of fidelity, hence cartoon dogs frequently called "Fido." Here we see the dog parked halfway between the bride and groom, indicating that it is their intention to be faithful to each other.

In the brass chandelier we find a single burning candle. This has two symbolic meanings. Broadly, a single burning candle in a painting of this period always makes reference to the burning presence of God, which reinforces the fact that this is a sacramental marriage with the Church's blessings, essentially the same message as the removed shoes convey. In a wedding portrait, however, it also offers a second meaning. You can identify that it is a wedding portrait (if there were any doubt) because the chamber has a wooden beamed ceiling. When a single burning candle is seen in a room with a wooden beamed ceiling, it signifies virginity of the bride. This is most often seen in a wedding portrait like the Arnolfini one, or in religious paintings with Mary, in which case the symbolism reinforces Mary as Virgin Bride of the Holy Spirit (often a small dove or teensy angel is there too standing in for the Holy Spirit). In this case the artist is recording that Giovanna was a virgin on her wedding day. That may come as news to you because she looks like she is about 6 months pregnant. Wrong! In fact, it is her dress that makes her look to the modern eye like she is pregnant. In her day fashionable women from wealthy families wore dresses with long trains in the *front*. The lady had to scoop up yards of fabric and lug her dress about whenever she wanted to move around, which pretty well became her full time job as opposed to doing anything productive. If wearing your classy clothes becomes a major job unto itself, then you can hardly be expected to wash a floor, or care for a child, or prepare a meal; you would need servants to do all those tiresome tasks for you. Only the richest women could afford the luxury of wearing such impractical dresses, so the fact that Giovanna is dressed this way makes it clear that she is a rich young lady who fully intends to stay that way after she is married. Behind the bride, by the way, is a wooden chair with a carved finial (next to the whisk broom) of Saint Margaret. Saint Margaret is the patron saint of childbearing, which in this case indicates that it is the couple's intention to raise a family. Unfortunately, there were no children recorded to this marriage so we must assume that Giovanna, for all her style and youth, was barren.

In the mirror on the back wall, which is only about the size of a silver dollar, the entire room is shown in reverse. We see the bride and groom, the bed and even the window, which is actually shown in greater detail with the tiniest city street scene outside. We also see two people standing in the doorway in front of the newlyweds, whom we may presume to be the witnesses to the wedding. One of them is apparently Jan van Eyck, given that he signed and dated the painting in the official manner of a legal document. We don't know who the second party might be. There are theories. Some authors have suggested that it might be the artist's assistant. While this is possible, there might have been more important people to the couple than some employee of the artist that the Arnolfinis may have preferred to witness their wedding vows. One possibility is a priest, given that there are multiple symbols indicating that the marriage was blessed by the Church. Another possibility might be the bride's brother. Although no relatives were evidently expected to be in town for the wedding, records have shown that one of Giovanna's brothers did in fact make an unscheduled trip to Flanders in 1434 to handle a business emergency. It isn't known whether he was in Flanders when the wedding took place, however, only that he briefly visited the country in the same year as the wedding.

Finally, you might have noticed that the groom seems to be conducting his end of the marriage ceremony all wrong. A groom was expected to shake hands with his bride while raising his left hand to repeat their vows, while here we see Arnolfini offering his left hand to his wife while raising his right hand instead. This unusual twist becomes all the more peculiar when we learn that infrared photography indicates that originally the black and white underpainting was done the correct way, and then it was changed before the tinted oil glazes were added. Why? What we have here is something called a "left-handed" or morganatic marriage. They were relatively rare, arising originally from feudal society in Germany back during the Middle Ages. Morganatic marriages were designed to protect a rich family (that is a family with lots of land back then) from a "gold-digger" – a girl of low station who might hoodwink an eligible bachelor into marrying her and then she winds up getting her husband's wealth and her child inherits the farm. During a morganatic wedding, the groom offers his left hand rather than his right. A morganatic contract means that the wife has agreed to relinquish all rights of inheritance against her husband's estate. In lieu of an anticipated inheritance one day (in feudal times it would be her son who inherits), the bride receives a morning gift the morning after the marriage is consummated (hence "morgan-atic – morgen means morning in German). The morning gift is a set sum of money negotiated before the wedding – kind of like a lump sum pay-off. As long as her husband remained alive and well, she could expect to live comfortably on his money. But when he died, neither she nor any children born to that union would ever inherit a penny. She and her offspring would have to make do on the money from the morning gift.

This raises the obvious question as to why Arnolfini and his wife would have had a last minute change of plans, opting for a morganatic contract. It was an arranged marriage after all, and in terms of net worth, her side was financially better off than her husband's family. You would expect that suggesting a morganatic union would be quite offensive to Giovanna's family. It turns out that Giovanni was considerably older than his new bride. In fact he was a widower, with pretty, young Giovanna becoming his trophy wife. The trouble was that Arnolfini's children from his first marriage were adamantly opposed to this wedding, business merger or not, because it was likely to have a negative impact on their own inheritance. Common sense said the new wife would outlive their father, and in a standard marriage agreement, she and *her* children would inherit everything, leaving his adult children from his first marriage out of the loop. In order to appease his children, the couple agreed to a morganatic marriage. Arnolfini would be responsible for supporting his wife as long as he lived, but when he died, her family would resume financial responsibility for the widow, presumably taking solace in the fact that business was better after the family merger, and Arnolfini's estate would go to his children by his first wife.

The last work by Jan van Eyck we will consider is the **Ghent Altarpiece**. Northern Renaissance paintings tend to be modest in size, so when a large altarpiece was required for the apse of a church, the custom was to create a huge frame and display a group of smaller paintings together. In smaller churches they might be able to get by with 3 panels hinged together, called a *triptych* (tri=three). If the altarpiece were destined for a large cathedral, they would create a big altarpiece out of many smaller panels, the large altarpiece being called a *polyptych (poly=many)*. Altarpieces were designed with hinges between the panels such that they could be opened and closed. The panels seen when it was closed tended to be bland, black and white or sepia and beige, almost monochromatic with little color. These are called *grisailles (pronounced greez eye)*. The inside panels seen when the altarpiece is open were the usual bright colors we expect to see in northern painting. The custom was to close the altarpieces during Lent so that the dull grisailles were presented. Lent is the 40 days prior to Easter, which is traditionally a time for fasting, sacrifice, prayer and reflection. Then on Easter Sunday the altarpiece was opened in all its brilliant glory to celebrate the Resurrection.

The **Ghent Altarpiece** was commissioned by a wealthy citizen named Jodocus Vijd (pronounced Vayd) for Ghent Cathedral, and it remains in its original location in the Cathedral of St. Bavon in Ghent, Belgium to this day. Jodocus Vijd and his wife, Isabella Borluut are depicted in donor panels on the grisailles (in fact, they are about the only colorful things on the grisailles). Serving as patron saints are Saint John the Baptist for the husband, and Saint John the Evangelist for his wife. Above them is an Annunciation scene where the Archangel Gabriel announces to Mary that the Holy Spirit will overshadow her and she will bear the Christ. In the background we see a Flemish town through an open window. The Holy Spirit is shown as a dove about to fly into Mary's head, and Gabriel holds white lilies, the traditional symbol of purity.

Inside the **Ghent Altarpiece** there are a variety of scenes, most revolving around the Adoration of the Lamb, a subject inspired by the Liturgy for the Feast of All Saints, which in turn comes from the Book of Revelation in the Bible. For our purposes, though, we are not going to detail all the iconography for the interior of the altarpiece, as that could be an entire course unto itself! Instead, direct your attention to the figures of

Adam and **Eve**. Nudes are rare in Northern Renaissance painting, especially in the 15th century which maintained strong ties to the modesty of Medieval art. Only with those subjects where nudity was unavoidable would it be considered proper and decent to show the human body nude. Notice that **Adam** looks believable as nudes go, but **Eve** looks completely unrealistic. Nude models were not readily available in Flanders during Jan van Eyck's time. He evidently used himself as the male model, which is why the figure looks like it was rendered from life. Producing a viable female nude was more problematic for the northern European artist. We know that Van Eyck was married (remember his lovely wife, Margaret?) and the two had several children, so one might wonder why he failed to have a more clear understanding of what a naked woman looks like. Social conventions at this time would have most well-to-do married men and women sleeping in different bedrooms, even if they had a close marriage that produced several children. A husband was obliged to make appointments to "visit" his wife, and more than likely she would be ready for him … wearing night clothes … under the covers … in the dark. He may have been able to locate what he was looking for, but that wouldn't mean he got a good look at what it was he found. Upon closer inspection of Van Eyck's **Eve**, it becomes clear that his model for the body was actually a clothed woman, possibly his own wife, wearing the same sort of elegant dress we see on Arnolfini's wife in their wedding portrait. The voluminous fabric gathered up in the front makes the women appear to have peculiar pear-shaped bodies, and this, translated into a nude, is what we see in **Eve**.

Hugo van der Goes

The second artist to be considered from 15th century Flanders is Hugo van der Goes. While Jan van Eyck is associated with the first half of the century, and with Philip the Good, Duke of Burgundy, Hugo was his successor in many ways during the third quarter of the century. He worked mainly in the neighboring city of Ghent, but also had ties to the Dukes of Burgundy, in this case, to Charles the Bold. Hugo's career was unfortunately much shorter than Jan van Eyck, with most of his work completed between 1467, when he became a professional master, and the late 1470's. It seems the painter was subject to bouts of depression, which eventually led him to take up a secluded life in a monastery in 1480. There he became increasingly despondent, and died two years later.

Like Van Eyck, he accepted commissions sometimes from Italian merchants whose business had stationed them in prosperous Flanders. One such client was Tommaso Portinari, a rich banker representing the great Medici banking family firm out of Florence, which was doing rather well on the interest made from financing foreign trade at that time. Portinari commissioned a gigantic altarpiece, a triptych atypically constructed out of whopping 8' tall wooden panel paintings, to be shipped back to Florence to adorn a family chapel in the Church of Saint Edigio. The **Portinari Altarpiece** had grisailles on the backsides of the two side panels depicting the Annunciation, like we saw on the Ghent Altarpiece by Van Eyck. Inside, the three panels are chock-full of major themes, as well as minor tidbits of other subjects that require a closer look for the viewer to take it all in.

In the central panel of the **Portinari Altarpiece**, the two principle themes are the Nativity, with baby Jesus in a manger flanked by Mary and Joseph off to one side, and also the Adoration of the Shepherds. Behind the large figures in the foreground can be seen two secondary themes. On the hill off to the right is the Annunciation to those same shepherds, who are visited by an angel and told to seek out the Christ Child. More to the center of the scene there are a pair of women conversing, representing the Visitation, where Mary, following her own Annunciation, goes to visit her kinswoman, Elizabeth who is six months pregnant with Saint John the Baptist. Behind the entire central scene is a large Romanesque church, symbolizing the Old Testament. In the tympanum over the central portal is a lyre, symbol of King David to comment that Jesus descended from the Old Testament lineage of the House of David, as it happens, on both sides of his genealogy. Joseph's line is traced back to David in the gospel of Matthew, as would be customary for a text prepared for a Hebrew reader of the first century, and Mary's line is traced in the Gospel of Luke, written originally for a Hellenized Jewish and Greek audience. The fifteen angels presiding in the scene symbolize the fifteen joys of the Virgin, and the sheaf of wheat symbolizes Bethlehem, considered the breadbasket of the Holy Lands in its day. The flowers in the still life in the foreground all have special hidden meaning. The purple columbine stand for the sorrows of the Virgin, while the red lilies stand for the passion of Jesus, and the three tiny red carnations probably symbolize the Trinity.

Equally laden with <u>Bible</u> stories and important information are the two flanking donor panels. To the left are Tommaso Portinari and his two eldest sons, Antonio and Pigello. Behind them are their patron saints. Behind the father is Saint Thomas, and behind the two sons is Saint Anthony the Hermit, who shared his namesake with the older boy and therefore must have been selected as his patron saint. But what about poor little Pigello, there without the benefit of a patron saint of his own to properly introduce him? The inclusion of Pigello helps scholars to date this painting as being produced in 1474-1475, which turns out to be significant as Hugo never signed or dated any of his work. The painting was obviously commissioned before Pigello was born, as the backgrounds for the two donor panels, including the towering images of patron saints, were initiated when there were obviously only 2 Portinari children, a daughter, born in 1471 and one son, born in 1472. Third-born Pigello, who was born in late 1474, evidently arrived after the painting was begun, but before it was completed, as the image of a second little boy was added, but it was too late to also squeeze in another giant patron saint. Furthermore, the later children, Maria (probably 1475), Guido (1476), and Dianora (1479) are not included, so obviously they had not yet joined the family. The fact that Pigello appears to be "old" should not fool you; even babies were often portrayed as older kids according to the artist's imagination of how they might look in a few years. In the background of the left panel is another Bible scene, in this case the Flight into Egypt. The right hand panel is dedicated to the Portinari women. Tommaso's wife, Maria Baroncelli is presented with her patron saint, Mary Magdalene (seen holding a jar of ointment), and the eldest Portinari daughter, Marguerita, is accompanied by Saint Margaret who predictably stands on the rather impressive head of a dragon. The three kings, or Magi, can be seen winding their way down a path in the background, presumably on their way to bring gifts to the Christ Child.

Hans Memling

The last of the Early Renaissance painters from Flanders that will be considered here is Hans Memling. Memling was the grand luminary painter in Flanders during the final quarter of the 15th century. Although not born in the booming port city, he first appeared on the citizen rolls in Brugge in 1465, and he became a member of the professional painter's guild in the following year. He wound up becoming one of the richest citizens in that city during his fruitful career, so much so that on occasion he was asked to pay additional taxes levied on the wealthy to help pay for special city expenditures. He owned three houses, and had a stable of apprentices in his studio. Memling appears to have married young, and was left a widower to raise three young children alone. As a city painter, rather than court artist, he was free to accept a wide range of commissions, and he was quite prolific during his career.

The Mystic Marriage of Saint Catherine Altarpiece, sometimes called the *The Saint John Altarpiece* was commissioned for the Hospital of Saint John, one of the largest and oldest hospitals in Brugge; it dates all the way back to the 12th century. Initially the hospital was run by laymen, but in 1459 the hospital was given "cloister" status under the monastic order of St. Augustine. The monks there answered to a master, and there was a bookkeeper. Adjacent to the monastery was a convent, run by a prioress and her assistant, the housekeeper. These four people in charge of running the cloister and hospital commissioned the altarpiece when a new choir and apse were added onto the older chapel. The triptych was for the main altar and at 5'8" tall, it is one of Memling's largest altarpieces.

In the central panel we see the Madonna and Child surrounded by saints and angels. Saint Catherine is the young lady to the left who is touching Jesus' hand. Catherine of Siena was a 14th century saint and very popular during the Renaissance because she was "current." The youngest of 25 children, she started having mystic visions at the age of 6. Catherine resisted all family efforts to have her marry so that she could devote herself to prayer and fasting. She became a Dominican nun at 16. Among her many visions was her mystic marriage to Jesus, where Christ placed a ring on her finger to claim her for himself. She apparently could see the ring all the time, but nobody else could. A lot of people thought she was either a fake or just plain nuts, but that didn't stop her from devoting her life to caring for the seriously ill such as lepers and plague victims that nobody else would go near. Catherine wound up becoming an advisor to the pope, who trusted her judgment and welcomed her criticisms. In addition to her claim that she was wed to Jesus, she also suffered from the stigmata, like Saint Francis of Assisi, remember? Saint Francis of Assisi's wounds were seen by many witnesses, however, but nobody could see any marks on Catherine ... until she died and at her death the wounds miraculously became visible to the shock of those who had doubted the saint's authenticity.

Here's the tricky part. What attribute seems to be associated with Saint Catherine in this painting? Do you see the wheel on the floor poking out from under her gown? The wheel is the attribute for Saint Catherine alright ... but the wrong one! The wheel is associated with Saint Catherine of Alexandria, who was a late third century woman. After annoying the pagan Roman government by insisting on being a Christian, that Catherine was sentenced to be executed through some torture involving a spiked wheel, but when the wheel broke, they lopped her head off instead. The correct attributes for Catherine of Siena can include a lily for her purity, a book since she was a learned advisor, a crown of thorns for her suffering or a visible heart since she changed hearts toward Christ. And of course her ring, don't forget the ring. We must presume that Memling meant for this to be Catherine of Siena since Jesus is placing a ring on her finger, but the artist appears to have made a boo-boo on the other attribute(s) and somehow conflated two Catherines into one... oops!

The lady dressed in green is Saint Barbara, a 4th century saint popular during the Middle Ages, although she may be 100% legend. She was yet another steadfast virgin who refused to marry so according to the story, her father locked her in a tower, then took her before a judge who tortured her, and finally, still not satisfied, her father took her up on a mountain and killed her, after which God struck old dad down with fire from heaven. At any rate, her attribute is the tower, which you can see tucked in behind Barbara in this scene.

Behind the female saints are the two Saint Johns to pay homage to the patron saints of Saint John's Hospital. The Baptist is accompanied by his attribute, the Lamb of God and John the Evangelist has his chalice with a snake in it. A chalice with a snake in it? The attribute comes from a story, true or otherwise, that a priest at the Temple of Diana took John prisoner in Ephesus and made him drink poisoned wine. John was unharmed although two people had died from the same cup. John laid his hands on them and they were resurrected. The chalice stands for Christ and his victory over Satan (the snake). Behind the Baptist we can see John preaching, John being brought before Herod, and John's headless body being burned. Behind the Evangelist are monks from the hospital measuring wine into barrels – wine sales being the hospital's most important source of income.

The left panel is dedicated to Saint John the Baptist. It shows his beheading, Salome's dance in the window in the upper left, and way back in the distant background is John baptizing Jesus in the River Jordan with God above. The right panel presents Saint John the Evangelist in exile on the island of Patmos envisioning the end times. The imagery is straight out of Revelations in the Bible illustrating John's vision of the tribulation and heaven.

The Mystic Marriage of Saint Catherine Altarpiece is a magnificent work of art, but it wasn't the only famous masterpiece Memling created for the hospital. The **Shrine of Saint Ursula** is an exquisite reliquary, or decorated box kept in a chapel to contain the relics of a saint. Memling designed the reliquary to resemble a Gothic church, standing 34" tall, measuring 36" long and a mere 13" wide. It is made of painted wood with gilt (gold) embellishment.

The Shrine of Saint Ursula was commissioned in 1489 by a pair of nuns, Josine de Dudzeele and Anna van de Moortele for the Hospital of Saint John in Brugge, and it is still in its original location. The reliquary holds the bones of Saint Ursula, an obscure Early Christian saint apparently from either Britain or Brittany, the daughter of a Christian king or otherwise a man of some importance; she was betrothed to marry a pagan prince from Germany. Ursula managed to postpone the marriage until her future husband agreed to become Christian. With ten ladies in waiting (the legend often ballooning this number to ten times ten ...), she set out to meet her fiancé, and proceed on a pilgrimage to Rome to seek baptism for her fiancé from the pope himself, and then to be married there. The reliquary depicts Saint Ursula at one end, accompanied by her ten ladies in waiting (like wee munchkins huddled about her gown), and the opposite end of the reliquary illustrates the two sisters who commissioned the box, shown humbly in the presence of the Virgin Mary.

Circling the box are six scenes telling the story of Saint Ursula, which is probably as much legend as truth. It starts with Ursula and her companions (chaperones), having arrived in Cologne to meet with her intended fiancé, and departing Cologne by ship to sail up the Rhine to Basel, Switzerland. In the first scene, if you look very closely at the building in the background, you might see in the window that there is an angel visiting a young woman while she sits in bed. This is to illustrate a vision, which Ursula purportedly had on the eve of their departure that she would be martyred. In the second scene, Ursula and her party disembark in Basel and set off on foot toward Rome. In the third scene, Ursula and her companions are in Rome, where the pope greets her and where her fiancé is baptized and they are married.

Around on the other side of the box, Saint Ursula is seen boarding her boat in Basel for Cologne, and it seems that the pope has also received a vision that Ursula might face some danger, so he has decided to accompany her on the journey in the hope of providing some protection. Alas, in Cologne they are greeted by Huns when their ship arrives. As the story goes, Ursula was such a ravishing beauty that the leader of the Huns found her irresistible. After disposing of all the extraneous people, he attempted to persuade Ursula to save herself by marrying him. Naturally she would rather chew glass than submit to such a vile existence, so the king butchered her too. In this last scene, the early start of what would eventually become Cologne Cathedral can also be seen in the background; remember that this Gothic church wasn't fully completed until the 19th century!

More than likely most of the story is romanticized fiction, although there *was* apparently a young woman of some station with an entourage of attendants who crossed the North Sea, then set out from Cologne en route to see the pope, and the ladies were all killed (shipwreck? Huns? Who can say?). Whoever she was, she was very highly thought of at the time because her remains were collected and kept over the centuries, even building a special church just so her bones could be venerated. The nuns who commissioned the reliquary during the 15th century were members of the religious order which had cared for Ursula's remains for at least ten centuries.

High Renaissance

The 16th century, or High Renaissance in Northern Europe saw the decline of influence of the Catholic Church, and gradually over the course of the century, the rise of the Protestant Reformation. In Rome there was a major campaign underway to rebuild Saint Peter's Cathedral, the old Early Christian basilica now having fallen into ruin. The popes were eager for the new church standing over the ancient shrine to be the grandest in Christendom, and the price tag for such a building campaign was prohibitive. The Catholic Church had lots of money coming in from tithes, but what must be remembered is that the Catholic Church also was the only charitable institution in Europe funding everything from monasteries and convents, to orphanages, to universities to hospitals to a multitude of other services that might be covered today by secular governments, but which in the past were provided by the Church. There wasn't the kind of money available to pay architects and artists to work for years on end for such a huge project without raising additional capital somewhere.

It was Pope Leo X who decided to rely on *indulgences* to help offset the cost of rebuilding Saint Peter's. The concept of indulgences was not new to the 16th century; it had been around about as long as the Church had been in existence. An indulgence is when a penitent person is offered an opportunity to reduce a penance by exchanging a substitute activity for the one originally assigned. Let me explain. From the early days of the Church, confessing one's sins and doing penance to show God that you were sorry was a regular part of Christian living. Let's say that a man had stolen his neighbor's horse. In addition to setting things right with his neighbor, he would visit his priest to confess the sin (John 20:23), and the priest would suggest an appropriate penance, let's say in this case it might be to fast and pray every Wednesday for 6 months to show God that he was genuinely sorry for what he had done. An indulgence might be offered, where let's say this same man might be offered a chance to make a one-month pilgrimage, and only fast and pray for 3 months after the pilgrimage instead of 6. He still must confess his sin, and he still must do penance, but part of his penance might be commuted if he substitutes another activity in its place.

The first time money had ever entered the indulgence equation occurred during the Crusades, where on occasion an indulgence was granted if a penitent made a financial contribution to support the Crusade – again after making a good confession and with every intention that he would still do penance, just a somewhat reduced version. Leo X decided to offer an indulgence for anyone who volunteered to make a contribution to the rebuilding of Saint Peter's Church. To get the word out, he contacted heads of state across Europe, who in turn contacted the bishops in their country who then made sure the local priests knew they could offer the indulgence. The donations poured in, except from Germany, where there was no central government, and therefore nobody in charge of communications with local clergy. The Archbishop of Mainz was asked to undertake the task of contacting German clergy, and he in turn gave the assignment to a local monk who had a reputation for excellent fundraising, Johann Tetzel. Unfortunately, Tetzel, in his zeal to support the building campaign, did not present indulgences according to Church tradition. He set prices on sins, as if to sell indulgences, and went so far as to claim that salvation might be linked to forking over cash for sins. Clearly this was not what the Church was teaching (then or ever), and it was not a problem in other regions, only in Germany under Tetzel's influence. One might wonder why the Pope didn't yank Tetzel off the job, assuming that eventually these problems must have been brought to his attention. One can only surmise that Leo X, perceiving it as a "German" problem, assumed that the Germans were clever enough to take care of these matters without the Pope having to intervene.

Sure enough, German citizens began to feel ripped off, and disgruntled because the new policies didn't seem to jive with the Christian faith as they knew it, they asked a scholarly monk at Wittenberg University to clarify the role of indulgences. That of course was Martin Luther, who in 1517 wrote his 95 Theses on indulgences, and nailed it to the doors of Wittenberg Cathedral. Some might suggest that this event started the Protestant Reformation, but in fact, this isn't so. While Luther was asked to retract some of his statements which were perceived as not quite in line with an historical understanding of indulgences, there was nevertheless no official response from Rome, given that what the 95 Theses did was simply get Germany back on track with the rest of Catholic Europe. Remember, the Pope had never sanctioned all the ridiculous shenanigans over indulgences going on there in the first place. It might be also mentioned that to whatever degree there was any flap over some of the statements Luther made in the 95 Theses, Luther wrote to the Pope himself and asked for his mercy in dealing with the fallout from the 95 Theses. This does not sound much like a monk bent on breaking away from the Catholic Church, and the Pope recognized as much. Over the next four years, however, Martin Luther wrote a number of articles and preached on other subjects, and it was these writings and lectures, not the 95 Theses, that triggered his eventual split with the Catholic Church.

Martin Luther addressed many different issues, some considered heretical and offensive to the Catholic Church, but *many* others considered benign. This chapter will cover a few of the "biggie" issues that finally led to the Pope asking Martin Luther to retract those statements considered heretical, he refused, and in 1521 Luther was excommunicated from the Catholic Church. The Lutheran Church was the first new denomination of the Protestant Reformation. For one thing, all Christians up to this point (Catholics and Orthodox alike) observed seven sacraments, defined as special gifts given by Christ through the Church as outward signs of internal grace: Baptism, Confession and Penance, Communion, Confirmation, Marriage, Ordination, and Anointing of the Sick (sometimes called Last Rites). Martin Luther indicated that while he agreed that many of these were good things to do, he believed that only two should be considered holy sacraments: Baptism and Communion. He also had different ideas about Communion. All other Christians at this point in history believed in something called "transubstantiation," which is to say, that when the priest or bishop consecrates the Mass or Divine Liturgy, that the bread and wine are transformed to the true presence of the Body and Blood of the risen Christ. Luther promoted a new theology called "consubstantiation," which suggests that the Holy Spirit is present, but the actual bread and wine undergo no transformation. These ideas were considered heresy in Catholic and Orthodox circles.

Beyond this, there were two popular battle cries of Luther's reformation: *Sola Fide* and *Sola Scriptura*. Sola Fide means that Luther promoted the idea that man is saved by God's grace through faith alone, while the Catholic and Orthodox position had always been that man is saved by God's grace, as evidenced by faith and deeds. Luther's point was what matters to God is whether or not a person believes; believers will be saved regardless of how they lived their lives, although this is not to be interpreted as carte blanche to live a bad life because it doesn't matter … Sola Fide presumes that one with faith will choose to be a good person in behavior also. All other Christians at this time believed that you had to have both faith and deeds – if one professed faith without trying to do the right thing, it was a hollow claim that God would not honor – you had to try to do what God expects of you in addition to believing in the Word. One without the other was a dead end; faith without effort to "do what Jesus would do," or doing good deeds without the faith to back them up – either one was incomplete.

Sola Scriptura was Luther's idea that the only authority for Christians was the written <u>Bible</u>. His argument was that the <u>Bible</u> had been in existence for many centuries by then, it was becoming more available through mechanical printing, and it contained whatever folks needed to know to gain salvation. Other Christians up until this time (Catholics and Orthodox) believed that it wasn't the Book that was the sole authority by itself, but the Word (Logos – the understanding of God's thoughts if you will), which included both the written text of the <u>Bible</u>, and Sacred Oral Tradition. Their argument was that the <u>Bible</u> was invented in the 4th century, largely in response to confusion over which written material was inspired by God and which was not. Ironically the primary litmus test used to determine what got included in the <u>Bible</u> was that a text had to conform without exception *to the sacred oral tradition*, which was a far larger body of information than what was available in written format. Christians outside Luther's theology agreed that the <u>Bible</u> was inerrant and inspired, they simply considered it the written part of a greater whole.

These new theological ideas did not spring up overnight. Luther appears to have come to his ideas gradually over a period of a few years. For example, at Augsburg in October, 1518, one year after the 95 Theses, he claimed that the <u>Bible</u> held authority over the Pope, but he claimed that the Church Councils were equal in authority to the <u>Bible</u>. The following year in July, 1519, at the Leipzig Disputation, he argued now that the <u>Bible</u> held authority over Councils too. Clearly Luther was not always in agreement with what the Pope or the Councils said, but it is a point worth noting, that the Pope and the Councils based what they said… on their interpretation of the Word, which is to say, their interpretation of the <u>Bible</u> in conjunction with Oral Tradition. It's not like the Pope or the Church Councils worked in a <u>Bible</u>-free vacuum any more than Luther did. In the end, what appears to be the issue here is not a book challenging a person, or group of people, but rather one interpretation of Scripture challenging another. In any event, these arguments eventually led Luther and Leo X into an official show-down, where Luther refused to amend his new theology, and the Pope gave him the heave-ho from the Catholic Church, thus officially starting the Protestant Reformation in 1521.

As a postscript on the Sola Scriptura question, fifteen years later in 1536 Luther issued his own <u>Bible</u>, which caused further heartburn between the new Protestants and Catholics. Luther's <u>Bible</u> was written in German, but it was not the first <u>Bible</u> written in vernacular language. In fact, by 1522 (much less 1536) there were already 14 German translations of the <u>Bible</u> that had been authorized by the Catholic Church. So what was it about Luther's <u>Bible</u> that caused such a tizzy with the Catholics? Luther's new <u>Bible</u>, among other things, reduced the number of books in the Old Testament. In 382 when the <u>Bible</u> was put together, the ***Septuagint Old Testament*** was "grandfathered" into the table of contents along with the roster of books accepted for the New Testament. The Septuagint was compiled in 200 BC, when 70 Jewish scholars in Alexandria were called upon to translate the Old Testament books from Hebrew into Greek. Remember, that Alexander the Great had conquered the Holy Lands during the 4th century BC, leaving that region of the world Greek speaking. Many people could no longer read the old Hebrew, so the Septuagint was a translation into a "vernacular" language that folks could understand since Hebrew had long been a dead language used only by rabbinical scholars. The Septuagint was the Scripture in place during the life and times of Jesus and all the Apostles, so that's what was used in the original <u>Bible</u>.

At the close of the 1st century, the Jews in Palestine held a special conference at Jamnia, where they restructured Old Testament Scripture. The most frequently cited date for this council meeting is 90 AD, so we'll go with that, although some authors place it as late as 100 AD, and others at dates in between. Jamnia was a center for rabbinical scholars (Pharisees), and this conference was specifically called to determine what to do about the "Christian problem" within Judaism, given that at that point in history, Christianity was perceived as a Jewish sub-cult. The Pharisees blamed the Christians for the destruction of their temple 20 years earlier (remember Titus during the Flavian period sacking the temple in Jerusalem?) – it seemed to the devout Jews that as had happened in the past according to Scripture, God was punishing His chosen people for worshipping false Gods. This Jesus guy had corrupted the purity of their faith, and worst of all, the followers of Jesus were using THEIR Jewish texts in their cult! All the New Testament books and letters were written originally in Greek, except the Gospel of Matthew which was originally in either Hebrew or possibly Aramaic as it was written originally for the conservative and scholarly Jewish Christian community in Antioch.

The Jews meeting at Jamnia decided to eliminate all Scripture that was not originally written in Hebrew as corrupted. This automatically disqualified any possibility that any of this Jesus = Messiah stuff would ever get taken seriously by "good Jews" (although I confess I do not know how they got around Matthew's gospel), but by default, it also meant that several books of the Old Testament Scripture that were written from the 4th century BC and later, originally in Greek rather than Hebrew, also got bounced from their list of accepted books. Their goal was to discredit any and all writings that supported Christianity, and if it cost them a handful of their original Old Testament, so be it. Most Jews today have a *Jamnian Old Testament* (Ethiopian Jews retained the Septuagint, however), and that's the Old Testament that Luther adopted in his <u>Bible</u>, and it is still the Old Testament used in Protestant <u>Bibles</u> today. Check it out sometime – Catholic <u>Bibles</u> are fatter than Protestant <u>Bibles</u> – they have more books in the Old Testament. Luther's position, and the subsequent Protestant tradition has been that the Old Testament was a Jewish collection of books, and the Jews ought to be able to determine for themselves what that canon should include. The Catholic and Orthodox position has always been to use the Old Testament books Jesus and the Apostles used, regardless of amendments made in the Jewish tradition after Jesus' time. The Old Testament books written originally in Greek are called (in the Catholic and Orthodox faiths) "Deuterocanonicals," or "second canon" because they were written later than the Torah, Prophets, Psalms and some of the older histories of kings and judges, which were originally in Hebrew (Deuterocanonicals were written between the 4th and 2nd centuries BC). These books include: Baruch, Judith, Tobit, Wisdom, Sirach, and 1 and 2 Maccabees, and parts of the Book of Daniel and also parts of Esther. Luther labeled these books as "Apocrypha," or uninspired books, placing them in the same category as books that never got in the <u>Bible</u> in the first place. He placed these books in an appendix, and eventually most Protestant Bibles dropped them altogether.

Additionally, Luther found fault with 4 books in the New Testament: The letter of James (which he nicknamed "the Epistle of Straw" in the preface of his 1522 translation of the New Testament – added to the Jamnian Old Testament in 1536 to become the new Protestant Bible) was especially problematic, and also Hebrews, Jude and Revelation. He set these books aside as another separated appendix, suggesting they were less inspired than the rest of the <u>Bible</u>, however after Luther died, his followers put the New Testament books back in the way they were. Finally, Luther tidied up the wording in Paul's letter to the Romans, by adding the word "alone" to Romans 3:28 so that it more clearly supported his Sola Fide theology. Needless to say, this did nothing to help mend differences between the Catholic and Lutheran Churches. The Catholics held yet another council (Trent) where they insisted that the <u>Bible</u> be restored to its original books and content, the Protestants kept their <u>Bible</u> as Luther had amended it, and the Reformation marched forward.

Germany rapidly accepted Martin Luther's new brand of Christianity, and across Northern Europe, pockets of the Protestant Reformation took hold during the 16th century. While Flanders remained predominantly Catholic (as did France and Spain), the Dutch in Holland moved away from the Catholic Church toward assorted branches of Protestantism. As rapidly as the Reformation began, it began to subdivide into splinter groups with one variation on theology or another, many of them disagreeing on fundamental issues of faith with each other as much as they disagreed with the Catholic and Orthodox Churches.

Pieter Bruegel

Pieter Bruegel was born, raised and educated in Holland during the 16th century, and accordingly he lived at exactly the time that all these changes were taking place in Europe, and in a region where the changes were making an impact on the lives of ordinary citizens. He was probably born in 1525, and he died young in 1569, leaving a young family behind. He studied painting as an apprentice in Breda, Holland, and after establishing his early career there, later moved to Antwerp, Flanders, right on the northern border shared with Holland. He lived there most of his short adult life, with only a brief stay in Brussels around the time of his marriage. We know that unlike many other artists of his day, Bruegel had the opportunity to travel some, taking a two-year trip in 1552-3 to France and Italy.

Bruegel serves as an interesting departure from the painting of not so many years earlier in the Netherlands. From Van Eyck to Van der Goes to Memlinc we find a consistency of focus on religious subject matters, but with Bruegel we discover an almost overnight shift away from faith as the source of inspiration, toward secular humanism, a phenomenon which is born during the High Renaissance in Protestant regions, and will expand over the centuries to eventually replace Christian themes in art almost entirely. **The Massacre of the Innocents** serves as a good introduction to this idea. Often in the Early Renaissance in Flanders, a Christian theme might be depicted with a domestic ambience, like scenes where donor figures are seen alongside Jesus and Mary in a setting that seems more familiar and cozy than it does lofty and religious. Be that as it may, there is never any question that Jesus and Mary are the grand pooh-bahs in the painting, and everyone else is shown in humble deference to the holy stars of the show. In Bruegel's sample of religious painting, it is pretty well impossible to find any clue that the scene has religious overtones at all. True, it does depict the threat of an army apparently bent on attacking wee children, but aside from the title, there is absolutely nothing that suggests anything out of the <u>Bible</u>. It may as well be some atrocity that took place last year in downtown Eindhoven. It looks more like a local event with local people.

Better still as an example of Bruegel at his best is the painting called **Netherlandish Proverbs**. The painting illustrates the movement in Holland away from

God and the mysteries of faith, toward an interest on secular "proverbs" as a way to instruct and manage one's affairs. In a way, Netherlandish Proverbs might be compared to the sort of catchy secular wisdom imparted by our own Benjamin Franklin in colonial America. It places the emphasis on man, and his own thinking, usually to the exclusion of God and religion ("a stitch in time saves nine," "early to bed, early to rise makes a man healthy, wealthy and wise" and so forth). Netherlandish Proverbs is brimming with clever little sayings, illustrated in such a way that a Dutch or Flemish person would have no difficulty finding all the hidden images, rather like a child finding the hidden pictures in a Highlights Magazine. Many of the sayings would be foreign to us in America, but others cross cultural boundaries easily. For example, on the roof of the house, there is a man shooting one arrow after another. This is tantamount to the saying you might hear of throwing away good effort after bad – fighting a losing battle long after you should have realized it is a lost cause. Or take a look in the lower left hand corner of the picture, and find the man who is butting his head against a brick wall – that one translates directly into our culture as a way of saying that one's efforts are futile. In the lower right hand corner of the painting there are a few images that should strike a familiar chord with American viewers. How about the man holding an orb topped by a cross – he has the whole world in the palm of his hand. And next to him is a distraught person crying over spilt milk. My personal favorite is the guy bent over a table trying unsuccessfully to reach between a pair of pancakes – he is trying to stretch to make ends meet. In all, there are 92 peasant proverbs included in this modest over-the-sofa sized painting.

Pieter Bruegel's preference for secular imagery frequently moved beyond art with meaning, if not religiously inspired meaning like Netherlandish Proverbs, to paintings with no particular meaning at all. Some good examples of this were a series of pictures commissioned by Niclaes Jonghelinck, a wealthy patron from Antwerp. They were landscapes produced to illustrate the seasons. **Hay Harvest** illustrates spring, **Wheat Harvest** illustrates summer, **Return of the Herd** is a scene depicting autumn, and **Hunters in the Snow** depicts winter. These pleasant pictures hearken back to the calendar pages found in Early Renaissance Books of Hours, where the whole point of the painting is to illustrate seasonal weather and activities. In these pictures, the artist attempts to improve the realistic representation of space through the use of diagonals employed to lead the eye into the background landscape, aerial perspective to make things in the background appear dull and more blue-grey by comparison to the foreground, and finally diminishing scale such that things that are far away are smaller than objects in the foreground.

Northern painters from Flanders and Holland during the 15th and 16th centuries made considerable progress in developing new techniques and ideas, many of which were not seen in Italy until decades after they were introduced in the North. Oil paint was invented here and widely used long before it was known or adopted in Italy. Likewise, there were advancements in the areas of portraiture, where the old-fashioned profile was replaced with the more challenging ¾ view. In the North, portraiture matured during the early 15th century, while in Italy we do not find comparable attention paid to portrait technique until the latter 15th century. Landscape, too, flourished as an interest in the North, with attention paid toward making scenery look as real as possible, while in Italy it was strictly the backdrop for "more important" subjects during the Renaissance. The word "renaissance" means "rebirth." The question, of course, is a rebirth of *what*? In

Italy, it will be the rebirth of antiquity, with artists looking back to Greece and Rome for ideas and images. In Northern Europe, examples of art from Greece and Rome were hard to come by, given that Greece and Rome as civilizations were found ... well ... in Greece and Rome! But this doesn't mean that the North was mothballed during the 15th and 16th centuries, without growth and development, and without a gradual shifting away from Medieval thinking, imagery, and techniques. In the North there was an emphasis on learning, and increasingly under the influence of the Protestant Reformation, a shift away from religious emphasis in art, toward a new focus on the ideas and activities of men, that is secular humanism.

12. **Early Italian Renaissance Art**

c. 1400 - 1500

The Renaissance in Italy was a much more dramatic and rapid departure from the Medieval world than what we saw across Northern Europe. That said, unlike the north where general statements might apply to broad regions, the Italian peninsula was populated by individual city-states during the 15th and 16th centuries, and when you speak of "Italian," you are really speaking of trends and accomplishments of selected cities rather than the whole country as we think of it today. Each independent city-state in Italy had its own government, and these might be a monarchy (ruled by a king) or a duchy (ruled by a duke), or a republic (ruled by elected officials). During the early Renaissance, the leader in art and other cultural pursuits was the city of Florence, which had long been a republic with warring political factions. Going all the way back to the 1200's, the two prominent political parties in Florence were the *Guelphs* and *Ghibellines*. The Guelphs tended to be the rank and file "regular people," middle class families with middle class values. The Ghibellines were the old landed nobility – the classy folks of yesterday's feudal social structure who wanted to hold onto power and control serfs while the Guelphs were predominantly guildsmen who lived in town rather than on the outskirts on estates. They were artisans and merchants who were more progressive in that they wanted to see power restructured to represent them more effectively.

In the middle of these political rivalries in Florence was the Medici family, who would rise to be the great rulers of Florence during the Early Renaissance. Giovanni di Bicci de Medici (1360-1429) started a bank to serve the rising merchant and craftsmen class, and he also established himself as banker to the papacy which in turn created a vast wealth for the Medici family. Giovanni was a modest patron of the arts, but his son, Cosimo (1389-1464), and his grandson, Lorenzo the Magnificent (1449-92) made Florence the cultural and art capital of the Early Renaissance. What separated the Medicis from other ruling families elsewhere was they frequently used their money to sponsor the arts in Florence such that public works given to the city were paid for privately by the family. Naturally their generosity helped to maintain Medici esteem in the polls, because the sort of project they underwrote engendered civic pride among the citizens, and lucky for the average guy on the street, paying for all the pretty stuff around town didn't come out of his pocket in the way of extra taxes. Their popularity prevailed, and by 1434 Cosimo had altered Florentine law such that the so-called Republic could only elect members of the Medici family to serve at the leadership level.

In 1401 the Medicis sponsored a contest that pushed the arts in Florence from Medieval to Renaissance overnight. First of all, the Medicis did not go in for the idea of a single court artist or town artist like we saw in Flanders. For one thing, if one of their primary motivations for sponsoring art was to maintain good public relations in Florence, then it made sense to draw as much attention to their charitable deeds as possible. If there were a court artist, it could become ho-hum routine that he was producing yet another goodie for the public to admire. On the other hand, a competition was exciting news. As it happened, the competition process had some beneficial side effects. For example, it opened the door for more artists to compete. It also tended to promote the notion that artists needed to be different from one another, and trying new things in order to get noticed. It assured the patron that he could expect to get the best person for the job, and also that he might expect to pay the best price as artists might be inclined to compete with their prices as well as their talent. The downside was that artists could not count on their popularity remaining stable, and sometimes this translated into not developing a promising idea (like a formula for oil painting in the north, or how to improve landscape painting) because the artist might be less inclined to work on the same idea for a period of time to perfect it.

The goal of the 1401 competition was to find an artist to create new doors for the town baptistery. Florence Baptistery had been built during the Middle Ages, originally with plain, wooden doors with the idea that later on these could be replaced with more expensive models. There were three entrances, north and south, and the main entrance facing east, directly across the street from the west entrance of the cathedral. The south entrance had already been upgraded with handsome bronze doors, and the Medici's plan was to commission a set of similar doors for the north entrance. The competition for the North Doors commission was open to all artists, and was set to be judged by the Imported Wool Refiners, which was the oldest and most prestigious *guild* in the city. Guilds functioned somewhat like unions, or professional societies. They provided opportunities for young people to apprentice and learn a trade, then join the guild and be respected as qualified pros in their field.

Lorenzo Ghiberti

To enter the 1401 contest, each artist had to submit a bronze relief sculpture panel depicting the **Sacrifice of Isaac**. The Sacrifice of Isaac is a Biblical theme from the Old Testament. Abraham, an ancient man by the time he finally had the son God had promised for many years, was asked to sacrifice the boy to prove to God that he would do whatever God commanded. He did not understand, but resigned himself to do what he had to do, and set out on a journey with Isaac who remained clueless about his destiny. At the appropriate time, Abraham had Isaac build an altar to offer a sacrifice to God, with Isaac still assuming an animal was to be killed. When Abraham raised his hand to slay his son according to God's will, God, now being assured of Abraham's sincerity, stopped the execution and provided a ram for the holocaust instead. The quatrefoil (4-lobed frame containing the scene) design as well as the figures and animals to be included were specified by the contest rules. In the end, the two top entries were the two artists least expected to win. The first runner up was *Filippo Brunelleschi*, who was a few years older and trained as an architect, but not especially a full-time sculptor. The winner was Lorenzo Ghiberti who was still an apprentice, and studying to be a painter at that.

What was it that Ghiberti and Brunelleschi did that captured the attention of the judges? Both depicted young Isaac nude. Nothing in the Biblical account would suggest that Isaac would be trooping around the countryside in the buff, so we can see this as an innovation both artists employed as a way to have their work be noticed. There is a striking difference between the two nudes, however. Brunelleschi's boy looks like a gawky youth, all elbows and knees. More than likely he used a real child as his model, perhaps an apprentice. Ghiberti's figure on the other hand was modeled after a classical Greek nude. It is the first time since antiquity (excepting a couple rare jamb statues at Reims Cathedral) that art from ancient Greece or Rome served as a prototype for current art, and therefore it marks the "renaissance," or rebirth of antiquity. Artists in Italy from this point forward will begin to focus increasingly on art from the classical world as an inspiration for their work.

A few years later, the Medicis arranged another sculpture extravaganza to improve downtown Florence. There was a huge building in downtown called Orsanmichele. Built in 1337, Orsanmichele served the city as a massive wheat exchange and granary to help citizens feel safe that there would never be a famine in their town due to natural disaster, famine or war, and the building also housed a small chapel. In 1339 fourteen decorative niches were created to improve the street level experience of having a big warehouse downtown in the heart of the city. The guilds were expected to each pony up for a larger than life sized statue to fill the niches, but by 1400 only three statues were installed. The Medici family now intervened to step up production by offering matching funds for project.

The Medicis persuaded all the guilds to commission a statue of the patron saint of their choice for a decorative niche, with these niches wrapping around the building exterior to dress the place up. Their family would provide matching funds for whatever sum of money each guild could raise so they could each afford twice as nice art than they might if they had to pay for it all themselves. The guilds that were rich could pick and choose what artists they liked, and those who could afford Ghiberti gave him their business. Ghiberti by now was the darling of the Florence art world, and he could charge whatever he liked and attract customers. **Saint John the Baptist** was commissioned by the Imported Wool Refiners for Orsanmichele. It was the first cast bronze statue of this scale (over 8' tall) produced since antiquity, and there were reservations over whether it was even possible. It is easy to identify images and statues of <u>Saint John the Baptist</u> because he usually wears animal pelts, as we can see here with the furry looking vest under his elegant toga-styled wrap. Ghiberti made his name as an expert in cast bronze, and his treatment of fabric, as we see here, often resembles dramatic fenders on a vintage car more than it looks like soft folds in a robe. The style is reminiscent of International Style like the Gothic jamb statue of the Archangel Gabriel from Reims Cathedral.

Donatello

Donato di Niccolo Bardi, called by the nickname Donatello was a contemporary of Ghiberti, although he trained initially as a goldsmith rather than in painting. Compared to Ghiberti, Donatello's career got off to a slower start. He wasn't as socially polished as Ghiberti, so in addition to not winning a big contest when he was still a student which gave Ghiberti's career an early boost, Donatello wasn't as suave, and therefore not as appealing in the social role of charming artiste. He was just starting out at the point when the Medicis introduced their project for Orsanmichele, and as a relative newcomer on the sculpture scene at that point, Donatello was also the bargain artist for any guild that could not afford the high-priced guys like Ghiberti. Two of the less wealthy guilds, the Linen Weavers and Peddlers found themselves too poor to compete with men like the Imported Wool Refiners. In fact, until they pooled their resources and decided to go in on one statue between the two guilds, they were priced out of the project altogether, even with matching funds from the Medicis. They hired Donatello to create for them a statue of **Saint Mark**. Like Saint John the Baptist by Ghiberti, Saint Mark is well over life-size, but the artist used a less expensive stone for this statue rather than pricey cast bronze. Throughout his career, Donatello excelled at customizing his statues for the patron; something Ghiberti was less interested in pursuing. Ghiberti developed his style, and when he made a statue, he produced "a Ghiberti," which presumably was what his patrons wanted. If you were to compare him to an actor, he would be the guy who tends to play variations of the same role in every movie because that's what the people pay to see. Think Jackie Chan. He does his schtick, and that's what the public expects. It was the same with Ghiberti. Donatello was the "character actor" of the sculpture world in that everything he did had its own character, and was a little different from anything else in his repertoire. Comparing him to the big screen, think of Billy Bob Thornton and Vincent D'Onofrio. These actors play roles so extremely diverse that you may not even realize who it is at first when you are watching the movie. Donatello's statues have that same level of individual character.

How can you tell that Saint Mark was commissioned by Linen Weavers and Peddlers? His clothes are a bit rough and shabby looking, so he might look poor. Beyond that, the fabric in his garments *looks* like linen. This is no accident, Donatello first made a miniature figure in clay … nude, and then dressed his small figure in wet, real linen robes (fabric soaked in "slip," which is a gooey mixture of clay and water that will dry stiff, so the little figure could be moved without messing up the robes). In addition to his interest in personalizing sculpture to suit the patron, he was also interested in paying homage to art of the past, by introducing accurate contrapposto.

One of Donatello's most famous statues is also one of his most ambiguous: **David**. The theme of David was popular in Florence, and visitors to the city even today find statues and images of David at every turn. Florentine affection for David dates back to the Middle Ages. During the 14th century, the Duchy of Milan in northern Italy posed a threat to Florence. The Lombard city-state had captured territories across northern Italy and began pressing south to encroach on Florentine sovereignty. In the process, Florence was cut off from her port facilities which compromised trade. Milan was poised to take control of Florence because to many old noble families across Italy, Florence posed a cultural threat with her middle class guilds and disdain for old feudal political systems. As luck would have it, the Duke of Milan died unexpectedly before the siege took place, which Florence saw as divine providence protecting their city from certain demise. After the challenge from Milan, next Naples to the south threatened Florence. Against the odds, Florence repelled the advances of her formidable foe, and defended her independence. The citizens began to liken their successes to young David winning against one Goliath after another, and so David became a freedom symbol for the proud city of Florence.

Donatello's version of David is a life-size cast bronze statue, and is credited as being the first life-size, freestanding nude produced since antiquity. That said, it is hardly a classical nude by Greek standards; why is the lad stark naked except for boots and a hat

... and what about that hat! It looks more like a fashionable Easter bonnet than something a Biblical shepherd would wear. The boy also does not have the anatomy of Greek nude – he is too young, physically immature, and too ... well ... effeminate. Ask yourself this: would *you* want this guy in charge of defending *your* city? Hmmmm ... maybe not. Given that the artist is Donatello, what would you most want to know to help you understand this statue of <u>David</u>? Probably you would want to know who paid for it, because with Donatello, this usually casts light on what motivated the artist to produce the work in a particular way. The problem is that there is no record of a commission.

The statue shows up in the inventory of Lorenzo de Medici in 1490, which is about 60 years after the statue was created. Many scholars are satisfied that it was therefore a Medici commission. Some, however, are not satisfied with that assumption. For starters, the Medicis were bankers by trade. Does it seem reasonable that a banker would forget to record money spent on a life-size bronze statue? We are not talking the cost of a bag of jellybeans here; life-size bronze statues cost a pretty penny. Beyond that, would there be any logical reason for the Medicis to desire a version of the city's freedom symbol looking less than heroic? What would they gain publicity-wise by having their city's pride in self defense reduced to a swishy kid wearing a flowered hat?

One scholar who was moved to look for an alternative explanation was the late Dr. Horst W. Janson. In the mid 1960's he proposed the theory that just maybe there was no commission for the work. How the Medicis got it 60 years later we do not know, but just suppose that the artist, who was doing well financially by the 1430's when we assume this statue was made, suppose Donatello created this statue for himself. It wasn't unheard of. Although artists as a rule did all their work for paying clients at this point in history, many artists occasionally made sculpture or paintings to suit their own tastes, not especially with an eye toward selling the piece. Then you have to ask: why would Donatello choose to make David look a certain way?

Few scholars would argue with the fact that Donatello was apparently gay; this was no secret to anyone studying the artist as he got in trouble with the guild for keeping on young apprentices who seemed to have been getting more of an education in the bedroom than in the studio. Okay. Could this be some sort of homosexual expression – turning the <u>Bible</u> hero into an object of affection? Donatello liked the boys, and on inspection, this boy is young (the age the artist apparently preferred), he is a bit effeminate with his peculiar attire, and the exaggerated contrapposto almost makes him look petulant. See how the bronze was polished? This is the only statue Donatello polished, hearkening back to Praxiteles and his subtle invitations to come pat the naked, sensual fellow on his tush.

Why David? Could the artist not have used Adam who was supposed to be naked in the <u>Bible</u>, or even Isaac who had already been depicted in his birthday suit by other artists, and who was a male about the age Donatello sought? Why did it have to be David? In 1 Samuel 18:1-3 and 1 Samuel 18:16 David is described as being much loved, not only by women but also by men after he killed Goliath. Look at Donatello's statue. Unlike most of the depictions of David at this time, our hero holds a sword, not a slingshot. He also stands on the head of Goliath, clearly indicating that the time sequence of Donatello's statue is *after* he killed Goliath. Now, it is unlikely that the authors of the Old Testament were suggesting that after David killed Goliath, that suddenly he was besieged with homosexual lovers! In the absence of an explained commission, it is impossible to discern whether this was Donatello's private interpretation and thereby the inspiration for this statue, or whether the theory is completely absurd. It is not uniformly supported by any measure, but then nobody else has provided a persuasive explanation either … do with it what you will.

Donatello is considered to be one of the greatest, if not *the* greatest sculptor of the Early Renaissance in Italy. His versatility is much admired, as well as the simplicity of his work which recalls the classic simplicity of ancient Greece, even when his actual subjects do not appear to copy Greek prototypes as closely as many other Italian artists.

Gentile da Fabriano

Painting lagged behind sculpture in Italy in terms of shifting gears away from Medieval styles in favor of something new. During the first quarter of the 15th century, most paintings followed along in International Style much like what we saw in northern Europe. The **Adoration of the Magi** by Gentile da Fabriano is a perfect example.

Gentile di Niccolo di Giovanni di Massio was one of the first painters to make a big name for himself in 15th century Italy. Although born in the small town of Fabriano (hence his nickname "Gentile from Fabriano"), he was first documented in 1408 as a painter working in Venice. He may have been trained in Venice, or Milan according to other scholars. In 1420 he settled in Florence where he rented a house and 2 years later in 1422 he entered the painter's guild living in the district of Santa Trinita Church. Gentile painted the Adoration of the Magi for that church in 1423 as a commission for Palla Strozzi, who at the time was possibly the richest man in Florence (considerably richer than the Medicis). He must have been since this 10' x 9' altarpiece was painted just for the sacristy (the room where priests put on their robes) – not even as the altarpiece for a chapel much less the main altar!

Like Italian Gothic painting produced about a hundred years earlier (think altarpieces by Cimabue or Giotto), Gentile's painting is contained by an elaborate, cathedral-inspired carved gold frame. The flattened and somewhat elongated figures are dressed in sumptuous, elegant fabrics and stand in an overcrowded, shallow space. These are characteristics that we associate with International Style. Think of the January page of the Tres Riches Heures du Duc de Berry for a comparable painting from the North, only in France the example of International Style is a small manuscript illustration, and here is it an enormous altarpiece The difference in scale alone speaks volumes about the early differences between the North and Italy. Whereas Northern Renaissance painting evolved out of a manuscript tradition, in Italy Renaissance painting can be traced back to icons and mosaics prototypes which were reinterpreted into large-scale altarpieces during the latter Middle Ages.

Masaccio

The artist who changed the face of painting in Italy is Masaccio, whose short career (he was a victim of Bubonic Plague in his mid-20's) was centered around the close of the first quarter century in Florence. Born Tommaso di Ser Giovanni di Mone Cassai, his nickname "Masaccio" can have different meanings, but probably it meant "Big Tom," as opposed to his teacher Masolino – also a nickname - meaning "Little Tom." Not sure if that was meant as a commentary of their relative physical stature, or perhaps in hindsight it was an observation that the student wound up becoming much more famous than his teacher.

The painting we will consider was produced when young Masaccio was still an apprentice working under Masolino, who employed International Style like most everyone else at the time. The **Tribute Money** is a fresco, so it is still in its original location, in the Brancacci Chapel (therefore commissioned by the Brancacci family, who were friends and supporters of the Medicis), in the church of Santa Maria del Carmine in Florence. The style of the chapel with its multiple scenes telling a story is not unlike the Arena Chapel in Padua produced over a hundred years earlier. The frescoes here all deal with the life of Saint Peter, which is a bit unusual for Florence, albeit more common in Rome.

You will recall that Florence had experienced some difficulties with her neighbors, Milan especially. The fresco series in the Brancacci Chapel was apparently an effort to flatter the papacy such that Florence might count on the pope's support if war broke out. The Tribute Money, which features Saint Peter three times in the scene, deals with taxation by conflating two passages from the Gospel of Matthew into a single scene. In Mt 22:17-22 the Pharisees have asked Jesus whether it is right for the Jews to pay their taxes to Rome, as they resent having to support a pagan government that represses the local people. He asks whose picture is one the coin, and they are obliged to admit it is Caesar, to which he responds that they are to render to Caesar what is Caesar's and to God what belongs to God (translated, pay your taxes whether you like it or not). In the scene, the Apostles have been substituted for Pharisees, but we see the Roman-attired tax collector twice as he asks for the money in the center of the scene, and then off to the right, Peter, begrudgingly it appears, pays the tax collector. The other Bible passage referenced here is Mt 17:24-27. Here, Peter comes to Jesus (which is what the fresco shows), but his question is about paying the Temple tax, which would not involve a Roman-attired tax collector. Jesus in this case suggests they should be exempt from the tax, but to set a good example by paying anyway, he sends Peter down to a steam to collect the tax coin from a fish's mouth (seen at the far left of the fresco). This choice of topic may have been related to a new tax passed to help offset the cost of defending Florence from Milan. There was debate on whether clergy should be expected to pay the tax.

The Tribute Money introduces two new ideas to Italian painting that would have a profound impact on painting during the Renaissance, and beyond. The first is *sfumato*. Sfumato is the fogging or hazing out of a background landscape such that it offers an illusion that there is a landscape in the background, but the weather is too foggy to see it in any detail. In Northern Europe, artists took great interest in experimenting with landscape. These artists came from a manuscript tradition, where artists took pride in laboriously painting minute detail. In Italy by contrast, most painting during the Middle Ages was inspired by mosaics and icons. An artist painted figures, and then opted to dispense with effort paid to a detailed background, usually painting the whole thing flat gold instead. Sfumato is somewhere in between landscape in the north, and the complete absence of landscape in Medieval Italy. Masaccio painted just enough landscape, a few trees, and some hills, to suggest that there *is* a landscape, but the foggy atmosphere excused the artist from having to paint the level of detail seen in the art up north.

The second new idea, and by far the more critically important, is *chiaroscuro*. Chiaroscuro is the contrast of light and dark, or highlight and shadow. Other artists, like Giotto for example, had experimented with this idea before, but Masaccio is the first to pull it off successfully. His objective was to make his figures look modeled and three-dimensional, figures with mass and weight, realistic, not flat. To accomplish this, he used the actual light source in the chapel, a window behind the altar, as the light source in his painting. All the figures are highlighted on the side of their bodies that face the window, and shadowed on the side away from the window. With highlights and shadows working consistently throughout the painting, the figures have a believable volume not seen in Italian painting during the Middle Ages.

Fra Filippo Lippi

Masaccio became the hero of Italian painting during most of the 15th century, and many artists followed in his footsteps. Filippo Lippi is a good example of one who held Masaccio in the highest regard. Filippo was born to a large family, and in a throwback to earlier times perhaps, his parents took young Filippo to a monastery to be raised by monks. Filippo Lippi became a brother in the Carmelite order, hence he is known as "Fra Filippo," or "Brother Philip." The Carmelite order is known for either attracting or producing more than its fair share of mystics, although Fra Filippo does not appear to have been blessed with such gifts. He had a talent for painting, and spent many childhood hours in front of the frescoes at the Brancacci Chapel marveling at Masaccio's work.

Unfortunately, Fra Filippo Lippi was not cut out to be a pious monk as early in his adult life he managed to get a local nun pregnant (it would appear that young Lucretia Buti was likewise ill-suited to her life of celibacy and obedience … ahem …). Both were chastised and assigned penance in the hope that they would turn their lives around, but alas, it didn't take long before Lucretia was pregnant again. Cosimo de Medici intervened and encouraged the Church to release both from their monastic vows so they could marry and raise their family. Fra Flippo and Lucretia married, and both did a better job living up to that vocation than either did to a celibate life.

Lippi's **Madonna and Child** is one of several portraits of his beloved Lucretia portrayed as the Virgin Mary, and their infant son, Filippino Lippi as Jesus (Filippino went on to also become a painter, by the way). Like Masaccio, Fra Filippo Lippi employed more landscape than earlier Italian painters, although Lippi's are usually richer and more detailed than his mentor's. He also modeled his figures in modest highlight and shadows to give his Madonnas a gentle life-like beauty. Incidentally, Fra Filippo continued to use his later unofficial title of "brother" throughout his entire career, long after parting ways with monastic life. Despite his inability to measure up to the strict rules of celibacy and obedience, he evidently still felt very strongly about the privilege of being a monk, and was loathe to relinquish the title even many years after he was married.

Fra Angelico

If Fra Filippo Lippi was the renegade monk of the 15th century art world, Fra Angelico was the perfect model of devout faith. Fra Angelico was born Guido di Pietro and later, after taking vows as a Dominican monk, was renamed Fra Giovanni da Fiesole. He was popularly called Fra Angelico, a name which seems all the more fitting today as he was beatified in 1983. Fra Angelico was trained as a painter before his calling and he was already working as a professional artist prior to making his monastic vows. Although Dominicans traditionally didn't have monasteries, by the 15th century occasional monasteries were built as Dominicans changed from being strictly mendicants to teachers. Fra Angelico started his life as a monk in the Dominican monastery near his home town of Fiesole. During this time, he frequently accepted commissions to paint in addition to his other duties as a friar.

His **Annunciation** painted originally for the cathedral in Cortona would be an excellent example of his painting at this time. Although a mid-century artist, Fra Angelico's style is like Jan van Eyck, the Limbourg Brothers or Gentile da Fabriano with textured detail and bright colors more than anything resembling Masaccio. Mary is seen inside a Romanesque interior. It should be quickly noted that no particular symbolism was meant to be implied since few Italian artists took an interest in hidden symbolism like they did in Flanders. There are no lilies here, although occasionally that is one symbol the Italians will include. The enclosed garden from Song of Songs is another, recalling Mary's virginity. Adam and Eve are shown in the background to remind us that sin was brought into the world when Eve disobeyed God, while Mary, the second Eve, brings Salvation by saying yes to God that she will bear the Christ. Unlike typical altarpieces from northern Europe, Italian altarpieces frequently include a string of small images running along the base of the frame called a ***predella***. The scenes incorporated into the predella usually dovetail into the main theme of the altarpiece, as if to tell the rest of the story. On this altarpiece for example, the predella scenes include the Birth of Mary, her Betrothal to Joseph, the Visitation when Mary went to visit her kinswoman Elizabeth, the Adoration of the Magi, Mary Presenting baby Jesus at the Temple, the Dormition of the Virgin where Mary died (fell asleep in the Lord), and finally her miraculous appearance to Saint Dominic.

Several years later Fra Angelico moved to the Monastery of San Marco in Florence. The Dominicans had been in Florence for some time, but during the 15th century another order of monks, the obscure Sylvestrines, had suffered diminishing numbers among their faithful, and they donated their monastery to the busy Dominicans who could now live as a community there. Given that Fra Angelico had demonstrated a gift for painting, he was asked to produce a series of frescos for the monastery's chapter house, corridors, and forty-four individual cells (bedrooms for monks) so that the men might be inspired by the frescos during their times of solitude and prayer. Dominicans hold special reverence for the Virgin Mary, and so many of the frescos focus attention on Mary, especially repeated images of the Annunciation. Many of these paintings were paid for by Cosimo de Medici who enjoyed a special affection for the Dominicans. He supported them well and often retired to the monastery himself, where the monks kept a bedroom "cell" set aside for his visits. There Cosimo could spend periods of seclusion and prayer away from politics and business as usual.

The **Annunciation** seen here is one of several frescoes of the same subject matter completed inside the walls of San Marco. Fra Angelico paid much less attention to Masaccio's innovations than most other artists working in the mid-15th century. His paintings seem to reach back to the serenity of medieval imagery, with more attention paid to the glory of faith, than to the realism of the world. The figures are contained in an enclosed, architectural space, as if the niche where Gabriel confronts the Virgin were adjacent to the monk's quarters, and there is little interest in chiaroscuro here. Incidentally, that's Saint Dominic in the background behind the Archangel Gabriel.

The **Last Supper** is also a fresco from a private cell at San Marco. Last Supper imagery will fall into one of two categories, and it's worth paying attention to which one is being presented. One way of presenting the scene is to emphasize the betrayal of Judas. The other places the emphasis on the institution of the Eucharist. Fra Angelico selected the latter concept which probably should come as no surprise since as a monk, he would have greater interest in the Eucharist as Christ's saving gift to the Church than in the particulars of the betrayal. In the scene, we see Christ offering communion to Saint John - like a priest would do at Mass - rather than a bunch of guys sitting around a table eating dinner. Saint Peter is off to the far right, and those Apostles who would have blocked our view have graciously left their stools and knelt on the floor. The Virgin Mary has also joined the party and can be seen off to the lower left.

Piero della Francesca

All the artists considered so far were Florentines working during the early to mid-15th century. Piero della Francesca wasn't from Florence, although for a time in his early career he visited the city and apprenticed briefly under a local master. Piero della Francesca came from a small town called Borgo San Sepulchro, and as an adult he became court artist in the Duchy of Urbino. Urbino isn't a big city today, so it may come as a surprise that during the 15th and early 16th centuries it was a lively art center, if not as famous as Florence, still ahead of many larger cities in Italy at the time. The Duke of Urbino, Federico da Montefeltro, was a celebrated general, and he was selected by the pope to train the papal army at an academy in Urbino. The Duke was an educated man, and from his point of view, it wasn't enough for the men being schooled there to simply develop good military skills, like citizens of Sparta, he expected the soldiers to be polished gentlemen as well, perhaps a little like Athens. Federico brought in scholars in a variety of fields to help round out the education of his pupils, and among the subjects emphasized, the arts were given considerable attention.

Piero painted portraits of **Federico da Montefeltro** and his wife, **Battista Sforza** sometime between 1472 and 1474 (scholars disagree whether these were completed in anticipation of the Duke's promotion from Count to Duke status or in celebration of the achievement). If they were completed in early 1472, Battista Sforza of the new ruling family in Milan was still alive, but by 1474 she had passed on, having died in childbirth in July 1472. If the portraits were completed after her death, then presumably a death mask was used to assure the Duchess looked like herself. Notice that both are profile portraits, a continuing tradition in Italy long past the introduction of the more challenging ¾ portrait in Flanders. There may well have been a particular incentive for Piero to paint the Duke in profile, regardless of popular styles, because Federico was missing his right eye, along with the bridge of his nose as you can see, both casualties of heroics in a tournament.

Piero often used landscape as a way to include additional information in his paintings. Some argue that the background in Battista's painting shows architecture from the sleepy town of Gubbio, which is where she and the children were staying in 1472 during construction on the palace at Urbino, and where she died during childbirth. Piero was not in the habit of signing his paintings, although he frequently included snippets of his obscure hometown in the background landscape in lieu of adding his name to the piece, and some scholars think that rather than Gubbio, elements of Borgo San Sepulchro are seen in the background. No matter, because that isn't the most interesting thing about the landscapes anyway. The landscapes in each portrait, both created mathematically with accurate perspective, appear to show slight curvature of the Earth, suggesting that decades before Columbus sailed the Atlantic and put to rest certitude that the world was flat, ideas of a round planet were already being discussed at the court in Urbino. Federico da Montefeltro was an intellectual man, and evidently so was Piero della Francesca as his status in court was in no small way enhanced by his ability to match wits with the Duke. At the same time period as these clever men, there was an Italian mapmaker named Paolo del Pozzo Toscanelli. Toscanelli believed the world was round, and despite this being a "scary" idea at the time, he created a map to illustrate as best he could this concept. It was this map that set Columbus on his course to prove Toscanelli's theory. Apparently Federico and Piero were familiar with Toscanelli as we see the influence of new scientific theory surfacing in Piero's art.

The **Brera Madonna** (also called simply the *Madonna and Child with Saints*) by Piero della Francesca, so named for its location in the Brera Gallery in Milan, is a curious painting. Like other Renaissance paintings, we expect to find the central subject in the center of the picture, and sure enough, there sits the Virgin Mary with the baby Jesus in her lap. What's odd about the mother and child, though, is that Jesus is not sitting up. Instead, he has been laid across Mom's lap. In Christian iconography, there are few circumstances where Christ is depicted in a prone position. First, when he is an infant in the manger, he is lying down. We do not see him lying down again until after he has been crucified. Typically, he may be shown lying at the foot of the cross with Mary, Saint John and others wailing over his death – this is called a *lamentation*, or he may be draped across Mary's lap, which is called a *pieta*. In this painting, Christ appears to be posed as a pieta, which raises questions as to why this might be. Let's look for clues. We see on the right side of the painting that the Duke has been included as a donor figure, along with a couple angels and a selection of patron saints. Across from the Duke, there are another couple angels and more patron saints, but a gaping hole where we would expect to find Battista.

Battista Sforza died during the summer of 1472. She was only 26 years old, with 8 daughters already, she died giving birth to their ninth child, Guidobaldo, the first and only son and heir to the Montefeltro realm. At the time, Federico had been consumed with work on a new palace, but he put those plans on hold and built a new church instead in honor of his wife for which he commissioned this altarpiece. The painting later made its way back to her family in Milan. The Brera Madonna then is a memorial to Battista, and a tribute to the birth of her son. The death is symbolized with the pieta, while the birth is symbolized by the peculiar ostrich egg suspended from the ceiling. The ostrich egg was part of Federico's coat of arms, aligning the belief that ostriches eat hardware (nails, bolts and screws etc.), the hardware angle being associated with soldiers. So on one level, any heir of a Montefeltro would be associated with the coat of arms and its ostrich egg. Further, like a pearl born of a shell (note the vaulting looks like a shell), the seed of the Montefeltro family was born of the late Battista. Still with me here? The ostrich leaves her egg to hatch in the warmth of the sun rather than babysitting her nest, so the ostrich is by nature an absentee mother. It certainly wasn't Battista's intention to abandon her son, but given that she died in childbirth, her child was left unattended nevertheless.

Piero della Francesca was rare in 15th century Italian painting for his interest in hidden symbolism. Themes of this sort were popular in Flanders, but in Italy the art was usually more straightforward. Piero was not widely known during his own day, and was not even documented by early art historians as a major figure of Italian Renaissance painting. He was rediscovered in the early 20th century, thanks largely to the artist Picasso's fascination with Piero's manipulation of space in his paintings.

Ambrogio Bergognone

Piero della Francesca was not the only artist from outside Tuscany to make a name for himself during the Early Renaissance period. Although not competitive with the great masters down in Florence, Milan produced a few artists toward the latter part of the 15th century who were considered masters in their region. One such artist was Ambrogio Bergognone. Bergognone was most famous in his day for a series of commissions completed for a convent in Pavia, but we are going to look at another painting by the artist. The **Virgin and Child with Saint Catherine of Alexandria and Saint Catherine of Siena** is interesting for another reason. Think back to Hans Memling's altarpiece featuring Saint Catherine. Recall how he mistakenly conflated two different Saint Catherines into one person? It is rare to see both Saint Catherines in a single altarpiece, so Bergognone's painting is a treat. On the left is the Early Christian Catherine of Alexandria who was tortured and killed by the Emperor Maxentius (contemporary to Constantine). She is shown as an aristocratic woman standing next to the wheel that was employed in her torture. On the right is Saint Catherine of Siena, the 14th century Italian woman who became a Dominican nun. Although Catherine of Siena is also shown as a beautiful woman in elegant gowns sometimes, here she is shown wearing her *habit* (nun's attire) and holding a simple lily as testimony to her purity.

Perugino

Another outsider was Pietro Vanucci, better known as Perugino as he was the premiere artist to hail from the city of Perugia. He became a famous artist not only throughout his native Umbria, but all the way to Rome. First, like Piero della Francesca, Perugino was familiar with art from Florence and even worked there for awhile, but he was never truly part of the Florentine art world. He eventually went on to work for the pope in Rome, as did a number of the artists from Florence of his generation although Perugino got there first. Also like Piero della Francesca, since he was not part of the Florence "in-crowd," he was often overlooked in early texts written on Italian

Renaissance painting other than a footnote that he happened to be Raphael's teacher (stay tuned, Raphael is a famous 16th century Renaissance painter).

Perugino's **Christ Delivering the Keys of the Kingdom to Peter** was painted in 1481, commissioned by Pope Sixtus IV for the Sistine Chapel. The chapel was a new addition to the Vatican (named after its patron, Sixtus), connecting two wings of the palace adjacent to Saint Peter's. Nowadays the Sistine Chapel is famous because it is used by the cardinals of the Catholic Church when they must meet to select a new pope. As a brand new building in the 15th century, it had no interior art at all and the pope set about finding the most talented artists to come to Rome to work on the frescos. The ceiling was initially painted solid blue with gold stars (not unlike the Arena Chapel) although many years later Michelangelo would be brought onboard to paint the famous ceiling as we know it today. The plan was to line the walls with a series of scenes illustrating the Old and New Testament, facing one another across the nave such that the art reinforced the Catholic understanding of Scripture that the Old Testament foreshadows the New, and the New Testament fulfills the Old.

The subject of this painting would be appealing to the pope as the Scripture reference where Jesus offers the keys of the kingdom to Saint Peter (Matthew 16:18-20) is referenced to the Old Testament (Isaiah 22:21-23) to relate the authority being conferred on Peter as being tantamount to that of Prime Minister, or leader in charge of the Church, hence the precedent for papal authority. Peter is shown in the center of a grand stone-surfaced plaza, not a real place but perhaps devoid of much landscape to emphasize Peter as the "rock" upon which Jesus would build his church. The building in the background is also not a real place, although it is a splendid example of Renaissance design. There are two triumphal arches like those incorporated in Early Christian architecture (like Old Saint Peter's Church which was still in Rome, if also in bad shape at this time) to symbolize the triumph of Jesus and Christianity in the world. Here the arches are inscribed to pay homage to Solomon and his glorious Temple, linking that great achievement to those of Pope Sixtus (no ego on the part of the pope there …). One wonders if this concept came from the pope himself, or if it was invented by Perugino who ironically perhaps was not an especially religious man (the art historian, Vasari said he was an atheist). Between the figures in the foreground and the architecture in the background there are two scenes. On the left is Perugino's version of the Tribute Money which we have seen before, painted by Masaccio for the Brancacci Chapel. On the right is apparently a scene from the Gospel of John where Jesus was under attack, but managed to hide himself then pass through the angry mob without being noticed (John 8:59).

Perugino's artistic contributions to the Sistine Chapel were soon joined by other artists, mostly from Florence, including Botticelli.

Sandro Botticelli

Our last Early Italian Renaissance artist grew up and established his career in Florence. While not the premiere favorite artist of the Medici family, he was awarded enough commissions to be taken seriously as an artist. Alessandro di Mariano Filippi was a late child born to aging upper middle-class parents, and was probably raised by his older brother who was a goldsmith. His nickname, "Botticelli" means little barrel and it remains a mystery as to how he came to be called that. He was apparently not very robust and considered sickly, which has often been attributed to problems arising from the advanced age of his mother (she was 40 when he was born - and his father 50 - which may not be ancient by today's standards perhaps, but in those days Mom would have been considered a dinosaur in the eyes of midwives). In any event, Sandro apprenticed under Fra Filippo Lippi, and when his master died, Botticelli took on the task of apprenticing Lippi's son, Filippino. By 1470 he had a well-established studio in Florence, and with the exception of his brief tour of duty painting in Rome, Botticelli was content to maintain his career in his hometown.

Botticelli joined Perugino in 1481-82 on the short list of artists selected by the pope to help decorate the Sistine Chapel. Over a nine month stretch Botticelli did three paintings in the chapel, all related to the life of Moses. The **Punishment of Korah, Dathan and Abiram** is considered the best of the three. Like we saw with Masaccio's Tribute Money at the beginning of the century, this fresco includes a cumulative story told through different scenes combined into one. The central scene in the narrative tells how the title characters have challenged Aaron's authority as a priest to make the appropriate sacrifices to God (Numbers 16: 1-40). Moses tells the men and their followers to offer incense in their censors (pots for burning incense) to see which prayers God answers. Aaron's incense burns and wafts up to heaven, while the others catch fire and burn the men; in Botticelli's depiction, fire seems to fall from heaven in the form of censors run amuck.

Moses is in the front raising his staff to heaven. See the gold rays shooting from his temples? After Moses saw God, the Bible says that light shone from his face; in fact, he had to cover his face so as not to blind the people. Artists have found a variety of ways to represent this phenomenon, everything from rays like you see here to what looks like horns, especially in sculpture where luminous light is more than a little difficult to represent. Aaron is behind to the right, also sporting white hair and a long beard like his brother, Moses. Aaron wears a pointy hat which at first glance may seem to resemble that of a wizard (Dumbledore?), but on closer inspection it is a papal tiara (see Rogier van der Weyden's Last Judgment to see another papal tiara). The allusion here is that Aaron, as God's choice to lead the faithful, is depicted as a pope reinforcing papal authority... just the sort of theme Sixtus would want to see in the Sistine Chapel.

On the far left side of the painting the earth has opened to swallow up the three evil men who led the rebellion. One man has presumably already fallen in and the other two can't seem to escape the gaping hole as Moses, staff in hand, looks on. On the far right Moses shields himself from angry Hebrews who want to stone him. Botticelli painted a superb rendering of the Arch of Constantine as a gateway between the action in the foreground and a serene landscape in the background. Landscape was still a relatively new interest in Florence, although by the last quarter of the 15th century artists were increasingly paying more attention to background detail.

In addition to religious themes, Botticelli also painted mythology which was becoming very popular toward the close of the 15th century in Italy. His mythological paintings were mostly Medici commissions, which coincided with Lorenzo de Medici's fascination with anything related to ancient Greece. In 1453 Constantinople, which had been the center of the Byzantine (Greek Orthodox) world, fell to the Turks, allowing Islam to dominate Christianity there. As a result large numbers of Greek immigrants flooded into Italy. The intellectual elite in cities like Florence suddenly took an interest in studying all things Greek, and new schools popped up in competition with traditional universities. Among those was the Platonic Academy, modeled after the ancient Platonic Academy in Athens. The school was started by a philosopher named Marsilio Ficino who taught Neo-Platonism. Plato was a Greek philosophy who lived in Athens from 428-348 BC. His philosophy emphasized the mystical more than concrete reality, believing that the idea (or what he called the "form") is what is real, and that what you can experience through the senses (hear, see, taste, smell etc) is a perception or copy of the reality which is more abstract and intuitive, and ultimately more "real" than "matter." Neo-Platonism was an updated version of Plato's original ideas, at the same time merging in all kinds of other influences.

By the time Lorenzo de Medici and Botticelli came along, the pooh bah in charge of the Platonic Academy in Florence was Pico della Mirandola, who was a glamorous and swashbuckling kind of guy that touched the romantic spirit of his followers. He wasn't one to follow the rules. For example, he fell in love with and kidnapped an unhappily married noblewoman which raised a few eyebrows. He also attempted to create a hodgepodge synthesis all purpose philosophy-religion. His *900 Theses* drew upon snippets of wisdom from a variety of sources including Plato, Christian and Jewish thought, Persian and Arabic sources and Eastern religions, along with tidbits collected from a few heresies that Christianity had discounted along the way. The Church was not especially amused, but that didn't stop people like the Medicis and their entourage from taking an interest in Pico and his teachings. He took an interest in magic, and believed that "good" magic could be achieved by manipulating talismans, herbs, gems and scents. He also supported the idea that music could be employed to attract positive magic, and he was attracted to astrology and the occult. Through all these ideas and ritual practices ran the concept that there was the "One," a sort of God-like unknowable force in the universe. From the One emanates the Intelligible (the Divine Mind) and the World Soul, which became corrupted by being bound to matter (as in bodies). In a nutshell, the physical world is ranked somewhere between being just plain evil and a mildly negative prison for the soul and intellect. The goal is for the soul and intellect to escape, which one does through self-knowledge, and perhaps ironically, by becoming immersed in beauty as a sort of reflection of the One.

Neo-Platonism was all the rage in Florence, with the Medicis at the center of this mystical philosophy that competed with Christianity. Some intellectuals of the day expressed the opinion that pagan philosophies and Christianity could be reconciled into one big, happy all-purpose religion, while for others it increasingly became an escape from faith altogether. *Humanism* with its preference for secular concerns and self-realization through reason over faith in a supernatural power was influencing all aspects of late 15th century life, and the art reflected this trend. By the close of the 15th century, mythology, the gods and tales from ancient Greece and Rome, rivaled Christian themes for popularity in Italian painting.

The **Birth of Venus** was painted on canvas which was very rare; probably it was used as a banner for a festival of some type originally. Notice that Venus is not realistic, although it is subtle. She is elongated with minimal shadowing used to make her appear life-like, in fact, outlines have been reintroduced almost like medieval art compared to the realism of Masaccio. Certainly Botticelli had learned techniques like chiaroscuro given that he studied under Fra Filippo Lippi, but he rejected those lessons as his career matured. Botticelli's point seems to be to reinforce a dreamlike quality in this scene; it isn't "real" because mythology isn't "real"... it is something one experiences intellectually. Mythological gods exist in our imagination. They are not physically tangible, so why should these subjects be painted like people next door? Beyond that, followers of Neo-Platonism were generally less interested in representing pure realism than artists who were strictly Catholic (without Neo-Platonism complicating their thinking) because Neo-Platonism presented "matter" as being somehow distasteful. The more you could escape "matter" (the physical world), the better. The Catholic Church taught that God created man (among all things), and that what God created was *good* (straight out of Genesis in the <u>Bible</u>). The Church didn't advocate getting overly caught up in the material world, but neither did it teach that the body or anything else created by God was less than good. As a true Neo-Platonist, however, Botticelli believed that it was more appropriate to create an alternative metaphysical dimension in art, rather than to try to copy nature directly. Even landscape has been reduced to imagination.

About the same time as Botticelli painted his <u>Birth of Venus</u> for the Medicis, a Dominican monk named Girolamo Savonarola arrived at the Monastery of San Marco. Savonarola disliked Lorenzo de Medici for being far too worldly with all this Neo-Platonism stuff and too power hungry also. The monk spoke publicly about the troubled leadership of Florence under Lorenzo, who admittedly was considerably less guided by his faith than his old grandfather Cosimo had been back in the days when Fra Angelico walked the halls of San Marco. Quickly the city became divided between supporters of Medicis and "weepers" – those who took Savonarola's preaching to heart and were moved to repent. The Medicis were not especially concerned that the new monk in town disapproved of their intellectual pursuits. While the Medicis were always concerned with their overall popularity with the citizens of Florence, an occasional malcontent wasn't something they fretted over. After all, you can't please all the people all the time, and the Medicis by nature seemed to opt more for a laissez faire attitude rather than ruling like iron-fisted despots, at least at this point in history. Perhaps they would have been wise to pay closer attention to Savonarola, because his speeches against the Medicis began to attract a wide hearing.

Savonarola prophesied the downfall of Florence as punishment for its sins and these prophesies seemed to come true, initially through no plan of Savonarola when French troops attacked the region in 1494. Many Medici family members were run out of town and killed (although Lorenzo himself appears to have died of natural causes). Savonarola then got directly involved with deposing the Medicis, and the family relocated to Rome where they sought protection from the pope. With that accomplished, the monk filled the political vacuum left in the absence of Medici rule by assuming control of the city government himself. By now he was also preaching against the new pope – Alexander VI – who was infamous for his personal immorality in the form of girlfriends and illegitimate children. The pope didn't appreciate the personal attacks one bit, so he sent papal envoy to check out this monk who seemed to be a troublemaker. By now, much of the Florentine public had turned on Savonarola, although he still had loyal supporters too. He was tried and tortured into admitting heresies (an odd position for a Dominican to be in!) and sentenced to death in 1498. He and his two top assistants were hanged and then their bodies were burned and the ashes dumped into the Arno River. All this upheaval left Florence without leadership and she never fully recovered.

Nobody knows for absolutely sure if Botticelli became a Savonarola supporter, but some of his later paintings strongly suggest that he felt the Church judged the zealous monk badly. **<u>Calumny</u>** a very good example. Botticelli's theme was taken from antiquity: a lost allegory painting by an ancient Greek painter named Apelles. Although the Greek painting was long gone, an ancient author named Lucian wrote about it, and his description would have been available to any interested Renaissance artist. We don't know who the patron may have been for <u>Calumny</u>, and of course when this is not known, there is always a chance it could have been painted by the artist as a personal piece (the painting may look as large as the Sistine Chapel fresco, but it is only 3' across, an over a chair sized picture - easily affordable to produce, patron or not).

In the scene, king Midas sits on a throne; he is the personification of the bad judge: corrupt, foolish, unjust. He is being advised by Ignorance on the left and Suspicion on the right – they lift his donkey ears to offer bad advice. This much could be interpreted as a worldly pope caught up in poor counsel. The victim, represented as a pious man clasping his hands in prayer, is being dragged in by his hair. Could this be Savonarola? Deceit, dressed in blue robes, is being assisted by Fraud behind in the task of bringing the victim before the judge. Meanwhile a graceful figure in red appears to be the influence of righteousness trying to intervene with no luck, while a scary looking man in black robes metes out his own judgment on Midas, confronting him with a menacing gesture. To the far left is a hooded <u>Dominican</u> nun (bear in mind that Savonarola was a Dominican) looks away. She is an old, weathered and beaten figure of penitence who points to the injustice before her, and turns her head to seek Truth – the nude reaching up to Heaven.

Following the demise of the Medicis and then Savonarola as well, Florence slipped quietly into cultural oblivion, becoming a political satellite of Rome. The Medicis had controlled the city for so long that nobody else seemed to have the insight or experience to take over the reigns of government. Instead, the charming Tuscan city was governed from afar on the advice of the Medicis, who decided to stay in Rome as they felt Florence was unsafe for their family. In time they would return, but Florence was never again the cultural heart of Renaissance Italy. During the 16th century, Florence was superseded by Rome and Venice for leadership in the arts.

13. **High Renaissance in Italy**

c.1500 - 1600

Leonardo da Vinci

Everyone has heard of Leonardo da Vinci; he and Michelangelo are probably the two most famous artists of the Renaissance. Leonardo is a celebrated genius, and perhaps in part because of this it is often difficult to stuff him into an art history slot with other artists of his generation. The bottom line is that Leonardo is a category unto himself. On the one hand, chronologically he was a late 15th century painter - a peer of Botticelli's – with whom he apprenticed for awhile together in the studio of an artist named Andrea del Verrocchio. The problem is, Leonardo doesn't fit any mold common to other Early Italian Renaissance artists. He is generally perceived as being the start of the High Renaissance, despite that he was a generation older than the rest of the artists we lump into that category. In the end, he isn't a comfortable fit there either, but we shall think of him as High Renaissance.

Leonardo da Vinci was born in1452, the illegitimate son of a wealthy Florentine. He grew up with every material blessing money could buy, but without a stable, close family. Perhaps as a result, Leonardo never trusted close personal relationships; he was the ultimate example of the guy who wants his space with plenty of elbowroom. Just the same, he was a brilliant young man, well versed in every possible subject and evidently charming company. Leonardo's genius was and is … the man and his mind. He was a talented painter, this is true, but his art is only a fraction of who he was in total; in fact, he completed very few paintings at all for being such a famous artist. He was also a gifted scientist. He kept journals all his life, which are easily identified since he wrote backwards from right to left in mirror image. He was left handed and apparently developed this writing style to avoid dragging his hand through wet ink and smudging the page - the pages are easily read by holding them up to a mirror - this explanation in contrast to some sensationalist authors who have attempted to make more of it than there is. In his journals he left behind drawings of all kinds of inventions from flying machines to submarines to conceptual hydraulic lifts to studies of human gestation. He was preoccupied with studying natural law, and while he developed a variety of inventions that foreshadowed later military equipment and engineering techniques, few were realized beyond his imagination. The man was a brilliant thinker. He was a bona fide genius.

Leonardo was enrolled as an apprentice to Verrocchio at age fourteen, where he would have become acquainted with Botticelli and Perugino who also studied there for awhile. Despite being from the metropolitan Florence area, Leonardo took little interest in the Medicis. He found "Lorenzo the Magnificent" rather dull and boring actually, which annoyed the Medicis to no end. He liked to travel rather than staying put, and in the end, his preferred court, to the degree he made close friends at all, was that of Ludovico Sforza in Milan. He moved to Milan in 1483 to work for the duke, gaining his position in no small part because he made great claims about his abilities as an engineer; his role as an artist was almost a postscript to his letter of application.

Leonardo held some odd ideas for his day. For example, most 15th century citizens were very proud supporters of whatever city-state they called home. Leonardo didn't think much civic pride, believing that if folks could get past all that and see themselves as citizens of the world, we might all enjoy greater peace. Further, most people in the 15th century were religious, or at least tried to be. Some were Jews of course, but most people in Italy were Catholic. Leonardo was certainly not an atheist, as he maintained there was intelligent design which could be attributed to God, but he wasn't an especially religious person and often saw religion as a crutch for those incapable of solving their own problems. Beyond these quirks of personality and belief, Leonardo also had the nasty habit of poor follow-through. He was especially notorious for leaving commissions unfinished, which is why he left so few completed paintings for an otherwise long career. One would think ideas and behaviors like these might alienate Leonardo from people, but in truth he was much sought after, suggesting what a witty, refined, distinguished, interesting and charming (and apparently drop dead handsome) man he must have been.

Leonardo produced a handful of religious paintings, although he was only given one commission officially from the Catholic Church, not because there was animosity between them (he was on friendly terms with more than one pope over his long life), but more because he was an unreliable employee. Popular fiction literature (and now a movie version too) has promoted more than a little false information about Leonardo's paintings, some of which were produced during his stay in Milan working at the Sforza court. There are two versions of the **Madonna of the Rocks**, which was commissioned for a chapel in the church of San Francesco in Milan by the Confraternity of the Immaculate Conception, a Catholic lay (non-clergy) organization of men (not women as some have mistakenly suggested) who like other confraternities came together to pray and do charitable works. The subject was to include the popular stars of so many High Renaissance paintings in Italy: the Virgin Mary, Jesus and John the Baptist, with God the Father included above overseeing the group. The painting was produced on wooden panel to be the centerpiece of a large triptych, although it was transferred to canvas when the triptych was not completed according to the particulars requested by the patrons. The scene Leonardo depicted was a popular legend, probably invented during the 14th century where the Holy Family meet up with Saint John the Baptist in the desert where the Angel Uriel keeps watch over him after Herod ordered the Massacre of the Innocents. The scene is unorthodox in terms of the setting in a dark cave, but otherwise it is not unusual at all in terms of the cast of characters who are easily identified through their attributes.

In the scene, Mary is centered as we would expect, creating a pyramidal form between her body and outstretched arms. Leonardo was fond of using geometry, pyramids especially, in his compositions, a technique that later artists of the High Renaissance borrowed from him as an easy formula to create successful compositions one after the other. Mary and Uriel appear almost as a couple of caregivers introducing two children to play. Mary coaches little John to come to Jesus by placing her maternal arm around the baby, as she raises the palm of her hand above Jesus' head in a traditional sign of parental blessing. John seem to intuitively understand that he is to worship Jesus as he clasps his hands in prayer, while Jesus offers his standard benediction blessing which we have seen in other paintings (see the Rolin Madonna by Jan van Eyck for a good example). For his part, the angel sitting near Jesus points to John as if to acknowledge his gesture of piety, sort of like a friend of the family pointing out to Jesus (and to us) that John's role is to worship his messiah. John sets an example for us all, and Uriah underscores as much with his gesture. Some have taken issue with the pointing, but this painting is not remotely unique; many Renaissance paintings have a saint or angel pointing to something the viewer is specifically supposed to notice and take to heart. Consider the figure of Saint John the Baptist in the Isenheim Altarpiece by Matthias Grunewald (High Renaissance, Germany) for a similar example.

The original painting, now in Paris, was quite large: 6.5 feet tall. The confraternity refused to pay for the painting, most likely because the artist had not followed all of the instructions of the contract (this was not the first or last time this happened with Leonardo). Eventually he and the painter who was commissioned to produce the side panels in the triptych sued, and the courts ruled in their favor so the confraternity had to pay up. The problem was, that it took years to sort out the squabble, and by then apparently the original Madonna of the Rocks had been placed with somebody else. Presumably that's why the artist painted a second version, stubbornly similar to the first now that the confraternity was obliged to accept it without God the Father overhead like they originally wanted. The later version of Madonna of the Rocks, housed in London, is almost identical to the first. The same cast of characters is present, in the same positions as before, with John praying to Jesus who offers a blessing for his cousin. Halos were added and Uriel doesn't point to John's faithful example for our benefit, but otherwise they are quite alike. John holds a cross here, but it should be noted that this was not part of the original painting; it was added some time later, and not by Leonardo.

Leonardo had a bad habit of frequently not finishing his paintings. He would become restless, or bored with a picture for one reason or another, or perhaps disenchanted with the patron. As often as not, the artist would pack his bags and be off, leaving his unfinished work to languish. At other times, we have paintings like the **Last Supper**, which was commissioned for the refectory (dining room) of the monastery of Santa Maria delle Grazie in Milan. Notice how the painting is in such poor condition today. Leonardo was a scientist, and his tinkering in this area frequently had a disastrous impact on his artwork. He was always experimenting with his paints to see if he could achieve a finished product that was more interesting. Unfortunately, these experiments often created more problems than successes. Leonardo couldn't abide fresco painting; it seemed so pedestrian painting on wet plaster and the artist had to work too quickly which compromised the quality of the work in his opinion. So he decided to experiment with producing an oil painting on the plaster wall, which turned out to be a disaster since the dampness of the wall seeped into the wet paint causing it do dry poorly and it was already deteriorating before the artist had even completed the entire scene. Sadly, there isn't so much as a square inch of Leonardo's original painting left on this wall. It had to be repainted several times during the 16th century, as no paint would properly adhere to that wall successfully after Leonardo's initial experiment. Since the Renaissance, the Last

Supper has been in a state of almost constant restoration; it is rare to visit Santa Maria delle Grazie and not find scaffolding in front of what is probably the single most famous painting in the world.

Many scholars have invested much time and effort to analyze the Last Supper, discussing Leonardo's use of perspective keeping us focused on Christ, the use of pyramidal groupings in his composition, and even the symbolism of dividing the Apostles into four (gospels) groups of three (trinity) men each. That's great, except that we really don't even know how much of what we see on the wall is true to what Leonardo originally painted. The difficulty is that until the 19th century, few artists thought the way we do today about restoration work. Nowadays when an artist signs on to restore the work of an earlier painter it is assumed that the task is to make the painting as true to what it originally looked like as possible. This would have been considered quite novel in earlier centuries. Artists who "restored" art frequently took liberties to "improve" it, leaving their own mark on another painter's work.

The Last Supper has now been restored to resemble preliminary sketches found in the artist's journals, but the fact remains that we do not truly know if it looks as Leonardo painted it, or even if we have inadvertently backed up his vision to an earlier prototype of what he actually painted on the monastery walls. Assuming for the moment that we have it right, and that what we see today is in fact close to what Leonardo originally painted, there are a few observations that can be made. First, the artist seemed more interested in focusing our attention on the betrayal of Judas rather than the institution of the Eucharist like we saw in Fra Angelico's version. Artists will usually focus on one or the other; it does not come as a surprise that a monk might find the Eucharist more fascinating, while an artist without such personal ties to the Church might prefer the drama of the betrayal. The artist has employed geometry in his composition again, with Jesus in the center conforming to a pyramid with his outstretched arms resting on the table. The group to Jesus' left is the most interesting as it contains Judas, seen in profile clutching the bag of silver coins. He is accompanied by Peter from behind, and young John, the clean shaven youthful fellow. John is always depicted next to Jesus, often resting his head against Jesus' chest. Here to preserve the central focus on Jesus, John has been shifted to one side, but perhaps to pay particular homage to John, his robes and pose mimic Christ's.

Milan was invaded by the French at the turn of the century, toppling the government of the Sforza family and leaving Leonardo without a stable patron there. His last years were spent moving around from Milan to Mantua to Venice to Florence, back to Milan and eventually to France where he died in 1519. It was during these later years that he painted the other painting that most people will immediately recognize: **Mona Lisa**. It is a small painting, which often surprises people who have not seen it at the Louvre Museum in Paris, because there is a tendency to want to make the picture larger to match its reputation. No portrait has ever commanded so much attention, and lovely as she may be, it remains a mystery to many *why* exactly this is the big kahuna as portraits go as opposed to a picture of somebody else. People have heard her eyes will follow you around the room. News flash: any time a sitter looks at the artist (or into the lens of a camera), the eyes will follow you around the room. Mona Lisa has no corner on that market. People have heard about her smile. It's a very nice smile. Is it the most remarkable smile you have ever seen? Maybe …

Part of the romance with the <u>Mona Lisa</u> is that the artist, whom most people hold in very high regard, obviously thought a lot of this little portrait, because he kept it with him until his death. Another element of intrigue is that we don't have a clue who this woman is. No record of a commission has been found for this painting. Conventional art history attributes the woman to be the wife of a Florentine banker and businessman named Francesco del Giocondo. Sometimes <u>Mona Lisa</u> is even nicknamed "La Gioconda" based on this assumption. Where did the theory come from? An Italian architect, painter and would-be art historian named ***Giorgio Vasari*** wrote a book called *The Lives of the Most Eminent Italian Architects, Painters and Sculptors* in 1550, in which he claimed the picture depicted Giocondo's wife. His evidence is flimsy, and is further compromised by the fact that he never interviewed Leonardo, who died an old man – living in a foreign country - when Vasari was only 4 years old! There was no record that Giocondo had hired Leonardo, which seems peculiar given that one might expect a businessman to keep half decent records, and even if the records were lost somehow, why didn't he and his wife demand to keep the painting after it was completed?

There are almost as many theories about the identity of <u>Mona Lisa</u> as there are creative imaginations. One of the au courant theories wafting its way around the Internet these days is that the portrait is not of a lady at all, but rather a self-portrait of the artist, done when he was an elderly gentleman, for some curious and unexplained reason deciding to present himself as a young woman. Assorted computer gurus have digitized Leonardo's **<u>Self-Portrait</u>** and that of <u>Mona Lisa</u> and found the two "aligned perfectly." It's possible. At the same time, it is no secret that artists frequently bring some of themselves to their portrait work, which is why two portraits of the same person by two different artists might both look remarkably like the sitter, and yet, the actual portraits look a little different from each other. Would Leonardo be inexplicably attached to a youthful portrayal of himself in drag? Maybe …

Other theories might be somewhat more credible. British scholar Donald Sassoon has published a book recently (2001) where he culls through some of the more credible possibilities about the <u>Mona Lisa</u>. For starters, the name "Mona Lisa" was not tagged to the picture until the 19th century, and that was taken from Vasari's writings where Giocondo's wife's name was affectionately dubbed "Monna Lisa" or "My Lady," or "Mrs." Lisa del Giocondo. It is also possible that the name may have even originally been a reference to the lady's personality (before Vasari?), and not to her proper name at all. Giocondo is also an adjective meaning witty, or playful, or even a tease. If it wasn't the wife of our Florentine banker / businessman, then who else might she be?

A painter contemporary to Leonardo named Gianpaolo Lomazzo, who was a personal friend of the executor of Leonardo's estate (Francesco Melzi) claimed the woman in <u>Mona Lisa</u> was from Naples, which would rule out Giocondo's wife. Another theory comes from scraps of evidence that predate Vasari. One is a diary record of a man named Antonio Beatis, secretary to Cardinal Luigi d'Aragona. Beatis evidently visited Leonardo's studio where he was shown 3 paintings, one of which sounds like the <u>Mona Lisa</u>, and according to the diary account, the lady was described, we presume by the artist himself, as a Florentine lady, requested by Giuliano de Medici (third son of Lorenzo the Magnificent). If this is true, then perhaps it is a portrait of Pacifica Brandino, Giuliano's mistress who was a widow, and who gave birth to Giuliano's child in 1511. It's been noted that Mona Lisa appears to have a black veil over part of her hair, which might be a reference to her being a widow. If it wasn't Pacifica, there were other ladies Giuliano might have commended to Leonardo; Isabella Gualanda and her cousin Cecilia Gallerani were both friends of Guiliano's who would have been in approximately the right place at the right time to have sat for the artist. Given that Giuliano married shortly after the picture was painted, if in fact the portrait was of one of these ladies done at his behest, he may have been just as glad that the artist kept the potentially embarrassing portrait to himself.

Perhaps the most persuasive possibility is that Mona Lisa may be a portrait of Isabella d'Este, sister-in-law of Ludovico Sforza, Duke of Milan and Leonardo's patron and friend. Isabella was the first person Leonardo paid a visit to when he left Milan for Mantua in 1500. During his stay he produced the profile **Sketch of Isabella d'Este**. If you compare Isabella to Mona Lisa, you will discover they share many common characteristics from facial features to the dress to the hands. Could Mona Lisa or La Gioconda (the witty, playful one?) be a portrait of Isabella, a gift from the young woman to the artist, or possibly a painting he created from memory and a sketch? Isabella d'Este and Leonardo da Vinci were quite good friends. Some have speculated that their relationship was romantic, although others have speculated that the artist was gay; although there is no proof of either. Regardless, however much everyone at the court in Milan may have enjoyed Leonardo, the fact remained that he was a bastard, and therefore he carried no title that he could offer a lady in marriage, be it Isabella or anyone else. Besides, Isabella had been engaged to a titled nobleman since she was six years old, and by 1500 when Leonardo came to visit, she was 26 years old and had already been married ten years. If Isabella sat for the portrait (she presumably at least sat for the sketch) for old time's sake or as a favor to her old friend, she may never have expected to take delivery of the painting, and it would explain why the artist held the picture so dear to his heart even into old age.

Many of Leonardo's paintings, like Madonna of the Rocks and Mona Lisa include landscape in the background, filtered through a smoky sfumato which he developed further from observing Masaccio and his followers, who initiated the technique. He also made good use of chiaroscuro, modeling his figures in highlight and shadow to make them seem real. Leonardo was a remarkable human being, but his art held less influence over artists to follow than three younger artists who shared the High Renaissance limelight: Michelangelo, Raphael, and Titian.

Michelangelo

Michelangelo Buonarroti was a true High Renaissance artist. He and Leonardo da Vinci are often spoken of together like matched bookends to the Italian Renaissance, but in fact the two men had precious little in common. With a 23-year head start on life, Leonardo was old enough to be Michelangelo's father. They came from the exact opposite social and family background. Whereas Leonardo grew up swathed in wealth but in an otherwise dysfunctional familial arrangement, Michelangelo came from a close-knit but poor family. Leonardo was lukewarm on religion. Michelangelo was a fervent Catholic, albeit with strong Neo-Platonist influence. Leonardo disapproved of national or civic pride. Michelangelo was proud to be Florentine. In terms of their art, Leonardo believed the best art was painting. It was a gentleman's vocation. A man could dress well, listen to music and carry on polite conversation while pursuing his craft. Michelangelo thought more highly of sculpture. While he did paint, he believed that a sculptor "creates" – his ideas are transformed into three-dimensional reality as opposed to mere flat copies of reality. The artists have in common that both were geniuses, but they were different types of geniuses. Leonardo had an IQ in the stratosphere – he was the definition of the Renaissance man, educated, erudite, witty and brilliant in many areas. Michelangelo in contrast was a child prodigy in sculpture, meaning that even as a child he could produce art more spectacular and beautiful than the statues of the greatest masters of his day, but his gift was in art, not in all subjects. Finally, both men were loners, but again there is a difference. Leonardo was clever and charming. People enjoyed his company, and looked forward to spending time with him. Michelangelo was often boorish and rude. He was a hothead whose temper got him in trouble more than once, and if he wasn't picking a fight, he was brooding. He was known to be so obnoxious at times that people often found him too difficult for polite company. Leonardo was sought by many, but it was he who eschewed close ties, preferring to keep his distance from others. Michelangelo in contrast seemed hungry for human contact and affection, while all the while driving people away with his temperamental personality.

Michelangelo was born in a countryside village near Florence in 1475, and he grew up in that city. Had he been born elsewhere, his talent may have gone undeveloped due to his parents' financial circumstances. At thirteen he was apprenticed to an artist named Domenico Ghirlandaio, but Michelangelo was capable of more than his master could offer. Fortunately, Florence was the land of the Medicis with their long-standing enthusiastic support for the arts. Ghirlandaio brought young Michelangelo to their attention when it was clear that he was truly gifted, but his family could not afford the best tutors to develop their son's talent. No problem, the Medicis graciously opened their doors and took the boy into their home, which is to say their palace, and he grew up alongside the Medici children receiving equal education and benefits as anyone else in the family. What an opportunity! Dinners at the palace were quite an affair. Lorenzo the Magnificent sat at the head of the table and would hold court with whomever sat in the chairs next to him. It was considered quite an honor, and frequently young Michelangelo would be given the seat next to Lorenzo, where he would be engaged in meaty dialogue all evening with the head of state … no small potatoes for a poor kid from the other side of the tracks. He was exposed to and absorbed much of the Neo-Platonism philosophy that was so popular at the Medici court, and in every way he was educated and trained to be a classical sculptor the likes of which would have made Perikles proud.

Lorenzo de Medici died in 1492 when Michelangelo was in his late teens. In the following years as Michelangelo passed from being a boy to becoming a man, he became involved with the Savonarola movement in Florence. Michelangelo was high strung, and devout in his Catholic faith despite his exposure to the varied philosophies discussed around the dinner table in the Medici household. Savonarola struck a chord with Michelangelo, and he may well have become involved with running the Medicis out of town, even after all they had done for him, and in spite of how well he knew them. After the Medicis fell from grace in 1494 Michelangelo skipped town for awhile too, so it is unclear whether he was directly involved with Savonarola's plans to upset the Medicis apple cart, or whether Michelangelo was simply an enthusiastic Catholic who perhaps heard merit in Savonarola's message, but at the same time, meant no direct harm to his adopted family.

Let's consider the artist's work. As testimony to Michelangelo's supreme gift as a sculptor, consider his **Pieta**, long considered one of the crown jewels of the Vatican. He was approximately the same age as a typical college student (early 20's) when he sculpted this statue of Jesus draped elegantly across Mary's lap. A French cardinal commissioned the piece to be set in Saint Peter's as a memorial to the tomb of Saint Peter below, where it remains until this day. Michelangelo was always quite particular in selecting his marble for statues, because he envisioned the finished statue as contained within the natural stone. It was less a matter of figuring out how to create the piece, as it was a matter of setting the figure free from the surrounding mass so its shape and form could be revealed. Mary is depicted as being ever youthful and beautiful. She contemplates Jesus, with both depicted as serene and at peace.

In 1501, probably close in time to when Leonardo painted his Mona Lisa, Michelangelo accepted a commission to sculpt a slightly larger than twice life-size statue of **David** for the city of Florence. The huge slab of marble had been partially sculpted by another artist, so it was quite a feat for Michelangelo to work around what was already carved to "find" the true figure within the stone, his David. Compared to Donatello's David, Michelangelo's is strong and heroic, and also a perfect classical nude in the tradition of Greek artists like Polykleitos. The time sequence is different too. David is not shown resting on his laurels after killing Goliath, but rather contemplating the pending battle. There is nothing fluffy about Michelangelo's hero – his facial expression is serious, even menacing as he calculates his strategy against the giant. Not surprisingly perhaps, the statue was awarded a position of great honor when it was completed, standing proud in the Palazzo Vecchio adjacent to the seat of city government (it has since been relocated indoors for protection, and a copy has been placed in the town square). It may have been no accident that the statue was positioned such that David glared toward Rome. A not so subtle message could have been directed toward the Medicis, those giants of the Florentine past, that they may feel secure under the pope's protection, but David, patron of Florence has not yet begun to fight. His pride is larger than life; he is strong and capable, and of course, everyone knows that David was the victor over Goliath. If this was the statue's intent, how ironic that Michelangelo was chosen to create this slap in the face toward the Medicis. They fell from grace in no small part because Savonarola disapproved of their preoccupation with antiquity, and he moved Florence to see the Medicis with disdain for this same reason. And yet, Michelangelo's David may well be the greatest testimony to the art of antiquity created during the entire Renaissance … it is the epitome of precisely the taste in art that Savonarola so loathed that in his zeal to eradicate this fascination with pagan antiquity, he lost his own life while destroying the Medicis.

Michelangelo sculpted his **Bound Slave** about a dozen years after David. Since the slave was never finished, and it serves as a good example of the artist's technique of removing marble to discover the statue hidden within. It is also worth noting that unlike earlier statues where Michelangelo exercised restrain, even if pent up energy was evident like we see in David, here we see a body twisted and struggling as if to free itself from the marble block as much as from the carved ropes that bind the figure. The Hellenistic Greek masterpiece, Laocoon had recently been discovered in 1506, and clearly

Michelangelo had seen the larger than life sculpture group of the tortured Trojan priest and his two sons being attacked by serpents. The <u>Bound Slave</u> moves beyond classical influence toward a more complex and emotional style of art. If we reflect once again on the cycles of development seen repeatedly in art and architecture in the West, Michelangelo fills a unique niche. On the one hand, he follows on the heels of the Early Renaissance when sculptors were in the early stages of rediscovering classical qualities in their art. Michelangelo offered the perfect classical perfection in statues like David. And then he moved on. His later work, like the <u>Bound Slave</u> more closely matches Late Classical style, foreshadowing Baroque art in the 17th century which completes the cycle of simple to complex once again.

Michelangelo always thought of himself as a sculptor, but he is equally remembered for his painting, perhaps in spite of himself. Michelangelo had come to the attention of Pope Julius II, who had recently succeeded Alexander VI (the one who executed Savonarola). Julius II was consumed with an interest in revamping Rome, both rebuilding Saint Peter's and also adding to the glory of the Vatican complex with a variety of other ambitious projects. Michelangelo was under contract to work in his hometown of Florence, but the pope had these obligations excused in 1505 so that the artist could come to Rome immediately and serve Julius as a court artist. Initially Michelangelo was to sculpt a marvelous tomb for the pope, which seemed like the kind of job Michelangelo might enjoy. No sooner had Michelangelo started on the tomb project when the pope reassigned him to be in charge of painting the Sistine Chapel ceiling. Michelangelo did *not* want *this* job, thank you very much, and he tried to wriggle out of it. Julius II kept the pressure on until Michelangelo relented. Both men could be ornery, bossy and temperamental; in a way they were made for each other as they took turns telling each other off, arguing, but in the end, respecting one another enough to get the job done.

Initially Julius tried to busybody, telling the artist what he wanted on the ceiling, but Michelangelo was such a disagreeable man to work with, that in the end the pope gave up and just told him to paint whatever he wanted … and despite rumbles of disagreement here and there between the two men throughout the project, that is apparently exactly what the artist did. The already completed walls in the Sistine Chapel illustrated scenes from the lives of Moses and Christ, painted by Botticelli, Filippino Lippi, Ghirlandaio, and Perugino, while the quilt of images that Michelangelo created to decorate the **Sistine Chapel Ceiling** focus on Old Testament narratives from Genesis. Looking at **The Creation of Adam**, we can appreciate that Michelangelo was a sculptor first, and a painter second. His figures are heroic and grand, but also more closely aligned to statues than to models in the flesh. The entire ceiling was completed in a mere four years, which was lightning fast for such a demanding undertaking. First there were the ups and downs of getting the whole shebang started at all since the artist didn't want to do it. Then consider the size of the project, 5,800 square feet of barrel vaulted surface, not to mention that the ceiling hovered almost seven stories above the floor of the chapel. The logistics alone must have been daunting; imagine the artist trying to figure out all the angles to make his figures look realistic from the all points at floor level. As if all this were not enough to make the project all but impossible, Michelangelo as a sculptor by trade had to learn from scratch how to paint in fresco … amazing!

After Julius II died, Michelangelo lost his position as court artist to the Vatican during the reigns of Leo X and Clement VII (stay tuned, more on that later), but when Pope Paul III came to power in 1534, Michelangelo was brought back to Rome in service directly to the Vatican. Among his commissions from the new pope, Michelangelo was asked to complete the Sistine Chapel with a gigantic fresco of the **Last Judgment** for behind the altar.

Holy Moly! Look at Michelangelo's Last Judgment! Christ is centered which may help you identify him, although he is barely distinguished from everyone else in the mayhem. He isn't larger than anyone else, he's naked, he's shaved, his hair is cut short, and he seems caught up in a stormy frenzy rather than presiding calmly over the end times. Christ is hardly the svelte king of kings, instead he looks more like a has-been wrestler who took too many steroids and ate too many doughnuts. His mother, Mary, is at his side; she is easy to spot because she remembered to wear her clothes. In the uppermost lunettes we see the symbols of Christ's passion: on the left is the cross and a figure holding the crown of thorns, while on the right several figures appear to wrestle with the pillar where Christ was flogged. As for the rest of the painting, what is going on here? Michelangelo offers little clarity on salvation and damnation compared to typical Last Judgment portrayals. If we look along the bottom of the scene, on the left where we expect to find those heading for heaven we can find a few relaxed looking bodies being assisted upwards, whereas the handful of bodies in the bottom right look less happy and they appear to be diving down rather than floating up. But the vast majority of the painting, which is to say most of what we would be able to see above the altar, is a writhing circus of naked bodies neither clearly being tormented by demons nor blessed by angels.

Amid the confusion there are some recognizable saints in the melee, although it isn't clear why these particular saints were included, and none of them appear to be offering any solace to the souls facing judgment. The most obvious is Saint Bartholomew, who is situated just below and to the right of Christ. He holds a knife and his own flayed skin (Bartholomew having been flayed alive). The saint appears to be a portrait of Michelangelo, although scholars are unsure why the artist may have selected this particular saint to sport his own likeness. To the right of Bartholomew and level with Christ is Saint Peter holding his key to the kingdom. Peter is a massive hulk of flesh like Christ, and he looks pretty grumpy too. On the right side of the painting there is a woman clad in green. That's Saint Catherine of Alexandria, seemingly flying out toward us through the broken, spiked wheel which is her attribute. And to the immediate right of Catherine is Saint Sebastian, holding up arrows which are his attribute (Saint Sebastian was a soldier martyred by being shot full of arrows).

When the painting was unveiled, the Last Judgment was severely criticized for the profuse nudity. There was already plenty of that to go around in Michelangelo's ceiling with scenes out of Genesis, but the Last Judgment was over the top with even Christ himself thrashing about in his birthday suit. There was something obscene about the prospect of a multitude of genitals flying about over the altar in the pope's private chapel, and so one of Michelangelo's assistants was called in to provide modest loin coverings for those figures considered the most offensive. Despite this apparent set-back in his approval ratings, Michelangelo went on to be appointed by Pope Paul III as chief architect on the project to rebuild Saint Peter's, so we will conclude our discussion of Michelangelo in the chapter on Renaissance architecture.

Raphael

Raphael is the third big name "old master" from the Italian High Renaissance. Born Raffaello Santi in 1483, he was 8 years younger than Michelangelo (31 years younger than Leonardo), and compared to either of the other two, he was the most "regular" as personalities go, and the least "gifted" in that he wasn't a brainy Einstein in terms of IQ like Leonardo, nor was he an amazing child prodigy artist like Michelangelo. That said, compared to the other two, Raphael is hands down the most important in terms of the lasting influence he made on art from his generation through all the generations that would follow right on up to World War I, and some may argue that his legacy is still just as profound today.

Raphael was the oddball in terms of his birth and childhood because he was not from Florence. He came from Urbino, where his father was a minor artist working in the duke's court. Raphael was only 11 when his father died. Under any circumstances this would be a tragedy, but with Raphael, every upset in his life seemed to have a silver lining. Somehow, even when bad things happened, it turned out well for this man; he must have had an angel perched on his shoulder looking out for him because he was chronically lucky. If his father had lived, he would have probably apprenticed his son himself, and we might conclude that this mediocre artist would have provided Raphael with mediocre training, so he would have gone on to become a mediocre artist. Instead, according to Vasari, Raphael was sent off to neighboring Perugia where he apprenticed under the regional big name artist, Perugino, with whom you are already familiar. More than likely this is a slight error (like Vasari's information on Leonardo?). Perugino was not in Perugia at the time Raphael's father died in 1494; he was away for twelve years and only returned in 1500 to take on a fresco commission in his home town. In all likelihood, Raphael did study briefly under Perugino after that date, but his early art training was apparently handled locally in Urbino. A sketchbook from Raphael's youth, completed between the ages of twelve and fifteen, was discovered in 1803 and purchased by the Academy in Venice. The sketches are mostly copies of art produced at the Urbino court by a visiting Flemish artist called Justus of Ghent (real name Joos van Wassenhove). More than likely Raphael produced these drawings in Urbino before venturing to greener pastures in his late teens.

All the same, Perugino's influence is apparent on Raphael's painting as a young master. Consider Raphael's **Betrothal of the Virgin**, an early work dating from 1504, which was commissioned as a small church altarpiece, compared to Perugino's <u>Christ Delivering the Keys of the Kingdom to Peter</u> (1481 – painted in the Sistine Chapel prior to Michelangelo's arrival to paint the ceiling – see the chapter on Early Italian Renaissance Art). The similarities in composition and even the background architecture are obvious. When Raphael had completed his studies under Perugino, he returned to Urbino for the summer, but decided not to stay. In addition to being lucky, Raphael never underestimated his worth. It occurred to him that if he were talented enough to win the praise of Perugino, then perhaps he was too talented to spend his career in Urbino, when it seemed to him that the going place in the art world was Florence.

Raphael arrived in Florence to begin his bright new career around 1504. He found commissions quickly, as the big name artists were all either out of town or otherwise engaged. Michelangelo and Leonardo made brief appearances given that they were pitted against one another in a contest to create a pair of frescos for the city (neither one was ever completed). But other than that, Michelangelo was already in Rome bickering with Julius II, and Leonardo was who knows where since he moved around a lot anyway. Other artists were likewise drifting away after the double whammy of first losing the Medicis as patrons, and then the fall of Savonarola. It just made the place seem less comfortable, and certainly less compelling as an art center than perhaps it had been a decade or two earlier. Undaunted by the changes in Florence, probably because Raphael had not experienced Florence during her zenith of culture anyway, the painter completed numerous modest commissions straight away for families who could afford art, but had few artists to choose from in those days.

The pictures painted during his years in Florence were simple Madonna and Child paintings and portraits. **Angelo Doni** and his wife, **Maddalena Strozzi Doni** were patrons at this time. Raphael's early portraits were like a marriage between Piero della Francesca's portraits, with an interest in background landscape, and Leonardo da Vinci. These two portraits would have been exactly contemporary to the Mona Lisa. While the background landscapes in Raphael's pictures are more like the familiar work he would have seen growing up in the Urbino court, unlike the hazy sfumato Leonardo preferred, the half-length ¾ pose, hands folded in the sitter's lap pose is just like Mona Lisa.

La Belle Jardinière and **The Alba Madonna** are also typical of his Florence period. Raphael was never one to make his job more difficult that it needed to be. There is a popular expression today: KISS, meaning Keep It Simple, Stupid! Raphael probably would have appreciated such a motto. While Leonardo might turn his painting studio into a chemistry lab, and create mysterious pictures people still ponder today (Mona who?), and while Michelangelo was desperate to learn all there was to know about anatomy so his figures would look so real it's tempting to check for a pulse, Raphael frankly just could not be bothered with any of it. He quickly developed a formula for cranking out attractive, simple and appealing Madonna and Child pictures. First, reduce the composition to geometry (he didn't think this one up of course – Leonardo gets credit for that). If he could reduce the basic forms in the picture so that his Mary with baby Jesus and often baby John the Baptist conformed to a pyramidal form, then plop that triangle into a rectangle or round (called a "*tondo*") picture plane … presto, instant composition. Why reinvent the wheel? It's easy to do, and it always looks good. KISS. And about those colors? Why make painting harder than it needs to be? The basic primary colors are red, blue and yellow. You have to do minimal mixing if you can stay close to these three, and they always look great together. Expect Raphael to prefer a tasteful primary palette to more complicated colors; except for background landscape, he tended to dress his figures in variations of rose, red, pink, royal blue, pale blue, teal, yellows and golds. KISS. Likewise, don't expect to learn much about anatomy looking at Raphael's early painting. His Madonnas are sweet, soft and motherly, and the babies are pudgy and adorable. Who needs more?

Everything was going along so well in Florence. Do you think Raphael was satisfied? Nope. It dawned on him after a few years that the famous artists were mostly down in Rome these days working for Pope Julius II. Raphael didn't want to be left behind, so he moved to Rome too, sometime around 1508. Much as he had tasted immediate success in Florence, it was unlikely that Raphael could catapult into the top echelon of great artists now that he was going up directly against Michelangelo. Just the same, he did well for himself, well enough to have Michelangelo start looking over his shoulder. It must have been doubly annoying to Michelangelo that Raphael was a pleasant fellow who got along well with everyone, including the grumpy pope – consider Raphael's portrait of **Julius II** to see just how grumpy … and this painted by the artist he *liked*! Julius II took a shine to young Raphael, and he liked the uncomplicated simplicity in his art too – it emulated the sort of simplicity Julius associated with antiquity and given that classical this and that was the pontiff's goal in redoing the Vatican, Raphael suited him quite nicely.

Julius II gave Raphael the commission to produce a series of frescoes for the Stanza della Segnatura, or Vatican apartments. The first of these frescos was the **Disputa**. The scene depicts the disputation (or better stated the "argument in favor" or the "defense") of the Eucharist. The iconography is not wholly original, although this is probably the best example in art of this theme. In the center of the painting we find God the Father at the top representing the *Salvador Mundi*, or Savior of the World as he holds the world in one hand and offers a blessing with the other. He is surrounded by gold rays ending in fluffy clouds, and if you look closely you will see that both the rays and the clouds are filled with *cherubim* (baby angels). The arc of gold rays and clouds is flanked by a cluster of (adult) angels paying homage to God. Below is a rainbow, symbol of God's covenant with man, and seated on a throne inside the rainbow, again surrounded by gold rays is Christ enthroned with his wounds visible. On Christ's right (our left) is the Virgin Mary shown praying to Jesus, and on his right is Saint John the Baptist, who points to Christ as the truth and the way. Below Christ, Mary and the Baptist is another bank of clouds, with the Holy Spirit immediately below Jesus represented by a dove encircled by more gold rays. Flanking the Holy Spirit are more cherubs holding four books to symbolize the four Gospels which tell the story of Jesus in the Bible. Finally below the Holy Spirit is an altar, and on that altar is a golden monstrance holding the Holy Eucharist to be adored by all present. So in simple terms, God takes on human flesh as Christ to bring salvation to man, Christ's teachings through the Word and his sacrifice on the cross release the Holy Spirit and through the miracle of the Holy Spirit, priests on earth consecrate the Eucharist that men may be one with God and be saved.

So that explains the symbolism in the painting, but what about the huge cast of characters on hand? While some of the faces are probably anonymous "extras," many of those present are easily identifiable. The grand pooh bah box seats belong to those guests of honor who are seated on the clouds alongside Christ. Starting at the far left is Saint Peter, who is always easy to spot with his keys to the Kingdom. Next to him is the mostly naked Adam, and then Saint John the Evangelist who is clean shaven and is busy writing, presumably one of his chapters in the Bible. Next to John we find King David wearing a crown and holding his lyre, and finally leaning over to speak to a figure almost entirely obscured behind the Virgin Mary is Saint Francis of Assisi in his brown robes. Continuing on the far side of Jesus, the clean-shaven saint in green who holds the palm frond of a martyr is most likely Saint Stephen, the first Christian martyr whose story is told in Acts of the Apostles in the Bible, and next to him is the readily identifiable Moses with his Ten Commandment tablets. The next fellow in his white robes holding a book is most likely Saint James, and next to him is Abraham holding a knife in his right hand. Finally the top row is completed with Saint Paul at the far end opposite Saint Peter. He holds a book to make reference to his letters, and a sword to indicate his death by beheading.

There's a frenzy of activity below, in contrast to the well-ordered dignity of the men perched up in the clouds. Among those flanking the altar are ordinary citizens, famous monks, bishops (tall pointy white hats) and popes (pointy white hats with three horizontal bands). Let's take a look at who is included. Starting again on the left, the further-most figure on the far left, an old monk dressed in black in Fra Angelico. The fellow leaning on the wooden railing looking over his shoulder back toward the altar is Bramante, an architect we will discuss a little later. Up close to the altar on the left is a bald, bearded man dressed in red who is reading a book; that's Saint Jerome, the guy who translated the Vulgate <u>Bible</u>. Next to him the pope (see the three-tier crown) is Saint Gregory of the Great. On the other side of the altar there is a prominent pope in gold robes and papal tiara; that's Pope Sixtus IV. To the left of Sixtus, the cardinal in the red hat is Saint Bonventure, and next to him is good old Pope Julius II who is the patron of the painting. Julius is chatting with Saint Thomas Aquinas, one of the preeminent theology scholars of the Middle Ages. To the right of Sixtus is Dante; see the laurel wreath on his head? And next to him is a surprise visitor, Savonarola! The previous pope may have convicted Savonarola of crimes and had him put to death, but Julius II thought better of it and posthumously reinstated Savonarola to the good graces of the Church for posterity.

The **School of Athens** is another fresco from this series. The figures are arranged either in rectangles or triangles and placed in a lunette (geometry in composition compliments of Leonardo), and the architecture detail allowed Raphael to show off his mastery of mathematical perspective (compliments of Brunelleschi who invented that technique). The subject centers on Plato and Aristotle, surrounded by all the great scientists and philosophers of antiquity, seemingly rediscovered and invited to the 16th century to teach one another along with men of the Renaissance. Plato and Aristotle are the stars of the show as they pass through the promenade of arches. Each holds a book to represent his writings. Plato raises one arm to illustrate his belief in God and heaven, while Aristotle's hand is extended forward, palm down, suggesting that his preference is to rely on empirical observations of the world. The artist had some fun with the characters in the scene. The figure of Plato is a portrait of Leonardo in his old age. One may wonder why Raphael selected Plato rather than Aristotle, since Leonardo's sympathies were perhaps more attuned to observing nature than they were directed at knowledge of the mysteries if God. Hunched over in the front, exuding a melancholy funk is Michelangelo, and off to the far right, Raphael tucked his own portrait in among assorted scholars.

Raphael's new status as an important artist and intellectual in Vatican circles enabled him to meet plenty of interesting, famous people. Among those was **Baldasarre Castiglione**, who wrote the <u>Book of the Courtier</u>, a popular primer on how to achieve the perfect manners of a courtier exuding nobility, military achievement, knowledge of the classics in literature and philosophy, and of course, an understanding and appreciation of the arts. Raphael's portrait of Castiglione is a masterpiece to be sure, but what is curious perhaps is the flat, plain background. It is a break from Raphael's earlier style, which like others from Italy since the latter 15th century included some element of landscape in the background (see his portraits of the Doni husband and wife, or the Mona Lisa by Leonardo). Where did Raphael get this plain backdrop? Northern Renaissance artists had used this style a century earlier, but would Raphael have seen any of these paintings? He was certainly familiar with the portraits of Justus of Ghent from his childhood, but Justus employed the more "modern" style of including some architecture in the background, sometimes with a window. The only northern artist who started using the plain backdrop a few years before Raphael, and who also visited Italy twice, once during the years Raphael was a student still in Urbino and then again when Raphael was in Florence ... was Albrecht Durer. Is it possible that Raphael might have seen a Durer portrait and borrowed the plain backdrop from the German master? Maybe so.

Julius II died in 1513. Michelangelo designed his tomb, and Raphael as the junior artist on staff got the job of creating a banner to carry in the procession. The banner, painted in oil on canvas instead of wooden panel, is called the **Sistine Madonna**. Once again we see a pyramidal group, consisting of a particularly pretty Virgin Mary holding infant Jesus flanked by Saint Barbara on the right (patron saint of the hour of death), and a portrait of Julius II on the left, being portrayed as Saint Sixtus, who was the patron saint of Julius' family, the della Roveres. Mary seems to float on clouds, which would be a clever first except that Raphael conveniently lifted the idea from Michelangelo's tomb design.

When a pope dies, another must be selected. The new pope was Leo X, whom we have already introduced back in the discussion of Martin Luther. Popes take on a new name when they enter their new office, in just the way that Simon was renamed Peter by Jesus (the only Apostle to be renamed in this manner). Before the pope became Leo X, he was ... Giovanni de Medici. The plot thickens. In fact, Giovanni de Medici was a contemporary of Michelangelo; he was one of the Medici "boys" with whom Michelangelo grew up at the Medici palace in Florence. The men knew each other well. Maybe too well. The pope maintained a cordial relationship with Michelangelo, *but* he was shrewd enough to understand that while Michelangelo was a tremendously gifted artist and someone from whom the Church would want as much art as possible, and while he was satisfied that Michelangelo was "family," if perhaps the difficult black sheep of the family in many ways, he was also somewhat wary that Michelangelo may have been involved with the Savonarola debacle that contributed to the fall of the Medicis in Florence, and therefore perhaps he should not be in a position where he had power and influence over others. So much for being court artist. Michelangelo was sent off to Florence, on friendly enough terms of course, to undertake the project of decorating the church of San Lorenzo where the Medici family tombs were located. Michelangelo wasn't happy about it, but the pope did his best to make it seem a plum assignment, while behind the scenes he could rest a little easier that Michelangelo was removed just enough from the mainstream that he could pose little threat to the pope. Leo X as far as we know was always cordial and friendly toward Michelangelo, if also careful to not let the artist create problems for the Medici family.

As Leo surveyed the prospects available to him, he quickly identified Raphael as the most suitable to succeed Michelangelo as leader of the arts in Rome. Was it because Raphael was the best of the best? Perhaps. Certainly Raphael had matured nicely and his paintings were excellent. Beyond that though, it certainly didn't hurt that Raphael was the only promising artist on staff who had not lived in Florence until after the demise of Savonarola. It was therefore impossible to suspect that Raphael could have had any sympathies with the anti-Medici revolt. With everyone who had been in Florence during the 1490's, there was always a lingering doubt over whether they may have contributed to the plot, and may even still harbor hostility toward the Medicis. Raphael became court artist to the pope. His picture of **Leo X** says it all. Leo is depicted as a luxurious man, and one who favors his own (the cardinal here whom Leo appears to be conniving with is his cousin, Giulio de Medici, who in not so many years would become Pope Clement VII). All things being equal though, Raphael was no less charitable to Leo than he was to Julius, who thought Raphael was an absolutely wonderful guy so perhaps the popes were pleased to be portrayed as dour fellows.

Leo X *was* an extravagant man and a worldly one too. He loved the arts, and he apparently loved a good laugh. He enjoyed animal tamers, circus acts and burlesque comedy acts – by burlesque we mean similar to the 20th century Three Stooges (as opposed to strippers!). He was also big on secular politics, especially as far as his native Florence was concerned. He forcibly reinstated the Medici family as governors of Florence, and while he was at it, he seized control of Urbino and made that city-state subject to Florentine rule against their wishes too. Aside from being a hardliner where Florence was concerned however, true to Medici temperament, Leo X was basically a tolerant, laissez-faire kind of guy in most matters. Or at least he was as far as he could be in the position of being pope. Consider that when Savonarola was drumming up trouble in Florence, did the Medicis arrest him and throw him in prison for subversion of the state? Naw. They figured it would blow over. It would seem that Leo X handled the indulgence problem up in Germany about the same way. Surely he got wind of the abuses being committed by Johan Tetzel. Now if he had been Alexander VI, he may have rushed right up there, arrested Tetzel and toasted him up extra crispy. That sort of knee-jerk response wasn't characteristic of the Medicis. Even after a few years of Martin Luther writing essays and delivering sermons that had others in the Catholic Church greatly offended, Leo preferred to write letters of warning to Luther rather than take drastic measures.

Ironically, by March 1517, several months *before* Luther nailed his 95 Theses to the doors of Wittenberg Cathedral, the Oratory of Divine Love had already been formed in Rome, with Leo X's approval, and coincidentally perhaps, Raphael was a member. The objective of this group of priests and laymen was to begin an earnest effort at reform within the Catholic Church, to rout out precisely the sort of corruption that was happening in Germany. They also demanded higher standards from the clergy as a whole, addressing many of the same issues Luther would write about, but doing so from inside the Church as opposed to eventually breaking away. One has to imagine that Leo X was under considerable pressure from the other bishops and cardinals to sanction Martin Luther for him to finally be moved to excommunicate the monk. Leo X was a longtime veteran of exploring interesting philosophies and pondering new ideas. Somehow, all that wallowing in Plato in his youth hadn't deterred Leo X from his Catholic faith. While some of Luther's teachings *were* heretical by Catholic and Orthodox Church standards, one has to wonder what *might* have happened if Luther had *not* been excommunicated in 1521.

Raphael died young in 1520 at the age of 37 following a brief illness; he passed away on Good Friday. At his request, his funeral was held at the Pantheon, and his body is interred there to this day. He was universally mourned. Leo X was not long behind him. He died in 1521 shortly after Luther was cut off from the Catholic Church.

Parmigianino

During the 1520's and 1530's an art movement surfaced in central Italy that was as unlike the rest of the High Renaissance as the Amarna Style was unlike the rest of New Kingdom Egyptian art. It has been nicknamed *Mannerism*. It is easier to describe what Mannerism looks like than it is to explain exactly why it came about. Taking a stab at the more difficult task, it may have been a reaction to the unsettled times in the Christian religion, with the advent of the Protestant Reformation challenging the Catholic Church in ways far more profound than any differences that had ever occurred centuries earlier between the Catholic and Byzantine Churches. Add to this, the people living in central Italy were also very disenchanted with the Medici popes, and with good reason. While Leo X may have been a jolly chap in some ways, he wasn't amusing at all when it came to politics, especially politics where Florence was concerned. He had a stern Medici government reinstated in Florence against the citizens' wishes. His kid brother Giuliano had already returned during the reign of Julius II, and had eased his way back into the old style of typically laid back Medici rule – Leo put an end to that and had their bully nephew, Lorenzo, take over, then he unseated the rightful heir to the Duchy of Urbino and expanded Florentine rule to include both regions, which pleased exactly nobody outside the Medici family. After Leo X died, there was a pious Dutch pope for a couple years who undid some of the political damage in Italy, and more importantly, made some progress in dealing with the Protestant Reformation. But he only lasted two years before he died under mysterious circumstances, and Clement VII, another Medici, became pope. Clement was far worse than Leo X, in that he carried on with the political intrigues which had marred Leo's tenure, and added to that personal immoral behavior, then tried to maneuver his illegitimate son into a position of power and prestige.

Small wonder a lot of people became discouraged! The closer they lived to Rome, the harder it was to fathom. Outside Italy the Protestant Reformation was going gangbusters during the reign of Clement VII. But the Italian Catholics loved the Church, and by and large had no interest in chucking it all for any of the new assortment of Protestant denominations, although they were certainly unhappy with how things were going in Italy as long as the Medicis were holding court at the Vatican. Mannerist art seems confused and even disrespectful of Christian faith, not because the artists were disenchanted with the Catholic Church, but perhaps more because they were distressed by the Medici popes and their disruptive and unpopular politics. It was as though the artists realized their art was lurching in the direction of being too trendy, self-conscious and different to be acceptable for a religious setting, but they pushed the limit anyway, almost as a backhanded insult to an overly worldly Church leadership (Medici popes) that would support religious art so obviously off-kilter.

A good example of Mannerist painting is the **Madonna of the Long Neck** by Parmigianino. It is almost hard to believe that this painting was commissioned for a church (Bologna Cathedral no less). It was never delivered, *not* because the patrons had a problem with it, but because the artist, in the end, wasn't satisfied with the final product. And so … how about this Madonna? First of all, Mary is a freak, and a sleazy freak at that. She could not possibly be hoisted into a standing position with those enormous hips serving as an anchor. Her appearance with movie star make-up and jewelry is certainly a departure from tradition (she looks more like a lady of the evening than a virgin!), and not only is she wearing some semi-sheer negligee fabric, but she is suggestively offering her breast to … what exactly? Jesus is about the size of a kindergarten child, and he looks dead. He is reclining across Mom's lap like a pieta, even recalls Michelangelo's Pieta pose, and his coloring is looking more than a little off. So … we have Mary decked out like a hooker, making a pass at the Messiah, who is actually a bald, dead kid. And people were going to pay for this. To hang in a church. Okay, what else? Who are those androgynous kids we see all clumped together off to one side, and why are they all half-undressed? And on the other side, why are there a series of column bases that disappear into a single, unfinished column at the top that fails to support anything? And who is that itsy bitsy little munchkin man standing off to one side reading a scroll … to some unseen audience that didn't even make it into the picture at all?

Obviously Mannerist art is more than just a little peculiar; much of it comes across as downright sacrilegious. It seems to have run its brief course during the decades when the Medici popes were in Rome, and then faded into oblivion with the arrival of true reform from within the Catholic Church during the latter part of the 16th century and on into the 17th century.

Sofonisba Anguissola

All the Italian artists we have considered so far came from central Italy: mostly Florence and to a lesser degree, Urbino during the 15th century, shifting over to Rome during the 16th century. Our next artist was outside the mainstream in more ways than one. First, Sofonisba Anguissola was from a noble family from Cremona, up in Lombardy not far from Milan. Secondly, Sofonisba Anguissola was a woman. You haven't heard much about women in art up until now, and with good reason. The historian Pliny suggests that there may have been a few women who contributed to the arts from Greece and Rome, but they were hardly big name artists. During medieval times again we seldom know the artists by name. Manuscript illustration was occasionally handled by nuns in convents, so presumably some nuns contributed to the arts just like monks, but again, we don't see much individual fame for the illustrators whether they were men or women during the Middle Ages.

During the Renaissance, for the first time since ancient Greece attention was paid to the individual artist allowing us to learn about the hand behind the art as well as appreciate the art itself. So why do all the artists seem to be men? The arts, like all careers in most European cities at this time, were regulated by guilds, or professional societies that oversaw apprenticeship programs for training students and which also provided a measure of guarantee to the public that guild members maintained professional standards. The problem was it was traditionally illegal for girls to apprentice under professional artists. Accordingly, the only way a girl could hope to learn to paint (you could pretty much forget about sculpture), was if Daddy happened to be an artist and he decided to take Petunia on as a student. And then, even if a father taught his daughter to paint, she was excluded from actually joining the guild, so she was pretty much stuck outside professional consideration as artists go. There had always been a small handful of women in this position, and they were limited to painting portraits of women and children for discount prices. Sofonisba Anguissola was the first to rise above the level of "second best girl artist" to be considered an equal to at least the minor professional painters of her day.

Sofonisba was the eldest of seven children, six of whom were girls. Perhaps because they were a prominent family in a smaller city not overrun with famous artists, Papa Anguissola was able to arrange for his eldest two daughters to be tutored by the leading painter in Cremona. Bernardo Campi came from a family of artists who for generations had served their hometown, and perhaps it was a combination of his respect for the Anguissola family combined with a father's desire to see his daughters receive an education when he had so many and only a single son in the family that brought about this arrangement. In any event, it was extremely rare for the 16th century, and probably would never have occurred had the family lived someplace like Florence or Rome. Sofonisba was the more talented of the two girls who apprenticed under Bernardo Campi, and she went on to become a portrait painter not just of local women and children, but of important people outside her hometown. Her most famous patron was the King of Spain who invited her to Madrid to paint portraits of his family, no small achievement at a time when most women of her class had no thought at all of a career, however modest.

Even as a painter of some renown, most of Anguissola's paintings were nevertheless pictures of her own family. **Portrait of the Artist's Three Sisters with Their Governess** illustrates Sofonisba's sisters playing chess. The painting combines the old fashioned profile portrait technique with the more modern ¾ view, and it combines an attention to each individual sitter with an attempt to show all parties interacting in a common activity. In this regard Sofonisba Anguissola foreshadows group portraiture that will be introduced in northern Europe during the 17th century as a popular art theme. Her treatment of the background landscape is an exaggerated version of sfumato (fogging out the details) combined with equally exaggerated aerial perspective (making objects at a distance appear more bluish grey than the foreground).

Giovanni Bellini

Venetian art during the Renaissance was almost a category unto itself. Venice was the maritime giant in Italy. The citizens there were much more involved with trade outside of Italy, be it with Northern Europe or the Middle East, than they were interested in all the politicking going on everywhere else in Italy. The Venetians were rich, somewhat glamorous, and somehow removed from a lot of the problems that seemed to rise and fall in central Italy. Painting here followed a slightly different path than it did elsewhere in Italy. Toward the latter part of the 15th century one family established themselves as the leaders in painting: Jacopo Bellini and his two sons, Gentile and Giovanni. The greatest of these was the youngest, Giovanni. He was a contemporary of Leonardo da Vinci, and therefore a bridge between the old style of the Early Renaissance and the guiding light for what was to come in the High Renaissance. Giovanni met artists visiting Venice who knew the painting traditions of in the North, and from them he developed an interest in oil paints where an artist could modulate color through building glazes. He also took an interest in landscape painting, which up until now had enjoyed only marginal exposure in Italian circles through the paintings of a few artists associated with the Urbino region.

Saint Francis in Ecstasy is an excellent example of Giovanni Bellini's style. It's a large painting (roughly 4'x 4.5') produced in oil and tempera on wood panel. The title suggests that the artist might be capturing the moment when Saint Francis received the stigmata. If you look closely you can see the wounds on his hands, but that doesn't seem to be what's captured the painter's imagination. In fact, not only is the artist less than impressed with the wounds, he isn't paying all that much attention to the saint at all. The detailed landscape offering a panorama view back miles into the distance is the real subject here. By manipulating color and scale, the artist has offered a foreground done in tans, blues and greys, where Francis plays his small role as the "subject" of the painting, and then an intermediate middle ground in browns and greens where the donkey stands. Behind there is the background village with small but detailed tan architecture set against a sienna reddish-brown ground, and finally way in the distance there are hills that fade into oblivion in their bluish-grey aerial perspective. Also like Northern painting of his generation, Bellini has included the occasional symbolic reference, something we don't see too often in Italy. Saint Francis has removed his sandals to indicate that he stands on holy ground. Grape vines, making a symbolic reference to the Eucharist, create a canopy over his wilderness desk. And the skull resting on his desk, a reminder of man's mortality, is a popular attribute of Saint Francis (and others) symbolizing a penitent saint.

Giovanni Bellini was the most famous artist in Venice when he died in 1516, but historically he is most famous today for being the teacher of his two most famous pupils, Giorgione and Titian.

Giorgione

We will briefly consider the elder of Bellini's star apprentices, Giorgio da Castelfranco (George from the village of Castelfranco), called "Giorgione," a nickname meaning "Big George." We know very little about this painter as he died young of the plague and left few completed paintings to his credit. Beyond that, he was apparently independently wealthy, and didn't have to work for a living, so for the most part, he didn't. Few of his pictures were probably commissioned. It seems he painted because he felt inspired, and to the degree that others wound up owning them, they were most likely given as gifts. Although Giorgione had a short career, he was a mentor and friend to Bellini's younger exceptional pupil, Titian, whose career spanned almost seven decades and who wound up being a significant influence on future generations of artists. So it is that we take a peek at Giorgione, because it was largely his mentoring, perhaps even more than Bellini's instruction, which helped to form the greatest artist from Venice during the High Renaissance, Titian.

Although scholars dispute the authenticity of several paintings attributed to Giorgione, one that is universally accepted as his work (although the landscape was completed by Titian after Giorgione's untimely death) is the **Sleeping Venus**. The subject matter alone offers insight to Giorgione's offbeat selection of themes. Mythology had become a popular subject throughout Italy by the late 15th century, and Venus had offered other artists an opportunity to paint a female nude. Consider Botticelli's Birth of

<u>Venus</u>. Going all the way back to Greek prototypes (like Praxitiles; remember the <u>Aphrodite of Knidos</u>?), Venus as the Romans called her, or Aphrodite to the Greeks was depicted as a beautiful young woman, having been born from the sea and discovering herself to be naked, she attempts to modestly cover herself. Well well well, so how about Giorgione's Venus? For some bizarre reason, Venus has emerged from the sea, apparently completely unconcerned that she is buck naked, and she has decided to take a nap out in the countryside in all her splendor. As viewers, we almost assume the role of peeping Toms; somehow there is an air of lurid sensuality here that exceeds the usual fare as Venus imagery goes.

The **<u>Pastoral Concert</u>** (often called ***Fete Champetre***) is another ideal example of Giorgione's style. It was painted shortly after the turn of the century, approximately contemporary to Leonardo's <u>Mona Lisa</u>, Michelangelo's <u>David</u>, and Raphael's Madonnas. There is no record of a commission, and accordingly there have been questions raised as to whether he even painted the piece (or was it Titian, or did Titian finish a painting started by Giorgione...), but let's assume that tradition prevails, and the attribution to Giorgione stands. What exactly do you see? Well, there are some men, dressed in contemporary clothing, and they are outdoors in a meadow playing musical instruments common to the late 15th / early 16th century. Now for some startlingly odd reason, some ladies have shown up for the concert, and they are all stark naked. Why? I have no idea, and despite however many scholarly papers have been written trying to turn it into mythology or a religious scene or anything else, the fact is nobody really knows what's going on here because the artist didn't leave behind an explanation. Taken at face value, as opposed to exercising our skills at revisionist history, this is one pretty weird scene.

There are some stylistic pointers worth noting about the artist's technique. First, notice that Giorgione employs plenty of chiaroscuro. His figures are modeled with the same earthy shadowing that we saw in Leonardo's paintings. Leonardo was in Venice, however briefly, when Giorgione was in his early 20's, and it is entirely possible that the younger artist was influenced by the famous master's style although there is no record that the two were acquainted. Like Bellini, Giorgione was much more interested in painting realistic landscape than the average Italian artist of his day. He may have been inspired by art in the North, given that Venice was a cosmopolitan city where trade connections brought the citizens into contact with people, places and things from outside their region. Or he may simply have pursued landscape on his own. Finally, notice that the artist was interested in full-bodied, natural color. He painted in tempera with oil glazes to produce luminous, transparent color unlike what was typically seen in other regions of Italy. Venetian painting will become known for its color during the Renaissance.

Giorgione excelled at painting odd little vignettes that defy logical explanations. Perhaps he had an offbeat sense of humor. Perhaps he was perverse. Whatever the truth of it may have been, Giorgione was Titian's teacher, so be prepared to find some of that wry twist of humor in some of Titian's paintings too.

Titian

Tiziano Vecellio, best known as simply "Titian," is the last of the truly great Renaissance Old Masters; in fact he was a major influence on later generations of painters. We don't know for certain when he was born, in no small part because he apparently put on airs that he was older than he was to impress people. The latest scholarship suggests he was probably born in the late 1480's, in a small town up in the mountains north of Venice. As a child he was brought to the city to learn the art of mosaics. He went on to apprentice under Giovanni Bellini, and it was in this studio that he met Giorgione who was apparently a few years older than he was and a little further along the learning curve in these early days of Titian's career. The two were dubbed the "modern artists" of their generation and their style, which was for all intent and purposes identical, was a departure from their master, Bellini. Giorgione was like a big brother to Titian artistically. When Giorgione died in 1510, Titian completed those paintings his friend and mentor had left unfinished, and then he went on to become the single leading artist in Venice for the better part of the century. He may have started his career humbly as Giorgione's assistant, but Titian wound up stinking rich while still young enough to enjoy it. In part this was because he was in demand for his superb painting, but it was also because Titian was a stable man, married and the father of four, endowed with both good work habits and shrewd business sense when it came to investing well. He owned a lavish palatial villa, traveled when necessary to accommodate his patrons but otherwise preferred being home in Venice to gallivanting about (he even postponed visiting Florence and Rome until later in his career), and he completed commissions for just about every important person in Italy who liked art during the 16th century.

Titian was a supreme colorist. Other Italian artists may have had quite nice color – deep and somber with Leonardo, or bright and perky with Raphael, but the so-called Venetian color which Titian popularized was rich, luscious even. In simplistic terms, think rose pink corduroy – that's Raphael. Titian is shimmering mulberry satin. It's not the same. Titian was the first artist to consistently paint with oil paint on canvas rather than tempera or oil on wood panel, and he had a clear concept of what he wanted to achieve with color and how to make it happen. First he would cover his canvas with a reddish ground color to improve the overall warmth of colors laid over the foundation. Then he would build up his colors through layering, often setting a canvas aside for awhile so he could come back to it with fresh eyes to reassess the colors. Finally, he would apply translucent, pearly glazes to even out the colors and give his paintings an overall luminous quality. In addition to his superb manipulation of color, Titian was the very first artist to decide it was okay to leave some of his brushstrokes visible. Everyone up to this time, and everyone else during the 16th century believed that a picture wasn't finished until all the brushwork had been smoothed away, so that you could see the subject matter, you could see the colors, and maybe you could see highlights and shadows. But you could never see how the paint had been applied. Texture was for sculpture perhaps, but not for painting. Titian was the first to leave texture here and there, a little glimpse into the artist behind the pretty picture. The rough canvas surface (as opposed to smooth wood panel) offered some *tooth* (rough texture) for the foundation, and from there he would build his images from brushstrokes rather than creating an outlined image and filling in the color. As time went on, he even used his fingers to scrub and blend the paint, often creating an *impasto* of thick, textured paint.

During his early career, Titian completed two monumental masterpiece commissions for the church of Santa Maria Gloriosa dei Frari in Venice. The first was the **<u>Assumption of the Virgin</u>**, commissioned by the Abbott of the monastery, and it is still found in its original location above the main altar in that church. Probably because it is so large (over 22' tall), the artist elected to paint on sturdy wood panel this time. The painting was produced just a couple years after Raphael's Sistine Madonna which also showed Mary floating on clouds, although there is no evidence that Titian saw that painting since he didn't visit Rome for another thirty years. Still, it's not impossible that the funeral banner could have been described to him by acquaintances that were in attendance and saw the funeral procession for Julius II. In Titian's painting, Mary rises up to meet God the Father, who dramatically flies out to meet her from an unearthly glow of pure golden light. Chubby cherubs hoist the rather substantial shelf of clouds up toward heaven while others clamor around the Virgin. The Apostles below flail about in an excited frenzy as they watch Mary being carried off to heaven. Titian seemed interested in communicating the thrill of such a moment through arm gestures especially, although his overall composition is as stable as other Renaissance art. As we have seen with other artists, the subject matter is front and center, and he also manipulated color, in this case shades of red, to create a triangular composition using Mary as the pinnacle and two Apostles as the base.

Just a few years later Titian created another major altarpiece for a side altar in the same church. The **Pesaro Madonna** (16' tall and on canvas this time) was commissioned by Jacopo Pesaro, who was the Bishop of Paphos, Cyprus although his family was Venetian nobility of longstanding. Bishop Pesaro was the admiral in charge of the papal fleet of galleys, and this painting was commissioned in thanksgiving for a successful campaign in 1502 when Pesaro and his fleet successfully won the Battle of Santa Maura against the Muslim Turks. While the Assumption of the Virgin remains conservative in composition, the Pesaro Madonna is highly innovative. First, the entire painting is designed to resemble a niche, which we have seen before (think of Piero della Francesca's Brera Madonna for example), but this time the niche doesn't mimic enclosed architecture, it gives the illusion of opening onto an expansive outdoor veranda. Further, all the usual tricks of composition have been altered to give the scene a dynamic quality not seen in other Renaissance painting. Presumably the Madonna and Child should be the central theme, but they are not in the center of the picture. Instead they are elevated onto a throne off to the right, accessed by a strong diagonal starting in the lower left, forcing us to "read" the painting from left to right rather than visually plop down in the middle and stay there. The patron, Bishop Pesaro, kneels in the lower left, with a turbaned Turk behind him (a token prisoner to remind us of the victory), and a soldier behind him, most likely Saint George serving as a patron saint to offer a suitable introduction to Jesus and Mary. Off on the right are additional members of the Pesaro family, all male (unlike Flanders, in Italy the men of the family frequently were depicted on behalf of the whole family instead of including the women), with Saint Francis of Assisi, in his brown robes and just barely visible stigmata wounds, serving as their patron saint since the church of Santa Maria Gloriosa dei Frari was served by Franciscan monks. Saint Peter, demonstrating the patron's loyalty to the pope, sits on the stairs with his customary yellow cape and his key to the kingdom spilling out from beneath his robe. To offer his composition stability, Titian relied on pyramidal forms: Bishop Pesaro and his brother clad in red form book end triangles, and Saint Peter between them forms another. The three together form a larger equilateral triangle, but where the artist departs from others is that the figures taken as a whole form a near right triangle. The spatial composition qualities of this painting foreshadow the Baroque period that will follow the Renaissance in the 17th century.

Titian was also highly respected for his portraits. Like Raphael, he was called upon to paint the popes, in his case, **Pope Paul III** (Alessandro Farnese) who followed the Medici popes in the mid-16th century. If you compare Titian's portrait of <u>Pope Paul III</u> to Raphael's portrait of <u>Pope Julius II</u>, you may be able to clearly see the difference in Titian's luminous (if also subtle) quality of color and texture compared to Raphael. Pope Paul III was an interesting transitional pope between the worldly if not especially pious popes around the turn of the century, and those who would follow into the Baroque time period. Paul III was the pope saddled with the aftermath mess of the early Protestant Reformation, and he was the pope who called the Council of Trent from 1445-1447 to try to get everybody back on the same page. He was completely earnest about reforms from within the Catholic Church, as well as serious about trying to mend fences with the Protestants so the Church could be reunited as whole, or at least as whole as it had been since the schism between the Catholic Church and Eastern Orthodox factions centuries earlier.

The pope was a faithful Christian to the end and truly wanted to restore greater faith and piety among all Christians. Curiously perhaps, his greatest failings as pope were linked to his own personal failings as a man. In his youth, Alessandro Farnese fathered a son, whom he named Pier Luigi after his own grandfather. By the time Alessandro became pope this was long in his past, but his attempts to look out for this son and the grandchildren who were born of Pier Luigi and his wife caused problems. He appointed two of his teenage grandsons to become cardinals, which drew criticism. He also struck a political deal to obtain the duchies of Parma and Piacenza for his son to govern, which drew further criticism. In the end this provoked a feud with the Gonzaga family who were the imperial governors of Milan now as well as Mantua and Pier Luigi was assassinated. All the nasty politics, which ended so badly for those the pope loved, broke his heart and he died at age 82 much saddened by the personal tragedy brought on through his own indiscretions.

Titian was especially sought after for his charming portraits of women. **Isabella d'Este**, probably the most influential and famous woman in 16th century Italy commissioned this portrait of herself when she was an old grandma ... as you can see, the artist was persuaded to use his imagination along with some sketches of Isabella in her youth to reconstruct the lovely young woman he ultimately painted. You might compare this portrait to Leonardo's sketch of her done during her youth. Odds are you will agree that Leonardo's sketch of <u>Isabella d'Este</u> looks more like his <u>Mona Lisa</u> than it looks like Titian's portrait here! Isabella d'Este was born to the Duke and Duchess of Ferrara (northeastern Italy between Venice and Ravenna) in 1474. She married Francesco Gonzaga in 1490, the Marquis of Mantua, and her whole family, which was quite close, followed her there. Mantua already had strong political ties to Urbino through marriage, and when Isabella's younger sister married Ludovico Sforza in 1491 and became Duchess of Milan it created a link of powerful political connections across northern Italy. Isabella was a frequent visitor in Milan, which was how she came to befriend Leonardo da Vinci. Her life was full ... full of glamour, but also full of political upsets and challenges, and personal disappointments within her family; her husband died of syphilis, and her eldest son who wound up assuming family leadership became involved in an affair with a married woman that strained relations with his disapproving mother.

Another "portrait" is Titian's **Girl with a Basket of Fruits** completed late in the artist's career. Traditionally the picture was believed to be a portrait of the artist's daughter, Lavinia, and while there are striking similarities in appearance, many scholars today doubt that Lavinia was the model for this painting. Perhaps the woman's identity is secondary to appreciating the artist's style, which is less formal than his earlier work. The lady's face is still captured in the now popular ¾ view, but the figure has been given an action pose, turning her body with her head tossed back as she glances over her shoulder at us, in order to show off the daring design of her gorgeous gown. The painting becomes so much more than a simple portrait of an attractive young woman. Also, given that we are not sure of the lady's identity, there is a possibility that it may not be a portrait of anyone in particular at all. If this is the case, then Titian once again proved to be an artist who foreshadowed what was to become popular in the 17th century: artists who painted anonymous scenes from every day life.

Perhaps Titian's most innovative work was outside the realm of religious themes and portraiture. The so called **Venus of Urbino** is a good example. The title was given to the work after the fact; we are not sure than Titian meant for it to be called "Venus." Just the same, Venus of Urbino was obviously inspired by Giorgione's Sleeping Venus; the similarities in presentation are clear, which makes it logical to presume the "Venus" association with this painting as well. This painting served as a springboard for a whole series of reclining nudes by Titian entitled as Greek and Roman goddesses, presumably all of them generic studies of well-endowed female pulchritude. The lady in *this* picture, however, was a portrait. It was commissioned by Guidobaldo della Rovere, Duke of Camerino, and later also of Urbino, and the woman depicted was apparently his mistress. Venus is supposed to be a virginal maiden who upon discovering her nakedness, makes every attempt to preserve some modesty, right? She is the goddess of love, chaste and pure. So who have we here? It's your goddess of love alright, wink wink. Not only is Venus staring at the viewer, making direct eye contact, she is brazenly lying on a rumpled unmade bed, and she seems to be anything but chaste or modest, and I wouldn't put my money on her virginity either. She isn't a classical nude; notice her bracelet, earrings and hair ornamentation. She holds a bouquet of flowers in her hand, which might just be a gift from her next customer, who would appear to be ... you! The painting is sensual, and textured between the cascade of tousled hair to her silky skin. And not to disappoint, Titian includes just a hint of whimsy, so much like Giorgione before him. See the dog on the foot of the bed? And what does a dog symbolically represent? Fidelity, right? Did you notice that the dog is napping? There won't be any of that fidelity business going on in this boudoir tonight.

The **Rape of Europa** is a late mythology canvas by Titian. It was commission by King Phillip II of Spain (the same king who also gave Sofonisba Anguissola some business); he brought Titian to Madrid to produce a series of mythological paintings, and the occasional portrait and religious scene to round out the royal art collection. The story line is typical of mythology fare: Jupiter as the grand pooh bah of the gods gets all worked up anytime a pretty girl crosses his path. This time it is Europa who has been hanging out with friends at the beach, minding her own business. Jupiter decides to trick Europa, so he transforms himself into a beautiful white bull which initially frightens

Europa, but the bull seems so tame and gentle that she comes around. She weaves a flowered wreath for the bull's horns, but then to her surprise, as she places the wreath on the bull he takes off out into the water with her barely able to hang on for her life. Meanwhile back at the beach her friends are freaking out. In all the commotion her clothes flutter half off exposing a breast here and lots of leg there, as wee cupids appear out of nowhere to seemingly conspire against Europa's chastity.   Titillating stuff. Despite the painting's size (73"x 81" – a very large over the sofa sized picture), you can probably see some of the textured brushwork even in a small reproduction image. Look around the hooves of the bull to see individual white dabs of paint to represent the water splashing as the bull's powerful galloping through the surf pulls him and his prize away from the shore and off to Crete where he will ravage the young beauty. You can see individual brushstrokes running down the flank of the bull's underside, including dabs of paint that together form a spiky-finned fish (Europa better be careful, if she slides off the bull's back… ouch!). Also, look at the distant landscape; the mountains, sea and sky fade away into a blended sunset of rich color and texture.

With Titian we come to a close in our look at Renaissance art. And perhaps it is well to save the Venetians for last, as more than any other art from elsewhere in Italy or Northern Europe, Venetian art foreshadows painting in the 17th century.

14. Renaissance Architecture

c. 1400 - 1600

Architecture during the Renaissance often exhibited an air of back to basics compared to the fanciful medieval conclusion of Gothic cathedrals, those complex and ornate skyscrapers of the Middle Ages. As we have seen before in both art and architecture, the West will start with simple ideas, develop them fully to an elaborate conclusion, then either return to a more simple style or opt for a new idea altogether. Church architecture produced during the 15th and 16th centuries offers considerable variety based largely on location. Italy now led the way in experimental church design having finally broken away from the strictly Early Christian model that had stubbornly held status quo throughout the Middle Ages while the rest of Europe fancied Romanesque and Gothic styles. During the Renaissance the Italians popularized something comparatively new in Catholic church design: large domes, often employed over crossings combined with the usual traditional basilica floor plan. Meanwhile across Europe the Renaissance ushered in an increased interest in secular architecture compared to the Middle Ages. It's not just about churches anymore with the rise of humanism and its emphasis on the individual and his accomplishments. Civic buildings took on greater importance as governments levied greater influence, as did magnificent homes for the glamorous people who had maneuvered their way to the top of society's social ladder.

Italy

Arnolfo di Cambio *(Gothic)*
Filippo Brunelleschi

<u>Florence Cathedral</u> was actually built mostly during the Gothic period, although its crowning glory, the magnificent dome, was designed by a great Renaissance master. It's not as elegant and ornate as most Gothic churches, but it makes up for that by its colossal scale; <u>Florence Cathedral</u> would dwarf plenty of other churches even from the Gothic period when bigger was considered better. Arnolfo di Cambio was the original architect of record, although it is generally agreed that the final design was a collaborative effort between several architects. Whether Arnolfo's baby or the brain child of a committee, the design exhibits greater fascination in the grand crossing of the nave and truncated transept than it does in the church as a whole. Although the nave is vaulted, it is not clear if this was part of the original design. The real crux of the building was the huge dome needed to span the crossing. The irony was that for as much as the whole building depended on that dome to work, when the church was designed, nobody

279

had no clue how on earth to pull off that little detail. The church was begun in 1294, but it was left unfinished with a gigantic hole in the roof where the dome was to go until Filippo Bruelleschi came along in the 15th century and figured out how to do it.

Brunelleschi got the commission to do the dome in 1417. The problems were complicated. The space was too big to attempt building the dome with traditional wooden centering (it was almost 140 feet wide) and beyond that, the way the crossing had been designed, there would be no support for the dome at its base from buttressed walls. Brunelleschi had to not only figure out a new type of dome (the old Roman hemisphere, like on the Pantheon, would not work here), he even had to invent special equipment to enable him to build it once it was designed. In the end, he constructed a tall octagonal drum over the crossing with round windows to bring light into the dome, then he created a tall octagonal dome with a thin double shell to reduce the weight, the first of its kind in history. The double shell was attached like a skin over twenty-four supporting ribs (the eight primary supporting ribs of the octagon can be seen from the exterior), which were then topped off by a heavy lantern on top that helped to stabilize the structure and keep the ribs from spreading apart at the top of the dome.

Bramante

Brunelleschi got the Italian Renaissance off to an impressive start with his humungous dome on Florence Cathedral, but perhaps one of the most influential buildings of this period was a tiny shrine created by one of the most gifted and most admired architects of the entire Renaissance generation, Donato Bramante. We know little about Bramante's early life and training. He was born near Urbino and apparently trained first as a painter, but we then have little information until he shows up in Milan where he served the Sforza family for over 20 years from the mid 1470's to 1499. He was in Milan around the same time that Leonardo was painting the Last Supper during the 1480's, and Bramante was apparently well acquainted with Leonardo. He was already over 40 by then. His career up to that point had revolved mostly around building churches following the styles of earlier architects – basilicas with barrel vaulting and some experimentation with domes.

Bramante left Milan for Rome in 1499 where he became the chief papal architect until the end of his life in 1514 (only a year after Julius II died). His most revolutionary building was the **Tempietto**, completed in 1502 shortly after his arrival in Rome. In many ways, the Tempietto is to Renaissance architecture what Ghiberti's Sacrifice of Isaac was to sculpture and what the Tribute Money was to painting. In each case, the artist or architect was for the first time clearly breaking away from medieval prototypes to seek inspiration exclusively from antiquity. Churches in Italy during the 15th century were beautiful to be sure, but the essence of the design process was a continuation of what had been produced during the Middle Ages: basilicas with barrel vaulting (sometimes ribbed groin vaulting, although the Italians never got as much mileage out of Gothic design as the French, Germans or English). The buildings were rectangles from the exterior with flat facades. The dome on Florence Cathedral was an exception to the rule, but otherwise most Italian churches still limped along reinforcing old fashioned models as design goes. The Tempietto was completely different.

First, it wasn't a church in the conventional sense, which undoubtedly freed Bramante to experiment more since he didn't have to concern himself with the usual considerations of who needs to be where during the Mass and how many people need to be shoehorned into the space at one time. The <u>Tempietto</u> was designed as a small shrine to mark the spot where it was believed that Saint Peter was crucified. It is a circular structure with a radius of only 15' in the interior space… almost more of a large 3-D sculpture than a building. Inside, there is a hole in the floor that allows visitors to view the shrine below. The round shape recalls some Roman temples that used that form, and the basic post and lintel circular peristyle employs a Roman variation on the old Doric order columns, complete with a frieze of triglyphs and metopes above. In fact, the lower level of the <u>Tempietto</u> takes its lead as much from Greek design as Roman. The round shape is more Roman; the notion that it was charming on the exterior, almost like an oversized sculpture, is more Greek. Above the entablature is a balustrade that encircles a sparingly decorated drum on which rests a dome, both the dome and drum being Roman design concepts. It was originally supposed to have a roomy circular courtyard around it which would allow visitors to step back and appreciate the wee temple from a 360 degree point of view, although nowadays it is tightly sandwiched into a small space. The <u>Tempietto</u> was revolutionary, and it impressed both architects and painters alike. Notice when you look at paintings from the period how many will include a temple-like structure in the background that seems to be inspired by the <u>Tempietto</u>.

Bramante's great claim to fame may be the <u>Tempietto</u>, but he was also court architect to the Vatican under Pope Julius II when the pope initiated his project to rebuild Saint Peter's Cathedral. You will recall that the original Saint Peter's was built during the early 4th century soon after Christianity was legalized in the Roman Empire. Although it started off as a shrine marking the burial site of Saint Peter, over time it became the seat of the Bishop of Rome (aka the pope). Like most Early Christian basilicas, Saint Peter's was in poor condition by the close of the 15th century. It either needed major repairs and refurbishing, or to be scrapped and replaced. Julius II chose the latter solution in no small part because he wanted an especially grand tomb built for himself set inside the cathedral, recalling (however majestically) the long standing tradition of church leaders being buried in the floor of this particular church since the beginning. And so… he tore the old mess down and set about a feverish building campaign to replace the old basilica with a wondrous new church. Bramante was the original architect on the project, which began in 1506 just a few years before he died.

Except for some interior details, all that remains of Bramante's contribution to the project is his **Plan for Saint Peter's**. Bramante's idea was to get rid of the long, skinny basilica plan, and replace it with a Greek Cross. It was Bramante's idea that there should be a huge dome floating directly above Saint Peter's tomb, and that part of the design was retained through fourteen architects and twenty popes until the church was finally finished and consecrated in 1626. Each arm of the Greek Cross plan was supposed to end in a round apse, with four smaller Greek crosses connecting the arms, each with its own smaller dome. It was destined to be a large church, but curiously perhaps, Bramante's design would have actually covered less ground than the old church did. Bramante's preference was for a plain exterior, and his design for the dome recalled the <u>Tempietto</u>, only somewhat more broad and squat (some have compared it to the Pantheon, although it was destined to be considerably more elevated than the old Roman prototype). Julius II died, and within a year, so did Bramante. Leo X took over the building campaign with the zeal of a true Medici, and the Saint Peter's building campaign continued.

Michelangelo

Before you go into shock imagining that Leo X put Michelangelo in charge of Saint Peter's ... no way Jose. Actually, he placed an architect named Sangallo in charge of the design, and court artist Raphael had considerable input also, and after Raphael, Sangallo the Younger. Sections of the building construction were completed during the reign of Leo X, as you might have guessed after all his efforts at raising money to fund the project (remember the indulgences?). Michelangelo didn't come on board as chief architect on Saint Peter's until 1546, long after Leo X was pushing up daisies. One of his first tasks was to tear down half of what was already built (most of Raphael's and Sangallo's work) in the hope of restoring it closer to what Bramante had originally designed. Michelangelo's **Plan for Saint Peter's** is actually a simplified version of what Bramante originally offered, and Michelangelo's design is the heart of the church to this day. Although the façade and interior were modified during the Baroque period (stay tuned, more on this later), when seen from the southwest, Saint Peter's still looks like Michelangelo's design. The crowning glory of Saint Peter's Cathedral is the dome, which was Michelangelo's handiwork. Inspired by both Bramante's design and taking construction cues from Brunelleschi's dome for Florence Cathedral, **Michelangelo's Dome** is tall and graceful. It was designed as a drum buttressed by pairs of attached columns, which correspond to supporting ribs inside the dome, and eventually paired columns again in the lantern.

Michelozzo di Bartolommeo

Saint Peter's is the definitive church built during this period, there is Saint Peter's and then there is everything else. Fabulous church architecture was a steady diet all through the Middle Ages. So don't architects design anything but churches? Well... yes, in fact they do. Back in Roman times you might recall, civic and religious architecture was important, but never more important than residential. There was increased interest in comfortable (and impressive) residential living during the Renaissance too.

We all have a feel for the Medici family at this point – the grand political power in Florence. The **Medici Palace** (later called Medici-Riccardi when another family purchased the home) was designed by Michelozzo di Bartolommeo. It is basically a big box, with exterior rooms enclosing an open courtyard in the center. Much hullabaloo has been made about how the texture of the masonry gets smoother as you go from the rusticated surfaces at street level and rise up to the third floor. Well, that's nice. Truth is, the basic design hasn't progressed far from the old insulae of ancient Rome, and maybe that's what the architect and his patron, Cosimo de Medici, intended. In ancient Rome, a whole city block was filled with an insula, or apartment building. The first floor was public – shops and public toilets - while the apartments were on the second through fifth floors. The building contained an enclosed peristyle garden where the residents could enjoy the outdoors in a private setting. Sounds a lot like this "palace," which looks more like a fortress (or department store?) than it does a luxurious home for the first family of Florence.

Palladio

Just as the Venetians developed a corner on the luxury market in painting, so did they also have a more clear vision of luxury in residential architecture (or any kind of architecture) compared to Florence. The real genius in this realm was Andrea Palladio. Palladio grew up in Vicenza, near Venice. He studied all the great masters of the Renaissance from around Italy as well as the architecture of ancient Rome in his quest to develop not only the most beautiful but also the most theoretically perfect architecture. Although he designed many public buildings and churches, his most influential work was residential. He designed a number of country estate homes for wealthy clients; the most famous is the **Villa Rotunda**. The patron was a retired clergyman who used the house as a retreat for entertaining and gardening. The villa stands on a ridge overlooking the architect's hometown. The home was designed around the concept of a classical temple portico (more Roman than Greek), or in this case, four porticos facing each of the cardinal points of a compass (north, south, east and west). The porticos radiate around the center of the structure, which supports a dome, modest from the exterior but quite impressive indoors as the center of the villa rises the full 2-stories with interior rooms opening off four central halls, each leading to the elegant domed heart of the home. Each portico was designed to offer a completely different view, and even to offer different atmospheric qualities at different times of the day.

The Medici Palace and Villa Rotunda are examples of Italian residential design for wealthy patrons. Perhaps we could say that the Medici Palace is the last hurrah for a residential style of the past, while the Villa Rotunda set new trends for architectural designs to follow; there will be plenty of Palladio-inspired design in our own country, especially in the South, as well as in Europe. What they have in common is that neither is knock-your-socks off huge and glamorous. For whatever reason, aside from Saint Peter's, which was to become the granddaddy of all churches in terms of scale, ornament and just plain WOW factor, Italian architectural design of the Renaissance errs on the side of understated and modest, even when the patrons themselves were anything but. If you really want to be impressed by architectural glamour, look outside Italy.

France

Domenico da Cortona

It is a curious irony of the period that one of the most famous and most glamorous homes of the Renaissance... not in Italy of course because that's not where you find the really spectacular spreads... was nevertheless designed by an Italian! Go figure. If you really want to be dazzled by the lifestyles of the rich and famous from this period, go to France. **Chateau de Chambord** was commissioned by King Francis I as a hunting lodge... one of several little getaways he kept in his real estate portfolio that he could visit when the mood struck. In fact, as stunning and as huge as this chateau is, nobody actually ever lived here, in fact, they didn't even keep it fully furnished. When the king was to visit, an entourage would be sent ahead with all the furnishings to make the palace ready for the king and his guests, and when they departed, everything was packed away and carted off again! Nobody ever lived here until a hundred years later when King Louis XIV fixed it up (it had fallen into disrepair having been abandoned), and eventually let his father-in-law, the deposed King of Poland, move in for awhile. For most of its history, though, Chateau de Chambord was a hunting retreat, and used infrequently at that.

So how big is it? Chambord boasts 440 rooms, 365 fireplaces and 84 staircases, one of which was the famous double helix open staircase where guests could go up and down the stairs without ever passing another headed in the opposite direction. It has been rumored that this clever double staircase may have been designed by Leonardo da Vinci, who was himself a guest of King Francis toward the end of the artist's life. As Leonardo's friend and admirer (not to mention his own personal greed), Francis tried to have the artist's famous Last Supper removed from the monastery in Milan and brought to France. That didn't work out, but he did get to keep the Mona Lisa, which Leonardo brought with him to France for those last years of his life. Chambord is the largest chateau in the entire Loire Valley, which is well-endowed with many fairy tale castles. Francis I was a contemporary of Henry VIII in England, and there was great competition between them. Francis invested enormous sums into fabulous chateaux sprinkled throughout the Loire to impress his "neighbors," not the least of which were the English.

Philibert de l'Orme

Chateau de Chenonceaux dates from the same era as Chambord, and the two are in the same Loire region of France. Francis didn't have this one built, but he did manage to pick it up when the previous owner fell behind on his taxes (oops). Chenonceaux is smaller and more intimate than Chambord. It was built on the site of an old mill on the banks of the River Cher. The chateau was never a favorite of Francis I, but after he died, his son and heir, Henri II decided to give the chateau to his favorite mistress, Diane de Poitiers. It's a tawdry tale of nobility lifestyle in generations past . Henri was betrothed to Catherine de Medici (yes, it's the same family) when the pair of them were kids; it was a politically correct match to smooth over wars between France and Italy. Both Henri and Catherine were all of 14 when they were married. Meanwhile back at the ranch… Diane de Poitiers was a stunning 35 year old widow, and a member of Francis' court due to her late husband's position in service to the crown. Well well well, it seems that Diane (35) and Henri (by then 16) hit it off and became a life-long item. Henri entrusted Diane with matters of state, and he gave her Chenonceaux as her private home. This didn't do much to foster affection with his wife, Catherine, who was a bit of a horsey heavy-set gal and not as drop-dead gorgeous as Diane. Catherine held no power, her husband was sleeping elsewhere, and the final insult was that Chenonceaux was Catherine's favorite of the family collection of chateaux. Grrrrrrr…. Diane de Poitiers had the spectacular bridge built across the river, and on the far side she created extensive gardens, both for flowers and vegetables. Here in her idyllic perfect little world she lived happily, but not forever after.

As fate would have it, Henri was an avid hunter and also a big fan of jousting. In 1559 he participated in a jousting tournament where a blade shattered and a piece of the metal pierced his eye and became lodged in his brain. He died a hideous, slow, painful death, leaving the ladies to sort out their relative positions at court. Finally it was Catherine's turn. She gave Diane de Poitiers the heave-ho out of Chenonceaux, banishing her to yet another chateau (it's always nice to have a spare), and Catherine moved herself and the kids to Chenonceaux where she finally got some respect. She ruled as regent and was known to put on a party or two at the chateau that would rival whatever opulence the relatives back home in Florence could muster.

As sort of a postscript on the saga, Henri II was King of France when the Protestant Reformation started making an impact in his country. The *Hugenots* were Calvinist (stay tuned, we'll cover that later) and Henri dealt with them severely. He thought nothing of having folks burned alive, and in general, it would be safe to say he was anything but tolerant. Catherine for her part was not a saint, but after Henri died, she made a better effort at negotiation and policies that promoted peace to resolve the Protestant Rebellion. Toward that end, she tried to marry off her favorite son to the young Protestant Queen of England, Elizabeth I in the hope of bringing greater political peace and religious unity to the region, but the marriage plans fell through.

England

William Cecil
Capability Brown *(gardens)*

William Cecil was not an architect by trade, but rather one of those truly rare "Renaissance men" who was exceptionally gifted in many fields of interest. We often think of Leonardo de Vinci as the ultimate example of this kind of "Jack of all Trades," (and in his case, Master of Most), but he wasn't the only fellow out there who seemed capable of doing almost anything he put his mind to. William Cecil was Privy Councillor (Secretary of State) to Queen Elizabeth I, he was her most trusted confidant, and in this important government capacity, he was awarded the honorary title of Lord Burghley. Desiring an estate home worthy of a man in his position, Cecil set out to design his own personal castle... himself. Obviously he managed rather well even without hiring a professional architect to create his dream home. The result was **Burghley House**.

English estate homes of this period were grand affairs that rival the chateaux of France, but when we compare Burghley House to Chateau de Chambord, we find some characteristic differences. Both are huge and cost a pretty penny to build, but the overall design and relation to the land is different. Chambord is very formal in design, with central halls dividing the "home" into four quadrants, not unlike the Villa Rotunda only much much larger. The home is "solid" in that there are no open courtyards inside the house, but perhaps to make up for that, the entire house is surrounded by a fancy perimeter "wall," complete with additional rooms inside the "wall" and quasi turrets at the four corners. This design is often refered to as *donjon style*, and it recalls old medieval castles that were built more for defense than hosting great parties, which was pretty much the sum purpose of Chambord. The walled fortress was then surrounded by a moat, again an idea borrowed from the past although at Chambord it doesn't have a thing to do with defense; it is purely decorative.

By comparison, Burghley House, although it has the same grand appearance as Chambord, is actually designed more like the Medici Palace in plan as it is a series of rooms designed around an open central courtyard in the heart of the building. Although grand, the layout of the house was also designed to be more comfortable as a real house that people live in, which Cecil's family has done since it was originally built in the 16th century down to the present day. The inner courtyard is surrounded on all four sides by a corridor, and off that corridor are the parlor, the library, dining room, kitchen, great hall and so forth, with most of these rooms having a pleasant view outward across the estate grounds as well as across the corridor into the courtyard. Burghley House had no fortress wall shutting off the house from the countryside, but instead put an emphasis on nature. Gardens played such an important role in English design that Cecil may not have hired an architect to design the house, but he did bring in a master landscape architect to design the gardens, "Capability" Brown. The French had gardens as well, but they were unlike English gardens which were carefully planned to look like they just happened to grow naturally that way – with rolling vistas that created a relaxed, outdoorsy feeling. French gardens were more formal, with flowers and trees lined up for inspection, or creating attractive patterns and designs, often with tidy pebble paths between rows of carefully pruned vegetation. English gardens invite casual picnics, while French gardens inspire champagne receptions.

Both Chambord and Burghley House are big boxes (albeit fancy big boxes), but again, you shouldn't confuse French design with English. Chambord, and other French chateaux of the Renaissance period, tend to have round towers topped with pointy party hats at the corners, and the overall sense of the roofline is spiky with lots of chimneys and lanterns poking up, and elaborately carved gables over windows. Burghley House, and other English mansions of the period, went in more for square towers at the corners of the building, crenellated walls with fewer spiky chimneys tucked in behind, and rather than pointy, elaborate gables defining the façade, Burghley House employed simple, rounded capped towers reminiscent of earlier English architecture.

Flanders and Holland

Herman van Herengrave

Not exactly a household name outside his own family, Herman van Herengrave is the architect of record for the **Town Hall in Nijmegen, Holland**. So far we have looked at a famous church and a few grand homes of the period, but up north in the "Low Countries" of Flanders and Holland, church and residential architecture during the Renaissance carried over much of the design attributes associated with the late Middle Ages. Gothic churches were still being built, and housing, estate-sized or otherwise was not distinctively different from what was built a hundred or more years earlier. Where we see the greatest innovation is in civic architecture. This particular town hall isn't the most famous or most important example, but it is typical of the period and is therefore introduced here to offer some basic insight to architecture in the North as it varies from building design elsewhere in Europe.

Architecture in Flanders and Holland employed steeply pitched rooflines. This is a common sense response to heavy snowfall in the winter months. Flat roofs or those with a shallow pitch are less expensive to build, so unless there is a practical reason for steeply pitched roofs, they are an expensive design feature that many architects in climates without much snow tend to avoid. The problem with flat roofs that don't shed snow effectively is they can suffer damage if the snowdrift on the roof gets too heavy. Flat roofs are also prone to leaking if they are subjected to heavy rain, or even just a lot of steady rain over time. In Italy this may not have been much a problem, but in Holland it rains probably more days a year than the sun shines. Accordingly, Netherlandish architecture usually features steeply pitched roofs that give even mundane, everyday buildings an almost gingerbread quality that is seldom seen in simple buildings in other regions. Notice especially the distinctive **stepped gables** on the town hall. This simple solution to getting rectangular bricks to conform to a steep angle is a common design feature in Dutch and Flemish architecture, and at the same time it adds a pleasant decorative quality to an otherwise simple building.

Cornelius Floris

The premiere architect in the North during the Renaissance was Cornelius Floris. His **Town Hall in Antwerp**, Belgium (Flanders) is hailed as the first Netherlandish building to exhibit Italian influence while retaining its distinctive Northern European character. Floris was well traveled, and his inspiration for the design was apparently an Italian piazza. The building was designed with four stories, with the lowest level being rusticated masonry punctuated by round, Roman arches not unlike what we saw on the Medici Palace. This level was completed first and reserved for shops, each with its own separate entrance onto the town square, and the revenue from these shops helped to pay the cost of constructing the rest of the Town Hall. The top story of the building offered a sweeping open veranda, and the building was topped with a "modern" *hip roof* rather than the more typical stepped gable like we saw on the Town Hall in Nijmegen.

Instead of the customary spire rising from the center of the roof seen on most buildings of this type in the North (see the Town Hall in Nijmegen for an example), Floris broke the façade with an enormous, decorative center gable rising from the street level to above the roofline. It is strictly façade; the structure does not correspond to any architectural feature inside nor does the roofline extend to meet the gable. It is purely aesthetic to break up the otherwise long horizontal quality of the building. On the second and third floors the rectangular windows give way to three arched windows per floor, and above, the structure is a series of decorative niches containing large statues. On what would be the fourth story level we find statues representing Justice on the left and Wisdom on the right, presumably good attributes to be associated with government. This level also features three crests: The left is the black field with a gold lion representing Brabant (which is the province where Antwerp lies), in the middle is the coat of arms for King Philip II of Spain, reminding us that the Netherlandish provinces were Spanish territories at this time, and on the far right is the crest of the margrave (local nobility) for the city of Antwerp. This level of the façade is bracketed on either end with obelisks, symbols of governing power since the days of the pharaohs in Egypt and borrowed by many societies ever since (consider the Washington Monument in our own national capital). On the upper level stands an oversized statue of a Madonna and Child, which was added later during the Counter-Reformation (a theme to be covered later). Originally there was a statue of the legendary Brabo, the mythical founder of Antwerp. Perhaps the mythical hero was seen as lurching toward paganism in the eyes of the Counter-Reformation, so good old Brabo was lowered to street level in the form of a bronze statue in the great market, and Jesus and Mary were given the elevated station at the pinnacle of the Town Hall.

Double engaged columns punctuate all the decorative features on this elaborate façade, giving the illusion of supporting a tiered wedding cake of frothy decoration. The columns follow the same pattern of rising fanciness with rising stories that appears in Imperial Roman architecture (the Colosseum in Rome would be a good example). The plainest style is reserved for the lowest level, and they become more ornate with each rising level on the building.

The Town Hall faced a huge open plaza where open markets were held. Flanking along one side were the great *Guild Houses*, owned by the professional societies in the city. These in Antwerp are spectacular to be sure, but perhaps not quite as remarkable as the Guild Houses built in Brussels during the 17th century so we will wait for the Baroque period to take a look at those instead. The town square was both the mercantile and social heart of the city, and is to this day where pubs and restaurants can be found, and where people mingle by day, and sometimes party by night.

The Renaissance was a period of growth and productivity that created burgeoning wealth from trade. Cities took pride in being cultural centers, and often merchant families parlayed their financial success into political clout, sometimes toppling the old guard nobility from power. Across Europe increased attention was paid to the individual, sometimes to the benefit of all, but also at times at the expense of the other guy. The stability of the Church suffered, both from corruption within and from dissent, and these influences are reflected in the architecture with as much money spent of civic and personal luxury as on churches, and in the art when secular themes began to rival Christian subjects perhaps for the first time since the Edict of Milan. The tug of war between faith and secular interests, and especially over authority, will reach a new zenith in the Baroque Period.

The Conflict of Faith, Authority and Humanism:

Baroque and Beyond

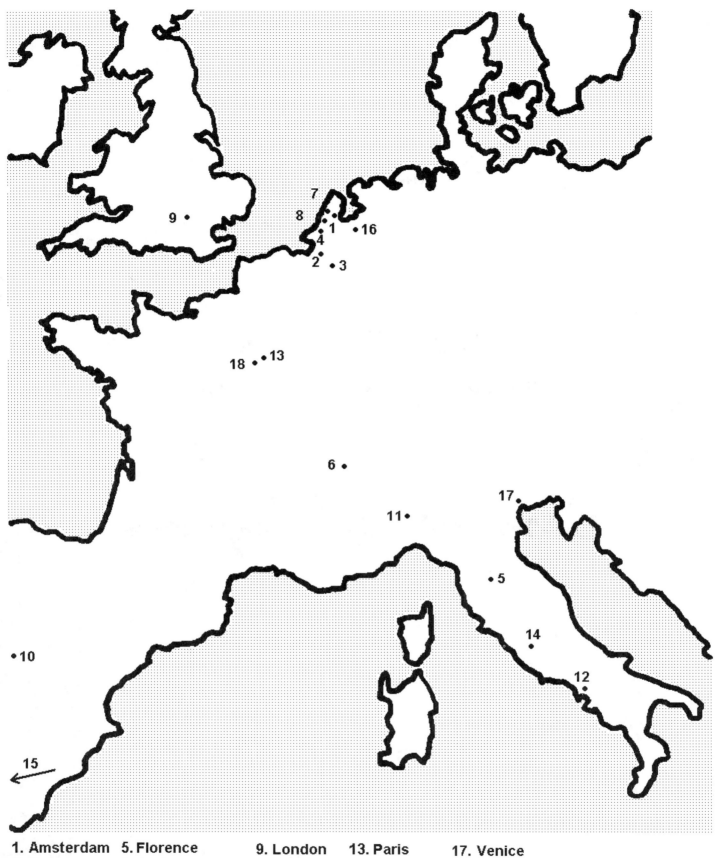

1. Amsterdam   5. Florence   9. London   13. Paris   17. Venice
2. Antwerp   6. Geneva   10. Madrid   14. Rome   18. Versailles
3. Brussels   7. Haarlem   11. Milan   15. Seville
4. Delft   8. Leiden/Hague   12. Naples   16. Utrecht

The Baroque World

Image List for Unit Four

BAROQUE: 1600-1700

ITALY

Caravaggio
1. Boy with a Basket of Fruit
2. Cardsharps
3. Bacchus
4. View of the Contarelli Chapel, Santa Luigi dei Francesi
5. Calling of Saint Matthew
6. Death of the Virgin

Artemisia Gentileschi
7. Judith and Holofernes

Gian Lorenzo Bernini
8. Cardinal Scipione Borghese
9. Rape of Proserpina
10. Rape of Proserpina (detail)
11. Apollo and Daphne
12. David
13. View of the Cornaro Chapel, Santa Maria della Vittoria
14. Ecstasy of Saint Theresa
15. Baldacchino
16. Cathedra Petri

Annibale Carracci
17. Farnese Ceiling Fresco
18. Triumph of Bacchus
19. Triumph of Bacchus detail
20. Flight into Egypt

Guido Reni
21. Aurora
22. Annunciation

Pietro da Cortona
23. Glorification of the Barberini

SPAIN

Jusepe de Ribera
24. Saint Andrew
25. The Holy Family with Saint Anne and Saint Catherine

26. The Martyrdom of Saint Bartholomew

Francisco de Zurbaran
27. Saint Serapion
28. Still Life with Lemons and Oranges

Diego de Silva y Velasquez
29. Water Seller of Seville
30. Old Woman Cooking Eggs
31. Feast of Bacchus
32. Portrait of Young Philip IV
33. Maria Teresa
34. Las Meninas
35. Sebastian de Morro
36. Rokeby Venus

Bartolome Esteban Murillo
37. Beggar Boys Eating Grapes and Melon
38. Two Women at a Window
39. Immaculate Conception
40. Assumption of the Virgin

FRANCE

Claude Lorraine
41. Embarkation of Saint Ursula

Nicolas Poussin
42. Assumption of the Virgin
43. Triumph of Poseidon and Amphitrite
44. Luna and Endymion
45. Funeral of Phocion

FLANDERS

Peter Paul Rubens
46. Raising the Cross
47. Rape of the Daughters of Leucippus
48. Helene Fourment
49. Landscape with a Rainbow

Anthony Van Dyck
50. Charles I

Foundations for Modern Art compares two paintings out of sequence; please study with their respective artists

51. Rape of the Sabines by **Poussin**

52. Rape of the Sabines by **Rubens**

HOLLAND

Frans Hals
53. Portrait of a Man
54. Banquet of Officers of the Civic Guard of Saint George
55. Archers of Saint Hadrians
56. Malle Babbe
57. Merrymakers of Shrovetide
58. Jonker Ramp and His Sweetheart

Judith Leyster
59. Self Portrait
60. The Proposition

Rembrandt van Rijn
61. Self Portrait
62. Self Portrait with Saskia
63. Polish Noble
64. Jewish Philosopher
65. Anatomy Lesson of Dr. Tulp
66. Night Watch
67. Bathsheba

68. Bathsheba by **Rubens** (group this with Rubens when studying)

69. Return of the Prodigal Son
70. Self Portrait as an Old Man

Pieter Saenredam
71. Interior of the Choir at Saint Bavo's Church

Johannes Vermeer
72. Kitchen Maid
73. Woman with a Water Jug
74. The Little Street

Jacob van Ruisdael
75. View of Haarlem
76. View of Haarlem
77. Windmill at Wijk

Aelbert Cuyp
78. The Maas at Dordrecht

Aert van der Neer
79. Fishing by Moonlight

ITALY

Carlo Maderno
80. Saint Peter's Cathedral

Gian Lorenzo Bernini
81. Saint Peter's Square

FRANCE

Jules Hardouin-Mansart
82. Les Invalides

ENGLAND

Sir Christopher Wren
83. Saint Paul's Cathedral

HOLLAND and FLANDERS

Lieven de Key
84. Meat Hall, Haarlem

(*architects unnamed*)

85. Guild Houses in the Grande Place, Brussels
86. FYI (*Renaissance*) Guild Houses, Brugge

Jacob van Campen
87. Mauritshuis, The Hague

FRANCE (*again*)

LeVau, LeBrun and LeNotre
88. Vaux-le-Vicomte

Mansart, LeVau, LeBrun and LeNotre
89. Versailles
90. Galerie des Glaces

ROCOCO: 1715-1790

FRANCE

Germain Boffrand
    91. Salon de la Princesse (Hotel de Soubise - Paris)

Francois Cuvillies
    92. Amalienburg Hall of Mirrors (Munich)

Antoine Watteau
    93. Pilgrimage to Cythera

Francois Boucher
    94. Madame de Pompadour
    95. Girl Reclining
    96. Resting Girl
    97. Odalisque
    98. Triumph of Venus

Jean-Honore Fragonard
    99. The Swing
    100. The Reader

Jean-Baptiste-Simeon Chardin
    101. The Silver Tureen
    102. House of Cards
    103. Prayer before the Meal

ENGLAND

William Hogarth
    104. Marriage a la Mode: Scene 1: The Marriage Contract
    105. Marriage a la Mode: Scene 2: Early in the Marriage
    106. Beer Street
    107. Gin Lane

Thomas Gainsborough
    108. The Blue Boy
    109. Mrs. Richard Brinsley Sheridan

NEOCLASSICAL PAINTING: 1775-1850

FRANCE

Jacques Louis David
    110. Oath of the Horatii
    111. Death of Marat
    112. Portrait of Napoleon

Jean Auguste Dominique Ingres
    113. Grande Odalisque
    114. Comtesse d'Haussonville
    115. Madame Moitissier

NEOCLASSICAL ARCHITECTURE: 1725-1850

ENGLAND

Richard Boyle
    116. Chiswick House

UNITED STATES OF AMERICA

Thomas Jefferson
    117. Monticello

James Hoban
    118. White House (front)
    119. White House (from south lawn)

William Thornton
Benjamin Latrobe
Charles Bullfinch
Thomas Walter
    120. The US Capitol

FRANCE

Jacques-Germain Soufflot
    121. Pantheon (Saint Genevieve)

Pierre Vignon
    122. La Madeleine

15. Baroque Art in Italy and Spain

c. 1600 - 1700

In broad terms, the Baroque Period dates from approximately 1600-1700, roughly spanning the 17th century, although in reality art and architecture starting changing before the turn of the century and in some places the period lasted longer than a hundred years. "Baroque" is a descriptive period name that has been assigned to the 17th century, give or take a few decades on either side. The name itself was assigned after the fact. Lower case "*baroque*" is an adjective meaning the opposite of lower case "*classical*." Things that are "classical" are understated, timeless, intellectual, simple or even stoic. Things that are "baroque" are complicated, exaggerated, dramatic, theatrical, gaudy or emotional. A plain, black evening dress or tuxedo is "classical" while a shocking pink and chartreuse Hawaiian shirt worn open to the navel with several pounds of gold chains around the neck is "baroque." A white Mercedes sedan is "classical; a fire engine red Ferrari is "baroque." The Classical period in Greece produced art and architecture exhibiting classical stylistic attributes. The Hellenistic period was little "b" baroque. Likewise, the Baroque period in Europe is so named because most of the art, architecture, music and more moved beyond the classical interests of the Renaissance to a more baroque presentation. That said, be forewarned that even within the Baroque period, some artists will be extremely baroque, while others will seem rather classical by comparison, if still more baroque than most artists working a 100 years earlier.

The seeds for the Baroque period were sown nearly half a century earlier at the **Council of Trent**, called in 1545 by Pope Paul III and finally concluded in 1563. This meeting of more than two hundred papal legates, cardinals, archbishops and bishops addressed issues raised by the Protestant Reformation, with the result being further clarification of Catholic Christianity. Keep in mind that Christianity began as a faith based on oral tradition, like Judaism before it, and information has only been formally written down over the centuries when it was deemed necessary because segments of the faithful were diverging in their beliefs and practices from the faith as it had been accepted from the get-go by tradition.

Protestant reformers were invited to Trent to present their positions that they might be considered more fully by the Council, but none within the Protestant movement chose to participate because they were barred from voting. It should be explained that this would be the norm, not an exception singling out Protestants for unfair treatment. The only voting members of councils, *any* council ever, are those who have received the apostolic blessing of an office within the clergy of bishop or higher. For example, priests and monks cannot vote anymore than outsiders to the faith can. To put this in secular terms by way of explanation, in the USA we have senators and representatives in congress who by the right of having been elected, can vote on issues affecting the general population. If a malcontent in society has an issue with the government, he or she might arrange an invitation to address congress and speak passionately about his or her concerns, but just because this person has a gripe with the system doesn't give that person a vote in congress.

Among the many outcomes of Trent was a mandate that Christian art should communicate its message clearly and with an emotional emphasis that the average guy on the street could understand and find inspiring. The Church wanted art to be for everyone, not just the educated elite. It should be moving and provide inspiration to the heart, not just the mind. The art ideals articulated at Trent encouraged a new movement within the Catholic Church to counter the impact of the Reformation: the Counter Reformation.

Italy

The biggest significant influence on Baroque art in Italy was the Counter Reformation. The popes of the Counter Reformation were deeply concerned over the impact of events that had transpired during the previous century. On the one hand, they were highly motivated to clean house from within, to move the Church away from the influences of secular humanism that had led to corruption during the tenure of some earlier popes. On the other hand, they were also very concerned with the state of the Christian religion splintering into a variety of factions as each reformer introduced a new spin on Christianity, pulling the faith apart. Observing this phenomenon from one viewpoint, one would note that the more people left the Catholic Church for one Protestant denomination or another, the more tithe money would be withheld from Catholic coffers, hence an assumption that money was the central issue. It is true this was a very real concern to the Catholic Church because there was less revenue coming in, yet the operating expenses of universities, hospitals, orphanages, monasteries and the like remained the same.

Observing the issue from another point of view, the Catholic clergy was deeply concerned for the salvation of people who chose to leave the Church. This may be difficult for many people to understand in a modern climate because nowadays most Protestants and Catholics get along fine and try to pay more attention to what they have in common rather than issues that divide. Back in the late 1500's and 1600's, though, the fact that the Protestant denominations were reducing the number of sacraments that had been universally observed in Christianity, and changing the nature of those sacraments they retained, was unthinkable to devout Catholics. Protestant churches were also disregarding the lessons of oral tradition, relying exclusively on the written tradition in the Bible, but then also not using the Bible that had been the accepted Christian text (for both Catholic and Orthodox alike) since it was first compiled in the 4th century. Furthermore, with no central authority within the Protestant movement, and with each reformer having his own personal interpretation of Scripture, the Protestants couldn't agree among themselves about central issues of faith. This created tensions not only between the Catholic Church and Protestantism as a whole, but also between rivaling factions within the Protestant community as well.

As we have often seen in the past, art is frequently employed to influence people's attitudes, and the Counter Reformation was no exception. Paintings and statues were commissioned to reinforce central tenets of the Christian faith, and to hopefully motivate viewers back to a strong appreciation of the Catholic Church. The art was aimed at two audiences. For one, it was presumably aimed at Protestants, of course, but for another, it was aimed perhaps much more at Catholics. Most Counter Reformation art was produced by Italian artists for Italian patrons to be displayed in Italy, and Protestants would have had to go out of their way to see any of it. It was important for Catholics to see art of this type, not so much because they were teetering on the verge of joining a Protestant church of one type or another, but more to strengthen the faith they already had since many had become relaxed about living a sacramental, Godly life themselves due to the influences of secular humanism during the Renaissance.

Caravaggio

The first Italian artist to make a career out of painting for the Counter Reformation was Caravaggio. Born Michelangelo Merisi in 1571 in Milan, the artist grew up in the neighboring town of Caravaggio, from where he got his professional nickname. He lived his life in the fast lane and was dead by age 38, but not before making a huge impact on the art world. Caravaggio completed his apprenticeship under a local artist in Milan, and many assume that during these early years he paid a visit to Venice and became familiar with the great masters of the High Renaissance from that region. Around the age of 20 he moved to Rome, penniless and in need of work, where he got by doing minor paintings of *genre* (simple scenes of everyday life), and still life, themes that didn't have much of a following in Italy at that time. **Boy with a Basket of Fruit** dates from this early period. Think back to Titian's <u>Girl with a Basket of Fruit</u>. The basic idea isn't new with Caravaggio, but the presentation is. Everything in Caravaggio's painting is "hyper-real." The fruit is painted in such luscious detail you can almost taste it, and the boy's presence seems both immediate and surprisingly sensual with his full lips slightly parted, his direct gaze and his shirt casually slipping off a bare shoulder. **The Cardsharps** dates from the same point in the artist's career. Here he shows an inexperienced, almost prissy young fellow who has gotten in over his head playing cards with a couple of cheats. Subjects like these were developing a following in Northern Europe, but they were pretty rare in Italy.

Let's take a look at Caravaggio's painting style. Caravaggio popularized the *earth tone palette*. This means that he preferred analogous colors similar to those we might see during autumn – brown, gold, green, red, rusty orange. What you will not see in Caravaggio's work is peacock blue and azalea pink. He used a *linear technique*. This means that he smoothed all his brushstrokes to leave a satin finish to his paintings. Most painters who came before Caravaggio also opted for the linear technique, although until the 17th century this would not be seen so much as a conscious decision as it would be just a matter of the way one was expected to paint. Lastly, but perhaps most significantly, Caravaggio developed the art of *chiaroscuro* beyond what anyone had done in the past. Masaccio is credited with inventing the idea of employing high contrast of highlight and shadow to model his figures 3-dimensionally, but it is Caravaggio who would take this idea and develop it into theatrical lighting where pictures are rendered as dark as night with spotlighting directed on the principal characters. The strong chiaroscuro added to the emotional expressions and gestures of the characters making the scene all the more dramatic. This exaggerated high contrast of light and dark in its most theatrical form it is called *tenebrism*.

The Cardsharps drew favorable attention to the struggling young artist. Dozens of copies were made by admirers, and best of all the painting attracted an important patron for Caravaggio, Cardinal Francesco Maria del Monte. The Cardinal was an art-loving connoisseur who was apparently pleased to let Caravaggio experiment with his developing style. **Bacchus** was among the canvases created for del Monte. Caravaggio has graduated from genre to a loftier mythological theme here ... but has much changed from his earlier Boy with a Basket of Fruit? Bacchus is the god of drink and all round party animal of mythology, but he's not usually decked out like a geisha in a brothel. Caravaggio's Bacchus flirts with his viewer like a pouty toy boy hanging around a sleazy bathhouse between romps with his "friends." He can't seem to keep his clothes on, and he offers us a fancy champagne glass brimming with rich red wine to get us in the mood. Notice his precious pinkie in the air; Bacchus is no doubt a creature of sensitivity and refinement. Although there is debate on the subject, most scholars agree that Caravaggio was almost certainly gay, or at least he entertained homosexual interests whether he was actively engaged in the pursuit of male companions like Bacchus, or merely fantasized about them.

The irony perhaps is that for an artist who painted effeminate males like the Boy with a Basket of Fruit and Bacchus, Caravaggio was a scrapper who spent most his short life getting in trouble for brawling. Always a man of great passion and uncontrolled temper, he was arrogant and aggressive, and the older he got, the worse his antisocial behavior became. He was accused of attacking a man with a sword, and assaulting a teacher (an incident connected with suspicions that the artist was molesting school boys). He was arrested for disrespecting an officer and for carrying a weapon without a permit. He assaulted a waiter, wounded another man in a fight over a prostitute and even wound up killing a friend over a lost tennis match. He spent nearly as much time dodging the law as he did producing art; fortunately he painted quickly which allowed him to complete about fifty paintings in between brawls before dying himself under peculiar circumstances.

With his violent personality, Caravaggio would seem an unlikely candidate for serving the Church in any capacity, much less as a spokesman for a movement to bolster a return to following the straight and narrow path. During his short career it is true that most clergy within the Catholic Church were highly critical of Caravaggio and of his art, although he did have a handful of supporters within the clergy. At the same time, he was wildly famous with the public and influential among young artists who deeply admired Caravaggio's simple, stripped down settings, emotionally charged tenebrism, and direct, almost in-your-face communication of the subject.

It turned out that in an odd way, Caravaggio may have actually been an ideal choice for unofficial spokesperson for the Counter Reformation. First, his art spoke for itself as it was full of emotional zeal. Beyond that, one of the central tenets of faith where the Catholic Church differed with some Protestant denominations (remember, it isn't one size fits all on Protestant theology!) was on matters of redemption. While the Catholic Church presumed to present an authoritative guide on matters of good and evil, the sacrament of reconciliation (confession and penance) offered a fallen man or woman the opportunity to try to set the record straight with God during this lifetime. This sacrament was eliminated in most of the Protestant world (the Anglican Church of England still has it on the books), and in some branches of Protestantism it was believed that people were either saved or not saved – a decision rendered by God before their birth, which rather tends to preclude notions of redemption as an ongoing process still available to those who manage to make a mess of things during their life. More on that later …

The Calling of Saint Matthew is an early example of Caravaggio's Counter Reformation painting. It was painted as a permanent installation for the Contarelli Chapel of the church of Santa Luigi dei Francesi in Rome, the commission probably coming through connections from his benefactor, Cardinal del Monte. In complete contrast to typical religious art from the Middle Ages or most of the Renaissance, the Biblical account of Jesus turning Saint Matthew away from his life as a wicked tax collector to become an Apostle is presented as a scene from everyday life. Gone is the grandeur of everyone looking holy and important in classical togas. The scene is played out in a simple interior space, a tavern in fact, with ordinary people. Caravaggio's intent was to make it seem probable that something like this could happen to anybody – even you and me! It isn't some Hollywood set; it is the real world, and the costumes and setting would have seemed quite contemporary to anyone viewing this painting in the 17th century. The men in the scene were real people from Rome; in fact the guy playing the role of Saint Matthew is probably the artist's tough guy buddy, Sicilian Mario Minniti, who modeled for his friend sometimes. In the Calling of Saint Matthew, it is suggested that not only might ordinary folks like you and me meet Jesus, we could be called to become Apostles. Furthermore, Matthew was a low-life scumbag before his conversion, which promotes our appreciation that no matter how badly we have lived our lives up to this point, the opportunity for conversion is always available. Best of all, once we have changed our hearts, we are not asked to "sit in the back" because of our past transgressions, but are offered a chance to be a leader in the faith. Conversion stories like that of the Saint Matthew or Saint Paul and others were popular themes for the Counter Reformation.

Caravaggio was so famous during his lifetime that he was flooded with commissions no matter where he went, and considering that he was frequently hop scotching about due to his scrapes with the law, he developed a following in Rome, Naples, Sicily and Malta. While he had no trouble attracting commissions, not all of the paintings he produced were happily accepted by his clients. Consider **The Death of the Virgin**. It was commissioned for a private Carmelite (monks) chapel, but when the artist delivered the finished painting, the horrified monks rejected it. Why exactly they were so offended was a matter of some debate as different accounts from the day offered different explanations, but the odds are all of these explanations were mitigating factors in the monks refusing the painting.

First, Caravaggio in a lapse of good judgment employed a well-known prostitute to pose as the Virgin Mary. Certainly this would not have impressed the pious monks. Beyond that, Mary looked so vulgar and common with her bare feet hanging out and her bloated body lying on the slab without any effort to make her look beautiful or special. Furthermore, she looks downright *dead*. Now that might seem reasonable enough since the end of her life was supposed to be the subject, but the doctrine of the Assumption of Mary stresses that Mary was taken up to heaven by Jesus at the end of her life … she simply fell asleep to life in this world and was transported to a glorified state in heaven with Christ. Presenting the Mother of Jesus as any old cadaver was simply beyond the pale of the very worst bad taste. As it turned out, one of Caravaggio's followers painted a replacement for the Carmelites and that one got the heave ho from the monks too; it showed Mary dying as opposed to being dead, but that was still considered offensive. Finally a third painting was done by yet another artist showing a true Assumption of the Virgin with Mary being raised to heaven by angels, and that one the monks liked just fine. Oh well, it didn't wind up cramping Caravaggio's style because no sooner had the monks rejected the original <u>Death of the Virgin</u>, than it was snapped up by the Duke of Mantua for his collection.

Caravaggio may have been fabulously famous during his lifetime, but his style didn't produce many followers after he died. There were a few in Rome, like Artemisia Gentileschi who we will cover next, but otherwise Rome quickly moved on to favor the painting of Annibale Carracci and his followers (stay tuned, he's coming up). Caravaggio didn't have the personality or stability to have a studio of apprentices working under him and learning his techniques, so perhaps it isn't surprising that his immediate influence seemed small. Although Caravaggio's style fell from favor in Italy, it was adopted by Spanish artists who became Caravaggio devotees while living in Naples, which at this time was a Spanish possession. Likewise, Catholic artists from Utrecht, Netherlands, traveled to Rome during the zenith of Caravaggio's fame and took his painting style back to Holland where it flourished briefly. Nowadays we understand the enormous influence Caravaggio had on future generations of painters, but the full impact of his unconventional style wasn't recognized until long after he was gone.

Artemisia Gentileschi

Up to this point we haven't heard much about women artists. Although the occasional woman made a name for herself in the arts during the Renaissance, for the most part female artists were extremely rare and their sphere of influence was usually so limited that one can't justify presenting their work as equal to the influential male artists of their generation. It was still illegal in most places for a woman to enter an apprenticeship under a professional artist, and then it was further against the rules for a woman who did manage to learn the artist's trade (almost always the daughter of an artist who studied under Pop) for a female artist to join the artist guild in her town. This meant that even with those rare girls who did learn to paint, far more common among women than sculpture, they were never considered "professionals." Thus, they were usually stuck painting only portraits of local women at a discount price, when the man of the house wanted pictures of his wife and daughters, but didn't want to pay for the expensive, famous artist in town.

A century earlier Sofonisba Anguissola managed to achieve limited fame, but she was a rare exception to the rule. She lived in a small town, the daughter of a prominent family that could pull some strings on her behalf. And despite her invitation to produce some paintings for the King of Spain, her expertise was strictly portraits, and most of her work is pictures of her own family. Artemisia Gentileschi is the first woman artist of significant fame whose reputation extended well beyond her local hometown of Rome. She was the daughter of a professional artist, who was himself inspired by Caravaggio's style, and she apprenticed in his studio alongside his male students. Unfortunately, Artemisia was raped by one of the young men in her father's studio, and the trial that ensued left as many deep scars on her as did the rape itself. In court she was tortured with thumbscrews until she would admit that the rape was her fault; had she not been in the studio tormenting all the young men, none of this would have happened. Her attacker received a modest sentence, and Artemisia's father, who was remarkably unsupportive, hastily married her off to a painter from Florence to get her out of town and spare the family further embarrassment. Her new husband turned out to be an abusive jerk, and in a bold move for her times, Artemisia divorced him and set out to establish her career as an independent woman. Artemisia Gentileschi went on to enjoy fame and fortune as a painter, accepting commissions from a broad-based clientele hailing from across Italy and abroad as well, especially France. She refused to limit herself to the customary portraits one expects from women painters of the Renaissance, instead preferring to paint large-scale religious scenes.

Judith and Holofernes is a typical painting for Artemisia Gentileschi. It is an Old Testament subject from the Bible, but don't be fooled into imagining that just because Artemisia was painting during the 17th century in Italy, and just because her paintings depict religious themes, that she was automatically a Counter Reformation painter! Artemisia wasn't so much interested in the Counter Reformation as she was preoccupied with religious subjects that focused attention on heroic women from the Bible. In the story of Judith and Holofernes, for example, Holofernes was the ferocious general in charge of the Assyrian forces under King Nebuchadnezzar. The king had ordered Holofernes and his troops to sweep the expanse of Mesopotamia and slaughter all those who refused to submit to Assyrian authority, which of course included the Jews. Holofernes' campaign was a roaring success as he wiped out one group of dissenters after another, until he reached Israelite territory. The Jews were terrified; they couldn't possibly win against such an opponent. Judith was a wealthy and attractive widow living in the Jewish community, a woman of spotless reputation. Seeing that somebody had to take charge of the bad situation, she had a plan. After much prayer, she put aside her traditional widow's clothing, bathed and decked herself out in her best clothes with all her jewelry so she evidently was looking like the Old Testament version of a movie star, and she and her maidservant set outside the city gates to let themselves get captured by the Assyrians. She made up a story about wanting to see Holofernes because she didn't want to die with the Hebrews. The men fell for her line and took her to Holofernes, who like the other men was hoodwinked into believing that this gorgeous creature was actually interested in him. Of course, she had it all well planned. Her maid carried a sack of tasty foods and skins of fine wine, which Holofernes enjoyed until he was drunk on his behind … then Judith took his sword and hacked his head off! The two women got away in the middle of the night as the army slept, with the head of Holofernes in the food sack. Holofernes' head was then hung outside the walls of the Jewish town. The next morning the Jews advanced on the Assyrians, who fled in fear once they realized what had happened.

It is easy to understand why subjects like Judith and Holofernes would hold a particular appeal to Gentileschi. It isn't so much pro-Catholic propaganda as it is pro-woman propaganda. Gentileschi's painting style is identical to Caravaggio's with an earth tone palette, exaggerated chiaroscuro and linear technique.

Bernini

The premiere sculptor of the Baroque period was Bernini. Born in Naples in 1598, Gian Lorenzo Bernini was the son of sculptor who provided his early training. Already as a young boy assisting his father, Bernini showed such talent that he attracted the attention of other artists, which in turn gained him the influential **Cardinal Scipione Borghese** as a customer. Cardinal Borghese's patronage supported Bernini during his early years allowing him to develop his gifts without having to scramble to make a living. Three statues, each as magnificent as the next, date from the 1620's while Bernini was working for the cardinal.

The earliest was the **Rape of Proserpina**, a mythological subject. Pluto, god of the underworld, was all by his lonesome hanging out in Hades when Venus, goddess of love decided to cut him a favor and sent Cupid to shoot him with one of his love-potion arrows. Feeling suddenly quite amorous, Pluto burst forth from the volcano of Mt. Etna on Sicily to find a bride, and set his sights on Proserpina, the daughter of Ceres (Mother Earth) by Jupiter, who as everyone knows, got around with the ladies. Poor Proserpina is then dragged off to Hades to spend eternity with Pluto. Ceres is distraught and makes her plight clear to Jupiter, who in time strikes a deal with Pluto for the return of Proserpina to her mother. Pluto tricks Jupiter though, and invites Proserpina to eat pomegranate seeds which will keep her faithful to him. So, Proserpina is doomed to spend all eterinity spending half the year in Hades (fall and winter when the earth is barren due to Ceres' sadness), and half the year (spring and summer) with her mother, who brings life to the earth as an expression of her joy. The sculpture group is just over life-size, and shows a writhing struggle similar to many Hellenistic Greek statues, which were an inspiration to young Bernini. Yet at the same time there is a softness to the figures that exceeds the exaggerated realism of ancient Greeks. See how Jupiter's grip on his prize dimples her flesh. The statue is marble, but the feeling is soft and pliable, like a living, breathing woman.

Apollo and Daphne was completed a couple years later. The subjects of both pieces are similar in that both mythological stories deal with a sex-charged god going after a reluctant babe. In this case, the chaste nymph, Daphne, got creative and turned into a tree, the amazing transformation taking place before our eyes. Lusty themes like these might raise a few eyebrows, wondering why a cardinal would commission art like this. In the case of Apollo and Daphne, there was an inscription on the original base that read, *"Those who love to pursue fleeting forms of pleasure, in the end find only leaves and bitter berries in their hands."* One could argue that the choice of subject was the marriage between the humanist preoccupation with mythology and all things ancient, so popular during the Renaissance, coupled with a moral to the story to keep the viewer's priorities (and libido) in check. With both sculptures Bernini offered exciting stories combined with dynamic action poses designed to stir our emotions. Understanding anatomy and producing the perfect nude as an end it itself was never enough to capture Bernini's imagination.

The third Borghese commission we will consider is Bernini's **David**. This subject was often explored during the Renaissance. Donatello created an immature youth almost coincidentally standing on the giant's head, apparently with little interest in projecting a strong heroic image. Michelangelo's <u>David</u> towered over his admirers while projecting a strong silent type persona as he contemplated the pending battle. Bernini's David gets down to the business of showing us why he's a hero; <u>David</u> is captured here in the act of fighting Goliath. Compared to the earlier two, Bernini's figure invites us to walk around the statue to see it from different points of view. Because <u>David</u> is not static - he's not just standing there in a contrapposto pose – the statue is more interesting from a variety of angles whereas both Donatello's and Michelangelo's statues would work just as well seen from a single point of view in a niche on a building as they do displayed in the round.

It's no surprise that Bernini would go on to produce the most remarkable religious sculpture of the 17th century, because in addition to being a talented artist, Bernini was a Jesuit. The Society of Jesus, commonly known as the Jesuit Order, was founded by St. Ignatius Loyola in 1534. Their rule calls for extensive education, religious of course but also scientific, literary and more, and they are known for their strict rules of obedience. Initially they directed their efforts toward the Counter Reformation, and in this regard, the Jesuits, in a way, picked up where the Dominicans left off. During the 13th century, the Dominicans were in charge of educating Christians about the faith, and then later on we find them mostly affiliated with education, more often than not at the university level. Similarly, in the late 16th and 17th centuries the Jesuits addressed educating Catholics, and Protestants when possible, about Christianity from a Catholic perspective. Their role expanded considerably during the era of colonial expansion, as they became the primary missionaries working abroad to convert native populations to Christianity. Nowadays you would be most likely to find Jesuits affiliated with institutions of learning, especially universities and Catholic high schools. As a Jesuit, Bernini was especially committed to the goals of the Counter Reformation, which can be easily seen in his work.

The Ecstasy of Saint Theresa was commissioned by the Cornaro family for their chapel in the Church of Santa Maria della Vittoria in Rome. The entire chapel was designed by Bernini to resemble a theater. The family is depicted filling box seats flanking the "stage" where the vision of Saint Theresa is played out; you and I are invited to witness the event from the equivalent of the orchestra pit. Saint Theresa, a 16th century Carmelite nun from Spain, was a mystic. Among her many written accounts, she recalled when an angel came down from heaven while she was entranced and punctured her heart and soul with a golden arrow, which in turn released an overwhelming pain, joy, and love of God. This scene, called the *Transverberation*, is what Bernini has chosen to represent. An appropriate question might be to wonder why this subject would appeal specifically to the Counter Reformation. Recalling that Saint Theresa was more-or-less contemporary, the message was that great miracles related to faith are not limited events that occurred during Biblical times, but rather they are ongoing … today … now. Naturally, it makes for convenient propaganda for the Catholic Church that the individual who happened to receive this particular gift from God was a faithful Catholic.

Bernini has captured the essence of physical, emotional and spiritual ecstasy in the transported facial expression of Theresa. Heavy robes swirl about her limp body while the angel, dressed in wispy light fabric, gently lifts Theresa up to be pierced again by God's arrow. Above the scene the ceiling was painted to resemble clouds in the sky opening to reveal heaven beyond, and shooting down from heaven are gold rays that serve as a backdrop for the ecstatic vision. All of this, the sculpture, the architecture and the painting, is Bernini's handiwork. The Ecstasy of Saint Theresa is not just an engaging statue designed to reinforce our faith. It is a 3-D experience involving art and the surrounding space where you and I become participants; we join the Cornaro family in their chapel to witness the wonder of a miracle. The art is not passive; it actively engages the viewer.

With Bernini's profound faith and intense dedication to the Catholic Church, it should come as no surprise that he made substantial contribution to new Saint Peters. The most remarkable of his interior projects is the **Baldacchino**. The Baldacchino is an enormous (over 10 stories tall) gold-plated bronze canopy which marks the place where Saint Peter is buried. It covers the main altar which in turn is situated over a hole in the church floor that reaches down through the ruins of Old Saint Peter's all the way to the old catacombs where Saint Peter's grave is located. The Baldacchino was designed to resemble a fabric canopy or tent, like the canopy or tent over the Ark of the Covenant in the Old Testament. The massive swirling columns came from Old Saint Peter's, and purportedly were originally from Solomon's Temple in Jerusalem.

Close to the Baldacchino, hovering above the high altar is Bernini's throne of Saint Peter. Called the **Cathedra Petri**, it reminds us that the pope is the leader of the Catholic Church. When a pope proclaims Christian doctrine on faith and morals with authority, he is speaking *ex cathedra*, or literally "from the chair." It's the same root word as we find in *cathedral*, which means a church that is the seat (or chair) of a bishop. Bernini's Cathedral Petri isn't a throne the pope can actually sit on, however; it is a magnificent, and massive decoration created in a variety of materials including stone, bronze, glass, gold, and stucco (plaster). The actual chair, which visually melts into the sculpture and golden glass, encases the original, considerably more humble throne from Old Saint Peter's (the original "Cathedra Petri") dating back centuries earlier. To give you a sense of scale, the original entire throne, now considered a relic, is contained inside a box situated beneath the carved cushion on the seat of Bernini's throne. The new chair, lifted effortlessly by four Goliath-sized Doctors of the Church, rises up into clouds toward heaven. Two gigantic putti flit above. Each is holding a key, the attribute of Saint Peter, in one hand and with the other they support the papal tiara, with its distinctive three horizontal bands, above the throne. The Holy Spirit, shown as an upward-bound dove surrounded by an aureola of back-lit golden glass, leads the way to heaven. Throngs of angels are caught up in the jumble of clouds and the rays of God's light shooting forth from the Holy Spirit. Bernini leaves no doubt that for him and millions of others, the heart of the Christian faith is here in the church of Saint Peter, a message dear to the Counter Reformation.

Bernini sculpted with the same gift for acute realism that we saw in Michelangelo. Both artists could make marble seem so life-like that statues almost breathe. The difference between them is quite simple. Michelangelo looked back to antiquity as a standard by which he and others should be measured. Most of his art has the dignity and quiet grandeur we might associate with the best of the Classical and Late Classical styles. Bernini was certainly aware of the art of antiquity, but he appears to have invested less energy attempting to mimic the past. For Bernini, antiquity was a point of departure. His art bears a stronger relationship to Hellenistic Greek, as opposed to Classical, but even at that, his work appears to be less of a deliberate effort to reiterate past ideals. Bernini created statues intended to pack a wallop – to WOW the viewer with emotions not so much because he wanted folks to appreciate his interpretation of art of the past, but more because he had something dynamic to communicate, right now, today.

Annibale Carracci

There were three Carraccis painting during the Baroque period, Annibale, his brother, Agostino, and their cousin, Ludovico. They began their careers working closely together, but as time went on, Annibale surged ahead of the two lesser talents. Annibale Carracci was a contemporary working in Rome the same time as Caravaggio, although the two painters followed very different paths in their art. Carracci was never interested in the shocking hard edge super realistic naturalism that so appealed to Caravaggio. Neither painter approved of Mannerism, but while Caravaggio was also blurting his discontent with Renaissance ideals in art, Carracci was extolling the virtues of Raphael and Michelangelo. Annibale was restrained and respectable in his personal life, and this is reflected in his likewise restrained and respectable painting. That said, he was no less innovative and revolutionary than Caravaggio.

Born in 1560 in Bologna, Carracci was a few years older than Caravaggio, but they both arrived in Rome around the turn of the century. By then Annibale Carracci had established a reputation as a successful fresco artist back home, and he was recommended to Cardinal Odoardo Farnese to complete a series of frescos for his enormous new Roman Palazzo Farnese (Farnese Palace). The Farnese frescos are considered today to be the great masterpiece of Carracci's career. Of these, the most famous of all is the ceiling of the gallery salon, which we will refer to simply as the **Farnese Ceiling Fresco**. The long gallery salon ceiling is a simple barrel vault which the artist decorated with a series of individual scenes representing mythological gods and love. The artist was inspired by Michelangelo's patchwork of Biblical scenes on the Sistine Chapel ceiling, but here he has taken the idea further by creating each individual story as if it were a framed work of art that has been installed on the ceiling. The pictures, the frames and the apparent carved plaster embellishing the patchwork design are all *tromp l'oeil* which literally means "trick the eye," that it is 100% of what you see that looks 3-D is painted illusion. In its day and for a couple centuries to follow this ceiling was considered a masterpiece to be studied by anyone undertaking a major ceiling painting project. While a few rare northern Italian artists had experimented with remarkable illusions in ceiling painting during the Renaissance, Annibale Carracci's <u>Farnese Ceiling Fresco</u> now set the standard for artists venturing into this relatively unexplored new type of painting.

The centerpiece of the ceiling is the **Triumph of Bacchus**. Let's take a look at the hero of the scene, Bacchus (see detail). So here he is, in the buff and hoisting up a bunch of grapes to remind us that he is the god of drunken revelry. Compare Carracci's Bacchus to Caravaggio's. This Bacchus isn't wearing a stitch of clothes but he seems far less lascivious that Caravaggio's sexy tempter. Carracci's version of Bacchus is a mythological god from antiquity participating in a parade of curious characters who seem to be having a good time but are otherwise behaving themselves. Caravaggio's Bacchus is a sensual, androgynous play thing, he's all alone, except for *YOU* being present. There is no context in the room, nothing to distract you from meeting Bacchus' mesmerizing gaze into *YOUR* eyes as he offers *YOU* a glass on wine. He is close, almost in your lap. He has adorned himself for YOU, and he lies on a rumpled unmade bed awaiting *YOU* to join him. There isn't a shred of lofty intellectual mythology from antiquity being presented in Caravaggio's <u>Bacchus</u>.

Carracci's painting, **The Flight into Egypt**, also commissioned by the Farnese family, illustrates another avenue of Italian Baroque painting. The title is a religious theme, but nothing about the story of the flight into Egypt promotes a pro-Catholic propaganda message especially. It is always important to notice this, because it would be incorrect to assume that every Catholic artist painting religious art during the 17th century is necessarily creating Counter Reformation art.

Closer inspection of the scene clarifies that what Annibale Carracci really wanted to paint was landscape. In his youth, Annibale Carracci dabbled in genre painting like Caravaggio, but little came of it. In contrast to this fleeting interest, the artist was a genuine trailblazer in the realm of landscape painting, and as such he influenced many painters from across Europe with scenes like this one. Landscape came into its own during the 17th century. Just the same, there were two informal schools of landscape painting, one for Holland, and one for everyone else. We will come back to the Dutch approach to landscape later; for now, let's consider Carracci's example which set the standard for landscape painting from the Baroque period in Italy … or France or England or Flanders and so on.

In [so-called] Catholic countries, landscape was popular to be sure, but there was a lingering notion that landscapes were supposed to be background painting, so therefore, it was necessary to infuse a "legitimate" subject matter into the scene, then title the work according to the legitimate theme. The legitimate subject matter identified by the title may be miniscule in relation to the magnificent effort applied to painting the "background" landscape, but that was okay so long as the subject matter was there. There were four categories of appropriate types of subject matters, all of which had enjoyed popularity during the Renaissance. The first was *religion*, like we see here. Second was *history* painting, followed by *mythology* and finally *portraits*. Any of these could be superimposed onto a landscape, and presto, instant legitimacy for landscape painting.

Another defining characteristic of landscape painting everywhere in Europe (except Holland) during this time was that the imagery did not represent individual real locations. The artist would keep a sketchbook of drawings done over time of assorted snippets of landscape from a variety of locations. He would then retire to his studio and create an idealized composite landscape using elements from several drawings done of different places.

Unlike Caravaggio who was a huge success as long as he was around to fan the fires of controversy and attract attention, but whose influence waned close to home after his death, Annibale Carracci was widely respected as an important master long after his death and his influence can be seen throughout 17th century painting in Italy. While Caravaggio was inclined to wing it, starting in directly on the canvas without creating preparatory drawings, Carracci was a stickler for planning his work ahead and sketching out all the details before ever picking up a paintbrush. He was a born teacher who trained the next generation how to paint.

Guido Reni

Annibale Carracci along with his brother and cousin established a large studio of apprentices whose individual styles ran the gamut from Renaissance-inspired classical to wildly flamboyant baroque. Guido Reni was one of their star pupils, and also among the most classical in his compositional restraint. Reni was born in 1575 in Bologna. He along with some of his classmates followed Annibale Carracci to Rome, and he may have worked the <u>Farnese Ceiling Fresco</u> as an assistant, although his contributions were probably minimal given that Annibale apparently didn't like Reni very much.

Guido Reni soon moved beyond the shadows of Carracci's studio to produce a masterpiece of his own, accepting a commission to decorate the ceiling of Casino Rospogliosi in Rome. A quick aside on vocabulary is called for here. Lest you incorrectly envision a Las Vegas style gambling venue, a *casino* is a small house, traditionally a country cottage or villa. "Small" is relative here in that a casino would be smaller than the family's regular home, which might be a palace; the average casino would dwarf where you and I live. The family casino was where they would let their hair down, play music, dance and have a good time on vacation. The entertainment might also include cards and gambling, which is how we today have seen that word come into use to describe "houses" that are strictly used for gambling.

The theme of Reni's ceiling is **Aurora**. Unlike Carracci's ceiling, Reni's is a single unified scene of <u>Aurora</u>, goddess of dawn, bringing light to the world and leading the way for Apollo, the sun god, who brings forth a fresh new day for the holiday-makers staying at the casino. Guido Reni's ceiling is composed of clean lines, less jumbled than Carracci's, and less challenging to paint too in that he didn't try to copy Annibale's ambitious efforts at fooling your eyes into believing that the ceiling encompassed stone and plaster relief carving. Instead the artist has focused on compositional simplicity by repeating classic lines – see how the arc of Aurora's body is repeated in the arc of the horses' bodies and again by the arc of the highlighted leg of the attendant in blue. Reni complimented the elegant lines of his composition with vivid lush colors especially the intense yellow, gold, and orange of the blinding sunrise that nearly absorbs Apollo on his chariot into pure light. Reni mastered the best of both Raphael and the Venetians with his carefully conceived composition combined with brilliant color.

Guido Reni eventually moved back to his hometown Bologna where he rose to prominence as the big-name artist of his generation painting religious and mythological subjects. He may not be considered a top propaganda artist for the Counter Reformation, but his religious paintings were all executed with the specific aim of engendering respect for tradition and reinforcing a conservative and very Catholic point of view. The **Annunciation** was a popular theme during the Renaissance; let's take a look at Guido Reni's treatment of the subject. Again notice the rich colors and overall simplicity of the composition like we saw in <u>Aurora</u>. Mary is represented with traditional dignity, shown humbly at her prie-dieu (kneeler) reading from scripture. Next to her we see the traditional white lilies to recall the Virgin's purity, just like artists in the past might have painted. What has changed is the emotionally charged supernatural quality of the setting. Mary is sitting in a simple chamber which is being engulfed by heaven. Thick, puffy clouds thunder into the room bearing the archangel and cutting off the natural world; see how the window with a view has been obscured by Gabriel's dramatic appearance inside the room? The clouds part to reveal God's light above, a window to heaven, where a couple of angels look on and the Holy Spirit, nearly invisible in the blinding light, hovers, shining down on the Blessed Mother.

Pietro da Cortona

Pietro da Cortona was born in Florence at the turn of the century (1596) where he apparently completed his early training before moving to Rome. Although not educated by Carracci, Cortona evidently saw the Farnese Ceiling and was impressed enough to desire a shot at creating a comparable masterpiece of his own. The opportunity arrived when the wealthy Barberini family hired Cortona to create a ceiling painting for the grand salon in their Palazzo Barberini (Barberini Palace). The family had reason to splurge on an extravagant show-and-tell depiction of their family credentials as one of their own, Maffeo Barberini, had been chosen as the new pope, Urban VIII. The **Glorification of the Barberini** ceiling fresco adorns a simple barrel vault with a dramatic scene so innovative and clever that many consider it to be the perfect embodiment of Italian Baroque ideals in art. Like Carracci, Cortona painted mock sculpted plaster molding, only instead of dividing the ceiling into a gallery of many pictures, Cortona instead decorated the perimeter of the ceiling with an illusion of cornicing where the artist introduced unframed allegorical scenes to brag about the assorted accomplishments of his noble patrons, but then reserved the center of the ceiling for one grand *tromp l'oeil* illusion of the vault opening up to heaven.

The centerpiece of the ceiling is much pomp and circumstance to glorify the new pope as a hero exceeding human proportions, and by extension make the rest of the family look pretty good too. Reading the scene from the bottom, the figure dressed in gold who appears to be radiating light represents Divine Providence. She lifts her arm to direct our attention to the hubbub at the far end of the ceiling, which is a tribute to the new pope. The three graces, Faith, Hope and Charity, hold an enormous laurel wreath high in the air, the laurel wreath making reference to peace, immortality and probably poetry as well (the new pope fancied himself a poet). Contained in the center of the laurel wreath are three humungous bees. The Barberini coat of arms contains three such bees, so the bees here are symbolically standing in for the Barberini family. The bees are directed toward the far end of the room, where we see that above the laurel wreath, a cherub assists in hoisting up the twin keys of Saint Peter that we often see in imagery associated with the Vatican, and above the keys the papal tiara is held high, making a direct reference to Pope Urban VIII.

The painting would lead viewers to imagine that Urban VIII was the most excellent pope since Peter himself, but that would be overstating reality. In many ways he was self-seeking, lining his own pockets and putting family favors ahead of more important concerns. Still, despite his personal shortcomings, not all was bad that came of his tenure at Saint Peter's. First, it was Urban VIII who commissioned and paid for Bernini's magnificent Baldacchino. In addition to getting high marks for his contribution to the arts, two important religious men were formally declared saints on Urban's watch, Ignatius Loyola, founder of the Jesuits, and Francis Xavier, who was instrumental in bringing Christianity to the Far East.

For as much as Guido Reni's <u>Aurora</u> ceiling painting exemplified a classical expression of Italian Baroque ideals, Pietro da Cortona's exuberant and complex <u>Glorification of the Barberini</u> is one of the most baroque works of art ever created.

Spain

Spain was closely tied to Italy during the 17th century. For one, the southern part of Italy encompassing Naples had been a Spanish possession since the 15th century, and for another, Spain was profoundly Catholic and therefore supportive of the Counter Reformation. Caravaggio's paintings were wildly popular in Spain, and most Spanish Baroque artists were inspired by his high impact, cutting edge style.

Ribera

Jusepe de Ribera (1591-1652) was born in Spain, but as a young aspiring painter he settled in Spanish Naples (by way of Rome) where he quickly became entrenched in the wave of Caravaggio enthusiasm. Caravaggio was already dead by a few years when Ribera arrived on the scene, but his persona and art were legendary in Naples, and while his popularity quickly dwindled in the rest of Italy soon after his death, Caravaggio's reputation and style were kept alive for another generation by Spanish artists in this region of Italy. Ribera's paintings became a primary conduit of Caravaggio's style from Italy over to Spain. The Spanish artist's subjects tend to be more conservatively presented than Caravaggio's more shocking themes, but Caravaggio's painting techniques were captured in Ribera's work. Consider his early **Saint Andrew**. Everything about the painting, except its conventional presentation of the subject, is a page out of Caravaggio's playbook. The palette is limited to earth tone colors, the brushstrokes have been smoothed to eliminate nearly all texture, the lighting has been heightened to a dramatic level, and the figure is placed against a nearly solid, dark background with only a hint of Saint Andrew's cross visible in the deep shadows.

The Holy Family with Saint Anne and Saint Catherine is quite similar, but notice here that Ribera has ever so slightly brightened his palette and softened the lighting on his primary figures in the foreground. The colors are still earth tone except for the Virgin's blue mantle, but we can excuse that departure given that the blue cloak by this time was largely recognized as an attribute of Mary, a clue the viewing audience had come to expect as a way to identify who's who in art. While the scene is painted in the style of Caravaggio, the figures themselves, especially Mary, look particularly Spanish making the people in the picture more accessible to Spanish patrons back home. To Ribera's audience, these folks looked like people from the old neighborhood, making it easier to feel like Mary is "one of us," which in turn made Baby Jesus feel like part of their lives in a special way.

The Martyrdom of Saint Bartholomew is a mature work by Ribera, and here we see his style as it moved beyond mimicking Caravaggio. Ribera presented the saint, who was one of the twelve Apostles, as a Spanish man to help his patrons relate emotionally to Bartholomew's plight (again, he's one of us). Ribera's colors got brighter and his paint thinner with increased texture as his career developed. He became particularly interested in painting weathered flesh, as we can see here on Saint Bartholomew. The artist also opened up the space more; see how Bartholomew's stretched arms almost seem to give praise to God and focus attention on the optimistic blue sky above.

Zurbaran

Francisco de Zurbaran was born in 1598 to a middle class family who recognized talent early in their son's childhood charcoal drawings. At 16 he was sent off to Seville to apprentice under a regional painter, and there he became familiar with Caravaggio's painting style, more than likely through copies rather than original work. Zurbaran took to Caravaggio's hard edge linear style, earth tone palette, and extreme tenebrism with gusto. The majority of his paintings are single figures, such as **Saint Serapion**, set against a plain, dark background. Zurbaran's special claim to fame was exquisite treatment of white drapery, which lent itself well to pictures of saints and martyrs dressed in white. As you might expect, paintings like these would be especially appealing to monastic orders and other religious patrons who derived great inspiration from pondering the uncompromising simplicity of a figure whose whole existence was dedicated to God. To make the saint more immediate and familiar to a Spanish audience, Zurbaran adopted Ribera's trick of taking Serapion, who was actually an Englishman, and turning him into a Spaniard so he seems "like one of us." Like Caravaggio's work and early Ribera's, Zurbaran's saint is shoved forward in the picture plane so he seems right in front of us. There is nothing to distract us from his suffering.

Although it might seem like an odd sideline for an artist known for his moving depictions of holy men, Zurbaran also painted still life pictures, like his **Still Life with Lemons and Oranges**. Still life as a subject category became quite popular in Holland during the 17th century, but in other countries like Spain it had only limited appeal. The artist may have been influenced by Caravaggio's still life imagery included in paintings like the Boy with a Basket of Fruit or Bacchus. Zurbaran's fruit isn't as lush as Caravaggio's though; he offers his lemons and oranges as starkly as he serves up saints. Also, the composition seems lackluster. The edible objects are arranged on a ledge like a police line-up of produce with a cup of tea on the side. Could it be that still life arrangements like these were meant to convey a religious sensibility, with the trinity being represented somehow by a selection of inanimate objects? Perhaps. In any event, Zurbaran's popularity ran its course, as happened with his mentor, Caravaggio in Italy. The difference was Zurbaran lived longer than Caravaggio, long enough to see his career fade into oblivion, and he died an impoverished has-been whose paintings had fallen out of fashion.

Velasquez

Diego Rodriguez de Silva y Velasquez (1599-1660) was a contemporary of Zurbaran's in Seville during their apprenticeship years, and like his peers, Velasquez was caught in the Spanish wave of Caravaggio adulation. Following in Caravaggio's artistic footsteps in more ways than one, Velasquez experimented with scenes of ordinary people participating in everyday activities. Like Caravaggio's Cardsharps, Velasquez painted scenes like the **Water Seller of Seville** or the **Old Woman Cooking Eggs**. All three paintings are *genre*, which is to say scenes from everyday life. Velasquez borrowed Caravaggio's deep earth tone colors, strong chiaroscuro/ tenebrism, and smooth, linear painting technique. Both artists were interested in painting inanimate objects. Caravaggio seemed to take particular delight in painting fruit, especially baskets of fruit, while Velasquez seems to have been keen on the textures of everyday objects like utensils, a glass or a clay vessel.

If we were to look for differences, Caravaggio often presented astute observation of human behavior, like the cocky boy getting drubbed in a card game because he presumes he is clever, but his deceitful companions have more street smarts and fewer scruples. In his early art, Velasquez seems more interested in portraying estrangement between human beings who interact out of necessity but without interest or affection. His early pictures lack the human complexity of Caravaggio's, and they do not aspire to comment on society so much as Caravaggio's foolish youths do. Both paint real people who would have been identifiable to local citizens who saw their work. Caravaggio frequently used friends as models. Observe that Velasquez used the same street urchin as his model for both of these early paintings too. Sometimes Velasquez' paintings pay direct homage to a specific Caravaggio painting. His **Feast of Bacchus** borrows Caravaggio's young, handsome god, but Velasquez isn't so much interested in manipulating Bacchus into an erotic tease as he is showing him as a down to earth god of drink enjoying happy hour with some of the local drunks. Velasquez' characters, with the exception of Bacchus, are working class Spanish guys who probably enjoyed seeing themselves in this slice of life painting.

Velasquez' skill exceeded many of his peers in Seville, and in time he attracted the attention of government officials serving the young king. In 1622 when the court artist to the king died, Velasquez was invited to Madrid to try his hand at producing a **Portrait of Young Philip IV**, whose unfortunate Hapsburg royal family likeness (they all looked alike) didn't give the artist much to work with. Still, Velasquez managed to make Philip look elegant and capable, if not exactly handsome. Velasquez was hired as the king's artist and brought to live at court, where he served the rest of his life painting mostly portraits of the royal family. Many of these are full length figures, like we see with young Philip, reminding us that the patron was super rich since full length portraits were expensive. Velasquez often preferred to present his sitter in a darkened room wearing dark clothing in order to focus out attention on the person's face. His later portraits, like the one of Philip's daughter, **Maria Teresa**, introduced occasionally brighter colors in the fancy clothes worn by the royal family, but there is still little to distract us from the sitter's direct gaze.

His most famous picture is called **Las Meninas**, which is a portrait of the petite kindergarten-aged Princess Margarita. The painting is huge, as would befit a royal portrait, and it is filled with a variety of people, most notably the princess and her entourage of assorted ladies in waiting. It should be emphasized that the portrait is of the princess; everyone else, and every*thing* else for that matter amounts to little more than "props" to make her look more important or to make the picture itself seem more important. This later, more sophisticated painting introduces something new in the artist's technique repertoire: visible brushwork. Velasquez was well traveled, thanks to his court position, and he had been to Venice where he had seen the work of Titian first-hand. He was also well acquainted with the painter Rubens, who was a guest at the royal court in Madrid in 1628, and who was quite keen on visible brushwork.

What makes Las Meninas an interesting candidate for study is the way the artist has manipulated his composition. We are looking directly at the wee princess and her attendants, but just off to the left we discover none other than the artist himself, apparently painting this scene! How could he be standing adjacent to the princess and be working on her portrait at the same time? Obviously he must have been looking in a large mirror unseen by the viewer somewhere out in the foreground. This would result in the entire scene being reversed in a mirror reflection. Note further that on the wall in the back of the room, about midway between Velasquez and the princess, we see a fuzzy image of … the king and queen. They are evidently standing in the foreground next to the large mirror, assuming the vantage place of the viewer. The parents are looking in on their daughter to see how things are going, and their presence has been captured in a mirror reflection on the back wall. Thus, the entire scene is depicted in reverse because it is actually a mirror reflection that we see. The king and queen are not backwards though, because they have been reflected in the back wall mirror, then turned right again in the big mirror in the foreground which is the view the artist is painting.

Complicated? You bet. Try mapping it out on a sheet of paper to determine where everyone was standing to create this scene. Now *this* is baroque Baroque! Las Meninas is the perfect example of 17th century sophisticated composition, used to engage the viewer by making us each part of the extended space encompassing an understood if also unseen foreground outside the work of art. Bernini's Contarelli Chapel achieves this by including the patrons in box seats watching the show, and by implying that as we enter the chapel, we take our place in the orchestra seats. Caravaggio's Bacchus does it too, as the androgynous god reaches forward to us offering a brimming goblet of wine. But perhaps none are as remarkable and even challenging as Las Meninas, where we assume the role of the unseen king and queen, conversing with the painter as he paints an unseen mirror reflection of a room full of people.

As a postscript on Las Meninas, notice that at least one of the princess' playmates happens to be a dwarf. During the 17th century, dwarfs and midgets were frequently kept at the royal courts of Europe as pets! They were not considered to be real people, and instead were kept on hand for the entertainment and amusement of others. It may seem hard to believe for us today, but often students of history discover one group of people or another at one point in history or another in one location or another being perceived as non-people, or at least, lesser people … be it women in ancient Greece, or for that matter, in many places in the world today, or African slaves, whether in colonial America or enslaved by different tribes back in Africa before they got here, or indigenous Indians in South America in colonial times, or in Central America today. Life isn't always fair. What is interesting here is that Velasquez, who was a bit of a social climbing snob himself, nevertheless took an active interest in the "little people" at the Spanish royal court, which by the way boasted one of the largest collections of midgets and dwarfs in residence. Although it was not politically correct within these circles to view these people with the respect due others at court, Velasquez made a project of producing individual full-length portraits of each of the dwarfs and midgets, portraying each as an interesting, dignified person, often with intellectual pursuits and talents probably overlooked by most people at court. **Sebastian de Morro** is a good example. The dwarf is given similar respect to other members of the royal court in that he is depicted full length, and further the artist seems to sympathize with Sebastian's plight as he is shown in full control of his intellectual faculties, as evidenced by the frustrated expression on his face being trapped in circumstances beyond his control.

The last painting we will consider by Diego Velasquez is nearly as famous as <u>Las Meninas</u>: the **Rokeby Venus** (also called *Venus at her Mirror*). It is a rare painting in the work of Velasquez in that as far as anyone knows, this is the only nude he painted. Nudes were quite rare in 17th century Spanish art. The Council of Trent had been critical of lewd art created for its titillating shock value (paintings like the <u>Madonna of the Long Neck</u> come to mind), but the arguments put forth at Trent specifically addressed nudity or overly sexualized content in *religious art*. While the Council of Trent certainly wasn't supporting pornography, the concern was over how religious art should be presented and what religious art should convey. Artists in Italy often got around the issue by saving their anatomical exercises and even sexy imagery for mythology, and for the most part so long as it wasn't blatantly offensive, the Church didn't get ruffled over nudes in art.

In Spain it was a different story. The Spanish Inquisition, which is sometimes incorrectly understood to be what the Counter Reformation was all about, was a movement sanctioned in Spain to deal with heresy. It was initiated by the Dominicans, the same monastic order who addressed the Albigensian Heresy in medieval times. Spain in many ways was more insecure about preserving the integrity of traditional Christianity at this juncture in history because unlike the rest of Europe, southern Spain had been occupied by Muslim Moors prior to the Crusades. Christians here were often more touchy than elsewhere in Europe when they perceived their traditional Christian beliefs being challenged. Curiously perhaps compared to other places in Europe, this protective attitude toward Catholicism had less to do with the threat of Protestantism, which wasn't so much of a big deal down in Spain compared to other countries since there were hardly any Protestants in Spain anyway, but more directed at threats, real or perceived, from Judaism and Islam. They burned books and prosecuted those who were judged to be insubordinate to Christian morals and values, however the purported wholesale executions villanized in literature have been largely discredited. Were some people executed? Yes. Was it a holocaust on a grand scale? Not according to recent scholarship. In any event, one very real outcome of the Spanish Inquisition was that the Council of Trent prohibition against indecent representations in *religious* art was generally accepted as a prohibition against nudity in art as a whole. So while you will see plenty of nudes in Italian art or Flemish art or French art in the 17th century, all countries supportive of the Counter Reformation, Spanish art steered clear of nudity lest it be considered immoral. Velasquez apparently was forgiven his foray into portraying a nude because he was the king's personal painter, and therefore excused a margin of artistic license.

The <u>Rokeby Venus</u> is a marvel of restraint. The palette is limited to brilliant red, cool white and bluish grey and a few dabs of pink, with even the woman's skin tones being a blend of these hues. The depiction of a naked lady flaked out on an unmade bed was almost certainly inspired by Titian's work, which Velasquez knew, although again we find the Spanish nude modestly presents her backside, and we are unable to make out her face. What's just as interesting is that the artist is introducing a mirror reflection again to include otherwise hidden information, in this case, the woman's face. The reflection has been softened so we can't identify our lovely lady, but perhaps she isn't meant to be anyone in particular, but rather a testimony to woman's beauty as a perfect ideal.

Murillo

The youngest of the "Golden Age" of Spanish Baroque painters was Bartolome Esteban Murillo who was born in 1617, also in Seville. His early works showed the expected Caravaggio influence, although Murillo didn't linger with that style very long. After visiting Madrid, where he had the opportunity to see Venetian Renaissance art as well as contemporary paintings by Velasquez, Van Dyck, and Rubens (stay tuned, more on Flemish Baroque art later), Murillo began to lighten and brighten his colors, he softened his highlights and shadows, and introduced softer brushwork to his paintings.

Like Velasquez, Murillo produced a number of genre scenes of everyday people, but unlike Velasquez' characters who seem so cold and indifferent toward each other, Murillo's people are always engaging, even lovable. **Beggar Boys Eating Grapes and Melon** and **Two Women at a Window** are both excellent examples of Murillo's genre paintings. The hungry <u>Beggar Boys</u> have discovered a basket of delicious fruit. The basket itself is a still life set into a larger picture, similar to what Caravaggio might have painted, but here it isn't so much the star of the painting as it is a prop to help the artist tell a little story about these two kids. The boys are gobbling up the fruit as fast as they can stuff it in their mouths. It's easy to imagine that these children don't enjoy fresh fruit very often and they are making the most of it while they can. They are simple, scruffy street kids, but somehow it's easy to like them as they share conversation over their feast. <u>Two Women at a Window</u> is equally inviting. The older woman might be a nursemaid, and she seems quite tickled about something as the giggles into her mantilla. The younger girl is smiling too. Have they just seen something amusing? They are looking right at you, did *you* say something funny? These women are peering out from behind shutters; they are engaging you the viewer, coming out from behind their protected world to enjoy your company. It's all kind of new and exciting to the older woman, while the younger girl looks like she's ready to take on the world. These images are positive affirmations of life.

Like Ribera and Zurbaran, Murillo was well known for his religious paintings, but unlike the other two, Murillo's work doesn't emphasize bleak scenes of nearly monochromatic suffering saints. Murillo's softer style was better suited to angelic Madonnas, and he produced numerous paintings of Mary floating with chubby cherubs in the clouds of heaven. These were not intended to be simple depictions of the Virgin for the sake of making pleasant religious art like we may have seen sometimes during the Renaissance. Most of Murillo's Madonnas were dedicated to two specific Catholic teachings: the **Immaculate Conception**, and the **Assumption of the Virgin**. If the pictures themselves didn't tell the story, the titles did. The <u>Immaculate Conception</u> is the teaching that God cleansed Mary of original sin at her point of conception to prepare her to be an acceptable ark of the New Covenant, that is, to prepare her to bear the Christ. The <u>Assumption of the Virgin</u> is the teaching that at the end of her life, Mary simply fell asleep in the Lord and was raised up to heaven by her son, body and soul to be with Christ. Neither of these teachings were new, but they were coming under attack in some

Protestant circles during the 17th century such that Catholic artists like Murillo chose to paint these subjects in support of the Counter Reformation, reaffirming their faith and offering it up to God as a sort of personal testimony.

As an interesting aside, we have seen how throughout history the attitude of the Church has usually been if it ain't broke, don't fix it. Nothing, not even which books comprised the <u>Bible</u>, was written down until there were enough people challenging the oral tradition that a council was called and the Church ***defined*** some aspect of the faith, which is to say they finally wrote it down with the understanding that it's in black and white now, so nobody has any excuse to not know the score. In response to challenges made against these two tenets of the faith, the Immaculate Conception was officially defined as dogma in the Catholic Church on December 8, 1854, and the Assumption of the Virgin Mary was defined as dogma in the Catholic Church on November 1, 1950. Curiously, these are the *only two times in the history of Christianity* when a pope has spoken ***ex cathedra***, or in plain English, the pope issued a proclamation "from the chair" in the context of being "infallible."

Italy and Spain were both actively engaged in the Counter Reformation, and while not every painter or sculptor in either country made a career of producing pro-Catholic propaganda art, most were supportive of the cause. Moving north of these Mediterranean countries we will find that the further north we go, the less the Counter Reformation will be the defining yardstick by which great art was measured.

16. Baroque Art in France & Flanders

During the Baroque period, most countries in Europe fell under the general category of "Catholic," although in most countries the Counter Reformation was not as big an influence as it was in Italy and Spain. France and Flanders were both predominantly Catholic, but in neither region was there much interest in producing specifically propaganda art to support reform within the Church. Neither were artists in these countries antagonistic toward the Catholic Church, which was an excellent patron of the arts, providing many commissions for lots of artists. In addition to Church commissions (altarpieces mostly), painters from France and Flanders generally worked for a wealthy clientele, just like artists from Spain and Italy did, and these patrons more often than not were Catholics. The types of painting subjects that sold well in France and Flanders were the same as what sold well in Italy and Spain, namely religious themes, history scenes, mythology subjects, and as always, portraits.

France

Claude Lorraine

Claude Lorraine is the best-remembered landscape painter from France during the 17th century, and possibly the most famous landscape painter in all Europe at this time. He grew up in the French countryside as a child, but then traveled to Rome as a young aspiring artist, and never left. Claude Lorraine had little interest in Renaissance painting with its intellectual scenes from antiquity, whether historical, mythological or religious. Claude fell in love with Italy the country, more than Italy the home of Renaissance art. His paintings reflect romantic, idealized pastoral landscapes, inspired by the Italian countryside, but created in the imagination of the artist's mind. They are not real locations, and compared to Carracci's <u>Flight Into Egypt</u>, they don't even pretend to be real. Claude's imagery is more imaginative and richer in color.

<u>The Embarkation of Saint Ursula</u> is a theme we have visited before in the reliquary by Hans Memling. For as much as Memling used the early Christian account as a springboard to show us architecture and costuming that looks more like Flanders and Germany during the 15th century, Claude Lorraine also updates the old story to include modern ships of his day, as well as a collection of fantastic architecture from an assortment of different periods in history. There is little interest in commenting on the story of Saint Ursula at all. Where is she? Can you even find the young woman and her ladies in attendance? Instead the artist is offering us a fairy tale. The steps in the foreground sweep right down to the water, looking perhaps more like Benares (Varanasi) in India than anyplace one might catch a boat in Cologne or Basel. The entire scene is a dream manufactured in the artist's imagination, and his link to reality is no more than finding the occasional model in terms of a ship or building to use in his lush scene.

Nicolas Poussin

By far the most influential artist from France during the 17th century was Nicolas Poussin. Of all the painters we will consider from this period, he is the most classical in temperament and style, albeit still very much a part of the Baroque period. He grew up in the countryside of Normandy, and as a teenager he moved to Paris where he evidently was permitted access to the royal collection of paintings and to the royal library. He studied the work of Italian Renaissance masters, initially finding a fondness for both Raphael and Titian. Poussin managed to save enough money to visit Italy twice, the second time almost on the heels of his first trip (he barely arrived back in France before packing to leave again), and the second time he stayed for good. As his career took form, Poussin gravitated increasingly toward an intense appreciation of Raphael. He established his studio in Rome to be close to Raphael's paintings so he could see them as often as he pleased, and his own painting emulated the style of Raphael.

Poussin's clientele was predominantly sophisticated, rich French people who would take vacations in Italy, visit the artist's studio to place their orders while on holiday in Rome, and then the artist would ship the final paintings back to France. Poussin had a stubborn, somewhat pedantic personality, fixated on classical interests that were not the height of popularity during his generation, and as a result he was not terribly popular in the big time circles where there was a lot of money to be made producing heroic great paintings: expensive commissions for popes, or kings or fashionable nobility. He only painted one large altarpiece, for Saint Peter's Cathedral, and he wasn't very satisfied with the painting when it was finished although others considered it a masterpiece. Most of his work was smaller, and appealed primarily to well-educated, upper-class French buyers rather than glamorous royalty from across Europe or the Church.

Poussin's **Assumption of the Virgin, Triumph of Poseidon and Amphitrite** and **Luna and Endymion** are very typical of the artist's style. The first is clearly a religious subject, while the latter two works are mythological presentations. The *Assumption* is a Christian theme better known in Catholic circles than Protestant. Oral tradition has it that when the Virgin Mary ended her days on earth, that like some rare Old Testament Bible heroes, Elijah probably being the most renown, Mary was taken up to heaven to be with Jesus instead of returning to dust in a grave. The Triumph of Poseidon and Amphitrite is largely a vehicle for portraying mythological gods as samples of anatomy arranged nicely in a simple geometric composition. Did you catch that the figure of Amphitrite was lifted from the famous Venus de Milo from antiquity? Poussin would expect you to notice this and appreciate the ancient Greek influence on this picture of a Greek subject. Both this picture and the Assumption of the Virgin show strong ties back to the painting of Raphael, both in concept and design. The story of Endymion is a mythological romance. Endymion was an ordinary shepherd, albeit a handsome one, and he caught the attention of the Moon Goddess, called simply "Luna" for "moon" in this work by Poussin. In any event, the goddess asked Zeus to make Endymion immortal, and he complied, but the catch was he made Endymion fall into a perpetual sleep. Somehow Luna managed to have children with her comatose husband just the same (creative romance…).

The style in all three paintings is linear; Poussin never allowed his brushwork to be seen, and the colors lean toward a primary palette, just like Raphael preferred a hundred years earlier. Poussin's figures look like mannequins frozen in time and space. The artist considered composition to be the most important aspect of painting, and he usually labored long on preliminary sketches before picking up his brushes to begin painting. Often he found models a nuisance as they don't appreciate hours upon hours of posing, so he would create for himself little sculpted figures he could fiddle with like toy soldiers until he got his design for the picture just the way he wanted it. Although most of his pictures were small in scale compared to what other painters working in Catholic countries at the time, the scenes themselves have a grandeur about them that would suggest they be appreciated as important pictures.

Poussin's **Funeral of Phocion** depicts a historical figure from ancient Greece during the fall of Athens after the days of Perikles. He was a student of Plato, a stoic and good man, one not given to putting on airs or talking big for the sake of being heard. He was practical and wise, and through most of his life and public career he was enormously respected both as a statesman and as a general. Philip of Macedonia held him in high regard, as did Alexander the Great, and he did a great deal to ameliorate the difficulties his fellow Athenians endured during the years when they were an occupied nation under Alexander. In the end, though, the fickle Athenians turned against him, and he was forced to partake of a poison cocktail in the tradition of Socrates. To add further insult to injury, the Athenians wouldn't let him be either buried or cremated on Athenian land, so here you see his corpse being carried away from the hometown he had served all his life. Like we saw in Annibale Carracci's Flight Into Egypt, this is a typical landscape picture for the time. The title tells us it is a history painting, and if we look closely we can actually find the figures in the foreground marching along in a funeral procession. Truly the real subject of interest, though, is painting the background landscape. Once again, it is not a real location, but rather a composite created from a collection of sketches done by the artist in a variety of spots. In the case of Poussin especially, the individual parts of the landscape have also been modified to suit the artist's requirements for making a pleasing composition, which is why Poussin's landscapes look somewhat less natural when compared to Carracci's work. Next to Claude Lorraine's shimmering color and dreamy romantic imagery, Poussin's landscape looks almost chalky and dull.

As a postscript on the art of France during the Baroque period, Poussin was not the most prominent painter from France during his lifetime, but he was elevated to that status rapidly after his death. Louis XIV came to the throne while still a child in 1661, just 4 years before Poussin passed away as an elderly gentleman painter. The "Sun King," as Louis was often called, grew up to be a strong-minded ruler with a keen vision for his country. It disturbed the king that France, which had been the center of the cultural universe for Europe from the days of Charlemagne through the Gothic time period, had slipped into artistic oblivion during the Renaissance, first falling behind the rising glory of Flanders, then ultimately kneeling before the grandeur of the High Renaissance in Italy. Louis XIV could not help but realize that even the best of the best of the most recent generation of French painters, Nicolas Poussin and Claude Lorraine, had somehow felt compelled to abandon Paris for Rome. Louis was determined to change this negative flow of talent away from their homeland, and to instead create a revitalized immersion into the fine arts in France, with Paris replacing Rome as the capital of the art world. He accomplished this turnaround in cultural fortune by establishing three interconnected French institutions that within a generation would change the art world forever.

The first new institution initiated under Louis XIV was the *Royal Academy*. Up until this time, if somebody wanted to study painting or sculpture the course to pursue was apprenticing under a reputable master in the local region. As a result, there tended to be regional styles, and one could normally anticipate that clients would be mostly local people of financial means or organizations like the Church or government. Seldom did artists have international exposure. The Royal Academy in Paris was a university style environment with a top-notch faculty in its art program, the *Ecole* (school) *des Beaux* (beautiful / fine) *Arts*. It was sponsored by the government instead of the Church which had traditionally backed most early universities, and students might be accepted from anywhere in Europe to study under the best talent together in a common environment. This was a way to standardize taste in a manipulated direction, since the French government oversaw the program and could influence who taught at the Royal Academy and the styles of art that would be promoted.

To make attendance at the Royal Academy / Ecole des Beaux Arts attractive, during the 17th century another new institution was introduced called the *Royal Salon*. The Royal Salon was a large, annual (sometimes biennial) international art show, the likes of which had never been seen before. Artists had to compete to get their work into the Royal Salon, but the bottom line was if they could achieve this goal, the tremendous positive exposure garnered from the experience would all but guarantee a lucrative career in art. It was no accident that the jury which selected the art to be accepted for the Royal Salon was composed of assorted faculty members from the Royal Academy. It doesn't take a genius to figure out that the best way to get your work accepted at the Royal Salon was to study at the Royal Academy and become familiar with the faculty.

In addition to the Academy and the Salon, there was a third institution, which encouraged young artists to flock to Paris: The *Prix de Rome*, or "Roman Prize." This was a contest sponsored alongside the Salon, where a young artist might win an all-expense paid scholarship to study art in Rome at the Royal Academy's own version of a study abroad program. It was a wonderful opportunity to travel and see the great masterpieces of the Italian Renaissance, but the real benefit was that winners of the Prix de Rome no longer had to submit their art to the jury for Royal Salon shows; they were automatically accepted. In all, these three institutions working together completely revamped how art was approached from the latter 17th century forward. There will be fewer examples of local artists apprenticing the next generation of local artists. Instead, more artists will be seeking a forum in an international arena through the channels available to them ... in PARIS!

For all this to work well, it was necessary from the beginning for the Royal Academy, the Royal Salon, and the Prix de Rome to endorse a common style of art as the official last word on good taste for any given generation. During the late 17th century, Louis XIV personally selected the work of the painter Nicolas Poussin to be the standard norm for fine art according to French taste.

Flanders

During the Renaissance period, Flanders was a northern province of Spain, and during the 17th century it remained so. Still affluent thanks to her role in international trade, Flanders was loyal to Spain, to the Catholic Church, and to continued prosperity. There were several painters who made good careers for themselves during the Baroque period, but none as famous as Peter Paul Rubens.

Peter Paul Rubens

If one were to identify the single artist who was the most influential, the most famous, the most sought after, the best educated and the wealthiest of the Baroque period, Rubens would win with scant competition. In many ways, Rubens is the definitive Baroque painter. Born of a titled, noble family, Rubens was raised with every luxury and the best education that money could buy. He was fluent in no fewer than eight languages, which didn't hurt his career any as he, more than any other artist, enjoyed the patronage of kings and queens across Europe as well as rank and file rich folks from all over.

Once he had completed his formal education, like many wealthy artists from Catholic countries, Rubens made a much-anticipated pilgrimage to Italy to see the paintings of all the great masters of the Italian Renaissance. Rubens visited Italy on several extended trips, and he always came back to the paintings of Titian as the most inspiring. Rubens found the lush colors of the Venetian painters as a whole appealing. With Titian in particular, he was moved by the visible brushwork. Taking his cues from the work of Titian, Rubens developed a style with rich colors, usually favoring a *primary palette* like that used by many High Renaissance painters, including Raphael and Titian among others. Rubens further developed Titian's interest in allowing brushwork to be seen. Rubens swirled the paint onto the canvas with animated strokes. He desired for his paintings to be appreciated not just for the narrative of the subject, and not just for the exciting colors, but also for the lively texture. We call this new appreciation of visible brushwork the *painterly technique*, and it is Rubens who is credited with developing it into a popular style.

Like other painters from Catholic countries, Rubens pursued commissions falling into the four popular topic areas: religion, history, mythology and portraits. **Raising the Cross** is an example of Rubens' religious painting. Rubens was raised as a Calvinist, although he was quietly Catholic (as opposed to being a Counter-Reformation activist) during his own adult life. The Catholic Church served him well as a steady client throughout his career. Compared to most Renaissance painters, Rubens put his emphasis on making the scene dynamic and dramatic, in this case through the use of diagonal lines in the composition as well as the colors and painterly style.

Aside from the Church, most of Rubens' patrons were wealthy aristocrats and nobility from across Europe. For these clients he produced a variety of themes. An excellent example of his mythological painting is the **Rape of the Daughters of Leucippus**. The subject is curious to be sure. Leucippus was born a girl, but raised as a boy given that her father had sworn he would kill the child if it were not a son. Mom, not surprisingly, was worried about the charade, and asked the gods to change the sex of

Leucippus to a boy. Her request was granted. In any event, Leucippus didn't marry, but managed to produce a pair of fine daughters named Phoebe and Hilaeira (one might wonder if this was before the sex change, or yet another convenient miracle after the fact). His daughters were fine young ladies of spotless reputation. One fine day while the fair maidens were out minding their own business, they were spied by two youthful dandies, the twins Castor and Pollux, who swept down on the girls and abducted them to become their wives. Castor married Phoebe and Pollux married Hilaeira. Of course, Leucippus didn't take this lying down; he rounded up his nephews and set out to avenge his daughters, and Castor was killed in the battle. Pollux then pleaded with Zeus for immortality, which he was granted, and he elected to share it with his twin such that they divided their time between Mount Olympus, hanging out with the gods, and Hades, land of the mortal dead.

What's wrong with this picture? The two chaste daughters appear to have been parading around stark naked … small wonder the guys found their beauty noteworthy. There is no shortage of flesh here either, as the girls are beefy heifers – no dainty little waifs for Rubens, thank you very much! Peter Paul Rubens is singularly responsible for shifting artistic taste away from the male nude, which had been favored since the days of ancient Greece, toward the female nude, which remains the more popular subject to this day. Rubens enjoyed painting nude women, although, in case you are curious, he was happily married with no evidence of philandering. He especially favored shall we say well-endowed, full-figured women. The artist often accepted commissions that allowed him to incorporate his trademark chubby beauties over commissions that failed to include naked ladies, and beyond that, Rubens frequently modified the storyline to include a buxom nude to make a painting more sensual and titillating than it might be with everyone fully dressed.

Like most of Rubens' paintings, this work is enormous. The sort of people who could afford paintings by Rubens lived in homes the size of one of those French chateaux. Rubens had a substantial clientele, and could afford to pick and choose what commissions he accepted. He ran a huge studio in his hometown of Antwerp, where numerous apprentices were trained to assist the master on important commissions.

Rubens lived a long, full life. After his first wife, Isabella Brandt, died, Rubens married a young girl of only 16 despite the fact that he was getting on in years by that time himself. **Helene Fourment** was the epitome of ideal beauty by Rubensian standards, as can be seen in his portrait of her. As we would expect with portraits from Catholic countries during the Baroque time period, Helene's portrait is full length. Only the wealthiest people could afford pictures of themselves, and the inclination was to pay a little more to get the very best. The sitter would be dressed in fancy clothes, and is shown either in an attractive interior room or out of doors in a garden or similarly appropriate setting. Although this portrait of Helene shows her quite alone, often portraits will include the sitter's children or pets, or a servant or two, all of which are included to enhance the status of the patron who is paying a hefty sum to look good in the portrait.

The last picture we will consider by Rubens for the moment (we will revisit Rubens later, comparing his work to other painters) is his **Landscape with a Rainbow**. Landscape painting was popular in Catholic countries, as we have seen, with the usual approach being to superimpose a religious, mythological, historical, or portrait subject matter to upgrade the importance of the picture. Rubens' painting has no additional theme, largely because his dabblings in landscape were predominantly done as a hobby for his own personal art collection, which adorned his country estate, the lovely and elegant Chateau Steen. His landscapes incorporate elements of the views on Rubens' estate, often including local peasants or even members of the artist's family puttering about, with an element of the artist's imagination thrown in for good measure.

Anthony Van Dyck

Anthony Van Dyck was Rubens' star pupil, and the most talented painter to emerge from Rubens' studio in Antwerp. Van Dyck was a child prodigy, like Michelangelo, who arrived on the scene a gifted artist as a child. He apprenticed under Rubens, and quickly demonstrated that he could duplicate the master's hand so closely that Rubens could effectively turn a big commission over to Van Dyck, who would paint most of the picture, then Rubens would come in, touch it up here and there with his own trademark brushwork, attach his signature and presto, instant expensive painting making a bundle of money for the master, while his flunky stooge who did a substantial part of the actual work gets paid at a student wage. Furthermore, Van Dyck was a quick study – despite the mastery of his execution, he could paint very rapidly and finish commissions, huge paintings, in record time. This was great for Rubens, but initially not so great for Van Dyck.

Van Dyck, whose style is very similar to Rubens with similar subject matters, similar palette and similar painterly technique, figured out early in his career that in order to get paid what he was worth, he needed to move away from Antwerp, in fact, he needed to move away from Flanders altogether. Had he stayed, he would have forever worked in the shadows of Rubens, the great master. By relocating, Van Dyck was able to establish his artistic presence abroad, and finally earn the kind of attractive salaries on commissions that his paintings were worth. He painted for nobility across Europe, taking his talent to them rather than asking the patrons to come to the master, which was more typical of Rubens. His greatest body of work was completed in England (although Van Dyck is still very much a Flemish painter), where he enjoyed the patronage of the royal crown under King Charles I.

Van Dyck's portrait of **Charles I** is the epitome of excellence in "Catholic" portraiture of the 17th century. Although Van Dyck painted a variety of different themes, the bulk of his best work is in the realm of portraiture. Predictably, we find Charles depicted full-length, donning fine attire. The artist has taken the time to include an attractive, pastoral outdoor setting; no expense is spared in making this the sort of impressive picture a king would be proud to display in his palace. Additional figures and animals, in this case his horse and hunting companions, have been included as props to flatter King Charles. The king was quite short, and while the painter has not lied about the king's stature, notice that his body proportions indicate a petite individual; there are no long legs here. He has made every effort short of dishonesty to make the king appear grand. Both his companions are shorter than he is (jockeys perhaps?), and his horse must be on the small side (a small Arabian probably, rather than a taller Thoroughbred), and the horse even has the good taste to bow before the king so that nobody's head is above that of Charles. Further, Charles stands on a slight knoll, with the viewer obliged to stand in a gully below, giving the viewer a "worm's eye" perspective – we look up at the king who glances down his nose at us. In reality, the king would have to look up to most people who would be taller than he without this convenient topography arrangement.

This picture was identified as an example of "Catholic" portraiture. True, Van Dyck was Catholic. But by this time, certainly the English royal family was Protestant. We will discover when we look at Dutch art, that the art of Holland was in every way different from painting seen anywhere else in Europe during the 17th century. Dutch art was "Protestant," while art from everywhere else is considered "Catholic" by default, whether the actual patron was Catholic, or Protestant as we see here with the King of England.

Foundations of Modern Art

Painting from the 18th, 19th and early 20th centuries is frequently best understood in the context of developments in painting during the Baroque period. During the late 17th century, Louis XIV personally selected the work of the painter Nicolas Poussin to be the standard norm for fine art according to French taste. Poussin was chronologically from the early 17th century and an exact contemporary of Peter Paul Rubens in Flanders, who would come to be seen as his arch-rival in painting, although the rivalry has more to do with later generations than it ever had to do with these men personally. Poussin and Rubens have in common that both were Baroque painters, both worked in a predominantly Catholic milieu for wealthy customers, and both gravitated to the same common themes: Religion, Mythology, History, and Portraits. There is no evidence that they paid particular attention to each other, although their followers in later generations were frequently artistic enemies. Rubens established his studio in Antwerp and attracted more clients from across Europe than he could process without considerable help from apprentices. Poussin, who was well-educated like Rubens and also from a reasonably well-to-do family, established his studio in Rome. Even so, his customers were almost exclusively rich French patrons. To illustrate the styles of these two artists, we will explore two paintings of the same subject matter, and that were completed within 24 months of each other during the mid-1630's:

The Rape of the Sabines	**The Rape of the Sabines**
by Rubens	by Poussin
Flemish Baroque (Flanders)	French Baroque (France)

It is critically important to understand the differences between Poussin and Rubens, as much of the painting from this point forward through the end of the 19th century and some might argue beyond will be subject to this litmus test: is it more *Poussiniste* (artists who favor Poussin's philosophy and style) or more *Rubeniste* (artists who favor Ruben's philosophy and style)? Here are two paintings done at exactly the same time, and portraying exactly the same history subject matter: a narrative from the early Republic in Rome.

Evaluate first which artist seemed to be more interested in *intellectual* art and which preferred *emotional* art. Poussin went to great trouble to make his painting conform to historical reality. He researched the costumes, the architecture, even the hairstyles to be sure it looked true to the Roman Republic; he was intellectual in his approach. Rubens might have been plenty intellectual in his day-to-day private life, but he had no interest in seeking an intellectual response in his art. He wanted to appeal to your emotions! Toward that end, sometimes he would take liberties with the subject matter to make it seem more exciting, or more sensual, or more exotic, more dramatic or even just more personal so the viewer could imagine being involved in the story narrative first-hand. In this painting, he has represented the women less as stale old Roman figures and more as Flemish beauties of his own day. This brings it to a level where it would appeal to the local market much the way sexy movie stars of today might entice more personal fantasy than seeing images of outdated-looking people in a picture.

In keeping with his intellectual interests, Poussin was primarily concerned with *composition*. He preferred to rely on *sculpture* rather than live models, either sculpture from antiquity or the Renaissance which he expected his educated audience to recognize, or miniature figures he would create himself so he could manipulate his figures until he had the composition perfectly arranged just so. Notice the arms in his painting all repeating the same diagonal pattern, repeated again in the diagonals of several swords. Often his figures look frozen in time, like neatly posed mannequins. Rubens in contrast placed greater emphasis on *color,* and he always opted for *live models* rather than sculpture. Poussin didn't use "bad" color - his colors are primary and quite lively. His philosophy, though, was that if the composition was perfected, the painting would be a success regardless of the color. Likewise, Rubens didn't use "bad" composition, although it is clearly not as laborious as Poussin's efforts. His compositions are usually more dynamic and spontaneous, and clearly secondary in consideration to the rich color.

Poussin, predictably preferred a *linear* technique where the brushstrokes were smoothed over into a satin surface without texture. Rubens was more excited about the *painterly* technique with lots of swirling strokes allowing the viewer to appreciate the texture of the paint as a medium alongside the color and the storyline of the subject matter. In choosing mentors, Rubens adored the paintings of *Titian*, while Poussin fell in love with *Raphael*; in fact, it was his affection for Raphael that kept Poussin in Rome most of his career. In the end, although both artists are from the 17th century Baroque period, Poussin's philosophy and style are more *classical* in taste, while Rubens was clearly a devotee of *baroque*.

17. Baroque Art in Holland

Holland was odd man out compared to other countries in Europe during the Baroque time period. The mood there was different, the market was different, the attitudes and priorities were different. During the Renaissance, Holland like Flanders had been a northern province of Spain. This arrangement began to chafe during the 16th century. Flanders and Holland were thriving economically as equals under an umbrella of international trade around 1500. Then came the Protestant Reformation, which had little impact on Flanders, but which took Holland by storm. Spain, appalled by the changes taking place in the religious climate of Holland, promoted trade through Flemish ports at the expense of those in Holland. Holland was viewed as the unruly child needing a lesson, but in the end, these sanctions motivated the Dutch to rise up against Spain and Flanders in a civil war that gained Holland her independence in 1609. To put this in proper perspective, one needs to understand why the rift over religion between Spain and Holland was so acute.

The brand of Protestantism adopted by Holland, at least initially, was Calvinism. The Protestant Reformation started during the 1520's when Martin Luther was excommunicated from the Catholic Church. During those early years, John Calvin was studying for the priesthood in France. As was true for most young men studying theology at that juncture in history, Luther's writings were a hot topic of discussion. Calvin found that the more he considered Luther's theology, the more he favored many of Luther's ideas. In the end, Calvin parted ways with the Catholic Church prior to his ordination in order to establish his own ministry. His church was first established in Geneva, Switzerland where he found a body of people willing to follow his teachings. His own particular brand of Christianity had its foundations in much of Luther's teachings, but could not be described as Lutheranism.

Like Luther, Calvin supported the idea that the Bible alone (Sola Scriptura) should be the only authority for Christianity, which differed from the Catholic and Orthodox position that it was the Bible combined with Sacred Oral Tradition. That said, even though they employed the same Bible, a shorter version than that used by Catholics and Orthodox Christians, Luther and Calvin didn't always agree on exactly what the Bible taught. Like Luther, Calvin agreed to toss out 5 of the original 7 sacraments practiced in the Catholic and Orthodox Church. What they kept were Baptism and Communion. What they eliminated as sacraments were Reconciliation, Confirmation, Marriage, Ordination, and Anointing the Sick.

Even with the two sacraments retained, however, the sacraments themselves changed. Baptism in the Lutheran faith was practiced much as it had traditionally been with children born into Christian families being baptized as infants. Within Calvinism, although the religion started with infant baptism, as the denomination further split into factions, some followers continued to baptize babies, while others believed it necessary to wait to baptize after a child was older, or became an adult. Communion, likewise, did not follow a common path. In the Catholic and Orthodox faith, communion was administered through consecrated bread and wine believed to be the transubstantiated

Body and Blood of Christ. Luther retained the bread and wine, but changed the concept to consubstantiation, which means that the bread and wine are not transformed, but that the Holy Spirit is present. Calvin replaced the wine with unfermented grape juice, arguing against having alcohol in church, and viewed communion as a remembrance of Jesus, no more, no less.

You should be noticing a pattern here. If Luther's theology was moving away from traditional Catholic and Orthodox Christianity, Calvin's was moving away faster and further. This was even more pronounced on the question of salvation. Prior to the Reformation, Christians uniformly believed that salvation was by God's grace through faith and deeds. In other words, you were expected to believe in the Christian religion, and you were expected to live according to that faith – one without the other got you nowhere you were hoping to go. Luther introduced his theology of Sola Fide, which said that people are saved by faith alone. Calvin's theology was different from either earlier model; he promoted **Predestination**. This concept is based on the premise that God is all-knowing and therefore knows even before you were born whether you will go to heaven or hell. By the way, no Catholic, Orthodox, Anglican or Lutheran Christian would disagree with that premise in its simple form. The question is one of **Free Will**, with all pre-Reformation Christians and many Protestant denominations at the end of the field saying people have maximum free will, and Calvinists at the opposite end of the field downplaying free will. According to Predestination, God decides who will be Elect (go to heaven) and who will be Damned (go to hell), the call being made before you were born, and in the end, you do not have the opportunity to affect the outcome of your own life. Those God loves are invited to salvation, which is irresistible. Everyone not chosen from the beginning of time to be Elect is outside the salvation loop. Accordingly, all the good deeds *and all the faith* in the world do not have an impact on your ultimate destiny. The assumption, of course, is that God will lead those he loves to live good lives filled with correct faith and good deeds – God's doing, not man's. If God has determined that a person is not to be Elect, then He will not lead that person to faith and good living, and therefore the inherently corrupt loser will live a life worthy of damnation. Other non-Calvinist Christians tend to see salvation as open to everyone by God's invitation, yet whether or not salvation is ultimately achieved depends at least at some margin on individual life choices, be it asking for and receiving the gift of faith, or coupling that faith with a conscious effort to live by God's precepts too. God knows from the start of time what choices you will make, but they are your choices nevertheless.

Finally, there was one last factor that separated Calvin's church from both the Catholics and most other Protestants of the 16th century, and that was something called **Apostolic Succession**. Apostolic Succession is like the Laws of Primogeniture. Under Laws of Primogeniture, the father passes down his inheritance to his firstborn son. In Hebrew Biblical tradition in the Old Testament, a father's blessing was also bestowed on the firstborn son. This involved a laying on of hands, such as one might read about in the story of Isaac, Jacob and Esau. Esau was the firstborn son, but God had determined that it was the younger twin, Jacob who should receive his father's blessing. It wasn't sufficient for Jacob to know God's Will, he still needed to receive his father's physical blessing to carry out God's plan. In Christian tradition, Jesus blessed the Apostles, and thereafter, future generations of bishops and priests were likewise expected to receive the laying on of hands. Many excellent examples of this can be found in the <u>Bible</u>, but perhaps one of the most moving is the story of the conversion of Saint Paul. Here was a man who encountered Jesus directly, and he was given a charge by Jesus, BUT he was unable to begin his ministry until he received a blessing according to the tradition; witnessing Jesus was not adequate to be a disciple, until he had been physically blessed by the local disciple who carried the Apostolic blessing to pass through the laying on of hands – Acts 9:1-18. At any given point in history, a bishop has been blessed by a bishop who has been blessed by a bishop tracing the blessing back to the Apostles and to Jesus himself. This act of receiving the blessing of Apostolic Succession is called Ordination. The Catholic Church practices unbroken Apostolic Succession, as do the Orthodox Church and the Anglican Church. Luther and his clergy were ordained themselves in the Apostolic Succession tradition, and while ordination was eliminated as a sacrament in their church, at least during the 16th century it was still in place, if by default, in the Lutheran Church. But Calvin was never ordained, so thus never received a blessing of Apostolic Succession, and therefore could not pass it on to anyone else either. As you would expect, the Calvinists believed it was no longer necessary to receive such a blessing; having a personal conviction was good enough. Other Christians questioned this relative to examples set forth in the Bible, as well as tradition in that things just had never been done that way.

The point of this discourse is to demonstrate that while today in the 21st century we may have become immune to noticing much difference between one Christian group or another, even between Christians and non-Christians, and we might wonder what all the fuss is about, but in the 16th and 17th century it was a BIG DEAL. Perhaps you can begin to appreciate why even other Protestant groups looked at Calvinists especially like they were way out in left field, as in many ways they were as different from other Protestants as they were from Catholics. Also, you may have an improved appreciation why Calvinists were not only anti-Catholic, they were inclined to lump other Protestant groups like the Lutherans and Anglicans in with those wine-drinking, baby-baptizing, ordained-clergy-type Catholics. As far as Calvinists were concerned, they were all caught up with aspects of religion that Calvinists considered damnable.

Now as if this were not enough to keep you on your toes, during the 16th century in Holland, the Calvinist religion fissured into 2 distinct camps. Are we having fun yet? A young Calvinist named Jakob Hermanzoon, who adopted the Latinized name of Jacobus Arminius (he was a professor at the University of Leyden, and it was common even in Protestant countries for academics to use a Latin variation of their name) initiated his own reformation of Calvin's theology. Arminius was a staunch Calvinist scholar who at the age of 22 set off for Geneva, where Calvin had led his ministry a half-century earlier, and where Calvinism was taught by the best of the best. As it turned out, though, the more Arminius studied Calvin's writings (*The Institutes of the Christian Religion*), the more he discovered he was not drawing the same conclusions from Scripture that Calvin did. He ventured off to Rome, and may well have come in contact with Jesuits there (certainly he was accused of this back home), but when recalled back to Amsterdam, he was quizzed on his faith and found fit to preach. In time, Arminius introduced his own theology, to reform the Reformation if you will.

Arminius' writings are called the *The Five Articles of the Remonstrants*, and the aspect of Calvin's theology he found most disagreeable was Predestination. In a nutshell, he still kept the sacraments in their reduced format, and he still argued for Scripture alone with no authority given to Tradition. He could not abide, however the idea that God made some people to be saved, and on these souls he lavished great love and blessings, while others were created for the express purpose of damnation. Arminius believed Christ died for all, and that being excluded from salvation was the result of failure to believe. In this regard, Arminius is much closer to both Luther and Catholic and Orthodox tradition. While he did not believe that man has saving grace within his own constitution (no Christian of any stripe would argue that point), he believed that it was by man's free will that he could choose to sin or not; grace is not irresistible, but at some margin, we choose to accept or reject it. Sounds quite a lot like Catholic and Orthodox on this point. He believed men had to be "born again." Catholics and Orthodox believe this also, only their understanding of the matter is a little different. Arminius saw this an unspecified renewal of spirit, understanding and affection for God. In the Catholic and Orthodox Churches, being "born again" is to be baptized, where the sins of this world as well as original sin inherited at birth are washed away, and you start with a clean slate. Calvin believed that once you were elect (as in before you were born), it was a done deal. Luther would have said it was negotiable only in so far as you had to maintain your faith. Curiously, Catholic and Orthodox Christians, *and* Arminius agreed that while being born again of [water and] spirit (sacraments and personal conviction for the former, just the conviction with the latter) was excellent armor against the powers of Satan and evil, that ultimately one could choose not to follow Christ's teachings by his or her unrepentant sinful actions, and poof ... all gone.

If you guessed that all this hubbub caused a religious ruckus in Holland during the late 16th century and 17th century, you would be absolutely right!!! The one thing they more or less agreed upon was that at least they weren't Catholics! If the Catholics could be construed as the enemy, that somehow made it alright, although in reality they were tearing each other apart. By the way, the bile from their arguments bled over to England and Scotland, where their churches also went through permutations such that the followers of Calvin – John Knox and George Whitefield - went one way, while the followers of Arminius – John Wesley – went another. In today's world, Catholics are still Catholics and Orthodox is still Orthodox, and Lutheran is still Lutheran, and Anglican is still Anglican. In our own country, the Calvinist position is most closely defined in the Presbyterian Church (although remember that the original Presbyterian Church has splintered into dozens of different denominations, some more Calvinist than others), while Free Will Baptists and most Methodists come in more on the side of Arminius, noting that the Baptists do not put much stock in liturgical worship and sacraments, while some branches of the Methodist denomination, originating from an Anglican background, do.

Well, that's nice. Holland was predominantly Calvinist, and while the true Calvinists hated Arminius, it was largely because he sounded a wee bit too Catholic. They especially hated the Spanish and Flemish, who in turn looked upon Calvinists as we might look at some new cult today. It did not auger well for a long term happy marriage, and when the Dutch parted ways with their Catholic neighbors at the turn of the 17th century there was an attitude of goodbye and good riddance! Holland became an independent republic with no royal family, no authoritative Catholic Church ... and no rich folks to speak of at least at the turn of the century as Holland had suffered financially in her struggle to gain freedom from Spain. It was a middle class country of staunch anti-

Catholic Protestants who were starting from scratch. You may be thinking… so what? Why is all this important; what difference did any of it make on the art?

Frans Hals

The first Dutch Baroque painter we will consider is not the most famous, but in many ways he IS the most typical. Frans Hals was a strict Calvinist from the small city of Haarlem. He was also a middle class man scrambling to make a living without the benefit of fancy rich patrons willing to pay lots of money for commissioned art. In Holland in the early 17th century, commissioned art was almost non-existent. People were struggling to make ends meet and they certainly didn't have a budget set aside for grand paintings. The only type of painting commission an artist might hope to secure was for a portrait. For better or worse people are vain, and the Dutch were no exception. Frans Hals was one of the top portrait artists in Holland during the 17th century. His **Portrait of a Man** is an excellent example of typical Protestant portraiture. The sitter was just a regular guy from Haarlem, nobody special and we have no idea today who it might have been. Compare it to the portraits by Rubens and Van Dyck, or the portrait by Velasquez. What a difference! The portrait is small, scaled to hang over a desk perhaps in a modest middle class home. It is a ¾ length portrait, which is cheaper than a full-length picture. The colors are drab, partly to economize (fewer paints to buy) and partly to reflect the decidedly "un-Catholic" way Calvinists in Holland dressed during the 17th century. It is painterly, not so much because Hals was making some artistic statement about technique, but because he could crank out the commission faster that way and move on to the next project in the hope that this month he might pay his bills (even with his painterly technique, evidently Hals tended to be a slow painter according to his impatient patrons). The artist has made every attempt to keep the price down so that middle class people can afford to hire him to paint their pictures. All of these little economies stemmed in part from the financial situation in Holland, but in part, they also reflect a conscious disdain for anything Catholic or even remotely similar to anything Catholic. As the century progressed, the Dutch became one of the wealthiest nations in the world by way of trade through the Dutch East India Company … but their thrifty and austere art remained the same.

It is also in Holland that for the first time we find the group portrait, like Hals' **Banquet of Officers of a Civic Guard of Saint George**, and **The Archers of Saint Hadrian's**. Group portraits were a specifically Dutch phenomenon during the 17th century because they made economic sense for both the artist and patrons. Many people could not afford to commission a nice portrait of themselves, even at Hals' comparatively inexpensive prices. So groups of people bound together by some common interest or common cause, like the military reserve unit seen here, would pool their resources and chip in to get one picture made with everyone included. It was a good deal for the painter too, because even though his canvas might be twice the size, and maybe the picture took twice as long to paint, the artist might make five times the money on a group portrait compared to an individual sitter. Middle class people could pay less for their share of a group portrait; a middle class artist could make more money producing a group portrait; everyone was satisfied that it was a good deal. Hals painted as many or more group portraits than any other artist in Holland; it was his bread and butter income. He mastered a formula of sorts to make the pictures look attractive without having to figure it out from scratch each time. The sitters would be arranged around a banquet table to where he could produce each face individually displaying the facial features, while employing a convenient formula composition that made the figures appear natural, not a police line-up of mug shots, but rather a social occasion where all the participants are portrayed as equals.

Painting discount-priced portraits was not likely to fetch enough income to support an artist and his family, so it was in 17th century Holland for the first time in history that we find the invention of the speculative market in art. Up until now, and still in other countries in Europe at this time, art was the luxury of the rich who commissioned paintings and statues for their estate, or the Church … whatever. In Holland, if an artist wanted to feed his family, sooner or later he figured out that nobody was going to become his sugar-daddy patron. He was obliged to go out and buy the paints and canvas out of his own pocket money, produce paintings then hope that after-the-fact someone might come along who both wanted to buy the painting and also had the money to do so. Speculative market art had to be modest in size both to keep the artist's investment small as well as to keep the sale price low enough to appeal to middle class people. It also had to represent a benign subject with broad appeal that would not offend anybody and that didn't require a buyer to be educated. The types of subjects that were popular elsewhere failed to meet these criteria. History painting wasn't popular because all history was perceived as Catholic and therefore bad. Mythology was even worse; not only was it popular in Catholic countries, it was pagan and nasty with naked people and other disgusting displays. Religious art was clearly a Catholic tradition, so not only did they not want to produce any more of it, they whitewashed what was already there out of the churches. Hmmm … what else is there? The answer is: *landscape*, which is nice to look at and incapable of offending anybody, *still life* (bowls of fruit, that sort of thing), and *genre*, which are scenes of everyday life.

Frans Hals was a portrait artist, a man who paints people, so to supplement his income, he turned to painting imaginary people in the form of genre for the speculative market. **Malle Babbe** might initially look a little like a portrait because it is a picture of a single sitter, but don't be fooled. The brushwork is loose, and the woman is hardly portrayed in a flattering way! She is depicted as an old crone, possibly drunk as she cackles over her stein of swill. She has an owl perched on her shoulder – a joke of sorts as owls are usually associated with being smart, but this gal looks a few cards short of a full deck. **The Merrymakers of Shrovetide** and **Jonker Ramp and His Sweetheart** are perhaps even more typical examples of Dutch genre painting by Frans Hals. A quick glance at the Merrymakers tells us these are not portraits because the colors are so much brighter. The reason for the brighter palette in many genre pictures is to attract passers by to the shop window where the painting would be for sale. What do we see in these scenes? There seems to be a group of men hanging out with a woman in the first, and a jovial couple three sheets to the wind in the second. They all appear to be drunk, probably in a tavern. The men are all flirting with the girl in Merrymakers in hopes that she might offer up some extra "fun" for the night. Jonker Ramp seems to have already hooked up with his cutie and they both look primed for a good time.

Excuse me, did we say genre was a scene from every day life? Do you suppose many Calvinists lived their lives this way – chasing drunk girls in bars in hopes of finding more than pleasant conversation??? Does this sound like the image of people who envision themselves as Elect, according to Predestination? No on all counts. And yet, paintings like this sold like hotcakes in Holland (otherwise Hals would have painted something else), while you would not have been able to sell a picture like this outside Holland in the 17th century even if you offered it at a Wal-Mart price. Ironically, the best-selling subjects in Holland included depictions of hookers, drunks, drug addicts and gamblers. It seems that people enjoyed these paintings because it clarified for them in a comfortable way, what "the Damned" look like. Unfortunately, Predestination or not, people in Holland were pretty much the same as people from anyplace else and not so different from you or me either. They weren't perfect. And yet every week the preacher reminded them that God leads the lives of the Elect toward strong faith and proper behavior. God is in charge. Everyone wants to believe he is on the shortlist of people selected for heaven, whether we're looking at Dutch people from hundreds of years ago or regular people living today. Most people are not looking forward to being served up extra crispy in hell. The problem is when you find yourself looking around and everyone else seems especially holy while you ponder what a crummy job you seem to personally be doing at living up to the ideals of being Elect. It was easy to feel insecure, to wonder if just maybe you weren't as Elect as you had hoped. And there wasn't a thing you could do about it. Paintings like <u>The Merrymakers of Shrovetide</u> and <u>Jonker Ramp and His Sweetheart</u> made ordinary people who may have felt insecure about their own salvation feel more confident that they were better than others who were far more sinful, and therefore probably they were among the Elect rather than hopelessly damned in spite of their imperfect lives.

Judith Leyster

Judith Leyster was a contemporary of Frans Hals during the early 17th century, working as an artist in the same city of Haarlem. Unlike the strict rules governing women in the arts elsewhere in Europe, in Holland women occasionally studied art as apprentices and became professional painters. Judith Leyster was the most accomplished of these. She apprenticed under Hals, and painted with a similar hand. Unlike Gentileschi who was building her career in Italy at exactly the same time, Leyster happily married a fellow student from Hals' studio, and eventually motherhood dampened her career. Nevertheless, during the years she painted she met with some critical success, so much so that Frans Hals became jealous and tried to steal a couple of Leyster's own apprentices at one point, and claim them as his own pupils. Leyster took Hals to court (basically she sued him!), and she won; he had to pay damages and publicly set the record straight.

Her **<u>Self-Portrait</u>** is a personal piece, but it illustrates the artist as a successful and happy individual. **<u>The Proposition</u>** is an example of a genre painting by Leyster. The theme is much like the <u>Merrymakers of Shrovetide</u> and <u>Jonker Ramp and His Sweetheart</u>, but notice how different the mood seems. Hals places his emphasis on the woman as the lusty object of the men's attentions. She looks like she enjoys being a lady of the evening. Leyster presents her woman as trying to ignore the improper advances of her insensitive suitor. She attempts to maintain her virtue, sewing quietly as if to hope that the boor pestering her will give up and leave her alone. One could make an amusing case here about how differently men and women might view the same situation. While the men are feeling pretty good about themselves, all the more after several drinks out with the boys, and flattering their egos about how much the women probably desire their company, the women are rolling their eyes and wishing Romeo would take a hike! Leyster's genre scenes tend to be more modest and less overt than most of Hals' pictures, yet both painters enjoyed good sales so there was a market for both varieties of genre scenes.

Rembrandt

Rembrandt is far better known today than Frans Hals and Judith Leyster, and yet despite being the most famous Dutch Baroque painter, he was not all that typical of the period in many ways. He was born to a comfortably middle class Calvinist family in the city of Leiden, but moved to Amsterdam to establish his career and shortly thereafter married the fashionable Saskia van Uylenburgh. His bride came from a wealthy family by Dutch standards. Saskia's parents worried about her marrying a painter, despite the fact that Rembrandt enjoyed early success as a portrait painter and was making a respectable living, and so they set up the newlyweds with a monthly financial stipend to cover their basic needs. This meant that unlike almost every other painter in Holland, Rembrandt didn't *need* to sell his paintings to keep a roof over their heads and food on the table.

Rembrandt had the luxury of painting what he liked, including loads of portraits of himself and his pretty wife just for fun. His **Self-Portrait as a Young Man** illustrates what a dashing young gentleman he was in the cosmopolitan environment of Holland's largest city. He may have been a practicing Calvinist, but Rembrandt hardly looks the dour role compared to most other portraits of the period. He also took great pleasure in painting images of himself and his wife playing characters from the Bible, or mythology, or even as the popular genre scene of a drunk making time with a prostitute, as we see in his **Self-portrait with Saskia**. Rembrandt certainly never intended for others to view this painting or others like it; they were private. In fact he kept them put away. Instead of decorating their home with his paintings, Rembrandt and Saskia hung costumes on the wall like tapestries instead. The latter scene captures Rembrandt's painting style, especially from his early career. He preferred an earth-tone palette and painterly technique.

Rembrandt was a popular portrait painter in Amsterdam during his early career, and most of his images of Dutch Calvinist patrons look similar to those painted by his rival, Hals. Not all of Rembrandt's portraits fit the mold, though. Consider his portraits of **The Polish Noble** and **The Jewish Philosopher**. Obviously these men are NOT standard issue Dutch Calvinists, yet both were residents of Amsterdam. Ethnic minorities were not well received in early 17th century Holland. People who were different were viewed with a certain amount of suspicion. Could they be among the Elect? It did seem unlikely, given that these East Europeans were either Jews or Catholics. Better to let them keep to their own kind. Most painters in Holland would not do business with ethnic minorities because it might reflect badly on them by extension, which could in turn have a negative impact on business. Rembrandt didn't especially care what people thought; he had the luxury of a private income … so what if someone got huffy and took their business elsewhere? It was worth the risk to him because he found these ethnic minorities fascinating. They dressed differently (always a plus for Rembrandt) and they had interesting stories to share. Rembrandt accepted commissions from Jews and Catholics, and on occasion he even asked for the privilege of painting an interesting face without pay.

Note as you look at these portraits that in addition to an earth tone palette and painterly technique, both typical of Rembrandt, we find very strong chiaroscuro. One could get the impression that Rembrandt had studied Caravaggio, but of course, no Dutch Calvinist painters were traveling to Rome to study the latest in Counter Reformation propaganda! Where did he get this Caravaggio influence? Rembrandt picked up the Caravaggio technique of strong chiaroscuro from a small school of painters working in the town of Utrecht, not far from Amsterdam. These painters, who happened to be Catholic themselves, deeply admired Caravaggio and copied his style as a sort of quiet tribute to the great master of the Counter Reformation.

Like Hals, Rembrandt was in high demand to paint pictures of groups. **The Anatomy Lesson of Dr. Tulp**, for example, illustrates a medical class at the local university. Unlike Hals who needed to produce his work as quickly as possible in order to pay the bills, Rembrandt with his private income had the luxury of spending more time with his patrons. His group portraits usually show more attention to portraying who the people were, as well as what they looked like. As the century progressed and more money was available in the thriving economy, one might imagine that the group portrait would become obsolete. After all, if more people could afford individual portraits, why economize? The Dutch group portrait remained an institution because it represented to the people a "republic" kind of mentality – a collective group effort that we are all working together. This sense of egalitarian camaraderie went hand in hand with an anti-authority attitude again in contrast to what they perceived as a Catholic mind-set of submission to the authority of the Church or the authority of a monarch ... none of that in Holland!

Rembrandt prided himself on painting not only what people looked like, but also who they were and what they were doing having a group portrait made together. Toward that goal, we have his much larger than usual group portrait called the **Night Watch**. The subject is theoretically a civic militia, rather like a National Guard unit. What Rembrandt has painted, however, is not so much a collage of individual portraits but rather an action scene depicting the men in a parade, complete with excited by-standers. Rembrandt fully expected this to be his greatest work. Unfortunately it was not well received at all; in fact, several of the men refused to pay their portion of the commission price. The patrons were offended because instead of fulfilling the terms of the commission, which was to paint the faces of the men in this group, the artist seemed more interested in "doing his own thing." The negative response to this painting snowballed into a tapering off of commissions as people reconsidered taking their business to Rembrandt lest he might produce a similarly unsatisfactory product for them as well. To make matters even worse, in the same year as Rembrandt painted the Night Watch, his beloved Saskia died. Rembrandt was left with a sickly son to raise, a public relations problem in his career, and a greatly reduced income given that Saskia's family scaled back his allowance now that their daughter had passed on.

For the first time in his life, Rembrandt had to work for a living, and for the first time in his life, he was not a sought after portrait artist. This left him with the speculative market, and he soon realized that he could not take that sort of pressure and be a single parent of a sick child too. Rembrandt hired a housekeeper named Hendrickje, who cared for his son, Titus … and in due course she became Rembrandt's mistress and gave birth to a daughter, Cornelia, by the artist. You can imagine the flurry of unpopular attention this created! Rembrandt was now the victim of uncharitable gossip with people speculating on whether he might even be Damned … oh my! If the locals didn't offer commissions after the <u>Night Watch</u>, they were reluctant to even buy his genre scenes and landscapes after Cornelia was born. Rembrandt was nearly destitute. He felt like he was between a rock and a hard place as the saying goes. If he didn't marry Hendrickje, his career was doomed because in Calvinist Holland he would be blackballed as an undesirable, immoral man. But if he did marry her, he would lose whatever pittance came in from Saskia's family since there was a clause in her will that cut him off if he ever remarried, and he couldn't guarantee that even if he did the right thing and got married, that society would be forgiving and bring him any business again.

So … since nothing much was selling anyway, he painted what he liked. He painted religion – a subject barely seen in 17th century Holland. In his **Bathsheba** he used Hendrickje as a model for the Old Testament paramour of King David who went on to become the mother of Solomon. Bathsheba was a happily married young woman whose life was swell, until one day David spied her in her bath and summoned her to join the ranks of concubines in his court. Like Rembrandt, Bathsheba had to accept that her happy life as she knew it was over. Rembrandt shows Bathsheba after she has read David's letter, and she has come to understand that no matter what she does, she can never have her old life back again. In contrast to this, see Rubens' version of **Bathsheba** painted about 20 years earlier. In Rubens' painting, Bathsheba has not yet read the sad tidings, so she remains blissfully unaware that anything tragic is about to happen. Rubens was not interested in moralizing; he was interested in finding an excuse to paint a voluptuous naked bimbo, and Bathsheba fit the bill. While Rubens would have had a wealthy client salivating for his expensive painting of Bathsheba, Rembrandt most likely did not. That said, many of his religious paintings WERE purchased (albeit not many were actually commissioned). The Jews and Catholics living in Amsterdam, those invisible ethnic minorities living on the fringe of society as social outcasts, bought them. They remembered that Rembrandt, the dashing young artist in his day had been their friend when few others would risk such associations. It was these East Europeans who supported Rembrandt, however modestly, in his old age.

Perhaps the greatest of these late paintings in Rembrandt's career is his **Return of the Prodigal Son**. It is a large painting for Dutch art – on par with the <u>Night Watch,</u> both of which could cover an entire wall in a stately home. The scene depicts a father welcoming home his younger son who has made a mess of his life and now is deeply sorry for his behavior. The prodigal son requested his inheritance early, then squandered it all on wine, women and song. After being reduced to a poor, starving swineherd, he determined to swallow his pride and return home to ask his father if he might become a servant at his childhood home where at least he would be given enough to eat. To his surprise, his father does not condemn him, but forgives him and celebrates his son's return with a feast. Ironically, this theme would have been a perfect choice for a Counter

Reformation painter (conversion, repentance, acceptance and forgiveness), but it is not a subject we would normally associate with Calvinist influenced art in Holland. Many scholars see this work as Rembrandt's reflections on his own life, and a hope that there would also be redemption for an old man who had likewise fallen from grace, but who placed his hope in a merciful Father. A final **Self Portrait as an Old Man** shows Rembrandt a broken, tired man, all but forgotten by the time he departed this world.

Pieter Saenredam

There has been a thread developed here between Hals and Rembrandt that the Calvinist Church determined much of the social as well as religious thinking in Holland during the 17th century, and Catholic anything was enough of a taboo that it could throw a damper in your ability to make a living and be accepted as a good citizen and good person around town. Hals was a Calvinist who played it straight, stuck with his own kind and made a good living. Rembrandt was a Calvinist with enough money in the beginning that he sometimes took chances with his reputation by associating with non-Protestant minorities. He got away with it for awhile, but once he made a mistake in his own personal conduct, it was easy for his Calvinist friends to look the other way while his career faltered. Although Holland became increasingly tolerant as time went on, to where nowadays it is one of the most permissive countries in the world, clearly this was not always the case.

The paintings of Pieter Saenredam serve as reminders of just how seriously the Calvinist community took their intentions to eradicate Catholic influences from their society. Saenredam was a loner, a hunchback who kept to himself, and his paintings are marvelous architectural perspectives of church interiors. He worked in Haarlem, the same city Hals called home, during the latter part of the 17th century. His **Interior of the Choir at Saint Bavo's Church** shows in great detail the Calvinist renovation of the lovely old Gothic cathedral in the heart of the city. Notice that all the art so typically seen inside churches of that era has been removed, right down to whitewashing the walls so no evidence of Christian art remains. There are no paintings, no statues, and not even stained glass windows. The dramatic change in the appearance of the church interiors in Holland was similar in many ways to the whitewashing and removal of Christian images in the Hagia Sophia when it changed hands from being a Byzantine Church to become an Islamic mosque. Catholic churches that were converted to Protestant use in Holland were uniformly given this level of "spring cleaning." It's interesting that while the Catholic Church was obviously not welcome in Holland, there were in fact still pockets of Catholics living there who continued to practice their faith. They were obliged to create secret churches to avoid problems with the authorities. One such church, called the Amstelkring can still be visited in Amsterdam today where is has been maintained as a museum. It is on the top floor of a private house built along one of the many canals. Visitors must slip in behind the walls through a secret passage on the lower level to locate the staircase that leads up to the small chapel, complete with altar and art just like churches from the past.

Jan (Johannes) Vermeer

Painting at the same time as Saenredam, but just a little to the south of Haarlem in the city of Delft was Jan Vermeer. Vermeer is perhaps the most gifted genre painter to come from Holland during the 17th century. Unlike Hals and Rembrandt, Vermeer did not produce commissioned portraits, instead painting all his work for the speculative market. He hailed from the city of Delft in the south of Holland, and all his customers were local. As a middle class man with a large family, Vermeer was unable to support himself, his wife and their children on the money he made painting, so he ran a modest art gallery to market his own pictures as well as paintings by other artists, and he was an innkeeper also. In the end, Vermeer painted fewer than 40 pictures, but they are highly regarded as among the best from Holland in the 17th century. **The Kitchen Maid** and **The Woman with a Water Jug** are typical of Vermeer's style. Unlike Hals, Vermeer took no interest in portraying drunks in bars. Vermeer was quietly Catholic – a convert in fact - in a Calvinist world; perhaps scenes devised to distinguish Elect people from the Damned did not appeal to him. Vermeer painted simple scenes, very small pictures of quiet people going about their ordinary lives. His style, like Saenredam, was linear, which was rare in Holland, and he preferred primary colors to earth tone (also rare), usually opting for understatement in his colors, composition and subjects. Most of his genre scenes follow a simple formula on composition. One or two figures are set in a simple Dutch interior room, with a window off to the left to provide a light source for the painting. His rooms often contain detailed still life set on a table; Vermeer was a personal friend of the scientist Anton van Leeuwenhoek (in fact Vermeer was the executor of Leeuwenhoek's estate when he died), and Leeuwenhoek's research with microscopes, which he invented, influenced Vermeer to look at objects in nature with a detailed eye.

The Little Street shows another side of Vermeer, where he took the idea of genre outdoors. Again we find the same quiet atmosphere and clear, even light. Perhaps best of all, we get a glimpse of real life as it must have been during a bygone era with real people (not imaginary, and not royalty either) going about the business of daily life.

Jacob van Ruisdael

The Dutch artist Jacob van Ruisdael was a landscape painter from Haarlem, though painting late in the century as opposed to early on like Hals and Leyster. Consider the pair of landscapes, both entitled **View of Haarlem**. Dutch landscape painting was unique in the world at this time. First, artists painted real locations instead of idealized composites. The actual paintings were executed in a studio setting (the idea of painting on location would not be invented for another 200 years), but they were made from a single, extremely detailed sketch with the intent that the finished painting would be almost photographically real if compared to the actual site depicted. Secondly, there is no superimposed additional subject matter to dress up the landscape and try to make it more than what it is. The Dutch thought their country was beautiful just the way it is, and it didn't need anything else to make it more presentable. The title of the painting will generally reveal exactly the location of the scene depicted.

Other characteristics common to most Dutch landscape include a low horizon, such that the sky fills more than half the picture, and a painterly technique employed both to save time and also to make the scene appear more fresh and natural. These two paintings were obviously done from a single sketch, with just enough minor changes introduced to make each picture unique, but not so different that a buyer might not hike out to the hills at Overdeen from where you can still almost duplicate this exact view with the Haarlem city skyline, which hasn't changed much, and Saint Bavo's looming above everything else in the center of town. The details make the picture a perfect copy of nature. Dutch artists, or at least this particular Dutch artist, evidently figured out that using one sketch for two or more finished paintings saves time, and therefore offers a higher financial return per painting than if the artist had felt obliged to do two different drawings to gain material for two finished paintings. It is testimony to the entrepreneurial nature of the 17th century Dutch to be sure, while at the same time it sets the stage for artists in the future who will undertake a series of paintings of a single subject, if not so much to make more money, to develop techniques on style.

Another picture by Ruisdael is his **Windmill at Wijk.** The Dutch love of painting outdoor scenes extended beyond conventional land-based imagery (houses, trees, streams and so forth) to include the sea. The Dutch reclaimed much of their land from the sea, in no small part by employing those famous windmills to generate power for such ambitious projects, and in Holland one is never far away from open water. The idea of painting the sea was novel at the time, but the Dutch were no strangers to artistic experimentation.

Aelbert Cuyp and Aert van der Neer

The Mass at Dordrecht by Aelbert Cuyp and **Fishing by Moonlight** by Aert van der Neer are wonderful examples of 17th century Dutch seascapes. During the 17th century, in addition to building a strong fishing industry they developed their Dutch East India Company to promote international maritime trade. The sea contributed substantially to the increasing wealth of this tiny nation, and the Dutch were justifiably proud of their maritime fleets. Like landscapes produced in Holland, there is usually an emphasis on "big sky" full of blustery clouds. Cuyp in particular seems to have studied art influences from outside his region, in addition to simply observing the comings and goings of boats from the harbor of his hometown, Dordrecht. His lighting and choice of golden colors on the water are reminiscent of paintings by Claude Lorraine. While Cuyp had probably never ventured down to Rome to see what the French master was producing in his studio, evidently some of those Catholic painters from Utrecht did. Not only did they return with influences in their work from Caravaggio (all that dramatic chiaroscuro), they also imported ideas about landscape from Claude Lorraine that in turn found their way to some of the great Dutch maritime paintings of this generation.

Dutch art of the 17th century is in many ways new and innovative compared to all that preceded it. With their antagonistic attitude toward Catholic Europe there was a push to invent new subjects that were not being produced elsewhere. Likewise, given the lack of official patronage in Holland at that time – no Church and no ruling family or wealthy upper class - the Dutch were the first to invent the notion of the speculative market where artists painted whether they had a patron or not. Dutch Baroque art is not necessarily better or worse than the art created in other regions at this time, but it *is* unique. Also for better or worse, the introduction of the speculative market in art will gradually grow as time goes on, increasing the distance between an artist's creativity and the public he may or may not hope to please.

18. Baroque Architecture and Rococo

c. 1600 – 1700 (all Baroque)

Baroque and Rococo architecture will complete the cycle of simple-to-complex once again, as we have seen consistently in the West. During the Renaissance, the elaborate styles of Gothic reverted back to simplicity; Bramante's <u>Tempietto</u> is the most pure example. As the Renaissance progressed and especially now as we move into Baroque and Rococo, look for architecture to become increasingly elaborate and complex once again.

Italian Baroque

Carlo Maderno

Carlo Maderno picked up where Renaissance architects left off on designing **Saint Peter's Cathedral**. He started his career as a stonemason, but entered and won a contest to become the chief architect on the Saint Peter's project under the direction of Pope Paul V. Maderno wished to complete the church according to the designs of Bramante and Michelangelo, but alas, the pope had other ideas. The problem with the original Greek Cross plan for the new church was that it failed to cover all the ground that had been originally consecrated for the church back in the 4th century; in essence, the new church was smaller than the original old church and that just didn't seem right.

And so, what started as a Greek Cross design was extended into a massive basilica by adding a nave and narthex to the original plan. The interior worked fine, but sadly the façade proved problematic for Maderno, as no matter how he approached the problem, from street level the new façade obstructed any possible view of Michelangelo's magnificent dome. Maderno elected to treat the new façade in a classical manner, as if to emulate the Pantheon, which also disguised the interior design by attaching a classical portico to a domed building. Even that clever idea was thwarted however because of how Saint Peter's is used. It is customary for the pope to greet the faithful congregated in Saint Peter's Square in front of the church from the balcony, but if a traditional classical portico had been applied to the design, the pope would have been visually obscured in shadow behind the freestanding peristyle porch fronting the building. Maderno was obliged to compromise by using engaged (attached) columns on an otherwise flush façade so the pope could be seen when he appeared on the balcony.

Finally, in order to offer some design interest to the exterior, Maderno planned to bracket the classical façade with two *campaniles*, or bell towers. This way the church would have a design that at least recalled other basilicas as seen from the square when the dome could not be seen. Unfortunately, he did not live to see these completed. His successor on the project, Bernini, was later commissioned to build the bell towers, only by the time he got the project, the towers had been enlarged and made more elaborate. One was built, but proved to be too heavy for the foundations so it was dismantled and the campanile part of the project was permanently tabled.

Gian Lorenzo Bernini

Bernini completed numerous contributions to the interior of Saint Peter's as we have seen. He also was responsible for the design of **Saint Peter's Square**. The objective of the piazza was to provide a gigantic open space where the faithful could gather in huge numbers to see and hear the pope give his blessing, either from the church or from his adjacent Vatican apartment. The challenge was to bring order and continuity to this humungous open space, to make it feel like it was a connected part of Saint Peter's without detracting from the church itself since, as colossal as the church is, the piazza is much larger. The square was already enclosed by the surrounding buildings, but without definition or continuity of design connecting it to the church. Bernini created the effect of massive arms reaching out from the Mother Church to embrace her children. The "arms" are covered colonnades employing Tuscan columns, a very plain Roman variation on the simple Doric style, so as not to visually compete with the more ornate columns employed on Maderno's church façade. There is an ancient Egyptian obelisk in the center of the great ellipse. The obelisk was brought to Rome as booty by Caligula in the 1st century AD, originally to decorate his circus where chariot races were held. It was moved to the square in front of Saint Peter's in the 16th century leaving Bernini with a centerpiece for his piazza, perhaps not of his choosing, but it was a master feat to move the obelisk to Saint Peter's in the first place, so why attempt to remove it now? Carlo Maderno had created a granite fountain off to one side of the obelisk, and Bernini added another flanking the other side to balance the design.

French Baroque (part 1)

Jules Hardouin-Mansart

Jules Hardouin-Mansart came to architecture through family connections. His grandfather was a famous architect who had enjoyed royal patronage in his day, and it was under Gramps that Jules apprenticed and learned the trade. He went on to become court architect to King Louis XIV and was one of the most famous architects in all of France. Mansart designed a church for a military veteran's hospital in Paris that may well be one of the best examples of architecture inspired by the original designs for Saint Peter's Cathedral in Rome. Mansart's church, today called **Les Invalides** has long been more of a museum than a church; in fact, it is the final resting place of Napoleon who lies in state beneath the grand dome.

Les Invalides was designed as a Greek Cross in the spirit of Michelangelo's contribution to Saint Peter's. The plan was simplified some and contained inside a square format, with an oversized dome dominating both the interior and exterior presentation. The façade was also modeled somewhat after Saint Peter's, only the vertical thrust of the building soaring up to the very tall, sleek dome is emphasized by creating a double classical portico, stacking one story on top of the other. Notice that Mansart employed double columns, an idea he borrowed from Michelangelo as a tribute to the great Renaissance genius. The dome itself was directly inspired by Michelangelo's masterpiece for Saint Peter's, only here a spectator standing before the building can see the dome clearly since the view is not blocked by a nave jutting out in front as happened at Saint Peter's.

The dome was and is something of a spectacle. From the outside it looks like a graceful, tall and slender version of Michelangelo's, but inside it is clever and complicated, creating an interesting illusion unlike the more simple design in Rome. The dome is actually three domes in one, with each one rising taller than the shell beneath it. The innermost and lowest interior dome rises up above Napoleon's tomb, but stops short of spanning the entire central space, ending instead is a wide *oculus*, or opening which allows folks to see up into dome number two above. That dome is lavishly painted with a scene of Saint Louis, patron saint of France, rising up into the clouds toward heaven. What is especially intriguing is that during daylight hours this magical scene is "miraculously" lit from below, making the image appear to be floating up to heaven. In reality, it is lit by windows cut into the two outer domes at their base, but obscured from view by the inner dome which does not share the windows. Finally, the outermost dome is the tallest by a substantial margin, but this is for our appreciation from outside the building, since it isn't possible to see up into that top dome from inside Les Invalides.

English Baroque

Sir Christopher Wren

Christopher Wren was a Professor of Astronomy at Oxford University when most of London burned to the ground in 1666. Although not primarily trained as an architect, he had an interest in building and wound up influencing the design of almost every church rebuilt in London during his lifetime following the Great Fire. Among these was his most famous and greatest church, **Saint Paul's Cathedral**. Saint Paul's was built at the same time as Les Invalides toward the end of the century, and both architects were heavily inspired by the architecture of Saint Peter's Cathedral in Rome. Like Mansart, Wren designed his Saint Paul's in a Greek Cross plan topped with a large dome. He constructed an enormous model to present his design, and the king was duly impressed and ready to build. Unfortunately, before giving his okay to proceed, the king submitted the design to the Anglican clergy for their approval, and the clergy balked at having a church that so clearly recalled the Catholic design of Saint Peter's Cathedral. They insisted that English churches had always been basilicas with very long naves, and as far as they were concerned, Wren's Greek Cross smacked of too much Catholic influence, even though traditionally the Greek Cross was a medieval Byzantine style, not Catholic (Catholic churches in Italy were customarily basilicas just the same as in England during the Middle Ages, but never mind this little detail getting in the way of the Church of England's objections to Saint Paul's).

In the end, just as Maderno had been required to do earlier in the century, Wren was obliged to amend his plan by adding a gigantic nave to his initial design, which as it had done in Rome, obscured the view of his beautiful dome from the street. Wren's dome, by the way, was tall like Michelangelo's and Mansart's, but the basic design harkened back more to Bramante's Tempietto more than it did to Michelangelo's dome at Saint Peter's. On the exterior it is simpler than either the dome at Saint Peter's or Les Invalides. Saint Paul's offers up a simple ring of single columns seemingly supporting a circular entablature and dome topped by a handsome lantern. The dome is a triple shell construction remarkably similar to Les Invalides, except without the painted illusion on the second inner dome. The façade shows two stacked stories of classically inspired design, more like Les Invalides than Saint Peter's, but unlike either of the other two, Wren finally added the pair of bell towers flanking the façade that Maderno had desired but never achieved on Saint Peter's.

Dutch and Flemish Baroque

Lieven de Key

All too often scholars pay great attention to church architecture from the Middle Ages through Renaissance and Baroque, and they patronize the designs seen in Italy and France especially, and to a lesser degree England also. Holland and Flanders are sometimes overlooked, which is a pity as this region produced some spectacular architecture during the Renaissance and Baroque period as well. Lieven de Key was born in Ghent and trained as a stonemason. He pursued his career abroad in England before returning to the Low Countries to accept a position as town architect in Haarlem, Holland, around the same time as Frans Hals would have been a prominent painter in that city. The **Meat Hall** in Haarlem is an excellent example of Key's work. It is a secular building, and not a gigantic one at that. The plan is a simple rectangle with a steeply pitched roof and stepped gable. In fact, the basic building is not unlike what we have seen in the Town Hall in Nijmegen built a century earlier. But look at how elaborately ornate the Meat Hall is by comparison! Key was a stonemason at heart and many of his buildings are embellished with beautiful stone carving. In this case the sculpted stonework is held to a minimum, but see the creative way he has employed simple brick to produce patterns and texture, adding a festive character to an otherwise unremarkable building.

[Assorted anonymous Architects]

The **Guild Houses in the Grande Place** in Brussels, Belgium (Flanders) are collectively one of the most elegant and impressive examples of secular architecture from all of Europe, not just the Netherlandish regions. Guild houses were like community centers associated with each guild or professional society in the city. They were normally built in the city square flanking the Town Hall, creating a commercial focus to the downtown area… not unlike financial districts in modern cities today. Compare the Guild Houses in the Grande Place to guild houses built in Brugge during the Renaissance.

Now remember that Brugge was stinkin' rich during the Renaissance, and yet, see how modest the guild houses were. During the Middle Ages when so many colossal cathedrals (and abbeys and pilgrimage churches) were built, religious architecture tended to dominate the skylines of cities and towns across Europe. During the Renaissance these churches continued to be respected as the Grandes Dames of their cities and towns. In some cases the grandest of the cathedrals were still under construction in the early Renaissance, and in other cases, beautiful new churches were commissioned.

During the 17th century we begin to see a shift in society, first in the north, especially in Protestant regions, and as time goes on, everywhere. Where the Catholic church had once been the most revered building in town – a sacred sanctuary the people were willing to support with whatever financial resources they had, gradually secular monuments to industry and trade crept in as the architecture masterpieces of a new generation. You see it first in the low countries: Holland and then Dutch influenced regions of Flanders. It is easy to understand that in places where the Catholic Church as an institution had fallen from favor that the citizens might not wish to glorify Catholic Church architecture. But they did not replace it with a grand Protestant Church building campaign so much as shift the focus over to expensive, ornate architecture that glorified man's achievements instead.

These palatial tributes to a flourishing economy sprouted up almost entirely over the span of a single decade – the 1690's – with each guild trying to outdo the others by impressing one another with the most expensive, fanciest and most pretentious displays of wealth and success. Collectively they dwarf many medieval churches in terms of their scale and elaborate display of what money can buy, and no medieval church sprang up out of nothing as fast as the architecture dedicated to secular prosperity.

Jacob van Campen

The **Mauritshuis** is a popular museum in the Hague nowadays, but it was originally designed as a small in-town palace for a popular general in Holland, Johan Maurits van Nassau, who in later life went on to become the Governor of Brazil. In any event, the general was a patron of the arts and he hired the fashionable architect of his day, Jacob van Campen to design a modest estate home for him. Jacob van Campen was a bit of a dilettante, dabbling in painting and sculpture as well as architecture. The **Mauritshuis** is a classical departure from typical Dutch stepped gable architecture, with its temple-like pediment perched above a modest entablature. Some have argued that van Campen's design recalls the work of Palladio. This is seemingly reinforced by the fact that the building has interesting elevations from all four sides, like Palladio's Villa Rotunda for example. The problem is there is no clear evidence that van Campen traveled to Italy to see Palladio's architecture. More likely he was familiar with architecture by Mansart from France. Mansart was certainly conversant with Italian design, but his work shows a certain classical restraint that would be appealing to the Dutch. Also, while Mansart was a Catholic architect working for a Catholic court, this isn't quite the same as being an Italian architect, who from the vantage point of a 17th century Dutch artisan would be perceived as not just Catholic, but directly tied to the pope himself somehow since he lived and worked in Italy.

French Baroque (part 2)

Louis LeVau (*architect*)
Charles LeBrun (*interior design and plaster work*)
Andre LeNotre (*landscape architect*)

Louis XIV ascended to the throne as a child after his father died, with his mother serving as regent until he came of age to rule. Assorted government ministers were expected to do their part to keep the country running during this time, and in charge of the treasury was his finance minister, Nicolas Fouquet. Fouquet used his position to accumulate considerable wealth (and not always through honest means), and he hired France's best design team to create for himself a grand country estate that would rival the likes of chateaux built during the days of King Francis I. The design team of LeVau, LeBrun and LeNotre created **Vaux-le-Vicomte**. Fouquet was understandably proud of his magnificent new estate, and to celebrate, he invited the young king and his mother along with an entourage of the rich and influential to spend a holiday at his elegant new mansion. No expense was spared to show his guests a good time.

Jules Hardouin-Mansart (*architect*)
Louis LeVau (*architect*)
Charles LeBrun (*interior design and plaster work*)
Andre LeNotre (*landscape architect*)

The young king was impressed alright... so much so that he observed that his underling was apparently living better than the king himself! Not wishing to be bested by an employee, the king arrested Fouquet, charged him with embezzlement, and threw him in prison. The king them confiscated <u>Vaux-le-Vicomte</u>, and set about hiring the same architecture team to design an even bigger house for himself. That would be the **Palace at Versailles,** built by the same three designers Fouquet had used, and adding in Louis' favorite, Jules Hardouin-Mansart to the architcture team also.

Versailles is enormous – a virtual city unto itself. And *why* did it need to be so colossal? Louis XIV was a clever fellow, and he determined early in his career as monarch that the best way to maintain absolute control over his nation was to maintain absolute control over anybody and everybody who had any shred of a possibility of wielding any influence counter to what the king wanted. And so it came to pass that the king "invited" all the rich and powerful people in France to come and live with him at the royal palace. This was an invitation that could not be refused, although Louis put a good face on the matter. The deal was these wealthy aristocrats and nobles were not allowed to work, on the argument that it freed jobs for the people who needed the money to support their families. Of course the real reason the king didn't want these people working away from <u>Versailles</u> was that he didn't want to offer them opportunities to influence rank and file citizens. They stayed home at the palace and partied with the king, while tax dollars supported the royal lifestyle. Children were not permitted at court, so the youngsters were shuttled off to the countryside to be raised by nannies until they were a presentable age to be introduced at court. The upper classes had no choice but to endure this life of imposed luxury and leisure, although most made the best of it. Meanwhile you might imagine that ordinary French citizens would resent picking up the tab for the richest among them to be indolent, but the king ran a rather tidy public relations campaign that kept criticism at bay. For one there was the issue of pulling out the richest citizens from the work force to open possibilities for others to get ahead. Besides that, Louis excelled at giving the people the illusion that he was accessible in a way that far exceeded your average ruler.

Versailles was much more open to the public than you might imagine, especially if you compare it to the situation we find in our own country where secret service personnel are everywhere and the White House is well guarded around the clock to keep out intruders. At Versailles for example, the king had a public audience every day for his official "*lever*" (getting up in the morning) and "*coucher*" (going to bed at night). The **Galerie des Glaces** is a great hall of windows and mirrors at Versailles where the public would congregate outside the king's bedroom to participate in these events. At the appointed times the bedroom chamber doors would be opened and Joe Lunchbucket would be ushered in to greet the king decked out in his pajamas and robe. In the morning, the king may have been awake for hours, but he would crawl back into bed to be "awakened" by an attendant to greet his public. Then at night, he would be tucked in before a crowd of admirers, but once they were gone, he might get up and play cards or read or gather with close friends as late as he pleased. The result was that average people frequently had an opportunity at some point in their lifetime to actually meet the king in an informal way, at his private home (if you can think of the palace as much of a private home). It gave people a feeling that the king was somehow approachable, perhaps the way you or I might feel if we got to meet a movie star we admired and s/he pulled up a chair beside the pool at some glorious Beverly Hills mansion and spoke to us for a few minutes as if we were important. It was a personal touch that smoothed over problems and made the public more forgiving than they would have been had the king been more remote.

French Rococo

c. 1715 – 1790

Germain Boffrand and Francois Cuvillies

After Louis XIV died in 1715, there was an immense sigh of relief among the upper crust of society that the baby-sitter was gone, and they could now enjoy the freedom that had been denied them during the Sun King's reign. Louis had been an absolute monarch, and he had maintained his authority over the aristocracy by controlling every aspect of their lives. Life at Versailles was splendid to be sure, but while Louis may have been happy living a fishbowl kind of lifestyle, most people preferred a little more privacy. Louis XV was a mere boy when Louis XIV died. In fact, Louis XIV was the new king's Great Granddad (!!!). Louis XIV outlived his own son, "Le Grand

Dauphin" who died four years before the king, leaving two sons of his own. The younger grandson, who was the better suited to rule, was also named Louis. He was then destined to succeed Louis XIV, but died a year after his own father of a severe fever at age 29. This left the wee great grandson as next in line. Given that it would be several years before the lad would be old enough to take over the reins of government, an interim government called the *Regency* was established. All the aristocrats immediately evacuated the palace at Versailles and returned to Paris where they chose to live in comfortable "hotels," which were not hotels like we might imagine (a Sheraton or Hilton Hotel) but rather gracious townhouses similar to what you might find in New York City's prestigious Upper East Side. The upper classes saw no reason to go back to work; they had grown lazy and accustomed to being supported by the labor and taxes of the little people. Instead, they spent their days languishing about, pursuing a frivolous lifestyle of intellectual soirees in fashionable parlors, clandestine sexual affairs, and expensive parties of every sort ... usually at taxpayers' expense.

Rococo as a style was first introduced during the Regency as a new interior design, which then expanded to include the building exteriors and the art that went inside these interior rooms as well. Rococo interior design emphasized smaller rooms than the grand ballrooms we might find at <u>Versailles</u>. Rococo interiors were scaled for a smaller home, and the rooms were more appropriate for quiet gatherings of a few friends rather than hosting an international symposium on global issues. Soft, pastel colors were preferred to garish bold color, with plenty of fancy gold trim on the moldings which in themselves tended to be ornate to the point of frou frou. Whenever possible lots of windows were employed to emphasize natural light and mirrors were commonly used to increase the bright, airy feeling inside. Rooms were often oval in shape rather than rectangular, and designers enjoyed including wall and ceiling paintings that were framed by intricate molding often undulating in and out in scallops; in fact, Rococo design was initially inspired by seashells, and you can often find shell-like shapes being incorporated into the interior design. Two excellent examples of Rococo interior design are the **Salon de la Princess** at the Hotel de Soubise in Paris, designed by Germain Boffrand, and the **Hall of Mirrors at the Amalienburg** in Munich designed by Francois Cuvillies.

When Louis XIV died, the influence of Poussiniste taste in painting died in France along with him. Rococo painting was created to compliment the new styles in interior design. It is first of all a rejection of Poussiniste art because the aristocracy was fed up with anything that recalled their days living under Louis XIV. The obvious choice was to pursue a style of painting opposite of Poussiniste ... Rococo art is the invasion of Rubenisme into the French Royal Academy and French Royal Salon.

Antoine Watteau

Pilgrimage to Cythera is a good example of the sort of painting that appealed to the Regency, and later to Louis XV during his reign as king. The artist, Antoine Watteau was originally from Flanders, which enhanced the authenticity of Rubeniste influence; after all, he was painting in the tradition of his own countryman. Although a large painting as compared to the modest works seen in Protestant art (art scaled for middle class homes), Rococo paintings like the <u>Pilgrimage to Cythera</u> were smaller than the colossal masterpieces commissioned for palaces and castles during the previous century.

They had to fit the lavish drawing rooms of Parisian townhouses, but not ballrooms at Versailles. Pilgrimage to Cythera is an example of a *fete galante* painting. These were romantic, fantasy genre scenes depicting elegant, aristocratic ladies and gentlemen in dreamy outdoor settings. Usually there is an underlying theme of illicit love; here for example men and women are paired up having sailed away to an imaginary island of love to spend an afternoon escaping the drudgery of daily life (not that the patrons had much of an idea of what drudgery might be like) with a romantic tryst ... or two or three ... so many lovers, so little time ... . All the people are dressed to the nines in expensive clothes; all are young, beautiful, and completely vapid. The stars of fetes galantes are insubstantial as heroes in art. Gone are the "great" paintings with subjects larger than life. Rococo paintings are facile, frilly lightweights in the grand tradition of art history. Clearly they were designed to appeal to the emotional wasteland of an idle rich class. They are painterly, featuring a palette of primary colors softened to pearly pastels.

Francois Boucher

Watteau may have been the man of the hour who established the new Rococo style during the Regency, but it was Francois Boucher who became the darling at the court of Louis XV once he took control of the government and moved back to Versailles. Louis XV was not the powerhouse ruler that his Great Grandpa had been, but he tried to maintain the same sort of royal court where the upper crust all hung out at Versailles and did the party scene, while the average Joe working out in the real world was supposed to be content with his lot in life and happy to pay the extravagant bills of the ruling class.

By nature this Louis was a more private man, perhaps a bit more insecure. He was married young to an available princess of some obscurity, Marie of Poland whose family was pleasantly surprised at the opportunity given that she was already getting a bit long in the tooth in her 20s to find a proper match, and Louis was still a teenager. All evidence is that the marriage started happily enough, but over the years their romance settled into a lifeless union. Was it the king's wandering eye that cooled his wife's enthusiasm for his company, or was it her withdrawal into her own world to avoid the social frenzy of Versailles that led to the king's infidelities? Either way, the king established a revolving door of young beauties (he preferred adolescent virgins) for his physical gratification. Ironically perhaps, although the king was known for his succession of bimbos in and out of the palace, his favorite paramour was not so much a teenage tramp as his equal in many ways. Madame de Pompadour was a bourgeois lady, married with a young daughter when she came to the king's attention. They remained an item for many years, although in the end she seems to have become more of a confidante and advisor, as their physical affair subsided to where she selected the little lovelies invited to sleep over in the king's bed.

It was also **Madame de Pompadour** who chose the court artist, Francois Boucher. This is one of his many portraits of her. As a Prix de Rome winner and an artist of some respect, Boucher was invited to paint portraits of all the who's who ladies of station who were in and out of Versailles. This isn't what got him the job, however. It was his pictures of nudie butt bimbos that made his reputation. There are dozens of paintings of young naked girls, some of them actually identified as real sex-playmates from the king's collection of dime-a-dozen quick scores. Not that the king really cared; it wasn't as if he invested any interest in the girls anyway beyond a one-night stand. **Girl Reclining** is a classic example. We actually know the name of this little sweetie; that's Louise O'Murphy (it apparently wasn't enough to work his way through all the young French beauties; Louis XV also sampled girls from abroad, many of whom it seems were eager to have a romp with a king to see what it was like). Girl Reclining was painted in 1751 … and the following year Boucher painted an encore "portrait" (if not so much of her face, perhaps her behind?) of Louise. This one is called **Resting Girl**. Evidently keeping company with the king was an exhausting pastime if Louise now had to rest … Now you'd think that old King Louis would have his fill of this pose, but apparently not since the following year again Boucher was obliged to paint **Odalisque**. This time though it's not Miss O'Murphy. Although it's not known for certain exactly who posed for this picture, a few critics suggested that the model resembled Boucher's wife, whom the artist did use on occasion in genre scenes a little less racy than this picture. The painting created quite a stir, and subjected Boucher to a measure of public criticism. The moral philosopher Diderot chastised Boucher for prostituting even his own wife to provide lascivious pleasure for the king.

Sometimes the paintings masquerade as mythology, although in reality nobody was fooled. There was never any interest in trying to introduce the slightest intellectual content to these; they were about as serious an art form as Playboy centerfolds are serious photography. The **Triumph of Venus** is about as cultured as these pictures get. The subject is the same as Poussin's Triumph of Poseidon and Amphitrite earlier in French art, and the colors are not unrelated. Boucher's has no reference to classical models, but substitutes intellectual references for sexy poses and a general frolic of cuties that is closer to a group bubble bath perhaps than a victory scene. The composition is casual, off-center and deemphasized, with lots of diagonal lines to make it exciting like Rubens might have done. Most of Boucher's paintings were pastel images of cuddly-soft young girls, completely nude and usually in a tantalizing, evocative pose, as often as not outdoors, and presumably just waiting to be ravished.

Jean-Honore Fragonard

Fragonard was a second-generation Rococo painter as he was almost thirty years younger than Boucher and had in fact briefly studied under the Court Artist to the King. Boucher later sent him over to study with Chardin (stay tuned, more on him later). As a young artist, Fragonard was attracted to noble religious themes in art, but he succumbed to the demand from Louis XV and his entourage to paint licentious romantic subjects that sold well to those with the money to buy art. **The Swing** illustrates a fashionably dressed young lady being pushed on a swing in a lush garden. Presumably that is her husband or at least her boyfriend in the shadows who is accommodating her pleasure by pushing her higher on the swing. All the while she is slyly flirting with another gentleman who is sneaking a peek up her dress while he hides in the bushes. See how she kicks off her shoe in his direction, by "accident" no doubt. **The Reader** shows another side of Fragonard. While The Swing looks back to the old fete galante style of the Watteau, The Reader is a quiet genre scene closer to what the artist's second teacher, Chardin would approve.

Jean-Baptiste-Simeon Chardin

The majority of Rococo period painting was in the vein of Watteau's and Fragonard's frilly flirtations or Boucher's plush pornography, but there is one rather stunning exception in French painting at this time, so much of an exception in fact that it is almost hard to group this painter in with the Rococo period at all. That artist was Chardin. Chardin painted genre and still life – real genre of middle class people with middle class values and ordinary everyday food and objects found around a country kitchen. Both of these subjects were not widely seen in France, although neither subject category was new; up in Holland they had been popular for some time. **The Silver Tureen** is reminiscent of the sort of painting pursued by many Dutch artists in the 17th century when Protestants were eager to find an artistic heritage apart from traditional Catholic themes. In sober earth-tone colors the artist has presented us with dinner; the wild game on the kitchen counter sits next to the tureen that will probably contain the tasty stew at supper time, while the family cat seems unsure whether that rabbit and bird are really dead or ready to bolt away giving kitty something to chase. **House of Cards** is a simple genre scene of a young boy amusing himself with a game. The composition is similar to Fragonard's <u>Reader,</u> showing Chardin's influence on his student. Chardin's paintings do not feature frolicking nudes; they are quiet snippets of how middle class people lived and as such, they emphasize the cultural and moral disparity between the French aristocracy and ordinary working people in France at the same passage in history.

His picture, **Prayer before the Meal** emphasizes the difference between the classes even more. It depicts a mother with her daughters, not fancy people in fashionable clothing and not even as well-to-do as our young friend playing with his cards. These are peasant folk, salt of the earth working class people asking the blessing before a humble meal. Chardin wasn't a big name painter during his own day, although he did enjoy some patronage and acclaim for his work. His scenes allow us to see behind the glitz, glamour and gutter morals of the upper class. Increasingly in France there was a gulf between the average man in the street and those who ruled over him. Kings had no concept of managing wisely. They bankrupted France while concerning themselves with their personal excesses. Meanwhile average people were working hard, and living simple lives that in many cases were still grounded in family values, faith and morals. It was only a matter of time until these parallel worlds collided.

England *(still Rococo more or less)*

William Hogarth

The height of the Rococo style was French, and it bled over into Germany in architecture in particular, but England also produced painters who dabbled on the fringes of the Rococo style or in some cases, poked fun at Rococo themes. William Hogarth fell into the latter camp. Hogarth was a satirist who produced several series paintings and engravings that mocked the lapsed morals of the upper classes. His most famous is *Marriage a la Mode*. The six paintings (which in turn served as models for later engravings on the same subject) trace the folly of an arranged marriage for money.

The story begins with **Scene 1: The Marriage Contract**.   The Earl Squander is arranging a marriage for his daughter to a rich merchant's son. He doesn't care that his daughter doesn't love her fiancé; all pops is concerned about is that his daughter marry into money. One lawyer presents the marriage contract to the Earl, with his family tree trailing onto the floor, and the merchant who wears his glasses so he can check out all the financial details in the agreement. Another lawyer tries to soft pedal the arranged marriage to the bride-to-be, while her brother and heir to the Earl's estate has nothing better to do than admire himself in a mirror.

The story moves on to **Scene 2: Early in the Marriage**. The husband and wife have evidently both been out partying, although not together. He's hung over and slumped in a chair, while his wife is looking quite pleased with herself, presumably no thanks to her husband. She stretches, legs spread as well, and looks upon her husband as a fool. The marriage is already in trouble, and to make matters worse, their lawyer is fed up because the couple isn't paying their bills. From there things go downhill further. Husband and wife both engage in affairs. The husband gets venereal disease and doesn't know which of his girlfriends is to blame. Meanwhile he comes home early one night and catches his wife in bed with her lover. A dual follows and the husband is fatally wounded. In last scene the wife, now destitute and alone commits suicide and her elderly father the Earl's first concern is to salvage her wedding ring because that's all there is left worth any money.

Hogarth's paintings may be tongue and cheek amusing, but his indictment of the aristocracy of the 18th century is unmistakable. His art was critical of the casual morals of society's wealthiest class, but he was equally hard on the working class and their affection for liquor. **Beer Street** illustrates Hogarth's recommended party beverage choice. Everyone is having a good time, but nobody is drunk out of their minds and folks who have work to do are still getting their jobs done. The moral of the story is that it's possible to drink and still live a productive, happy life … so long as you stick to beer rather than hard liquor. Compare that message to **Gin Lane**, where a nursing mother is so pie-eyed that she drops her baby over a railing. The man sitting next to the drunk mother is starving because he'd rather drink than eat; meanwhile in the background people pick fights with one another and some poor soul has hung himself on his balcony. Hogarth used his art as a vehicle for social commentary, an idea that would become more common in the future. But most of his peers during the English Rococo period were more conventional in their choice of subjects.

Thomas Gainsborough

Most English artists the 18th century were more preoccupied with portraits and landscape than they were political satire. Thomas Gainsborough is one of the best examples. The son of a teacher from Suffolk, by age fourteen Thomas was allowed to leave home to go study art in London. Although he trained as an engraver (working for awhile under Hogarth in fact), and while he enjoyed painting landscape best of all, Gainsborough is best remembered for his portraits. He was inspired by Van Dyck's portraits of British nobility done a century earlier, and he frequently had his subjects situated in a landscape setting just as Van Dyck had done. **The Blue Boy**, so often reproduced nowadays, was most likely a portrait of Jonathan Buttal, a wealthy hardware merchant's son. The story is that Gainsborough did the painting not so much as a grand commission, but more on a wager that he could use the color blue successfully as a central color in a portrait.

More typical of the artist's career is his portrait of **Mrs. Richard Brinsley Sheridan**. Like Boucher, Gainsborough attracted commissions from all the elegant ladies in high society. Having now settled in Bath, England, which was rapidly becoming the up-and-coming place for fashionable people to live or at least visit on holiday, Gainsborough enjoyed a steady stream of social climbing lovely women who were eager to have their portraits painted. Mrs. Sheridan sits outdoors in a landscape that recalls Van Dyck's work, but it is also not unlike the romantic breezy settings for Watteau's or Fragonard's imaginary beautiful people. Eighteenth century portraits are less formal than typical Baroque fare. Like Madame de Pompadour by Boucher, Mrs. Sheridan sits off-center within the picture frame, her body is relaxed and there is an attempt to make the viewer feel as though we just happened upon these ladies by accident as opposed to seeing sitters posing for the artist like their 17th century counterparts. Gainsborough preferred a pastel palette like most Rococo painters in France, and he likewise employed a feathery light painterly technique.

In 1768 England launched its new Royal Academy of Art to compete with the French institution across the English Channel. Their objective was to encourage English artists to study the great masters from the past and to promote fine art in Britain. Classical art did not have a longstanding tradition in Britain, while Van Dyck and the Rubeniste painting style did, so painters like Gainsborough were promoting the established British ideal.   The opposite was true of France. By the final quarter of the 18th century the French drifted back to their love of Poussiniste formal order and images of intellectual substance.   But the door had been opened in France for artists to experiment with new ideas, and during the 19th century, war would be waged in the halls of the Academy and Salon between the loyal followers of Poussin, and devotees of Rubens' more expressive style of painting.

19. Neoclassicism

c. 1775 - 1850 (painting)
c. 1725 – 1850 (architecture)

Neoclassicism is the stylistic and cultural link between the past generations of great Renaissance and Baroque masters, and the future modern world. It is at once both the past and future. Everything about Neoclassicism is tied to change: changes in government, changes in attitudes toward religion, and social changes as well.

France

David

Louis XV died in 1774, which set the stage for change in France. Neither he nor his successor, Louis XVI was a charismatic leader capable of ruling France as Louis XIV had done during the previous century. Louis XVI and his wife, Marie Antoinette, were vain and self-indulgent to a fault, which led the country to near bankruptcy while taxes spiraled out of control. Jacques Louis David, a young artist originally trained in the studio of Boucher in the Rococo style, saw an opportunity to capitalize on the king's vanity for his own personal gain. Like many young, ambitious artists, David desired to win the Prix de Rome. He cleverly decided to buck the current trend in art by producing a painting employing the old Salon style of Poussin, explaining with his entry how much he admired the king and how Louis XVI deserved a more weighty, important style of painting like the great "Sun King," Louis XIV. The king was flattered, and David won the Prix de Rome.

On his departure for Rome, David received a commission from the king himself to create a noble history painting for the crown in this new *Neoclassical* style, classical art like Poussin's revisited after three quarters of a century of Rubeniste "foreign" style painting in France. The picture was to be completed while David was away on his scholarship in Italy. David obliged with his **Oath of the Horatii**. The painting tells a story from Roman history in which two families assume the responsibility of settling a feud between their two cities, by having three sons from each family fight to the death to determine victory (or defeat) for their hometowns. The scene depicts the Horatii father distributing arms to his sons, who are to battle the Curatii boys. The women off to one side do not appear to be pleased with the prospects of the impending fight, and we learn that one of the sisters is engaged to marry one of the Curatii boys. In the end, the Horatii won the day, but when the victor returned, he was annoyed to discover his sister weeping for her lost fiancé, so he murdered her too. Everything about the painting reiterates Poussiniste philosophy in painting; it is linear with an emphasis on composition and the subject is adequately obscure that it requires knowledge from a reasonably sound classical education to be appreciated and understood.

The painting was exhibited in the Royal Salon of 1785, and given all the laurels one might expect for a royal commission. As it happened, the painting offered particular appeal to French citizens who advocated revolution, and it was adopted as a call to arms for those who were fed up with the monarchy and wanted to overthrow the government. In all likelihood, these ideas did not reflect David's initial intentions; he would have been a fool to paint a deliberately revolutionary painting, which might offend his patron, the king, and land him in jail (if he was lucky) as a result. Just the same, David was a shrewd man, and throughout his career he excelled at second-guessing history and landing himself on the right side of the government du jour at this time of great political instability in France. He determined, correctly, that if Louis XVI and Marie Antoinette were pitted against a nation of hungry and angry citizens, the forces of revolution would prevail. Thus, he maneuvered his position to where he publicly stated his support for the revolution when it was convenient to do so, and slid from his position in line to become court artist to the king, to becoming court artist to the revolution instead.

The Death of Marat is an excellent example of David's official paintings for the French Revolution. Dr. Marat was in charge of masterminding the underground communication network for the Revolution, which in no small part contributed to their success against the royal government. None of King Louis XVI's supporters could figure out how the revolutionaries were getting their information past barricades in the city. Of course, they were running their messages through the city sewers. Dr. Marat had developed a serious skin affliction, which was exacerbated by his new career in the sewers, so when he worked in his office, he did so from a medicated bath in which he could soak while he kept up with correspondences. A Counter-Revolutionary named Charlotte Corday discovered the location of his office, and determined she would risk sacrificing herself in order to assassinate Marat. She presented herself as a Revolution supporter who had special information for Marat's eyes only, and gained admittance to his office. Once inside, she stabbed him. David was called in before the body was moved to do preliminary sketches for a tribute painting to memorialize Dr. Marat. David chose to play down the blood and gore, which may have indirectly paid the greater homage to Charlotte and her victory over Marat. Instead, he reduced the colors altogether and tinkered with his composition to make a statement about Marat the martyr, more than Marat the victim. Poussiniste artists frequently look to the past, especially to sculpture for inspiration. David's pose for Marat was lifted unmistakably from Michelangelo's famous Pieta. By asking us to make this parallel, David is also asking us to view Marat and his legacy as being of the same moral fiber and profound significance as the life and legacy of Jesus ... pretty high praise indeed!

David was a master at looking out for number one. Not only did he manage to wiggle from being a wannabe court artist for the king into the good graces of the Revolution, he repeated this feat of political chamelionship again when Napoleon challenged and then toppled the government of the Revolution. When others lost their heads to the guillotine or found themselves in exile, David found himself serving as the first court artist to Napoleon. His elegant, full-length **Portrait of Napoleon** is one of the most famous images surviving of the emperor.

Needless to say, an artist like David with such skillful abilities in both painting and politics would be a custom fit for the Royal Academy and Royal Salon. It was David who turned the art world of France away from Rococo to a revitalized appreciation of their original love, Poussiniste art, in the form of the new official style, Neoclassicism. David's work is very similar to Poussin's painting. It was his star pupil's art, Jean-

Auguste-Dominique Ingres who nurtured Neoclassicism into a mature period of painting that surpassed 17th century thinking and style.

Ingres

Ingres was a child prodigy, an accomplished painter and musician (violin) by the age of 13, and he was consumed with love for his Neoclassical heritage through David back to Poussin and back further still to Raphael. He was an intellectual man, one content to match his hours in the studio with hours of study. Ingres was more inclined than David to push the envelope when it came to intellectualizing his art, and a particularly good example of this is his early painting, the **Grande Odalisque**. It was produced in 1814 as a Salon piece. One might mistakenly believe that such an exotic subject as a harem girl might smack of Rubeniste sensuality, and at some margin this might be true, but in fact reclining nudes were a staple item at Neoclassical Salons as they had an established tradition dating back centuries by this time. Even so, when this particular nude was exhibited, it caused an uproar. Critics were alarmed that the woman in the painting appeared to have three vertebrae too many. They lamented how such a gifted young artist could make such a stupid mistake. Look closer. That elongated back isn't all that is amiss with this young lady! Her left leg isn't attached to her body - it hovers in space above, and if it were attached, it would be growing out of her navel and be several inches longer than her right leg. Best of all perhaps is the woman's breast, which miraculously defies the laws of gravity and floats up under her armpit. What is going on here?

Ingres pointed out that all the Neoclassical artists showing at the Salon paid lip service to being intellectually detached and placing the lion's share of their energy into composition. When they actually put brush to canvas, though, they were loyal to their ideology for inanimate objects like buildings and even elements of landscape, but the human body was somehow sacred and could not be rearranged to suit composition. In the Grande Odalisque, Ingres treated the human form with impersonal detachment. It is a composition of lines, shapes and forms, no more, no less, with some parts beings stretched or rearranged to suit the artist's design. Additionally, Ingres noted that while Neoclassicists were keen to say how much composition should outweigh color, they continued to employ the same bright primary colors seen in Rubeniste painting. Ingres reduced his palette by eliminating bright colors and warm colors, opting for a palette emphasizing blues, beiges, golds and white. In the end, Ingres was more Poussiniste than Poussin himself!

Ingres quickly rose to prominence and became the leader at the Royal Academy and the yardstick by which artists were measured at the Royal Salon. He taught his students to "draw lines, lines and more lines," always emphasizing the importance of excellence in composition above all else in the best art. Despite his great success, he was not an especially happy man. He would have appreciated being independently wealthy, but alas, although he certainly lived well, he had to work for a living and sometimes this meant accepting commissions he did not enjoy. Ingres is famous for his many portraits of society's upper crust women. The ladies flocked to Ingres for his accomplished paintings that flattered with subtle finesse. Unfortunately, Ingres always felt these paintings were a compromise on his talent, perhaps in the same way Michelangelo held the much admired Sistine Chapel in disdain because he thought himself a superior sculptor to painter.

Ingres managed to remain true to his interest in composition, even in his portraits. The **Comtesse d'Haussonville** is a good example of just how subtle his compositional nuances can be. A lovely young lady dressed in blue stands before a mirror, which is situated at an oblique angle to the picture plane. It seems so simple, until we notice that the mirror reflection has been shifted ever so slightly to the right, allowing us to see more of her hair in the reflection. A portrait done about a decade later of **Madame Moitissier** illustrates the artist furthering this concept of playing with mirrors in his composition. (Note that Madame is wearing a dress with *red* flowers ... one might envision the heartburn this caused Ingres as it would seriously conflict with his philosophical disposition!) The model now sits directly in front of a mirror, in which her reflection should be completely obscured by her head and body. But no! Her reflection has been shifted off to the right, *then* the artist twisted her head sideways to view a profile of her face and hair, *then* he *cropped* the image, which is to say he sliced part of it off, the way photographs sometimes do by accident. Artists working 30 years later during the infancy of photography will begin to manipulate composition in this fashion, but in the case of Ingres, we have a child prodigy artist who remained a gifted genius of composition - decades ahead of his time - and well into his old age.

England

Although the dates 1775-1850 appropriately cover Neoclassical influence in art, Neoclassical style drifted into architecture decades before it appeared in painting. At the beginning of the 18th century, you will recall that Louis XIV died in France, and the aristocracy escaped from Versailles to Paris. The insubstantial, fluffy Rococo style was born in the fashionable drawing rooms of elegant Parisian townhouses during the Regency. The upper classes were tired of the old Baroque style, and their new love was a lighthearted, whimsical art and architecture that reflected their own vacuous lifestyle.

Curiously, at the same time as this artistic upheaval in France, a similar change in taste occurred in England, and for the same reasons although the outcome was quite different. King George I came to the throne in 1714 and with his new reign came a general discontent with the old Baroque style of his predecessor. In England, though, the frilly Rococo style never appealed much to the British sensibility, and they moved in the direction of greater restraint. Instead of getting fancier than the already ornate Baroque, they opted to get back to basics with a look to the past for inspiration. In 1715 a Scotsman named Colen Campbell published a book called *Vitruvius Britannicus* that reintroduced the architecture of the Italian Renaissance and in particular, the book created a revival of interest in Palladio.

Richard Boyle

Richard Boyle, third Earl of Burlington was an amateur architect who was deeply inspired by Campbell's book. As we have seen with others in the past in England, this amateur saw no reason to locate a professional architect when he desired a new addition to his estate in the form of a guest house where he could accommodate a few visitors, but mostly where he could host receptions and entertain. **Chiswick House** was built in 1725, adjacent to Boyle's estate home (now gone). It was deliberately inspired by Palladio's famous <u>Villa Rotunda</u>. The modest "home" is a large central rotunda- salon where soirees were held, capped by a dome. On either side of this large, central room there were two suites of apartments where guests might stay over while visiting Lord Burlington.

Although obviously similar to <u>Villa Rotunda</u>, <u>Chiswick House</u> has some modest adjustments designed either to accommodate its setting, or to improve upon the original design. For one, <u>Villa Rotunda</u> was perched overlooking lovely vistas from each side of the house. To make the most of this opportunity, Palladio treated each side of the house as its own main entrance with verandas to take advantage of the pleasant views. <u>Chiswick House</u> in contrast did not have fabulous picture postcard scenery out every window, so the architect settled for one primary entrance and the other three sides of the building are de-emphasized in the design. Also, while <u>Villa Rotunda</u> has a shallow, round dome, Lord Burlington set out to improve on the old design by elevating the dome, which was an octagon rather than round by the way, up onto a drum-base so large windows could be employed to make the interior salon brighter with natural light.

United States of America

Thomas Jefferson

Half a century later, around the same time as Neoclassical design was gradually filtering its way into French art and architecture, America's own Thomas Jefferson likewise was experimenting with Palladian architecture design. Like Richard Boyle, Jefferson was not an architect by training so much as he was an enthusiast who mastered architecture as a sideline to his many other interests and areas of expertise. Jefferson had read Palladio's treatise on architecture written back in 1570, and he was also familiar with <u>Chiswick House</u> near London. He designed his estate home, **Monticello**, with these earlier prototypes in mind. Like <u>Villa Rotunda</u>, <u>Monticello</u> enjoyed fabulous scenery from all four sides so it was designed with multiple verandas to capture the views. Like <u>Chiswick House</u>, <u>Monticello</u> was designed with an octagon dome elevated onto a drum to allow for more windows that the earlier Italian model. It differed from either <u>Villa Rotunda </u>or <u>Chiswick House</u> in that Jefferson actually lived in this home as his full-time residence. Both the other houses were more like grand guest cottages designed for entertaining. At <u>Monticello</u>, a mere round room for parties flanked with minimal living quarters was not likely to make do. <u>Monticello</u> fans out to either side of the central domed building with additional rooms to make the house more comfortable for day to day living. It is also constructed out of locally produced brick rather than stone like <u>Villa Rotunda</u> and <u>Chiswick House.</u>

James Hoban

Most of us are so accustomed to seeing images of the **White House** that we don't even stop to think if it might be architecturally part of some period of design; we almost presume it is a category unto itself. When the nation's first president took office, there was no official capital, much less an elegant residence for the head of state. In the Residence Act of 1790, George Washington was given the honor of selecting the site for the "presidential palace," and together with his Secretary of State, Thomas Jefferson they established what would become the District of Columbia. In 1792 a contest was held to select the architect who would design the presidential palace, and James Hoban, an Irish immigrant to America won. He designed a simple 3-story Palladian-style mansion made of very pale grey sandstone. The corner stone was laid on October 13, 1792. Ironically, George Washington died before the White House was completed, and John Adams was the first president to actually live there.

The War of 1812 followed, and two years into the war, the British set fire to much of the capital, including the White House, which sustained severe damage. James Hoban was called in to help restore the home, and Benjamin Latrobe, who was responsible for much of the design of the neighboring Capitol, assisted. It was apparently Latrobe's idea to add attractive Neoclassical porticos to both the front entrance and to the south lawn entrance, although Hoban was ultimately responsible for seeing the project through to completion.

William Thornton
Benjamin Latrobe
Charles Bullfinch
Thomas Walter

The design and building of the **US Capitol** was a more complicated and involved project than the White House. The story starts off the same as the White House though... George Washington and Thomas Jefferson were brainstorming on how the new "Federal City" should be designed, and as they determined with the White House, a competition seemed to be a reasonable route to choosing the best design. Incidentally, the prize for the contest winner was $500 and a plot of land in the city (same prize Hoban won for the White House). Unfortunately, unlike the White House contest where a winner was easily selected, none of the seventeen entries for the US Capitol pushed any of the right buttons. After the contest was closed, a letter arrived from Dr. William Thornton, a Scottish trained English physician living in the British West Indies, asking if he might submit a design. The commissioners overseeing the contest figured they had nothing to lose letting the doctor send in his entry, and it wound up being the design Washington recommended they accept for the project. The cornerstone for the US Capitol was laid by George Washington himself on September 18, 1793.

Unfortunately Thornton, while well-intended with good ideas, really had little experience with architecture, so assorted professional architects were brought in during construction to aid the good doctor and keep the project moving along. In fact, James Hoban, who was working across the Mall on the <u>White House</u> was called on from time to time to assist with trouble-shooting on the <u>US Capitol</u>; he wound up being responsible for getting enough of the north wing adequately designed and built so the first session of Congress could meet there on November 17, 1800. By 1803 Benjamin Latrobe was onboard as the new lead architect. He was largely responsible for designing the south and north wings. After a decade on the job Latrobe departed, leaving the two wings connected by a temporary wooden passageway.

By then, of course, the War of 1812 was underway, and on August 24, 1814 the British troops burned "Federal City." Like the <u>White House</u>, the <u>Capitol</u> was badly damaged. Some consider it divine providence that on the day the capital was set to blazes, a heavy rainstorm moved through the region dousing much of the fire and preventing the complete destruction of the nation's capital. Latrobe returned to Washington the following year to start repairing the damage on the <u>Capitol</u>. He stayed on two years, both reconstructing what was lost and making changes to the design and to the materials used (he introduced marble to the project). In the end, he got frustrated with delays and rising costs and resigned as chief architect in 1817, and Boston architect Charles Bullfinch was awarded the grand pooh-bah position in charge of the project. Bullfinch designed the Senate and House chambers and the Supreme Court. He also redesigned the central section of the building and added a higher dome than what was previously envisioned.

The <u>Capitol</u> remained primarily the product of Thornton, Latrobe and Bullfinch until 1950. By then the sheer numbers of senators and representatives had outgrown the original facility. Another competition was held (with another $500 prize) for the best plan to expand the building. Although five architects were chosen to work on the design, ultimately Thomas Walter, a Philadelphia architect, was chosen to supervise the whole project and complete the work. Extensions were made to exterior walls, which were then sheathed in marble instead of the original sandstone which had deteriorated badly over time. With the new length of the building more than doubled, the original dome looked too small. The crowning glory was the new dome, designed by Walter and completed by his assistant, Edward Clark. In addition to being bigger, taller and more beautiful than the squat dome it replaced, it was also cast-iron and hence, fireproof. No doubt you can see the design pedigree of domes from the past, from Saint Peter's to Saint Paul's and Les Invalides.

France

Jacques-Germain Soufflot

Having recovered from their sojourn into Rococo style, the French embarked on producing Neoclassical architecture as well. The **Pantheon** was built originally as a church dedicated to Sainte Genevieve, the patron saint of Paris. King Louis XV commissioned the church in thanksgiving for his recovery from an illness, and it stands on the site where an earlier medieval abbey dedicated to the same saint once stood. Like other churches before it, Sainte Genevieve was designed as a Greek Cross plan with an enormous dome at the crossing. This time Bramante's dome design was favored over Michelangelo's. What makes it Neoclassical rather than Baroque like Les Invalides, aside from the dates, is the uncompromised Roman-style classical portico slapped on the entrance. Small wonder it got nicknamed the Pantheon early on. Like the original Pantheon built in Rome by the Emperor Hadrian in the second century AD, the oversized classical façade seen from the street disguises the interior shape and space of the building, plus both are crowned by domes.

It may have started off as a church but it didn't end up that way. The king vowed to build the church in 1744, but it wasn't actually begun until 1758. Apparently once the king recovered his health he felt less pressed to make good on his promise to God to build the church. There were also financial setbacks that contributed to the delay. In the meantime, in 1774 the king died, and in 1780 the architect died, leaving the church incomplete. By the time it was finally finished, Louis XVI was gone also, and the government in France was now the French Revolution. The Revolution had no love of the Catholic Church, in fact no love of religion of any stripe. It promoted a nationalistic agnosticism (I am being generous… some might say the Revolution was downright atheistic). The last thing the Revolution wanted to see was another church, so the government ordered that the building be rededicated from a church to a secular mausoleum for great Frenchmen: a temple to men as opposed to a temple to God.

Twice there have been movements to convert the Pantheon back to a church, but it remains more of a museum to honor dead secular heroes to this day. Among the many notables buried in this modern-day necropolis are Voltaire, Rousseau, Marat, Victor Hugo, Marie Curie, Rene Descartes, Louis Braille, Alexandre Dumas, and Soufflot, the architect. Naploeon, of course is not buried here… he apparently considered it slumming to be laid in state with a crowd and reserved Les Invalides for himself. The fact that Les Invalides was a former military hospital chapel undoubtedly factored into the decision to inter Napoleon, the great military hero, at Les Invalides instead of the Pantheon.

Pierre Vignon

Neoclassical design frequently looked to the Renaissance for inspiration, but occasionally architects took their inspiration directly from antiquity. Consider the Church of **La Madeleine** in Paris, which was commissioned by Napoleon himself. This was another church project that Louis XV envisioned but never got around to building, rather like Sainte Genevieve. La Madeleine was to replace an earlier church that had fallen into disrepair, and the king did manage to get around to laying the cornerstone before he abandoned the project. Then came the Revolution, and they certainly didn't want to see another church built. For years there was debate on whether to turn what little there was constructed into a library or a bank or stock exchange. Anything but a church!

In 1806, Napoleon tore down what there was onsite, and decided to build a Greek temple, or perhaps more correctly a Julio-Claudian style Roman temple heavily influenced by Greek design. It seems his initial idea was to dedicate it to himself and the soldiers of his grand army: a temple of glory (or ego…). With the volley of power that transpired in France at that time, first Napoleon was strong, then King Louis XVIII challenged Napoleon and the two took turns controlling the nation and languishing in exile. The church / temple of <u>La Madeleine</u>, meanwhile, sat unfinished much as the Pantheon had a few years earlier. Finally it was decided that the building should be converted to a church as had been originally planned (Napoleon being somewhat less hostile toward Christianity than the Revolution government), and with the exception of one brief threat years later when it was nearly turned into a train station, it has remained a church ever since.

Photos of the church can be deceiving, in more ways than one. For starters, it is huge. Presumably you can tell that it is bigger than Roman temples, like Temple Fortuna Virilis, but it might surprise you to realize that it is also considerably larger than the Parthenon in Athens. That pediment, by the way, depicts the Last Judgment with Mary Magdalene playing a prominent role given that the church carries her name. The second surprise after its size is the interior. It seems straightforward enough... a Greco-Roman style temple... no hidden rotundas behind a classical façade or any of that design chicanery. But when you walk in the front door expecting to find a gigantic cella with a flat, post and lintel ceiling, instead you find a regular church, albeit a dark one since there are no windows allowing daylight to brighten up the place. Above the long nave there is neither the flat ceiling we might expect, nor a tidy barrel vault which might make sense, but rather a series of three modest domes, each with a cupola designed to function like skylights to offer at least some light to the church interior.

Neoclassicism brings the cycle of development that had been in progress since the Renaissance full term back to a new beginning. Following the extravagant cathedrals of the Gothic time period, Renaissance artists looked to antiquity for a more simple style in both art and architecture. In time, during the late 16th and 17th centuries these ideas were perfected and were erring again on the side of bigger is better, and a little extra complexity just makes it more interesting. Rococo was the last hurrah for fabulously frothy style in this cycle before everyone intuitively sensed that enough is enough and it's time to get back to basics. Neoclassicism marks the conclusion of 18th century art and architecture, and also the dawn of the 19th century which will see many changes in the art world, and a faster pace of change as well.

Unit Five

Toward a Secular Society:

Art in Modern Times

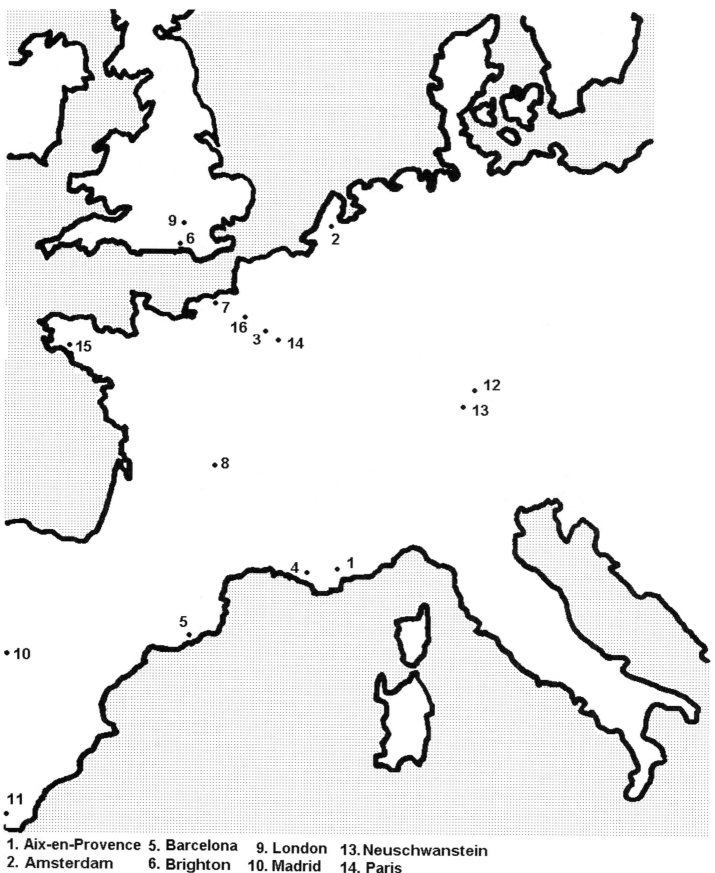

1. Aix-en-Provence
2. Amsterdam
3. Argenteuil
4. Arles
5. Barcelona
6. Brighton
7. Le Havre
8. Limoges
9. London
10. Madrid
11. Malaga
12. Munich
13. Neuschwanstein
14. Paris
15. Pont Aven
16. Rouen

The Modern World

Image List for Unit Five

ROMANTICISM: 1800-1863

> **Francisco Goya** *(Spain)*
> 1. Third of May 1808

> **Theodore Gericault** *(France)*
> 2. Raft of the Medusa

> **Eugene Delacroix** *(France)*
> 3. Massacre at Chios

> **John Constable** *(England)*
> 4. The Haywain

> **John Nash** *(England)*
> 5. Royal Pavilion at Brighton

LATE 19th CENTURY ARCHITECTURE: 1860-1900

> **Sir Charles Barry** *(England)*
> **A. Welby Pugin** *(England)*
> 6. Houses of Parliament, London

> **Ludwig II of Bavaria** *(Germany)*
> 7. Neuschwanstein

> **Richard Morris Hunt** *(USA)*
> **Frederick Law Olmstead** *(USA) gardens*
> 8. Biltmore House

> **Petrus Josephus Hubertus Cuijpers** *(Holland)*
> 9. Rijksmuseum

> **Charles Garnier** *(France)*
> 10. Paris Opera House

> **Louis Sullivan** *(USA)*
> 11. Wainwright Building

REALISM: 1820s-1880s

> **Jean-Francois Millet** *(France)*
> 12. Gleaners

Gustave Courbet *(France)*
    13. Funeral at Ornans

Edouard Manet *(France)*
    14. Dejeuner sur l'Herbe
    15. FYI: Raphael's Judgment of Paris
    16. Olympia

Manet out of sequence

    21. Gare Saint Lazare
    22. Boating (@ Argenteuil)
    23. Boating (detail)
    24. Bar at the Folies Bergere

IMPRESSIONISM: 1863- 1920s

Claude Monet *(France)*
    17. Dejeuner sur l'Herbe
    18. Impression Sunrise
    19. Regatta in Grey Weather
    20. Gare Saint Lazare

Monet out of sequence

    25. Rouen Cathedral
    26. Rouen Cathedral
    27. Haystacks
    28. Haystacks
    29. Water Lilies
    30. Water Lilies

Camille Pissarro *(France)*
    31. Boulevard des Italiens

Monet out of sequence

    32. Boulevard des Capucines

Pierre-Auguste Renoir *(France)*
    33. Le Moulin de la Galette
    34. Detail of Le Moulin de la Galette
    35. Luncheon of the Boating Party

Edgar Degas *(France)*
    36. Spartan Boys and Girls Exercising
    37. The Rehearsal
    38. The Rehearsal

39. Race Horses
40. The Tub

POST-IMPRESSIONISM: 1880-1906

Georges Seurat *(France)*
41. Bathers at Asnieres
42. Sunday Afternoon at the Island of the Grande-Jatte

Paul Cézanne *(France)*
43. The Temptation of Saint Anthony
44. Mont Sainte Victoire
45. Mont Sainte Victoire
46. Mont Sainte Victoire
47. Basket of Apples
48. Bathers

Paul Gauguin *(France)*
49. Breton Village
50. Martinique Landscape
51. Vision After the Sermon: Jacob Wrestling the Angel
52. Shuffenecker Family
53. Nafrea Faaipoipo (When Are You Getting Married?)
54. Te Arii Vahine (Woman With Mangoes)

Vincent van Gogh *(Holland)*
55. Potato Eaters
56. Vegetable Gardens in Montmartre
57. The Harvest at Le Crau
58. View of Arles With Irises

Gauguin out of sequence

59. Landscape at Arles
60. The Night Café

61. The Night Café
62. Starry Night

SYMBOLISM: 1890s

Edvard Munch *(Norway)*
63. The Scream
64. Death of Marat

EXPRESSIONISM: *1900 – WWI*

Wassily Kandinsky *(Russia)*
65. Improvisation # 30

CUBISM: *1907-WWI*

Pablo Picasso *(Spain)*
66. Les Demoiselles d'Avignon
67. Ma Jolie
68. Three Musicians

DADA: *WWI*

Marcel Duchamp *(artist from France, career in USA)*
69. Nude Descending a Staircase
70. Fountain
71. LHOOQ

ASHCAN SCHOOL: *1908-1920's*

Robert Henri *(USA)*
72. Smiling Tom

John Sloan *(USA)*
73. Backyards in Greenwich Village
74. Sun and Wind on the Roof
75. South Beach Bathers

PHOTO-SECESSSION: *1902-1917*

Alfred Stieglitz *(USA)*
76. New York Street
77. The Steerage

GROUP OF SEVEN: *1912-1933*

Tom Thomson *(Canada)*
78. Byng Inlet of Georgian Bay

Arthur Lismer *(born in England; career in Canada)*
79. September Gale

JEH MacDonald *(born in England; career in Canada)*
80. The Falls at the Montreal River

Lawren Harris *(Canada)*
    81. Beaver Swamp
    82. Mountain and Lake

AMERICAN REGIONALISM: *1920's – 1940's*

Grant Wood *(USA)*
    83. American Gothic
    84. Stone City, Iowa

Thomas Hart Benton *(USA)*
    85. Lewis and Clark
    86. FYI - Murals at the Missouri State Capitol

John Steurat Curry *(USA)*
    87. The Baptism

PHOTOGRAPHY BETWEEN THE WARS: *1920's – 1930's*

Ansel Adams *(USA)*
    88. Half Dome

Dorothea Lange *(USA)*
    89. Migrant Mother

MEXICAN MURALISTS: *1920's – 1950's*

Diego Rivera *(Mexico)*
    90. The Arsenal
    91. Man at the Crossroads

Frida Kahlo *(Mexico)*
    92. Broken Column

AMERICAN REALISM: *1920's – 1950's*

Edward Hopper *(USA)*
    93. Chop Suey
    94. Nighthawks
    95. Hotel Lobby
    96. Rooms by the Sea

PRECISIONISM: *1920's – 1930's*

Charles Sheeler *(USA)*
    97. American Landscape

98. Upper Deck

CONCEPTUAL ART: *1960s – present*

Yves Klein *(France)*
Nothing to show!

Joseph Kosuth *(USA)*
99. One and Three Chairs

Douglas Huebler *(USA)*
100. Site Sculpture Project: 42nd Parallel Piece
101. Crocodile Tears: Howard
102. Crocodile Tears: The Great Corrector

ENVIRONMENTAL ART: *1960s – present*

Richard Smithson *(USA)*
103. Spiral Jetty

Andy Goldsworthy *(UK)*
104. Reconstructed Icicle

PUBLIC ART: *Early Examples*

Frederic Auguste Bartholdi & Alexandre Gustave Eiffel *(France)*
105. Statue of Liberty

Gutzon Borglum (and others) *(USA)*
106. Stone Mountain
107. Mount Rushmore

Korczak Ziolkowski *(Poland/USA)*
108. Crazy Horse Memorial

PUBLIC ART: *1960's – present*

Blue Sky *(USA)*
109. Tunnelvision

Claes Oldenburg *(Sweden / USA)*
110. Floor Cake
111. Clothespin
112. Flying Pins

CONCEPTUAL + ENVIRONMENTAL + PUBLIC ART

Christo *(Bulgaria / USA)*
Jeanne-Claude *(France / USA*

20. Romanticism &
19th c Architecture

Romanticism *c. 1800 - 1863*

Romanticism as an art movement appeared across Europe around the turn of the century, and was in part a reaction against Neoclassicism, which had established a following about a quarter century earlier. Since the days of the ancient Greeks we have discussed the concept of cycles of development in Western culture, where we begin with a simple idea, which is developed and perfected over time. Eventually man becomes bored with perfection and what was once a simple idea is made more complicated, fancy, dramatic, or emotional until it reaches its most elaborate expression. Up to this time, these cycles developed in an orderly fashion with one stage leading to the next in time. While it is true that Poussin (classic simplicity) was concurrent with Rubens (baroque complexity), they lived in different regions and did not overlap clientele. With the establishment of the Royal Salon in Paris, and an effort to systematically standardize world taste in art, clearly only one style dominated at a time. Around 1800, for the first time in history, we find that even within the world of the Royal Salon, the cycle in art reduced in time to where the "early" stage, Neoclassicism with its classic simplicity, had not yet run its course before the "late" stage of Romanticism with its baroque complexity was introduced. For the first time, Poussiniste and Rubeniste were competing directly in the same venue.

Goya (Spain)

Romanticism appeared first outside France, and this should not come as a surprise. In France, the Royal Salon at this time was controlled first by David and then by Ingres. Both painters were avid supporters of Poussin's philosophy in art, and since the Royal Salon and Royal Academy functioned like Siamese twins, it was very difficult for anyone affiliated with either one to break with Neoclassical tradition. Outside the pomp of late 18th century Paris, however, artists were more free to experiment so long as their customers were satisfied with the artistic results. One of the earliest painters to produce art in a Romantic vein was Francisco Goya in Spain. His early career was spent working for the king of Spain as a court artist. He painted official portraits of the royal family as well as "light" subjects designed to please aristocratic tastes. This came to an end when Napoleonic forces invaded Spain in 1808. The Spanish people responded with patriotic resistance, and were horrified when, on the third of May, 1808, Napoleon sent his troops into Madrid to round up civilians and systematically shoot them dead in the streets. It was a barbaric atrocity that shocked the people, and certainly made a strong impression on Goya as well. He produced several series of engravings and etchings detailing with the horrors of war, but his grand masterpiece was his painting of

The Third of May 1808.

The painting was actually completed a few years later in 1814, but the memory of the horrible massacre was obviously still fresh for the artist. The scene shows a faceless caterpillar of French soldiers gunning down frightened Spanish victims. We are not invited to see the French army as people at all - no faces are visible - while the Spanish are animated and expressive. It is a moving scene promoting any number of emotions favoring the Spanish plight. It must have attacked raw nerves when it was first shown in its day. There wasn't a family in Spain left unaffected by Napoleon's reign of terror in their land, and Goya made sure the citizens of Spain would not soon forget this infamous day in Spanish history. Toward this end, the artist placed more emphasis on an expressive, painterly technique rather than laboring too much on the composition, and he manipulated the color to draw our attention to his central Spanish victim who assumes a Christ-like pose at his execution.

Goya's painting demonstrates a stronger affinity for Rubeniste philosophy in art than Poussiniste. Was this deliberate? Certainly as court artist to the king, Goya would be familiar with Rubens' paintings. Remember that during Rubens' day, his native Flanders was a northern territory of Spain, and Rubens himself had been no stranger at the royal court in Madrid. Goya knew the art of Rubens, but this does not necessarily mean that paintings like The Third of May 1808 were created as tributes to the great master, Rubens. Goya was motivated by his own emotions and the need to share these feelings with his fellow countrymen. In the end, his art carries on the tradition of Rubens by default. This points up a significant distinction between Neoclassicism and Romanticism. With the former, artists are by nature working in an intellectual manner with an eye toward their artistic pedigree, and it is reasonable to assume that each painter was well aware of those who came before him and to whom he owed his artistic influence. It was different with artists who followed in the line of Rubens. Since the nature of their art is personal and emotional, *sometimes* an individual artist might have been consciously aware of his Rubeniste heritage and be deliberately trying to develop this style. Then again, other painters in this camp were consumed only with their own feelings and inner expression, and they were unaware of how their art fit into the greater scheme of artistic development over time, or they just didn't care.

Gericault (France)

In France, meanwhile, Romanticism got off to a slow start. The year Goya produced his painting The Third of May 1808, coincided with Ingres' production of The Grande Odalisque ... clearly France was not ready for Romanticism just yet. The first artist to broach Salon protocol and exhibit a painting that would be classified as Romanticism was Theodore Gericault. In 1819 he painted **The Raft of the Medusa**, which like Goya's work before him could be described as a current event subject. It was a huge painting, approximately life-sized, recounting a hot story in the news about a shipwreck. The frigate *Medusa* wrecked off the coast of Africa, and the captain and senior officers took the lifeboats for themselves, leaving their passengers to die at sea. When they reached the safety of land, these men concocted a story to make themselves look like martyrs in their unfortunately unsuccessful attempt to save everyone else before saving themselves. What they hadn't bargained on was having any of these passengers survive to tell the truth. Of the 149 passengers who strung together a makeshift raft, only 15 survived the dreadful ordeal, but survive they did. When they returned to France and their story went public, there was an enormous outcry from the public to end government corruption. The ship had been staffed with a captain and senior officers who received their commissions through government favoritism, and it was generally accepted in 20/20 hindsight that it was faulty judgment on the part of these improperly appointed seamen that caused the accident in the first place.

Gericault's painting offered up a Romantic subject, but his approach to producing the painting was systematic and in keeping with Neoclassical sensibilities. For example, he studied dead bodies at the morgue to guarantee that his figures would look correct, if not too upsettingly real; there are no decayed bodies or evidence of cannibalism which would have made the work considerably more shocking. He had the shipwright, who was one of the survivors, reconstruct a replica of the raft so the artist could experiment with how it appeared on the water. In general, Gericault's approach to this emotional theme was more detached and intellectual compared to Goya's work. Perhaps this is why the painting was accepted at the Salon. In any event, it created quite a stir, but was passed over by the state for purchase which was something of a snub for Gericault; he had hoped it would receive higher acclaim than it did.

Delacroix (France)

Gericault's student, Eugene Delacroix would be the man to finally promote Romanticism in France to an equal footing with Neoclassicism. Like Gericault, Delacroix came from an independently wealthy family, which was advantageous for anyone bucking the official system of art in France. Because the Royal Academy and Royal Salon had a stranglehold on the artistic taste of the French, artists who chose to disregard the popular style found they didn't receive many commissions, and their work didn't sell well on the speculative market either. Delacroix was a bit of a dandy, and by disposition disliked the regimented austerity of Neoclassicism. He appreciated the work of Rubens, and made a deliberate point to follow Rubeniste style in direct opposition to Ingres' Poussiniste, classical perfection.

Ingres loathed Delacroix. Gericault had been annoying as well, but at least Gericault had the decency to die young. In contrast, Delacroix outlived Ingres, and remained a poison arrow in his soul for decades. To make matters more unbearable, Delacroix had connections in high places within the government (he was rumored to be the illegitimate son of Tallyrand, an important government official with whom his mother had an extramarital affair and whom the artist physically resembled) and Delacroix managed to obtain commissions, often important commissions, and he was rich already. Meanwhile Ingres had bourgeois roots and found that despite his considerable success in leading the Royal Academy and Royal Salon, he had to stoop to doing portrait commissions in order to maintain an affluent lifestyle. Ingres spent enormous energy maintaining his animosity toward Delacroix. He was known to make a public display of his disapproval whenever Delacroix visited the Academy or Salon, at times to the point of being absurd. On one occasion, he went so far as to turn his back to the loathsome Romantic upstart, and stumble down the steps of the Salon sideways like a crab in order to avoid making eye contact with Delacroix who was coming up the same flight of stairs. Ingres couldn't keep Delacroix from exhibiting at the Salon, although he certainly tried, but he did manage to keep his nemesis blackballed from the faculty at the Royal Academy; Delacroix did not receive a teaching post until after Ingres died.

Delacroix, like Gericault and Goya before him, often selected current event themes charged with emotions to spark his audience response. One such example is **The Massacre at Chios**. The subject is from the Greek war of independence against Turkish rule; this particular battle having caught the attention of the press as the celebrated English poet, Lord Byron, whose work was enormously popular in France, died at Chios fighting for the Greek cause. Delacroix produced a large canvas to immortalize the plight and suffering of the Greeks, all of it painted in full Rubeniste tradition to reinforce the mood of the piece. Normally the Salon was quite prickly about hanging large Romantic scenes, but as always, Delacroix was the singular exception because of his influential friends in the government. He went to the Salon to personally supervise where his masterpiece would be hung (he insisted on the best gallery for important historical paintings). While he was there, he decided to walk among the paintings being hung to see what the competition looked like that year (1824), and it was here that he discovered a painting that would change his technique even further into the realm of Rubeniste style than even Rubens had dreamed of himself.

Constable (England)

Delacroix discovered John Constable. Constable was an English Romantic painter, accordingly not much admired by the French Salon and delegated to a back gallery for unimportant works. England had not suffered through the brunt of Napoleon's ego, and perhaps this is why current event paintings with political overtones did not carry much appeal there. Instead, landscape painting was popular. After all, England was a Protestant country rather like Holland, and simple art devoid of historical baggage felt more comfortable. Constable had made a career of painting scenes of the countryside near his home in just the same manner as Dutch artists had been doing for 200 years. One of these paintings, **The Haywain** had been accepted for the Salon of 1824 as one of those token "foreign" works just to show the world how open minded and accepting the Salon was. Not really of course, but inclusions like this were designed to create that illusion. In The Haywain, Constable had experimented with a new concept coined the *broken brushstroke* technique. Constable had followed the Dutch approach of using painterly brushwork, but increasingly he was dissatisfied that mere visible brushstrokes didn't adequately capture nature. He wanted to show the freshness of leaves after a spring shower, or dew on grass. Mixing a suitable shade of green and dabbing stroke after stroke of the same color was not achieving the level of freshness Constable desired. So he tried something daring. He mixed several shades of a color (green for example), along with white and occasional adjacent colors (blue and yellow would be adjacent to green) and he dabbed on the mish-mash of colors a few strokes at a time, such that when the painting is seen from a distance the colors blend together, but up close it is possible to see flecks of different colors.

Delacroix was beside himself with excitement when he saw Constable's Haywain. Although Constable had created his broken brushstroke without any regard for Rubens whatsoever, to the educated eye of Delacroix, here was an artist who had outdone Rubens at being Rubeniste! If color and texture were important, here was a technique that drew more attention to both than any art of the past had ever done. Delacroix was so impressed that he scurried back to his studio with his own <u>Massacre of Chios</u> in hand, and he hastily repainted the background of the scene in the new broken brushstroke technique. The paint was still wet when it was finally hung for the show in the Royal Salon of that year.

An interesting thing happened when the jury judged the paintings. John Constable received an honorable mention, while Delacroix was so severely chastised that one critic even nicknamed <u>The Massacre at Chios</u> "The Massacre of Painting" because it was so bad. Why? Constable was a foreigner, and therefore nobody expected much of his work so it was permissible to offer him a little award with the same sort of condescending charity that one might compliment a child just learning to play a musical instrument on how wonderful it sounds. Besides, Constable was painting landscape, which had never been a subject category that anyone at the Royal Salon took very seriously. Delacroix was French, and by his birthright should know better than to paint sloppy mush in a painting when everyone else painstakingly kept to a linear technique. Here was the real coupe for the Salon, though, a triumph of French snobbery over Delacroix's independent spirit. Delacroix had insisted that his work be hung in the best gallery for *history* paintings. After all, he didn't want to be a second rate hack artist, and there was no official category for current events because they were so new. The jury at the Salon argued with a certain malice against Delacroix that if he had been willing to admit that his silly current event paintings were nothing more than glorified *genre*, then he could have had his work hung with others (foreigners no doubt) who were not held to the same high standards as the finer French artists.

Delacroix went on through the 1820's, 30's, 40's and 50's to pummel his Romanticist preference into the sensibility of French art until finally, despite the intense opposition of Ingres, it was accepted side by side with Neoclassical work. He was the leader of Romanticism in France and indirectly for the world since the world continued to look to France for artistic leadership.

The Romantic movement in painting died with Delacroix in 1863.

John Nash (England)

At the same time as painters were challenging the prevailing Neoclassical taste of the Royal Salon, there were also designers who were bored with classical buildings and who wanted to see their fantasies expressed larger than life in architecture. **The Royal Pavilion at Brighton** stands alone as perhaps the most Romantic building of its generation. The architect was John Nash, who started his career as a business real estate developer in London. When the market went sour, he turned his talents toward designing one-of-a-kind country estates for those who could afford his services.

One such patron was The Prince of Wales (affectionately or otherwise known as "Prinny"), Prince George IV of England. As so often happens in royal families, the next in line to rule has to cool his heels while his reigning parent lives on… and on and on… with the crown prince finding himself a grown man without a career. He will be king eventually, but in the meantime he has no particular job other than to hang around and wait his turn. So it was with George IV, and he was rather gifted frittering away both his time and the nation's wealth on frivolous pastimes and expensive hobbies. The family indulged his excesses, given that there wasn't much productive he could be doing in the meantime anyway.

It seems that the prince was a bit of a ladies' man, which raised fewer eyebrows than one might imagine in those days, until he managed to go and fall in love. Indiscreet liaisons were to be winked at, but serious love was another matter. Worse yet, the lady in question was a devout Catholic and a few years older than the future king. The woman George adored was Mrs. Maria Fitzherbert, a charming lady who until now had been unlucky in love, having been widowed twice, each time very soon after the wedding. Maria took her faith seriously, and while she was likewise smitten, she refused to enter into an illicit affair with the heir apparent. Good Catholic girls get married, and that was her take it leave it offer to George. The man was in love to be sure, but what is the future king of England to do? The Law of Succession dated back to the days of Henry VIII and the mess he made of things with his revolving door at the altar leaving behind one daughter each of the Catholic and Protestant persuasion. In addition to that law which banned a Catholic from ever ruling, another law had since been imposed called the Royal Marriage Act which forbid a royal from marrying a Catholic. So how did George handle his dilemma? He married his Catholic sweetheart anyway, in a secret ceremony. He was 23 at the time; she was 29.

Well… as you might guess, this didn't sit well with the folks back at the palace in London, which is why George and Maria spent their time away from official royal life in the holiday resort town of Brighton. A modest farm was acquired there, to which John Nash was set to work remodeling and changing until in the end, the farm completely disappeared and the Royal Pavilion at Brighton was created in its stead. There is no other building on the face of the earth quite like it. Scholars at a loss for words to describe the design have developed a broad vocabulary of invented adjectives, although perhaps the most often cited is "Hindoo Gothic," which is amusing given that presumably their point of reference is the Taj Mahal in India as inspiration for the onion domes on the Royal Pavilion, but the Taj Mahal is a Mughal design, Islamic, not remotely Hindu. Oh well…

In any event, George spent a small fortune (actually, a large fortune) making the Royal Pavilion the architecture spectacle of its day. Since he didn't have any real source of income, he incurred colossal debts, further enhanced by his penchant for gambling. In the end, the family won. They struck a deal with George that he needed to separate from Maria and marry a horsey relative (who evidently also had rotten body odor according to George's memoirs – he loathed the woman), Caroline of Brunswick. It was not altogether tidy given that the pope declared that George's marriage to Maria was valid, but the English Royal Family determined that it was an "unapproved marriage," and therefore was null and void. Hmmmm. Maria did go to France for awhile as it all seemed just a wee bit too complicated, and George did his duty as Prince of Wales and managed to produce one child by Caroline (Charlotte, who died young) before pretty well cutting Caroline out of his life. After separating from Caroline, George arranged his affairs so that he left his entire estate to Maria, and while they resumed their relationship, they respected his position in society just enough to refrain from sharing the same home. She was provided with a home in London, and never returned to her husband's beloved estate in Brighton, although their love letters to and fro are now on display at the Royal Pavilion. And it doesn't get much more romantic than that!

Late 19TH century Architecture *c. 1860-1900*

From the 1860's to the end of the century, architecture style was about as close to anything goes as in any period of history. A relatively small number of architects were forward thinking and produced designs that would influence our world of modern skyscraper boxes in the 20th and 21st centuries, but most architects were into "revivals." The deal was you could revive just about anything that had been there and done that, jazz it up a bit and presto, new design that would have the world gawking your way with tongues wagging. This is not meant to denigrate architecture of this period (if only they could have imagined something new and more clever?); not so at all - some of the most glorious buildings of "modern" times were built during this historical window. They may not be as "modern" as glass boxes, but they are spectacular.

Sir Charles Barry (England)
A. Welby Pugin (England)

Charles Barry was the primary architect for the **Houses of Parliament** in London. The old "Palace of Westminster," as the Houses of Parliament were affectionately known by the locals, was completely destroyed by fire in 1834 (London has had more than her fair share of devastating fires). Charles Barry, a distinguished architect of his day, was selected to undertake the task of rebuilding the Palace of Westminster. He may have won the contest… but there was a problem. Barry was a Neoclassical enthusiast, and while he *was* the architect selected, the conditions of the competition dictated the new Houses of Parliament were to be designed in the newly fashionable Neo-Gothic style, as much as anything to flatter and incorporate old Westminster Abbey (which actually *was* Gothic) into the meld of buildings since the old church was next door and was already a famous building in the neighborhood.

Barry didn't feel comfortable stretching his expertise into Gothic design which was pretty foreign to his work, so he teamed up with another architect who served as a "second fiddle" on design, A. Welby Pugin. Pugin functioned as an advisor of sorts since his expertise was Gothic Revival architecture design. In the end, the final product was a blend of Neoclassical and Neo-Gothic… pretty unlikely bedfellows to say the least. The Gothic contribution is easy to spot: all those spikey, sculpted finials poking up, and the tall, English Gothic-looking square towers recall medieval churches. The Neoclassical elements wind up being more subtle. Notice that the buildings are long and horizontal, which is much more typical of Classical architecture than pointy tall Gothic. Also, although individual photographs do not always show this, there was an effort on Barry's part make as much of building as possible symmetrical with *formal balance* (formal balance is where things are even on each side of the building – a column here, one there, a pediment at one end, and a matching one on the other end and so forth). Classical inspired architecture design almost always favors conservative formal balance over more experimental, asymmetrical designs.

Ludwig II of Bavaria with help (Germany)

Neuschwanstein is the ultimate fairy tale castle. It served as the model for every prince and princess castle in Disney animated feature films and also it was also the model for Cinderella's castle at Disneyland and Disney World. It would be easy to presume that such an idyllic, perfect castle perched so precariously in the midst of craggy mountains must surely have been a real place... a real castle built during the Middle Ages as a fortress. How romantic! It's a bit of a disappointment initially to realize that the most perfect "medieval" castle ever built was actually constructed during the late 19th century, but if we can get past pooh poohing its lack of historic authenticity, it still comes out ahead as one remarkable building, even if we would have to create a special category to describe the place (what? Neo-Medieval? Neo-Castle? Neo-Rococo? Perhaps Neo-Romantic... like the Pavilion at Brighton, only done half a century later, it defies a conveniently simple shoebox category).

Neuschwanstein was the brainchild and also the design of King Ludwig II of Bavaria, although he did require professional advice here and there to actually get the place built. Poor old Ludwig. Here he was, ruler of a naturally beautiful kingdom. Then in 1866 Bavaria and her friend, Austria found themselves at war with Prussia. Prussia won. The net result was that Bavaria as a nation lost its independent identity. It was absorbed into Prussia, which a few years later became Germany compliments of Prussian prime minister, Bismarck (Germany was created from a collection of former small states; Bavaria once upon a time was one of the largest of these). Ludwig became a king without a kingdom. His solution was to create his own fantasy kingdom in the form of castles tucked away in the Bavarian Alps, with Neuschwanstein being the crown jewel. As Lugwig (aka "Crazy Ludwig") withdrew more and more from reality, he focused increasing attention on his favorite composer, Richard Wagner. Neuschwanstein's design inspiration was heavily influenced by Wagner's music, with many rooms designed more like elaborate (and expensive and wholly original) stage sets for Wagner's operas rather than regular rooms in a regular home (or even a regular castle).

It is worth mentioning as a postscript to this unique building, that Ludwig's great inspiration, Wagner, had his own unique concept of what an opera should be. Unlike Italian or French operas, where there is a story dealing in general terms with the human condition (love, infidelity and death being favorite themes), and the production is a mix of ballet, arias and duets, Wagner believed that opera should be more like Greek drama. He emphasized mythological legends translated into a German national experience, and made much of this cultural influence on the life, thoughts and emotions of the Germanic people. He was a lot less interested in pleasant musical entertainment than he was in serious drama and hammering home his themes. The nationalistic bent evidently appealed to Ludwig in a profound way, although not everyone found Wagner so enjoyable. One of Mark Twain's amusing anecdotes was that "Wagner's music isn't as bad as it sounds."

Richard Morris Hunt (USA) *architect*
Frederick Law Olmstead (USA) *gardens*

The <u>Houses of Parliament</u> and <u>Neuschwanstein</u> may not appear to have a lot in common, but both are romantic buildings designed to resemble very grand and elaborate architecture from the past. <u>Neuschwanstein</u> may be the most obviously blatant example of this, but even the more staid <u>Houses of Parliament</u>, while being boring old government buildings, manage to look more like a fabulous old castle, or even a castle crossed with a cathedral. Both of these buildings reach all the way back the Middle Ages for design ideas, but others built during the latter 19th century achieved much the same effect by looking back only as far as the Renaissance and Baroque.

A good example of this is the **Biltmore House** built in Asheville, North Carolina. The architect, Richard Morris Hunt has the distinction of being the first American architect to receive his formal education and architecture training at the Ecole des Beaux Arts (Royal Academy) in Paris. His patrons, the Vanderbilt family, could afford the best and they wanted a true American castle / palace / chateau as wonderful as anything built in Europe. Given that Hunt was fresh off the boat from France it was a natural leap of faith for him to borrow heavily from French chateaux, looking to Renaissance examples with some Baroque flair thrown in for good measure. <u>Biltmore House</u>, in keeping with the traditions of old European chateuax, was designed to be completely self-sustaining with everything from farming to orchards to stables to its own winery, much of which is still in place today. The Vanderbilts not only hired the best architect money could buy, they went all out on selecting Frederick Law Olmstead to mastermind the landscape architecture. Olmstead is perhaps best known as the designer of Central Park in New York City.

Petrus Josephus Hubertus Cuijpers (Holland)

For as much as <u>Biltmore House</u> looks like a French chateau built in the late 19th century on American soil, the **Rijksmuseum** designed by Petrus Cuijpers looks a lot like a French chateau in the heart of downtown Amsterdam. The <u>Rijksmuseum</u> houses the national art collection (paintings like Rembrandt's <u>Night Watch</u> are there). The architectural masterpiece was built early in Napoleon's reign, commissioned at his directive by his brother who served as regent in Holland at the time. Napoleon had a very clear vision of a Europe that would be a united empire, and among his priorities was the preservation and enhancement of cultural achievements, including art. Holland at the time had a willy-nilly system of collecting and exhibiting her art treasures. Napoleon wanted a grand, national museum that would both store and display Dutch art properly. Cuijpers was sent to France to study French architecture design, and then encouraged to employ what he had seen in the marvelous chateaux of France combined with indigenous Dutch design featuring steeply pitched roofs.

Charles Garnier (France)

The last two examples were non-French buildings that were clearly inspired by French architecture of an earlier generation. So what was being built at the same time in France? The most spectacular building of this generation is the **Paris Opera House** designed by Charles Garnier. Once again the building is one-of-a-kind, but it recalls the best of what past architecture has to offer. The Paris Opera House might be best described as "Neo-Baroque," although it is considerably more baroque than anything ever produced in France during the actual Baroque period... in fact, it pretty well out baroques anything else built period (although Neuschwanstein and the Royal Pavilion may compete on the fringe).

The Paris Opera House was built during the era of Napoleon III, called "the Second Empire." Although potentially confusing, Napoleon III was not Napoleon's grandson, nor was he his nephew as some books occasionally claim, although that better describes their age difference. Rather he was Napoleon's step grandson, and not so much younger than the original Napoleon. Some cliff notes on the family tree here: Napoleon married an older woman, Josephine, who already had two nearly grown children by a former marriage. She was apparently past childbearing as the two of them never had children. Much as Josephine was the love of his life, for political reasons several years later Napoleon was persuaded to divorce Josephine and marry a young Austrian princess. The princess had a son by Napoleon – that is Napoleon II. But he died young, leaving Napoleon without a legitimate heir. Napoleon III was actually Josephine's daughter's son. After Napoleon was deposed and the royal government was briefly reinstated and failed, Napoleon III gained control of the government as heir apparent to Napoleon. Well that's nice.

The era of Napoleon III was a time when new moneyed industrialists were flexing their financial muscles in France (and elsewhere – think of folks like the Vanderbilts in America). This new aristocracy was rapidly displacing the old nobility; new money held new influence over old money as never before. Traditionally, old money tends to be more quiet than new money. The real flashy stuff is more likely to belong to a Johnny Come Lately than it is a rich guy who is accustomed to having deep pockets. New money defined the Second Empire. The ostentatiously wealthy industrialists wanted the glitz ladled on in heaping portions, and they got just what they wanted in the Paris Opera House. This was someplace to see everyone on the who's who list and be seen yourself. The main salon was inspired by the Galerie des Glaces at Versailles, but Louis' palace isn't anywhere near as ostentatious as the opera house, and the grand staircase made those pretentious grand entrances of every self-ordained VIP an event that rivaled whatever performance was delivered on stage. Curiously, the *real* nobility, descendants of the old royal family and their peers disliked the Paris Opera House because they found it too gaudy and gauche. The new money wealthy loved it, however, because it made them feel like what they imagined being kings and queens was like. As an aside, the Vanderbilts (Biltmore House family) also commissioned another house by Richard Morris Hunt called the Breakers, which is located in Newport, Rhode Island and which was modeled quite a bit after the Paris Opera House.

Louis Sullivan (USA)

Everything we have seen from the latter 19th century thus far has had an element of retro to it with architects looking over their shoulders to the past for inspiration. That's not necessarily a bad thing, and we got some rather amazing architecture as a result of architects looking to the past, but reinterpreting old ideas to make them new. This last architect, however, put more energy into forward thinking, with minimal nostalgia for the past. Louis Sullivan is associated with the early origins of the skyscraper, which was to become the hallmark of modern architecture in the 20th century. His **Wainwright Building** is an excellent example. The Wainwright Building stands nine stories tall, which nowadays might barely qualify as a dormitory-sized building on any college campus, but at the close of the 19th century, that was a big deal.

There were two important construction inventions that allowed architects to design skyscrapers, whether modest like this example or monumental like the Sears Tower in Chicago. For one, they learned how to build a skeleton frame for the building out of steel girders (called *steel-framed construction*) which were then sheathed in a curtain of non-supporting building materials (brick, stone, glass, whatever). In the past, the walls of the building were *load-bearing*, which means that the building materials of the wall had to support the wall. For example, the Colosseum in Rome is made of stone doweled together, and each of those stone arches had to support itself and whatever weight was stacked on top. Steel frame construction is much stronger, plus the steel does the work of holding the building up without relying on the exterior brick or stone to carry the load. Post and lintel, arches and vaults seen in the building's "skin" will now be more likely decorative rather than structural. The second invention that allowed architects to build taller buildings was the elevator, allowing people to soar between multiple stories without having to hike up and down numerous flights of stairs.

Despite being so modern in its construction, the Wainwright Building remained fairly conservative in its visual presentation. Although windows abound (why not? It doesn't weaken the structure), there are still wide, decoratively carved stringcourses making each floor. The building is also topped by a heavy, decorative cornice that almost recalls old Renaissance palace designs, like the Medici Palace from Renaissance Florence.

21. Realism & Impressionism

Realism *c. 1820's – 1880's*

Realism is a difficult art movement to define, precisely because it never was an organized art movement. Loosely then, Realism encompassed a variety of artists who on the whole were less than impressed with both traditional Neoclassicism and Romanticism, as both seemed artificial to the common man. One style may have been presumed to be more intellectual and one more emotional, but in reality both were elitist and appealed mostly to educated patronage. As the French moved toward the middle of the 19th century, many painters longed to see the subjects pursued by their foreign neighbors, namely landscape and genre painting, gain approval within Salon circles. These artists were not organized activists, but they did share certain common traits. Realists tended to be educated artists who erred on the side of being upper middle class to well to do as opposed to working class. They uniformly admired the Royal Academy and Royal Salon, even if they found themselves disgruntled with the pompous art exhibited there. They all would have preferred Salon success, but in the end found that they were unwilling to compromise their art to meet the official taste of the day. Many went to great lengths to re-educate the French people about art, mostly through writing articles, and eventually by exhibiting their painting independently from the official Salon.

Millet (France)

A typical Realist painter would be Jean-Francois Millet. He was a country boy who grew up on a farm, and held a warm nostalgic affection for the pre-industrial countryside with its simple people and simple vocations. His picture **The Gleaners**, painted in 1857 is well known and loved as an outstanding example of peasant virtue. The poor women comb the harvested fields for any leftover usable grain. There is nothing grand or heroic about their actions beyond the quiet nobility of character of these simple, good women. Millet was a conservative Catholic of strong convictions, and he was more interested in communicating the humbled state of mankind than he was in dazzling society's elite with grand paintings of "important" subjects at the Salon. Although he had studied art in Paris, he didn't take well to city life, and in the end took greater pleasure studying nature rather than studio models and plaster casts.

Courbet (France)

Another genre painting enthusiast was Gustave Courbet. At heart Courbet was a bit more impressed with himself than Millet was; his love for the common man was less motivated by the Bible, and more inspired by his liberal politics, alternately described as Socialist, Democrat and Republican. When he made political commentary, he appeared to be embarrassingly less well informed than he let on, which tends to obscure where his actual political sympathies lay. In any event, his ego was enormous, and it seems in retrospect that Courbet was more fascinated with the challenge of bucking the system and proving that he could still be considered an important painter than he was inspired by anything especially noble like Millet.

Courbet's painting, **Funeral at Ornans** is an excellent example of his work. It depicts his grandfather's funeral, which was a simple enough subject although hardly the sort of theme to take an award at the Salon. It wasn't the simple genre theme that raised the most eyebrows, however. For starters, the picture is immense, measuring over 10' by nearly 22'. Most painters who did genre scenes were a bit more modest; The Gleaners by comparison measures just 33" x 44." Courbet's heroic scale wasn't so much a moving tribute to Grandpa as it was a puffed up tribute to his imagined stature as a painter, and perhaps the critics could see through his vanity. Beyond that, the composition was considered to be less than fascinating; instead of relying on the old tried and true rules of geometry, he merely lined up the cast of characters like a stiff and lifeless parade of faces. This scene was painted in 1849.

By 1855, Courbet had grown impatient waiting for success at the Salon, which he of course considered his due. Given that he was a man of means, when his pictures were again rejected from the Salon, he elected to put up his own art show next door to the Salon called the *Pavilion of Realism*. Courbet invited other genre and landscape painters to exhibit their paintings also, and he wrote essays to explain to the unenlightened public why Realist painting should be given the same respect as Neoclassicism and Romanticism. It didn't change the world overnight, but the Pavilion of Realism did open the door just a crack to the possibility that the Royal Academy and Royal Salon might not be the only venues where good taste could be established.

Early Manet (France)

Edouard Manet is a complex artist who defies an easy slot into one art movement or another, and for this reason he is sometimes included in with the Realists, and at other times with the Impressionists. He is not a perfect fit in either camp, but perhaps he fits Realism better. For one, throughout his life he preferred painting genre (albeit not always the simple genre of his Realist peers) to more typical Impressionist themes. He also took an interest in manipulated, formal composition like many other Realists. Finally, although he did meet with the Impressionist artists and on occasion painted with them, he never ever exhibited with their group. He longed for the official success of the Royal Salon, although it proved to be elusive, sadly until shortly after his death when he was "discovered" and became somewhat of a hero after the fact in French art.

Edouard Manet was born to an upper-middle class family in Paris in 1832. He received an excellent private school education, but was an average student. His parents had high hopes that he would become an attorney, which was considered a prestigious position for a young man of his social standing. Instead, Manet grew up hoping to become a painter. When his parents finally relented to allow him to study art, he sought traditional ties with the Royal Academy. Failing to meet the high academic standards for admission, he instead apprenticed under Thomas Couture, who like other painters of the period, pursued art in the Neoclassical tradition of Ingres. During his years in Couture's studio, Manet developed a deep respect for the art and theories of Ingres and Poussiniste tradition. As time passed however, he became increasingly disenchanted with the annoying boredom of copying classical images, and eventually departed Couture's studio.

Although he had no interest in producing shocking art that would offend the public taste, that is nevertheless what he proceeded to do. In 1863 he painted **Le Dejeuner sur l'Herbe**, which translates to Luncheon in the Grass, although the painting continues to be known by its French title. The painting depicts a well-known model of that day, young Victorine Meurand enjoying a picnic in the park with a pair of gentlemen friends who also happen to be easily identified: Manet's friend, the author Baudelaire and the artist's brother, Eugene. The problem is, the men remembered to dress appropriately for the luncheon, while Victorine is naked! Where would the artist get such a bizarre concept? He was familiar with all the great Renaissance art in the Louvre, including the Pastoral Concert painted in the early 16th century by Giorgione. In that painting, we likewise have young men dressed in clothing appropriate for their time and place, seen outdoors playing musical instruments (presumably an ordinary activity for the time), while for whatever reason, their lady friends have shown up for the impromptu concert buck naked. Why? Who knows?

The point is that for generations artists had admired the Pastoral Concert. Neoclassical artists, who prided themselves in being ever so intellectual, had long copied artists like Titian and Giorgione, but what they painted was Renaissance looking ladies scampering about with men decked out in leotards and tunics. Manet noted that this did not show that they *understood* the Venetian Renaissance, but only that they could copy it. How intellectual is that? His goal was to understand the paintings of the past, and in his own time re-create the same concept as what had been done. In reality, Giorgione had produced a highly unorthodox genre scene, not some sentimental picture depicting people from another era. To copy it, with Renaissance women and men, showed no true understanding of what the original artist had intended. Manet sought to paint what the Venetian had meant to convey in the original work. To make his painting even more of an intellectual exercise, Manet lifted his compositional arrangement directly from Raphael's engraving of The Judgment of Paris (see the 3 figures in the lower right of the engraving), assuming that this link would be as evident to the critics at the Royal Salon as his new and improved rendition of Renaissance inspired subject matters.

Manet submitted Le Dejeuner sur l'Herbe to the Royal Salon of 1863, fully expecting it to win the top laurels of that year. To his shock and dismay, the painting was rejected! How could this be? As it happened, many paintings were rejected that year, and Manet and others complained that they were not getting a fair shake from the jury. The government responded by doing something completely unorthodox; they decided to sponsor a second art show called the **Salon des Refuses** (show of refused works), where artists who were so inclined could hang their work and let the public decide for itself whether they were any good. Manet decided to participate, and hung his Dejeuner sur l'Herbe. Unfortunately for Manet, the French public was no more prepared for his innovative art than the jurors at the official salon, and he was the laughing stock of the show. Critics wondered why he seemed to feel the need to create such a scandal with his art ... was he suggesting that Victorine was an immoral tramp having affairs with these two men at the same time? What was the point of it? Manet was amazed and saddened that nobody seemed to grasp what his intentions had been, despite how obvious they seemed to him.

In the same year, Manet painted a companion piece to the Dejeuner, once again employing Victorine as his model. The work is titled **Olympia**, and like the Dejeuner, its point of artistic departure is the Venetian Renaissance. The parallels to Titian's Venus of Urbino are painfully obvious. Again a contemporary, recognizable woman is shown lying on an unmade bed with an air of expectation as you enter the room assuming the role of her next customer.

Manet had championed the same ideas as he developed in his Dejeuner. He used a famous Renaissance painting as his prototype, but rather than merely copying it, he made an effort to understand it, and then re-present it as a contemporary piece. Manet chose to hold back Olympia with the idea that if he waited until the next Royal Salon in 1865, he might fare better with the jury and earn the recognition and glory he deserved for his art which was, after all, more intellectual than what the Salon was peddling.

Remarkably, the Salon of 1865 *did* accept his Olympia. But alas, it was not because they now understood and admired Manet's work. They had discovered two years earlier that the Salon des Refuses had attracted so much attention away from the legitimate Royal Salon, that this go-round they decided to accept a few buffoon paintings to draw in the crowds who were more interested in a good laugh than in viewing "good" art. Manet was the laughing stock again. The public was aghast that the artist seemed determined to destroy the reputation of this poor girl, now showing her as a common prostitute after his apparent attempt to suggest she was the star in a ménage a trois two years earlier. Furthermore, with Olympia there were additional criticisms about how flat the painting appeared, and how dull the colors were, almost monochromatic. Why it was hard to get emotionally involved in this nude at all as she lacked any sensual feeling. Who does this sound like? Reducing the palette, reducing the painting to lines, lines and more lines, treating the figure like little more than a detached compositional exercise? Ingres, of course. Manet had learned his lessons well. He admired Ingres immensely, but as with everything else in his career, he was not satisfied to just copy, he wanted to re-create. Manet outdid Ingres at his own philosophy in painting, just as a generation earlier, Ingres had outdone Poussin himself at producing Poussiniste painting.

Frustrated by his lack of Salon success, Manet traveled to Spain to escape, and became familiar with the art of both Velasquez, whose superb, complex compositions he admired, and Goya, whose painterly brushwork he enjoyed for it had a life of its own. After his return to Paris, he became better acquainted with Berthe Morisot, a painter who was to be his link to Impressionism, and later to become his sister-in-law when she married his brother, Eugene. She encouraged Manet to accept the admiration of a group of younger painters, their leader being Claude Monet.

Impressionism *c. 1860's-1920's*

Early Monet (France)

Claude Monet was born in 1840, the son of a prosperous, yet decidedly middle-class grocer in Le Havre, France, a town on the coast in the Normandy region northwest of Paris. He was not a city boy like Manet, and without the high society connections, he received a standard public education. Monet was not much of a student, preferring instead to doodle unflattering caricatures of his teachers and prominent townspeople which he arranged to show in the local pharmacist's shop windows. He had the reputation of being anything but serious. It was assumed that he would grow up to become a grocer like his father. Monet had other plans, however, and petitioned the city for a grant to study art in Paris. He was turned down for insufficient talent, perhaps illustrating that the folks who knew him in his youth did not see much promise in this undirected kid who, despite natural drawing talent, was not likely to make much of himself.

He proved them all wrong. After saving enough money, young Monet ventured off to the big city. He was not in a position to be accepted at the Royal Academy. He didn't have the grades to get in; he didn't have the connections, and he didn't have the financial resources to afford the tuition. Perhaps most of all, though, he didn't have the discipline to languish in a studio copying classical art. Instead, he gravitated to the Montmartre neighborhood of the city, home of the "starving artist," the bohemian district where there were cafes, brothels, racy nightclubs, and cheap flats. Second-string painters ran studios here to apprentice young wannabes who were themselves outside the mainstream milieu of the Royal Academy and the Royal Salon. Monet enrolled in different studios in succession, where he met other painters like himself: young men who hailed from small towns, as opposed to the city, who had little hope of getting in with the "in crowd" at the Salon and who were mostly allergic to the concept of being told what to do and how to make their art. Montmartre suited them fine. The studios provided minimal instruction, instead relying more on the relationships of the painters and their informal critiques to move young artists along a learning curve in their work.

Monet was a leader by temperament, and others found in him a spokesperson for their group. These young men and the occasional woman enjoyed painting outdoors in the fresh air, often drawing attention to themselves with the public who was more accustomed at this time to artists working inside the studio. Most relished their role outside the Salon. Although they may not have enjoyed the idea of being without financial success, they were not inclined to want to play the game in order to fit in with established art tastes. They were rebels, and they liked it that way.

Putting it into perspective, these years when Monet was a fledgling painter in Paris corresponded to the same time that Manet, a somewhat older and slightly more seasoned artist was painting his Dejeuner sur l'Herbe and Olympia. Monet and his friends heard all about this rebel painter upsetting the status quo first at the Salon des Refuses, then at the Royal Salon with his shocking art. Everything about Manet sounded like their kind of guy. In 1866 Monet was so impressed with the legend of Manet as it was told in all the bohemian cafes, that Monet produced a huge canvas entitled **Le Dejeuner sur l'Herbe** as a tribute to his new hero. It takes no more than a passing glance at Monet's painting to realize that Monet was infatuated with the myth of who he imagined Manet to be, and not the real artist at all. Monet's painting illustrates ... well ... a luncheon in the grass plain and simple. Gone is the tension between a naked lady and her clothed companions. It would be reasonable to assume that not only had Monet never seen Manet's painting of the same subject, he had no clear idea of why exactly it was controversial. That said, what Monet's early painting does illustrate is the natural talent of a gifted landscape painter. He had an eye to see the subtle nuances of natural light as it filters through the trees, and an innate sense of color that enabled him to capture a fleeting moment in nature.

During the early 1870's Monet and his friend and fellow painter Camille Pissarro (not to be confused with the Camille he will marry!) traveled to England where they were introduced to Romantic landscape painting. Monet developed a deeper appreciation for texture and color in painting from observing the broken brushstroke technique popularized in England where artists like Constable had begun to dab on strokes of different colors such that the eye would mix them at a distance. Upon returning to France, in 1874 these men staged a modest art show where they hung their assorted landscape paintings. Thirty artists participated. Among the paintings shown was a blurry river scene known today as **Impression Sunrise** (1872), which Monet produced during his tenure in London painting foggy versions of the River Thames. An art critic panning the show and its dreadful art seized this particular picture as an example of all that was wrong with this newfangled art, stating that it was all just an impression of real painting. The title stuck, and from that point on these artists referred to themselves as Impressionists, creating their own exhibitions completely outside the system of the Royal Salon, and without much interest in official success through old-fashioned channels like the Academy and the Salon.

Monet and many of his friends found they preferred life outside the hubbub of Paris, and they tended to settle in small towns along the River Seine where the countryside was pleasant and where they felt at home painting outdoors producing mostly landscape paintings. Monet and his family settled in Argenteuil. The painting **Regatta in Grey Weather** is a good example of mature Impressionist style painting from the 1870's. It is a seascape, and these along with landscapes, which took little to no interest in figures, became the standard subject and style of the Impressionist painters. It was painted on location, with attention to capturing the natural light and color seen by the artist. In order to keep the colors true to nature, black is all but eliminated from the palette. Black is the absence of all color, and therefore viewed as being unnatural; dark blues, greens and browns will normally substitute where another artist might fall back on employing black. The brushstrokes are short, thick and choppy. There is little interest in thinking about composition; objects are not so much thought of as solid objects at all, but rather as masses of light, color and texture.

Mature Manet (still France…)

During the mid-1870's Manet teamed up with Monet on a few occasions to paint together. A good comparison of Realism and Impressionism is their two versions of **Gare Saint Lazare**, which is a train station in Paris. Presumably the two men visited the station together, but they obviously saw the scene through different eyes. Manet focused on people, and saw opportunities to play with composition. In the end, he produced a studio painting (he was not in the habit of hauling all his art supplies out in public, thank you very much). He employed good old Victorine again, posed this time with a little girl at a gate where the pyramid of Victorine's black dress plays nicely against the pyramid of blue and white in the child's dress. For his part, Monet barely noticed the people at all. He was more preoccupied with all that steam and the affect it had on light and color. The solid masses of locomotives seem to evaporate into billowing clouds of smoke. Manet was also cajoled away from the city on a couple occasions to visit Monet in the country, and to be exposed to the great outdoors and open air painting, which Manet condescended to try, at least a little to appease his admirers. Manet's painting, **Boating** dates from this period. His colors are brighter, which is clearly the influence of Monet and his friends, but otherwise Manet will always remain on the fringe of true Impressionism ... a mentor to the movement, but not a true devotee to their painting philosophy and style. When you observe a detail from the painting, note that while it is very painterly, the brushwork is more like Goya and Romanticism than it is like Impressionism. The solid objects never really melt into the texture of the paint. No matter how close you get to a Manet, you can still see the subject matter. Manet also preferred genre scenes to straight landscape, which differentiated him from mainstream Impressionism.

The last painting completed by Manet before his premature death in his early 50's (apparently of Multiple Sclerosis - it is described as "locomotor ataxy" in biographies) was **The Bar at the Folies Bergere**. This painting perhaps best sums up all that the artist was as a painter. It is a genre scene, but not sentimental, more of a catalogue of modern, urban life. The masses of people at the nightclub are little more than foggy blobs of paint; they are nameless, faceless entities devoid of personality and without meaning or attachment to the lonesome and bored barmaid in the foreground. She stands in front of a mirror which reflects the scene she views, including a portrait of YOU who assume the role of the gentleman ordering a drink, and perhaps pitching her some cliché in a lame attempt at flirting. Notice that your reflection has been shifted off to one side, in order to offer the viewer a painfully direct confrontation with the barmaid, while also including the chap perhaps responsible for her ennui. Where have you seen mirror reflections used to include a room in reverse? Velasquez. Where have you seen a mirror reflection shifted off-center in order to include additional information? Ingres. Where have you seen this heavy use of black in the palette, and the scrubby texture of brushwork? Goya. Manet perhaps better than any other painter of his generation was able to see art of the past in a new way, and reinvent it into a completely modern understanding. In many ways, he stands as the father of modern painting.

Mature Monet (also still France)

While Impressionism remained a second class art in France for most of Monet's life, Americans found it very appealing and many collectors on this side of the Atlantic became avid patrons of Monet and his fellow Impressionists. In his later years, after reaching a comfortable level of financial success, Monet turned to painting series of common theme canvases on a variety of subject matters. One such series, dating from the 1890's was **Rouen Cathedral**. His goal with these paintings was to capture the ultimate fleeting sense of varying light and color. To begin, he stretched a number of like canvasses, all ready to go at the same time. Over the course of a year or more, he would sit daily at the same window in a rented studio in Rouen across the street from the cathedral to paint the same scene over and over again. For example, on a bright sunny morning in autumn he might begin to paint, but by midday, he would be obliged to set that canvas aside for another day, as the light and shadows would be changing as the sun traversed the sky. After several hours he would have to switch paintings again to accommodate the late afternoon light and so on. If the next day were dreary, he would resort to an entirely different round of canvasses. When the autumn sun passed to a crisp winter scene he would be working on new paintings again, as would he when winter passed to spring and so forth. In the end, he had a whole collection of paintings of the same scene, but no two are quite alike.

Another series of pictures done around the same time as the cathedral pictures, and called simply **Haystacks**, pushed his manipulation of color in new and exciting directions. Traditionally, painters had always known that to portray an appropriate darkened shadow for any given color, the way to achieve the proper effect was to mix a small amount of the color found opposite on the color wheel. For example, if a painter wished to shadow an orange, the best way to get a pleasing darkened shade to make that orange look real would be to mix a small amount of blue (the opposite of orange) into the orange to create a good shade. These opposite colors are called *complementary*. With Monet's later work, frequently the basic color of an object is highlighted or shadowed with pure complementary color. Look at the Haystacks. They are painted basically yellow, with some orange highlights, and the shadows are rendered in a mix of pure purple and blue. Just as Monet had always asked the spectator's eye to mix the colors and brushstrokes together to see objects (up close the paintings often disappear into a blur of blotchy color and the actual scene cannot be discerned until you step back several feet), now he asked the spectator's eye to read highlights and shadows where only pure colors existed, the relationship of the colors tricking the spectator's eye and brain into making sense of what is seen.

Finally in his later years, Monet's paintings became so large that it is impossible to determine what they represent (beyond a tangle of pure color and texture) until one stands 50 feet or so away. The best example of this phenomenon is his **Water Lilies** series. In the early 1900's he began painting the water gardens at Giverny, his glorious estate out in the country, which became his private and personal Garden of Eden in his old age. The paintings began in a normal scale, but continued to grow until they became so enormous they require a huge museum setting for display.

Manet and Monet played important roles in the development of modern art. Both were associated with Impressionism, although with Manet it was perhaps more of a loose social connection than a stylistic one. He never took to the theme of landscape painting, never eliminated black from his palette, never gave up his hope of Salon success, deeply admired many more traditional artists, and never chose to exhibit with the Impressionists. He was urban and urbane, and retained a disposition more akin to Realism. Despite this, he remained the hero of Impressionists like Monet. Monet was the true ringleader of Impressionism, and in many ways the herald of the independent-minded artist who snubs the notion of society approval at some margin while demanding freedom to do his own thing.

Pissarro (born US Virgin Islands, career in France)

Monet's primary ally in the Impressionist group was Camille Pissarro. Pissarro was older and more mature, which didn't hurt as Monet was an irresponsible youth (imagine that), and Pissarro and his wife helped keep the group together with their stability ... for that matter, they kept Monet from completely messing up his life by taking care of his pregnant girlfriend and the child born of that union until Monet got his act together and married his sweetheart, Camille. Pissarro was not French, having come to Paris from Saint Thomas in the US Virgin Islands, so when the Franco-Prussian War broke out, Pissarro was as keen as Monet to get out of the country, and it was the two of them who went to England, pursuing *plein air* painting (painting outdoors on location).

Pissarro was less arrogant than Monet. He was more inclined to learn from others, most notably Realist landscape painters, and he was also better than Monet about working with young wannabe painters who gravitated to the Impressionists for advice and instruction. Monet was the chief public advocate – the man people saw and the name they knew, but in many ways, Pissarro was the backbone to the movement – less visible, but contributing more than the others behind the scenes. Like Monet, Pissarro was fond of landscape themes. Many of his paintings were produced in the countryside, but others were studies completed in Paris. One such work is his **Boulevard des Italiens**, completed on location in an upper level Parisian studio. Monet painted a similar urban landscape: **Boulevard des Capucines**. You can observe the similarities in the concept, and also slight differences in the actual painting technique with Pissarro offering a thicker impasto of choppy, distinct brushstrokes compared to the softer touch of Monet. It's hard to believe that Monet's picture predates Pissarro's by nearly 15 years! Monet painted his version of a Paris city street seen from above during the early 1870's – at just the time when Impressionism was fresh and new, while Pissarro's street scene, however similar in concept, was painted during the 1890's around the time Monet was renting his city studio in Rouen to paint the cathedral.

Renoir (France)

Pierre-Auguste Renoir is very much associated with the heart of Impressionism, although he was less of a landscape purest than Monet and Pissarro. Renoir came from a working class background, the son of a tailor from Limoges. He dabbled in the china painting business before moving on to Paris where he met Monet and Pissarro, and his early training in the Limoges china industry gave him a flair for Rococo-style figure painting that he never completely left behind. Renoir was uncomfortable making a spectacle of himself painting landscape in public. He did it to please the others, but in truth, he was a chubby fellow and somewhat shy, and not naturally inclined to exhibitionism like the dashing and daring Monet. Renoir also was not as hostile toward the whole Salon scene as most of the others. On occasion when he could afford it he took classes there, never as a full-time student, but on the fringe of the socially elite in-crowd.

Renoir's favorite themes in art were pictures of the fashionable bourgeoisie enjoying themselves in the company of good food, good wine and most of all, good friends. Two excellent illustrations of Renoir's good life are **Le Moulin de la Galette**, and **Luncheon of the Boating Party**. Notice in each case the marvelous use of filtered light and color, both captured with a feathery brush stroke, softer and less deliberately vigorous than what we typically see in either Monet's or Pissarro's work.

Degas (France)

The last of the Impressionist painters to be discussed here is Edgar Degas. Degas is another unique character in the Parisian painting world at the close of the 19th century, and perhaps his closest match might be Manet. Both men were from the social upper crust unlike the rank and file Impressionists. Both men were well educated; in fact, Degas' family also preferred that he study law, and so he did before switching careers to art. He was a graduate of the Royal Academy and a strong advocate for the work of Ingres, whom he admired. He also preferred genre subjects to landscape, and he made no bones about criticizing aspects of the Impressionist movement that he did not approve. There were two things that separated Degas from Manet, and suggest that he might be considered an Impressionist even though, like Manet, much of his artistic career would seem to support Realism at least as well. For one, although he initially dreamed of success at the Royal Salon, just like Manet, once the Salon abandoned him as a great artist, Degas set that dream aside and assumed the attitude that if the Salon didn't like his work, it was their loss, whereas Manet never gave up the dream of being recognized through official channels as a great painter. Secondly, Degas rolled up his sleeves and exhibited in the Impressionist shows, even though his pictures looked different, and even though he was often snobby in his opinions about his colleagues' work. Manet may have occasionally painted alongside Monet, but he never showed his pictures in the "off-Broadway" type venues that the Impressionists created in direct competition to the real Salon.

As a young artist, Degas tried his hand at producing history paintings of the sort he believed the Salon would approve. A good example is his **Spartan Boys and Girls Exercising**. It deals with a Greek subject, which should be safe enough, and employs nudes too for good measure, but the painting isn't very persuasive somehow. It seems obvious that Degas painted the picture because he felt he should, but perhaps not because the theme interested him very much. His failures with pictures of this type corresponded with the same time frame as Manet's early disappointments. Like Manet, Degas took a vacation from the Paris painting scene –

Manet went to Spain while Degas went to New Orleans to visit family on his mother's side. Upon his return, Degas came to terms with his apparent fate in the eyes of the Salon, and decided to paint subjects he enjoyed, assuming he would find ways for his work to be seen outside the Salon.

The themes that Degas loved were gentleman pastimes of the urban idle rich: the ballet, the opera, the racetrack, although in each case, he was more intrigued with behind the scenes images than polished performances. **The Rehearsal** (two different versions seen here) is a good example. Degas was always interested primarily in composition, and although he produced his work in the studio from sketches made on location, he also expanded his horizons to appreciate Impressionist light and color. **Race Horses** is a good example of bright Impressionist color although like many of his mature works, this picture is a pastel drawing. Degas lived to a ripe old age, but lost his eyesight to macular degeneration. In his later work he often found he could control his art better by drawing in color rather than painting. Notice how the picture is cropped, with horse and rider being chopped off abruptly on one side. In part this interest in cropping comes from his hero, Ingres - remember Madame Moitissier? With Degas there is a second influence, however: photography. Photography was in its infancy, and largely a hobby of the rich as it was expensive to pursue. Degas often photographed his subjects as well as sketching them, and allowed the arbitrary cropping in the photographs to influence the final composition of his work.

A final work by Degas is **The Tub**, a pastel produced late in his career. He created a series of similar drawings, by "renting" baths for women who might not otherwise be able to afford the luxury. We take daily bathing for granted, but in 19th century Paris, most apartments did not have private baths, and one would secure a tub from a vendor who would deliver the tub, heat the water, then arrange to stop by later to pick up his tub. It was normal for the entire family to take advantage of a single tub of hot water, so it was more often than not a rushed affair, half the time in tepid dirty water after others had already bathed. Degas was well to do, so he used his personal financial resources to buy baths for women who in turn would allow the artist to peek through the keyhole and sketch them while they bathed. Sounds pretty kinky, but the reality was that Degas was less interested in being a perverted peeping Tom, and more interested in getting models who were natural and not posing like they self-consciously did in typical studio situations. Degas didn't want to crank out the typical bosomy glamour girl like other painters; he wanted real women who were less than perfect hoisting themselves about in unflattering positions. He also used these late works as an opportunity to tinker with composition in ways little seen before. In The Tub for example, although the artist was undoubtedly watching his model from the next room, and therefore seeing her either from the side, or back or front, he could not possibly have seen her from an oblique angle above, as if hanging from a chandelier! He has altered his point of view of the model, but beyond that, different objects in the room are seen from different points of view. We see the shelf next to the model from directly above, but the objects on the shelf are seen head on. Ingres first introduced this idea, however subtly in his portrait of Madame Moitissier. Degas is developing the idea much further to where manipulating composition has now become as important to the picture as the subject matter. Degas was the first painter to routinely show different points of view for different objects within a single scene.

The Impressionists were a tight-knit group during the 1870's, and on into the early 80's. They worked outside the mainstream of official French art, and were the first group of painters to not really care about Salon success. There were a number of painters who drifted toward the

Impressionists during the 80's and 90's who were never fully integrated into the group, but who were clearly influenced by their style, and also by their attitude. These were the Post-Impressionists.

22. Post-Impressionism & Early 20th Century Art

Post-Impressionism *c.1880-1906*

During the 1880's and 1890's a second string of painters appeared on the Parisian art scene; the Impressionists influenced them, yet they never fully participated in that art movement. The Post-Impressionist period spans the last 2 decades of the 19th century, and by the turn of the century it had pretty well run its course. These painters were not a unified group like the Impressionists. While some of them knew each other and may have even been friends for awhile, it is reasonable to say that each artist was doing his own thing without feeling obliged to belong a group bigger than himself. Each painter is unique, taking lessons learned from Impressionism and reinterpreting art in an individual way.

Seurat (France)

Georges Seurat was short-lived, dying at age 31 in 1891. He was trained by a disciple of Ingres at the Ecole des Beaux Arts under the greater umbrella of the Royal Academy, and while he applauded the freshness of Impressionist painting, he also thought the group had thrown the baby out with the bathwater. They had some good ideas to be sure, but they had dumbed down painting to where the great intellectual qualities for which French art had been hailed for generations were lost to feel-good simplicity. Seurat's goal was to retain the fascination with color seen in Impressionist, but to turn back (or forward?) to a more intellectual analysis of the color. He developed his own style of painting called *pointillism*.

Two excellent examples of this new technique are companion paintings **The Bathers at Asnieres** and the more fashionable **Sunday Afternoon at the Island of the Grand-Jatte**. Both are large – about twice the size of a Millet but still half the size of a Courbet! These simple, stylized genre scenes, one paying homage to the working class and the other to the bourgeoisie as they seek weekend entertainment, were vehicles for the artist's new pointillism technique. Impressionist painters had sought to intuitively dab on blobs of paint according to their fleeting senses painting on location. Seurat in contrast, sought a more rational, deliberate way to play with color. He studied relationships between one color and the next, reading theses like Ogden Rood's Modern Chromatics which had only recently been translated into French, and assorted treatises written by his fellow countrymen, Charles Blanc and Eugene Chevreul. He was interested in how colors affect one another, such as complementary colors receding or popping out when placed next to each other. He developed his own theories on how color should be used with shades adjacent to the color in question as well as the opposite hue on a color wheel. In short, he broke his brushstrokes down to a multitude of tiny dots, with each one calculated to have a particular relationship to the dot next door.

Seurat's pictures are not as painterly as mature Impressionism in that you never lose sight of the subject matter, no matter how close you get to the painting. At the same time, while the texture is not as prominent as it might be with Monet or Pissarro, the vibrance of color and intricate smorgasbord of every shade in the rainbow comes alive the closer you get to the surface of the canvas. His style is sometimes called "*Neo-Impressionism*," and it attracted a few followers into the turn of the century.

Cézanne (France)

In many ways, Paul Cézanne was the most important artist of the Post-Impressionists; he stands as a link between masters like Manet and Degas of the latter 19th century, and intellectual experimentation in the early 20th century. Cézanne was not a city boy like Seurat; he grew up in the South of France near the Italian border in Aix-en-Provence, the only son of a self-made banker who expected Paul to follow along in Papa's footsteps and take over the family firm he had worked so hard to build. Unfortunately, Paul was a total disappointment to his family. He had this cockamamie notion that he wanted to become an artist, although he did not show the slightest promise in any of his creative endeavors; in fact, the only subject he failed in school was art! Trying to ride out Paul's adolescent fantasy, his parents ponied up the money to buy him a house in the countryside which he had permission to paint however he saw fit. He all but ruined the place, producing murky, dark murals of rape scenes and other violent themes that might be appealing to manufacturers of computer games nowadays, but were hardly the sort of thing anybody wanted to see a hundred plus years ago. An example of his early painting can be seen in the **Temptation of Saint Anthony**. The composition is ill considered, the colors are muddy and poorly defined, and about all anybody might find that is good about the work is that Cézanne seemed to be a natural when it came to rich texture – it's right up there with Frans Hals or Manet. Cézanne's parents frequently get a bum rap in art history books as being the noodle-heads that didn't see the genius in their own son, but to be fair, in his early years, frankly Cézanne didn't show any genius. Small wonder his parents were concerned that he would waste his life chasing an elusive dream.

Cézanne squandered his youth getting nowhere. Finally as a grown man he received grudging permission from the family to travel to Paris to pursue his art. His boyhood friend, Emile Zola was there as well, and the two of them managed to gravitate to the seedier side of Parisian lifestyle, which enraged the folks back home (talk about prophesy fulfillment that it was a bad idea for Paul to leave home…), and in the end, his father moved to Paris for a spell to baby-sit Paul's apparent irresponsible behavior. Amid these family struggles, Cézanne connected with Camille Pissarro, the most patient and helpful of the Impressionists, and it was Pissarro who encouraged Cézanne during two years of personal tutoring to keep his painterly texture, while moving on from his dark themes. Pissarro suggested the fledgling painter try his hand at still-life and landscape, forcing him to paint the colors found in nature instead of the foreboding gloom he seemed to be dredging up from his mind. Pissarro's advice opened Cézanne to a whole new world of exploration, as color would become central to his work.

Cézanne spent most of his career back in Aix-en-Provence, living a rather lonely life away from other artists, working long hours in solitude, and locked in a so-so marriage (compliments of his own difficult personality; his wife was a remarkably patient woman) that brought him little happiness. He was a grumpy fellow, given at times to a bad temper alternating with moody silences. Small wonder he was a social stick-in-the-mud. The one thing he cared about was his art. His favorite landscape subject was **Mont Sainte Victoire**, a mountain not far from his home that he painted over and over and over again. Ironically in a way, Seurat's pictures seem so precise and yet he worked fairly quickly, considering the tedious pointillist technique, while Cézanne's work gives the illusion that he simply slapped the paint on the canvas with carefree abandon, while in reality each stroke was painfully considered. His landscapes are remarkably spare, with just the number of strokes needed to convey the artist's intentions, but no more. Cézanne's landscapes are also intriguing because he deliberately eliminated atmospheric perspective, such that colors in the background are the same intensity as those in the foreground rather than fading as they recede into space. In the end, Cézanne created landscapes that fool the eye. One moment they read as three dimensional spaces because old tricks like diagonal lines, or overlapping objects, or even just the familiar outline of the mountain convince us that the space is real. Then a moment later, you can look at the same painting and barely read the landscape at all – the picture is a series of flat planes of color and texture. If you are unable to break free of the subject matter reading 3-D, try this little trick. Take a Cézanne landscape reproduction and rotate it – it will lose the connotation of landscape while retaining its other visual qualities because the background and foreground were painted as if sharing the same plane. Sometimes this helps a newcomer see Cézanne's work in a new way. Truly, his paintings are more phenomenal in person than in reproduction. When seeing a gallery full of Cézanne landscapes, the viewer *will* experience the tension (dare I say deliberate confusion?) with pictures reading as flat and 3-dimensional at the same time, but sometimes when all you have is an isolated reproduction, you have to nudge yourself a little to see it.

His **Basket of Apples** is a still life that also moves painting in interesting directions not quite seen before. Again his approach was tediously painstaking as he contemplated every single stroke. In fact, while many of us might think of still life as being the student exercise one masters before moving on to more challenging exercises, Cézanne invested so much time into his still lifes, even as a mature artist, that the fruit actually rotted before he could finish the picture and he would replace the apples one by one with artificial wax fruit in order to maintain his unhurried study of the subject matter. As he manipulated color and space in the landscapes, so he does with still life also. Remember that Constable was considered quite bold when he first used his broken brushstroke and allowed different shades of a color to be applied in individual strokes so your eye could mix them. Then later on, the Impressionists took this idea much further by using pure complementary colors to serve as highlights and shadows. Cézanne is also using a variety of colors here, but instead of following the rules, where an opposite color is the highlight or shadow, he is jolting the eye by using "surprise" colors – bright for highlights and dull for shadows, but outside the conventions of traditional color mixing.

Something even more remarkable is going on here too, this time with perspective, or one's point of view. Remember that Ingres was considered quite innovative when he shifted Madame Moitissier's reflection over to the side and turned her head in order to let us see the lady's coiffeur, although it was subtle and you may have even missed it if you didn't know to look for that level of detail. Then along came Degas, and in The Tub he managed to show his viewers a variety of different points of view: we see the bather from an oblique angle, while the shelf is seen from directly above, yet the pitcher on the shelf is seen head on. Cézanne is outdoing them all! Look at the table. Can you see that one side of the table is seen from the side, while the other side is viewed from above? And what about that basket? You can see the side of the basket, and then it is as though the artist pulled it around like rubber so you could also look down into the basket. He does the same with the plate of bread, stretching it to show you the object from different vantage points at the same time. Cézanne was the first painter to give his viewers multiple points of view *of the same object*. In this regard, Cézanne was very clearly the link between painting of the 19th century, and Cubism in the early 20th century.

Bathers is a very late painting by Cézanne, completed the year before he died. Cézanne was never a figure painter, but in a way, his nudes foreshadow the distorted anatomy seen in many early 20th century paintings. Obviously the scene was not done from life; in 1905 it wasn't the norm for ladies to congregate on the banks of rivers and hang out naked. The painting is a compositional exercise, using the female nudes as props. Recall that Ingres introduced this concept way back, almost 100 years earlier with his <u>Grande Odalisque</u>. Cézanne's <u>Bathers</u> pays homage to Manet, with the three figures in the foreground setting up a picnic – they reference the <u>Dejeuner sur l'Herbe</u>, set as they are in a group around what appears to be a blanket or table cloth, and with a stream behind them. Cézanne has taken the practice of employing geometry for composition to an exaggerated conclusion, such that many of the individual women are scrunched into a pyramidal form, the stacking of bodies creates larger pyramidal forms, and even the trees force nature into a grand, albeit contrived pyramid resembling the vaulting in a Gothic cathedral.

Cézanne's art perhaps more than any other Post- Impressionist is the marriage of Poussiniste and Rubeniste thinking and tradition. He was quoted often as saying, "I want to do Poussin over again, from nature," and "I wish to make Impressionism something solid and durable, like the art of the museums." He was devoted to color (once he learned from Pissarro), he enjoyed painting landscape and other subjects no one considered lofty and important, and he had an expressive love of texture in his paintings ... so he is Rubeniste, right? Then again, he painstakingly addressed composition in his work, and manipulated color with the express intent of creating illusions within the composition; he was methodical in his technique, and very aware of all the artists from the past who contributed to his own style ... which are predominantly Poussiniste characteristics. Cézanne was masterful at bringing together the best of both artistic worlds, and in the process, he set the stage for 20th century art more than any other single painter. He died in 1906, at just the point when Picasso was beginning to translate Cézanne's lessons on manipulating form into Cubism.

Gauguin (France)

Paul Gauguin was a far more romantic personality than either fussy Seurat or stodgy Cézanne. And nobody appreciated Gauguin's romantic charisma more than Gauguin himself. Unlike most of the others of this generation, Gauguin didn't start pining away to be a painter in his youth. Not at all! He was a stockbroker, happily married to a lovely Danish wife and the father of a houseful of charming children. He enjoyed living a comfortable bourgeois life. He took up painting as a fashionable hobby with as much serious intention as the average businessman might give to golf. Sure there was an element of pride in learning a few pointers and doing a decent job of it, but just as nobody expects the average businessman who owns golf clubs to be the next Tiger Woods, nobody gave Gauguin a second thought that he might aspire to be anything more than a Sunday painter. He submitted pictures to the Impressionist Exhibitions as an amateur, but so did a lot of people who never made it to be big, famous artists.

Then in the early 1880's the stock market crashed and Gauguin lost his cushy job. To the family's shock and dismay, he announced that he was going to become a full-time painter (mid-life crisis? Probably that was exactly how this career move was perceived). He flitted about Paris learning this and that from other painters, while gradually going broke, and soon decided that he would never be a great artist with the burden of his wife and all those kids, so he packed the family off to his in-laws in Copenhagen, where he visited them on occasion until that too became more than he could bear.

His first big move was to the village of Pont-Aven in Brittany (along the coast, just southwest of Normandy) where he hooked up with a small artist colony there that was attracting some attention in Parisian circles as being very "au courant." His **Breton Village** was painted at this time, and shows the influence of the Impressionist landscape painting tradition. But somehow Brittany wasn't doing the trick for Gauguin. It wasn't exotic enough, picturesque and quaint, yes, but not a dramatic and abruptly different departure from the rest of his life in France. Gauguin's mother was originally from Peru, and Gauguin held a great infatuation for what he imagined to be the perfect life of the native, removed from all the hypocrisy of civilization. In 1887 he traveled to the Caribbean in search of this great nirvana, but was disappointed. He worked for awhile on the Panama Canal project, and spent 6 months in Martinique, but it wasn't the Garden of Eden he imagined. Gauguin painted **Martinique Landscape** on this visit, which hints at the imaginative colors and painting style he would develop in his mature work, while retaining the loose brushwork from his early days of following the Impressionist lead.

Upon returning to France, somewhat disillusioned that he had not found what he was looking for in the Caribbean, he drifted back to Pont-Aven to see if there was anything shaking there that might inspire him. A new batch of artists were in residence by then, and one in particular, a guy named Emile Bernard, was experimenting with color in ways Gauguin had never considered before. Gauguin's, **Vision After the Sermon; Jacob Wrestling the Angel** was painted at this time. Hopefully you can see that this picture is a far greater departure from Impressionism than the work of either Seurat or Cézanne. The Breton women with their distinctive hats are not blurred into abstraction, but are rather featured in great clarity against a vivid red ground. His inspiration came from Bernard, who was experimenting with a *cloisonné* approach to applying paint in blocks of flat color. That explains the hard edge style with outlines and minimal shading. The choice of arbitrary colors, like the red field for example, was symbolic. The artist would select the color that best communicated the mood of the scene, rather than the actual colors seen in nature. Here presumably the women are quite moved after a Sunday sermon, so much so that they witness <u>Bible</u> heroes playing out the pastor's message before their very eyes. This would be a profoundly moving experience, and accordingly the artist has staged the event on a red field, suggesting hot emotions, rather than a using a more relaxing green.

The Pont-Aven experience opened new doors for Gauguin, but it was still boring old France, and before long wanderlust got the better of him. Gauguin longed to once again seek a magical land of natives and tropical wonders. He set sail for Tahiti in the South Pacific, and finally found his paradise. The colors were spectacular, the women were easy, and he could dispense with modern culture and wallow in the laid-back island lifestyle. Gauguin set up housekeeping with one young girl after another, his "vahines" which were tantamount to middle school aged common-law wives (he and Mette never divorced), and except for occasional trips back to France to try, usually unsuccessfully, to sell his paintings, he lived out his last years in the Polynesian South Pacific. He had a gallery in Paris that promoted his paintings, and the generous gallery dealer, **Shuffenecker**, invited Gauguin to stay with his family, who he painted on at least one occasion on these return trips. Dear Shuffenecker even loaned Gauguin money to keep on with his painting. Gauguin repaid this kindness by going to bed with Shuffenecker's wife, which naturally soured the relationship.

Most of his Polynesian pictures favor the figure, either clothed, as in **Nafrea Faaipoipo (When Are You Getting Married?)**, or nudes like **Te Arii Vahine** (commonly called **Woman With Mangoes** in English, although it isn't a direct translation of the native tongue). The second painting depicts one of Gauguin's assorted live-in girlfriends, this one being 14-year old Pau'ura. The pose was borrowed from Manet's <u>Olympia</u>, which Gauguin had copied earlier. Gauguin's mature work emphasizes flat patches of arbitrary color with a more linear approach to brushwork such that the figures retain their solid mass.

For all Gauguin's romance with the South Pacific, it is curious that he never learned the local dialects and except for giving his pictures exotic titles from the local language, did most of his communicating in French, which he expected the locals to master enough for him to be understood. Likewise, for all his contempt for the bourgeois trappings of marriage, he continued to send letters to his estranged wife in Denmark, who seems to have resigned herself to the reality of having married a philandering husband and deadbeat dad, and for her part she got on with the business of raising their brood as best she could with no expectations of help from her husband. By the end of his life, Gauguin was an impoverished wreck with few friends, no money, and trouble with the local authorities over a libel suit after Gauguin wrote a scathing letter criticizing corruption in the French governance of Polynesia. He was also seriously ill, having contracted venereal disease from a prostitute back in France (the man never could keep his pants on), which he generously spread among the local young women on the island. He was going blind, had open sores on his feet such that he could barely walk, and no money to pay for medical treatment. Gauguin died of complications from advanced syphilis in the Marquesas Islands in 1903, one month shy of his 55th birthday.

Van Gogh (Holland)

Perhaps the most tragic of all the Post-Impressionist soap operas was the life of Vincent van Gogh. Born into the large family of a Dutch Protestant minister, Vincent was a sensitive, if also unstable soul from the start, and as such, he was a huge disappointment to his rigid, disciplined father. Vincent's only solace was his kid brother, Theo, whose love of his skittish big brother was the only thing that kept Vincent semi-sane and able to cope with life at all. Vincent tried his hand at being a language teacher in England, where he failed miserably by falling in love with his landlord's daughter, or at least becoming infatuated with the girl to whom he had barely spoken. The would-be Romeo created quite a stir by writing lewd love letters to the poor girl, for which he was promptly sent home to Papa in disgrace. From there he decided to straighten up and fly right by following Dad into the ministry. His assignment was to pastor a poor mining village in Belgium, and it was here that he first began to paint, with canvasses like his famous **Potato Eaters**. The genre scene reflects Dutch painting from 200 years earlier, with a dull, dark palette and thick painterly technique that are closer to Hals than to the current styles seen in Paris at that time. His health failed him, and after collapsing from exhaustion, poor nutrition and general self-neglect, Vincent was again sent home to Papa, who by now perceived Vincent as a chronic loser.

Theo, meanwhile, had moved to Paris and obtained a job working as an art dealer, and he invited his brother to come spend time with him in the big city where he could paint and pick up some pointers from other artists. In 1886 Vincent arrived in Paris for what would be a two-year stay. He fell in love with Impressionism, and also with Japanese prints, which were all the rage with the art dealers of that era. **Vegetable Gardens in Montmartre** dates from this period.

Theo lived near Montmartre, so views of this type would have been readily available. See how van Gogh's palette brightened compared to **Potato Eaters**, and notice the choppy brushstrokes recalling Impressionism. Yet even with the support of his loving brother, Vincent seemed to be suffering from chronic depression (he may have also had epilepsy), and they decided together that perhaps the sunny south of France would be just the ticket to perk him up. He set off in 1888 for Arles in the Provence region, ironically not far from Cézanne's stomping grounds although there is no evidence that the two men associated at all. During the next two years, which would be his last, he painted with prolific energy; sometimes completing an over-the-sofa sized oil painting per day.

Van Gogh produced landscape paintings inspired by the bright light and colors in Provence, especially compared to the grey skies of Paris, and even gloomier weather in Holland. **The Harvest at La Crau** is a good example. Van Gogh's style is similar to Cézanne's in that each artist has eliminated atmospheric perspective by keeping the intensity of color consistent between background and foreground. Both artists were painterly, but van Gogh's palette is more brilliant and his brushstrokes were applied in rapid, thick, straight strokes, while Cézanne's brushwork is more mottled and spare, sometimes even allowing raw canvas to be left without paint at all in spots. The end result is that Cézanne's landscapes are more abstract, while van Gogh's pictures like The Harvest at La Crau resemble a cheerful patchwork quilt of color; they are more expressive and cohesive.

Van Gogh moved to Arles in February 1888. By June of that year, he had written to Paul Gauguin, inviting him to join him in Arles. He had met Gauguin while staying in Paris, Gauguin being a high-profile, colorful character flitting from one creative opportunity to another. Van Gogh was bamboozled by Gauguin's apparent glamour as a true artiste, and just as Vincent had deluded himself that he was in love with the landlord's daughter, a girl he had barely met during his stay in London, so too he imagined that Gauguin was his friend. He pleaded with Gauguin to come and paint the fabulous light and color in Arles. Finally in October Gauguin did relent to join van Gogh and partake of his generosity of a free place to live and work (Theo, of course, was paying the rent), but what sealed the deal was neither his affection for Vincent, nor an interest in Provence. What persuaded Gauguin to go was that Theo basically bought him off by cutting him a deal to show his work in respected Paris circles if Gauguin would be kind to Vincent and not spurn his invitation. Sad really. The two men had a short and feisty stint of working together. Van Gogh was like a child with a newly found best friend, while Gauguin was just marking time with a mildly annoying acquaintance in exchange for favors.

The two artists worked side by side painting landscapes during their brief time together in Arles. Van Gogh's pictures, like his **View of Arles With Irises** show a keen eye for the bright light and colors of the Provence countryside coupled with animated, thick brushwork. Gauguin's paintings, like his **Landscape at Arles** are considerably less representative of the actual visual experience of Provence, and seem to recall the colors of Polynesia. It seems safe to suggest that Gauguin was homesick for the islands, and not much invested in Van Gogh's dream of starting an art colony in Arles. Gauguin's work is also less painterly, again emphasizing the broad areas of comparatively flat, arbitrary color that he first explored in Pont-Aven. All in all, the trip to Arles didn't seem to impress Gauguin nearly as much as Van Gogh had hoped. The two men also dabbled in genre painting, in some cases painting the exact same theme. Consider their two versions of **The Night Cafe**. Gauguin's is a fairly straightforward representation of the café, complete with some of the local people going about their business. Van Gogh's is more unsettling. His Night Cafe seems to magnify the jarring colors of acid green and tomato red, and the bizarre radiation oozing from the relentless glare of the overhead lights leaves the viewer wondering if such dens of evil pastimes could take their toll on one's sanity.

In the end the two quarreled, and Gauguin decided he had suffered quite enough of his zealous host, and he moved out to a local hotel. In a fit of rage or despair (???), Vincent cut off part of his ear and delivered it to a local prostitute he knew and had been trying to "save" in his own way. Needless to say, the bizarre gift shocked the young woman, who reported the incident to the authorities. Gauguin was then summoned to look in after Van Gogh who had clearly gone mad. Gauguin found him unconscious in a puddle of blood. His solution to the situation was to contact Theo to come take care of the mess, while he excused himself from the scene, and while he was at it, from Van Gogh's life altogether.

Theo arrived in Arles to pick up the pieces, and he and Vincent together agreed that perhaps Vincent needed special care. He was committed to an asylum in Saint-Remy, by his own choice, where he could receive medical treatment, not that they had much of an idea of what to do for him. It was during this last year of his life that Vincent painted his famous **Starry Night**. Although it has been confirmed that the basic elements of the picture were real – the cypress trees and distant church are pretty much true to the view he would have had from his hospital window – the scene is hardly a realistic presentation of nature. The sky swirls about in a turbulent display of neon bright moon and stars, and the air itself seems to visibly come to life like pounding surf. The painting pretends to be a landscape, but in reality it was the turbulent mood swings of the artist that was being portrayed. Through all of this, Theo remained the loyal brother, visiting Vincent and paying all his bills, even though Theo himself had recently married and was embarking on building a family of his own. This worried Vincent enormously. How could he continue to be such a burden on Theo? He felt jealous of his new sister-in-law while at the same time, he felt sorry that her life and Theo's too were held hostage by his own mental illness.

In 1890 Vincent had taken leave of the asylum to spend time in the personal care of his physician, Dr. Gachet, at his home in Auvers. Dr. Gachet specialized in nervous disorders, although Vincent noted in his letters to Theo that his host may have taken a special interest in the subject primarily because he himself seemed to battle the demon of depression. Vincent often compared himself to Gachet, seeing similarities physically in their mutually uncommon red hair, and also emotionally with their uncontrollable mood swings. On July 27, 1890, Vincent happened to be home alone, waiting for news from Theo, which was a day or two delayed from what Vincent expected. Suddenly plummeting into a pit of despair that Theo had turned away from him in favor of his new bride, Vincent wandered out into a nearby field … and shot himself. He died two days later, only 37 years old. Van Gogh died thinking himself a complete and total failure. He had only sold a single painting, and that money he had given to charity. It is sadly ironic that the person most responsible for Vincent van Gogh's meteoric rise in notoriety and fame such that today his pictures are well known and loved, the person who devoted a lifetime to collecting all Vincent's paintings, documenting them, and showing them so the artist's life was not lived in vain … was Theo's wife.

Symbolism *c. 1890s*

Munch (Norway)

A postscript to the Post-Impressionists, and a link to early 20th century art is Symbolism. The most remarkable artist of this genre is the Norwegian painter, Edvard Munch (pronounced moonk). Coming from a tense family background, with a strict Protestant pastor for a father, and burdened with the trauma of watching both his mother and sister die slow, painful deaths, Munch was about as jolly a young man as Vincent van Gogh. In fact, Munch admired Van Gogh only slightly less than his real hero, the master of well-adjusted life, Paul Gauguin. What Munch liked about the paintings of these men was their expressive quality. With Van Gogh, the paint itself oozed emotions, while with Gauguin, the arbitrary choices of color intrigued Munch. He developed a style that was more painterly than Gauguin, although not as textured as Van Gogh. Munch's paintings retained elements of the flat cloisonné that Gauguin adopted during his tenure in Pont-Aven, but his themes were more troubled than either of his artistic heroes..

Probably the most famous painting from Munch's repertoire is **The Scream**. How many Halloween masks have been modeled off this image? It doesn't portray anybody in particular, nor does it tell a story. Instead the imagery is expected to convey a mood, and a distressing mood at that! Munch's paintings usually deal with unhappy memories from his own youth and the dismal state of his chronically troubled soul, which he enhanced through excessive alcohol consumption. Although most of his paintings hold no reference outside the artist's own melancholy life, **The Death of Marat** is a theme we have seen before. Recall the original masterpiece by David, where Dr. Marat, though stabbed to death in his bath, is portrayed as a heroic martyr, even to assuming the pose of Christ from Michelangelo's <u>Pieta</u>. None of that glory here! The emphasis is on the morbid victory of Charlotte Corday, who is not only present, but stripped naked to add a twisted sexual component to the story. Further, Marat is not only dead (and a bloody mess at that), he has also been castrated by the evil woman … which has absolutely nothing to do with the truth of the story. Clearly Munch had his own problems to preoccupy his mind, and he has used only the skeleton of the story (a woman killed a man) to set himself off on a journey of emasculating and mutilating the man at the hands of the vile temptress. Most of Munch's paintings deal with death, pain and suffering, sexual humiliation and rejection, and in general, being miserable. Munch had few friends (now there's a surprise), but he did find common ground with Norwegian playwright Ibsen, whose characters seem haunted by a malevolent force bent on dooming their fate. They must have been some fun company.

Expressionism *c. 1900-WWI*

Expressionism is a name assigned to a variety of smaller art movements, or groups of artists experimenting with modern interpretations of emotionally based art. In the interest of brevity, this chapter will only address one of these many painters, one who made a particularly substantial contribution to moving art forward into a completely modern style.

Kandinsky (Russia)

Wassily Kandinsky was born in Russia, and grew up in Moscow where as a young man he became a law professor. It wasn't until he was nearly 30 that he saw one of Monet's <u>Haystack</u> paintings at an exhibition, and he decided he would like to become a painter himself. Kandinsky emigrated from his homeland to Munich, Germany to study art in 1896. Throughout the next fifteen years he studied art, dabbled in psychology, and traveled to Paris to get a feel for the new styles of art emerging across Europe during those pre-war years. In 1911 he organized a group of 9 artists in Munich, which called themselves *Der Blau Reiter* (the Blue Rider). Different scholars have attributed different meanings to the offbeat name, but for our purposes, we are going to focus on the art.

Kandinsky is often credited as being the first completely abstract artist, although it might be overstating his painting given that he himself warned others – in his own book entitled <u>Concerning the Spiritual in Art</u> - not to abandon their subjects entirely lest their art become nothing more than superficial decoration. A good example of his painting from this period is **Improvisation 30**. Kandinsky named this series of paintings as one might name uninhibited experiments in music, and it is quite possible that they were directly inspired by music. The cannons seen in this piece in the lower right corner might recall themes like Tchaikovsky's <u>1812 Overture</u>, which includes bellowing cannons as part of the music, and which debuted in 1882 and would have been well-known and admired by a fellow Russian artist. Kandinsky said that the Improvisation paintings were unplanned, "largely unconscious, spontaneous expressions of inner character, non-material in nature." The question might be then, while he was spontaneously brushing all that colored paint around the canvas, what was he thinking about (or listening to) at the time – what was his inspiration, conscious or otherwise?

The painting may also have strong roots in Kandinsky's Russian heritage. <u>Improvisation 30</u> clearly has cannons in the lower right hand corner, and there seem to be tall buildings which appear to be toppling over in the background. There is a centuries old tradition in Russia that was popularly revived around 1900 that Moscow would become the new capital of the world, associated with the Second Coming of Christ, during the third millennium. Could it be that Kandinsky, surely aware of the looming probability of a major war on the horizon, wondered if this meant the beginning of the end? Some scholars believe apocalyptic imagery can be interpreted into a number of Kandinsky's seemingly non-objective "abstract" paintings; might there have been more to them than a bunch of pretty colors? It was a popular idea in Russia at the turn of the last century that the first center of Christianity was Rome, the second "Rome," according to Eastern tradition, was Constantinople, and the third and final "Rome" they predicted would be Moscow, this according to the vision of a 16th century monk. Ivan the Terrible was the first to call himself a Czar, Russian for "Caesar" in anticipation of this great future event. Perhaps Kandinsky was influenced by such ideas, but for whatever reasons, kept the true meaning of his work to himself.

Cubism *c. 1907-WWI*

Picasso (Spain)

At the same time as artists like Kandinsky were transforming a Rubeniste approach to painting into a completely new kind of art never seen before, artists like Pablo Picasso were doing the same complete overhaul of the more intellectual Poussiniste philosophies of line, composition and reduced palette. Picasso was born in Malaga, Spain, the son of an artist who taught at the School of Fine Arts. He was artistically precocious, developing quickly as a teenager into a competent young artist himself. By the time he was 19, he was traveling back and forth to Paris to keep up with the latest trends, and 4 years later in 1904, he packed up and moved there.

He became actively involved in politics, eventually joining the Communist Party, and studied the work of many artists, trying out different styles himself during these early years. His first experiment with Cubism came in 1907 when he painted **Les Demoiselles d'Avignon**. The influences for the painting were several. For one, he had recently become interested in ancient Iberian art from regions near his birthplace, and this combined with a fascination with some primitive carvings Gauguin had done in Polynesia and African masks, which were a recent novelty in the Parisian art scene gave Picasso a nudge to produce a painting with distorted faces. Beyond that, he had studied the Neoclassical images of Ingres, and decided to remake Ingres' odalisque paintings into an updated study. Instead of harem girls he shifted gears into the brothel to depict common prostitutes. "Demoiselles" – the ladies – is a euphemistic way to refer to ladies of the evening, and Avignon was referring to a street in the red light district of Barcelona where Picasso had spent some rowdy years before heading off to Paris. Just as Manet once took respected art from the past and updated into a contemporary understanding, so Picasso did with Ingres' work. Further, he had observed Cézanne's experiments with shifting planes, and flattened space, and reduced his own ladies into lines and chopped up, flattened forms. It may not be Picasso's best work, but it was clever, and he was definitely on to something. His peers didn't think so. Some of them even thought he was poking fun at modern art.

Straight Cubism quickly developed into the logical conclusion of the concept: *Analytical Cubism*. **Ma Jolie** is an example. Here the artist has broken down every facet of a woman's face and body into forms, which have then been further reduced into flat planes, which could be shifted around here and there to improve the artist's composition. Color, too, has been completely reduced to variations on a monochromatic theme. Analytical Cubism was no longer about the original subject, which presumably in this painting was a woman. The woman was nothing more that the raw material for a cubist reconstruction, which then in turn became the model for the further fractured and manipulated analytical piece. The artist could now be completely divorced from any connection with humanity, and spend his time slicing up planes of flat space into endlessly interesting bits of grey or beige flat forms. Hmmmm. Fascinating concept, and perhaps the ultimate conclusion of good old Poussin's ideas on art, but ultimately not terribly satisfying for the artist. It was a flash in the pan experiment that was intellectually cool, but actually kind of boring to keep on with it after a couple years.

The next step was *Synthetic Cubism*, like the **Three Musicians**. Synthetic Cubism was exactly what the word synthetic implies: it was fake cubism because it wasn't really cubist at all. In these paintings and *collages* (pieces of paper and other materials pasted on paper, canvas, cardboard or wood) there is a visual relationship with traditional cubist art in that there are geometric shapes and all, but in fact, the shapes do not represent a breaking down of the original image. They are simply shapes of color or texture that have been arranged in an interesting way, such that they resemble a final subject matter. It is more a process of building a theme out of random shapes and color, as opposed to starting with a theme and breaking it down into a series of random bits and pieces.

Dada *the years associated with WWI – c. 1913+*

Dada was a short-lived movement during the years of World War I, sprouting up first in European centers like Zurich, Berlin, Paris and London, then eventually coming to New York City. In fact, it was during the atrocities of World War I that the focus of the art world shifted from Paris, which had been the grand dame for centuries, to New York, and thus far, New York remains the cultural center for the arts with the greatest gravity into our own times.

In many ways, Dada is a critical movement to understand, as the thinking behind it had a profound impact on the development of *all* subsequent art during the rest of the 20th and now also into the 21st century. If you can grasp Dada, you'll have a better shot at making sense of art you see being produced around you nowadays, which let's face it, doesn't seem to have a lot in common with Michelangelo for the most part.

First of all, we need to get some perspective on how artists were changing in terms of their self-awareness, especially as it relates to patronage. In the beginning, the artist and the public had a cozy relationship. The public decided what it wanted to see, and the artist learned his trade in order to meet that demand. This doesn't mean that the artist had no latitude to "create," but it does imply that at the heart of his masterpiece was the desire to please whomever was paying for the art. This mutually supportive system was the backbone of most of the art produced in history. ALL ancient art was produced in this manner. ALL Medieval art was produced in this manner. ALL Renaissance art was produced in this manner. And then along came the 17th century. In most places, the old tried and true system continued to work as it always had, but in Holland, the absence of a wealthy upper class, plus the absence of the Church requesting commissions left wannabe artists without their traditional patronage.

Their solution was to produce spec art. The artist desperately wanted to please his patrons, he just didn't know up front who the "patron" was going to be. Without the clarity of a commission, painters tried to second-guess what themes would sell on the open market. The point is, the artist still wanted to create art that the public would appreciate, but he was at a slight disadvantage because he didn't have traditional patrons placing orders for specific works of art. Speculative art became increasingly the norm over the course of the 18th and early 19th century, whether it was a simple landscape painter trying to get by in England, or a history painter hoping to land a prize at the Royal Salon in France.

The Realist movement was the first shift in attitude where the artist, really for the first time wanted to be successful in traditional terms, but he wanted to do things his way rather than meeting public demand. These artists wanted to get in to the Salon, be famous and make lots of money, but they were not willing to compromise on what types of subjects they would paint in order to achieve that goal. They wanted the public to change their preferences to meet the artist's personal taste. Impressionism took this independent thinking a step further, in that they were so intent on painting whatever they wanted to, in whatever style they liked, that these artists no longer really cared whether the public liked their work or not. Sure, they preferred to make enough money to live well as opposed to being destitute, but their higher priority was doing their own thing – in other words, putting themselves ahead of the public, which is to say, their potential patron. This is a complete change of priorities from anything in the past.

The attitude that "I the artist am the creative genius, and you the public need to get with the program" grew with Post-Impressionism. It was here that the notion of *avant-garde* crept into the thinking of artists. The goal increasingly became to produce art that was on the cutting edge of something new and challenging, dare I say even a little jolting to the public taste. Not all artists were equally caught up in this thinking, but some of them took it quite seriously. Seurat, for example, could be quite arrogant about how superior his painting theories and techniques were, and there was sometimes an air of superiority that well, you just can't expect Joe Lunchbucket to understand how brilliant we artists are. Increasingly there was a circle of artsy in-crowd types who made it their business to be enlightened. They would go to the independent art shows and make it a point to understand and appreciate art that was generally obtuse to the average guy on the street; it became an endorsement of their superior intellect and finely tuned sensitivity if they could discover the merit in whatever to newest art trend du jour might be and hail it as genius before others figured out what they were looking at.

And then along came Dada.

Duchamp

We will consider only one Dada artist, although there are many to choose from. Like many European artists, Frenchman Marcel Duchamp wound up coming to New York during World War I To escape the brunt of the war. He had been an established painter of some reputation in Paris, producing canvasses in the latest buzz style called Futurism, which was a derivation of Cubism. In 1913 there was huge art show in New York called the Armory Show. The ambitious exhibition was coordinated by a pair of artists, Walt Kuhn and Arthur B. Davies, and it included more than 1600 original works of art from both American and European artists.

Duchamp entered a painting entitled **Nude Descending a Staircase**. Now had he shown this work in Paris, the odds are by 1913 he would have received high marks as a genius painter, but New York was somewhat more provincial and Duchamp's painting was panned by the art critics. In fact, one critic described the piece as an explosion in a shingle factory, and cartoonists had a grand time poking fun at the ridiculous picture.

This got Duchamp to thinking (something at which he excelled). What exactly IS art? Could it be defined? And if so, whose definition was valid? You might be inclined at first blush to say that art is something beautiful – something created as a work of beauty. But is it? Were the Egyptian funerary statues created to be beautiful? And besides, who decides what is beautiful? Delacroix produced splendid paintings, but would Ingres have found them beautiful? I think NOT! So what IS art, if it isn't something that can be uniformly agreed to be beautiful? After great pondering, Duchamp decided that the single quality that all art had in common was that art was produced by an artist. In the end, the artist decided what art was. Taking that analogy a step further, if there is no true definition for art, but you in your delusion insist on believing in art, then you must accept what the artist tells you art is. By extension then, if you put legs on a Rembrandt canvas and use it as a card table, it becomes a card table. But the flip side of the argument must then also be true, if an artist identifies anything at all as art, then the believers in art are obliged to accept the artist's opinion, and accept it as art.

This line of thought led to *Readymades*. Readymades were ordinary objects which Duchamp selected for display as art. The most famous of these was his **Fountain** of 1917. The object, as anyone can plainly see, is a urinal. It is not a sculpture of a urinal, or a photograph of a urinal, or a painting of a urinal. It is a real porcelain urinal purchased from a plumbing supply company, set on its backside and signed R Mutt for no particular reason other than to give it a signature. Duchamp entered his Fountain in a liberal non-juried show (which meant they couldn't reject it) in New York, but it was considered so controversial that the sponsors of the show determined that even the artsy elitist chardonnay and brie crowd might be offended, so they "displayed" it behind a curtain. Those who did see the Fountain tried in vain to understand the work in traditional terms – the flowing lines of the piece, or the smooth texture of the porcelain – as if Duchamp had exhibited Fountain as an exercise in broadening the aesthetic appreciation of the avant-garde public. HA!!! It confirmed to him that the art believed in by the bourgeois values of the public, even the elitist "informed" public, was an illusion.

On the heels of Fountain Duchamp produced **LHOOQ**. The piece is a cheesy copy of Leonardo's Mona Lisa to which Duchamp had added a penciled-in mustache and goatee. What's the point? This work is perhaps the ultimate insult to popular "good taste." He has taken what is probably the most famous, most revered painting in history, the one image pretty much everybody can recognize, and completely desecrated it. First, he used a crummy copy, not a decent reproduction of the real painting, then in case the viewer still thought it was great art, he doodled on the mustache and goatee like so much graffiti. The final insult is the title. Now at first it makes no sense … LHOOQ … what's that? Aaaahhh, remember that tricky intellectual, Duchamp was French! When the letters are pronounced in French (el ahsh oh oh koo), and then run together slightly (el ah shode oh koo), they spell out the brief statement: Elle a chaud au cul, which translates into the vulgar remark that "she has a hot ass."

Dada manifested itself a little differently in other locales. In some places it was as much a literary and theater movement as it was art. Also, in many of the European centers, Switzerland especially, it was heavily charged with politics and anger directed against established middle class values which they blamed for the problems of the world. In all, Dada was a nihilistic anti-art that sought to tear down established understandings of what creativity was in the first place. Dada challenged aesthetic sensibilities. It sought to make fools of people who held firm to ideas of the past.

The long-term fall out from Dada is that from that point forward, the old framework for understanding art had been undermined. Artists still had the option of producing beautiful art that would inspire the public, but many artists chose to pursue a different path. In fact, during the 20th century, really for the first time, it became fashionable in some circles to produce art that the general public would NOT like or understand. There developed a certain attitude that if the average Wal-Mart shopper could relate to your art without excessive intellectual programming, that perhaps you weren't producing "real" art. Artists who appealed to the common man, like Norman Rockwell who was made famous for his covers on The Saturday Evening Post (and later LOOK magazine) were sneered at as mere "illustrators". Never mind that much of the great art of the past was also illustration. Much of the art being produced in our own times eludes the average guy on the street, and many of the artists working nowadays don't especially care. Their art is produced as an extension of themselves. To the artists' credit, many are happy to explain their influences and motives, but two facts remain. One, a lot of the art *has* to be explained because otherwise a substantial segment of the planet would never *understand* it. Secondly, since much of the art produced no longer makes "beauty" a high priority, without a grounding in what motivated the artist, it is unlikely that a spectator will *enjoy* the art as he might have in centuries past, even if he were ignorant back then of anything beyond his own senses.

23. Early 20th Century Art in North America

Small wonder so much of the art filtering into the gallery shows in New York from Europe during the early 20th century was poorly received. North America was on a completely different wavelength from Europe. In some ways this phenomenon continues into the present. Europe is a very old culture and artists had been working along a continuum of developing ideas for a very long time. Now you might say to yourself that this means that Europe was established and wise, and therefore the newest and latest modern art coming out of Europe must surely be quality stuff exuding centuries of development along the path to perfection. Maybe so. On the other hand, North America was the fresh new land of pioneer spirit, and that has merit too. If we can take a step back, there is almost a dual perspective that creeps into art the closer we get to our own times. On the one hand, there is the educated elite, the chardonnay and brie crowd who often see European heritage as highly prized whether it happens to be in cars, wine or art. Distinctly American anything is viewed with a certain disdain. The steak and potatoes side of the opinion poll suggests that a lot of what the elite crowd fawns over as great art doesn't communicate much of anything meaningful to the average guy on the street. The educated elite sometimes have a condescending attitude toward the steak and potato crowd, viewing them as a bunch of know-nothing bumpkins. At the same time, the regular Joes also hold the chardonnay and brie elitists in contempt for selling out on traditional Western values.

The Ashcan School *USA ± 1908-1920's*

At the turn of the 20th century America was searching for an artistic identity. It was common practice for aspiring young painters to make their way to Paris to immerse themselves in the trendy art world that had been flourishing there since at least the days of Louis XIV. Meanwhile back home, the American response to the Ecole des Beaux Arts (Royal Academy) in Paris was the National Academy of Design in New York City which promoted very conservative, academic art.

Robert Henri

An artist named Robert Henri was to initiate the first truly American 20th century art movement. Born Robert Henry Cozad in Cincinnati in 1865, Robert had the misfortune of having a professional gambler for a father who shot and killed a man in an argument when Robert was eighteen. The family skipped town and moved east, where Robert and some of his siblings decided it might be a good idea to change their last name. Robert opted for "Henri" which was a French spelling of his middle name. He attended the Pennsylvania Academy of Arts and traveled to Paris where he enrolled at the

Academie Julian. During his time in Europe, Henri checked out the great masters of painting, and he developed an appreciation for the loose, painterly technique of Velasquez, Hals, Goya and Manet. He spent some time in Brittany around the time Gauguin was there, and for a couple decades he popped back and forth across the Atlantic painting and teaching in both Paris and Philadelphia. In time he was elected a member of the National Academy of Design, which sponsored juried art exhibitions similar to the Royal Salon in Paris. Henri wanted the National Academy to become more liberal, and after some heated squabbles over the issue, in 1908 he was not reappointed to serve on the jury for their big art show. Furious at this development, Henri decided to initiate his own independent art show called simply *"The Eight"* because he and seven fellow painters, most of them friends from Philadelphia, joined together to put on their own show. The Eight was the first independent art exhibition in the USA, in much the same spirit as the Pavilion of Realism had been a half century earlier in France.

What separated The Eight from the National Academy was that Henri and his friends were promoting 100% American art. True, painters like Henri had lived abroad and had been stylistically influenced by European painting techniques, but what mattered to Henri was that his subjects be slices of real life within the urban reality that was home to these painters. They never called themselves the "ashcan" school, although it was dubbed that after the fact because so many of their themes focused on the gritty, unglamorous cityscapes, activities and people of inner-city poor neighborhoods. Robert Henri enjoyed painting portraits, especially of children perhaps because he and his second wife were childless (his first wife died young shortly after a miscarriage). **Smiling Tom** is a good example. The painting style could easily be Manet or even Hals, but the child looks as American as apple pie.

John Sloan

Curiously, although Henri started the Ashcan school, his art probably isn't the best example of the urban themes the group promoted as all-American art. That laurel probably goes to John Sloan, as you can see in his paintings called **Backyards in Greenwich Village** and **Sun and Wind on the Roof**. These pictures both capture the most mundane activities of regular working class families living in Greenwich Village in the early 20th century. In the first, children play inside their chain-link fenced yard in the middle of winter making a snowman while one family cat climbs up the snowdrift to check out the action and another perches on a wooden fence keeping an eye on us instead. Inside their smiling sister peers out a window, but she is also more interested in you and me as spectators than she is in her brother and sister and their snowman. It's apparently laundry day and even in the dead of winder clothes flap in the wind on the clothesline overhead. The second painting also deals with laundry day, but this time it's summer and Mom is barefoot up on the roof catching a little sunshine in the warm breeze as she hangs out the clothes to dry. **South Beach Bathers** offers us a glimpse of how the urban working class enjoyed a summer afternoon at the beach with family and friends. Sloan was almost like an updated Renoir of his day. The people in his pictures weren't elegant or important but they were happy and satisfied that their life was pretty good just the same.

John Sloan was born and raised in Pennsylvania, and also a graduate of the Pennsylvania Academy of Art, which is where he met Robert Henri who became his mentor. Sloan started his career as a cartoonist and an illustrator working for the *Philadelphia Inquirer* before moving to New York to participate in The Eight and then become one of the founders of the Ashcan school. He married young and never had much money to his name, but that didn't seem to stop John Sloan from taking an optimistic view of people and life in humble circumstances. He always showed an affection for everyone in his genre scenes, whether it was children playing happily, families enjoying time spent together, or simply the satisfaction of enjoying a pleasant day doing routine chores. He and the others in the Ashcan school have sometimes been labeled as having socialist tendencies, but Sloan for his part described himself as a man without a political party, although he was forward-looking and usually welcomed change.

Photo-Secession USA *1902-1917*

Alfred Stieglitz

At the same time that the Ashcan school was making a splash in New York, another artist of the same generation was establishing his own alternative art scene in the Big Apple. Alfred Stieglitz was born in Hoboken, New Jersey in 1864 (making him a year older than Henri). The family moved soon after to the fashionable Upper East Side, then to Germany for awhile where Alfred studied mechanical engineering before switching to photography, which at this time was still quite new.

He returned to America with a young wife and the luxury of not having to work for a living since both his own father and his wife's were rich, and they kicked in a hefty allowance to provide for their grown "kids." In the 1890's he decided to enlarge his photography interests by working as the editor for *American Amateur Photographer* magazine, but his arrogant attitude offended readers and he was asked to resign. Stieglitz moved on to the New York Camera Club and upgraded their newsletter into a more serious art journal, but that still wasn't what he really wanted to do as a career in photography.

In 1902 he organized a group he called the ***Photo-Secession*** in New York. He only invited people he wanted in the club to join, and together they organized their own exhibitions (it helped to be independently wealthy when it came time to pay the tab). They also collectively published a quarterly photographic journal called *Camera Work* which attracted favorable accolades among serious photographers. The photo **New York Street** dates from 1903 during these early years in his career. Stieglitz was interested in capturing the essence of New York just like the Ashcan school was, and yet he had little regard for the pedestrian themes that Henri and Sloan painted. He thought it was much more important for painters to keep pace with European styles in art rather than documenting the humdrum of American city dwellers. Stieglitz was captivated by composition and mood in his photographs, along with the mechanical techniques of photography, and he believed that the realism provided by photography now relieved the painter of any obligation to produce anything but abstract art.

Between 1905 and 1917 Stieglitz opened his Little Galleries of the Photo-Secession at 291 Fifth Avenue, which soon became known simply as *"the 291."* His famous photo of people boarding an ocean liner called **The Steerage** dates from this time. He was attracting a wider circle of artist friends and admirers by now, and in the process he managed to mess up his marriage. Seems his wife didn't appreciate coming home and finding Stieglitz taking nude pictures of another woman. Hmmmm. She threw him out, but after his divorce, he married the other woman, a young Georgia O'Keeffe who also went on to become a famous artist. Of course, she likewise came home one day and found him taking nude pictures of yet another woman (what goes around comes around). Although they stayed married, from then on Stieglitz and O'Keeffe lived apart for months at a time with him in New York and her out in the American Southwest.

As a true advocate for modern art and a pioneer in one of the most avant-garde new art forms of his generation, photography, Stieglitz was instrumental in helping coordinate the International Exhibition of Modern Art at the New York Armory - better known simply as the Armory Show – in 1913. You already know all about that fiasco; that's the show where Duchamp's Nude Descending a Staircase was derided as looking like an explosion in a shingle factory. Most of the artists represented in the show were Americans, although a number of Europeans had been invited in the hope that they would make what was being produced by American artists (and what was being taught at the National Academy of Design in New York) look hopelessly provincial.

Curiously, some who review the results of the Armory Show in 20/20 hindsight have suggested that it was a turning point in American art, suggesting that now American artists were more eager to gobble up European ideas and model their own art after European styles. This author doesn't see that happening much at all. For starters, both the press and public opinion on the Armory Show were hypercritical of the "foreign" art from Europe. In fact when the show traveled to Chicago there was flap about creating a special committee to determine if some of the art was morally respectable enough to be placed on display. Further, it would take decades before abstract art would become the norm in North America the way it had in Europe.

Group of Seven CANADA c.1912-1933

New York wasn't the only place in North America where artists were trying to establish a fresh identity for an artistic style that was all their own and not just a second class replica of what was the "in thing" in Europe. Canadian artists also struggled to find an artistic tradition all their own at the turn of the century. Perhaps the issue was all the more sensitive there, given that Canada had only recently gained her independence from Great Britain. English landscape artists harkening back to the glory days of Constable, and the even earlier Dutch landscape schools which were the inspiration for the English master, continued to be admired in Canada almost like a sacred tradition.

In the early years of the 1900's a group of painters in Toronto decided it was time for something new. Most of the young men were graphic designers by trade, and they became friends while working together at the same graphic design firm and hanging out after hours together at the Arts and Letters Club in Toronto. Their individual backgrounds varied, but they shared a common belief in the importance of having a national vision for Canada that could be expressed in art.

Tom Thomsom

Tom Thomson was one of the original ringleaders of this loosely knit group of painters seeking to define Canadian art. He was trained as a commercial artist in Seattle, but Thomson had never pursued fine art painting before, unlike some of his friends who had traveled and studied in Europe. Thomson was an outdoorsman, and it was he who initially encouraged the men to get out of their city studios into the great wilderness up north to find their Canadian identity in the rugged forests and lake country of northern Canada. The guys began taking vacations up to Algonquin Park where they would paint, and make oil sketches and drawings for later paintings they could work on back in their Toronto studios. Thomson was a naturally gifted painter despite his lack of training; his **Byng Inlet at Georgian Bay** is a good example. The colors are bright, the planes of space are flat and the paint is thickly applied in choppy brushstrokes. His style is closer to Post Impressionism, like Van Gogh's, than it would be to early 20th century painting in Europe. The trees are more simplified than we would see in Van Gogh's work though. The painting seems stylized, showing the graphic designer's influence perhaps from Thomson's training in commercial art.

Sadly, Tom Thomson died at the age of 39 in a canoeing accident, ironically at his beloved Algonquin Park. There were suspicious circumstances surrounding his drowning, although nothing was ever proved. Thomson's death devastated his friends. The accident occurred in the spring of 1917, three years before the group held their first exhibition, and so technically Tom Thomson died before the "Group of Seven" became a formal reality. Still, it is important to remember him because much of what the group became was due to the inspiration of Tom Thomson. By the time the artists felt ready to exhibit their paintings, there were seven in the group, which is where "Group of Seven" comes from, although over the years painters would drop out or come on board so the actual number of artists in the group fluctuated up and down over the years.

Arthur Lismer

Arthur Lismer was one of the original participants in the Group of Seven. Like Thomson, he adored the great outdoors up at Algonquin Park, so much so that he brought his wife and daughter along with him. His enthusiasm is expressed through brilliant color and rough brushwork responding to the rugged environment out there in the Canadian wilds. **September Gale** shows a blustery sky lashing down at the torrent of water while trees are whipped about in the wind. If you compare Lismer's painting to Thomson's, it is apparent the influence the artists had on one another ... the thick impasto brushwork, the style of the trees, elements of composition, and choices of colors.

Arthur Lismer was originally from Sheffield, England. He moved to Toronto at the age of 26 and took a job at Grip Engraving Company, where he met Thomson and his cohorts, and took up painting the Canadian wilderness. Although he continued to paint throughout his life, in the end Lismer is best know for his interests in art education, especially for his tireless efforts to develop art education programs for children.

JEH MacDonald

Another of the founding members of the Group of Seven and a close friend of Tom Thomson's was James Edward Hervey MacDonald. JEH Macdonald was born in Durham, England of Canadian parents, and James was a teenager by the time the family moved back to Canada. He studied art first in Hamilton, Ontario before moving on to the Central Ontario School of Art in Toronto. MacDonald also got a job as a graphic designer at Grip Engraving Company where Thomson was working around 1907 (before Lismer arrived on the scene), and along with others they began taking their sketching trips up north together. In 1912, MacDonald and another friend in their circle, Lawren Harris, took a trip down to Buffalo to see an exhibition of Northern Painting by Scandinavian artists. Both were impressed with what they saw. Scandinavian terrain is similar to Canada, as is the light, and so MacDonald and Harris were able to appreciate the way Scandinavian artists used broad, flattened areas of color in their paintings because that's what seemed to work for the Canadians too. It reinforced their artistic experiments with rendering Canadian landscape, partially capturing the likeness of the land, but at the same time expressing the intangible emotional impact vast wilderness has on the human soul through color, texture, and manipulated composition. **The Falls at the Montreal River** is one of MacDonald's most famous paintings. The style is similar to Thomson's and Lismer's, but you probably wouldn't get them confused. MacDonald's palette is softer, as is his brushstroke.

Lawren Harris

Lawren Harris was born and raised in Ontario, but unlike the others in the group, he was the only one who came from an independently wealthy family. He was sent off to Germany to receive his formal education, and while he was hardly a big devotee of all that was European, he was probably more familiar with Impressionism and Post Impressionsim first hand, and he had read Kandinsky's book, *Toward the Spiritual in Art*, so he was coming from a slightly more elite academic background than his buddies in Toronto. Since he stood to inherit his family's fortune, he wasn't compelled to learn commercial art and he didn't have to worry about making a living in the meantime either. He was one of the boys to be sure, but for whatever reasons, his paintings were the most unique (better or worse can be a debate supported on either side of the argument, but different to be sure).

Beaver Swamp is an example of his early style. The basic elements of the picture are similar to Thomson's, Lismer's and MacDonald's – the stylized trees set against a simplified landscape and plenty of texture on the paint. But the colors are darker and duller overall, and the mood of the painting seems almost sinister compared to his friends' pictures which "feel" optimistic and welcoming. When the painting was shown at the first exhibition of the Group of Seven in May 1920 it was perceived as subversive and some folks wanted assurances from the government that art like that would never be shown abroad since it might scare people away from coming to Canada!

While the others in their group seemed content to develop their newly discovered "Canadian" national style over the next several years, Lawren Harris never stayed with the same approach to his art for very long. He became fascinated with the stark simplicity of the Arctic and began traveling farther north to paint there, making his landscapes more dramatic and surreal. **Mountain and Lake** shows a cold, lifeless landscape of flat, drab mountains rising from a mesmerizing emerald pool. It seems hauntingly quiet and still compared to the robust scenes painted at Algonquin Park. In the end, Lawren Harris abandoned landscape painting altogether and after the Group of Seven disbanded, he reached the conclusion of his path toward simplicity through non-objective abstract painting.

The Group of Seven hosted their first exhibition in May, 1920, and their last in December 1931. JEH MacDonald died in 1933, and after that the group disbanded. At first they were constantly criticized for their paintings. In fact, when the National Gallery of Canada purchased Arthur Lismer's September Gale in 1926, there were protests in Ottawa that it was "the greatest abortion of a work of art ever seen" there. Within a decade, however, their popularity grew to where paintings by the Group of Seven became associated with a newfound Canadian national pride.

American Regionalism USA *1920's-1940's*

The United States had been an independent nation considerably longer than Canada, but there was still a sense here that what America needed was its own art as opposed to themes and styles hijacked from a European mindset. Although there had been for some time a current of avant-garde art styles competing for attention in New York City, outside New York Americans were not enthralled with abstract art during the years between World War I and World War II. During the Depression of the 1930's especially there were strong sentiments that we needed to pull together to find the good in America and stand proud of our country. It was during this time that American Regionalism painting touched the hearts of Middle America.

American Regionalism was a naïve, sometimes even primitive style of pictorial illustration that focused on rural life in the Midwest. It was similar to the Ashcan school a decade or so earlier in that the artists were adamant about producing a wholly American art that was less interested in keeping up with the Joneses in Paris, and a lot more concerned with expressing the American life experience in art. It also had common roots with the Group of Seven up in Canada in that it avoided urban visuals, preferring instead a slice of rural life that communicated something more basic about the national identity. American Regionalism tried to offer to the average guy living a no frills life in small town America the same kind of pleasant recognition and affirmation that the Ashcan school gave to residents of Greenwich Village. It was wholesome and appealing, if sometimes also a little corny.

Grant Wood

Is there anyone in America who doesn't recognize **American Gothic**? This painting may not be admired as highly as the Mona Lisa, but it has probably been reproduced as often in North America as Leonardo's mysterious lady. You may know his double portrait best, but most of Wood's paintings were farm country landscapes like

Stone City, Iowa. Like the Group of Seven, Grant Wood found the essence of America in its land, only for him it wasn't unbridled wilderness so much as rolling fields of plenty.

Grant Wood was born and raised in Iowa, and he devoted his life to painting themes aimed at an American sensibility. Now you might take a look at his work and imagine that the man had no professional training as an artist because his art seems almost childlike … but you would be wrong. Grant Wood had more art training than most painters in the Ashcan school and the Group of Seven combined, and he could pretty much top the best of the Impressionists and Post Impressionists too. He trained as a designer at the Minneapolis School of Design, then studied at both the University of Iowa and also the Art Institute of Chicago. After serving in the military during World War I, Wood moved to Paris for two years where he enrolled at the Academie Julian just as Henri had, and he visited Italy as well. He took a second trip to Europe a few years later and traveled around Holland and Germany, which is where he discovered German primitive painting … and that's where he got the inspiration to produce his paintings in a certain distinctive way back home. Wood felt so strongly about what he believed American art should be that he wrote a manifesto called *Revolt against the City* in 1935 that instructed painters to find a new style that was particular to America and get away from copying European styles in modern art.

Grant Wood was a professor at the University of Iowa, and he was also awarded the honor of heading up the *WPA (Works Progress Administration) Federal Arts Project* which hired artists to produce art for the government as a way to help unemployed civilians get back on their feet during and after the worst of the Great Depression. The bottom line is that Grant Wood's art may seem simple to us today, but it would be a mistake to write him off as unimportant. He was a major contributor to the art world in America between the wars.

Thomas Hart Benton

Thomas Hart Benton declared himself to be the "enemy of modernism," and like Grant Wood, he built his career in the Midwest painting country scenes of America. The grandson of a Missouri senator (after whom he was named), Benton grew up spending as much time in the nation's capital as he did back home. His family hoped he'd follow in his grandfather's footsteps, but from an early age Thomas wanted to be an artist. He studied at the Art Institute in Chicago a few years ahead of Grant Wood, and like Wood he also rounded out his education with an extended stay in Paris where he enrolled at the Academie Julian. When he arrived back in the USA, Benton initially settled in New York where he taught at the Art Student's League which had been created in 1875 to broaden the offerings at the National Academy of Design.

Although he was anything but famous during his early career, he landed an important commission to paint a series of murals about Indian life for the Century of Progress Exhibition in Chicago in 1933. His murals created quite a stir, and he wound up on the cover of *Time Magazine*. This prompted Benton to leave New York and return to his Midwest roots. He secured a teaching position at the Art Institute in Kansas City, Missouri which enabled him to focus on rural America as a theme, both as it was in his own day during the 1930's and also nostalgically looking to the past as we see in his

Lewis and Clark. The artist was also much in demand for his public murals which can be found in the Missouri State Capitol and the Harry S. Truman Presidential Library.

John Steuart Curry

The third dominant figure in the American Regional painting movement was John Steuart Curry. Like the others, Curry was born and raised in the Midwest. A native of Kansas, he was drawn to rural farm life as a theme in art throughout his life. Curry studied art at the Kansas City Art Institute, the Art Institute of Chicago and Geneva College in New York, and like his fellow American Regionalist cohorts, he spent time in Paris where he admired the work of Rubens and Courbet especially. Although Curry exhibited at the National Academy of Design in New York, he never moved to the city like Benton did. Instead he settled into an academic post teaching at the University of Wisconsin in Madison which enabled him to remain close to the landscape and people memorialized in his art. One of his most famous paintings is **The Baptism** which offers a quaint view of life in conservative 1930's rural and predominantly Protestant America.

Photography Between the Wars USA *1920's-1930's*

Ansel Adams

American Regionalism was a movement promoting national pride confined to painting during the decades between World War I and World War II. The same attitude of pride in America's beauty appeared in photography at the same time, with Ansel Adams leading the way. Adams was a California boy, hailing from San Francisco. Born in 1902 to a well-heeled family, Adams became interested in photography as a child. When he was 15 young Ansel got his first camera as a gift, and his family took a vacation to Yosemite National Park so he could try his hand at taking photographs rather than just admiring them in books. He had already decided to leave school and educate himself in the things that interested him, and first on the list had been mastering the piano. For years Adams alternated between working as a concert pianist and pursuing photography as a career.

The majesty of the US National Parks inspired Adams to join the Sierra Club at age 17, and he went on to become an environmentalist using his photography to document the beauty of pristine nature, especially in the National Parks. Yosemite was always a personal favorite; not only was Yosemite his first experience photographing nature, but he also met his wife, Virginia, there. His photograph of **Half Dome** communicates the spectacular beauty of America as well as Ansel Adams' talent at capturing nature at its best.

Adams was a voracious writer as well. He wrote a series of three technical manuals so other photographers, amateurs and professionals alike could learn from his experience, and he was one of the founders of *Aperture*, a foundation and accompanying magazine which is dedicated to advancing fine art photography. Adams also invented the *zone system*, a technique photographers use to translate light into specific densities on negatives and paper which gave photographers more control manipulating the highlights and shadows in their finished photographs. In 1932, together with several of his photography buddies Adams formed **Group f/64** devoted to exhibiting and promoting new directions in fine art photography. They became the West Coast equivalent of Stieglitz' Gallery 291 in New York.

Dorothea Lange

Dorothea Lange was a contemporary of Ansel Adams, but they could not have been more different. She grew up in Hoboken, New Jersey, the product of an unhappy childhood. She suffered polio at age seven which left her with a gimpy leg, and then a few years later her father abandoned the family leaving her destitute mother on her own to raise Dorothea and her brother at a time when opportunities were scarce for a single mother. Dorothea was a lonely girl with no friends and not much interest in school. At 18 she decided to become a photographer, and through her own independent efforts she created her own self-styled two-year apprenticeship program by working part time at portrait studios and befriending photographers who were willing to teach her their craft.

Once she determined that she had enough experience to go it on her own, she took off for California and settled in San Francisco. California suited Dorothea better than New Jersey. She opened a photography portrait studio, made friends for the first time in her life, and even met and married a painter with whom she had a couple children. The economic instability of the Depression clobbered her career since there was little demand for portraits after the economy collapsed, and Lange responded by wandering the streets documenting the personal strife of the people she saw.

These pictures came to the attention of Paul Taylor, who was an economist at the University of California at Berkeley. Taylor was working on reports for the California State Emergency Relief Administration documenting the hardships of migrant workers who suffered dreadful working and housing conditions. It occurred to him that a picture is worth a thousand words as the saying goes, so he hired Dorothea Lange to photograph the people and their circumstances to include in the reports. **Migrant Mother** says it all. The images Lange produced were so compelling that on the basis of the first Taylor / Lange collaboration report alone, the federal government ponied up $20,000 (which was a lot of money in those days) to build two new migrant worker housing projects in California … the first government funded public housing in US history. Incidentally, as a postscript on Lange, she and Taylor wound up collaborating on more than government reports. By the end of that first year working together they both divorced their respective spouses and married in December of that year. Dorothea Lange became the visual voice of people living on the margins. Perhaps more than anyone else she offered a counter-balance to the optimistic art produced by other artists between the wars.

Mexican Muralists MEXICO *1920's-1950's*

Meanwhile down in Mexico, the country had just been through the 1910 Revolution. Mexican politics were profoundly different from whatever was happening in the United States or Canada. Canada had recently gained her independence from England, but never had the citizens felt abused. They may have been eager to establish a sense of national pride, but they weren't crawling out from under a rock of oppression.

Likewise, during these decades many American artists were seeking to establish an artistic tradition that was independent of the salons of Europe, but it was a matter of national pride more than a need to overthrow some hideously awful status quo. Even Dorothea Lange who documented the poverty of migrant workers did so in the spirit of everyone working together to make the country better. Nobody in Canada or America was a revolutionary struggling to overthrow the past in favor of an all new society. But south of the border, that's exactly what was happening.

In Mexico, a military general doubled as "president" (in effect he'd been dictator since 1876), and while General Diaz had been busy promoting industry in his country to keep pace with the West, it was mostly at the expense of the working peasant class. So while a few fortunate families enjoyed wealth, power and education, most Mexicans were left out of the prosperity loop. In 1910 Diaz allowed an election, feigning a spirit of being a modern, democratic country like her northern neighbors, but then had his opponent's supporters arrested so they couldn't vote, effectively guaranteeing that their guy, Francisco Madero, would lose. The aftermath of the rigged election was that Diaz was forced to resign amid rebellion, but it didn't end there. Mexico suffered topsy-turvy political upheaval over the course of many years.

Diego Rivera

Diego Rivera was a contemporary of the American Regionalist painters in the USA, but his motivations and interests ran along different lines. He was ethnically Jewish, although he might be better described as atheistic, and in general he was openly hostile toward Christianity and especially the Catholic Church. His politics were left-wing, and his private life was undisciplined and self-indulgent. As a young man, Diego traveled to Paris where he connected with the avant-garde left. He slept around and fathered several children, all of whom he abandoned.

When Rivera returned to Mexico in the early 1920's he quickly became a spokesperson for left-wing politics, creating large murals in public places to promote his propaganda message. A handful of other artists followed him, creating the Mexican Mural Movement. He employed bold, bright colors, which were traditional in Mexican art but which also helped attract attention to his paintings, and he employed large, simplified figures ostensibly presented as "typical" members of Mexican society, although the context of the message in Rivera's work was always anything but traditional.

Check out **The Arsenal**, which Rivera painted in 1928. Okay … the figures may have the simplicity associated with pleasant peasant pictures from Mexico, and in the background we do see some typical looking Mexican men on horseback, wearing the stereotypical bandanas and hats. But what's going on here? Men dressed as proletariat workers looking for all the world like they just stepped off the boat from Russia are unpacking a crate of guns and distributing them to their comrades. There's a hammer and sickle flag waving in the middle ground of the scene, and some men are wearing red stars on their clothing. This isn't just some social commentary on how sorry everyone is about the plight of poor people and how mean all the boss men are at the top of the food chain, this is an invitation to Communist Revolution. See the woman in the center of things taking charge of handing out guns … the one in the r-e-d shirt? That's Frida Kahlo. She was a young Communist activist in Mexico, and the following year after this painting was completed she married Diego Rivera.

Man at the Crossroads is an especially interesting mural by Rivera, especially for American viewers. During the 1930's when Americans were actively pursuing public art in the form of murals (think WPA and artists like Thomas Hart Benton for example), Diego Rivera received invitations to visit the United States to produce murals here. Americans identified with the Mexican's desire to be free of tyranny, and so it seemed reasonable that an artist producing famous murals supporting the cause of freedom would have an appeal here. Nelson Rockefeller, the famous New York politician and philanthropist, hired Diego Rivera to paint a huge mural for the Rockefeller Center in New York City. Man at the Crossroads is what Rivera painted. The scene shows a man caught between the past on the left and the future on the right. The past shows a few orderly looking upper middle class types sitting in front of an enormous statue of a god-like figure (notice that the statue wears a Christian cross) who is strangling himself with his own beard. Behind them police with Billy clubs are barging in to beat everyone up. Overhead there are bomber planes attacking, and soldiers wearing gas masks. The inner circle close to our man at the crossroads is filled with aristocratic types sitting around playing cards and dancing. This is Rivera's perception of the corrupt past: Capitalism and Christianity. His vision of the future is on the right. On this side the god-statue has been decapitated, so religion has no place in modern society as Rivera sees things. Aside from the Olympic-style nymphs who are allegorical of "good," everyone is depicted as a proletariat working class Communist. They march along with banners singing a slogan to support their cause. The inner circle close to our man at the crossroads features Lenin as the star of the show, the father of the Communist Revolution in Russia and this artist's inspiration for man's future. Just outside the inner circle, Trotsky hoists a red Communist flag.

All in all, somehow this wasn't exactly what Rockefeller had in mind. He insisted that Diego Rivera make some adjustments to his painting, at the very least remove Lenin as a hero since there was no way such Communist propaganda would sit well in America. Rivera refused. In the end, Rockefeller paid the artist off just to get rid of him, and then promptly shelled out more money to have the entire offensive mural destroyed. All the negative flap over Man at the Crossroads sent out a shock wave across the US that what Diego Rivera celebrated as "freedom" and the sort of freedom Americans held dear were two entirely different ideals. The artist's invitation to create a mural for the Chicago World's Fair was canceled, and Rivera returned to Mexico where he was able to reproduce his defunct mural from the Rockefeller Center in the Palacio de Bellas Artes in Mexico City. The second version is titled *Man, Controller of the Universe*.

Frida Kahlo

Frida Kahlo was not actually a muralist, but since she defies any other category we will group her in with her husband since their lives and work were closely interrelated and her sympathies were certainly with the leftist politics espoused by Rivera and his followers. Kahlo was born in 1907, the daughter of Romanian-German Jewish immigrants to Mexico. Her life was a catalogue of suffering and miseries, partly through the misfortune of illness and injuries in her youth, and partly through her own poor choices as an adult. Like Dorothea Lange, Frida Kahlo was the victim of childhood polio which left her with one poorly formed leg. Also like Lange, Kahlo didn't let polio get the better of her and it may have just made her more determined. As a teenager, though, she was involved in a severe accident that caused her considerable physical pain for the rest of her life. Frida was riding on a bus which collided with a trolley car. The impact impaled Frida Kahlo on an iron handrail, breaking her spine and nearly killing her. Although in time she learned to walk again, she was never without physical pain.

Kahlo decided to pursue a career in art, which is how she came to admire and eventually marry Diego Rivera. She also got involved in the Communist movement; in fact, she recruited Rivera who didn't take a whole lot of persuading since his politics leaned in that direction anyway. Rivera was a lousy husband, as anyone might have guessed he would be given his womanizing coupled with a violent temper ... he would cheat on Frida and then slap her around ... great guy. They divorced. But then against all common sense she married him a second time. Go figure. Frida Kahlo seems to have thrived on her "victim" status, which in turn became the primary theme of her art.

More than a third of all her paintings star Frida as the subject, usually coping with pain and suffering in some capacity. **Broken Column** is a good example. It is a portrait of Frida, cut away so we can see her spine is depicted as a damaged column (an obvious reference to her broken spine in the trolley/bus accident) and she is pierced head to toe with nails to illustrate her pain. Some scholars have tried to suggest that Frida Kahlo was a surrealist painter since some of her paintings resemble those of artists who called their work "surreal," but Frida herself dismissed that label pointing out that what the surrealists painted was dreams while she painted the reality of her life.

American Realism USA *1920's-1950's*

Edward Hopper

This category is half bogus in that the one artist included here needs a category unto himself, and even then there's debate on what to call his art (Social Realism? Urban Realism?). The artist is Edward Hopper. Everyone agrees on the realism part, but the question is how to distinguish him from the Realist movement in France a hundred years earlier. "Social" doesn't describe Hopper very well since most of his art emphasizes loneliness which hardly seems very social. He WAS an urban artist and he painted mostly urban scenes ... but not exclusively urban scenes. Hopper was, however, every bit as 100% authentic American in his choice of themes as the American Regionalists, albeit not the slightest bit interested in down home country Americana as his Midwestern compatriots. So "American Realism" it will be.

Edward Hopper was contemporary to Wood, Benton and Curry, but unlike these painters, Hopper was an East Coast fellow. Born in Nyack, New York in 1882, he was educated first in commercial art before switching over to painting at the New York School of Art, where he studied under Robert Henri. Like so many other artists of his generation, Hopper traveled abroad and spent extensive time in France, but he was completely unimpressed by European art. Like Henri and his followers, Hopper lived in Greenwich Village, although he was a generation younger than the Ashcan school. His paintings frequently focused on urban themes similar to those of the Ashcan painters, but

Hopper's communicate a very different mood. Consider paintings by John Sloan. They unapologetically and optimistically pay homage to the urban, working class lifestyle of early 20th century America. It may not be glamorous, but we get the feeling that the people in Sloan's paintings are happy and satisfied with their life.

Let's look at Edward Hopper's view of life in the city. **Chop Suey** is an early work. City life looks inviting here with a pair of attractive women conversing over tea in a cheerful, bright restaurant. Even so, it seems clear that while the couples at each table are content to carry on conversations, unlike Sloan's images there is no sense of community where everyone present is on friendly terms. It's a room full of anonymous people whose contact with humanity is limited to the one person sitting directly across the table. Fifteen years later Hopper painted his most famous painting, **Nighthawks**. Once again people are in a restaurant, but the mood of the painting is increasingly lonely. The scene is bleak, with three strangers eating their lifeless meals in isolation from one another. Even the man and woman who appear to have come to the restaurant together apparently have nothing to say to one another. The painting communicates lonely people living lives of dull solitude; even when they are with others they seemed locked inside their own thoughts.

Edward Hopper didn't have an unhappy life, although he was apparently teased for being tall and gangly as a teenager, and some scholars suggest the teenage taunting may have caused Hopper to withdraw socially. He grew up in a middle class family; his father owned a dry-goods business which provided comfortably for the family and even gave Edward a part-time job as a teenager so he had pocket money to enjoy himself. He got a good education and traveled abroad when many other Americans were less fortunate. He exhibited in the all-important Armory Show and even sold a painting from that exhibition. He got around to marriage a little late (both he and his wife were over 40), but Jo had been a longtime friend who was devoted to him. But somehow as an adult, even though he enjoyed a successful career and had every opportunity to create a satisfying home life, Hopper extracted minimal joy from the blessings that came his way. For example, Hopper was jealous of Arthur, the family cat, who in his opinion got too much attention from his wife (they never had children; one wonders how much he might have resented their intrusion had the couple raised a family). So he was ornery and obstinate around home to spite his wife, the squabbling was constant and the two apparently made each other miserable.

By the time Hopper painted Nighthawks, he and his wife had plenty of money and they traveled often, although not outside the country. Sometimes vacations away from New York provided new material for his art, but the mood of loneliness and solitude prevailed even when the artist got out of the city. **Hotel Lobby** says it all. The space seems oddly constricted, and even the elderly couple who appear to be sorting out their plans don't seem to be having a very good time being on holiday together; notice how the wife leans as far away from her husband as is physically possible within the confines of her armchair. Hopper's genre scenes are as moving and real today as they were decades ago because each picture tells a story about people we know; perhaps the scenes even seem like a slice of our own lives.

Edward Hopper's career extended beyond World War II, and his very late work occasionally moved beyond genre scenes with people to focus on simple planes of space found in architecture design, light and abstract shapes created by sunlight reflected off flat architecture surfaces, as seen in **Rooms by the Sea**. Edward Hopper's paintings never moved completely away from the structure of an architectural setting, but a few of his late works in the 1950's move in the direction of abstract art.

Precisionism USA *1920's-1930's*

Charles Sheeler

For as much as Edward Hopper captured an impersonal modern world, Charles Sheeler took the idea much further. Sheeler was a photographer who used his hard-edge photographic realism as a springboard for a new style of painting that he dubbed "precisionism." Sheeler studied at the Pennsylvania Academy and then departed for Paris which had become a pretty common educational path for most aspiring young American artists in the early 20th century, but unlike most, he was very impressed with the art of Cezanne and especially Picasso (by comparison, Hopper, who was an exact contemporary of Sheeler, said that he didn't recall hearing about Picasso at all while he was in Paris around the same time). On his return home, Sheeler took up commercial photography to make a living, while doing painting on the side. Among his assignments were documentation photos of industry in America.

Charles Sheeler became completely immersed in the enthusiastic industrialization of America, at times going so far as to suggest that the machine was the new messiah for modern man, displacing God and conventional religion of the past. He became the darling of Big Industry, and industrialists like Henry Ford were quick to tap into Sheeler's almost evangelical appreciation of the new America they envisioned. **American Landscape** was painted on the heels of doing a stint of photographs and paintings for Henry Ford of his River Rouge Plant in Dearborn (greater Detroit) Michigan. Henry Ford had revolutionized automobile manufacturing. By moving the car along a line of workers, each skilled in only one aspect of the production, instead of a few men building a car from the ground up and doing it all, Ford was able to efficiently produce the Model T for the remarkably affordable price of $490 in 1914. After further improving the system, Ford got the price even lower, down to a mere $219 per car in 1919 so that almost everyone could afford to own a Model T. Like Henry Ford, Charles Sheeler saw industry as the future of America. His American Landscape illustrates a very different vision of the country than the American Regionalists had at the same time. Gone is the bucolic countryside with citizens who live in harmony with God and their picturesque homeland. Most of Sheeler's paintings show no people at all, and the "landscape" is more likely to be a factory spewing smoke out to the heavens as if to let God know that we are all doing fine down here on our own thanks, we don't need any interventions from above.

Sometimes his paintings reduce the imagery further, chopping "landscape" out the picture altogether in order to focus our undivided attention on those wonderful machines that do the job more efficiently than men. For example, **Upper Deck** was painted following a commission to photograph a new ocean liner, the *USS Majestic*. Think back to Aelbert Cuyp's Maas at Dordrecht (17th c Dutch). That's how pictures of ships had been rendered in the past. Sheeler bypassed any sentimental attachment to the beauty and grace of a glamorous ocean liner, and instead fawned over the mechanical equipment that gets a ship from point A to point B now that boring old-fashioned sails are obsolete. Although the painting continues to have identifiable objects and is therefore not truly abstract art, it is also true that the machines seem decreasingly compelling as a theme while the emphasis on forms (mostly geometric) and composition increasingly become a subject unto themselves.

Few artists in North America during the early 20th century were eager to jump on the European bandwagon and copy Cubism, Expressionism and the host of other art movements making news on the Paris art scene. Following World War I the focus of the international art world gradually shifted away from Paris toward New York City, in no small part because the Great War left Europe exhausted, and America energized. World War II further established New York as the new center of the cultural universe, and while other urban centers in North America and Europe continue to have a culture of the artiste elite, from now on people will keep an eye on New York the way they did on Paris centuries ago.

24. Contemporary Art Outside Museums

In the beginning there were no art museums. Art was produced for patrons who had enough money to pay an artist to create something the patron wanted. Most art produced in ancient times was created for political rulers who used art to promote their authority, impress the lower social classes, or in some other fashion to improve the ruler's status or circumstances. Ancient art also served to reinforce the local religion, which more often than not also benefited those in charge, who frequently used religion to enhance their own position. In medieval times art was often created to support and teach religion, regardless of local politics. During the Middle Ages and on into the early Renaissance the primary patrons were still either wealthy heads of state, fabulously rich noble families or the Church. Regular people didn't have the resources to commission art, so they either viewed art in church, or in the town square, or some other place where the government, local upper class citizens or the Church had selected to make art available to the common man.

Along came the Protestant Reformation in the 16th century and the relationship between art and the average guy on the street began to change. In regions where the people divorced themselves from the old Catholic society they had neither the Church, nor in many cases a ruling class to commission art. Sometimes this resulted in the art market drying up with very little art being made at all. In other locales, entrepreneurial artists created modest art without the benefit of any patron in the hope that the art might appeal to some middle class individual who could afford to buy it. Artists in this circumstance no longer had any guarantees that anybody would pay them for their work, unlike the old days when a patron placed an order and the artist knew what his buyer wanted. So artists guessed. They chose to paint simple subjects likely to have a broad appeal, and their art was smaller and less expensive so that any number of average Joes could hopefully afford to buy the picture. The artist was now slightly disconnected from the public, second guessing how to please mystery buyers. Further, once a painting was bought, it was squirreled away in the buyer's small house where nobody else in town was likely to see if unless he was invited over for dinner.

As time went on, more and more artists found themselves producing speculative art. It started in the late 16th and 17th centuries in northern Europe, but by the late 18th and 19th centuries art had become competitive through the Royal Salon, and many artists submitted art they created specifically for the show in the hope that their painting or statue would be a ticket to fame and fortune. In the early days of the Salon, fortune was still perceived as a shot at government commissioned work, or the chance of attracting some ritzy patron who would order enough expensive paintings to keep the artist living the good life off in a comfortable villa someplace. Artists went to a great deal of trouble to please their "patron" of a sort, only in this case there was no benefactor paying the bills, artists were frantically trying to please the jury of the Royal Salon. It was tough on the artists to be sure, but at least the art was openly available to the general public at the Salon shows in a way that it hadn't been so much since the advent of the speculative market in art.

Now up until this point, artists had been attentively trying to produce art that buyers wanted. There were the occasional grumpy artists who picked fights with their patrons (Michelangelo on the Sistine Chapel ceiling?), and by the early 19th century there were a couple different schools of thought on what good painting was supposed to be (Poussiniste vs/ Rubeniste), but individual artists by and large desired to produce art that others would appreciate. Artists felt entitled to public respect, and they expected their art to "fit in" to the norms of their day. The Realists were the first group to rock the boat in that they still wanted to be respected and they still expected people to like their art ... but the glitch was they didn't feel like painting the sort of subjects that "fit in" for their day. They weren't producing weird or offensive art; in other words they weren't trying to be hell-raiser rebels so much as they were hoping to have their cake and eat it too. If they could just nudge public taste to understand and appreciate the sort of subjects they felt like painting, then everyone could be happy.

Along came the Impressionists, and for the first time we have a number of artists who not only wanted to do exactly what they felt like doing, they didn't care whether the "patron," in this case the Salon, liked their work or not. It's not that they were trying to offend public taste, but they weren't much interested in accommodating it either. Many of the people who decided to buy Impressionist art were collectors, a new breed of consumer who wasn't buying the art so much to hang in a specific room in his house as he was buying the art just to have it. Kings were like this in the past, but kings had palaces that could hold an awful lot of art, and they passed their art collections on down through the family. Collectors don't usually live in huge palaces and more commonly they donate their art to museums, which were now becoming increasingly popular. By the time we get to the early 20th century, few works of art were being produced on commission anymore, some were produced for big art shows in the hope they would attract favorable accolades, but many were produced primarily because the artist felt like it; there was a nearly complete breakdown in the traditional relationship between the artist and the public.

Increasingly too, among the art elite there was an attitude that if country bumpkins could look at your art, understand it and enjoy it, well maybe you weren't up to snuff as an artist. By then, generations of artists we consider great dating back a hundred years or more were frequently misunderstood in there own time, creating a sense that animosity from the general public toward your art might even be a litmus test as to whether you as an artist were on the right track. The net result has been that frequently the general public will not understand or appreciate the art that artists feel like making, leaving it to be housed in museums the public often won't bother to visit. People feel alienated by the art, and artists are sometimes torn between contempt for the "bad taste" of the general public, while also being frustrated that their art is unappreciated and isn't supported by the public. It's a vicious circle.

This "crisis" in the fine arts was captured with clarity in the Dada art movement and by a number of shows dating around the same time, like the Armory Show. Artists like Marcel Duchamp questioned whether art even existed; how could it be defined when nobody seemed to agree on common standards? He determined that art was whatever the artist says it is, but the general public didn't jump onboard. The gulf between artist and public widened. Many artists in the Dada movement now produced art aimed at deliberately confusing or even offending public taste. Where was all this going?

Conceptual Art *1960s to Present Day*

The logical conclusion (or perhaps illogical conclusion) to Dada has been Conceptual Art. It was formally recognized as an art movement in the 1960's, enjoyed it's heyday in the '60s and '70s, and continues on to the present day in assorted permutations. The first rumblings that something new was just around the corner occurred in the 1950's.

Yves Klein

French artist Yves Klein was on the cutting edge. In 1957 he announced that his paintings were now invisible and he invited the public to an exhibition of his latest work, which was in fact just an empty room. And people showed up to see what there was to see … which of course was … nothing. Is it art? Well now, that is the $64,000 question. On the one hand, it is in keeping with Duchamp's assessment that art is what the artist presents as art. On the other hand, Klein's exhibit is also a modern version of the timeless story of the Emperor's New Clothes. The Hans Christian Anderson tale goes like this:

There was once a very vain Emperor who liked to dress in the most elegant clothes. Two scoundrels decided to take advantage of the Emperor, so they presented themselves as being gifted tailors who had invented an extraordinary weaving method that produced fabric so fine that it was invisible to all but the most discerning eyes. They claimed they had designed patterns in exquisite colors just for the Emperor, which of course average people would be unable to appreciate because they are too stupid. The vain Emperor was so impressed he ordered a new suit, paid the scoundrels and provided them with looms, silk and gold thread. The Emperor was pleased because not only would he have the most glorious new clothes in all the land, he would be able to tell who was stupid among his subjects because they would be unable to appreciate the beauty of his new clothes. The scoundrels of course pretended to weave while pocketing all they had received.

By and by the Emperor asked his prime minister to check on the progress of the special fabric. There was nothing to see, but the prime minister was afraid to admit he was stupid, so he fibbed and told the Emperor how marvelous the fabric was. Eventually the scoundrels finished their weaving, and brought a bolt of the non-existent fabric to the Emperor, gushing with pride over how magnificently beautiful the fabric was. The Emperor was horrified to realize that he could not see or feel anything. His prime minister could see and feel it; did this mean that he, the Emperor was stupid? Not wishing to admit such a glaring personal flaw, the Emperor pretended to be impressed. The scoundrels suggested the Emperor remove all his old clothes so he could try on the new outfit. The Emperor was embarrassed because there he stood in his birthday suit looking into a mirror, but to his relief everyone in the room, not wishing to been perceived as stupid, raved at how glorious the new clothes were.

The people of the kingdom had heard rumors about this exquisite new fabric, and they had rallied for a chance to see the Emperor's new clothes. And so, the Emperor agreed to a ceremonial procession to show off his new attire. All the adults were shocked to see the Emperor in the buff, but knowing that this implied they were stupid, they pretended to see the clothes and complimented the Emperor on how fine the fabric was, lest they lose their jobs. But a small child, who neither had a job to lose nor guile enough to understand why everyone else was lying, blurted out that the Emperor was naked! A ripple shot through the crowd, and little by little others admitted that they too could see nothing except their naked Emperor. The Emperor now suspected that he'd been had, but he was too proud to admit it so he carried on with the procession, trying to persuade himself that he really was wearing clothes that only stupid people were unable to see.

And so ... was Yves Klein's 1957 exhibition art that only stupid people could not comprehend? While you ponder that one, let's consider what this art movement is all about. The underlying premise of Conceptual Art is that the true genius of an artist, what separates him or her from the rest of us is not so much what the artist produces, but rather the vision of the artist – the ideas (as in c-o-n-c-e-p-t-s = "conceptual") in his or her mind and the physical product we call art, is little more than a tangible documentation of the artist's creative genius. If artists could figure out a way to telepathically transmit the genius of their creative minds to others, we'd all own their art and the artist would never have to make physical art again. Needless to say, this definition of art rather precludes museums as a venue for display since there isn't much to see. Beyond that, even if there is some detritus used to explain the artist's vision, it is not supposed to be evaluated as the art itself, which is conveniently housed inside the artist's head, so even if there is an exhibition of *something*, whatever is on display cannot be assessed using traditional vocabulary related to aesthetics. It isn't intended to be "beautiful" or "inspirational" ... it just "is."

Joseph Kosuth

Joseph Kosuth (born 1945 and still kicking) was a prominent figure in the Conceptual Art movement in the 1960's. To quote his own words, Kosuth believed that, "The value of particular artists after Duchamp can be weighed according to how much they questioned art." In other words, what separates "good" art from the mediocre, in Kosuth's opinion, is how much the artist has questioned what art is supposed to be in the first place. By this standard, most of the modern art we have covered so far would be dismissed as so much toady work produced by guys who were decent at craftsmanship, but who may not have measured up as "artists." A famous example of Kosuth's work is **One and Three Chairs** from 1965. Now what you see here *was* shown in a gallery setting, but remember this is *not* the art; the art is the artist's idea which he tried to communicate using these props. Kosuth wished to share with us his understanding of a chair. Now had he been Leonardo, or Rubens, or Vermeer, or Gauguin he might have painted a chair – any kind of chair – and we would have gotten the picture of what the artist wished to convey. Kosuth preferred to offer us the real chair, combined with a photo of the same chair, and a written definition of a chair copied from a dictionary and enlarged for viewing. He has given us three ways to understand the one chair.

Douglas Huebler

Douglas Huebler (1924-1997) was even more abstract, if also less pedantic than Kosuth with all his written dictionary definitions, so dear to Kosuth's heart. Huebler's famous one-liner sums him up pretty well, "The world is full of objects, more or less interesting; I do not wish to add any more." In 1968 Doug Huebler created his **Site Sculpture Project: 42nd Parallel Piece**. The artist's idea was to document the existence of the 42nd parallel (latitude). You can't touch it, see it, or hear it, but we all know that in the abstract, it exists. Huebler laid out a map of the USA and selected a series of towns along the 42nd parallel. He then sent off mailings with return postal receipts to random addresses these towns. In the end he got 21 returned postal receipts, proving that these places were real, and he exhibited the postal receipts along with the map and a written explanation of his project. Once again, the stuff put on display in the museum was not the art, the art was finding a way to share the 42nd parallel with his viewing audience.

Doug Huebler was a generation older than most of the other Conceptual artists, and he received critical comments from some others in the movement (like Joseph Kosuth for example) for being "too old" to really be taken seriously as an *avant-garde* (trendy, really cool, contemporary) artist genuinely contributing to the movement (ask yourself: which is more truly abstract and conceptual, the 42nd parallel ... or a chair? Uh huh ...). Perhaps in response to whatever snooty digs other artists tossed his way, Huebler produced a series of cartoons called Crocodile Tears that are pretty funny; the man certainly did have a sense of humor. **Crocodile Tears: Howard** tells a story of a struggling Expressionist artist who is excited to discover his style of painting has been recycled and is popular again as a "neo" movement ... but alas Howard discovers he's now too old to be cool. As a postscript on Doug Huebler, he was Dean of the California Institute of Arts for twenty years. Keeping that in mind, check out his **Crocodile Tears: The Great Corrector**.

Environmental Art *1960s to Present Day*

Around the same time as Conceptual Art became big news in elite art circles, a sister art movement called Environmental Art also appeared on the scene. It is similar to Conceptual Art in that it doesn't fit the typical museum mode for modern art presentation. Environmental Art is a new twist on sculpture in that the artist might select materials found in nature to create objects, or sometimes the artist manipulates nature to present art in an outdoor setting. Sometimes the art is a permanent installation created in sturdy materials, and at other times it is fragile, left to disappear over time. Some artists manipulate the natural environment creating permanent "damage" in that their art is irreversible (they alter the environment), while others might use found twigs, leaves, snow or whatever is available to create a temporary display that doesn't disturb the natural environment at all.

Richard Smithson

A famous example is Richard Smithson's **Spiral Jetty** built in 1970. It was constructed out of bulldozed rocks and earth on the northeastern shore of the Great Salt Lake in Utah. The environmental sculpture of rocks and mud forms a giant 1500-foot long and 15-foot wide counterclockwise coil jutting out into the lake from shore. When Smithson constructed <u>Spiral Jetty</u> the water level in the lake happened to be low. When it returned to its normal level the following year the jetty wound up submerged under water, and there it remained for almost thirty years. Then it reappeared in 1999 when the water levels dropped again and except for the occasional spring submersion when the lake levels rise due to melting snow from the mountains, it has been visible since. The artist, who was born in 1938, died just three years after completing his <u>Spiral Jetty</u> project.

Andy Goldsworthy

British sculptor and environmentalist Andy Goldsworthy (born 1956) creates sculpture using elements of nature, but without compromising or permanently changing the environment like <u>Spiral Jetty</u>. Many of his works are fragile and temporary, like his **Reconstructed Icicle** which could hardly have been displayed in a museum even if this had been the artist's lifelong dream.

Public Art *1960s to Present Day (sort of)*

Okay, the truth is public art wasn't invented in the 1960's. Public art has been around since forever. Statues like the <u>Augustus of Prima Porta</u> was public art dating all the way back to ancient Rome, and it's not like the Roman emperors were the first guys to think it would be a good idea to sprinkle the landscape with lots of nice statues of themselves. Michelangelo's <u>David</u> was public art too in that the statue was commissioned to be placed in a public location with the understanding that everyone in town would see it on a regular day-to-day basis. But as the centuries wore on, and commissioned art increasingly became the exception to the rule, grand public art projects dwindled too. During the Great Depression the WPA (Works Progress Administration) promoted public mural projects so there was a brief flowering of public art then, but otherwise it had become almost antiquated – a type of art associated with a lost age when patrons like the Church, or a powerful ruler, or city council felt inspired to spend a lot of money on art to impress or edify the people.

Late 19th / Early 20th c Public Art in America

Before we look at the contemporary version of Public Art, let's get up to speed on some examples of public art in America that would be considered modern, if not contemporary. The **Statue of Liberty** is a perfect example. This magnificent colossus standing at the mouth of the Hudson River in New York City harbor has become the symbol of the United States of America as much as the bald eagle or Uncle Sam. She stands defiant against a harsh world to welcome the downtrodden to America, the land of plenty. American poet Emma Lazarus summed up the Statue of Liberty with these lines from her poem entitled *The New Colossus*,

> *Give me your tired, your poor,*
> *Your huddled masses yearning to breathe free,*
> *The wretched refuse of your teeming shore.*
> *Send these, the homeless, tempest-tossed, to me:*
> *I lift my lamp beside the golden door.*

The Statue of Liberty was a given to the USA from France in 1886 as a gift to celebrate the centennial (100 year birthday) of the Declaration of Independence. *Frederic Auguste Bartholdi* was the sculptor, and *Alexandre Gustave Eiffel*, who designed the Eiffel Tower, engineered the complex internal structure. The gift was supposed to be here for the big occasion in 1876 but it arrived late – oops – due first to the artist getting a late start, and then funding ran out so they did a fundraiser sending her giant arm with the torch on a road show where for fifty cents a pop curious people could see the arm.

The statue is 151 feet tall, boosted another 154 feet into the air on her giant pedestal. She has broken shackles at her feet to symbolize that that America has broken free of the tyranny and oppression that plagues so much of the world, and the seven spikes on her crown signify the seven seas and the seven continents, which is to say that people of the whole world are welcome here.

Stone Mountain, located not far from Atlanta, Georgia, is supposedly the largest relief sculpture in the world, covering more than 3 acres. The carving is a tribute to the Confederacy, and it depicts Stonewall Jackson, Robert E. Lee and Jefferson Davis. The idea for the project is credited to Helen Plane, who as a member of the United Daughters of the Confederacy, wanted to see a lasting monument to the Southern Cause. Stone Mountain became associated with Ku Klux Klan activities, as the owner of the mountain, Samuel Venable, was a sympathizer and allowed the KKK free reign over the mountain for their meetings and activities. To be fair though, Helen's idea for the tribute to Confederate heroes predated Klan activity on the mountain by at least a few years.

The idea was born around 1910 (some sources date it is a little before and others a little later). The Venable family deeded the north face of the mountain for the project in 1916, and the project was turned over to sculptor *Gutzon Borglum*, but work was delayed until 1923 due to money crunch problems caused by World War I. In 1925 Borglum had a falling out with those in charge of the project, and he blew out (stay tuned, he moved on to an even more famous public art project). The project was turned over to a series of other sculptors over the years until its final completion is 1972, which was celebrated by the Ku Klux Klan burning 60-foot crosses on the mountain at the Venable family's invitation. The state of Georgia, considering the inflammatory nature of such activities at what was now a significant monument worthy of national pride, condemned the land and then purchased the mountain so that the memorial could be managed by the state of Georgia, and visitors could learn about the Confederacy and see the magnificent relief without fear of the Klan marring their experience.

Meanwhile, where did sculptor *Gutzon Borglum* go after bugging out of the Stone Mountain project? He was hired to create **Mount Rushmore**. Located in the Black Hills of South Dakota, Mount Rushmore was conceived as a monumental project to at once reinforce national pride by honoring four presidents who were each instrumental in establishing and protecting the sovereignty of the United States of America, while also bolstering tourism (and hence the economy) in South Dakota. The name, Mount Rushmore, preceded the project as the mountain had been so named in 1885 after a prominent New York lawyer who led a prospecting expedition there. Prior to that, the mountain had been known by a variety of names among settlers, and predating those monikers the Lakota Indians called it Six Grandfathers. Anyway, the four presidents honored in Borglum's sculpture are George Washington, Thomas Jefferson, Theodore Roosevelt, and Abraham Lincoln.

Mount Rushmore (or in its longer name: Mount Rushmore National Memorial) was commissioned in 1925. By 1933 the site was placed under the jurisdiction of the National Park Service as tourists were already flocking to South Dakota to see the project in progress. Borglum died in 1941, after dedicating Washington's completed face in 1934, Jefferson's in 1936 and Roosevelt's in 1937. His son took over for awhile but the funding ran out with the advent of World War II depleting treasuries. Lincoln's head was completed in time, but the project was still considered unfinished for many years as the original plan, now abandoned, was to complete all the figures to their waists instead of just being the four heads. Curiously, although the site, still considered to be in progress was listed on the National Register of Historic Places in 1966, it wasn't officially dedicated until 1991, by George H. W. Bush.

The heads on Mount Rushmore are enormous, each measuring 60 feet tall. But they are dwarfed by the last public art project in this early modern category: The **Crazy Horse Memorial**. Mount Rushmore was created in old Lakota Indian territory, land that had been granted to their tribe in the 1868 Treaty of Fort Laramie. Many Native Americans were offended by Mount Rushmore, seeing the monument as an encroachment on their land and their culture by a European America. Their response has been to commission an even bigger public art sculpture close by (only 8 miles from Mount Rushmore) dedicated to honoring a great Indian leader, Crazy Horse, who led the Lakota at the Battle of Little Big Horn in 1876. The project was started in 1948 by sculptor *Korczak Ziolkowski*, a Polish American who worked on Mount Rushmore under Borglum. After Ziolkowski won first prize for sculpture at the 1939 World's Fair, the Lakota determined that his ability combined with his familiarity with working in the Black Hills of the Dakotas made him the right guy for the job.

Planning was began soon after the World's Fair, but the actual sculpture didn't get underway until after World War II as the artist served in the Army and was wounded at Omaha Beach during the Normandy invasion. Although the original artist died in 1982 the work is ongoing but far from complete. The Lakota have been offered federal funding to pay for the monument, but they have refused to accept any money from the "white man's" government, which of course contributes to the pokey rate of progress. When and if the sculpture is ever completed, the Crazy Horse Memorial will be the biggest sculpture in the world. As it is now, only the face of Crazy Horse is complete, and it is 87 feet tall, compared to the 60 foot tall heads on Mount Rushmore. It should be noted that while the Crazy Horse Memorial is dear to the heart of many Native

Americans, just as many are furious about the project and do not support it at all. The controversy is centered on the offensive notion of taking sacred Indian land and converting it into a park for tourists, especially because it involves "defacing" a wild mountain into a sculpture. They argue that Crazy Horse would be disgraced by his own people treating nature in this way.

Public Art Today

All the public art projects mentioned here so far have in common that they were envisioned as tributes and memorials destined to instill pride in the viewing audience who, hopefully, share common ideals. Public Art as a movement in more contemporary times is different. These displays are also placed in settings where presumably thousands of people will see them every day, but what's changed is that the art is something the artist felt like making and sharing with the public as a matter of personal expression, rather than the artist being commissioned to produce a project others wanted to support their cause.

Blue Sky

An excellent example that would be familiar to many South Carolinians would be **Tunnelvision** by Blue Sky. Blue Sky was born Warren Edward Johnson on September 18, 1938 in Columbia, South Carolina. He won his first art competition in 1954 while he was still in high school, which encouraged him to pursue art after graduation and following a stint in the National Guard. He attended the University of South Carolina, pursuing more art competitions during his student years and he was eventually invited to study at Art Students League in New York. By 1966 he was back home in Columbia where he returned to USC for grad school. Finally in 1974 he legally changed his name to Blue Sky, the moniker by which he has established his art career.

Blue Sky painted <u>Tunnelvision</u> in 1975 on a blank wall on the side of AgFirst Farm Credit Bank, at the time the Federal Land Bank, in Columbia, South Carolina. The bank agreed to let Sky paint their building, on the provision that he wasn't a communist, but they refused to pay for it so the artist had to apply for a grant to cover his expenses on the project. The mural turned a blank wall into a tromp l'oeil of a street cutting under a tunnel then stretching out into a dawn vista in the Blue Ridge Mountains. The artist intended the mural to have a spiritual impact as well; a 'window' to transcendental reality (consider when the painting was created … the mid 1970's … enough said). Blue Sky has restored and fully repainted the mural five times, and each version has featured at least one new element to extend the metaphor; for example, the most recent addition is a street sign which reads, "One Way." Blue Sky is one of many artists who turned to outdoor murals as a way to bring their art to the people rather than house their work in a museum where the public might never see it.

Claes Oldenburg

Claes Oldenburg was born in 1929 in Stockholm, Sweden, but moved to New York as a child in 1936, then later to Chicago, where he studied at the Art Institute of

447

Chicago. His specialty is large scale sculptures of ordinary everyday objects, and while he is often grouped in with Pop Art, he is being included here since most of his mature works are permanent installations in public settings. He began as many artists of his generation did by producing large pieces for museum shows; his 1963 **Floor Cake** is a perfect example. The 9 foot 6 inch long slice of cake is an assemblage constructed out of painted canvas and foam, hardly the materials that Bernini or Michelangelo used in their day.

Oldenburg soon moved his sculptures out of museums, employing more durable materials that could withstand the elements, and accordingly he joined the ranks of artists creating their art in a public milieu rather than hoping people might stop by a museum to see contemporary sculpture. His early public sculptures were whimsical to be sure, but relatively uncomplicated as composition and logistics go, like **Clothespin** from 1976, located in Centre Square Plaza, Fifteenth at Market Street in Philadelphia. Constructed of Cor-Ten and stainless steel, the sculpture stands 45 feet tall. More recent pieces stretch the imagination with their complexity, like **Flying Pins**, located at the intersection of John F. Kennedylaan and Fellenoord Avenue in Eindhoven, Netherlands. The sculpture, created in 2000, is made of steel, fiber-reinforced plastic, foam, and epoxy, then painted with polyester gelcoat and polyurethane enamel. There are ten bowling pins total, all flopping every which way and some appearing to be partially buried into the earth. Determining dimensions of this piece is tricky, so just look at the sculpture in relation to the surrounding buildings, vehicles and people to get a sense of the scale.

Now where is this discussion of post 1960 Conceptual, Environmental and Public art leading?

Christo and Jeanne-Claude

Christo Javachev, better known by just "Christo" is a contemporary artist, alive and well and living in New York City. Born in Bulgaria on June 13, 1935, he studied art at the Fine Arts Academy in Sofia, Bulgaria. Under Communism, however, there was no future for an aspiring young artist, so he arranged to escape to France. Christo is a small man, and with the help of friends, he was actually packed in a crate marked "medical supplies" and shipped out by train without the armed guards at the border becoming wise to the ruse.

Once in Paris, Christo fit the bill of "starving young artist" and it was in this capacity that he developed a trade in painting portraits for the upper class. One of his commissions was for a prominent French general who desired a picture of his wife. At their estate, Christo met all members of the family, as he was often their guest. The general's daughter, who by the way was born the exact same day and same year as Christo, couldn't resist this charming and unpretentious foreigner, and the two quickly became a couple. Jeanne-Claude married Christo and moved away from the elegant life of her youth to the more bohemian art world of her still-unknown husband. Even during his early years of painting to make ends meet, Christo had already started wrapping small objects. Jeanne-Claude tells stories of not being able to find her shoes, and discovering her husband had transformed them into wrapped art! Christo saw promise in his wrapped creations, but discovered there was no market to sell these pieces in Paris. So after only a few years in Paris, Christo, Jeanne-Claude and their son, Cyril moved to New York. That was in 1964. In the early years Christo was the lone driving artistic force behind the art. The creative vision is his, and he creates all the preparatory drawings and determines how the art will look. Over the years, however, his wife played an increasing role in *producing* the projects, and in 1994 they decided to officially become known as the artists Christo and Jeanne-Claude to acknowledge her contributions to making these monumental projects come to life.

The Christos' work straddles all three art movements: Conceptual Art, Environmental Art, and Public Art, and to this end, Christo and Jeanne Claude are unique. Nobody else does what they do. The husband and wife team create **HUGE** outdoor environment-scaled projects where they wrap, drape, surround or otherwise employ tens of thousands of yards of fabric to alter the appearance of some aspect of the local landscape. It takes them *YEARS* of cajoling local authorities to obtain the permits, clearances, and the good wishes of those whose permission they need to undertake their projects. Then after all the years of meetings and politicking and begging and schmoozing, the project goes up in a matter of weeks, stays up only a short time, and then is completely removed such that no trace of it can be found! Their objective is to create a vision from Christo's mind – a new way to see something – in such a way that the fleeting physical reality brings together as many people as possible to participate in the actual process of creating the masterpiece. Then after this has been accomplished, they take away the physical reminders so that it remains only in our memories … in our minds, which is where it all started for Christo in the first place.

The projects are Conceptual art in that the true vision is in Christo's mind. With Jeanne-Claude's help he brings his vision to life and shares it with others, but then it disappears again such that all we have is documentation and memories. The projects are Environmental Art in that they encompass the natural environment, temporarily altering it so we can see it in a new way, and then everything is returned to its natural state. Environmental concerns run high for the Christos, and they leave the environment as they found it, or improved by removing garbage that was distracting from the beauty of nature before they got there. They are also Public Artists in that all of their installations are produced on a massive scale out in the open, and could not possibly be avoided by anyone passing through.

Let's start with some early examples of their work, starting with **Valley Curtain**, created in Rifle Gap, Colorado near Denver in 1972. After two years of planning, 35 construction workers and 64 helpers, many of them college students, secured 142,000 square feet of orange woven nylon fabric across a valley between two ridges. The curtain was visible for miles. The project took 28 months to plan and was in place only 28 hours before gusting winds forced them to start removal. On the heels of this "success," in 1972 Christo and Jeanne-Claude started working on **Running Fence** which was realized four years later in 1976. The huge project spanned Sonoma and Marin counties in California with an 18 foot high white fabric fence that meandered along almost 25 miles from north of San Francisco down to Bodega Bay where it trailed off into the Pacific Ocean. The fence crossed the private properties of 59 ranchers who all had to be persuaded to participate by allowing the Christos and their entourage and workers to troop through their pastures and fields in the name of art, something most didn't care tiddly winks about. The project took 42 months of collaboration meetings, public hearings, a 450-page Environmental Impact Report and even three sessions of the Superior Courts of California before all the permissions were in place to finally carry out the project. The project was up only 14 days, and then dismantled so that not a trace remained.

Why do they do it? The objective is to first imagine the physical world altered through artist's use of fabric on a grand scale. Then Christo goes to work on the preparatory drawings and solicits the help of engineers and other experts needed to figure out the construction. All the while they are involved in the necessary negotiations to have others agree to let them produce the work at all (and more projects have failed at this stage than have been completed). Finally they use their art as an opportunity to bring together many interested people to help turn the project on paper into a larger than life visual remastering of the environment, but rather than leave it in place, it is quickly removed creating an urgency on the part of the public to see it while it is here, like a beautiful sunset which quickly fades away, but afterwards lives on forever in the minds of those who shared the experience of being there.

You might be wondering who pays for this extravaganza. Christo and Jeanne Claude raise all the money to produce their installation projects 100% by themselves. No tax dollars, or corporate sponsors, or donations are accepted. Christo produces drawings and mixed media renderings (artworks in their own right), which serve as working drawings for the projects while they are underway. Jeanne-Claude then raises millions of dollars to fund the projects by marketing these drawings in a unique fashion to collectors and investors. It works like this: if a collector or investor buys the drawing *before* the project is undertaken, s/he may get it at a substantial discount, but s/he only receives an IOU until after Christo is finished with the drawing's contribution to getting the project completed. By the time the project is over, the drawing is worth many many times what the purchaser paid, so s/he can either resell it for a handsome profit (none of the profit going to Christo), or hold onto it and see an immediate increase in the net worth of his art collection.

Christo is very insistent that the projects themselves make NO profit – he refuses to sell any part of an actual project and gets annoyed when others want to make money off his genius, although there are times when he has allowed *others* to sell posters and the like, if it was the only way to get final permission to do the project at all. The projects all cost millions of dollars to create because they are so large, because all the fabric must be custom made to meet whatever criteria are needed for that particular set of conditions, and because Christo must incorporate large numbers of people to make it all come together, and everyone from the chief engineer to the stooge making sandwiches is paid. There are no unpaid volunteers on a Christo project – he pays minimum wage for the first 40 hours in a week and overtime beyond that.

So why are we focusing the grand finale of the book on Christo and Jeanne-Claude? I have now been on hand for three Christo Projects, and on a personal note, it is an opportunity to share first-hand experience with my readers. On the first project, Surrounded Islands, I was a paid worker involved with the production of the project over a three week period. On the second, The Pont Neuf Wrapped, I was on hand as a guest for a week, although not officially working on the project, and for the third, The Gates, I flew in for the unfurling but was otherwise a tourist like millions of others who made the pilgrimage to be there. I was sorry to miss another, <u>The Umbrellas</u>, but I was expecting a child at the time and the project culminated too close to my due date to travel.

<u>Surrounded Islands</u>, Miami, May 1983

Back in 1983 I had a grad student who had done his undergraduate studies in Kansas City and he was there when Christo did his Wrapped Walkways project (not featured here, sorry). Steve wanted to go down to Miami for <u>Surrounded Islands</u>, but it was smack during final exams and he figured he couldn't make it. My grad assistant, Petra, mentioned this to me, and I immediately asked Steve to inquire if Christo would take all three of us. The word out of Miami was that Christo was short-handed and could use all three of us. Within 24 hours I had both Steve's and Petra's final exams commuted, I had my exams written and delivered to a third party to be done in my absence, I had farmed out my only child at the time to his grandparents and Steve, Petra and I were on the road to Miami, where we would work for Christo for the full three weeks of the project installation. Since we got there on the first day of check-in, we were available to participate on some behind-the-scenes work before the actual installation began. The divers already had all the submerged anchors and tether lines in place around the 14 islands to be surrounded with glorious pink petticoats, like giant water lilies. Think of Monet's Water Lilies … Christo did! There was concern that the submerged tethers could be a threat to the habitat of certain marine life, especially manatees, so the islands had to be patrolled around the clock to keep an eye out for any animals caught in the lines. We were glad to get involved early and pulled a few all-nighters cruising around Biscayne Bay in motorized rubber rafts as troubleshooters.

Pelican Harbor Marina in Miami was base of operations for <u>Surrounded Islands</u>. Over the course of several days, over 600 people from all around the world arrived to work on the project. Each person had to be checked in which included offering a body of information recorded on 3x5 cards, and having a picture made. Christo and Jeanne-Claude maintain enormous files in their loft in New York City, and they periodically keep in touch with people who have participated on a project; I still occasionally get invitations to their openings around the world. Everyone also got a pink t-shirt screen-printed with the Surrounded Islands logo which we were expected to wear at all times once the project was underway, and we got French Foreign Legion style hats to wear in the sun.

Christo and Jeanne-Claude began the project by holding a press conference interview at Pelican Harbor. They go out of their way to be cordial and helpful with the press. In fact, before any project begins all the workers are gathered together for an orientation program and the Christos make it very clear that while the project is underway, every worker is 100% representing both the art and by extension, the artists, 24 hours a day, 7 days a week. There is no such thing as being rude to someone – be it passers by, tourists, or reporters or anyone else, even if the *other* guy is being rude or even hostile to you. Being on the team means acting like the entire success of the project rests on your own behavior, and it doesn't matter if you are tired or sore, you WILL be helpful and polite, especially to folks who are not directly involved with the project.

Once everyone was checked in and Christo and Jeanne-Claude had done their orientation program, we were sorted into island crews that were identified by a color and number; I was on Green 9. The first real job was to move bundles of underlayment to the islands by motorboat relays. The underlayment was designed to serve as a protective buffer between the abrasive beach (sand, broken shells, bits of coral etc.) on each island and the real pink fabric that would be floated over it. Once we had the underlayment anchored in place, we had to roll it up onto shore and sandbag it in place for several days while we got the rest of the puzzle pieces in place.

The next step was to move the "booms." Christo was there the entire time, offering demonstrations on how the process would work once the unfurling was underway, and in general supervising not only our entire crew of workers, but also a substantial number of hired day labor Haitians who came on board just for this segment of the project. The booms were very long, fat Styrofoam "logs" that were wrapped with fabric then covered with a protective bunting that could be easily slipped away during the *unfurling*, which is the term they use for pulling the fabric out from a rolled-up state to stretch over the surface they intend to cover, in this case, the water. There were hundreds of booms, they were all extremely heavy and they had to be moved carefully such that no part of the boom was bent or stressed as they could break. We started at 4am (yawn) and worked until about 3am the next day (beyond yawning) to get those babies all in the water. On a Christo project, you get used to going full-tilt for days on end. The bottom line is you do what you have to do to get the job done. There is no such thing as breaks and quitting because the clock says it must be time to go. There was 24 hour food delivery of unlimited sandwiches and apples and we were all expected to carry gallon jugs of water with us at all times ... and, well, you just keep on going. I must admit that was the day with the most frayed nerves, though as we were all shot ... no, beyond shot. One of my funniest memories was of Christo and Jeanne-Claude, who are usually a super team together, standing about 5 feet apart, each with a bull-horn screaming at each other in French. What a day!

The booms were pulled by boat to the respective islands where they were then attached to the submerged anchors, which were already in place. As always, Christo was right there in the middle of everything, checking on details and spending time with the workers. It may seem remarkable, but I can honestly say that Christo is one of the most unpretentious people I have ever met. By 1983 I can assure you he was already a huge internationally known artist (I did a paper on him when I was in college over 10 years earlier), and yet he stayed at the same string of inexpensive art deco hotels where he put up all the crew, which is to say, people like me. He took all his meals at Denny's. I only saw him wear 2 shirts in the 3 weeks I was there – he'd wear one, evidently until it needed to be washed (probably in the hotel sink), then rotate to the other, then back again. He went out of his way to talk to just about everyone involved and paid just as much attention to the lowest guy on the totem pole as he did to titled nobility when they showed up wanting a tour. He made a point of emphasizing that everyone on the project was as important as anyone else. If the sandwiches don't get made and delivered it can be just as much of a crisis as if an anchor laid by the best engineer wobbled loose. Everyone does what he or she does best to make the project work as a whole. He may handle millions of dollars to make his art, but he only pays himself $25,000 a year beyond travel expenses (or at least he did in 1983, I hope he has given himself a raise since then!) and Jeanne-Claude works for free – all the money goes into the art, or buying apples to feed the crew, or even buying t-shirts and hats for the crew, as it is more a matter of working *with* him than it is working *for* him.

To illustrate the transformation Biscayne Bay would soon undergo, I have included a couple good aerial views of one of the islands, not "my" island, but one of the smaller ones. You see it first the day all the booms were anchored in place. Notice how you can see the submerged tether lines. The fabric was custom designed to float on the surface of the water, but just the same, the fabric was pulled over these tether lines to assist buoyancy. The second photo is how it appeared the following day after the unfurling ... quite a change, yes?

Once the booms were in place we had to remove the sandbags and roll the underlayment back onto the beach. Ah for the BIG day!!! The unfurling took only a matter of a few hours it was so well orchestrated. There were boats anchored off each island "connected" by walkie-talkies. At precisely the same moment all the buntings were stripped away and the crews, all stationed on their respective islands, p-u-l-l-e-d the fabric in using more tether lines that had been run in by rubber rafts the day before from the booms. We had to keep the fabric low to the water. One island crew got casual about that rule and they got a big airlift under the fabric carrying several people skyward 30 feet or more until dozens of people jumped on the fabric to get the air out! Once the fabric was in to shore it had to be secured by anchors on the beach, then workers had to shimmy out onto the fabric and lace the panels together into unified "lily pads". All you can see from the islands was pink. Most folks never saw the view from on the islands themselves, but the scale of it was overwhelming.

After the unfurling, everyone working on the islands saw nothing but pink for as far as the eye could see, especially on Green 9 since our island and Green 10 had a sandbar running between them and the two were surrounded together as a figure-eight. People *not* involved with the project, however, saw clips on the news featuring aerial shots of the project. Most air traffic out of Miami International was routed over Biscayne Bay for the three weeks that the fabric was in place. Many people also hired helicopters to fly over the islands. I was lucky because my island captain happened to be one of the engineer divers responsible for anchoring the tether lines under water, and as I was able to do triangulations myself, I assisted with some of the tech work, usually putting in long hours after most of the regular rank and file workers had knocked off for the day. As a result, I got to know a lot of the behind the scenes people better than the average person on the project, and because of this, I was offered a chance to fly over the islands myself. They slid me in with some Earl of Something or Other (I forget!) and his wife visiting from England (very charming older couple) and I got to go as a tour guide of sorts on behalf of the project. Not only was it my first time in a helicopter, but it meant that I got to see the project from above which was particularly interesting after being soooo close to it for weeks up until that moment.

After the project, I coordinated my efforts with the Christos up in New York to produce a written documentary on all the workers on the project, which was later published as part of the monograph on Surrounded Islands. I sent questionnaires to the almost 700 people who had participated on the project, and I was pleased that a substantial number wrote back to me. Combining that data with the statistics the Christos had collected on each worker from the start, I was able to write about the individuals who worked on the project and made it what it was. One of the observations I made, which still stands today all these years later, is that many people (myself included) commented that working on a Christo Project had in some way changed their life. Many (many many!) of the workers are "repeat offenders" – they come back time and time again to work with Christo, and I am not talking about just hippy skippy artsy types. I am talking about professional people with lucrative careers who put their lives on hold when Christo gets the green light to do another project. All kinds of folks from all over. It's special. People seem to discover something in themselves – a "can do" attitude that rubs off on the workers after hanging around with Christo and Jeanne-Claude for awhile. We all noticed that there are never any "problems" with Christo – there are only "situations," and situations generally find solutions. The Christos are the most ordinary, humble people, and yet, look at what they accomplish! And somehow, by just being part of it, many of us have gone on to do more than we might have ever dreamed possible – because we discovered that we could.

Pont Neuf Wrapped, Paris, September 1985

Despite its name as "the new bridge," the Pont Neuf is the oldest bridge in Paris and as such has a sentimental spot in the hearts of all Parisians. Situated such that it connects the Louvre to Notre Dame (Paris) Cathedral as it spans the Seine River, it is picturesque under any circumstances. Christo's dream was to enhance this beauty with shimmering maize-gold fabric, if only for a couple weeks to bring thousands of people together at this landmark of old Paris.

In 1985 I was doing post-graduate doctoral work at the University of Saint Andrews in Scotland. I hadn't taken time away from my studies to go to Paris to work on the Pont Neuf Wrapped because we Americans had all heard the word that one of the provisions the French had put on the project was that there could only be paid FRENCH employees, and we knew that Christo would not let anyone work who was not on the payroll, except his wife. Even so, I knew when the unfurling was scheduled to take place, and packed up my son, Jacob who was 9 at the time, and we made the pilgrimage over to Paris for a week just to be there for the unfurling. Many of the old, familiar faces were there, folks I had met in Miami, many of whom I was still in touch with on a regular basis.

As with Surrounded Islands, much of the effort goes on in the days before the actual unfurling when all the press is on hand for the big event. We arrived in time to see the professional mountain climbers getting the arches of the bridge strung up with the fabric booms, which were running under the arches then secured just along the edge of the exterior ready to be pulled up over the bridge on the big day. The unfurling went so fast on The Pont Neuf Wrapped that it was breathtaking to watch, all the more when you are a tourist and not sweating out the labor of doing the work yourself! Within minutes the arches were completely covered and the climbers had moved on to securing the fabric around the great piers. The finished product was absolutely beautiful. The bridge glistened in the early autumn light (a lovely time of year in Paris), and the entire street above, lamplights and all were covered.

I had seen the Christos briefly, but not like in Miami given that I was there as a tourist and not as a worker. The evening after the unfurling there was to be a big party for all the crew workers, just as we had in Miami after Surrounded Islands. Christo had hired a big bateau mouche, those barge-like boats you see along the Seine, and he was putting on cocktails and dinner for all the workers - fortunately a much smaller crew than we had on <u>Surrounded Islands</u> as 600-700 people would never have fit on one boat! That afternoon I was chatting with one of the participants I met in Miami, Ted Dougherty. Ted had been a regular on Christo projects ever since Valley Curtain, and one of his sons was an island captain on the Miami project. Ted was always easy to spot because he is confined to a wheelchair, not that this stopped him from being a key person on projects. He asked if I was planning to go on the boat that night. I said I had not been invited given as I was not on the crew this time around. He gave me a sly look, and said, "Are you sure? Have you checked the guest list?" At that I strolled over to where these two particularly snooty Parisian girls had been working the check-in desk all week, usually acting huffy and telling people what they could and couldn't do with an air of presumed authority. I inquired whether my name was on the list for the party that evening. They looked down, and said that why in fact, the woman I mentioned WAS on the list with 4 stars. I asked what the 4 stars meant, and one girl said with a look suggesting this had been hammered into her pretty little head at orientation, that they were to treat this woman as a very very very very important guest. I must have looked surprised, because it dawned on one of them that perhaps, just maybe I might be that person. Uh oh … they had been rude to me all week, but suddenly you would think I had just been personally made queen as they stumbled over themselves to get our reservations made for the dinner cruise.

The party was fun, but the very best part was that Christo spotted Jacob, my 9-year-old little boy whom he had never met on <u>Surrounded Islands</u> since Jacob stayed with his grandparents watching the project unfold on television. Christo pulled up a chair and chatted with Jacob for the longest time – about what he thought of the art, how he liked going to school in Scotland, and a variety of subjects covering just about every base. Here he was, the famous artist in his hour of glory on the heels of a successful project, surrounded with enthusiastic admirers, and he spent time talking to a 9 year old kid about soccer. Christo truly is one of a kind.

<u>The Umbrellas</u>, Southern California and Japan, October 1991

I regretted missing **The Umbrellas**, but I had friends who were there. What was particularly intriguing about this project compared to the others was that it combined twin projects on two separate continents simultaneously. All of Christo's large environment-scaled projects encompass time and space issues coordinating a number of people over a very large area all working together on a carefully orchestrated event, but with Umbrellas, the unfurling was happening simultaneously across time zones.

Christo selected California on one side of the Pacific Ocean, and Japan on the other, and designed over three thousand large umbrellas (19' 8" diameter) to all pop open simultaneously, remain open for a total of 18 days, then be closed and dismantled. On the California side, there were 1,760 bright yellow umbrellas scattered across an 18 mile by 2.5 mile valley in southern California about 60 miles north of Los Angeles. In Japan the selected valley was 75 miles north of Tokyo, and it was a little smaller at 12 miles long by 2.5 miles wide. The umbrella color for Japan was blue, and 1,340 umbrellas were installed. Given that the California valley was a little larger than the location in

Japan, it's interesting to compare how many landowners had to be persuaded to cooperate with the artists, their entourage and workers trooping across private property. In California, only 25 landowners factored into the negotiations, whereas in Japan the artists had to win over a whopping 459 private property owners in order to undertake the project. It took a core team of 500 staff to work out all the logistics, obtain all the permissions and get everything good to go, along with 960 workers in California and 920 workers in Japan to make The Umbrellas become a physical reality.

The Gates, Central Park, New York City, February 2005

The Gates is the Christo's most recently completed project, although the idea and long, long battle to get permissions predates other projects completed sooner. Way back in 1979 the artist became inspired to create a series of fabric gates for Central Park. When landscape architect Frederick Law Olmstead designed the park back in the mid-1800's, he enclosed the space with walls that were supposed to have beautiful entrance gates. Sadly the gates were never completed, but it was the idea of these lovely gates greeting the public as they entered Central Park that inspired Christo. After years of disappointment and frustration to where he might have wondered if the project would ever come to pass, at long last it was approved, all the permissions were signed and this long time dream-project of Christo's was finally going to happen.

I knew about the project of course, but I'd been out of the loop since The Umbrellas and between teaching, writing textbooks (like this one) and juggling a family of one husband, five kids (albeit only four still at home), two dogs and a cat, I had my hands full. I hadn't planned to go to New York for this Christo project … especially in February … brrr! Then one afternoon in January the phone rang, and unexpectedly it was Petra, my former grad assistant from 20 years ago and roommate on Surrounded Islands. She asked if I was ready for The Gates and wondered if I wanted a roommate again, because she was planning to come into the city for the unfurling. So as it was with Surrounded Islands, within hours the decision was made, plane tickets arranged and a hotel room booked.

We arrived about an hour apart from our mutually different states, settled in at our economy hotel on the upper West Side just a couple blocks from the park, and headed off on foot to check out the day-before-the-unfurling preparations. Neither of us was working on the project so we had the luxury of just being informed tourists. The park was buzzing with workers in grey vests sporting walkie-talkies as they checked and rechecked the installed frames for the fabric panels, all 7,503 of them covering 23 miles of walkways, that would the following day transform Central Park into a sea of fluttering golden orange. We stayed out wandering the park until long past dark, then stopped by the boathouse where some of the workers had kicked back after a long day in excited anticipation of what was to come tomorrow.

This time around Petra and I were the veterans, not the new kids on the block, and after so many interim years since Surrounded Islands, I actually had former students since Petra's day who were on the project. One, Annie, had pursued a career in New York at an art museum in part hoping she'd get to work on The Gates, so we had plans to tag along with her team the following day during the unfurling, giving us the luxury of having an insider's view without having to do any work! No sooner had we rendezvoused with Annie the following morning, than my cell phone rang. It was yet another student, this one still in college. She had skipped out of school for a few days in order to be in New York for the unfurling so she was in the park too, and the four of us spent the day being part of the amazing event, with Annie scrambling around doing all the work, and Petra, Jes and I along for the ride. The unfurling was thrilling to see, as it always is. We saw celebrities we recognized hanging out with everyone else just for the chance to be part of it all. News teams were everywhere broadcasting live. Christo and Jeanne-Claude spoke briefly from a podium, and the atmosphere was electric. After the unfurling, we walked around for hours covering miles upon miles of the park to see the spectacle from every possible angle. There were people everywhere, and everyone was in a happy mood, pleasant, friendly and having a great time just being there. I think maybe that's what Central Park was always intended to be, but it took a few thousand fabric gates to make it happen.

That evening the four of us went out to dinner at a cozy Italian restaurant not far from Annie's place in the city. Except for having taken classes with me and learning about Christo among other things, none of these three women had ever met one another before that day, and before taking art history, only one (Petra) was an artist or had any particular interest in art. And yet there they were, chattering away like best friends about art and how amazing The Gates experience had been, and making plans already to be part of the next project. For future reference, that will be **Over the River**, currently scheduled for no earlier than 2011. The project will span 6.7 miles of the Arkansas River in Colorado with shimmering waves of translucent fabric suspended 8 - 25 feet in the air above the water. Boaters should be able to see through the fabric to the sky above, and people flying over should be able to see through the fabric to see boats on the river below.

I was only in New York for a couple days, but after I returned home I received a steady stream of messages from students I'd had over the years. I was impressed with how many took it upon themselves to get to New York to be part of The Gates. By 2005 I had been teaching online for awhile and my students, former and present were from all over. I think my favorite photo of those sent my way was of a group of cadets from the US Merchant Marine Academy in full uniform, grinning like a bunch of Cheshire cats in front of a long path of bright orange gates ... I am not sure what brightened the obviously cold, dreary grey day more, the gates or the men's smiles.

The Gates was up for 16 days, and then *POOF*, it was gone. And now, so is your tour through Art History from Prehistory to Contemporary. I hope you have learned a thing or two along the way, and that knowledge has brought you greater understanding and appreciation of the world around you, as it was in the past and as it is today.

Glossary

A

abbey – church for monks or nuns

acropolis - "high city" usually used in reference to Greek temple district

additive architecture – buildings built on top of the ground

aerial perspective – making objects in the background appear to recede in space through dull, bluish-grey colors

aesthetics – comes from philosophy, relates to the nature of art and beauty

aisle – the portion of a church that flanks the nave, commonly used for circulation

altarpiece – religious art situated on or hanging above an altar in a church

ambulatory – a passageway behind the apse (and sometimes choir) of a church

amphitheater – a double theater – round or elliptical such that people sit around an arena

amulet – an object or charm worn to ward off evil or bring good luck

Anastasis - Resurrection

Annunciation – when Archangel Gabriel visits Virgin Mary (Gospel of Luke)

apocrypha – Writings not considered authentic; early writings not included in the Bible

Apostolic Succession – A blessing passed on through the laying on of hands from Jesus to the Apostles on down through the generations of bishops and priests in an unbroken commission.

apse – the east end of a church – the holy sanctuary, or in a pagan Roman basilica, a semi-circular room customarily used as a courtroom

arch - a curved or pointed structure that spans a space in lieu of a flat lintel. Created from wedge-shaped blocks called voussoirs; produces outward thrust when carrying weight from above

architrave – the lower of two lintels in an entablature

arena – central space in amphitheater where combats or violent sports were staged

Arianism – Early Christian heresy that denied that Father, Son and Holy Spirit were equal in the Trinity

asceticism – self discipline and self-denial

atrium – 1) enclosed courtyard in front of a church, 2) living room in Roman house partially open to the sky

attribute – an object or particular color used to help identify the identity of an individual in art

avant-garde – adjective or noun referring to artists or styles (19th c or later) that are innovative, challenging to the established public taste

B

baptistery – building adjacent to a Christian church used for baptizing

baroque – dramatic, theatrical, exaggerated, complex, emotional

Baroque – the 17th century

barrel vault – ceiling design based on the round, Roman arch. Popular 11th & 12th c

bas-relief – low (shallow) relief carving

basilica – 1) Pagan Roman – building used for public assemblies, court and commodities exchange, 2) Christian architecture – rectangular church

beehive tomb – Mycenaean tomb built by corbelling then buried

book of hours – manuscript containing prayers for different hours of the day

broken brushstroke – a painting technique of dabbing strokes of different colors and allowing the viewer's eye to mix the colors as opposed to the artist mixing all colors in advance and applying strokes of a single mixed color.

buttress – masonry support to brace outward thrust from arches or vaulting

C

campanile – bell tower adjacent to church

canon – system of proportion

canon law – Church law of conduct derived from Scripture, Tradition, and Councils

capital – 1) top of a column that identifies architecture order (Doric, Ionic etc), 2) money

cartouche – oval frame containing hieroglyphic letters to create a word

caryatid – a statue used in architecture as a supporting column

casino – Italian word for a modest vacation home in the country

catacombs – underground galleries and chambers used to bury the dead

cathedra – the seat of a bishop. When used **ex cathedra** refers to the rare occasions when a Pope speaks with official authority; **cathedral** is a physical church building which is the seat of a bishop

Catholic Church – Christian Church in the West that grew out of the Early Christian Church

cavea – auditorium seating, can be in a theater or amphitheater

cella – chamber in a Greek temple where statue of deity is housed

centering – wooden frame used to stabilize an arch while under construction

central plan – round, oval or octagon shaped church

cherubim – angels depicted as chubby babies in art

chiaroscuro – high contrast of light and dark (highlighting and shadow) to model figures

Chi Rho – Symbol for Christ with an X (Greek letter for chi = C) overlapping a P (Greek letter rho = R) – the first two letter's in <u>CH</u>rist

choir – extension of the nave east of the transept, normally reserved for clergy, monks, and nuns

city-state – independent, self-governing city

classical – simple, plain, understated, timeless

Classical – refers to 5th and 4th century BC, or Classical antiquity refers to ancient Greece and Rome

clerestory – windows located above a nave arcade

cloisonné – term from jewelry-making – narrow wire or fine metal strip soldered to contain enamel or other material. In painting refers to flat areas of color contained by outlines that resemble cloisonné jewelry

cloister – in the context of architecture, an enclosed garden usually attached to a monastery. Can also to a monastery or convent where nobody from outside the religious community is allowed to enter.

coffered ceiling – decorative ceiling with recessed panels

collage – composition by combining various flat materials (paper, cloth, text etc)

colonnade – rows of columns

column – vertical upright in classical architecture, cylindrical, decorative post

complementary colors – opposite colors on the color wheel, such as red and green, blue and orange, yellow and purple

composition – arranging shapes and forms in art and architecture

connoisseur – an expert on art appreciation (identifying and understanding style)

contrapposto – shifting the weight in a statue from 2-feet to 1-foot to make the figure appear relaxed

corbel – arch: cantilevering stones gradually in construction over posts to alleviate weight on a lintel, or dome: cantilevering stones in a circle such that the stacked walls bend into create a beehive-shaped structure

Council - meetings in the Christian Church to confirm issues of faith or resolve heresies

Corinthian order – most elaborate Greek order, popular in the Hellenistic period

cropping – slicing off the edge of a picture as a means of altering the composition

Crusades – Medieval wars with Christians trying to reclaim their Holy lands from Muslims

cubicula - bedroom in Roman house

cuneiform – Mesopotamian written language

D

Delian League - Political treaty between Athens and her Greek neighbors during the reign of Perikles

Divine Liturgy – the religious service of the Byzantine / Orthodox Church

dome – hemispheric vault

donjon style – taken from the word "dungeon," it refers to a castle style that resembles a walled fortress

donor figure – image of the patron

Doric – simple and early Greek order – capital resembles cereal bowl

E

earth-tone palette – autumn colors in painting

Ecole des Beaux Arts – the school of fine art within the greater umbrella of the Royal Academy in France

elevation – head on flat view of a wall

engaged column – half column carved on wall; decorative pilaster

entablature – double lintel on top of columns in classical architecture

entasis – the artificially created appearance of swelling in a stone column slightly above its base

Eucharist – Consecrated bread and wine consumed during communion

F

façade – front, or "face" of a building

fete galante - Rococo imaginary romantic outdoor genre of the upper classes

fetish – object believed to carry special powers, excessive preoccupation

feudalism – Medieval socio-economic system where status is based on landholdings

flying buttress – supporting arm that carries outward thrust from a vault to a buttress

foreshortening – shortening the perspective to make objects appears to project forward or recede rapidly into space.

form – an object's shape and structure

formal balance – seen in architecture when a building is designed to be symmetrical. In art refers to composition that is centered with even number of figures or equivalent on either side.

freestanding sculpture – statues

fresco – applying paint pigment to wet plaster

friars – monks that are not tied to an abbey; mendicants

frieze – second lintel in an entablature – usually decorated – or any ornamented band of sculpture

G
gallery – upstairs area over an aisle

Gallery of Kings – a band of sculpted figures commonly found on the façade of Gothic churches in France

gilded – gold-plated

Gospels – New Testament books of Matthew, Mark, Luke and John that tell the life story of Jesus

Greek Cross – variation on the central plan such that in addition to the apse and narthex forming arms, 2 perpendicular chapels are added such that the central nave has 4 approximately equal arms

grisaille – outer panels on an altarpiece produced in subdued colors such that altarpiece can be closed during Lent to show the somber images, then opened at Easter to show bright colors

groin – the crossing between 2 vaults

guild houses – buildings used by trade guilds - usually found along the perimeter of a town square

H
Hiberno Saxon – Celtic influenced early Medieval art found in Britain and Ireland

hieroglyphics – Egyptian writing system

high relief – carved relief images approaching full, rounded character

hip roof – a roof that slopes on all sides (there is no pointed gable)

Holy Spirit – Third person of the Christian Trinity – often depicted in art as a dove

hue – color

humanism – starting in the Renaissance, emphasis on education and relying on potential of man's thinking, often in contrast to relying on God and Faith

hypostyle hall – Egyptian temple architecture – roofed area supported by many columns

I
icon – image of Apostle, saint, or scene from the life of Christ. Used in Eastern Orthodox Christianity as catalysts in prayer

iconoclasm – also **inconoclast movement** - destruction of religious images – particularly between 726 and 843 due to government ban on sacred images

iconography – the study of the meaning of art. Includes understanding narrative themes and iconology

iconology – within iconography, the specific study of symbolic meaning of objects in art - understanding hidden religious content or themes in art

iconostasis – large screen located in the apse of an orthodox church with icons. Visually separates the back of the apse from the rest of the church

impasto – thick, textured paint brushstrokes

impluvium – pool of collected rainwater in center of Roman atrium

indulgence – an opportunity to commute part or all of a traditional penance with an alternative sacrifice of the part of the penitent

informal balance – in architecture, a plan or elevation design which is deliberately asymmetrical. In art, a composition that emphasizes asymmetrical, off-center composition

in situ – in place

inscription – text written on the surface of the picture or carved into the stone on a statue

insula – multi-story apartment building

International Style – popular style seen across Europe around 1400 characterized by elongated, flat figures, bright color, heavy patterning, gold, and overcrowding in a shallow field of space

Ionic – Greek order with capital that resembles a scroll

J

jamb statues column-shaped statues located on the door jambs at the entrance of Gothic churches to greet the public

Jamnian Old Testament – an abridged version of the Old Testament dating from 90 AD that eliminates all Scripture not originally written in Greek. Originally designed to discredit Christian writing as "Scripture." Employed by Jews (except in Ethiopia) and Protestant Bibles

K

ka – Egyptian soul

keystone – top voussoir in a Roman arch

kore – Archaic Greek statues of young women

kouros – Archaic Greek statues of young men

L

lancet windows – a narrow window with either a rounded or pointed arch at the top

linear technique – no visible brushstrokes – associated with Poussiniste art

load-bearing wall – a wall that supports weight from above

lunette – a semi-circular area above a window, door, or on a manuscript calendar page

M

magi – The Wise Men

mandorla – almond shaped halo – usually surrounding Christ

Mannerism – 16th century art movement in central Italy associated with tenure of Medici popes. Irregular presentation of religious subjects to the point of apparent parody

manuscript – historically it means a hand-written book (nowadays it may also refer to a draft of an unpublished work)

martyrium – a church that is built over the grave or death site of a martyr

Mass – the religious service in the Catholic church

mastaba – house for the dead in Egypt

medium – the material something is made of

megalith – big stone

mendicants – monks who have renounced worldly goods, including abbeys, and wander – teaching, begging and serving others

menorah – a 7-branched candelabra or lampstand used in Jewish worship

metope – space between triglyphs on Doric frieze

monochromatic – reduced to a single color

monolithic - large, single block of stone

monotheism – faith in one god

mosaic – small pieces of glass, stone or ceramic tile attached to wall, ceiling or floor to create picture or pattern

mummification – Egyptian technique to embalm body as permanent home for soul

Muslim – follower of Islam religion

N

narthex – lobby or vestibule area in church

nave – large hall space where congregation stands during church service

nave arcade – columns or piers supporting arches that separate a nave from aisles

nave colonnade - columns or piers supporting a flat lintel that separate a nave from aisles

necropolis – city for dead people – a district of tombs

Neoplatonism – a study of Plato's philosophy modified by Aristotlelian philosophy and additional other influences from the orient. Allows that the world comes from God (or the "One") and that man can be mystically reunited with this One. Devotees often tried to blend Christian principles with pagan philosophy and Oriental philosophy.

nomad / nomadic – people who move around

O

oculus – round opening at the top of a dome

onion dome – dome that comes to a point – looks like a Dairy Queen ice cream cone ☺

opisthodomos – bogus back porch on a Greek temple

orchestra - circular center of Greek theater where performance took place. Comparable location in Roman theater used for seating dignitaries while performance shifted onto a stage

ordination – sacrament that confers the blessing of Apostolic Succession on priests and bishops

Orthodox – the Eastern Christian Church which evolved from the Byzantine Church

P

pagan – worship of many gods or having no religion at all, often associated with hedonism

painterly – visible brushstrokes – often associated with Rubeniste painting

palette – term used to describe colors, also a slab or board used for applying color

Pantocrator – large mosaic or fresco image of Christ in either a dome or half dome inside a church

parchment – prepared lambskin used for a writing material

pastels – light colors, or can mean a type of colored chalk

patriarch – highest religious leader in the Eastern Orthodox Church (regional)

patrician – upper class Roman citizen

patron – person who pays for art or architecture

patron saint – saint selected at confirmation into Catholic or Orthodox faith

pediment – the gabled end of classical architecture

pendentive – triangular supports used to support domes, especially over oval or square spaces. See Hagia Sophia for example.

penitent – somebody who is sorry for offending God

Pentateuch – Christian term to describe first 5 books of the Old Testament (same thing as Torah)

peplos – a simple belted woolen dress worn in Greece

peristyle – a roofed area supported by columns usually around a cella or a covered porch

perspective – any method of illustrating 3-dimensional space
(mathematical, one point, two point, atmospheric etc.), also one's point of view

pictograph – picture used as early form of written communication

pier – masonry post

pieta – Mary mourning dead Christ across her lap

pilgrimage – a journey (usually arduous in some way) to a religious shrine

plan – map of a building

plebian – lower class citizen in Rome, either lacking pedigree or landholdings

plein-air – painting outdoors

pointillism – Seurat's painting technique of using tiny dots of color

polyptych – altarpiece made of many individual parts

polytheism – belief in many gods

pope – leader of the Catholic Church. Another name for the Bishop of Rome

portal – entry (doorway)

post and lintel – an architectural building principle based on a pair of uprights supporting a cross beam

Poussiniste - followers of Poussin's style – intellectual, linear, composition, classical

predella – a narrow decorated ledge at the bottom of some altarpieces that rests directly on the altar

Predestination – religious principle that God knows whether an individual will go to heaven or hell. In Calvinist theology this is extended to include that it is by God's decision before the individual is born whether one will go to heaven or hell

presbytery – square shaped sanctuary on English church architecture, comparable to an rounded apse

primary colors – palette based on red, blue and yellow

primogeniture – One's birth order dictates one's station in society – usually associated with the eldest male inheriting a particular birthright

Prix de Rome – prize awarded by the Royal Academy in Paris for a 1-year study abroad scholarship in Rome

pronaos – front porch on a temple

proskenium – the stage in an ancient theater, originally the flat topside of props storage behind the scenery. Later it jutted out in front of the scenery, although the stage still customarily included storage area underneath

provenance - the origin or source

psalter – Book of Psalms

pylon – massive gateway to Egyptian temple with sloping walls

Q

quatrefoil – a cloverleaf shaped emblem

Qu'ran – Holy Book for Islam religion

R

readymades – everyday found objects presented as art

refectory – dining room in a monastery (abbey)

relics – Objects associated with Christ or a saint or Apostle – robe or bones for example – often kept as inspirations in faith

relieving triangle – area above the lintel in a corbelled arch

religious – when used as a noun it refers to monks, nuns and friars

reliquary – a box designed to contain relics; **reliquary chapel** – the chapels located off an ambulatory or transept where relics are kept

ribbed groin vaulting – vaulting based on pointed arches where weight is distributed to pressure points along the nave wall. Associated with Gothic churches and some late Romanesque design (Norman churches especially)

rose window – round stained glass window, usually interpreted to symbolize the Virgin Mary and/or God and the Church

rotunda – round building covered by a dome

Royal Academy – government sponsored higher education in France initiated by Louis XIV

Royal Salon – juror-selected international art exhibition in Paris; a big deal during the late 17th, 18th and 19th centuries

Rubeniste – followers of Rubens' style – emotional, painterly, color, baroque

S

sanctuary – the holy of holies – most sacred place within a temple or church

scale – relative size of one object compared to another

scriptorium – large room where manuscripts are produced

Septuagint – Greek translation of Hebrew Old Testament dating to 200 BC. It was the Old Testament used by the Jews until 90AD It was the original Old Testament used in Christian Bibles, and is still used in Catholic and Orthodox Bibles

Serf - peasant

sfumato – fogging or hazing out of a background landscape

shatter – tall pointy tower usually mixed in with onion domes on Russian Orthodox churches

skene - the backdrop in a theater which is customarily decorated with scenery (skene in Greek = scene)

Sola Fide – Protestant theology that one is saved by faith alone originating with Martin Luther

Sola Scriptura – Protestant theology that the written Bible is the only source of the Word of God, usually combined with the assumption that it is self-explanatory by way of the Holy Spirit. Concept originated with Martin Luther

Steel-framed construction – steel girders are employed to create a skeleton for taller buildings such that outer walls no longer support the weight of the structure

stepped gable – steeply pitched gable where the line of the gable conforms to the brickwork resembling steps

stigmata – the wounds of Christ as they appear in rare instances on a saint

stringcourse – a raised band of brickwork, often employed to mark the division between floors or levels on a building exterior

stylobate – floor of a Greek temple

subtractive architecture – removing dirt or stone to create a cave or tunnel into the earth

T

tabernacle - box in which the consecrated Eucharist is stored; originally the term described the tent where the ark of the covenant was kept

tablinum – room in Roman house where busts of ancestors were kept

tempera – a paint medium with an egg base

tenebrism – exaggerated chiaroscuro – very high contrast of highlights and shadows

terra cotta – baked clay used as a medium in art

tesserae – small pieces of glad or tile used to create mosaics

tholos – buried corbelled dome used as a tomb

Torah – in Hebrew, the first 5 books of the Old Testament, which is the Hebrew Law (same as Pentateuch)

transept – open hall between the apse and nave in a basilica plan church. Normally communion is distributed here

triforium – fake gallery in Gothic churches

triglyph – alternate with metopes in a Doric frieze – recall butt ends of wooden rafters

triptych – an altarpiece with two narrow outer panels that can close over the central panel

tromp l'oeil – trick of the eye – a painted illusion usually making a space appear to open to something beyond. Sometimes used in reference to painting a flat surface to resemble plaster molding or sculpture.

triumphal arch – huge freestanding arches erected by emperors to recall their victories

tympanum – lunette above the lintel over a door

V

vassal – small scale landowner beholden to nobility

vellum – treated calfskin used for writing manuscripts

veneration – profound respect

voussoir – wedge-shaped stones used to build an arch

W

wattle and daub – sticks and mud or clay used as a primitive building material

westwork - west entrance to a church with flanking towers; entrance leads to a vestibule smaller than a narthex with an upstairs view of the nave

wet drapery technique - statues that look like their clothes are wet to show anatomy under fabric